Seanchaidh na Coille
The Memory-Keeper of the Forest

Anthology of Scottish-Gaelic Literature of Canada

Michael Newton, Editor

Seanchaidh na Coille
The Memory-Keeper of the Forest

Anthology of Scottish-Gaelic Literature of Canada

Michael Newton, Editor

CAPE BRETON UNIVERSITY PRESS
SYDNEY, NOVA SCOTIA

Do dh'Eòin G. MacFhionghain
Caraid nan Gàidheal Canadach

Portrait from the archives of the Beaton Institute, Cape Breton University. 79-1005-3985. ca.1910. Photographer Unknown.

Praise for Seanchaidh na Coille
The Memory-Keeper of The Forest

An t-Ollamh Roibeart Dunbar
Cathair Chànanan, Litreachais, Eachdraidh agus Àrsaidheachdan Ceilteach, Ceannard Roinn na Ceiltis agus Eòlas na h-Alba
Oilthigh Dhùn Èideann

'Se an cruinneachadh saoibhir seo de bhàrdachd agus rosg Gàidhlig à Canada na chruinneachadh as iomlaine dhen litreachas sin a bha againn a-riamh, agus bidh e na ghoireas sònraichte, gun choimeas fad bhliadhnaichean mòra san àm ri teachd. Tha an t-Oll. Newton air obair shuaicheanta a dhèanamh ann a bhith a' lorg agus a' mìneachadh gu gleusta an uiread de stuth taitneach, agus anns an dòigh sin a' sealltainn dhuinn cho iomadh-fhillte is a bha agus a tha beatha nan Gàidheal anns gach àite air feadh Chanada anns am faighear iad. Bidh na h-eadar-theangachaidhean ealanta aige air leth feumail do leughadairean gun Ghàidhlig. Bidh an leabhar barraichte seo cho feumail is a ghabhas do sgoilearan agus oileanaich, do luchd-rannsachaidh, agus do dhuine sam bith aig a bheil ùidh anns a' phàirt chudromaich seo ann an eachdraidh de dh'ioma-chultarachd agus ioma-chànanas Chanada, agus ann an cultar na Gàidhlig san fharsaingeachd.

Dr. Robert Dunbar
Chair of Celtic Languages, Literature, History and Antiquities,
Head of Celtic and Scottish Studies
University of Edinburgh

This extremely rich collection of Gaelic poetry and prose literature from Canada is the single most comprehensive collection of such material we have ever had, and will be an outstanding and unique resource for a long time to come. Dr. Newton has done a remarkable job in retrieving and expertly contextualizing a large amount of fascinating material, showing the rich variety and national extent of the Gaelic experience in Canada. His sensitive and skillful translations open up this material to an English-speaking readership. This outstanding book will be of inestimable value to students, researchers and anyone interested in an important strand in Canada's multicultural and multilingual identity and in Gaelic culture more generally.

Lodaidh MacFhionghain, Tagraiche dha na Gàidheil, Ceannard Iomairtean na Gàidhlig is Bàrd

Tha an co-chruinneachadh seo a' toirt am follais ann am faclan is an cànan nan Gàidheal fhéin – aig a' robh tùs ann an Gàidhealtachd na h-Albann – an eachdraidh cho-fhillte, mì-bhreithnichte, dhoilleir fad linntean anns a' Cho-chomann Chanéideanach agus an làmh a bh'aca air Uachdaranachd Chanada. Tha e a' sealltainn do mhuinntir Chanada cho fada is farsuing 's a bha tuineachadh nan Gàidheal aig àm a' Cho-chaidreachais: na suidheachaidhean poileataigeach, sòisealta is eaconamach a mhùchaich cha mhór an cànan agus an dearbh-aithne chultarach; agus tha e a' sònrachadh na h-aon mhór-roinneadh 's an dùthaich 's a' là an diugh far a bheil Gàidheil agus a' Ghàidhlig agus a cultar a' leanaid agus a' fantainn mar choimhearsnachd bheò; is mar a 's urrainn dhan roinn seo a bhith 'na goireas do fheadhainn a tha airson ceangal ás ùr a dhèanadh ri'n dualchas Ghàidhealach ann an roinntean eile na dùthcha. 'S ann 's a' leabhar seo goireas eireachdail do dhuine sam bith a tha 'sgrìobhadh neo a' bruidhinn air, no a' cur an gnìomh, iomairtean a bhuineas dha na Gàidheil is an cànan is an cultar anns a' cho-theacsa Chanéideanach.

Lewis MacKinnon, Poet, Gaels' Advocate and Executive Director of Nova Scotia Office of Gaelic Affairs

This anthology brings to light in the words and language of the Gaels themselves – whose origins were the Highlands and Islands of Scotland – their long, complex, misunderstood, obscure history in Canadian Society and their role in the Canadian State. Newton demonstrates to Canadians how far and widespread the settlement of Gaels was at the time of Confederation: the political, social and economic circumstances that almost smothered their language and cultural identity. The only remaining jurisdiction in the country, Nova Scotia, is where Gaels and their language and culture persist in a vestigial and active communal sense, and can be an asset to those who want to reconnect with their Gaelic heritage in other regions of the country. For anyone who is writing on, speaking of or establishing initiatives pertaining to Gaels and their language and culture in the Canadian context, this book is an excellent resource.

Dr. Silke Stroh,
Assistant Professor of English, Postcolonial and Media Studies,
University of Muenster (Germany)

Presenting a wide range of Gaelic poetic and prose texts, along with English translations and information on biographical, historical, socio-cultural and literary contexts, this excellent anthology significantly enhances the accessibility of important primary sources. It also contains analytical commentary which, despite its necessary brevity, includes many thought-provoking observations, making this book an important intervention in contemporary criticism linking Gaelic Studies to wider comparative debates on North American multiculturalism, minority identities, international diaspora studies, colonialism and postcolonialism. While promising to become an important reference for scholars in literary and cultural studies—as well as for historians—this anthology is also of interest to the general reader, being very successful in explaining complex matters in a jargon-free, succinct and compelling manner. It not only contributes to a more nuanced understanding of Canadian colonial and postcolonial identities, but also has implications for contemporary debates about future cultural and educational policies.

Copyright © 2015 Michael Newton

All rights reserved. No part of this work may be reproduced or used in any form or by any means, electronic or mechanical, including photocopying, recording or any information storage or retrieval system, without the prior written permission of the publisher. Cape Breton University Press recognizes fair dealing uses under the *Copyright Act* (Canada). Responsibility for the research and permissions obtained for this publication rests with the author.

Cape Breton University Press recognizes the support of the Province of Nova Scotia and the support received for its publishing program from the Canada Council for the Arts Block Grants Program. We are pleased to work in partnership with these bodies to develop and promote our cultural resources.

Cover image:: Governor of Rupert's Land on a tour of inspection [Governor George Simpson]. HBC's 1926 calendar from a painting by L.L. Fitzgerald (from a photo of a painting by Cyrus C. Cuneo) - HBCA P-390. Hudson's Bay Company Archives. Provincial Archives of Manitoba.
Cover design: Cathy MacLean Design, Chéticamp, NS
Layout: Mike Hunter, Port Hawkesbury and Sydney, NS
Copyediting: Katie Yantzi, Toronto, ON; Catriona Parsons, Antigonish, NS.
First printed in Canada.

Library and Archives Canada Cataloguing in Publication
 Newton, Michael Steven, 1965-, author, translator
      Seanchaidh na coille = The memory-keeper of the forest : anthology of Scottish-Gaelic literature of Canada / Michael Newton.

The author contextualizes specific Gaelic works, recounts them, and offers a translation.
Includes bibliographical references and index.
Issued in print and electronic formats.
Text chiefly in English; some text in Scottish Gaelic.
ISBN 978-1-77206-016-4 (paperback).--ISBN 978-1-77206-017-1 (pdf).--
ISBN 978-1-77206-018-8 (epub).--ISBN 978-1-77206-019-5 (mobi)

     1. Canadian literature (Gaelic). 2. Canadian literature (Gaelic)--History and criticism. 3. Canadian literature (Gaelic)--Themes, motives. 4. Canadian literature--Scottish Canadian authors. 5. Canadian literature--Scottish Canadian authors--History and criticism. I. Title. II. Title: Memory-keeper of the forest.

PS8089.5.S26N49 2015   C810.9'89163   C2015-903574-0
                                                  C2015-903575-9

Cape Breton University Press
1250 Grand Lake Road
Sydney, NS B1P 6L2 CA
www.cbupress.ca

Contents

Acknowledgements	xii
Foreword	xiv
1 – Introduction	1
A Multitude of Solitudes	1
Gaelic Perspectives, Gaelic Sources	8
Reading Gaelic Literature	13
Transmission and Transcription	21
About this Volume	28
2 – The Subjugation of Gaeldom	32
1: A Song in the Wake of Culloden	40
2: The Tacksman of Griminish	44
3: The Lament of the North	52
4: Glencalvie Clearances	59
5: A Gael's Lament	62
3 – Militarism and Tartanism	68
1: The Song of the Gaels	78
2: The Renown of the Gaels	83
3: The Gaels at War and the Gaels at Peace	91
4: Antigonish Highland Games	95
5: Address to Hamilton and Toronto Gaelic Societies	100
6: Speech by Niall Mac na h-Innse at Lochiel	108
7: The Scots of Canada	116
8: The Gaels of Nova Scotia	118
4 – Migration	121
1: "That is the Way I Would Go"	129
2: "It was on Sunday Morning"	132
3: The Song of the Big Sheep	138
4: Coming to America	142
5: MacNiven and the People of Uist	147
6: Sailing to Prince Edward Island	150
7: From Kilmartin to Tiverton, Ontario	154
8: Gaelic Guidebook for the Emigrant	161
9: From the Isle of Lewis to Quebec	167
10: Dòmhnall's Testimony about Manitoba	170
11: In Praise of the Canadian Prairies	175

5 – Settlement — 184

1: "I Am Dejected In The Bog By Myself" — 189
2: Clearing the Forests — 193
3: "I Am Vexed Today" — 194
4: "I am Gloomy" — 196
5: Curses on the Mice — 199
6: The Bear's Song — 201
7: An Account of Prince Edward Island & Cape Breton — 203
8: The Song of the Fire — 215
9: The Gaelic Communities of Megantic, Quebec — 219
10: Immigration to Saltcoats, Saskatchewan — 221
11: Gaelic Communities in Prince Edward Island — 224
12: The Gaels in Cape Breton — 227
13: The Song of Clandonald — 246
14: The Gaels of Winnipeg — 250
15: The Song of the Reaper — 256

6 – Love and Death — 261

1: Elegy to Tòmas Friseal — 263
2: Elegy to Bishop Uilleam Friseal — 268
3: Ontario Love Song — 274
4: Elegy to Iain MacGilleBhràth — 275
5: Seònaid's Lullaby — 282
6: "The Great Hearts of Generosity" — 285
7: Lament for Edith and Dòmhnall — 286
8: Elegy for Father Niall MacLeòid — 289
9: "My Heart is Agonized" — 295
10: Lament for Gilleasbaig MacEalair — 298
11: Eulogy to a Horse — 302
12: The Macdonalds of Bailey's Brook — 305
13: "The Journey that I Took from the Town" — 308
14: Elegy for Iain Alasdair MacLachlainn — 311

7 – Religion — 315

1: Odes to Assist the Faith of the Gaels — 322
2: The Dissemination of the Scriptures — 323
3: A Song to Bishop Cailean MacFhionghain — 333
4: A Morning Hymn — 338
5: A Song about the Presbyterian Church of Canada — 340
6: The Farmer's Thanksgiving Hymn — 347
7: "That is the Drink I Would Imbibe" — 349
8: The Bible — 353
9: The Missionary on Lake Winnipeg — 357

10: About the United Church of Canada	361
11: National Hymn	369

8 – Language and Literature 371

1: New Year's Eve near Lake Huron	387
2: A Song to the Traveller	389
3: In Praise of the *Young Highland Traveller*	395
4: In Praise of Gaelic in Hamilton, Ontario	398
5: A Portrait of Eóghann MacColla	401
6: Salutations to Eóghann MacColla	405
7: In Praise of Gaelic and of Echo	406
8: "A Toast to the Gaelic Mothers"	411
9: Silenced Voices in Saskatchewan	413
10: News of *Awakening*	417

9 – Identity and Associations 421

1: An Ode to the Gaelic Society of Toronto	431
2: A Song to the Glengarry Highland Society	434
3: An Ode to the Celtic Society of Montreal	439
4: A Letter from Glengarry	442
5: An Ode to the Antigonish Highland Society	444
6: The Scotch Gathering of Alexandria	450
7: A Song to the Gaels of Vancouver	456

10 – Politics 463

1: Election Rally of Pictou	469
2: Gaelic in the Nova Scotia Assembly	474
3: The Election of John Thompson	477
4: The Death of the Repeal of Canadian Federation	480
5: A Letter from the Gaelic Society of Bruce County	484
6: A Speech about Gaelic in the Canadian Senate	487
7: A Song about the Glengarry Election	493
8: Scorn for the Bolsheviks	496
9: A Song about the Nova Scotian Election	499
10: A Song about the General Election	502

Conclusions	504
Biographies	515
Maps	524
Notes	530
References	551
Index	564

Acknowledgements

The Gaelic title *seanchaidh* has no exact equivalent in English. A seanchaidh is a professional custodian of seanchas: communal memory, history and experience, often in the form of literature, especially song-poetry. The title of this volume alludes to an attempt to restore this largely neglected storehouse of material to its rightful place in the historical annals and literary archives of Canada. The title is also an homage to the work of the Rev. Dr. Alasdair MacGill-Eain Sinclair, an indefatigable Gaelic scholar from Nova Scotia who produced a series of volumes of Gaelic literature around the turn of the 20th century, two of which included the word "coille" (forest). The image of the forest is a dominant one in the Gaelic literature of North America which refers to the continent with such kennings as "Dùthaich nan Craobh" (The Land of Trees) and "A' Choille Ghruamach" (The Gloomy Forest).

I have been aware of and engaging with the heritage of Scottish Gaels in Canada to some degree since the mid-1990s, when I was conducting research in Celtic Studies at the University of Edinburgh. The core of the texts in this collection began in earnest in 1999 when the late Kenneth McKenna of Glengarry, Ontario, bequeathed photocopies of newspaper cuttings from his area to me. I accumulated much more material and a heightened motivation for publishing it while teaching Celtic Studies at St. Francis Xavier University. The absence of any substantial body of primary texts in Gaelic about the immigrant experience, despite the prominence of the iconography of Highlandism in popular Canadian history, became quite apparent to me in the course of research and teaching.

My efforts have been aided by the help and cooperation of many individuals and institutions. I am especially grateful to the staff of the Angus L. Macdonald Library, St. Francis Xavier University, the Archives of Ontario, the National Library of Scotland, the library of the School of Scottish Studies and the Special Collections of the University of Edinburgh for enabling me access to rare and important materials as well as permission to print them. Permission to reprint items that have appeared in previous publications has also been graciously granted by *Comann Eachdraidh Tholastaidh bho Thuath* and the *Stornoway Gazette*. A digital image of the frontispiece portrait of Gilleasbaig MacFhilip (in his book *Collected Verse: The Blind Bard of Megantic*, 1913) was kindly provided by the Rare Books and Special Collections of McGill University Library. Thanks to the Beaton Institute of Cape Breton University for permission to use the portrait of Eòin G. MacFhionghain, to Jocelyn Gillis of the Antigonish Heritage Museum for the portrait (presumed to be) of Iain Boid (John Boyd) and to Laurinda Matheson at the Angus L. Macdonald Library for scanning the image of Alasdair MacGill-Eain Sinclair.

Many individuals have been generous in sharing their knowledge and materials with me: Sister Dr. Margaret MacDonell volunteered historical references and much encouragement to me; the late Dr. Kenneth Nilsen provided me with his photocopies of *Cuairtear nan Coillte*; Margaret Bennett gave me a photocopy of the booklet of songs by Cailean MacÌomhair; Susan Cameron and Kathleen MacKenzie of Saint Francis Xavier University aided me in finding and accessing many rare sources; Professor Robert Dunbar of the University of Edinburgh shared his research on the Bard MacGill-Eain and Dr. Michael Linkletter his thesis on Alasdair MacGill-Eain Sinclair; David Anderson of Williamstown, Ontario, furnished notes about some Glengarry authors; Alexander MacLennan of Carleton University was able to track down information about several Cape Breton poets on my behalf.

I am grateful for comments, corrections and suggestions on drafts of chapters from James Ambuske, Matthew Dziennik, Steve Johnston, Stephanie Johnston, Sarah McCaslin, Lodaidh MacFhionghain (Lewis MacKinnon of Antigonish/Halifax), Iain MacFhionghain (Iain MacKinnon of Skye), Silke Stroh and Wilson McLeod. I am particularly indebted to Alexander MacLennan for his copious comments and suggestions. Friends who kindly provided help in several points of translation and cultural nuances include Michael Bauer, Robert Dunbar and Donald Meek.

Cape Breton University Press has been very supportive in the development of this volume and I am grateful for bringing it to fruition.

Thanks are due, finally, to my wife Stephanie and my daughter Róisín for their patience as I spent nights, weekends and holidays completing this extensive project.

M.N.

Foreword
Diana Gabaldon

What a privilege to be asked to introduce such a fascinating, elegant and invaluable book!

My own experience with Gàidhlig (Scottish Gaelic, the Irish form is "Gaeilge") began in 1988, when I began to write a novel for practice, and chose (on the basis of seeing a young man in a kilt on a "Dr. Who" re-run) to set it in the Scottish Highlands of the 18th century. A modicum of initial research revealed that the language of the Highlands at that time was almost exclusively Gaelic, and – conscientious writer that I was – I thought I must both make that fact clear in my novel, and somehow contrive to give an actual flavour of the language.

All I can say is that if you think it was easy to find a Scottish Gaelic/English dictionary in Phoenix, Arizona, in 1988 ... think again. The Internet, as we now know its illimitable quantities of information, contacts and sources, didn't exist. The local Caledonian Society, while very friendly, had no Gaelic speakers. I had never met a Gaelic speaker, native or otherwise, and was not infrequently informed that it was a dead or dying language – who cared?

I persevered and was eventually able to acquire a slender Gaelic/English dictionary from Schoenhof's Foreign Books, in Boston. Even they appeared somewhat bemused by my exotic request, but they did manage to find the book and ship it to me at fantastic expense (no Amazon Prime back then, either).

I used this book to cobble together bits of spoken Gaelic for *Outlander*, my first novel. Much to my surprise, this novel was not only published, but resulted in a three-book contract, at which point I said to my husband, "OK. I really must go and see the place." Scotland, that is. And on my list of Things to See and Do was #3: Find a better Gaelic dictionary. (#1 was "Look at Everything" and #2 was "Eat Haggis."[1])

I did find a much bigger and more comprehensive dictionary, and with that, made further forays into quasi-Gaelic while writing *Dragonfly in Amber*. That novel, too, was well received, and I began to get fan-mail (real letters; email didn't exist, either). Among these lovely letters was one from a gentleman named Iain MacKinnon Taylor. Mr. Taylor praised my books, saying how wonderful it was to see Scottish history handled so well, and how much he enjoyed the story. He then coughed metaphorically and said delicately that he had just one observation: he had, he said, been born on the Isle of Harris, and was a native Gaelic speaker. And, "I think you must be getting your Gaelic from a dictionary."

It wasn't, he said, so much that the words I was using were wrong, as that I had no grammar, voice, or idiom with which to arrange them. Might he, perhaps, offer his assistance?

To which my response was a fervent, "Mr. Taylor, where have you been all my life?"

Iain – with the assistance of his twin brother Hamish and other family members still living on Harris – helped me with the Gaelic for the next three books. Health issues unfortunately stopped him from further involvement, but good fortune (and an internet friend named Cathy MacGregor – by this time, there was an internet, with email, no less) introduced me to the redoubtable Catherine-Ann MacPhee, native Gaelic speaker from Barra, and a well-known radio and TV presenter in the U.K. The two Cathys – and much more recently, the delightful Àdhamh Ó Broin (Gaelic tutor and consultant to the *Outlander* TV show) have made the Gaelic in my novels ever more plentiful and authentic – and given me the barest smattering of familiarity with that amazing language and its history.

Language is the first thing that defines a culture. Nothing else is more important to a people than a shared tongue. Even though language is an ever-living, ever-flexible thing, the fact that it binds human beings in an immortal chain, binding them together. And even though that chain may be stretched and twisted by time and distance, it endures.

One day my husband came back from a short motorcycle trip, and told me that while parked at one rest-stop, he'd been approached by two Spanish tourists, asking directions. He does speak Spanish, but isn't truly fluent, and was pleased when another man, a local monoglot Spanish-speaker,[2] overheard the tourists and asked if he could help. The conversation was going well, my husband said, but ran into a sudden snag. The man giving directions asked the men where they'd turned, off the main road and they replied that it was at a "semafora." A what? My husband and the local man exchanged baffled looks. "A semafora," the tourists repeated, looking anxious. "Describe it," my husband suggested, in Spanish. "What does a semafora look like?"

xvii

They did, and my husband and local man laughed in revelation. "Es un alto," the local man informed them. A stop sign.

Divergence in geography or time results in difference – but not in basic identity. Gaeilge and Gàidhlig have very obvious commonalities, though the Irish and Scottish branches of the language diverged long ago.

To track such divergences, to identify the ancient commonalities and to preserve the more recent past for the benefit of present and future, is the blessed job of a scholar and a lover. Someone so in love with a language and a culture that the largest themes are easily apparent and the smallest details treasured. Luckily for us and for the history of the Gaelic tongue and diaspora into the New World, Michael Newton is just such a one.

This book is as elegantly and passionately written as a novel, while providing enough detail to satisfy the most exacting academic sense of curiosity.

It modestly purports to be an anthology of Canadian Gaelic poetry – and certainly it's that. It's much more, though: a stunning description of a culture, both in situ and in transition, and an analysis of the enduring themes in Gàidhlig literature and poetry.

It's also remarkable for its discussion of matters literary, and the durability of the Celtic oral tradition, with its emphasis on the warrior as a common central figure. I found that most interesting myself, as I'd noticed exactly that emphasis in my historical research. The Scottish Highlands were a tribal culture; this is why emigrant Highlanders in America often had no trouble joining or dealing with Native American groups – they identified with both the group dynamics and traditions, the value of a warrior and with the strong oral culture. Stories and songs are paramount in such a culture, because these are the chief means of preserving not only history, but also language.

As I noted above, when I began my research some twenty-five years ago, I was routinely told that Scottish Gaelic was a dying tongue. In fact, Iain Taylor expressed just such a fear to me, saying that he was afraid it wouldn't last past his own generation in the Highlands.

Moved by his letter, I wrote back and said, "I tell you what, Iain; if the Gaelic language dies, it won't be because neither you nor I tried."

Language is the first thing that defines a culture. Sometimes, it's also the last. Many of the smaller Native American tribes have disappeared – because there is no longer anyone who knows their tongue.

A few years ago, I was invited to a book festival in Lithuania; a fascinating experience, the more so as Lithuanian has no perceptible common links to any of the few languages I have a passing familiarity with. I hastily learned "exit," "push," "pull," "toilet," and "ice machine" (the latter by accident), but was for the most part dependent on the kindness of multilingual strangers.

These Lithuanian strangers were very kind indeed. At one point, my hosts took me (with the translator of my books, the only person there who spoke fairly fluent English) to Vilnius University, an ancient and venerable establishment. There isn't much left in Lithuanian that is ancient and venerable any more, save the buildings. Lithuania was occupied for most of the last century, by waves of invaders: the Russians, the Germans, and then the Russians again. Each wave of plunderers receded with the valuables – and much of the tangible history – of the country.

The last wave of Russians tried to take the intangible, too. The invaders forbade Lithuanian to be spoken in public. Only Russian could be used.

But the Russians have been gone for nearly a quarter-century[3] and the Lithuanians have begun stubbornly salvaging their history. One small room at the university contains a small bronze monument, a slab set in the floor, called "The Grave of the Balts," which shows a supine woman in prehistoric costume and lists the contents of a traditional Baltic burial. The walls of the room are painted with figures illustrating one of the classic myths of Baltic history.

Above the monument is a window, made of small diamond-shaped panes. Some are stained glass and some are clear, and the design is intricate. Alone, I would never have seen what my host pointed out: on one of the small, clear panes of glass, someone had painstakingly written with a diamond, "They are trying to kill us. They can't...." In Lithuanian.

We owe a great debt to the stubborn faith of people like the person who wrote that – and people like Michael Newton. People who have kept faith with the past, the singers of songs, the record-keepers, who will not let love or language die. The seanchaidhs.

March 15, 2015
Scottsdale, Arizona
Diana Gabaldon

1 – Introduction

A Multitude of Solitudes

Since the 19th century, the standard means of celebrating the legacy of Scottish immigrants and their descendants in both Canada and the United States has been to compile and embellish a list of influential people of Scottish descent widely known because of their political power, financial success, entrepreneurism or artistic accomplishments. It is not hard to find numerous examples of people who meet these criteria: catalogues always include such luminaries as Sir John A. Macdonald, Sir Alexander Mackenzie (explorer of the Pacific northwest), Hugh MacLennan (novelist) and so on.

There are a number of problems and shortcomings with this formulaic approach, however. The importance and prominence of the mainstream Scottish "heroes" is generally determined by their ability to work within the confines and standards set by anglophone society. The recognition of their success is ultimately a celebration of anglophone culture rather than the culture in which they themselves or their ancestors originated.

Even the notion of Scottishness needs further refinement to be meaningful. Like Canada, Scotland consists of at least two solitudes, one of which is rooted in the Highlands and Western Isles, speaks Gaelic and has a long history of conflict with the anglophone world, including the Scottish Lowlands. This segment of the Scottish population invested as much as any other in the formation of Canada: recent research has revealed that Scottish Gaelic was the third-most spoken

European language at the time of Confederation.¹ And yet today, apart from scattered homesteads in Nova Scotia, not only has the language receded from the immigrant communities that once spoke it, but it has practically disappeared from public memory. The descendants of Gaels, who once described themselves as bitter enemies of English speakers, are now categorized as "English Canadians" with only occasional nods to the many distinctions that once divided them.²

The linguistic limitations of scholars have often confined the materials used to tell these stories to sources written in English. These constraints coincide with the willingness of many Gaels and their descendants in North America to reduce their ancestral culture to the set of colourful symbols in favour with the dominant culture—tartans, kilts, bagpipes, etc.—and to abandon the rest. Yet, there are ample sources available in their native language, Gaelic, to construct much more complex narratives that do not concur so neatly with Anglocentric triumphalism, tales that occupy the marginal spaces shared by other subaltern peoples. If we examine the materials produced by Gaelic immigrant communities, we can find a different set of heroes and accomplishments that are more relevant from their own cultural perspectives. The texts in this volume may help restore some balance to the list of who has been celebrated and who has been ignored and forgotten in the conventional Scottish-Canadian "Hall of Fame."

Although some of the memories preserved in this volume could be described as heroic or celebratory, some are not. Canadians of Scottish descent, who do not want to challenge the status quo, or question their position and privilege within it, may not wish to embrace all of these memories. They are crucial, nonetheless, if we are to understand the story of Scottish Gaelic immigrants in its fullness and complexity. The reconstruction of historical experiences is always complicated by the selective process of highlighting the aspects that meet the approval of contemporary opinion and purging the elements that are less seemly or favourable.

The stories of how and why Scottish Gaels came to Canada and what happened after they arrived has been obscured not only because of the shortage of trained scholars who can read and interpret the sources, but also because the immigrants themselves and their descendants have sometimes suppressed or altered elements that proved awkward or embarrassing to retain in public view. Rusty Bitterman has noted, for example, that while the first generation of immigrants denounced the disenfranchisement and poverty that they endured in Scotland, these radical critiques could be easily repressed once the immigrants were drawn into the forces of commercialism and could prosper from it, whatever its negative impact on other peoples.

> Although members of the upper echelons of Highland society helped to construct an anti-commercial critique of the agrarian transformation of the Highlands and to transfer it to the New World, they and their descendants would over time distance themselves from key aspects of this construction. Having arrived in a new environment and assayed some of the possibilities of the New World, many, like Murdo MacLeod, must have found certain aspects of their past inconvenient and dispensable.[3]

Immigrant Gaels in Canada found themselves enmeshed in systems willing to harness their energies to advance the Anglocentric agendas of the British Empire, but resistant to any notion of the inherent value of cultures and languages, and the identities expressed by them, that did not align with imperial priorities and pretensions. By assimilating to dominant identities of "Britishness" and "whiteness," when they were available, Gaels could gain access to the highest levels of privilege and power in Canadian society, but at the cost of trivializing and distancing themselves from their ancestral inheritance.[4]

Many popular books about the legacy of Scottish immigrants in Canada treat Scotland as if it were a homogenous country populated by people whose differences in customs, language, social structure, and religion were of little consequence, if worth discussing at all. This is a convenient fiction that disregards one of the most fundamental facts of Scottish history, that of the division between Highlands and Lowlands. This partition, and the social processes that caused and perpetuated it, conditioned both sets of people for the experiences they were to have in Canada and informed their perceptions of themselves and others. While relations and exchanges between Highlands and Lowlands were complex and in constant flux, the general trends and emergent attitudes leading up to the 18th and 19th centuries are clear enough.

To Lowlanders, the Highlands[5] were a wild place populated by uncouth and uncivilized people who spoke a detested alien language. Being lazy and treacherous by nature, they preferred to steal and plunder rather than produce wealth through their own effort and industriousness. Lacking civility and refinement, they obeyed no laws of morality or political principle but were inveterate rebels against authority and rationality. The use of ideas from classical texts depicting the opposition between civilization and savagery suggest that Lowlanders were anxious about the implications of growing linguistic, religious and political ties between themselves and England while the unconquered Gaelic "barbarians" defied demands for assimilation and the presumed "laws of progress."[6]

The native inhabitants of the Highlands and Western Isles, for their part, saw the people of the Lowlands as incomers and interlopers who usurped the fertile plains as well as the royal court, disenfranchising Gaels from the independence and prestige that they had once enjoyed as the founders of the Scottish nation.[7]

Anne Grant of Lagan (in the Central Highlands), a woman who spent parts of her life in British North America, Lowland Scotland and Highland Scotland during the late 18th and early 19th centuries and who spoke both Gaelic and English, relates to us that antipathy and distrust were mutual:

> No two nations ever were more distinct or differed more completely from each other, than the Highlanders and Lowlanders; and the sentiments with which they regarded each other, was at best a kind of smothered animosity. ...
>
> The Highlanders, again, regarded the Lowlanders as a very inferior mongrel race of intruders, sons of little men, without heroism, without ancestry, or genius ... who could neither sleep upon the snow, compose extempore songs, recite long tales of wonder or of woe, or live without bread and without shelter for weeks together, following the chace. Whatever was mean or effeminate, whatever was dull, slow, mechanical, or torpid, was in the Highlands imputed to the Lowlanders, and exemplified by allusions to them...[8]

These animosities were carried forward into Canada just as much as any common sense of "Scottishness," especially when Highland immigrants did not conform to the ethnolinguistic norms and expectations of anglophones. In a survey of Gaelic traditions in Prince Edward Island conducted in 1987, for example, John Shaw remarked,

INTRODUCTION

"A small portion of PEI Scots had come from the Scottish Lowlands and according to reports they demonstrated naked hostility to Gaelic—more so than any other ethnic group."[9]

Such prejudices have characterized fraught relationships between many different ethnic groups, but negative stereotypes about Highlanders have proven particularly resistant to deconstruction. With the collaboration of Lowland Scotland in the British Empire and the triumph of an Anglocentric master narrative, derogatory caricatures of Gaels are still often taken at face value.

Many Scottish Canadians did not want to challenge or offend what appeared to be the unassailable dominance of the anglophone ascendency: they only wished to ingratiate themselves with it and be included within its bounds. Pleas for respectability and acceptance called for highlighting the cultural practices and features held in common with anglophones and suppressing or silencing the rest. Take, for example, a speech delivered at the St. Andrew's Day celebration on November 30, 1857 to the St. Andrew's Society of Montreal:

> In these things we seek besides to illustrate and adorn the common brotherhood which knits us to those of our own land, kindred and tongue. It cannot be said of Scotchmen that they have ever been indifferent to the wants or the sorrows of their countrymen. None of us, I believe, can hear the Doric familiar language of our native home, speaking the words of distress or telling the tale of suffering, without feeling the liveliest sympathy with the sufferer. ...
>
> Since the time of the Reformation, Scotland has not simply been a Nation represented by a king and government, but it has been a people and a commonwealth. The interests of the country after that date pertained not to the aristocracy alone, but also to the democracy; hence our Colleges and Seats of Learning have for ages been open to all. ...
>
> As a nation we stand foot to foot with the bravest and the best, and of right we have become sharers in the common glory of United Britain. ...
>
> From England, it is certain, we have derived Saxon, Anglo-Saxon, and Norman elements to a very considerable extent, and

to these we are doubtless, somewhat indebted for our manly independence and love of liberty. ...

It will thus be seen that the elements which make up our Nation are of the best kind, and form a composite of high organization, capable of the highest culture. ...

The very differences that exist among us are on comparatively minor points, and such as could only arise among a people acutely intelligent in religious principles and deeply impressed with a sense of religious obligations. It has, we hesitate not to say, been righteousness that has exalted our Nation. [We] will have the high honor of sending forth intelligent and hardy sons to subdue new and unexplored regions of the earth, and to plant among the Nations of the future the seeds of learning, of true religion, and of a manly national character.[10]

Missing from the ten pages of this "patriotic" propaganda is any acknowledgement that the Doric of the Lowlands was a foreign language to the many Gaelic monoglots who lived in Scotland and Canada during that era, that there were still native Scots who clung to their Catholic faith despite ongoing economic and cultural pressure to convert them to Protestantism, and that Gaels had little if any opportunity for formal education in their own language. Modern scholarship has revealed and condemned the presumptions of racism and colonialism in similar tracts about other peoples, but these same basic claims have been recycled continuously by popular writers staking a claim for Scots in the formation of Canada and the (so-called) modern world.

The texts in this volume show that while some Gaels were willing to reconcile themselves to Anglocentric assertions about identity and history that obscured traditional Highland norms, others continued to conceptualize their ethnicity and sense of belonging in much more conservative terms, employing ethnonyms and literary formulations that derive from medieval Gaelic practice.[11]

At the core of Gaelic perceptions of ethnicity was the opposition between us and them. The ethnonym "Gàidheal" in Gaelic means both a Gaelic speaker and an inhabitant of the Scottish Highlands or Western Isles, given that there was no distinction between the two concepts before the late 19th century. The ethnonym "Gall" essentially means "non-Gael" but was applied most specifically to Scottish Lowlanders. Gaelic speakers in North America extended its meaning to include anglophones as a whole, although it sometimes seems to apply to anyone outside of the Gaelic speech community. There are also Gaelic terms that denote the communities constituted by each sort of people: "Gàidhealtachd" corresponds approximately to the geographical Highlands and Western Isles when situated in Scotland, or any Gaelic-speaking community of significant size; and "Galltachd" corresponds roughly to the geographical Lowlands when situated in Scotland, or any non-Gaelic-speaking community in general.[12]

A song-poem composed by Donnchadh Niall MacDhòmhnaill of Kenyon, Ontario, apparently while he was a student abroad in late-19th-century Edinburgh, offers a typical example of Gaelic ethnic consciousness. Despite being a native-born Canadian, Donnchadh identified strongly with the Scottish Highlands and fell in love with a young woman there on one of his visits. The song he composed is introduced in the Glengarry newspaper in which it appeared as "moladh a leannain, agus a dhùthcha féin" (praising his sweetheart and his own homeland). His affinity for the Highlands and aversion to the Lowlands, despite receiving education in the latter, is clear in his composition:

...Air fhad m' fhuirich an Dùn Éideann,
Cumail comann ri luchd Beurla,
Bheir mi 'n t-soraidh seo gun tréigsinn
Dh'ionnsaigh m' éibhneis anns na gleannaibh.

Ged a thàrladh dhomh bhith 'n taobh-sa,
Gur beag mo thlachd dha na Dubh-Ghoill;
Is bidh mi nis a' cur mo chùil riuth'
Is a' dèanadh an iùil air na beannaibh.

Gur eutrom mo ghleus is m' impidh,
Is neo-lòdail mo cheum o'n fhonn seo
Gu tìr àrd nan sàr-fhear sunntach
Is a' tréigsinn Galltachd 'nam dheannaibh. ...[13]

While I reside in Edinburgh, keeping company with anglophones, I will send this greeting steadfastly to the source of my joy in the glens.

Although I happen to be on this side [of the Highland line], I take little pleasure in the utter non-Gaels; and I will now turn my back on them and set my course for the mountains.

My mood and anxiety are lightened, my step is carefree, leaving this soil for the high land of the cheerful heroes and deserting the Lowlands in a rush. ...

Gaelic Perspectives, Gaelic Sources

By the late 18th century emigration and exile became nearly universal experiences for the natives of the Scottish Highlands and Western Isles, and have remained so to the present day. Although some communities have managed to remain in or close to their ancestral grounds, it is not an exaggeration to state that not one has had the luxury of taking anything for granted about its own survival or continuity.

The centrality of emigration and exile has made a corresponding impression upon the literary expressions and repertoire of all Gaelic communities, whether in Scotland or elsewhere. Song-poems in particular are more than just the records of events that are performed within the specific populations that experienced them: they are powerful literary resources that have become a means for all Gaels to reflect on what it means to belong to a particular place, to negotiate between internal desires and external demands, and to deliberate over the unresolved historical injustices to which Gaels as a whole have been subjected.

The song-poem "A' Choille Ghruamach" (The Gloomy Forest) composed by Iain MacGill-Eain in Nova Scotia before 1820[14] continues to be popular in Scotland; "Guma Slàn do na Fearaibh" (Farewell to the Men), composed in the central Highlands to men leaving for Australia in 1838,[15] was popular in Bruce County, Ontario, in the early 1900s;[16] the song "Chì Mì na Mór-Bheanna" (I See the Great Mountains) was composed by Iain Camshron when returning home to his native Glencoe from Glasgow, but was popular in many Canadian communities, including Glengarry County;[17] and there are many other such examples. If it were possible to recapture the céilidhs in the homes of immigrant Highlanders in Calgary, Ottawa, Vancouver, Moosomin, Montreal, Winnipeg, Antigonish, and elsewhere in Canada, we would observe a kaleidoscope of texts produced by communities reflecting and refracting layers of each other's experiences as they constantly fragment and relocate across countries and continents. Songs have proved to be very effective emigrants themselves, able to find host communities willing to welcome and sustain them on their own merits.

Gaelic literature has a long and illustrious lineage, one that is even older than exists in English. Gaelic literary expressions which have continued to develop in Canadian communities to the present day have their roots in early medieval Scotland and Ireland and display remarkable continuity and resilience. Despite this, Scottish Gaelic literature composed in Canada has received very little serious attention from scholars, whether in Scotland or North America.

Some societies invest their cultural and intellectual resources in constructing monumental architecture, or in contriving sophisticated culinary delights, or in exploring the heavens or earthly territory. Gaeldom put a great deal of its talent and energy into literary production. Verbal forms of cultural expression may be harder to recover and appreciate than material manifestations of culture, but the activities, accomplishments and perspectives of Gaelic communities, whether in Scotland or Canada, cannot be properly understood without taking these into account. The general neglect or, at best, mishandling of these sources has often resulted in both misrepresenting the distinctiveness of the Highland immigrant experience in Canada and the issues that were of importance to Gaels.

Scholars have understood for decades that it is of crucial importance to tap the sources created by the people whose history they are writing to ensure that their own experiences and perspectives are taken into consideration. This is particularly crucial when the subjects of research are a minoritized group that has been ignored in, or distorted by, the official national narratives. Without sources such as those in this volume, conclusions about a range of issues are at best premature and incomplete. Some of the most consequential issues, in terms of collective memory and cultural survival, include the variety of ways that communities engaged with the dominant anglophone hegemony, whether in terms of resistance, critique, avoidance, compromise, accommodation, complicity or assimilation. These strategies, in turn, had ramifications on Gaelic perceptions of and relations with First Nations as well as other immigrant groups.

North American scholars have in many cases been instrumental in exposing and critiquing the social injustices inflicted on indigenous and minoritized people during the expansion of empires in the Americas. Gaeldom has seldom benefited from such analytical studies, however, because it has been largely excluded from the halls of learning and because differences of race have played a greater exclusionary role in the construction of privilege than culture or language, which can be erased with little trace.[18] This does not nullify the social and psychological impact of these attacks on Gaelic communities in the past, nor does it delegitimize the study of nascent colonialism in a Gaelic context. To the extent that it is recognized as an entity at all, Gaeldom is often portrayed implicitly as being an inarticulate, undeveloped peasant culture waiting to be educated and enlightened by the anglophone world. The triumph of assimilation and deference to Anglocentric norms is such that few Canadians of Scottish descent have the incentive or critical apparatus necessary to question this master narrative.

There are documents written in English about Highland immigrants, but these do not cover the breadth of social classes, mentalities, experiences or viewpoints of the community as a whole. For this, Gaelic texts are a vital and underutilized resource. The late Eric Cregeen, folklorist at the School of Scottish Studies, remarked on the unique value of such materials:

> Songs are crucial to understanding life at all times in the Highlands and Islands, far more so than in England, and are one of the prime sources for the historian, for they mirror the concerns of everyday life. ... In the historic reconstruction of social and cultural life the value of oral tradition is perhaps even more important, for written sources are rarely able to illuminate the mental activities, spiritual values and customary practices of Highland communities. They belonged to a world beyond reach and interest of the English-speaking traveller, official and improver.[19]

There are many accounts from Gaelic communities in Canada that attest to the strong feelings and opinions that people had about their experience as individuals and as a community which deserve to be investigated and incorporated into the historical record, even if such sources need to be nuanced, complemented, and analyzed critically.

INTRODUCTION

Take, for example, this description of the historical representation of Patrick Sellar by Gaelic communities in 19th-century Nova Scotia:

> Bha Pàdruig Sellar 'na chulaidh-ghràin do'n t-sluagh leis an obair uamhasaich a bha e a' dèanamh. ... Oir gus an latha andiugh tha an t-ainm aige a' lobhadh ann an Cataibh, agus chan e mhàin sin, ach tha seann mhuinntir ann an Abhainn Bhàrnaidh a thàinig á Cataibh d' am bheil an t-ainm aige fhathast 'na ghràin agus 'na uamhas. Tha seann bhoireannaich aig Abhainn Bhàrnaidh a nì dannsadh le mire-chatha agus le cridhealas, a' seinn luinneig-aigheir, aoiridh no òrain-càinidh a rinneadh air Sellar ann an Cataibh. Shaoileadh tu gum buaileadh na cinn aca na sparran, no cliath mhullaich an taighe, leis an leumartaich agus na sùrdagan a bhios iad a' gearradh air an ùrlar; agus iad a' seinn mar smeòraichean feadh nam preas air madainn Chéitinn.

> Patrick Sellar was detested by the people for the awful work that he did. ... To this day his name is putrid in Sutherland. Not only that, there are old people at Barney's River who find his name loathsome and disgusting. There are old women at Barney's River who can dance with ardour and mirth, and who sing a humorous, satirical and vituperative ditty composed about Sellar in Sutherland. You would think their heads would hit the rafters or the ceiling as they leap and spring from the floor while singing like thrushes in the bushes on a May morning.[20]

The primary sources in this volume provide similarly compelling evidence about historical events and persons, albeit inflected through literary expressions. I have provided translations of these texts, but rendering Gaelic into English is an inexact process: a translation is a particular interpretation of words into another system of thought and expression, and certain types of information are inevitably lost. I have offered a modicum of literary analyses for some texts in the hopes of highlighting the amount of useful information and insight that can be gleaned through careful and sensitive handling of these sources.

If incorporating these materials can greatly enrich our understanding of Gaelic communities and their universe of discourse, neglecting them has had a corresponding detrimental effect on the development of scholarship about Canadian Gaeldom. Take, for example, a recent historical study of the life of Margaret Macdonald, a nurse from Nova Scotia who played a leading role in the development of Canadian military nursing (Margaret's family is featured in text 6.12). The author of the study chose Macdonald as a subject because of how she "personifies the point at which gender intersects with the overlapping contexts of ideology, structure and institution in the late nineteenth and early twentieth centuries," especially in terms of such major themes as imperialism and the military.[21] Macdonald was raised in a Nova Scotia community where Gaelic was still the language of most people even though they had been under tremendous pressure for generations to bow to Anglo-conformity.[22] Despite the scope for exploring the ironies of how someone who had been raised in a community and family whose historical experience had been one of domination by an anglophone hegemony became a fawning anglophile, there is hardly any reference to the Gaelic language or culture in the volume.[23] Instead, there are vague references to Jacobitism and "a brooding past."[24]

While I do not mean to demean or devalue the important contributions that this and many other studies have offered, this presumed "brooding past" symbolizes the frequent lack of knowledge about Gaelic history and culture on the part of scholars researching Highland immigrant communities, and people descended from those communities, that often results in the projection of stereotypes and clichés inherited from the anglophone literary imagination. One is very hard pressed to find actual evidence of this "brooding past" in the Gaelic materials composed and transmitted by real immigrant communities.[25]

Some of the texts included in this collection are prose accounts of events or experiences that would not seem to be appropriate to include in an anthology of literature, but even these frequently contain oral formula, literary flourishes, allusions to proverbs and references to song. Gaelic song-poetry in particular was deeply embedded in an oral "corpus" to which all Gaels had common access and this cannot but have coloured the way in which they perceived the world and expressed their experiences. Such sources also provide rare internal evidence about the communities who were the audiences for Gaelic literature and whose lives and traditions formed the context for their composition and reception.

INTRODUCTION

Reading Gaelic Literature

The Celtic-speaking peoples of Britain and Ireland produced the earliest surviving literature of western Europe in their own vernacular languages, generations before Anglo-Saxons were writing down their compositions.[26] Throughout the medieval period, Gaelic scholars produced literature and accumulated learning on a range of topics—politics, theology, law, medicine, geography, etc.—that met the needs of religious institutions and secular leaders in both Ireland and Scotland. The professional Gaelic intelligentsia established a guild-like system in about the 12th century to institutionalize the literary practices that they had developed, to regulate the training of new scholars, and to ensure that the poetic order would be intimately bound up in the privileges and concerns of the native aristocracy. Poets legitimated the authority and advanced the interests of their patrons—and criticized them, when necessary—and aristocrats rewarded the men of letters in kind.

This system of sponsorship and entitlement provided stability for the Gaelic intelligentsia and enabled a highly ornate and carefully regulated body of creative expression to flourish. It changed little from the 13th century to the 17th century from the south of Ireland to the north of Scotland—a singular accomplishment in the history of European literature. Although professional poets produced a majority of the most polished and sophisticated texts that survive, non-professional aristocrats also participated in the production of literature that has proven popular and influential throughout Gaeldom. Not only did such lay-people share a great deal of the educational and cultural background with the literati, they too were drawn to the elegant and elevated means of expression that the classical Gaelic tradition offered them.[27] The high status and prestige of the poets and their work caused their literary conventions, styles and use of language to "trickle down" throughout the social ranks of Gaeldom and influenced the literary and verbal expressions of even the most humble, albeit aspiring, poets.

Many of the most accomplished Gaelic poets who immigrated to Canada came by their literary aptitude from being only a few generations removed from either the native Highland nobility or the professional literati. Canadian Gaels steeped in the history and traditions of their people retained a reliable communal memory of the historical origins and social roles of the Gaelic literati, as reflected in

Figure 1.1 – Alasdair Friseal (Alexander Fraser), Gaelic scholar and founder of Archives of Ontario. Portrait from The Celtic Monthly, *no. 1 vol. xx, January 1912.*

this account by Alasdair Friseal in late-19th-century Toronto:

> Am measg nam fineachan Gàidhealach bha na bàird àrd-inbheach agus ann am mór-mheas. Cha b' e cogadh is creach a-mhàin anns do ghabh na laoich tlachd; bha iad treun ann an cath ach bha iad suairce, caomh ann an sìth. Bha mór spéis aca do cheòl na clàrsaiche agus gu sònraichte do dhuain fhonnmhor nam bàrd. Bha am bàrd 'na sheanchaidh: b' esan a chum cunntas air gnìomharan nan laoch, aig fleadh an fhìona dh'aithris e an cliù, agus an déidh am bàis chàirich e an carra-chuimhne 's an dàn. ... B'e miann gach triath agus treun-fhear a bhith air a mholadh ann am marbhrann agus bha dreuchd nam bàrd, air an adhbhar sin, cha b' e a-mhàin deacair, ach ro urramach.[28]

> Among the Highland clans the poets had a high status and were greatly respected. Warfare and raiding were not the only things from which the warriors derived pleasure: they were brave in battle but they were civil and kind in peace. They greatly enjoyed the music of the wire-strung harp and the melodious song-poems of the poets in particular. The poet was a memory-keeper: it was he who kept an account of the deeds of the warriors, at the wine-feast he recited their feats, and after death he immortalized them in poetry. ... It was the desire of every chieftain and champion to be eulogized in an elegy and the office of the poet, for that reason, was not only arduous but highly honoured.

INTRODUCTION

Song-poetry has arguably been the most respected and admired form of literary expression in Gaelic society and the poet one of the most influential figures in any Gaelic community. As native Nova Scotian Pàdraig MacNeacail stated of this ubiquitous cultural role, "Chan eil clachan 's am bheil Gàidhlig air a labhairt nach do thog bàrd no dhà" (There's no village in which Gaelic has been spoken which did not produce a poet or two).[29]

Some of the compositions celebrating the lives and accomplishments of the native nobility during the medieval and early modern eras were transcribed into family poem-books for posterity, but Gaelic poetry should be understood primarily as song meant to be performed for, and heard audibly by, a live audience. The "oral-dominant mode" of Gaelic literature remained a defining feature until fairly recently and the transmission of texts through oral performance had important consequences for the style and conventions of Gaelic song-poetry. Although some poetic metres facilitate extended commentary of an expository nature, content could be most effectively communicated in the form of concise verbal units that could be immediately comprehended by listeners, often evoking compelling visual images or strong emotions.

> Once these conventions were established, even an oblique reference would be intelligible in the very same terms. The commonplaces work thus for anyone who through song has known the rhetoric from childhood. ... What the bards have produced here is therefore a coherent system of rhetoric of great resonance and evocative power.[30]

Gaelic literature consists of many distinct genres and subgenres with their own characteristics, each of which may have been brought into being for a particular purpose by a specific social group. Literary practice has sometimes perpetuated these defining traits and associations, but in other cases genres and styles have become hybridized and blurred over long periods of time. Songs in dàn metre, for example, have their origins in the high-register literary culture of the élite and are different from the "sub-literary"[31] labour songs of the peasantry (such as òrain-luaidh). At the same time, it is clear that a number of songs that had originated in higher-register genres were pulled "downwards" into use as labour songs (and their linguistic norms and metres adapted accordingly).[32]

> The oral tradition common to all Gaels which was transported intact to the [Canadian Maritime] region and survives to the present includes among other things story-telling, songs, proverbs, historical legends, prayers and religious lore, prophecies, witch lore, second sight, cures and weather lore.[33]

Gaelic literature suffered for a long time under the burden of being judged by the standards of English literature. The crucial breakthrough in understanding Gaelic poetry, in particular, came in an article by John MacInnes in 1978. In this extended study, MacInnes relates the historical experiences, social structures and cultural signifiers of Gaeldom to a consistent and coherent set of symbols, images, ideas and themes in vernacular Scottish Gaelic song-poetry which he calls the "panegyric code."[34] The employment of this analytical framework has enabled Gaelic literature to be analyzed and evaluated on its own terms, rather than being constrained by the norms that govern anglophone literary criticism.

> MacInnes's work represents not an act of discovery but of recovery—although it had never previously been laid out in writing, the principles and topoi of the panegyric code were well known to poets, patrons and céilidh-house audiences of the past, and indeed this familiarity allowed traditional verse to be highly allusive and succinct in expression. The corollary is that with the decline of the tradition, rhetorical sophistication ceased to be an advantage and ultimately came ... to be seen as a drawback.[35]

Due in particular to the social capacities of the Gaelic literati and the system of patronage that sustained them, the rhetoric developed for and embodied in the practice of poetry can be understood as primarily intended to express praise or dispraise. The convergence of thematic, aesthetic, cultural and political concerns aided in consolidating literary expression across class, gender and geographic divisions. That is to say, the Gaelic professional poets and their patrons, who were also often practitioners of literary pursuits, created an art form and set of common literary resources that was shared by all Gaels, even if they were inflected through various local lenses and social strata.

> Different social levels had, of course, different types of poets and audiences, and therefore we have different types of poetry. Yet all the various categories were linked to each other by what John

MacInnes, writing in the seventies, defined as the "panegyric code," the set of conventions which can be found throughout Gaelic literature in all its genres and social categories. It is probably the fundamentally oral character of the transmission of poetry that provides the reason for this all-encompassing literary conformity, and this conformity, or consistency, must be seen as aiming to preserve social order and cohesion. And this is no surprise, for whether in the complex metrics of the professional *file* or in the accentual verse of the nurse to the household children, and even in the yet humbler waulking song, we find echoes of the principles for the government of society established in the ancient Gaelic laws.[36]

The message of validation (when praise was due) or censure (when criticism was necessary) in Gaelic poems is formulated in a dense, interlocking weave of metonyms, metaphors, similes, kennings, analogies and literary allusions, usually directed toward a noble subject who is depicted as central to the survival of his or her community. Poets were able to draw upon and effectively deploy a mammoth pool of symbolic resources by drawing from the large repertoire of literature with which Gaels were familiar:

> Specific virtues and characteristics are emphasised: nobility, wisdom, strength, generosity, beauty, and so on. Distinct tropes, figures and metaphorical associations and rhetorical figures are used again and again, almost as if reshuffled from poem to poem. ... Classifications, hierarchies and dichotomies permeate the system: a chief's eyes, mouth or hand might be praised, never his nose or ears, he might be likened to an eagle or salmon, never to a sparrow or pike, to an apple-tree or an oak, never to an alder or elm.[37]

Decoding the message of a song-poem may entail unravelling references to mytho-historical characters that feature in the folk tales, clan sagas, and other forms of oral narrative that have survived in Gaelic communities virtually to the present day. Canadian Gaelic song-poetry features such characters as the medieval poet Maol Ciarain[38] (see text 2.1) and the members of the legendary warrior band the Fian (see texts 3.6, 4.7, 7.1, 8.2, 8.9, 9.1 and 9.5). Probably the most prominent character of the Fian in Canadian Gaelic verse is the poet Oisean, transformed by James Macpherson into "Ossian" (see texts 2.1,

8.2, 9.1, 9.3 and 9.5). With the increasing penetration of the Protestant Evangelical movement in the Highlands in the latter part of the 18th century, Biblical characters and scriptural allusions assumed a greater prominence in Gaelic literary production, especially in the poetry of Presbyterians.

Gaelic literary techniques and styles reflect a social environment and cultural worldview that is difficult for modern anglophones to appreciate without adjusting their assumptions and expectations. Recent analysis of 17th-century Gaelic poetry, for example, reveals the degree to which it relies not upon metaphors but metonymies and the reasons for these preferences:

> Metonymy is arguably the literary equivalent of a closely-knit social structure where individuality, as opposed to connectedness, is not overly promoted and where the poet's role is to remain more or less within the status quo, rehearsing in persuasive and polished ways versions of the familiar. ... What is distinctive in the Gaelic tradition is the extent to which it prefers to express praise in a manner which is metonymic both in its subject matter (connections with others through warfare, generosity, bloodline or sexual attractiveness) and in its technique, which is primarily the use of synecdoche.[39]

The metre, air and chorus chosen by a poet are further considerations for the interpretation of Gaelic song-poems. Particular metres came to be associated with specific topics and functions and some are better suited for certain kinds of phrasing and modes of expression than others. Poets seldom concocted their own melodies or choruses from scratch but chose from a wide selection of models circulating in oral tradition. Knowing the original song-poem used as the foundation of a new one can add to the message of the poet by either augmentation or contrast.

John MacInnes's study of the panegyric code demonstrates that Gaels reacted defensively to centuries of conflict with an expansionist anglophone hegemony—both England and Lowland Scotland—bent on dominating and assimilating them. This experience encouraged the kin-groups of the Highlands and Western Isles to build and maintain networks among themselves, and, until the 17th century, with Irish Gaels, to defend their language and culture against such threats.

These social strategies for survival are reflected in the function and conventions of Gaelic literature.

> Gaelic panegyric is not merely the direct celebration of great men in life and death, although it is of course that. It is also a system which reflects the entire Gaelic experience in Scotland and the siege mentality which that experience created as the Gaelic nation strove to maintain an identity. The historical realities of this precarious situation ensured that an artist was honoured in proportion as he celebrated those qualities and those values that were necessary for the survival of the nation. That is the reason why the warrior's role is the apex of the panegyric code. We can see how the system works with centripetal compulsion, ever bringing us back to this central symbol: the warrior who is protector and rewarder.[40]

A close reading of the Gaelic texts composed by immigrants in Canada reveals that this siege mentality was not left behind in Scotland: indeed, many Gaels continued to seek out each other for support and assistance in Canada in order to maintain their identity against a hostile anglophone world which they saw as being responsible for their eviction from their homeland in the first place. The precarious and vulnerable situation in which they found themselves triggered a sort of existential crisis that drove some Gaelic poets and intelligentsia to create some explanatory narrative about their catastrophic experiences and to seek out what solace they could from the past. It drove many others into abandoning their language and culture in order to escape stigmatization and to secure the privileges available to anglophones professing allegiance to the British Empire.

Poets caught up in the experience of exile, migration and resettlement essentially produced two varieties of literature: a strain attempting to explain what happened in the past and why, and a strain that celebrated the contemporary life of the community by employing traditional themes and conventions, especially the praise of people and things that resonated with Gaelic sensibilities.

> Gaelic poetry was used by the poets of the emigrant generation in much the same fashion as it had traditionally been used in the Old World—to define and reinforce the values of their society, particularly at times of crisis—and for the poets of the emigrant generation, there was no greater crisis than that brought on by

the departure from the Old World and the challenge of rebuilding Gaelic communities in the New. ... The emigrant poetry, then, is a poetry of community building.[41]

Gaelic immigrant poets could draw on a literary genre of exile at least as old as the 10th century,[42] but the mood of calamity and urgency had probably never been more severe. In compositions trying to make sense of the challenges that Gaeldom faced after Culloden, culminating in Clearance and emigration, poets often draw a clear binary opposition between the old Highland order and the new one being imposed by the anglophone world. These dualities were sometimes extended into personal life by contrasting youth (in the idealized birth community) with old age (in a non-Gaelic environment), "traditional" Highland virtues with "unnatural" non-Gaelic corruptions, and revered Gaelic symbols with unwanted foreign imports.[43] These polarities depict a world turned upside down. It was particularly after Gaelic communities re-established themselves securely in Canada that poets could return to the traditional forms and functions of the literature.

The role of the poet was not just to produce a verbal record of what had transpired in reality in the past, (s)he was also expected to persuade listeners to take one side or another of an argument and to influence actions in the future. One anecdote about the song "A' Choille Ghruamach" (The Gloomy Forest), in which Iain MacGill-Eain laments the difficulties he encountered when attempting to colonize new land in Nova Scotia, relates its ability to discourage potential emigrants from leaving the Highlands:

> Tha e air innse gun deach an t-òran seo a sheinn aig banais ann an Tobar Mhoire, beagan an déidh do'n bhàrd a dhèanamh 's a chur a-nunn gu 'chàirdean. Cha chualas am Muile e gu sin, agus mar chaidh am fear-seinn air adhart, dhrùidh an dàn air an luchd-éisteachd air dhòigh 's nach robh sùil thioram 's a' chuideachd nuair bha e ullamh. Chan eil teagamh nach do chuir "Òran na Coille Gruamaich," mar a theirte ris, tilleadh air iomadh teaghlach bho thighinn air imrich do'n dùthaich seo. Is òran e is dearbh fhiach a chumail air chuimhne.[44]

> It is said that this song was sung at a wedding in Tobermory, a little after the poet had composed it and sent it over to his friends.

It had not been heard in Mull until then, and as the singer went on, the poem made such an impression on the audience that there was not a dry eye in the company when he was finished. There is no doubt that "The Song of the Gloomy Forest," as it was called, caused many families to reverse their decision to migrate to this country. It is a song that is truly worthy of keeping in memory.

Gaelic texts open windows into the internal life of their composers and the wider community, but they pose their own challenges: handling them rigorously requires fluency in the Gaelic language, knowledge of the conventions of the Gaelic literary tradition and its specific genres, familiarity with the larger corpus so as to recognize intertextual allusions, sensitivity to variations, omissions, and elaborations of the standard conventions, and an awareness of how the local context and agenda of the author has conditioned the text. A poet may indulge in understatement, exaggeration or even falsehood in order to earn the sympathy of the audience or sway them to a particular side of an argument, although the use of poetic license is usually transparent.

The aforementioned song-poem "A' Choille Ghruamach" again provides an ideal case study. From the very first stanza MacGill-Eain complains that exile has disoriented him so much that he has lost his command of the Gaelic language and is unable to compose a song properly, even though he manages to produce a massive text of 144 long lines. Gaelic texts contain much truth—objective and subjective—but we must always be careful to condition our analysis with the caveat that they are ultimately products of the literary imagination and not necessarily literal records of the past.

Transmission and Transcription

The academies in Ireland created for the training of the Gaelic intelligentsia came tumbling down in the early 17th century with the wholesale conquest of the native aristocracy. The extinction of the Irish nobility abolished not only the poets' sources of patronage but their social purpose. Parallel processes intended to assimilate and subsume Scottish Gaeldom into an Anglocentric imperium were less violent and abrupt, and took longer to achieve, but were just as inexorable. Composition in the classical Gaelic literary tradition came to an end in Scotland in the first half of the 18th century.[45]

Highland gentry and churchmen were instrumental in maintaining elements of the higher registers of Gaelic literature, but to a large extent the peasantry became the de facto heirs of the bulk of this enormous corpus of material. Although largely lacking the formal institutions that the native intelligentsia had used to maintain learning in the past, communities continued to meet together in each other's homes to create, reproduce, transmit and celebrate their literary inheritance in evening céilidhs during the wintertime:

> It is conventional to say that until the Society in Scotland for the Propagation of Christian Knowledge was set up in 1709 there were virtually no schools in the Highlands. Technically that is true. What is overlooked however is that the céilidh-house was an educational institution. Like the schools of the time, it operated on a seasonal basis (during the winter months, when children could be spared from domestic and agricultural labour), but in other respects it had much in common with the educational values of today. Children were not whipped or humiliated for speaking Gaelic or failing to remember their lessons. Children and adults learned together. Girls and boys learned as equals. And the quality of learning did not have to depend upon the strengths and weaknesses of an individual, for the visitor to the township—the stranger who told his "tale until dawn"—was eagerly listened to.[46]

Accounts from the 19th century about the céilidh[47] support the notion that it was not only responsible for sustaining oral tradition, such as song-poetry, it was an exercise in social cohesion and cultural solidarity.

> The young man would go away from the céilidh elevated from the knowledge he had acquired there. He knew he was not a stray atom in creation. He had listened to the tales told of his clan, and felt that the halo encircling their brows reflected a glory upon him. ... But though proverb, tradition, and story served to educate the young Highlander at this wonderful institution of the céilidh (at which dance also had no mean place), the great source of knowledge and of culture was in the poetry of the country; and if it is a sign of superior culture in the homes of rank and

fashion to be able to quote the poets, it must necessarily be so also in our lowly Highland cots.[48]

The positive reinforcement offered by the céilidh was often in sharp contrast to official schools where children could be humiliated and punished for speaking Gaelic and made to defer to the authority of the anglophone world rather than their local community and ancestral traditions.[49] Indeed, as this column from a Nova Scotia newspaper in 1937 attests, many Gaels have long considered schools to be weapons put in the hands of their long-time enemies to strike a fatal blow at their language and identity:

> Bha na Gàidheil a thàinig a-nall a Cheap Breatann glé fhileanta 's a' Ghàidhlig agus cuid mhór dhiubh, rachadh aca air a' Ghàidhlig a leughadh; gu sonraichte muinntir Eaglais Shaor na h-Alba a chleachd a bhith leughadh a' Bhìobaill 's a' seinn na[n] Sailm an Gàidhlig moch is an-moch 'nan adhradh spioradail. Ciamar a chum iad greim cho daingeann air cànain a sinnsreadh an déidh an tàir a fhuair iad bho na Goill, agus an oidheirp a thug iad gus a dubhadh ás gu buileach an déidh an cumail fo chuing fad còrr agus dà chiad bliadhna?
>
> An uair a fhuair iad uachdranachd air Alba, b'e cheud ni a rinn iad, a Ghàidhlig a chur ás na sgoiltean Gàidhealach. Maighstirean sgoile Beurla a chur a theagasg na cloinne an cànain céin nach b' aithne dhaibh a gnàths. ... Bu léir dhaibh gun robh e na b'fhasa an Gàidheal a chìosnachadh le cànain a chridhe thoirt bhuaithe na le faobhar a' chlaidheimh....[50]

The Gaels who came over to Cape Breton were very fluent in Gaelic and a great many of them were able to read Gaelic; especially the members of the Free Church of Scotland, who were used to reading the Bible and singing the Psalms in Gaelic morning and night in their worship services. How else could they keep such a firm grip on the language of their ancestors after all of the contempt that they got from the non-Gaels, and the effort that they made to wipe it out entirely after they had been subjugated by them for over two hundred years?

After they achieved dominion over Scotland, the first thing that they did was to banish the Gaelic language from the Highland schools. Anglophone school-masters were sent to teach children in a foreign language whose standards they did not know. ... They realized that it was easier to conquer the Gael by wresting the language out of his heart than by the blade of the sword....

Oral traditions could be performed and shared in contexts other than the céilidh. The bee of North American pioneer communities offered an opportunity for putting Gaelic labour songs to good use, as described in an anecdote about the early days of Glengarry, Ontario:

> Anyone who ever saw the reaping "bee" by moonlight was likely never to forget it; a singer would, sickle in hand, follow the bent forms of the racing reapers (women and men) leading the solo part of a song which they, or their forbears, had learned in the Highlands, while the workers took up the chorus with great glee and good time; for example—
>
> Mo ghille dubh, buidhe, bòidheach
> Tha mi deònach as do dhéidhsa
> O mo ghille 's tu mo laochan.
>
> Chorus:
> Mo ghille dubh cridheil gaolach,
> O mo ghille 's tu mo laochan.
>
> Although young men did not handle the needle at quilting bees, they generally put in an appearance in the evening when the girls had accomplished that feat, but at fulling bees both sexes participated and the fulling could not be properly carried on without the songs to regulate the time for the beating of the cloth with hands and feet.[51]

The communal nature of oral tradition and the nature of transmission via close personal contact encouraged people to value and memorize not just individual texts but the lineage of transmission through which they received them. The person who transcribed song-poem 2.2, for example, supplied the following details about its pedigree:

> Chaidh an t-òran seo a sgrìobhadh air pàipear bho aithris Ghilleasbaig MhicGill-Ìosa ann an Albainn Nuaidh; dh'ionnsaich esan e aig bràthair athar, Iain MacGill-Ìosa, a dh'fhalbh á Uibhist a Tuath; dh'ionnsaich Iain an t-òran aig

seann cheistear a fhuair e, a-réir aithris, aig a' bhàrd ainmeil Iain MacCodruim.

This song was written down on paper from the recitation of Archibald Gillies in Nova Scotia; he learned it from his father's brother, John Gillies, who emigrated from North Uist; John learned the song from an old catechist who received it, according to report, from the famous poet John MacCodrum.

The oral nature of the sources of communal memory made it very vulnerable to loss. Gaelic scholars of the 19th century were keenly aware of the hemorrhage of oral traditions and lore incurred by the large-scale loss of population in the Highlands. The pioneering folklorist Iain Òg Ìle (John Francis Campbell) stated in the year 1860, for example:

> I have inquired, and find that several Islanders, who used to tell the stories in Gaelic, are now settled in Australia and Canada. … There are hundreds in those distant lands whose language is still Gaelic, and to whom these stories are familiar, and if this book should ever remind any of them of the old country, I shall not have worked in vain in the land which they call Tìr nam Beann, nan Gleann 's nan Gaisgeach.[52]

Highlanders who had been dispersed across the empire formed a variety of social and communications networks that conveyed information about families, spread cultural developments, carried new songs between settled communities and fostered a sense of international Gaeldom. Books and periodicals formed a sort of mobile media, connecting literate Gaels across Canada, Scotland and elsewhere to each other for the sharing of tales, song-poetry and other forms of lore. Remarking on a mid-17th-century song contributed to a Scottish newspaper by Alasdair "the Ridge" MacDhòmhnaill in Nova Scotia, for example, Dr. Keith MacDhòmhnaill noted:

> If the whole of Oban were to turn out and walk to Glenfeochan, I very much doubt if they would find any trace of the above lament. They would be more likely to meet with the last music-hall ditty, and broken Gaelic, than the vigorous language and music of their forefathers. … We have to go to the Colonies for these long lost things.[53]

Despite the strong MacDonald biases harboured by the Ridge family, the song that they preserved in this case was composed by a Campbell woman lamenting the death of her husband, brothers, foster-siblings and son after the Battle of Inverlochy. We should not underestimate the active curiosity and pan-Gaelic sympathies of many tradition-bearers.

Probably more influential in the dissemination of Gaelic materials than printed matter were human travellers. Some of them were migrants themselves, often moving in stages from one community to another, sometimes returning to their original birthplaces after a period of time. Others had employment which required travel: sailors, soldiers, railway workers and so on. Such people were ideal conduits for oral traditions, new and old, and ensured that no immigrant community was truly isolated from the developments occurring in others.[54]

Travellers were expected to share the news and lore they carried from community to community, and they were sometimes sent with messages from one individual to another at a far remove. This is reflected in a Gaelic song composed after the Second World War by Donnchadh Ruairidh a' Chùbair of Beàrnaraigh, in the Outer Hebrides, who asked his nephew to communicate his greetings to relations in Vancouver.

> Nuair ruigeas tu Vancouver thall,
> 'S an àm, toirt dhaibh do sgeul:
> Dèan innse dhaibh gum bheil sinn slàn,
> Is na dh'fhàg thu ás do dhéidh. ...[55]

When you arrive in Vancouver over yonder, relate your news to them at that time: tell them that we, and everyone you left behind, are well ...

Carriers of oral communication were particularly important for the many Gaels who, due to the assimilationist policies of official educational institutions, did not have the opportunity to learn how to read and write in their native language. A mid-19th-century poet on the Isle of Lewis mourned not only the loss of his brother to Canadian emigration, but the inability to communicate directly with him:

> Sinn cho fada bho chéile 's tha 'n cruinn-cé 's e cho farsaing
> Sinn gun sgrìobhadh gun leughadh, och, gu sgeul a thoirt ead'rainn.

INTRODUCTION

> We are as far apart as the world is wide; we cannot write nor read to give each other news.[56]

With a full translation of the Bible into vernacular Scottish Gaelic finally complete and in print in 1807, religious schools were established and promoted in the early-19th-century Highlands that allowed for record numbers of Gaels to become literate in their native language.[57] At least some of the immigrants to Canada benefited from the education that they received in them.

> One of the first Presbyterian missionaries to travel among the Highland settlers of Cape Breton estimated in the eighteen-thirties that not more than one-fifth of the heads of families could read, although he noticed that most of those who were young enough to have attended the Gaelic schools in Scotland before they emigrated were at least literate in their own language.[58]

The forward momentum being made in favour of Gaelic in Highland schools was nullified when universal education through the medium of English became effectively mandatory in Scotland and Canada in the later part of the 19th century.[59] Despite institutional limitations, we should not underestimate the number of Gaels who acquired literacy by one means or another and their impact on the transmission and documentation of oral tradition. It is due to their efforts, after all, that so many texts were preserved and cherished, including many of those in this volume.

When examining the Gaelic literary tradition we should also be careful not to draw too great a distinction between oral and written forms of literary expression and transmission. Books and newspapers were often read aloud at céilidhs by literate members of the community, bringing new material into oral circulation. At the same time, the transcription and publication of oral literature boosted its perceived prestige and slowed down the inevitable mutations and variations brought about by oral transmission:

> No corner of the Gaelic world was immune to the influence of print, which soon began to displace the oral medium in the very centre of Gaelic cultural life itself—the traditional céilidh-house. ... Once the concept of the book had been internalised, Gaelic printed texts after 1800 became a vital means of stabilis-

ing the Gaelic language and its culture in an age of considerable change.[60]

The injection of texts read aloud from newspapers into the aural medium of the céilidh is described in an account from Sagart Àrasaig (Raonall MacGilleBhràth, 1835-1892) of Nova Scotia, who describes how a Gaelic newspaper was used to enhance the evenings:

> The *Cuairtear* was read with great delight and avidity by the Gaelic-speaking people of this county. The writer being then five years of age, remembers still the pleasure and delight the advent of the *Cuairtear*, month after month, brought to the family. When the *Cuairtear* arrived in the evening, the neighbours gathered in, the candles were lit, and the old man began to read out its contents from the first to the last page, while the audience listened to its tales, songs and stories with the most intense interest and pleasure.[61]

I have done my best to discover the identity of the authors of these texts and, when analyzing them, sometimes allude to the voice of the author. Sources that have been in oral circulation, or that are oral compositions modelled on previous texts, create complexities for speaking definitely about "authorship" (see in particular texts 2.2, 4.2 and 4.3). This should actually be seen as an asset when looking at the cultural importance of these materials. The poet was expected to voice concerns, encapsulate experiences and values, and advocate positions exactly because they were in the interest of his or her community. Songs continued to circulate in oral tradition because performers and audiences continued to value them, but they could mutate and accumulate contemporary resonances in the process of transmission. Such texts, then, are an important record of the ideals that met with the approval of at least a significant segment of the wider community.[62]

About this Volume

I used several criteria in choosing the sources in this volume: breadth of topics, geographical coverage, literary merit and intertextual allusions. In other words, I have tried to represent a wide diversity of subjects and viewpoints that have been expressed by Gaelic spokespeople in as many different locations as possible across Canada, giving extra weight to literary merit, texts that are enmeshed in dialogues with

INTRODUCTION

other Gaelic literary expressions, and unique historical testimony. The texts herein stop in the period between the World Wars, at which time most immigrant communities experienced a terminal decline in the number of Gaelic speakers and literary activity essentially ceased everywhere except for Nova Scotia.

This volume exposes just the tip of the proverbial iceberg and I hope that it will inspire others to follow the trails I have discovered and pursue even further other texts which I have not been able to include. This can only help to improve our understanding of the history and development of Gaelic immigrant culture in Canada. Others will no doubt build upon my efforts by improving my translations, augmenting information about the authors and contexts of the original texts, and offering new insights into these sources as literary and cultural expressions.

It is only very recently that Gaelic song-poems have been given titles as a regular practice, and these were usually assigned for convenience by editors rather than authors. I have honoured any assignments designated by authors in this volume and acknowledged them in context. I have indicated with quotation marks the titles for sections that are comprised of extracts from the original text. Whenever I have used an English translation from a source along with the original Gaelic text, the bibliographic reference is placed at the end of the English text; most translations in this volume are my own and thus the reference is placed after the Gaelic text, which always precedes the English.

Rendering both sound and sense from a Gaelic source into an English translation in a complete and consistent manner is an all but impossible task. There are, for example, many Gaelic words in these texts that convey the general sense of the English adjective "beautiful" but with a greater range of associations and intensities than is available in English and, interestingly, hardly any are gender-specific in Gaelic. The people addressed and described in the song-poems in the volume are often referred to with terms and names that liken them to animals, plants, parts of trees and legendary heroes. The lexicon of Gaelic poetry is full of deep and rich resonances from oral tradition, medieval literature, the natural environment and spiritual practice that have no clear contemporary equivalent in modern English.

I have made silent emendations to the original text only when these are merely a matter of updating the orthography or correcting mistakes to the spelling of a word whose meaning is reasonably certain. Some of the sources used for the texts were illegible or damaged, leaving parts missing or hard to read. I have marked with <angle brackets> any letters or words that could not be read in an original Gaelic source, forcing me to reconstruct or speculate on the text. If, on the other hand, a source could be clearly read but it contained non-trivial mistakes that I have corrected, I have marked those emendations with [square brackets]. I have sometimes supplied the original text in an endnote. I have also marked with [square brackets] any words in the English translation that I have inserted to extend or elaborate on the original author's meaning.

A radical interpretation of the Gaelic Orthographic Conventions (GOC) has become the de facto standard for writing Gaelic in Scotland since the 1990s. It is a significant break from aspects of the written forms of Gaelic of the past and, in some respects, favours dialectic features of the Outer Hebrides, the part of the Scottish Gàidhealtachd where Gaelic has remained strongest to the present.[63] Although I have applied most of the aspects of GOC on the historic Canadian texts in this volume, I have chosen not to impose the extreme forms of these Scottish conventions.[64] I have retained a somewhat more conservative orthographical standard that is closer to the original texts and is a better representation of the dialects of Gaelic that remain strongest in Nova Scotia.

It has sometimes been necessary to make minor changes to the English text to render it more natural to anglophone habits of expression. Gaelic texts can make sudden shifts in pronouns or persons addressed, or allude opaquely to people or things mentioned or implied previously. The definite article may be present or absent in Gaelic in cases that contrast with English. I have sometimes changed the order of words or clauses (dictated by considerations of metre and rhyme in the original texts) to make the translation easier to parse. I have not, for the most part, carried the vocables (syllables of non-semantic content) into the English translations, and I have italicized them in those cases where they are present.

I have arranged the texts in this volume into chapters according to theme; the items within each chapter have been placed in chronological order (according to time of composition) insofar as surviving evidence allows them to be dated. Each chapter begins with an introductory section which provides an historical overview and interpretative framework for the materials included within that theme. Each section in the chapter thereafter consists of an individual song-poem or prose account prefaced by as much contextual information as I could locate and as many interpretative notes on the text as seems appropriate. These sections are referred to in the text of the volume with numbers such as 3.2, which indicates section two of chapter three.

Giving Gaelic authors the opportunity to speak for themselves in their native language through their own voices has also encouraged me to maintain their real names wherever possible rather than to use the translated forms of their names by which they were known to the anglophone world. I have retained the personal names, clan names and place names in their proper original Gaelic forms except when translating texts. The biographical section at the end of the book provides the various forms of the names of the authors of the texts in this volume, in English translation as well as in original Gaelic form.

2 – The Subjugation of Gaeldom

Successive kings and central governments of Edinburgh and London made formal efforts to control and assimilate the Scottish Highlands from the beginning of the 17th century, particularly by passing legislation that required the obedience of the native nobility and their integration into the educational, social, political and economic systems of the anglophone world.[1] This did not necessarily have an immediate and adverse effect on the lives of the common people of the Highlands: To the contrary, the 17th century can be seen in many respects as an era of renewed vigour and vitality for Scottish Gaeldom in general.

> The conventional approach of writers and historians to seventeenth-century Scotland has for too long led with the sorry story of civil and religious wars, interruptions to trade and commerce, economic stagnation and famines and epidemics. In the same context, intellectual or artistic endeavours (including, say, music) are ignored before the "sunburst" of the Enlightenment. We might usefully compare the Highlands and Gaelic society in the post-Reformation and post-Union of the Crowns period—a period when Scottish Gaelic society was undoubtedly at its most confident, successful and assertive and the Highlands, arguably, the most decisive factor in seventeenth- and eighteenth-century British history. Gaelic culture and society has tended to be omitted from the discourse, apart from the briefest of aperçu when the Highlander rudely invades the stage of British politics, and too often viewed retrospectively through the defining lenses of economic determinism, "Clearance" and Romanticism.[2]

Regardless of the verve and resilience Scottish Gaeldom enjoyed, the Anglocentric hegemony was fast closing in, particularly in the aftermath of the conquest of Gaelic Ireland. By the early decades of the 18th century some Highland leaders were anticipating the restructuring of their estates and tenantry so as to expend less on the maintenance of their dependents and to accrue greater financial profit for themselves. The soft target for their stratagems was the Gaelic middle class, the fir-bhaile (tacksmen), who were usually sons of chieftains who had not inherited the mantle of clan leadership or cadet branches descended from such sons. The tacksmen—essentially minor gentry—had long been entrusted with managing the interests of the clan on dispersed small holdings that could potentially cover a great deal of territory and contain significant populations but their interests often conflicted with those of the chieftains.[3] They were aware that they were an increasingly vulnerable group but since they had the administrative skills needed to negotiate the terms of passage and settlement in North American colonies, they had an incentive to escape preemptively. The first community emigrations were led by tacksmen to the provinces of New York and North Carolina in the 1730s.[4]

Gaelic sources remind us time and again, however, that the real watershed moment in Highland history was the Battle of Culloden on April 16, 1746. In the aftermath of that event, the government made a concerted and systematic effort to intrude into the lives of all Highlanders and impose its norms upon them, breaking the social bonds between the ranks of Gaelic society and the cultural values and practices that had kept it distinct from anglophone Britain. So bad was the punishment meted out to some areas by vengeful government troops that Gaelic tradition designates 1746 as "Bliadhna nan Creach" (the Year of Plunderings).

Those Highland leaders who were left after the post-Culloden shakeup were quick to adapt to and comply with the anglophone establishment to survive in the new order. Many of them had already been enmeshed in British political and social life for generations, and had accrued financial debts that took increasing precedent over their traditional commitments to Highland bonds of kinship and collective stewardship. Profit and individual self-advancement were now the overriding concerns of those in charge of estates and tenants, and such landlords retained the unchecked power of feudal lords over the peasantry. The Highland population did not have recourse to legal, political or parliamentary mechanisms—including the right to vote—that could ensure their own interests and concerns were taken into account in this era of rapid change. They were, instead, left exposed to the ill-will of the wider anglophone world and the neglect and exploitation of their landlords.

Highland society was quickly unravelling and tacksmen led others also desperate for an alternative to certain poverty. Although the early waves of emigration are often described by modern commentators as "voluntary," it is clear that Gaels felt that duress and intolerable conditions of oppression led to this so-called choice. While touring North America in 1791, Patrick Campbell relates the complaints of many compatriots who were driven to leave the Highlands not because they were unable to sustain themselves there but from top-down economic and political pressures that made it impossible for them to do so:

> Every inhabitant has innumberable resources of wealth furnished by nature at his door, were they permitted to make the proper use of them. But being deprived of that by the impolitic salt laws, and other oppressions, must drive them to despair, and ultimately tend to make them seek an asylum in the wilds of America.[5]

By the 1770s, if not earlier, landlords began to forcibly evict tenants from their homes. Top-down restructuring of estates expanded in scale and scope in the 1780s, causing widespread dispossession and disquiet.[6] By the early 19th century, as the old caste of landlords fell into bankruptcy or were physically absent due to their military missions and profiteering enterprises, the running of estates came into the hands of lawyers and accountants in the Lowlands who felt little empathy for Highlanders, whom they believed to be a subordinate race to be disposed of accordingly.

> In common with 19th century projects for the oppression of indigenous peoples it is likely that accountants were insulated from feelings of remorse by adhering to prevailing assumptions about the inferiority of Highlanders and Gaelic civilisation, and the superiority of their own ideologies. ... Accountants were therefore, not simply applying their craft in a neutral, value free manner. While their decision-making was founded on the cold logic of maximising estate revenue and rendering property more saleable, it was also conditioned by prevailing ideologies about the

progress of the capitalist economy, "improvement" and social morality. In exercising their professional judgement in ways which dispossessed the impoverished crofters and cottars of the Highlands and Islands, senior Edinburgh accountants advanced the commercialisation of the landed estate and entrenched landlordism. Accountants were effectively agents in the acculturation of Scottish Gaels. Their activities were in accord with the contemporary "Establishment" who "treated the Highlands like colonies to be exploited."[7]

Gaels were dispossessed not only of the land on which they lived but of the resources and access to resources that made life possible. Some of the most economically vulnerable and lowest ranking social orders in the old Highland order were goat-herders. Stray verses from the island of Jura depict the distress of people whose goats were taken from them as they were divested of their lands and livelihoods:

'S fheudar dhomh bhith beò:
Chaidh na gobhair dhìom,
Ciamar gheibh mi 'n smuairean
Seo chumail dhìom?
'S fheudar dhomh bhith beò:
Chaidh na gobhair dhìom. ...

'S ann an uamh MhicMhàrtainn
Thog iad creach an tàilleir ...

'S ann an Lag nan Capall
Fhuair iad grunnan Eachainn ...[8]

I must survive: the goats are gone from me; how can I keep away from this sorrow? I must survive: the goats are gone from me.

It was in MacMartin's cave that they looted the tailor['s goats]...
It was in Lag nan Capall that they took a few of Hector's [goats]...

The Highlands were described by fieldworkers investigating social conditions at the beginning of the 19th century as "an entire region seething with discontent."[9] If we are to understand the historical context for the Highland Clearances properly, we must comprehend the anglophone world's sense of moral and cultural superiority over Gaeldom and its belief that Anglo-Saxons were the master race destined to rule over the inferior races, including those labelled "Celtic."

Gaelic communities were powerless to negotiate the terms in which supposed "improvement" was dictated to them. The Clearances on the Sutherland estates offer one of many illustrative examples. Patrick Sellar, the factor on the estates, stated in defense of himself and his landlord employers:

> I presume to say that the proprietors humanely reordered this arrangement, because it surely was a most benevolent action to put their barbarous hordes into a position where they could better associate together, apply to industry, educate their children, and advance in civilization.[10]

In the past, the close interdependence between the Gaelic aristocracy and the lower social classes in the Highlands had been a source not only of economic sustenance but of social capital and psychological reassurance. Being abandoned by their former leaders as well as exposed to and dominated by their former rivals—anglophones, including Scottish Lowlanders—left Highlanders feeling humiliated, angry, ashamed and profoundly disoriented. This is a common theme in the songs in this volume and one that helps to explain other subtle cultural developments that follow from this experience of subjugation in Gaelic life. An 1803 report about the rage for emigration in the Highlands concurs with this view, noting that "rash plans of Improvement" had the effect of "disgusting and alienating the People" who saw few alternatives but seeking refuge in a distant colony:

> [T]he Highlanders were accustomed to be caressed and cherished by their Lairds, and used to look up to them for protection and comfort, in all their distresses; the Lairds had an absolute command over them, not coercive but paternal; the people would never offend their Chiefs or Chieftains; they prided themselves in being taken notice of by them, they gloried in the great qualities of their superiors, and themselves possessed an innate spirit incapable of mean and inglorious actions.[11]

Some Gaels consciously or unconsciously blotted these debasing episodes of eviction and the associated shame from communal memory, even if they were left with emotional scars and cultural traumas that were difficult to resolve. Some made an effort, especially through oral tradition, to create a heroic emigration narrative that could turn the experience of defeat and dispossession into a triumph of self-determination and success. Many others, however, were left with an inferiority complex that not only encouraged them to seek the external validation of the anglophone world but to ultimately assimilate to its norms as thoroughly as possible in order to gain its status and privileges.

Those who left early could hardly recognize the Highlands after its transformation under the self-appointed "improvers." Such is the import of an anecdote featuring Bishop Alasdair Mór MacDhòmhnaill (Alexander Macdonell), who was a leading figure in the Gaelic community of Glengarry, Ontario.

> Air fear dhe na tursan a bha e 's an Roinn Eòrpa an déidh dha faighinn a bhith 'na Easbaig, thadhail e an Albainn a choimhead air a chàirdean 's air an dùthaich. An déidh dha tilleadh dhachaigh an-seo [gu Gleann Garadh, Ontario], thubhairt e air latha Dòmhnaich ann an Eaglais Naomh Raphaels, gum biodh e glé thoilichte an ath Dhi-Dòmhnaich naidheachd a thoirt dha'n t-seann shluagh air an t-Seann Dùthaich, nam biodh iad cho math is gun tigeadh iad do'n Eaglais.
>
> Cha mhór sean na òg a bha 's an dùthaich nach do chruinnich, is an déidh dha'n t-seirbheis a bhith seachad, thòisich an t-Easbaig air innseadh dhaibh mar a chaidh an dùthaich air h-ais, 's an t-atharrachadh mór a thàinig oirre bho'n dh'fhàg iad i, nach robh taigh no fàrdach no leithid siud 's no leithid seo de ghleann as nach do dh'fhalbh iad air fad nan dùthchanan, is an àit' an t-sluaigh a bh' ann, gum bheil e fo chaoraich 's fo riaghladh Ghall.
>
> Nuair a sguir an t-Easbaig, dh'éirich sean duine 'na sheasamh air a bhata an teis-meadhan na h-Eaglaise, is thubhairt e, "A Rìgh! Cobhair mise, an e an fhìrinn a th'agad, Alasdair?"
>
> "'S i, Iain."[12]

On one of the trips that he took on the continent of Europe after he had been installed as Bishop, he visited Scotland to check up on his relations and on the country. After he returned home [to Glengarry, Ontario], he said on a Sunday in the church of St. Raphael that he would be very glad to give news about the Old Country to the older population on the next Sunday, if they would be so good as to come to church.

There was hardly anyone in the area, young or old, who didn't assemble, and after the service was over, the Bishop began to tell them how the country had deteriorated, and about the immense changes that had come upon it since they had left it, that they had visited practically every house and habitation in this glen and that glen throughout the region, and that instead of the people who had once been there, the territory was now populated by sheep and under the rule of the Lowlanders [or non-Gaels].

When the Bishop concluded, an old man stood up on his cane in the middle of the church and he said, "O God, help me! Are you telling the truth, Alexander?"

"I am, Iain."

Although the Clearances have attracted a great amount of controversy and commentary, the voices of Gaels who experienced these events and expressed their horror and frustration have been given inadequate space or consideration in the pages of many histories. This was particularly true before the 1990s, when a significant corpus of materials was made available to a wider, non-Gaelic speaking public. One of the most industrious Gaelic authorities, Donald Meek, has drawn attention to the resistance of mainstream scholars to integrate Gaelic sources about these events.

> Yet, in spite of the potential value of this body of verse in illuminating the perceptions of those who experienced the nineteenth-century Clearances and the Land Agitation, it has been little used by modern historians. There seems to be some reluctance on the part of certain historians to allow the Gaelic evidence to speak for itself, even when part of that evidence is available in translation.[13]

Michael Kennedy's study of Highland emigration to the Canadian Maritimes contains an even stronger condemnation of scholars whose reliance upon anglophone sources inevitably biases their interpretations against their subjects.

> By ignoring virtually the entire body of historical commentary supplied by Gaels, the wealth of evidence is supplied, by default, by English observers. Even were it not for the long history of conflict and prejudice between these two groups, such an externally derived framework makes the remaining evidence selected for

examination extremely volatile and as vulnerable to becoming a mere reflection of the common preconceptions of the past observer and the latter-day analyst as it is likely to be a source of clear, unequivocal data. ... Even with much accessible evidence demonstrating that the Gaelic community could act rationally, positively and consistently, historians have had great difficulty in fully realizing the scope and meaning of such proof and incorporating it into their analyses, since it so dramatically contradicts the English concept of the Gaelic world.[14]

David Craig spent decades collecting the accounts of Highlanders dispossessed during the Clearances, not just from the written sources of the 18th and 19th centuries but from the descendants of survivors who have kept memories of those unreconciled atrocities alive in their families. He notes the grip of these stories through the generations and the uneasiness that they cause to modern British historians.

In Skye and Tiree and Yell, in Ardnamurchan and Sutherland and Harris and Mull, I have again and again been brought close to the evictions, and the later fight-backs against them, as I have listened to crofters and teachers and retired people as they recalled their forebears' experiences, often in words passed down through anything from one to six generations. ... This sort of discomfiture at heartfelt speech seems to spring from the habits of managerial and academic persons. They incline to the official and the dispassionate because they are used to the orderly and comfortable and they benefit from it in their own lives.[15]

If Gaelic perspectives were taken seriously, they might highlight the injustices perpetrated in the past that have created one of the most concentrated and unjust landholding patterns in the world, one in which native Highlanders are still disenfranchised. They might suggest that reparations are in order. As Dòmhnall Iain Dòmhnallach has recently argued, the Highland Land Agitation of the 1880s deserves to be celebrated and its agenda pressed forward in the present:

A century and a half ago, the people of Gaelic Scotland were forced from their homes, 2000 people a day at the Clearances' height, and sent overseas or settled in reservation-style crofting communities on the poorest land. But because of this the Highlands and Islands can claim a proud history of direct action against landlordism. I hope I've shown that the Gaelic crofters were radicals on par with the Chartists, and the Trade Unionists, and Suffragettes. But with inequitable patterns of landownership persisting and conservationist ideologies striving to keep the Highlands an economically-dependent backwater, the work of radical land reform remains unfinished.[16]

Many historians of the Clearances simply treat these events as the inevitable calculus of economics and the irrepressible march of modernity. The resistance of some scholars to take these Gaelic perspectives seriously could be interpreted as an attempt to maintain the authority of an Anglocentric master narrative that asserts that the British Empire was an unstoppable force for civilization, progress, and enlightenment. If such conceits no longer hold water in other colonial outposts where the treatment of native peoples and cultures is concerned, why should they in the Highlands?

All but the last song-poem in this chapter were composed in Scotland about these events by people who witnessed them. All but text 2.3 are known to have been brought by emigrants to Canada and passed on to their descendants to explain and commemorate their exile experience.

1: A Song in the Wake of Culloden

This song-poem was composed by Iain mac Theàrlaich Òig MacGill-Eain of Inbhir Sgathadail (Inverscadale) in Ardgour and brought to Nova Scotia by Ailean "Ridge" MacDòmhnaill, who left Lochaber in 1816.[17] It was sung by at least three successive generations (spanning over a century) of this Canadian family: John L. Campbell recorded it from Aonghus "the Ridge" in 1937 and Pàdraig J. MacNeacail recorded it from him in 1950.[18] This surely suggests that it said something worth remembering about the Gaelic experience.

The legislation referred to on line 2 is the *Act of Proscription* enacted in 1747 to demilitarize the Highlands by making it illegal for a civilian male to wear the kilt and own weaponry, regardless of which side, if any, he had taken in the Jacobite Risings. Gaelic poets from Hanoverian areas express the resentment that all Highlanders were placed under the same punitive and demeaning measures. Plaids and weapons were utilitarian goods as well as symbols traditionally associated with masculinity, so the legislation was also a strong statement about the Crown's claim over Gaeldom's cultural assets and its right to appropriate them for its own military aims. This song echoes many other Gaelic sources that appraise the defeat of the Jacobite Rising of 1745 as a turning point in the history of the Highlands.

Like many other post-Culloden poets, MacGill-Eain emphasizes the disparities between the old order and the new by drawing sharp contrasts between traditional Highland clothing (lines 3-5) and Lowland clothing (lines 7-8); the beauty of the forests, streams and mountains (lines 12-15, 20, 22-4, 36, 45 and 68-9) and the filth of farms and cities (lines 9, 55 and 71-2); heroic weaponry (lines 3, 12, 47 and 49-51) and the tools of hard labour (lines 48 and 55); and noble Highland customs (such as music and hunting in lines 18, 15-40, 46 and 70) and the drudgery of agriculture and urban industry (lines 9, 53-57 and 70-71).

Iain's despair is not only born of his personal economic decline, but of his identity as a Gael and his consciousness of the subservient status of the group to which he belongs. The Lowlanders, whom the Highlanders had long held in contempt as a torpid and unimaginative people debased by menial toil[19] (lines 61-62), have now won the upper hand over the Gaels in their own homeland and lord over them (lines 63-64). This imposition of alien values denies and undermines Gaelic cultural fundamentals (lines 1-2 and 53-54). Iain compares this experience to death (lines 41-44) and contrasts it with the freedom and vigour he enjoyed in youth, likening himself to Gaelic literary characters who have witnessed traumas and survived to describe them (lines 41-42).

Iain's song idealizes Highland life by asserting an essential connection between Gaelic culture and the natural environment in which Gaels lived, which is a common response of many subjugated peoples. This song is a lament for a language and way of life endangered by the supremacy of the anglophone world.

Original Text

    1   'S ann leam nach eil tlachdmhor
         An t-achd a rinn Deòrsa,
         Thug ar n-airm uainn, is ar n-aodach,
         Bha daonnan 'gar còmhdachadh;
    5   'N àite breacain an fhéile,

Anns bu ghleusta fir òga,
Gun ach briogais, is casag,
Agus bata 'nar dòrnaibh.

Cha b' e cadal 's an smùraich
10 'S na chuir mi ùidh an tùs m' òige,
Ach éirigh gu sunndach
Air an driùchd is breith air mór-ghath;
Bhiodh a' choill' air gach làimh dhomh,
Cur deagh àile 'am phòraibh,
15 Is mi dìreadh nan creagan,
Is tric a leag mi damh cròic ann.

Is an uair a thigeadh an Dàmhair,
Cha b' i 'chlàrsach bu cheòl domh,
Ach bùirich nan làn-damh
20 Ann an àird nam beann móra;
Bhiodh ar mìol-choin is ar gadhair,
A' cur faghaid an Conaghleann;
Bu tric agh, is damh cabrach,
Mu na h-aisridhean gorma.

25 Chluinnte cuach anns a' choille,
Bu bhinn a ghoireadh an smùdan,
A' toirt teisteanais làidir,
Mar bha nàdar 'gan stiùireadh;
Gheibhte liath-chearc 's an doire,
30 Is bu toil leam a ciùcharan,
Is an coileach mu coinneamh
Air toman a' dùrdail.

Gheibhte broc ann is taghan,
Capar-coille 's boc-earba,
35 Agus bradan glé lìonmhor,
Air na linnteanaibh garbha,
Snàmh air buinne sruth fìor-uisg',
'S e gu h-inntinneach tarra-gheal,
Is gu crom-ghobach ullamh,
40 Leum ri cuileig 's an an-moch.

Ach 's e dh'fhàg mi mar Oisean,
Is mar choltas Mhaoil Ciarain,
Dh'fhàg mo chridhe air a dhoch'neadh,
Is mo dhosan air liathadh,
45 Bhith gun ghiùbhsaich ri choiseachd,
No bhith 'm fochair na fiadhach,

>   Is gun de dh'airm chun mo choisneadh,
>   Ach corcag bheag iarainn.
>
>   Ann an àite an daga
> 50   A' chlaidheimh is na sgéithe
>   Is a' chuilbheair chaoil ghlaic
>   Chuireadh stad air mac éilde –
>   Nach cluinn mi guth aca
>   De dh'eachdraidh, no sgeulachd,
> 55   Ach cuibh'lean is *factory*,
>   Beartan is Beurla.
>
>   Gun iomradh air dualchas,
>   Air cruadal no tapadh;
>   Chuir a' Chuibheall mun cuairt di
> 60   Car tuathal agus tarsainn;
>   Sliochd nam bodachan giùgach,
>   Bha 's na dùnaibh 'gan cartadh,
>   Seòladh àrd os ar cionn-ne,
>   On a thionndaidh a' bheart oirnn.
>
> 65   Mìle marbhphaisg ort, a shaoghail,
>   Tha thu caochlaideach cealgach;
>   Bha mi uair nach do shaoil mi
>   Teachd ás eugmhais a' gharbhlaich;
>   Mis' a chleachd bhith 'n Àird Ghobhar
> 70   Am bu tric gleadhar bhoc-earba,
>   An-diugh an Sòrn odhar
>   Air todhar a' mheanbh-chruidh.[20]

Translation

(1-8) I do not at all like the act that King George has proclaimed that has taken our weapons and our clothes from us that had always covered us; instead of the tartan kilt in which young men were vigorous, we have only breeks, a cloak and a staff in our fists.

(9-16) From my earliest youth I took no interest in sleeping around muck; I preferred to arise merrily in the morning dew, grabbing a great spear; the forest would be all around me, filling me with fresh air as I climbed the crags; often did I fell the antlered deer.

(17-24) When the rutting season would come, the harp was not my music but rather the bellowing of the mature stag on the pinnacle of the great mountains; our hunting hounds and our dogs would execute the pursuit in Conaghleann; many were the hinds and the antlered stags around the green passes.

(25-32) The cuckoo would be heard in the forest, the melody would call sweetly, giving powerful testimony as nature was conducting them; a female black grouse could be had in the thicket and I enjoyed her cooing with the black cock in front of her, murmuring on a hillock.

(33-40) A badger and a pine marten could be found, a capercaillie and roebuck and plentiful salmon on the turbulent waters, swimming in a rapid stream of pure water, excited, white-bellied, with a bent mouth, at the ready, leaping for a fly in the twilight.

(41-48) But what has left me like Ossian, and like Maol Ciarain—what has left my heart damaged and my locks greyed—is the absence of the pinewoods when I walk, and not to have the company of the hunt, and having no weaponry to earn my keep except for a little iron sickle.

(49-56) Instead of the pistol, the claymore and the shield, and the slender, gripped musket that would stop the stag—I hear nothing from them about history, or oral narratives, but only factory, gears, machinery and English.

(57-64) There is no mention of heritage, of sturdiness or heroic feats; the Wheel [of Fortune] has turned counter-clockwise and crossways; the bent-back little churls who would muck out the middens [now] hover high above us, since the cards turned against us.

(65-72) A thousand curses on you, o world, you are fickle and deceitful; there was a time when I never thought that I would live outside of the craggy land, being accustomed to living in Ardgour in which there was often the clamour of the roebuck; but today I am in anemic Sorn around sheep manure.

2: The Tacksman of Griminish

Iain MacCodruim of North Uist composed the following song-poem, which has something of a complicated history. By the late 19th century it was known in the island of North Uist in Scotland by the title "Òran Fir Ghriminis" (A Song of the Tacksman of Griminis), a position held by Aonghus MacDhòmhnaill in the post-Culloden period. His heavy-handed personal style made him highly unpopular among his peers.

They subsequently decided to trick him into emigrating to North Carolina in 1766 by convincing him that a large-scale migration was underway, loading large amounts of fake baggage at the port from which the ship would be leaving. Aonghus seems to have unravelled the plot but sailed off in any case.[21] It is more likely that Iain MacCodruim composed this song between 1769 and 1773 as large numbers of the tenants of Sir Alexander MacDonald in North Uist and Skye migrated to North Carolina.[22] A letter written by Allan MacDonald of Kingsborough, husband of the renowned heroine Flora MacDonald, echoes many of the sentiments in this song about the declining state of Highland society on these estates during the time.

> The only news in this island is emigration; I believe the whole will go for America—in 1771 there shipped and arrived safe in North Carolina 500 souls. In 1772 there shipped and arrived in said place 450. This year they have already signed and preparing to go, above 800 souls and all those from Skye and North Uist. It is melancholy to see the state of this miserable place; the superior summoning the tenants to remove for not paying the great rent, etc. and the tenant the superior for oppression, for breaking the condition of his tacks, and for violent profits. The factor, tenants at law, for iniquities and wrong accounts and them out of their lands in the month of May and June without previous warning— No respect of persons, as the best are mostly gone, stealing of sheep etc. constantly, and picking and thieving of corn, garden stuffs, and potatoes perpetually, lying, backbyting and slandering—Honesty entirely fled, villainy and deceit, supported by downright poverty in its place. When this next emigration is gone, only Àird and other three old men, will lease, that will be in Slate and Trotternish of the name of MacDonald.[23]

The variant of the song printed here was transcribed from oral tradition in Nova Scotia and was known by the inauspicious title "Òran Aimearaga" (The Song of America). It consists of fifteen verses, much longer than the ten-stanza variant recorded and published in Scotland. Due to the fact that it was transmitted orally for generations before being transcribed, it is not possible to state definitively if the people who sang it in Scotland had forgotten or combined several of the stanzas, or if the people who sang it in Nova Scotia elaborated and extended the original text. The latter scenario seems most likely, but even if that is the case, it is a strong indictment of the treatment of the Gaels.

Like many other Gaelic poets, MacCodruim celebrates the prestige and successes of the Clan Donald in the Highlands and in Scotland as a whole (lines 41, 49 and 90), harkening back to their role as the stalwarts of the old Gaelic order.[24] He laments the loss of valued members of the community who were models of cultural excellence and contrasts the virtues and social obligations of the old chieftains with the upstarts who no longer steer by the same moral compass and no longer recognize the humanity of their own people. The unworthiness of these pretenders is demonstrated by the negative effects they have had on the territory and climate (lines 105-106).

As in the previous song, the Wheel of Fortune is turning itself against the Gaels (line 58); they feel shame that they are now under the thumb of their old rivals (lines 22 and 47) who restrain them from access to the privileges and activities they once enjoyed proudly (lines 81-84). The Gaels have been driven out of their land unwillingly (lines 17-19) and are now exiles. He predicts that the time will come when people will not agree about the events of which he speaks and dismiss his account as rubbish (77-80)—a prophecy which has been largely fulfilled.

Original Text

1   Moch is mi ag éirigh fo sprochd is fo éislean
      Gur bochd mo sgeula, is cha bhreug mo chainnt;
      O, sgeul tha fìor e, sgeul as cianail'
      A chualas riamh an Innse Gall;
5   Sgeul tha mór e, o, sgeul a' bhròin e
      Air bheagan sòlais, gun cheòl, gun fhonn –
      O, sgeul as cruaidhe a chuala cluas e,
      Air bheagan buannachd is gur buan a chall.

      O, is bochd an sgeula seo bhith 'gar tréigsinn
10 Na connspainn threubhach, iad fhéin is an clann –
      Na daoine maiseach, na daoine gasta,
      Na daoine tlachdmhor gun dad de mheang;
      Is iad air falbh bhuainn an dùldachd aimsir
      Ri ùpraid fairge as aingidh greann;
15 Gun fhios an d' ràinig, gun fhios nach bàs dhaibh,
      Is nach b' ann le àilgheas a chaidh iad ann.

O, sgeul as cruaidh leinn a bhith 'gur fuadach,
Ar sàr dhaoin'-uaisle, gun ghruaim, gun sgraing;
Is gun do ghabh iad fògradh, is nach b' ann le'n deòin bhuainn
20 Do'n tìr nach b' eòlach an seòrsa thall;
Is tha sinne leòinte, air cnoc 'nar n-ònrachd
'S e luchd ar fòirneirt a bhuinigeas geall;
Is gun ann ri fhaotainn de bhrod ar daoine
Ach seann daoin' aosta is an t-aog 'na mheall.

25 Na daoine fialaidh, bha cliùiteach ciatach,
Nach d' fhuaireas riamh ann am fiar, no foill;
Gu fearail feardha, gun bhleid, gun anabharr,
Gun tnù, gun fhearmad, gun chealg, gun sannt;
O! sgeul as cràdh leinn sibh bhith 'gar fàgail
30 A' dol thar sàile, air bharr nan tonn;
'S e smaointinn ànraidh ur mnathan 's ur pàistean
Is goirt a ràinig gach cridh' tha 'n com.

Na daoine fìnealt', bha socair sìobhalt',
'Gan robh pailteas rìoghail gun strì gun staing;
35 B' e mais' ur beusan bhith sgaipteach gléidhteach
Bhith tapaidh gleusta, gu cur 'na cheann;
A reic ur n-àirneis is ur n-àite-tàmhachd
A dh'fhàg ur càirdean gu tùrsach trom;
Na bheil an làthair gu falbh a-màireach
40 Gun tuilleadh dàil ach gun tig an long.

Bu bheachdail mórdhalach, neart Chloinn Dòmhnaill,
An àm nan sròldan a chur ri crann;
Cuid d' ur fasan, ceòl is caismeachd
Is gur i ur bratach bu sgairteil srann;
45 Is gur e an cruadal bha dhuibh an dualchas –
Ma leig sibh suas sinn, is ar guaillean fann;
Ach is éiginn strìochdadh do luchd ar mì-rùin
Is ar càirdean dìleas dol fad' bho làimh.

An fhine b' ainmeil' bha riamh an Alba
50 Nach d' fhuaireas cearb orr' an àm advance;
An fhine dh'fhalbh bhuainn, an fhine 'shearg sinn,
Gur goirt a dhearbh i dhuinn siud 's an rann;
'S e sgeul tha tùrsach, mu'n fhine mhùirneach,
Is an fhine chliùiteach 'n àm rùsgadh lann;
55 A sheasadh làidir air chùl nan Spàinnteach
Is nach traoight' an àrdan gun bhàs nan Gall.

An nì tha cinnteach, a-réir na h-innse,
Gun do bhuail a' Chuibhl' oirnn an tuinnse teann;
Bhon chaidh beul-sìos oirnn, gun dùil ri dìreadh,
60 Is gun laigh am mì-fhortan air ar ceann;
Is mu'n fhine phrìseil bu mhisneach rìoghail
An àm dol sìos is a bhith cruinn an camp;
Sinn nis neo-thàthail nuair thig an nàmhaid
Gur lag ar pàrty is an àireamh gann.

65 O is bochd an sgàthan bhith triall gu'r fàrdaich
Ur n-ionad-tàmhachd 'na làrach lom;
Ur taighean gasta, far am biodh am pailteas,
A bhith 'gan sgapadh, gun chlach, gun chrann;
Far am biodh a' chòisir gu mùirneach ceòlmhor
70 Na taighean móra, bu dòigheil greann;
Bhiodh còmhlan ùr-ghlan a' danns' air ùrlar
A' lìonadh bulla is gun chaomhnadh dram.

Ged is bochd ri smaointinn, dh'fhalbh brod ar daoine
Ceann-stoc ar caonnaig, is chan ioghnadh leam;
75 Bu neartmhor gaoirdean, bu sgaiteach faobhar
Mu'n caisgt' an t-adhbhar, neo-chlaon an dream;
Nuair thig an fhàistinn, bidh fear ag ràdhainn
Is fear ag àicheadh gun robh sibh ann;
Dh'fhalbh reachd Chloinn Dòmhnaill nan cath is nan
    còmhrag
80 Tha dreach mo stòiridh mar sheòrsa rabhd.

O, seach mar b' àbhaist, cha chluinnear làmhach,
Is bidh cadal sàmhach aig damh nan eang;
O, caidlidh earbag bheag nan gearra-chas
Is cha chluinn i farbhas no fuaim 's a' ghleann;
85 O ghluais Clann Dòmhnaill nan sgiath is nan ròiseal
Bhith dian 's an tòrachd, bu nòs do'n dream,
Is na dh'fhalbh a' cheud uair is na bheil gu triall bhuainn
Ri ùine bliadhna, chan fhiach sinn taing.

Ar n-armailt uaibhreach a dhearbh an cruadal
90 Rinn Alba 'bhuannachd le cruas an lann
A sheasadh làidir, b' e dreag ar nàmhaid
An cinn bhith gearrte is an cnàmhan pronn;
Ged thuit is a chnàmh sibh gu luchd a' bhàta
Gur beag am bàta, ma bhios e trom;
95 Cha seas sibh duty rìgh no crùin dhuinn,
Gur bochd is gur tùrsach a sgiùrs sibh ann.

O 's ann a tha sinn mar uain gun mhàthair
Gun tàinig cearr oirnn gu gearr an t-àm;
Gach peacach gràineil a' briseadh barr oirnn
100 Mar bha fuil Àbail air Cain dall;
Is tha cùis ri'r n-aodann cho cruaidh is a dh'fhaodas
Tha fearann daor oirnn, gun saorsa plaing;
Tha 'n t-sìde air caochladh le gaoith is le caonnaig
Is an t-uisg' air maomadh air taobh nam beann.

105 Dhubh na speuran is ghuil na reultan,
Dh'fhalbh teas na gréine is chan eil e ann;
Tha dosgaidh dhaoine is croisean saoghalt'
Am bun gach aon fhir is tha 'n taod cho teann;
Gun iochd aig uaislean, gun mheas air tuath
110 Ach a' dol mun cuairt, mar gum biodht' am fang;
'Nar daoine truagha is tha 'chùis cho cruaidh oirnn
Gun dùil ri fuasgladh an luath no mall.

An nì tha 'mhiann orm is tha 'rùn air m' inntinn
Chan fhaod mi innse dhuibh, o cheann gu ceann;
115 Gach lasgair' ùr-ghlan a chaidh do'n taobh sin
Is nach eòl dhomh chunntas có as diùbhaidh ann,
Ach is mór an dìth air a' cheann seo de'n rìoghachd
A' mheud na h-ìre seo thog sibh thall,
Is na rinn sibh triall bhuainn l'ur cliù is l'ur ciatadh –
120 Ach beannachd Dhia bhith 'gur dìon 's gach àm.[25]

Translation

(1-8) It is early as I awake, feeling dejected and struck with grief; my tale is a wretched one but my words are no lie; it is a true and most woeful tale, saddest that was ever heard in the Outer Hebrides; it is a substantial tale, a sad tale, with little joy, music or mirth; the harshest tale that an ear ever heard, with little profit and with enduring loss.

(9-16) Wretched is this tale that the mighty heroes and their children are abandoning us—the elegant people, the excellent people, the favoured and unblemished people; they are leaving us in the gloomy season for the turmoil of the ocean with most angry countenance; there will be no way of knowing if they reach their destination or if they die, and they did not leave through their own desire.

(17-24) Oh, the tale of our pre-eminent nobles—good-humoured and genial—being dispossessed is very hard on us;

they have been exiled and they did not leave us willingly for a land where their kind are not known; we are wounded, left alone on a hillock; it is our oppressors who have gained a victory; the finest of our people can no longer be found here, but only old people and death in heaps.

(25-32) The generous people who were renowned and seemly, who were never found deviant or deceptive, who were manly, brave, honest, temperate, unmalicious, trusting, forthright, generous; oh, it is a painful story for us that you are leaving us! Going across the ocean on the crests of the waves; it is the thought of the distress of your women and children that has made each heart sore upon the hearing of the tale.

(33-40) The elegant people who were gentle and civil, who had royal comfort and did not create conflict or barriers; the beauty of your virtues—generosity and frugality, accomplished and skilled, in summary; who sold your possessions and homes and who left your relations heavy-hearted and sad; those who remain are to leave tomorrow and will not linger after the vessel arrives.

(41-48) High-minded and magnificent was the power of Clan Donald when the ensigns were lifted up the mast; part of your custom was music and war-song, and your banner made a mighty fluttering; your heritage was to be hardy, although you have left us when our shoulders were weak; but we must submit to our antagonists while our faithful friends depart far away.

(49-56) The most renowned clan that was ever in Scotland who were never deficient when the troops advanced; the clan that has left us, the clan that has diminished us, it has proved that to us sorely in verse; it is a mournful tale about the beloved clan and the clan that was renowned when it came to brandishing blades, who stood strong behind the Spanish claymores and whose wrath could not be quenched until the non-Gael was killed.

(57-64) What is certain, according to report, is that the Wheel of Fortune has struck us a terrible blow; ever since ill-will overcame us, with no hope that we can ever overcome it, so that misfortune will fall on our heads and around the precious clan that was the hope of kings when it was time for combat and to gather in the camp; we are now lacking unity when the enemy comes, our party is weak and small in number.

(65-72) Oh, it is a sad sight to journey to your homesteads, for your residences are a bare ruin; your lovely homes, where there was plenty, have been strewn apart, lacking stones and joists; the

THE SUBJUGATION OF GAELDOM

great houses of fair countenance where the merry, melodious company was once found, and there would be a pure company dancing on the floor, filling up a drinking vessel that never lacked a dram.

(73-80) Although it is painful to contemplate, the cream of our people have departed, the greatest champions of our battles, and it does not surprise me; their arms were mighty and their blades were sharp, and they did not waver until the cause was won; when the prophecy is fulfilled, one man will assert and another man deny that you ever existed; the rule of Clan Donald of the wars and combats has departed and my story will seem to be just gibberish.

(81-88) Unlike in the past, gunshots are not heard and the hoofed stag will sleep soundly; oh, the little doe of the short feet will sleep and she will hear not a trace or a sound in the glen; since Clan Donald of the shields and the banners, who was intense in the chase—as was that people's custom—has moved on as well as all of those who have and will depart from us in another year's time, we will not retain any merit.

(89-96) Our proud army who proved their ruggedness, who won Scotland with the hardness of their blades, who would stand strong—you were our enemy's death omen, signifying that their heads would be cut and their bones pounded; although you have now degenerated to the point of being merely a boat's cargo; the boat will be small, even if it will be heavy; you will not defend the duty of the King or Crown for us, you were exiled sadly and pitifully.

(97-104) We are like a lamb without a mother, very quickly has injustice fallen on us, every hideous sinner is overpowering us like the blood of Abel over blind Cain; the matter before us is as difficult as possible, the land is priced beyond our reach, without any room for negotiation; the climate has deteriorated, with winds and squalls, and floods bursting across the mountain sides.

(105-112) The skies have darkened and the stars have wept, the warmth of the sun has departed and no longer exists; human misfortune and worldly afflictions are distressing every single man and the noose is exceedingly tight; the gentry have no compassion and do not respect the tenantry but simply go around them, as though they were in a sheep pen; we are wretched people and the matter is so hard on us, and there is no hope that it will be resolved slowly or quickly.

(113-120) The thing that I wish, and the agenda that is on my mind, I cannot relate to you from start to finish; with all of the youthful lads who have gone abroad, I cannot surmise who is the worse off, but it is a huge loss to this part of the kingdom given the huge number of them that have been lured away; you have taken away with you your prestige and your happiness—but may God's blessing protect you always.

3: The Lament of the North

Coinneach MacCoinnich composed this song-poem in 1783, the year that the American Revolutionary War concluded and not long after Clearances began in Inverness-shire,[26] and provided the title himself. Although there is no surviving evidence that this composition was brought to Canada, it is one of the most detailed and discerning analyses of the condition of the Highlands to have been composed in Gaelic in the 18th century. It describes the many consequences of the assimilation of the upper echelons into anglophone society and their increasing alienation from their former clansfolk.

MacCoinnich alludes to a very common literary device at the beginning of this poem: the ship of state. Rather than extolling a praiseworthy chieftain who is steering his adherents effectively, however, MacCoinnich depicts a shipwreck that has left passengers and crew floating at the mercy of the seas, many of them destined to drown. He suggests that the only escape from further destitution and thralldom available to Gaels is emigration to North America (lines 132 and 145-52). Gaels were outraged at the number of restrictions imposed on them by the tightening grip of landlords, including constraints on hunting (lines 69-72). Foxes were banned (line 67) in order to protect the sheep being moved onto the hills by the incoming sheep farmers, an observation with a similar social connotation made by the contemporary poet Donnchadh Bàn Mac an t-Saoir (Duncan Ban Macintyre).[27] The poet expresses his sympathy for the American rebels openly and condemns the misrule of King George and other aristocrats (lines 73-90).

THE SUBJUGATION OF GAELDOM

Original Text

1   Is mi 'g amharc le dìcheall
    Gum bheil mulad air m' inntinn is pràmh;
    Is mi bhith sealltainn mun cuairt domh
    Is mi faicinn na tuath air an t-snàmh;
5   Ma tha cuid diubh ni 'bhuannachd
    Tha cuid eile nach buannaich an tràigh;
    Gum bheil móran diubh 'briseadh
    Is chan ionghnadh leam idir mar thà.

    Chan ionghnadh leam idir
10 Gar an dèanadh iad piseach no stàth,
    On là dh'inntrinn an saoghal
    Cha robh 'm fearann cho daor is tha i 'n-dràst';
    Tha 'n Taobh Tuath air a leadairt
    O dh'inntrinn an greadadh seo th' ann;
15 Thug iad uath' an cuid daoine
    Is iad nas moth' ann an saothair gach là.

    Is iad nas moth' ann an saothair
    'S iad na h-uaislean a dhaoraich a' mhàil;
    Dh'fhalbh truas o na daoine
20 Is tha fuaralachd a' taomadh 'na àit';
    Cha sheas facal duin' uasail,
    Is dona 'n teist tha ri luaidh orra 'n-dràst';
    'S ann tha fìrinn is ceartas
    Na linne seo an itean nan geàdh.

25 Fìrinn is ceartas
    Chaidh iad clì o chionn fhada 's an àit';
    Tha sannt agus mì-rùn
    Cho pailt 's nach téid dìth air gu bràth;
    Dh'fhalbh gaol o gach duine
30 Is bochd a' ghaoir th' aig a' chumant gach là;
    Tha na h-uaislean 'gan spealadh,
    'S iad 'ga mhun' ann an Lunainn an àigh.

    'S iomadh fear a chaidh 'Lunainn
    Is a chaith a chuid uile gun stàth;
35 Nuair a thigeadh iad dhachaigh,
    Gun cuireadh iad sac air a' mhàg;
    Is iad cho sanntach gu tarraing
    Ri coin a bhiodh tamall gun tràth
    Is a' chuid a dh'fhuirich aig baile,
40 Tha iad cho lùbach is cho carach ri càch.

Tha iad cho lùbach is cho carach,
Is adhbhair cùraim do'n talamh an-dràst'
Gum bheil breitheanais Dhé oirnn,
Ge b'e b' urrainn a leughadh le dàn;
45 Tha mi 'faicinn is a' léirsinn
Luchd-seasamh na cléire 'dol cam,
Is iad an aghaidh a chéile
'G am bu chòir a bhith teumach le gràdh.

Chuir gràdh rinn a chùl-thaobh
50 Is tha uaislean ar dùthcha cho crost';
Iad a' caitheamh cho stròdhail
Na tha milleadh is a' leònadh nam bochd;
A' toirt uath' an cuid stòrais
Gar an cuir iad dheth móran mu seach;
55 Is air a' mheud is gun cruinnich iad fhéin deth,
Cha bhi beannachd Mhic Dhé ann am pac.

Cha bhi beannachd Mhic Dhé ann
Is cha dèan E bonn feuma le tlachd
Aig a' mheud-sa tha 'shaothair
60 'Ga thional aig daoine fo'n t-sac;
Cha toir iad an déirce
Do na bochdan, ged théid iad a-steach;
Is adhbhar mulaid ri éisteachd
Na th' agam ri leughadh d'an lochd.

65 Is olc an naidheachd da-rìreabh
Tha air uaislean na tìre seo nis;
Chuir iad bac' air an t-sionnach
Is mur feairrde sinn fhéin e, cha mhist';
Ma bhios gunn' air mo ghiùlain
70 Their iad uile gur diùlannach mis',
Is fiù is coileach nan stùc-bheann –
Chan fheud mi mo shùil a chur ris.

Chan fheud sinn bhith spòrsail:
Tha smachd aig Rìgh Deòrs' oirnn gu léir;
75 Chuir e achdachan mór' oirnn
'S e 'gam meudachadh oirnn gach ré;
Tha e fuilteach is cha dheòin leis,
Is e 'toirt dhaoine gach lò uainn gu 'fheum;
Is e 'toirt uainn ar cuid stòrais
80 Is e 'ga chaitheamh ri gòraich is bu bheud.

Is e 'ga chaitheamh ri gòraich –
Is léir a bhuil 's an Roinn Eòrpa gu léir –
Ri Aimearaga còmh-strì
Is nach fhaigh e ri bheò iad da-réir;
85 On tha ceartas is còir ac'
Tha am Freastal a' cur leò anns gach ceum
Agus chum e iad dìleas
On a' cheud là dh'inntrinn an streup.
Ach a-nis on a ghéill e
90 Is gun d' rinn iad an réite an àrd,
Mo dhòigh, nach miste sinn fhéin e,
Is gun leasaich e fhéin sinn 'nar call
Aig bochdad na dùthcha
Is iomadh neach a chuir cùl ris an àit';
95 Tha 'm peice-min air a mhionaid
Fichead sgillinn is a trì 's an taigh-gheàird.

Is iomadh neach tha mun cuairt duinn
Air a ghlacadh le cruadal 's an àm,
Agus neach tha air faontradh
100 Bha 's a' bharail nach aomadh iad ann;
Chuir a bhlianas iad suarach
Is chan urrainn iad gluasad ach mall
Is iad a' ceannach am beò-shlàint'
Is iad air acras an còmhnaidh 'na cheann.

105 Chan ioghnadh sinne bhith falamh
Is a liuthad uair bha sinn a' gearan gun fhàth
Nuair bha pailteas mun cuairt duinn
Gun robh sinn ro uaibhreach air fàs;
Chuir a' bhliadhna seo cruaidh
110 Ris gach neach nach do bhuannaich am barr,
Is chuir i sac air an guaillibh
'Chumas cudthrom mun cuairt doibh gu bràth.

Chan eil feum anns a' ghearan,
'S ann as còir dhuinn bhith toilicht' a ghnàth
115 Leis na bhuilicheas Dia oirnn
On as E am fear-riaghlaidh as àird';
'S ann as dòcha sinn dìreadh
Ged a tha sinn cho ìosal air làr;
Is ged [bha] sinn air ar bualadh
120 'S E 'cheanglas sinn suas ann an gràdh.

Ach nam falbhadh a' chabhag-s',
Ged a tha sinn cho falamh is a tha,
Nuair thig barr ás an talamh
Tha mi an dùil nach bi 'ghainne 'gar cràdh;
125 Ge cruaidh oirnn an t-Earrach
Tha na h-uaislean gun ghainne 'nan dàil;
Cha bhi cuimhn' air mu Nollaig
Tha mi an dùil gum bi 'chomaidh nas fhearr.

Ach ma dh'éireas sinn idir,
130 Is ma théid sinn air phiseach gu bràth,
Bidh sinn treun ann am misneach
Is théid na ceudan a thiotadh air sàil;
Bidh ar n-uaislean gun chùram
Is an cuid fearainn gun sùgh is e fàs;
135 Mas e fìor na thuirt mise
Gum bi biadh aig na big a nì tàmh.

Chan ionghnadh sinn bhith gun stòras
Is a liuthad nì a tha 'n tòir oirnn gach là;
Cha bhi coinneamh no còmhdhail
140 Nach bi caitheamh gu leòr air an sgàth,
Ge b' e aighear no sòlas
No mulad no bròn bhios 'nan dàil;
Gach tì chluinneas an t-òran,
Bithidh iad uile ag òl mo dheoch-slàint'.

145 Is mithich dhuinne bhith gluasad
Fhad is tha beagan mun cuairt do ar làmh;
Mun toir iad uainn e
Is mum bi 'bhochdainn an dual do ar clann;
Is olc air mhath le'r cuid uaislean
150 Gheibh sinn fhathast làmh an uachdar gun taing,
Is théid sinn a-nunn air na cuaintibh
Do dh'Aimearaga shuairce seo thall.[28]

Translation

(1-8) As I look steadfastly, my mind is troubled with sadness and dejection; as I gaze around me, I see the peasantry adrift; if some of them will gain, others will not reach shore; many of them are broken, the situation does not surprise me at all.

(9-16) It will not surprise me if they do not recover or recoup; land has never been so expensive, ever since the world began; the North has been massacred, ever since this current oppression began; [the landlords] took their people from [the lands] and each day their toil is increased.

(17-24) Their toil increases: it is the nobles who have raised the rents; people no longer feel pity, and frigidity is taking its place; a noble's word no longer stands and currently it carries an ill reputation; the truth and justice of this era are to be found in the goose's quill.

(25-32) Truth and justice, they were perverted long ago in this place; greed and ill-will are so plentiful that they will never run out; kindness has departed from everyone and the cry of the commoners is wretched every day; the nobles are mowing them down, as they learn to do in luxurious London.

(33-40) Many men went to London and spent their wealth uselessly; when they returned home, they placed a burden on the farmland; they are as greedy to extract it as a dog who has fasted for awhile; and those who stayed home, they are as wily and deceitful as the rest.

(41-48) They are wily and deceitful, and it is now a cause for the land to be concerned; God's judgement is upon us, whomever may understand it in verse; I see and comprehend the defenders of the clergy becoming crooked as they fight against each other when they ought to be lovingly diligent.

(49-56) Love has turned its back on us and the nobles of our land are so disagreeable, spending so recklessly all that ruins and injures the poor; taking their assets away from them, even if they had not put much aside; and with all of it that they have accumulated, the blessing of God's son will not be theirs.

(57-64) There will not be the blessing of God's son and He will not gladly help one bit given all of the toil that is accumulating as people's burden; the nobles will not distribute charity to the poor, even if they come inside; it is a cause of grief to hear all that I have to read about their faults.

(65-72) The current news about the nobles of this land is atrocious; they have outlawed the fox, and if we ourselves are not the better for it, we are none the worse; if I carry a gun, they will all say that I am a champion, when I cannot even aim at the moor grouse.

(73-80) We have no enjoyment, King George has dominated us completely; he has enacted overwhelming laws against us and he is constantly augmenting them; he is violent and he is not good-intentioned, as he takes people from us every day for his own purposes and takes away our wealth, and spends it foolishly, and it is wrong.

(81-88) He spends it foolishly and the effect is clear throughout Europe as he struggles with America and he will never be able to make them comply; since they are on the side of truth and justice, Fortune sides with them in every step and it has kept them faithful from the first day that the contention began.

(89-96) But now that he has yielded and they have come to a resolution, indeed, we are the worse of it and he will make it to our own loss through the poverty of the country and the many people who have turned their backs on the place; the weight-measure at this moment is twenty-three pence in the guard house.

(97-104) There are many around us who have been seized by hardship at this time, and many who have gone astray who had believed that they would not be able to grow old there; the insufficiency has left them worthless and they can only move slowly as they earn their livelihood but are always hungry nevertheless.

(105-12) It is no surprise that we are destitute since we often complained needlessly when we were surrounded by plentitude, for we had grown too arrogant; this year has given hardship to all but the upper classes and it has put a burden on their shoulders that will keep them encumbered forever.

(113-120) There is no use in complaining, contentment ought to be our habit with all that God has bestowed upon us, as He is the highest sovereign; it is most likely that we will overcome even though we have been brought down to the ground; and although we were struck, he is the one who will unite us with love.

(121-128) But if this hustle would depart, even if we are as destitute as we are, when the harvest grows from the soil, I expect that scarcity will not afflict us; although the spring is hard on us, the nobles do not experience scarcity; it won't be remembered by Christmas, as I expect that our shared food will be better.

(129-136) But if we prevail at all, and if our condition ever improves, we will be strongly self-confident and hundreds will go overseas immediately; our nobles will be heedless as their lands wither and empty; if what I have said is true, the lesser ranks who stay behind will have food to share.

(137-144) It is no surprise that we have no wealth given everything that is constantly hounding us; there is never an assembly or forum that does not involve expenditure, despite whatever joy or solace, grief or sadness accompanies it; everyone who hears this song will drink a toast to my health.

(145-152) It is time for us to be going while we have at least a little wealth; before they take it away from us and before our children will be heir to poverty; despite the opinion of the nobles, we will gain the upper hand regardless, and we will traverse the oceans to arrive in bountiful America over yonder.

4: Glencalvie Clearances

Although many brutal evictions were carried out in the 19th-century Highlands, some of them gained greater notoriety than others because of the presence of journalists who reported on the events in major metropolitan newspapers. The Glencalvie Clearances of 1845 were amongst those that shocked readers for its cruelties, broadcast most widely in *The London Times*:

> One of these clearances is about to take place in the parish of Kincardine, from which I now write; and throughout the whole district it has created the strongest feeling of indignation. ... It is the inhabitants of Glencalvie, in number 90 people, whose turn it is now to be turned out of their homes, all at once, the aged and the helpless as well as the young and strong; nearly the whole of them without hope or prospect for the future. The proprietor of this glen is Major Charles Robertson of Kincardine, who is at present out with his regiment in Australia; and his factor or steward who acts for him in his absence is Mr. James Gillanders of Highfield Cottage, near Dingwall.[29]

In the book *The Highland Clearances*, Alexander MacKenzie graphically depicted the dejection and helplessness of the tenants driven from their homes to the shelter of a graveyard:

> Great cruelties were perpetuated at Glencalvie, Ross-shire, where the evicted had to retire into the parish churchyard. There for more than a week they found the only shelter obtainable in their native land. No one dared to succour them, under a threat

Figure 2.1 – Eaglais na Cròic (Croick Church), where the cleared natives of Gleann Cailbhidh took shelter in 1845. Image from Douglas Beck and used with his permission.

of receiving similar treatment to those whose hard fate had driven them thus among the tombs. Many of them, indeed, wished that their lot had landed them under the sod with their ancestors and friends, rather than be treated and driven out of house and home in such a ruthless manner.[30]

Pàdraig MacNeacail, the editor of the Gaelic column in *The Casket* newspaper in Nova Scotia where this song appeared, received the text anonymously, suggesting that the shame and trauma of the events may have still had an effect on those who had experienced it or had family members who had been involved. This may be the only surviving Gaelic source related to the Glencalvie Clearances. It bears a strong resemblance to a song cursing Patrick Sellar, the assistant factor to the Countess of Sutherland who forced tenants out of their homes in 1814.[31]

Original Text

<pre>
 1   Is dhearbh Seumas a dhùthchas
      Bhith 'na shiamarlan brùideil
      Mar bha 'sheanair bho thùs
              A' creach is a' rùsgadh nam bochd;
 5   Am fìor ainmhidh gun chùram
      Gun Dia, gun chreideamh, gun ùmhlachd,
      Gun chliù, gun tuigse, gun diùlam,
              Ach 'na ùmpaidh gun tlachd;
      Gheibh e breitheanas dùbailt
10   Air son na Rosaich a sgiùrsadh
      Á Gleann Cailbhidh le dhùrachd
              Na daoine ionraic gun lochd;
      Bha riamh onarach sùmhail
      Gun sgilinn fhiachan air chùl orr'
15   Is na màil pàight' aig gach aon diubh
              Is gach cìs shaoghalt' bha orr'.
</pre>

>   Bu truagh cianail a dh'fhàg e
>   Gleann Cailbhidh 'na fhàsach
>   An sluagh sgapt' anns gach àite
> 20   Gun cheò, gun làrach, gun taigh;
>   Air an ruagadh le tàmailt
>   Is olc a fhuair iad an càradh
>   Gun àite-fuirich no tàmh ac'
>   Gun truas, gun chàirdeas, gun iochd;
> 25   Chaidh cuid a chòmhnaidh fo sgàil dhiubh
>   Ann an cladh Chinn Chàrdainn
>   Thug siud masladh is tàire
>   Do'n t-Siorrachd Ghàidh'leach seo 'm feasd;
>   Is bidh Seumas Mór air a phàigheadh
> 30   An latha ghairmeas am Bàs e
>   Is cha bhi bròn air na Gàidheil
>   Nuair a théid a chàradh fo lic.
>
>   Rinn am buamastair grannda
>   Obair eile bha gràineil:
> 35   Chuir air ruaig Clann 'ic Theàrlaich
>   Bha pàigheadh màl Choire Bhuig;
>   An tuath chothromach làidir
>   Nach d' fhuair masladh no tàire
>   Gus an tàinig an nàmhaid
> 40   Nach dèanadh fàbhar air bith;
>   Chaidh an sgaoileadh 's gach àite:
>   Cha robh tròcair 'na nàdar-s';
>   Fear gun chogais, gun nàire,
>   Air an laigh an càineadh as mios'!
> 45   Is iomadh athchuinge àraidh
>   Chaidh a ghuidhe d'a chnàmhan
>   Is chan urrainn esan bhith sàbhailt
>   Ann an àite sam bith.[32]

Translation

(1-16) James [Gillanders] proved that his inherited character is to be a brutal steward, as his grandfather originally was, plundering and fleecing the poor; a true animal lacking compassion, Godless, creedless, arrogant, without good repute, awareness or shame, an unpleasant boor; he will receive a double judgement for intentionally scourging the Rosses out of Glencalvie, an upright and blameless people who were always honourable and peaceable, never a penny in debt; every single one of them had paid their rents and every worldly toll.

(17-32) He left Glencalvie a wretched and lonely desert, with the people scattered everywhere without the smoke of a fire, a ground for occupation, or a house; routed out with humiliation, they found themselves in horrible circumstances, lacking a residence or resting place, denied compassion, kindliness or mercy; some of them went to find shelter in the graveyard of Kincardine: that has brought everlasting disgrace and reproach to this Gaelic district; Big James will be paid back on the day that Death calls him and the Gaels will feel no sadness when he is buried under a gravestone.

(33-48) The hideous blockhead has done another deed that was hateful: he banished Clann 'ic Theàrlaich who were paying the rent for Coire Bog; the honest, strong tenantry who never had disgrace or reproach until the enemy came who would not grant any favour at all; they were scattered everywhere, he had no mercy in his nature; a man without conscience or shame on whom the greatest reproach will fall; many special curses were invoked on his bones and he will not be safe in any place.

5: A Gael's Lament

Only the pen name of the author of the next song-poem[33] survives: "Gille Braonach." This name suggests that he or his family may have originated in Loch Bhraoin (Lochbroom) in Scotland or the community in Pictou County, Nova Scotia, of the same name. In the preamble that accompanied the song, the author states that he was living in the Northwest Territories in Canada when he composed this song and it is possible that he went to the Yukon during that region's gold rush 1896-1899 (lines 3 and 31-32). He also added that he went to visit the Gaels of Nova Scotia as often as he was able. Although he states that he is well supplied with silver and gold, he is dissatisfied with his life because he lacks the companionship he preferred (lines 21-24 and 29-32).

The author is keenly aware of the betrayal inflicted on the Gaels by the nobility, despite the loyal service that the tenantry offered to their former chieftains, regiments and government (lines 65-72). He seems to be haunted by scenes of brutality that happened during the Clearances (lines 34-36, 41-48 and 57-64). Wishing to escape the poverty and humiliation at home, Gaels are easily beguiled to emigrate with hyperbolic praise of the New World (lines 81-88). Although he is grateful for the material wealth he enjoys in Canada, he is saddened by the devastation inflicted on the Highlands by its enemies, now being nothing but an empty playground for rich English plutocrats (lines 97-104). He fears that the damage has gone on for so long and has been so thorough that it may never be undone, even though the land and its resources were capable of providing the Gaels with all that they needed (lines 37-38 and 101-102).

Original Text

1   Bitheadh cuid a' seinn mu Chanada
      Gur maiseach grinn an t-àite e;
      Bitheadh iad ag innseadh dhuinn mu'n òr a th'ann
      Mu choilltean agus mu'n phràiridh;
5   Ach ged is maiseach uile iad –
      Chan urrainn neach 'ga àicheadh –
      B' e mo mhiann-s' a bhith 's a' Ghàidhealtachd
      Far an cluinninn fuaim na Gàidhlig.

      Ach ciod a chuir 'nam chlaigeann-sa
10 Nochd bhith tòiseachainn air dànaibh
      Is mo chompanaich 'nan cadal trom
      Ach dhomhsa, chan eil tàmh innte;
      Ged tha mo leaba socrach
      Is i gleusta air a càradh,
15 Chan fhaigh mi fois no cadal innt',
      'S ann tha m' inntinn thall thar sàile.

      Is gur iongantach is gur mìorbhaileach
      Is gun tuigse dha a tha mi;
      Mar tha mi air mo chruthachadh
20 Is na buadhan tha 'nam nàdar;
      Tha biadh is deoch is aodach agam
      Is obair mhath is pàigheadh;
      Is gidheadh chan eil mi riaraichte
      Is nach cluinn mi facal Gàidhlig.

25 Ged tha àitean ann an Canada
      Far am bheil sliochd nan àrmann
      Chaidh 'fhuadach dhe'n cuid fearainn fhéin
      Is na féidh 'gan cur 'nan àite;
      Chan eil iad anns a' cheàrnaidh seo

30   Ach tearc a labhras Gàidhlig,
       Is tha mis' mar sin air seachran
       Measg Ghall is Gheangach grannda.

       Is ged nàraicheadh na h-uachdarain
       Bho bhith sgiùrsadh Clann nan Gàidheal
35   Is a' losgadh an cuid taighean orra
       Is nach faigheadh iad cothrom tàmh annt',
       Gun d' fhuair iad ruith cho fada leis
       Is gum bheil na glinn a-nis 'nam fàsaich;
       Chan fhaicear ceò ag éirigh ást'
40   No maighdean dol gu àiridh.

       Is tha eachdraidh 'g innseadh sgeula dhuinn
       Gum b' uamhasach 's gum bu chràiteach
       Bhith faicinn daoine le'n teaghlaichean
       Air cladach nuadh 'gam fàgail;
45   Gun bhith rompa ach coille 's dorchadas
       Is muir bhith teann ri'n sàilean
       Is gum bu chruaidh air cridhe màthar sin
       Is an leanabh ri rànail.

       Ach ged bu mhór an fhòirneart sin
50   'S e na dh'fhàgadh as motha fhuair tàir dheth,
       Is iadsan 'chaidh do Chanada,
       Cha robh factor orra no bàillidh;
       Is gun do thòisich iad air clìreadh,
       Cha robh rompa ach obair nàdair
55   Is an-diugh tha taighean-còmhnaidh ac'
       Is fearann gu bhith 'ga àiteach.

       Ach na truaghanan nach d' fhuadaich iad
       A-null thar muir mar thràillean;
       'S ann dh'fhàg iad air na creagan iad
60   Is bu choma beatha no bàs dhaibh;
       Is chan fhaodadh iad aon cheum a thoirt
       A-mach thar crìochan àraidh:
       Nach robh fear le gunna 'g éigheach riu
       "Ciod nì sibh seo an-dràsta?"

65   Is gur truagh mar chaidh an duaiseachadh
       Ged bu lìonmhor anns na blàir iad;
       Is ge liuthad fear 'chaidh 'mharbhadh dhiubh
       Is iad gléidheadh cliù nan àrmann;
       Mar chuala an saoghal uile e
70   Cha do theich iad riamh ro nàmhaid,

Is gun do choisinn Breatann rìoghachdan
Le treubhantas nan Gàidheal.

Ach an-diugh, chan fhaigh i saighdearan
No daoine air feadh na Gàidh'lteachd
75   A bhitheas mar bhunait dòchais dhith
An aghaidh cumhachd nàmhaid;
Is na féidh, cha ghabh iad ceannsachadh,
Cha robh iad cleachdte riamh ri hàrness
Is ma chreideas sinn na pàipearan
80   [ ].[34]

Na gillean òga th' ag éirigh
Anns na bailtean feadh a tràghad:
Chan fhaigh iad là de chosnadh ann
Is gum feum iad an t-àite sin 'fhàgail;
85   Is thig agents null á Canada
Is emigration ac' air clàraibh,
Is gum meall iad sinn do'n dùthaich seo
Le geallannaibh bhios àraidh.

Ach chan eil mi dol a chàineadh dhuibh
90   Na dùthcha seo an-dràsta,
Bhon nochd i tomhas de chaoimhneas dhuinn
Nuair chuir iad ás ar n-àitean sinn;
Ach tha reothadh cruaidh 's a' gheamhradh innt'
Is pàirt de phlàighean Phàraoh
95   Is tric thug orms' bhith cuimhneachadh
Air tìr nan laoch is nan àrmann.

Is gur h-e a chum gun chadal mi
Bhith faicinn tìr nan Gàidheal
'Na àite spòrs aig Sasannaich
100   An uair air bith as àill leò:
Na beinn is na glinn is na h-aibhnichean
Bheir biadh is deoch is blàthas dhuinn,
An-diugh a bhith cho aonaranach
Ri fàsaichean Sahàra.[35]

Translation

(1-8) Let some people sing about Canada, about how it is a gorgeous place; let them talk about the gold there, the forests and the prairies; although all of those things are beautiful—no one can deny it—my desire is to be in the Highlands, where the sound of Gaelic is heard.

(9-16) What has put it in my head tonight, to start composing poetry while my companions are deeply sleeping? There is no rest for me; although my bed is comfortable, and it is well made, I can get no rest or sleep in it, for my mind is over across the ocean.

(17-24) It is wondrous, it is marvelous, and it challenges my comprehension; how I have been created with the gifts that are part of my being; I have food, drink and clothing, good work and livelihood, but regardless, I am not satisfied for I cannot hear a word of Gaelic.

(25-32) There are places in Canada where the descendants of the heroes reside who were expelled from their own land while the deer took their place; in this corner there are only a few who speak Gaelic, and I therefore find myself gone astray among vile anglophones and Yankees.

(33-40) Even if the landlords could be shamed because of expelling the Gaels and burning their houses on them so that they could not take the opportunity to live in them, they have gotten away with it for so long now that the glens are now deserted; no peat smoke can be seen rising from them or maidens going to the sheiling.

(41-48) History relates the news that it was horrifying and painful to watch people with their families being left on an unfamiliar beach; with nothing before them but darkness and forest, with the sea close at their heels, and it was hard for a mother's heart when the baby was crying.

(49-56) And although that oppression was bad, those who were left behind had the worst humiliation, while those who went to Canada had no factor or magistrate over them; they began to clear the land without the use of machinery and today they have dwelling-places and farmland to cultivate.

(57-64) But the pitiful ones they did not evict over the oceans like slaves, they were left on the rocks and no-one cared if they lived or died; and they could not take a single step beyond designated boundaries without an armed man yelling at them, "What are you doing here now?"

(65-72) Ill were they rewarded even though many of them went to battle, and even though many men were killed as they perpetuated the fame of warriors; as all of the world has heard, they never retreated before an enemy and the bravery of the Gaels conquered many lands for Britain.

(73-80) But today she cannot find soldiers or even people throughout the Highlands who will act as the basis of her hope; the deer cannot be domesticated and they were never accustomed to a harness, and if we can believe the newspapers, [ ].

(81-88) The young men who are growing up in the villages along the coast: they cannot find a day of work there so that they have to leave that place; and agents come over from Canada with emigration on their agenda, and they lure them to this country with extravagant promises.

(89-96) But I'm not going to disparage this country right now to you, since it has displayed a good measure of kindness to us when we were put out of our homes; but it freezes hard in the winter and has some of the plagues of the Pharaoh, and that has often made me think of the land of the heroes and warriors.

(97-104) What has kept me awake is the sight of the land of the Gaels used as a playground for the English any time they wish; the mountains and glens and rivers that can provide food, drink and warmth to us are today as lonely as the deserts of the Sahara.

3 – Militarism and Tartanism

In perhaps no other domains of the immigrant experience are the ironies and contradictions of Gaelic history more manifest than those of military triumphalism and tartanism.[1] The Highland soldier became an icon of British imperial supremacy and earned the accolades of the anglophone world so long as his energies and ambitions were directed toward imperial ends. Gaels proved in Canada and elsewhere that they were capable of attaining privilege and power by deferring to anglophone norms, but once they renounced the legitimacy of their own language and culture there was nothing left but a hollow shell of tartanism. Canadian Gaelic literary texts were beginning to embrace tartanistic clichés by the early decades of the 19th century, demonstrating that Highlanders were aware of these stereotypes and willing to conform to them to win approval. They thus could play the role of gallant, manly champions capable of conquering any country and yet were incapable of defending their rights on their own turf.

The manipulation of the images of tartan and military service does not imply that they were entirely fabrications of the anglophone world, however. Charters and land titles granted by kings and earls did little good to the clan chieftain of old if he did not have the military might and local political clout to assert his right. In the pre-Culloden Highlands, a clan's wealth and power ultimately depended upon the amount of productive territory under its control, although productivity was measured in terms of social value rather than surplus export.[2] In his 1805 *Observations on the Present State of the Highlands of Scotland*, the Earl of Selkirk (Thomas Douglas) suggested that the chieftain's need to maintain a large number of tenants had kept the cost of rents low:

> Every person above the common rank depended for his safety and his consequence on the number and attachment of his servants and dependents: without people ready to defend him, he could not expect to sleep in safety, to preserve his house from pillage, or his family from murder; he must have submitted to the insolence of every neighbouring robber, unless he had maintained a numerous train of followers to go with him into the field, and to fight his battles. To this essential object every inferior consideration was sacrificed; and the principal advantage of landed property consisted in the means it afforded to the proprietor of multiplying his dependents. ... The Highland gentlemen appear to have been so anxious on this subject, that they never ventured to raise their rents, however much the circumstances of any case might make it reasonable: the tenant in fact paid his rent not so much in money as in military services.

Although economic pressures were already starting to mount before the Battle of Culloden, the rapid integration of Highland estates into the British economy and the debts that many landlord-chieftains had accumulated in their appetite to live luxuriously turned this logic on its head. Many of the Gaelic poems composed in the 18th century criticize chieftains for betraying this social contract which valued the human capital on their estates, particularly as employed as military forces to protect local clan interests.

The common myth that the Highland regiment was the organic and predestined successor to the military arm of clan life was, however, an artifice carefully crafted and nurtured by the 18th-century land-owning elite for their own benefit. In reality, armed conflicts between clans within the Highlands plummeted in the 17th century as the grip of the central government grew ever stronger. Any military capacity possessed by clan chieftains was directed toward international conflicts and civil wars.

> Clearly, the military aspects of clanship had been in long-term decay since well before the end of the seventeenth century. ... Appreciable decline in clan militarism warns against the assumption that the later high-profile Highland presence within

Britain's imperial military was in some way natural and inevitable.[3]

The opponents of the Stewart kings exaggerated the stereotype of the wild Highland warrior to whip up fear and opposition to Jacobite armies and those prejudices persisted long after the defeat at the Battle of Culloden. The vestiges of the old Gaelic elite successfully exploited these stereotypes to their own advantage. The British Empire's ability to expand the territories under its control from 1756 to 1815 owed much to the fact that it spent from 75 per cent to 85 per cent of its budget on military enterprises.[4] Landowners sought to tap these vast financial resources and enhance their own social rank by selling their Highland tenantry as natural-born soldiers who could be recruited in large numbers by leveraging their hereditary clan relationships. Highlanders of many social ranks seemed to believe that they could gain favour with the London government and dispel any lingering suspicions of Jacobite sympathies by a conspicuous demonstration of their loyalty in military service.[5] Thus, the economic-political interests of the land-owning elite and the military ambitions of the empire conspired in the Highlands' specialization in military recruitment, a specialization justified by recourse to obsolete and ethnocentric myths about supposed Gaelic "savagery."[6]

In 1756 the young chieftain Simon Fraser of Lovat—son of an executed Jacobite "rebel"—successfully petitioned to raise a regiment to fight against French forces in North America and within two months about 2,000 Highlanders were mobilized for action.[7] Some 12,000 Highland soldiers in total were involved by the end of the Seven Years' War in other regiments as well. Gaels perceived themselves to have proved their mettle and their loyalties prominently by their efforts, not least on the Plains of Abraham. These contributions are saliently marked in Gaelic verse commemorating the war, and Highlanders seem to have allowed themselves to become much more heavily invested in British imperial enterprises thereafter and to become more confident of that investment. "Quebec served as explicit proof of the merits in fashioning a self-imagery around the British Empire that helped many Highlanders to embrace the triumphalist discourse of imperial hegemony."[8]

During the Seven Years' War, the Scottish elite regarded their military contributions to the empire as helping to counter-balance what might have otherwise been seen as an unequal partnership with England.⁹ Popular representations of Scottish history throughout the 19th century emphasized the importance of national heroes who preserved Scotland's independence long enough for it to enter into a voluntary union with England as a collaborator, rather than as a vanquished colony; at least, these were the tales and interpretations of history that gave solace and comfort to the realities of empire. Foremost of these national heroes was William Wallace.

> But the Wallace cult was not designed to threaten the union or inspire political nationalism. ... Rather, the cult reminded the Scots of their own history in which the union had been achieved because of Wallace's struggle for freedom. Wallace had ensured that the Scottish people had never been conquered. As a result of their own courageous fight for independence in medieval times a fruitful union between equal partners had become possible in 1707. ... The national devotion to Wallace demonstrated that pride in Scottish nationhood and loyalty to union and empire could be reconciled.[10]

Other events in Scotland's national past—such as the confrontation with the Romans in Scotland at the Battle of Mons Graupius, resistance to the Viking invasions and the victory of Robert the Bruce at the Battle of Bannockburn—were also interpreted so as to paint the Scots as an indomitable people tenacious of their freedom and irrepressible in their national pride. Such characters from Scotland's history and their functions in expressing these values appear in a number of the texts in this chapter and demonstrate the degree to which Gaels also wanted to find consolation in popular myths of national sovereignty.

It was not necessarily easy to reconcile the value placed on Highlanders as military assets with the wider Scottish pretensions of civility as accentuated by the Enlightenment of the 18th and 19th centuries. Some items in Gaelic oral tradition reflect the contradictions facing Highlanders as a people who were co-opted as warriors into a system that both valued them for their presumed "barbaric virtues" and disparaged them when those capacities appeared to contradict or threaten Anglocentric agendas. One exemplary tale is set in the 1650s when Oliver Cromwell made General George Monck commander-in-chief in Scotland and put him in charge of an army of occupation in the Highlands. Whether or not the tale accurately represents an actual historical event is not as important in this discussion as what it tells us about what Highlanders thought that the people in power believed about them.

According to the tale, Cameron of Lochiel refused to capitulate to General Monck's orders, so Monck selected and ordered troops to go into Cameron territory to force them into submission. The Camerons, however, successfully overcame the government forces. Lochiel himself was ambushed by an English officer and was locked in a violent struggle with him, fighting for his life. As the Englishman made a sudden lunge to get the better of his opponent, he exposed his neck; Lochiel bit into his windpipe and killed him.

> Many years afterwards, when attending at Court in London, Lochiel went into a barber's shop to get his hair and beard dressed, and when the razor was passing over his throat, the chatty barber observed, "You are from the North, sir?"
>
> "Yes," said Sir Ewan, "I am; do you know people from the North?"
>
> "No," replied the irate barber, "nor do I wish to; they are savages there. Would you believe it, sir, one of them tore the throat out of my father with his teeth? I only wish I had the fellow's throat as near me as I have yours just now."
>
> Sir Ewan afterwards said that it was the only time he ever experienced the sensation of fear, as he felt the edge of the steel gliding over the part so particularly threatened.[11]

Cameron of Lochiel—like Highlanders in many other circumstances—resorted to a desperate tactic to protect himself and his kinsmen against forces bent on punishing him for defying authority. Once outside of his own territory, however, Sir Ewan was subject to the prejudices of Englishmen who assumed that all Highlanders were savages. Ironically, he had gone to a barber to make himself presentable to the "civilized" members of the king's court (hair styles symbolize the supposed distinctions between "civilization" and "savagery" in most cultures). His own throat could now be easily cut out of a desire for revenge by the son of the man who had tried to kill him, despite the fact that Sir Ewan acted in self-defense against Monck's aggression. Such stories in Gaelic oral tradition demonstrate that Highlanders were aware of the paradoxes surrounding Highland integration into British society.

Despite the popular image of Highlanders as fearless and zealous serviceman, most were less enthusiastic about joining regiments than is usually presumed: the "decision" was sometimes a matter of socio-economic pressures or even coercion, as relayed in numerous Gaelic songs about press gangs and dishonest deals in taverns. Soldiers had a high mortality rate and little if any control of where they would be posted; "generally, Gaels were reluctant rather than willing recruits."[12] Even more disconcerting to the elite was the fact that the population in the Highlands had declined so severely by the 1790s—through emigration, dispossession and over-recruitment—that landlords could no longer yield a large harvest of fresh recruits for military employment on demand.[13]

It is exactly at this time of crisis, when landlords feared that their facade of clannish pretensions would crumble away and expose the degree to which their hereditary roles and relationships had become meaningless in contemporary Highland life, that the colourful pageantry of tartanism and Highlandism began to be constructed in full. These facades acted as fig-leaves to cover the insecurity of the Scottish elite whose rapid absorption of English norms left them with an inferiority complex about their culture and identity.

> They were conscious to a painful degree of their backwardness, their poverty, their lack of polish, their provinciality. They adopted a mentality of emulation, a catch-up ideology of imitation and self-improvement that, though it may have predated the Union, became more urgent by the 1720s. There was, therefore, a candid acceptance of inferiority in economic life, in cultural attainment, and in manners. The consequence was, not a stolid stoicism, but a concerted effort, almost a collective mission, to reach forward toward the standards set by London and by England. ... Encounters with the English in the early and mid-eighteenth century were less than edifying for the maintenance of a sense of Scottish nationality. The redefinition of Scotland after the Union entailed a deliberate contraction of its language, identity, and pride.[14]

Whatever else it may be from other perspectives, tartanism is a phenomenon which reflects the subordinate status of Gaeldom as a whole in the British polity and its corresponding inability to maintain its own cultural resources on its own terms. It was also a testimony to the psychic vulnerability of the Scottish elite who became willing to plunder Gaeldom's cultural assets in order to emphasize their distinctions from other anglophones by the salient display of Highland symbols. The popularity of the anglophone literature written by Walter Scott in the early 1800s and the exhibition of exoticized, tartan-clad clansmen for the visit of King George IV to Edinburgh in 1822 are often seen as crucial steps in the creation of Highlandism as we now know it.

> Highland dress provided landowners who had military interests with a recognizable brand in a lucrative marketplace. ... The military symbolism of Highland dress allowed elites to define the Highlands as a military region par excellence, and thereby to benefit from the political capital this gave them as consummate supporters of British expansion.[15]

The romantic image of the Highlands as a repository of ancient Scottish tradition and masculine, martial virtues also began to take the form of rituals and artistic performances at social gatherings orchestrated by the landowning classes. Despite spurious origin myths asserting their antiquity, the first Highland Games were not held until after the defeat of Napoleon at the Battle of Waterloo, supporting the hypothesis that they were part of the gentry's effort to create an artificially archaic picture of Highland life to protect their own role as the natural leaders of Gaelic society and to underscore their commitment to the British Empire by endorsing a narrow role for Highlanders as loyal soldiers.[16]

The actual spectacles and competitions at Highland games were crafted to highlight Gaels as brawny, macho and

Figure 3.1 – A sketch of Highland Games at Montreal's Decker Park in 1872. Image from a print from Kenneth McKenna).

militaristic rustics eager to win the approval of their superiors, to the exclusion of their other cultural achievements or traditions. Had Highland games been run by Highlanders for the purposes of maintaining Gaelic culture, they might have featured the many aspects of oral and literary tradition; commitment to such internal touchstones were instead compromised to provide entertainment for anglophones. In other words, Highland games were part of a series of measures designed to transform selected elements of Highland tradition into palatable commodities agreeable to the tastes and fantasies of the "respectable" classes of British society, and to orient Gaels toward meeting the demands made of them by the British State and away from their own development as a separate and independent ethnic group. Some Gaels were only too relieved to find themselves the subjects not of loathing but of adulation, however misguided, and delighted in the cachet afforded by tartan and the military tradition.

Gaels themselves remarked on these inconsistencies. A dialogue used to teach Gaelic in the late 19th century, portraying a conversation between two Gaels outside of the Oban Highland Gathering, delivers a sly commentary on the counterfeit nature of these extravaganzas:

A: An robh an t-éideadh Gàidhealach air móran dhiubh?
B: Bha e air a' chuid a bu mhò de luchd na farpais is air corra h-aon de na h-uaislean. ...
A: An innis sibh seo dhomh? An robh duaisean air an toirt ann air son bàrdachd Gàidhealaich?
B: Cha robh.
A: Cha b' ionnan a' chùis ri linn Dhonnchaidh Bhàin Mhic an t-Saoir. ...
A: Nach iongantach nach eil na h-uachdarain a' toirt misnich do na bàird againn fhéin?
B: 'S eadh, is gur h-i 'Ghàidhlig cainnt an t-sluaigh![17]
A: Were many of them wearing Highland clothing?
B: The majority of the competitors wore it and a few of the aristocrats. ...
A: Will you tell me this? Were prizes offered there for Gaelic poetry?
B: There weren't.
A: The matter was very different in the time of [Gaelic poet] Duncan Ban Macintyre. ...
A: Isn't it strange that the aristocrats aren't encouraging our own poets?
B: Indeed, given that Gaelic is the language of the people!

These two characters subtly reveal their displeasure that the aristocrats who conduct the events dress up in kilts but neglect Gaelic, the actual language of the common people, and its literary expression. Donnchadh Bàn Mac an t-Saoir (Duncan Ban Macintyre) was one of the most popular Gaelic poets of the late 18th century and won the prize for an original Gaelic poetry composition in praise of Gaelic and the bagpipes in the competitions held at the Falkirk Tryst from 1781 to 1783.[18] The Tryst is considered by many as a precursor to the Highland Games and was organized by the London Highland Society. Its short-lived fidelity to Gaelic, and quick transition to tartanism, was paralleled by most other cultural organizations.[19]

The contradictions and ironies surrounding militarism and tartanism were experienced by Gaels in Canadian immigrant communities as well and local histories captured from Gaelic oral sources provide testimonies that can supplement, and sometimes challenge, the conventional stereotypes. A series of tales circulating in the oral tradition of Cape Breton about Captain Dòmhnall Gorm MacDhòmhnaill, for example, express an implicit criticism of British military regiments and the violence meted out in conflict:

> In spite of his impeccable Gaelic pedigree and central role in the Eastern Theatre of the war, Gaelic legend is consistent in emphasising his demonic aspects rather than the qualities of bravery and military valour recorded by his British masters. Storytellers convey a grudging respect for his cunning and effectiveness as a soldier, but the most striking characteristic of the oral accounts is the unbridled savagery that he loosed upon the French-speaking Acadian population of the island.[20]

Indeed, there is other evidence of Gaelic Canadian soldiers who regretted the part that they played in the brutality that is an inevitable consequence of military conflict. A biographical sketch of Iain Dòmhnallach, a native of Àrasaig who migrated to Pictou County about the year 1790, suggests that he was haunted by his memories of warfare and experienced what we would now call "post-traumatic stress disorder":

> In earlier years he, like many other Highlanders, was for a time connected with the English Army, and as such, happened to form a unit in the British force, detailed to enforce the edict resulting in the "Expulsion of the Acadians." In the first instance,

he was, no doubt, an unwilling actor, in not only disturbing but utterly destroying for ever, the happy homes of the unfortunate Acadians of the beautiful "Land of Evangeline." ... Did John MacDonald know that he should ever have to witness such a scene, he would have never entered the army. In his advanced years, his grief of heart swelled anew, as he related with tremulous voice and subdued tones, the sad scenes as he recalled the piercing cries of the broken-hearted peasantry.[21]

Local historian Micheal MacMhurchaidh of Gleann MhicMhurchaidh in Cape Breton remarked that the founders of the Gaelic community in Nova Scotia first arrived in the region as combatants but that at least some of them were less than enthusiastic about their duties:

> We all know that the first Highlanders came to Cape Breton in 1758. They landed in Louisbourg, marched through the country to St Peter's, where they burned a church in which some French fugitives had taken refuge. And this act of British warfare was very unwillingly performed by some of them.[22]

Very seldom do the official histories, which only valorize Highlanders as loyal soldiers, admit to the moral ambivalences or objections felt by those who engaged in warfare or to any negative repercussions of British domination. Jingoistic strains are parroted, however, in the Gaelic song-poems and tales in praise of Highland regiments, individual soldiers or battles which were endorsed by nearly all of the Gaelic elite, who remained strongly committed to the British Empire. Their goal—one much easier than critiquing an apparently invincible superpower—was simply to carve out a niche for Highlanders as the choice warriors of the Crown. Poets were able to leverage and extend a large repertoire and long history of Gaelic literary tradition to that end. A global theatre of war gave military-minded Gaels expanded heroic opportunities and poets a new range of contemporary subjects to which they could apply old literary conventions.

> Initially at any rate the Gaelic response to military service was direct, naive, and enthusiastic. As in other parts of the Empire, a warrior tradition was given a new setting, with enough in the way of military trappings and emblems to maintain a feeling

of continuity. ... From within Gaelic society [these songs] are charters that reflect and endorse a new security. Their aesthetic power is inextricably bound up with the assertions they make.[23]

This obeisance became a straight-jacket, however, which did not afford any space for opposition to imperial dictates when they were not in the interests of the Gaels as a distinct cultural and linguistic group. The power over other peoples that Gaels could access as collaborators in empire building and the approval that they garnered in the exercise of that power, however, offered forms of compensation for the powerlessness they otherwise experienced. The texts in this chapter testify to the degree to which the Gaelic elite deferred to anglophone authorities for approved social roles and cultural standards.

The elite of any society usually have a disproportionate effect on the self-image and aspirations of that society, and it is no surprise that the adoption of militaristic values and tartanistic imagery would have a ripple effect on the consciousness of Highlanders of all social levels. It would be overly simplistic to argue that these were artificial fabrications given that they are amplifications of features that had a long presence in Gaelic culture. The important point in the present discussion is that this is a small subset of Gaelic cultural elements that was selected because of its appeal to the dominant anglophone majority; an exclusive focus on these facets on account of their ability to provide external validation to upwardly-mobile Highland elite had the effect of undermining Gaelic communities' confidence in the integrity of their culture as a whole and creating a pattern of dependency on the endorsement of anglophones for their accomplishments in a narrowly circumscribed role in the empire.

1: The Song of the Gaels

The following song-poem was composed by Iain MacGilleBhràth to the tune of an older song, "A Bhean an Taighe, Fàg an Sìola." Iain was well educated and closely connected to the Highland elite of the early 19th century (see song-poem 6.4), so it is little surprise that this poem incorporates the tartanistic themes of the period. It is not clear who titled this text or when Iain composed it, although, according to one source, he did so as a response to one of his sons who refused to buy tartan clothing.[24] This may indicate a growing gap of perceptions or habits between Gaels born in Scotland and their descendants born in North America.

At the beginning and end of the poem, Iain states explicitly that he is resident in Nova Scotia and that he considers Scotland to be the natural home and inheritance of the Gael, the land in which Gaelic identity is rooted. He concludes with a toast to the Gaels, drinking the waters of Nova Scotia rather than the Old Country (lines 61-64). His allusion to the string being stirred (line 62) seems to be a reference to the playing of harps in the halls of the chieftains of old. Iain appears to be attempting to extend the territory of the Gaelic community but to also assert the continuity of the tradition.

Gaels are praised in their military capacity by drawing on a number of conventional literary tropes that add an archaic air to the text: the chorus contains the kenning "fir shuaiceanta nam breacan" (distinguished men of the tartans, line 2), recalling a metonym that came into usage no later than the Battle of Killiecrankie;[25] he refers to Highland soldiers by the kenning "garbh-bhuillich" (rough-strikers, line 34) and likens them to "coin gharg" (fierce hounds, lines 35 and 51) that were used for hunting; Highland troops have become so close and protective of King George as to become his "còta cruadhach" (steel coat, line 44), invoking older Gaelic terms for the chieftain's bodyguard such as "léine-chneas."[26]

Iain employs popular 19th-century ideas about Scottish history to depict Scots in general as unbeatable champions. He begins by alluding to the resistance of the Caledonians to Roman occupation (lines 13-16) and moves forward in time by mentioning the ultimate defeat of Norse power (lines 17-20). It becomes more clear that his eulogy is not limited to the Gaels but extends to all of Scotland when he refers to the subjects of his praise as "na Tuathaich" (the Northerners, line 24) who beat the English at Bannockburn. These particular historical references, as discussed in the introduction to this chapter, enhance a positive self-image for Gaels by recourse to their military prowess but betray the influence of anglophone learning. They also attempt to avoid any hint of ethnic division within contemporary Britain. The kenning "na Tuathaich," for example, used when discussing the Battle of Bannockburn, gives the Scots a topographical rather than an ethnic designation.

He alludes to Jacobite episodes in the past in his reference to the Gaels' dislike of King George "and his sort" in previous times (lines

41-42), but does not name specific events or people. Nevertheless, Iain reassures us that the Gaels are now as faithful to King George as they were to the other kings of the past, defending him and fighting on his behalf. This is the "acquaintance" that he refers to (line 43): the knowledge of warfare, particularly in the theatres of North America.

He proceeds in the following three verses to enumerate the recent battles of the British Empire, without differentiating Scottish from English troops. He puts particular emphasis on the French as enemies, as this prolonged struggle provided a strand of continuity in the Gaelic involvement in British regiments and was, in fact, instrumental in bringing early Highland emigrants to British North America. The kenning "luchd na foille" (infidels, line 56) for the French provides moral certainty to the victors and distance between Gaels and their former French associates.

Original Text

1 Soraidh bhuam thar cuain air astar
   Gu fir shuaicheanta nam breacan,
   Chumadh suas gu buan an cleachdadh
   Anns an riochd bu dual dhaibh.

5 Soraidh bhuamsa nunn thar sàile
   'Dh'fhearann dùthchasach nan Gàidheal
   Far am bheil na suinn 'gan àrach
   Ann an sgàth nam fuar-bheann.

   'S iad nach tréig le uaill am fasan –
10 An t-éileadh cuaiche is an gartan –
   Na suinn chruaidhe chuanta sgairteil
   Th' anns na batail buadhach.

   Ciod i 'n tìr anns an Roinn-Eòrpa
   Nach do chìosnaich feachd na Ròimhe,
15 Ach sliochd dhìleas Chaledòni,
   Chum an còir le'n cruadal?

   Is ged bha Lochlannaich le'm feachdaibh
   'G iarraidh an dùthaich a chreachadh,
   Thill iad na dh'fhan beò dhiubh dhachaigh,
20 Sia no seachd de dh'uairean.

   Is ged bu dianmhor gaisgich Shasann,
   Is lìonmhor sliabh 's an deach an sgapadh;
   Riamh bho dheuchainn Allt nam Breacag
   Sheachainn iad na Tuathaich.

25 Is caoimhneil, macanta 'nan sìth iad,
    Fiosrach, ceart, dha'm facal dìleas;
    Borb, do-chaisgte 'n gleachd no 'n strì iad
    Ge b' e dh'ìocadh gruaim dhaibh.

    Is lìonmhor sluagh dha'n tug iad greadan,
30 Is neach nach cuala riamh an eagal –
    Am fuil uaibhreach théid gu beadradh
    Cluinntinn fead na luaidhe.

    Nuair dh'éireadh meanmna 'nan spiorad,
    Bhiodh na garbh-bhuillich gun ghiorag,
35 Mar choin gharg an sealg a' mhillidh,
    Ann am mire an fhuathais.

    Bonn, cha tais iad ri uchd stàilinn
    Dol a chasgairt leis na clàidhean;
    Beòthail, ladurn' agus làidir,
40 Builleach, sàthach, ruaineach.

    Is ged bu bheag orr' aon uair Deòrsa,
    Is iad gun chaoimh aca r'a sheòrsa,
    Nise, bhon a fhuair e 'n eòlas,
    'S iad a chòta cruadhach.

45 B' eòlach Bonipart is na Frangaich
    Air an spailpearrachd 's na campaibh;
    Is tric a dh'fhàg iad àrach fann,
    Is a dh'fhàg iad gann de shluagh e.

    Cha robh streup 's an robh 'chuid armailt
50 Eadar an Éiphit is a' Ghearmailt
    Nach robh lomhainn threun na h-Albann
    Le'n cuid calg 'ga bhualadh.

    'N Waterloo bha 'n tùrn ro shoilleir:
    Fhuair iad cliù bho'n Diùc mar thoilleadh;
55 Choisinn iad gach cùis o'n choireach
    Is luchd na foille 'fhuadach.

    Nise, chan eil ceàrn 's an t-saoghal,
    Is nach eil meas orra mar dhaoine;
    Is balla làidir do'n luchd-gaoil iad,
60 Is aognachadh luchd-fuatha.

    Is ged tha mise 'n-dràst' an taobh seo,
    Tha'n teud nàdarra 'na dùsgadh;
    Dh'òlainn ur slàinte le dùrachd
    Ge b' e bùrn an fhuarain.[27]

Translation

(1-4) Greetings from me far across the ocean to the distinguished men of the tartans who would always keep up the tradition in the semblance which they have inherited.

(5-8) Greetings from me over the salt-water to the native land of the Gaels, where the warriors are raised in the shadow of the cold mountains.

(9-12) They will not let arrogance cause them to abandon their fashion—the kilted plaid and bonnet—those tough, handsome, energetic warriors who are victorious in the battles.

(13-16) Is there any country throughout Europe that the Roman legions did not conquer, except for the loyal people of Caledonia, who kept their rights through their resilience?

(17-20) And although the Norse, with their armed forces, wanted to pillage the land, those who survived were sent back home six or seven times.

(21-24) And although the warriors of England were ardent, they were routed on many a hillside; ever since the trial of Bannockburn, they have avoided the Northerners.

(25-28) They are kind and gentle in peacetime, intelligent, in the right, and true to their word; they are savage and invincible in conflict and strife, regardless of who might be surly to them.

(29-32) They have given a thumping to many a battle host, no one has ever heard them speak of fear—their proud blood will proceed excitedly while hearing the whistle of bullets.

(33-36) When they are inspired by courage, those rough-strikers are as valiant as fierce hounds hunting down destruction in a battle frenzy.

(37-40) They do not cringe one bit in the face of steel, going to slaughter with the swords; lively, daring and strong, dealing blows and thrusts, ferocious.

(41-44) And although at one time they disliked George and they had no love for his sort, now that he has become acquainted with them, they are his steel coat.

(45-48) Bonaparte and the French came to know their boasts in the camps; often did they weaken [the troops of] a battlefield and leave it nearly empty.

(49-52) There was never a skirmish that included their army between Egypt and German in which the brave hounds of Scotland were not striking blows with their blades.

(53-56) Their achievements were very clear in Waterloo: they earned renown from the Duke as they deserved; they triumphed over the criminal at every encounter and routed the infidels.

(57-60) Now there is no corner of the world where they are not esteemed as men; they are a strong wall [of defense] to those who love them and the omen of death to those who hate them.

(61-64) And although I am currently on this side [of the ocean], the hereditary string is stirred; I would drink to your health with sincere wishes, regardless of the source of the spring's water.

2: The Renown of the Gaels

The following article appeared in the bilingual newspaper *Cuairtear nan Coillte* (The Forest Traveller) published in Kingston, Ontario,[28] in 1842 under the title "Cliù nan Gàidheal." The Gaelic text is shot through with awkward compound words that were probably coined by someone translating an original English text that does not survive. In any case, it is an early example of a North American Gaelic text indulging in Highlandism and romantic clichés in order to reassure Gaels that they have qualities—almost all militaristic—that anglophones admire or even envy. This need for external validation through unrealistic stereotypes only reinforces the vulnerability and dependency of Gaeldom and its dissociation from some idealized past. At the same time, the text deplores that the younger generation is as-

Figure 3.2 – The masthead of the newspaper Cuairtear nan Coillte *from Kingston, Ontario. The central logo depicting a Highlander was borrowed directly from the Scottish newspaper* Cuairtear nan Gleann. *Image from a photocopy provided by Kenneth Nilsen.*

similating to anglophone norms and abandoning the language and customs of their ancestors. It attempts to convince them to take pride in their own culture, however, by seeking the same external approval of the anglophone world. The author creatively interprets the Gaelic diaspora as a means for Highlanders to propagate to other supposedly barbaric people the "civilizing mission" to which they have been subjected.

Original Text

Chan eil eachdraidh a leughas sinn mu shluagh air an domhain a bheir de thoil-inntin dhuinn na eachdraidh nan Gàidheal bochda. Tha an eachdraidh làn nithean fiùthail tha ro eiseimplearach do ghinealachd an latha an-diugh. Cha bheag an t-adhbhar uaill is toileachais do neach air bith a fhreumhaich bho'n t-seann stoc seo, a bhith leughadh chunntasan urramach mu'n timcheall ann an obraichean seanchaidhean fhineachan eile a bha foghlamaichte, gaisgeil, mór agus cumhachdach. Anns na h-eachdraidhean ud a tha toirt cunntas orra an linnibh céin agus dorcha, chì sinn iad eadhan ann an staid bhorbh agus aineolach a' dearrsadh fo shubhailcean a chuireadh tuilleadh onair air na fineachan as foghlamaichte agus as àitichte ann an àrach inntinn.

Chì sinn iad gaisgeil treun do-cheannsaichte neo-dhìbreach air son an saorsa fhéin a ghléidheadh mar shluagh. Chì sinn iad bàigheil tìorail teò-chridheach càirdeil dhoibhsan aig an robh feum air cobhair, eadhan do'n nàimhdean nuair a thuiteadh iad gu dìblidh neo-chomasach 'nan còir. Chì sinn iad a' tuireadh os cionn cuirp laoich thapaidh threuna an nàimhdean a thuit 's a' chath le'n làimh agus a' feuchainn comhfhurtachd a thoirt do'n dìlsean a bha brònach air son am bàs ana-abaich. Chì sinn iad fìrinneach do'm facail—dìleas do'n uachdaranan laghail a bha fiùthail air taic agus maitheanasach tròcaireach dhoibhsan a rinn coire le cumhachd dhoibh nuair a dhèanadh iad ceartas riutha agus a' leigeil an dì-chuimhne seann eucoirean nuair a thionndadh iad an càirdeas cinnteach seasmhach do'n ionnsaigh. Chì sinn iad a' seasamh gu neo-fheolltach ri còrdadh no réite air bith a dhèanadh iad r'a nàmhaid, nì a thug meas orra anns gach rìoghachd a chunnaic iad no a chuala mu'n déidhinn.

Chì sinn iad gu h-onarach urramach duineil a' cumail bho dhìoghaltas a ghabhail le fealltas air an ana-càirdean—nì air bith a dhèanadh iad anns an dòigh seo, is ann le faobharaibh claidheimh an cath fosgailte—cha bhiodh mort an-fhiosach ri chur as an leth. Chì sinn iad ro thìr-ghràdhach dùthchasach eadhan gu oirthir amaideis; chì sinn an sùilean, nach sileadh deur leis an dòrainn bu mhò, a' taiseachadh agus a' fliuchadh air faicsinn sealladh de bheanntaibh an rùin eadhan ann an dealbh agus ri cluinntinn crònan agus nuallan na pìoba dosraich. Le fìrinn, gun leth bhreth, cha mhór gun do leugh sinn riamh mu shluagh a b' eireachdail agus a b' urramaich is bu ghloine càil na iadsan.

Bha iad mar leòghannan an cath agus mar uain ann an sìth. Bha iad umhal mar ìochdaranan agus pàrantail a chuid bu trice mar uachdaranan. Bha iad iriseal 'nan gluasad agus àrd-inntinneach 'nan dèiligeadh agus 'nan giùlain—ro eudmhor mu chliù an cuideachd agus an dùthcha—toirm-builleach mu chuimhneachan an sinnsearan agus an ainm fhéin mar dhaoine leis nach bu diù gnothach tàireil no maslach. Bha iad truacanta ri coigreach agus pàirteach ris an aoiseach; adhartach an deuchainnibh agus fulangach ann an dòchas. Bha iad ealamh am foghlam nuair a leigeadh iad an inntinn ris, saidhbhir an cruitheachd-inntinn agus an dealbh-bheachdan; ro shoirbheasach an ealantachd is an cruth-ghnìomh—cridheil eutrom agus fearas-chuideachdail, déidheil air ceòl is àilgheas is cleasachd neo-lochdach; furas[ta] ri bhith air am buannachd thairis, gu math agus mór-bheachdach mu nithean spioradail, eadhan gur ann mu nithean nèamhaidh no saobh-chreideach a bhitheadh e.

Bha am beachdan farsaing agus an smuaintean domhain gabhaltach mu nithean dìomhair no do-thuigseach agus toradhail an cruth-aigne. Bha iad àrd-urramail 'nam beachan mu uachdaranaibh agus mu adhradh, ciod air bith seòrsa do'm buineadh e, agus h-àraidh do neach sam bith a bha airidh air a leithid de dh'umhlachd—agus faodaidh sinn co-dhùnadh le ràdh air chinnte gun robh buaidhean làidir co-shuainte riutha bha comasach air bhith air a thionndadh gu bhith 'na inneal ro chumhachdach gu math no gu olc a-réir mar a rachadh an àrach suas, buaidhean air nach robh an saoghal eòlach aig iomadh àm, agus air an adhbhar sin, neo-chomasach air meas a chur orra gu'n tarraing a-mach air faiche fharsaing an t-saoghail gu'n éideachadh suas gu feum ceart, agus an àite measa, 's ann a bha iad 'gan cur fo dhìmheas, agus le fòirneart agus le tarcuis, 'ga lasadh suas an teine 'na nàimhdeas is 'na corraich nuair a dh'fhaodadh iad an toirt gu soillseachd ghlòrmhor ann an speur na càirdeas agus nan urramachd.

Is iomadh linn anns an do dhéilig Sasann riutha le aineolas anns an dòigh seo gus an do phàigh iad gu daor sin, agus am b' fheudar dhaibh an càirdeas a chùirtealachd, gus an d' fhuair iad air an aonadh riutha fhéin iad, aonadh de'm bheil a' chuid thuigseach dhiubh a' dèanadh taice móire, agus uaill nach gann os ìosal, seadh eadhan iadsan a chunnt iad 'nan leth-bhrùidean is 'nam borbanaich is 'nam feall-daoine. Nam b' oil leis an t-saoghal, dh'éirich iad suas is chrath iad dhiubh duslach an dìmeas anns gach rìoghachd air domhain an càs na Rìoghachd sònraichte; is shiubhail an cliù air sgiathaibh na h-ainmeileachd gu iomall an t-saoghail air son gach buaidh a bhuineas duibh agus an ùrnaighean air sgiathaibh ainglean gu cathair rìoghail a' Chruithfhir ann an nèamh agus tha an ùrnaighean a-nis dol suas 'nan cànain binn drùidhte fhéin (leis, math dh'fhaoidte, an do dh'aslaich ar ceud sinnsear beannachd an Tighearna) anns gach ceathramh de'n t-saoghal far am bheil iad a' sgapadh do thaobh a-nis, ach theagamh an amharc Dhé a chum craobh-sgaoileadh nam feartan ud a bhuineas do'n nàdair air àrdachadh le eòlas nèamhaidh gu inntinnean meallaichte nan cinneach ana-bàigheil a shlugadh a-steach gu sìobhaltachd agus eòlas diadhaidh.

Tha cuid de dh'òigridh ar dùthcha am measg an t-sluaigh anns an dùthaich seo leis an tàir iad fhéin a chluinntinn a labhairt na cainnte a dh'ionnsaich am màthair dhoibh, an t-éideadh a chaitheamh, an cluais a chumail ris a' cheòl sin a b' uaill agus a b' urram le'n sinnsearaibh bhon d' fhuair iad an t-saorsa a th'aca agus am beagan measa tha air a chur orra. Labhraidh sinn gu h-aithghearr riutha agus theagamh anns a' chànain as measail aca, ann an dòigh a chumas iad a' cnàmh na cìre air a' cheann-labhairt seo beagan làithean.

Tha mo chridhe air a chràdh nuair a chì mi an fhuaralachd a tha ag éirigh suas anns a' ghinealach òg, cuid dhiubh a thionndaidheas an sròn gu tarcuiseach air neach a chì iad a' caitheamh an éididh sin, no labhairt na cànain sin air an robh iad fhéin a-mhàin eòlach an làithibh an òige agus a bu mhiann, roghadh, agus uaill am pàrantan. Ach tha aon adhbhar sòlais againn nach fhaca sinn aon de'n t-seòrsa seo riamh air nach robh na Goill fhéin a' sealltainn le gnè de tharcuis, a thaobh bonn-stéidh bho'm bheil an t-àrdan aineolach seo ag éirigh.

Tha fios aig na Goill gu math air urram nan Gàidheal agus is tric air làithibh féill, no co-chomainn, a chì sinn iad a' tionail fo shuaicheantas na h-Alba ann an làn earradh nan Gàidheal ged nach urra dhoibh an cànain a labhairt, nì bu mhiannach leotha; agus chan fhaca sinn Gall riamh do'm b' urra a labhairt nach d' rinn uaill aiste agus air chinnte, chan eil nì as coireach ri Gall air bith a bhith a' cur tarcuis air Gàidheil an-diugh, ach nach urra dha aonachadh riutha an cànain no an éideadh, agus nach urra dha smàl a chur air an ainmeileachd an dòigh air bith eile.

Chan aithne dhuinn nàmhaid an-diugh air thalamh as motha a th' aig na Gàidheil na cuid diubh fhéin a tha le aineolas a' saoilsinn gur tàir dhoibh a bhith air an coltachadh ri'n sinnsearaibh. Ach nan sealladh iad ri sinnsearaibh nan Gall, chitheadh iad na bu mhotha de dh'adhbhar tàir, a bhith air an ainmeachadh orra; ach cha mhór feum a bhith ri leithid seo de mhuinntir nach eil ri leughadh facal mu eachdraidh an dùthcha no an cinnidh ach a tha mar phoca-saic le'm beul fosgailte gu gabhail a-staigh gach nì a shéideas gaoth fuadain air adhart do'n ionnsaigh.[29]

Translation

There is no history that we can read about the people of the world that gives us as much delight as the history of the hapless Gaels. Their history is full of valuable ideas that are exemplary for today's generation. Everyone who is descended from this ancient stock has a great reason to be proud and pleased to read noble accounts about them in the works of the historians of other people who were learned, heroic, great and powerful. In those histories that give an account of [the Gaels] in ancient and obscure eras, we can see them even in a state of barbarity and ignorance shining with moral virtues that would give higher honour to people whose minds have had greater opportunities for learning and cultivation.

We can see them heroic, brave, indomitable and steadfast in preserving their own freedom as a people. We can see them kind, genial, warm-hearted and friendly to those who had need of assistance, even to their enemies when they happened to fall despairing and helpless at their mercy. We can see them keening over the corpses of the brave and triumphant warriors of their enemies whom they felled with their own hands in the battle, trying to provide comfort to their companions who were saddened by their untimely deaths. We can see them true to their word—loyal to their legitimate superiors who were worthy of support, forgiving and merciful to those who offended them when they would do justice to them, allowing old injuries to be forgotten when they would ruin their dependable and trustworthy kinship. We can see them honestly defending any agreement or compact that they would make with their enemy, a thing that has earned them respect in every country that ever saw them or heard about them. We can see them with honour, dignity and manliness keeping themselves from seditiously exacting vengeance on their adversaries—anything of this nature that they would do would be done in open combat with the blades of swords—they would never be accused of covert murder. We can see them passionately attached to their native land to the point of foolishness; we can see their eyes, that would not shed a tear from the most severe torment, becoming wet and moist from seeing the sight of their beloved mountains, even in a picture, and from hearing the croon and bellowing of the multi-droned bagpipes. In truth, without any bias, we have hardly ever read about a people more striking, more esteemed, or more pure in constitution.

They were like lions in war and like lambs in peace. As subjects, they were obedient and as lords, they were most often parental. They were humble in their actions and noble-minded in their dealings and in their behavior—very zealous about the renown of their companions and their country—adamant about the remembrance of their ancestors and their own reputation as people who would not tolerate a disgraceful or shameful matter. They were merciful to a stranger and generous to the elderly; diligent in tribulations and patient in hope. They were quick to learn when they set their minds to do so, rich in creativity and in imagination; very successful at the arts and creative production—a heart that was merry and humorous, fond of music and pleasure and harmless entertainment; easily won over, well and strongly informed about spiritual matters, whether they were truly holy or superstitious.

Their ideas were expansive and their thoughts deep and capacious about the mysterious and inscrutable matters of the mind. They were highly reverential to nobility and about worship, whatever denomination it might belong to, and in particular to anybody who was deserving of special obeisance—and in conclusion we can say with certainty that great powers were attributed to them that were capable of being turned into very effective tools for either good or evil, according to how they had been brought up, powers with which the world was not always familiar, and for that reason, it was incapable of respecting them until they were drawn out on the vast battlegrounds of the world to be fitted up to good avail, and instead of respect they were held in contempt with oppression and scorn, kindled into a blaze of enmity and wrath when they could have been brought to glorious enlightenment in the heights of friendship and honour.

England dealt with them ignorantly in this fashion for ages until they were paid back dearly, and until they had to court them for their friendship, when they were united with themselves, a union of which those who are perceptive are greatly supportive and take tremendous pride confidentially, indeed even those who regard [the Gaels] as being half-brutes and barbarians and traitors. Despite everything, they arose and they shook off the dust of contempt in every country of the world in the cause of one particular kingdom; and their renown travelled the world on the wings of fame to the ends of the earth for every victory that belongs to them and in the prayers on the wings of angels to the royal throne of the Creator in Heaven and their prayers are now ascending in their own melodious and penetrating language (with which, it may well be, our first ancestor entreated for the blessing of the Lord) in every quarter of the world to which they are now scattering, although perhaps this is God's plan to distribute those qualities that belong to their character so that will be advancing the deluded minds of the hostile Gentiles with Heavenly knowledge for their assimilation to civility and godly knowledge.

Some of the youth of our area are among those people in this country who feel disgrace if they are heard speaking the language that their mother taught them, wear the clothes or turn their ear to listen to that music that was considered a source of pride and honour by their ancestors, from whom they inherited their freedoms and the little esteem that is granted to them. We can speak briefly to them and perhaps in the most highly regarded language that they have, in a way that will cause them to contemplate this topic for a while.

My heart aches when I see the coldness that is developing in the young generation, some of whom turn their noses up contemptuously at anyone who wears that clothing, or speaks that language with which they themselves were conversant in the days of their youth and which was the desire, preference and pride of their parents. But we have one cause for solace as we have never seen a person of this sort that the Lowlanders themselves did not look upon without a kind of contempt regarding the basis from which this ignorant arrogance arises.

The Lowlanders know well the dignity of the Gaels and often on holidays or in society meetings we see them gather under the ensign of Scotland in full Highland regalia even though they cannot speak the language and would like to be able to; and we have never seen a Lowlander who was able to speak it and was not proud of it, and indeed, there is no reason for any Lowlander to hold Gaels in contempt today except that he cannot be equated with them in language or in clothing, and he cannot tarnish their renown in any way.

We do not know of any greater enemy to the Gaels on earth today than those among themselves who with ignorance think that it is a disgrace to bear a resemblance to their ancestors. But if they would look to the ancestors of the Lowlanders, they would see that being named after them would be a greater reason for disgrace; but there is little use in engaging with these sort of people who do not read a word about the history of their country or their people but are like sacks with their mouths wide open, letting in anything that a stray wind blows their way.

3: The Gaels at War, and the Gaels at Peace

Gilleasbaig MacFhilip was living in Montreal when he composed the following ode for the Canadian Highland Society's 1859 poetry competition. He was awarded first prize for his efforts and included the text (the Gaelic original as well as a literal English translation) in his first anthology of poetry. All of the other texts in his book are in English and promote the Temperance movement, causing MacFhilip to state self-consciously in the preface, "The English reader will excuse the insertion of the Gaelic Poem...."

In this piece, MacFhilip celebrates the supposed unbeatable power of Highland soldiers using the stock conventions: tartan, kilts, bagpipes and the alleged lack of an equivalent for the word "retreat" in the Gaelic language. Beginning the catalogue of Highland victories in Quebec (lines 15-16), where MacFhilip himself was living,

Figure 3.3 – Gilleasbaig MacFhilip (Archibald MacKillop), the Bind Bard of Megantic, in his old age. The frontispiece portrait from the book Collected Verse: The Blind Bard of Megantic *(1913), provided by the Rare Books and Special Collections of McGill University Library.*

underscores Gaelic participation in the British domination of the province.

Despite the poet's intention to valorize Highland warriors, the poem stumbles on the contradictions of the "civilizing mission" of empires: as the title (which he provided himself) indicates, the Gaels have to be efficient killing-machines when called into duty, but are otherwise meek and submissive subjects in peace-time. While the violence committed by the sepoys during the Indian Rebellion of 1857 is condemned as barbarity (lines 27 and 31), their defeat by the Highland regiment is described as a kind of vengeance (line 32) leaving thousands dead (line 40), perhaps prompting the poet to reassure us that the Gaels are "compassionate, well-mannered and noble" (line 43).

The poem ends with a hint of the paradoxical nature of the Highland participation in empire. Although MacFhilip states that no has ever conquered their land (lines 4 and 56), his own life story, as well as that of many other Gaelic emigrants, contradicts such rhetoric. He admits, after enumerating military victories, that he had long pined for Scotland and would have given the sight of his eyes for one more view of his homeland (lines 49-50). He seems to have become resigned to his blindness, however, and by extension his powerlessness to change circumstances. He says that now he will take consolation in the prestige that Highland regiments have acquired (lines 51-52), perhaps also finding compensation in the vicarious celebrity that poets enjoyed by virtue of their association with their subjects.

In concluding the song by reiterating a portion of its beginning—the entire first verse, in fact—MacFhilip is drawing on an old structural feature of Gaelic poetry called the dùnadh (closure).

Original Text

1   'S e mo rùn a bhith cantainn air mórachd nan Gàidheal!
Cho treun ann an cath, is an càirdeas cho fìor,
Cho dìleas mar bhràithribh is an aonachd cho làidir,
Is nach d' rugadh an tì sin 'thug buaidh air an tìr.

5   Na saighdearan Gàidhealach an éididh ro àlainn,
Bha misneachail dàna is gun eòlas air fiamh;
An claidheamh mór 'nan dorn, is a' phìob a' dèanadh ceòl dhoibh –
Cha b' aithne dhoibh teicheadh, is cha d' strìochd iad a-riamh.

Is chan iongnadh nach teicheadh na daoine as treise
10 Is gun fhocal 's a' Ghàidhlig, ged tha i cho deas
Mar a deirear le daoine "retreat" anns a' Bheurla
Ach is focal "retreat" nach bi feum air am feast.

O is mór tha ri innseadh le aiteas is fìrinn
Mu ghaisgich a' bhreacain is nam boineidean gorm' –
15 Chaidh ceud bliadhna seachad is bu ghlórmhor an latha ud
Nuair thug iad Quebec o na Frangaich le stoirm.

Bha Bonaparte uaibhreach is a Fhrangaich ro bhuadhach
Is an dùil iad thoirt sgrios air an talamh gu léir;
Aig Waterloo chòmhdhail na Gàidheil an t-ollach
20 Is mharbh iad a Fhrangaich is ruaig iad e féin.

Is choisinn iad cliù bhios cho maireann r'an dùthaich,
Ri darach nam beann is ri sléibhtean an fhraoich;
'S iad Gàidheil na h-Alba, aig cogadh mór Alma
'Chuir saighdearan Russia mar cheò leis a' ghaoith.

25 'S na h-Innsean teth grianail, bu ghoirt is bu chianail
An strì a thug saorsa do phrusunaich thruagh;
B' an-iochdmhor is bu ghràineil mar chleachd Nina Sahib
E féin, mun tug Breatann is na Gàidheil air buaidh.

Ach rug iad air Delhi, le cabhaig is starram,
30 Is rinn greim air an Rìgh nuair a b' àill leis dol ás;
Is air na daoine gun nàire, 'mhort fir agus mnathan
Is naoidheanan maoth, rinn iad dìoghaltas gu cas.

Nuair chuala Cailean Caimbeul gun robh Lucknow an teanntachd
Ghrad-tharraing e suas iad ri guaillibh a chéil';
35 Cha robh cridh' ann a dh'fhàilnich, 's ann dh'fhalbh iad gu gàirdeach
Is "Tha na Caimbeulaich 'teachd!" bha a' phìob 'cur an céill.

Is chual' iad 's a' bhaile am fuaim mar mhac-talla
Mun d'ràinig na Gàidheil an teàrnadh o'n bhàs –
Ach ruig iad gu grad iad is shaoraich air fad iad,
40 Is na cinnich 'nam mìltean bha sìnte air a' bhlàr.

Nuair a dhealraich a' mhadainn le cloinn agus mnathan
'S ann dh'fhalbh iad 'gan stiùireadh gu ionad na dìon,
Oir th' an Gàidheal ro thruacant deagh-bheusach is uasal:
Ro threun ann an cath, agus ciùin ann an sìth.

45 Ciod e a' ghnè dhaoine bha 'marbhadh nan ceudan?
Cha tuigeadh na h-Innseanaich dh'aindeon an cridh' –

Bha iad sgeadaichte mar mhnàthaibh is bha ceòl tighinn
o'm meadhan
Is cha robh duine anns na h-Innsean nach ruitheadh iad
sìos.

O Albainn! Mo dhùth[aich]! air son fradharc mo shùilean
50 Bu tric bha mi 'n dòchas gun rachainn thar cuan –
Ach dall is mar a tha mi, biodh cliù nan Gàidheal
A' sìor dhol am meud, is bidh mo ghàirdeachas buan.

Mar seo, tha mi cantainn air mórachd nan Gàidheal!
Cho treun ann an cath, is an càirdeas cho fìor,
55 Cho dìleas mar bhràithribh is an aonachd cho làidir
Is nach d' rugadh an tì sin 'thug buaidh air an tìr.[30]

Translation

(1-4) It is my intention to speak about the greatness of the Gaels! So brave in battle, and so true in friendship, as loyal as brothers and so strong in unity, and no one has ever been born who has conquered their land.

(5-8) The Highland soldiers in most striking clothing, who were courageous and bold, unacquainted with fear; the great claymore in their fists, and the bagpipe making music for them—they did not know retreat, and they never surrendered.

(9-12) It is no surprise that these strongest of men did not flee; although Gaelic is elegant there is no equivalent to "retreat" in English, but "retreat" is a word for which there will never be a need.

(13-16) O, there is much to be said, with joy and truth, about the warriors of the plaid and of the blue bonnets—one hundred years have passed, and that day was glorious when they took Quebec from the French with a storm.

(17-20) Bonaparte was haughty and his Frenchmen quite triumphant and they expected to completely destroy the land; at Waterloo the Gaels met the great warrior, and they killed his Frenchmen and put him to flight.

(21-24) They earned renown that will be as enduring as their country, as the oak of the mountains, and as the heathery hills; it was the Scottish Gaels at the great battle of Alma who dissipated the soldiers of Russia as the mist by the wind.

(25-28) In hot, sunny India, the struggle that brought freedom to the wretched, oppressed people was sore and painful; Nina

Sahib behaved mercilessly and cruelly before Britain and the Gaels defeated him.

(29-32) But they seized Delhi, with a rush and clamour, and they seized the King when he desired to escape; and they brought severe reprisals on the shameless people who murdered men and women and tender infants.

(33-36) When Colin Campbell heard that Lucknow was in dire straits, he quickly drew his men together in solidarity; there was no heart that failed, indeed, they departed cheerfully as the bagpipe proclaimed, "The Campbells are coming!"

(37-40) In the town they heard the sound as an echo before the Highlanders arrived to rescue them from death—but they arrived suddenly and they were all saved, and the heathens were laid low on the battleground in their thousands.

(41-44) When the morning shone with women and children, they departed, guiding them to a haven of safety; for the Gael is compassionate, well-mannered and noble: very brave in battle, and gentle in peace.

(45-48) What manner of men were killing the hundreds? The Indians could not understand, despite their hearts—they were clothed like women, and music came from their centre, and there was no one in India they could not run down.

(49-52) Oh Scotland! My country! For the sight of my eyes, I had often hoped that I could travel across the ocean—but blind as I am, may the renown of the Gaels constantly increase, and my rejoicing will be everlasting.

(53-56) Therefore, I am speaking about the greatness of the Gaels! So brave in battle, and so true in friendship, as loyal as brothers and so strong in unity, and no one has ever been born who has conquered their land.

4: Antigonish Highland Games

Uilleam mac Dhòmhnaill mhic Ruairidh Mac a' Phearsain (William MacPherson) of Loch an Fhamhair (Giant's Lake) in Guysborough County, Nova Scotia, composed the following song-poem in 1871 after he returned home from the Antigonish Highland Games. About three thousand people attended the Games that year, including the 78th Highlanders of Halifax. Dòmhnall Eóghain, a native of South

River, Antigonish County, transcribed the song onto paper much later and sent the song to *The Casket* newspaper along with this note about the circumstances of its composition:

> Bha pìobairean agus dannsairean ann anns an deise Ghàidhealach a bhuineadh do na 78th Highlanders; 's iad a' gabhail puirt ann an clùithean Gàidhealach, agus chòrd an sealladh cho math ri Uilleam 's gun do rinn e an t-òran mun do chaidil e.

> There were bagpipers and dancers there in Highland clothing who belonged to the 78th Highlanders; they were playing tunes in Highland clothing and William enjoyed the spectacle so much that he composed the song before he went to sleep.

A great deal of the poem is spent reassuring the Gaelic audience that as Scots they have a long tradition of military might and autonomy of which they can be proud. Allusions to Bannockburn (line 24) and William Wallace (lines 41-56), like the references to the resistance of the Caledonians to Roman occupation (lines 79-80) and the repeated reminders of Gaelic victories over (anachronistically described) red-coats (lines 20 and 47), reveal the influence of 19th-century anglophone texts.

There are some elements of the poem that may derive from a knowledge of Gaelic history and literary tradition, however. During his own lifetime Rob Roy MacGregor (lines 57-72) became the subject of oral traditions in Gaelic and Scots, as well as written literature in English. King Malcolm III of Scotland left a significant mark on history and Mac a' Phearsain demonstrates that he understands the meaning of the king's epithet (Cenn Mór, "Big Head") by giving it another form in Gaelic (line 19). The medieval Gaelic origin legend claimed that Scots were named after a daughter of the Pharaoh of Egypt, from whom the Gaels themselves were descended, and Mac a' Phearsain shows us that he knows her name, "Scota" (line 75).[31]

Original Text

1   Mi ag amharc air clùithean nan Garbh-Chrìoch
      Fasain Alba tighinn am follais;
      Comann sunndach nan cas meanmnach,
      Cha robh dearbhadh air an leithid;

MILITARISM AND TARTANISM

5   Cha robh coimeas dhoibh ri fhaotainn
    Anns an t-saoghal dhe na rinneadh;
    Dhe na chinnich de shliochd Àdhaimh,
    'S i 'n fhuil Ghàidhealach mo roghainn.

    Comann sunndach, lùthmhor, loinneil,
10 Nach cuir cùl ri dùthaich eile;
    Nach gabhadh o nàmhaid ruaigeadh
    Dh'aindeoin luaidhe, fuaim an teine;
    Fir mo ghaoil nach aomadh teicheilt:
    Siud na laoich nach fhaoidte leadairt,
15 Bhiodh an nàimhdean marbh air raointean
    Mar gun tigeadh gaoth na beathrach.

    Daoine starbhanach, làn spionnaidh
    Làidir, calma, àrd 'nan spiorad
    Bho linn Chaluim a' chinn tharbhaich
20 Is iomadh còta dearg a sgrios iad;
    Daoine càirdeach, làidir, loinneil
    Dhèanadh air an nàmhaid pronnadh;
    Fhad is a' bhios anail beò 's a' Ghàidheal
    Cliù là bràch dha Allt a' Bhonnaich.

25 Cuiream an Gàidheal 'na dheise
    Air paràd cho àille is a sheasas:
    Boineid ghorm agus it' àrd innt',
    Osan gearr is féile preasach;
    Sporan á calg a' bhruic mhollaich,
30 Pìob na nuallanaich le dosaibh,
    Claidheamh cruadhach á deagh stàilinn –
    Buaidh no bàs, biodh iad air thoiseach.

    Nuair a sheinnteadh pìob nam feadan,
    Ghluaiseadh uabhar smuais nam fleasgach;
35 Bhiodh gach buille 'dol an luaithead,
    Is iad cho cruaidh ri fuaim nan dreagan;
    'S i 'n Réisimeid Dhubh gun teagamh
    'Choisinn cliù an ioma teth-chath;
    Nuair a ghluaiseadh iad na faobhair,
40 Chuireadh iad an taobh gu leth taobh.

    Cuimhnichibh air eachdraidh Uallais,
    Is air an neart a bha 'na chlaidheamh:
    Fhad is a bha Alba fo chobhair
    Liuthad s[ad]adh[32] thug e 'Shasainn;

45 Bhiodh iad 's an àraich 'na dheaghaidh
    Marbh air todhar ris an adhar;
    Bhiodh an còta ruadh mu'n dronnaig,
    Luchd nam boineidean 'gan sgathadh.

    Có bha beò an Eòrp na Cruinne
50 'Chumadh comhstrì ri Sior Uilleam?
    Cha ghlacadh Sasann ri bheò e
    Mur biodh mealltaireachd Chloinn Chuimein;
    Chuir iad cuireadh foill do'n Fhraing air
    Chumail aimhreit ris an Leòmhann;
55 Shrac e an cridhe nuas o sgòrnan
    Is shlaod e 'n claidheamh mór troimh dhronnaig.

    Cuimhnichibh air Rob MacGriogair:
    Liuthad bristeadh thug e dh'Athall;
    Cuimhnichibh na deich thar fhichead
60 Thàinig ga shireadh á Sasainn;
    Seallaibh a-nis air an spiorad!
    Thug e dhoibh a làmh gu bhrathadh
    Nuair a thug e bhuapa an t-airgead
    Sgiùrrs e na cealgairean dhachaigh.

65 Òlaibh a-nis slàint' an armainn
    A [b]ha tàmh am Bràighe Raithnich:
    Am Bail' Chuidir, ghabh e 'thathaich
    Far am faigheadh càirdean fasgadh;
    'Fheara, lìonaibh suas gu stràic i,
70 Òlaibh, tràighibh i gu h-ealamh –
    Bha Rob Ruadh an airm a' Ghàidheil
    Nuair a thug am Bàs e dhachaigh.

    Hó, ged leanainn seo air adhart
    Thigeadh sgeul as ùr gu m' mheomhair
75 Mu shliochd gineal Ghàidheal Scòtia
    Bhiteadh leis an òr gun cheannach;
    Cha robh nàimhdean riamh ri faotainn
    Sheasadh le faobhar mu'n coinneamh;
    Comann rìoghail Chaledòni
    Chuir sliochd nan Ròmanach fodha.[33]

Translation

(1-8) I gaze at the clothing of the Highlands, the fashion of Scotland on display; a lively group with high-spirited feet, they seek no approval; in all of creation, no equal to them can be found; of all of the descendants of Adam, the blood of the Gaels is my favourite.

(9-16) A lively, athletic, elegant group who will not retreat from any land; who cannot be defeated by any enemy despite bullets and the sound of gunpowder; my beloved men who would not yield to flight; those are the champions who could not be walloped; their enemies would be dead on fields as though lightning wind had come.

(17-24) Robust men, full of energy, strong, brave, high-spirited; ever since the age of Malcolm the large-headed, they have destroyed many a red-coat; friendly, sturdy, elegant people who would give their enemies a beating; for as long as the Gael has breath, the [Battle of] Bannockburn will always be acclaimed.

(25-32) Let me put the Gael into his attire, on a parade as lovely as can be: a blue bonnet with a long feather in it, short hose and a kilted tartan; a sporran made from the spiky pelt of the furry badger, the bellowing bagpipes with its drones, a steel claymore of excellent metal—victory or death, let them lead the charge.

(33-40) When the chanter-full bagpipe would be played, the pride in the marrow of the young men would be aroused; each finger-movement would accelerate and be as harsh as the roar of the dragons; it is the Black Watch that has indeed earned renown in many a heated battle; when they would brandish the blades, they would turn aside the enemy.

(41-48) Remember the history of [William] Wallace, and the strength that was in his sword: for as long as he assisted Scotland, he gave many a thrust to England; they were left dead, exposed to the air, decaying on the battleground in his wake; the red coat would be around their back as the people of the bonnets cut them down.

(49-56) Who lived in Europe who could challenge Sir William? England would have never captured him alive if it weren't for the treachery of the Cummings; they sent a deceitful invitation to France in order to cause disturbance to the Lion; he tore the heart out through his throat and he heaved the claymore through his back.

(57-64) Remember Rob [Roy] MacGregor: he gave Atholl many a defeat; remember the thirty who came from England to find him; look at their spirit now! He gave his hand to them for betrayal; when he took the money from them, he routed the traitors homewards.

(65-72) Drink now to the health of the hero who dwelled in Brae Rannoch: he lived in Balquhidder where his relations would find shelter; o men, fill up [the toast] for pride's sake, drink it and empty it nimbly; Rob Roy was kitted out in Highland gear when Death took him home.

(73-80) *Hó*, even if I were to continue this, some new story would come into my mind about the Gaelic offspring of Scotia who could not be bought with gold; no enemy could ever be found who could withstand, with blades, their challenge; the royal company of Caledonia who threw down the Roman people.

5: Address to Hamilton and Toronto Gaelic Societies

In the summer of 1891, D. J. Campbell, a resident of Hamilton, Ontario, addressed the members of the Hamilton and Toronto Gaelic societies who gathered together for an inaugural outdoor assembly.

> A very pleasant event occurred on Saturday last at Oakville when the Gaelic societies of Hamilton and Toronto met for the first time to picnic and enjoy themselves together. The old motto Clanna nan Gàidheal an guaillibh a chéile was exemplified in a friendly manner and it is safe to say that the acquaintance begun under the favorable auspices which prevailed on Saturday will prove lasting and beneficial to the societies. ...
>
> Until the arrival of the afternoon boats the visitors enjoyed themselves by picnicking on the green sward and engaging in friendly games. The Hamilton contingent were the first of the late arrivals to come in. They were met at the wharf by Piper Munro and some of the officers and escorted to the grounds. Immediately thereafter the Modjeska steamed up, and from four to five hundred Toronto Highlanders and friends were landed amid the cheers of their Hamilton brethren. ...
>
> It was meet that they should assemble at Oakville, the first settler of which was a sturdy Highlander named Mr. Chisholm, who,

for aught he knew, at that time owned all the land on which Oakville was subsequently built.[34]

Campbell's talk was originally delivered in English and was translated into Gaelic[35] before it was printed in *The Scottish Canadian* newspaper. His claim that there were millions of Scottish emigrants in Canada at the end of the 19th century is obviously exaggerated, although Campbell's declaration of 250,000 Gaelic speakers in Canada was mirrored by a contemporary tally by Canadian church officials. It is well above a recent estimation of 90,000 Gaelic speakers based on census records, however.[36]

The text applauds Gaels for their loyal service in securing North American territories for the British Crown. Campbell clearly endorses deference to anglophone norms in opposition to the contesting claims of the Francophone community. His stance that Gaelic is more deserving than French as a second language in Canada is merely rhetorical, given that he also states that Gaels make no complaint or protest that their language gets no recognition or usage in the formal institutions of the nation. His depiction of Gaelic as only a musical language of emotion and familial ties implies that it is not suitable for such official or high-status purposes.

Campbell claims that world peace will be achieved by the dominance of the British Empire and the meek submission of others to that authority. The Gaelic language, like other elements of Highland culture, he implies, must not challenge or cause discord for an anglocentric hegemony. Within this system of logic, Highlanders are paragons of humble and loyal service that other subjects of the British Crown should follow.

Original Text

> A chinn-suidhe is a chàirdean Gàidhealach bho bhailtean Thoronto agus Hamilton: Anns a' chiad àite, tha e 'toirt móran toileachais-inntinn dhomh gum bheil na h-uiread bho'n dà bhaile chomharraichte seo a tha neadaichte air bruach Loch Ontario, agus bho'n dùthaich mun cuairt, air cruinneachadh an-seo, air an latha chiùin shamhraidh seo a dh'fhaotainn eòlais air aon a chéile, agus dh'ùrachadh seann chàirdeas; agus tha mi 'cur an céill an dòchas anns na tìmean a tha 'teachd, gun coinnich sinn gach bliadhna a dh'ùrachadh agus a chomhphàrtachadh ar

deagh ghean aig coinneamhan sunndach càirdeil de'n t-seòrsa seo.

Air dhomh a bhith sealltainn thairis air eachdraidh an t-sluaigh a thàinig do'n dùthaich seo, tha mi 'faicinn nam muillian de dh'Albannaich a thàinig do'n dùthaich seo, gum bu Ghàidheil dà-thrian diubh. Tha e air a dhèanamh a-mach gum bheil corr agus 1,000,000 de Ghàidheil agus d'an gineal an Canada aig an àm seo, agus gum bheil air a' chuid as lugha ceathramh dhiubh seo a thuigeas agus a bhruidhneas Gàidhlig. B' e seo an sluagh a bha 'nam prìomh mheadhon air an uachdaranachd oirdheirc seo againne a chur mar phàirt dhi fhéin ri oighreachd ghlòrmhor Breatainn.

Cha ruig mi leas a chur 'nar cuimhne gum bheil mìltean do Ghàidheil anns an dùthaich seo a tha dìleas do'n dùthaich, do'n Bhan-Rìgh, is d'a Crùn; is ged nach deach an cànain altram, no a cleachdadh an cùirt, no am Pàrlamaid, cha chualas riamh an dragh no an iorgaill. Ach their mi seo: ma tha tuilleadh agus aon chànain feumail an cùirt no am Pàrlamaid, gu dé a' chànain as coraiche air an urram sin 'fhaotainn na cànain nan treun-laoch, a sheas guala ri gualainn air Còmhnard Abrahaim, am pìobairean a sheinn binn-cheòl na h-Alba, is an claidhmhnean móra a' deàlradh an grian na h-òig-mhaidne an latha a chaidh an dùthaich oirdheirc seo againne a chosnadh do Chrùn Bhreatainn. 'S ann do ghaisge gun choimeas nan saighdearan Gàidhealach a tha sinn fo fhiachaibh, gum bheil agus gun robh an t-Arm Breatannach buadhach anns gach dùthaich 's an robh dleasnas agus onair 'gan gairm.

Agus an-diugh, tha bratach Bhreatainn gu bòstal a' snàmh thairis air an t-siathamh cuid de raon an domhainn, agus thairis air a' cheathramh cuid de 'sluagh. Tha mi gu h-onarach a' creidsinn is ag ràdh gur ann an tomhas mór tro mhisneach agus ghaisge Chlann nan Gàidheal, a thàinig Breatann gu bhith 'na rìoghachd cho làidir glòrmhor is a tha i an-diugh. Tro ghaisge ghreimeil threun-laoch Albann, cha deach riamh a chìosnachadh, chaidh an earrann mu thuath seo de Aimearaga a spìonadh bho chumhachd choigreach agus air a tàthadh ri rìoghachd Breatainn. Aig facal na h-àithne, air Còmhnard

Sliabh Abrahaim, le mór-ghaisge, bhrùchd fir làidir a' bhreacain is an fhéile air an aghaidh gu buaidh ghlòrmhor agus bu leinne Canada.

Air an adhbhar sin, tha mi a' cur an céill gur ann do Chlann nan Gaidheal a tha sinn am fiachaibh air son gur dùthaich Bhreatannach Canada an-diugh. Cha choigrich na Gàidheil 's an dùthaich ach daoine nach gabh seachnadh. Bho òg-mhadainn an latha a streap iad suas Àirde chreagach Sliabh Abrahaim gus an uair seo, bha aig Gàidheil ann an iomadh dòigh gnothach ri uachdaranachd na dùthcha. Bha Ceann-feadhna Chlann Dòmhnaill, An Ridire Iain Dòmhnallach nach maireann, a-nis 'na riaghladair anns an dùthaich dlùth air dà fhichead bliadhna. Duine aig an robh comas gun choimeas mar cheannard agus mar chomhairliche rìoghachd. Duine a chomh-éignich mór-mheas eadhon bho na daoine a b' eascàirdiche ris. Duine a rugadh 'na Bhreatannach, agus 'na Bhreatannach chaith e 'bheatha gu latha a bhàis.

An t-Onarach Alasdair MacCoinnich, duine eile a bha mìorbhuileach ann an comas; bha 'uile fhacail agus 'ghnìomhan a leigeil ris a ghràdh d'a dhùthaich is bidh a reachdan glice agus a ràideanais air an gléidheadh air chuimhne le ginealaich a tha ri teachd. Agus gun iomradh air na h-onaraich O. Mowat agus Deorsa Ross, daoine beaga am pearsa, ach cho tapaidh is a sheas riamh ann an làrach bhròg, no air móran tuillidh de dh'ainmean a tha gràdhach leinn a tha 'soillseachadh air iomadh dóigh ann an eachdraidh Chanada. Ainmean a tha 'dearbhadh gum bheil na Gàidheil 'nan sluagh nach gabh seachnadh, a tha, agus a bha, a' cleachdadh uachdaranachd chumhachdach a chum math. Coma gu dé an t-anacothrom a bhios iad fodha, no am bacadh a théid a chur orra, gheibh iad an làmh an uachdar orra air fad.

Cha labhair mi an-dràsta air na bàird a rinn a' chànain Ghàidhealach glòrmhor; no air fir agus mnathan gaisgeil treun a rinn naomh i le briathran bàis; no air na martaraich a dhòirt am fuil ann an seirbhis agus an adhbhar am Maighstir. Iadsan nach d' fhoghlaim air tùs aig glùn am màthar, iadsan nach d' fhuair solas orra ann an cagarsaich gaoil, ann am mànran blàth, no ann an caoidh mhuladach ri àm trioblaid, no ann an athchuinge dhùrachdach an anama beò: chan urra dhaibh tuigsinn na faireachdainnean agus an gluasad-inntinn leis am bheil na Gàidheil a' meas an cànain mhilis cheòlmhor bhrìoghail fhéin.

Anns na blàir-chath a bu chruaidhe air an cleachdadh có aca a b' ann air Còmhnard Sliabh Abrahaim no ag imeachd le feachd-cheum ann an teas nan Innsean gu Lucknow, no anns an t-sreang chaol dhearg aig an Ridire Cailean air mullaichean Bhala-clabha no air gainmheach theth na h-Éiphit aig Tel-al-Keber, is anns gach ceàrn de'n t-saoghal 's ann bu chruaidhe bha gaisge Bhreatann air a feuchainn. An-sin, àrd thairis air fuaim nan inneal-cogaidh, àrd os cionn toirm lagalach a' chath, chluinnte srannraich gheur na pìob móire, measgte le gairm nan Gàidheil: "Clanna nan Gàidheal an guaillibh a chéile," is iad a' brùchdadh air an aghaidh gu buaidh. Faodaidh mi seo a chur an céill, ged a shaoileas cuid agaibh gur iongantach e, nach eil pìobaire an-seo an-diugh, no air son na cuid sin deth an àite sam bith eile, a dh'ionnsaich riamh a' phìob a chur air ghleus ri àithne an ruaig a ghabhail; agus 's e an t-adhbhar, nach eil a leithid de cheòl, na de chaismeachd-shiubhail, 'na fhoclair, agus coma a bhitheadh, cha robh riamh feuma aca air a leithid; oir b' e cleachdainnan Ghàidheal anns gach linn, leigeil leis na nàimhdean an teicheadh a dhèanadh.

Ach feumaidh mi tighinn gu co-dhùnadh, oir lean mi tuilleadh is fada cheana, ach is éiginn domh seo a ràdh mun dèan mi suidhe: gum bheil a' chàirdealachd agus an caoimhneas a tha air am faicinn an-seo an-diugh, a' toirt adhbhar dhuinn a chreidsinn gum bheil na tìmean a' greasad, na tìmean glòrmhor sin, nuair nach bi buaireas gach dream, gach buidheann, is gach creideamh a' dèanadh mì-riaghailt no aimhreit air an dùthaich àlainn agus thorach seo. Nuair a thig an latha glòrmhor sin, mar as cinnteach gun tig, agus a bheachdaicheas sinn air Canada, an té as òige is maisiche de rìoghachdan saora, ceangailte ri chéile ann am bannaibh gràidh; bho chladach na h-Atlantic ann an Albainn Ùir, gu claon-bhruachaibh tràighe na fairge Shèimh ann an Columbia àlainn, an-sin chithear bonaidean Gàidhealach, àrd 's an adhar, agus cluinnear àrd-iollach an cànain mhilis ar dùthcha, a' cur an céill "Ciad mìle fàilte" do'n reul as deàlraiche is as àille ann an Crùn Bhreatainn.[37]

Translation

Dear president and Highland friends, from the cities of Toronto and Hamilton: firstly, it gives me great pleasure that there are so many people from these two notable cities that are nestled on the banks of Lake Ontario, and from the outlying areas, who are gathered here on this peaceful summer day to get to know one another and to renew old friendships; and I would like to express the hope that, in the times to come, we will meet every year to renew and share our goodwill at friendly, merry meetings of this sort.

After looking over the history of the people who came to this country, I see that of the millions of Scots who came to this country, Gaels made up two-thirds of them. It is reckoned that there are more than 1,000,000 Gaels and their descendants in Canada at this time, and that at the very least a quarter of them can understand and speak Gaelic. It was this people who were the means by which this illustrious dominion of ours was added as her own entity to the glorious heritage of Britain.

I needn't remind you that there are thousands of Gaels in this country who are loyal to the country, to the Queen, and to her Crown; and although their language has not been nurtured or used in court or in Parliament, no complaints or outrage have ever been heard about it. But I will say this: if more than one language is useful in court or in Parliament, what language most rightfully deserves to get that honour than the language of the champions, who stood shoulder to shoulder on the Plains of Abraham, their bagpipers playing the sweet music of Scotland, and their great claymores shining in the early morning sun on the day in which this illustrious country was won for the British Crown. It is to the peerless heroism of the Highland soldiers that we are indebted, that the British military was and is victorious in every country to which their duty and honour are called.

And today, the British flag proudly flies over a sixth part of the surface of the world and over a quarter of its inhabitants. I honestly believe and assert that it is in great part through the courage and heroism of the Gaelic people that Britain came to be a kingdom as strong and glorious as it is today. Through the tenacious heroism of the champions of Scotland, who were never defeated, this northern portion of North America was seized away from the command of foreigners and fused with the kingdom of Britain. When given the command on the Plains of Abraham, the strong men of the plaids and the kilts burst forward with great heroism to glorious victory and Canada was ours.

It is for that reason that I am declaring that it is to the Gaelic people that we are indebted for Canada being a British land today. The Gaels are not foreigners in this country but people who cannot be ignored. From the early morning of the day on which they ascended the craggy height of the Plains of Abraham to this very moment, the Gaels have had a hand in the leadership of the country in many ways. The MacDonald chieftain, the late Sir John Macdonald, was the leader in the country close to forty years. A man who had matchless competence as a leader and as a nation's counsellor. A man who demanded great respect even from the people who were least friendly to him. A man who was born a Briton and who spent his life as a Briton until the day that he died.

The Honourable Alexander Mackenzie is another man who had marvellous capacities; his every word and deed demonstrated his love of his country and his wise laws and pronouncements will be preserved in the memory of generations to come. And that is without mentioning the honourable O. Mowat and George Ross, small men in stature but as formidable as any men on two legs, or many further names which are beloved to us that shine in many ways in the history of Canada. Names that prove that the Gaels are a people who cannot be ignored, who are and were exercising powerful leadership for the best. Whatever the disadvantages they may suffer, or the obstacles that are placed before them, they will gain the upper hand over all.

I will not speak at present about the poets who made the Gaelic language glorious; or about the brave, heroic men and women who made it holy with the words of [their] death; or about the

MILITARISM AND TARTANISM

martyrs who spilled their blood in the service and cause of their Master. Those who did not originally learn it at their mother's knee, those who did not experience it in whisperings of love, in playful talk, or in emotional outpourings at a difficult time, or in the sincere supplication of their living soul: they cannot understand how their own sweet, melodious, musical, efficacious language can move the feelings and the mental state of the Gael.

In the hardest battles fought, whether it was on the Heights of the Plains of Abraham or travelling with infantry in the heat of India to Lucknow, or in Sir Colin's thin red line on the Heights of Balaclava, or on the hot sands of Egypt at Tel-al-Keber, and in every corner of the world, the battle-mettle of Britain was tested even harder. There, high above the sound of the war machines, high above the thundering din of war, the piercing drone of the bagpipe would be heard mixed with the battle-cry of the Gaels, "Highlanders, shoulder to shoulder," as they burst forward to victory. I can say this, although it may surprise some of you, there is no bagpiper here today, or for that matter in any place at all, who ever learned how to use the bagpipe in order to signal a retreat; and the reason is that there is no such music or march in his repertoire, and that doesn't matter, as there was never any need for it; for it has always been the custom of the Gaels in every age to allow their enemy to retreat.

But I must come to a conclusion, for I have already gone on for too long, but I must say this before I sit down: that the friendship and the kindness that has been seen here today gives us reason to believe that the times are hastening, those glorious times, when the troubles of every population, group and religion will not cause disorder or upheaval to this beautiful, fertile country. When that glorious day arrives, as it certainly will, and we think about Canada, the youngest and most exquisite of free countries, united together in bonds of love; from the shore of the Atlantic in Nova Scotia to the winding sea-banks of the Pacific Ocean in lovely [British] Columbia, there will be seen Highland bonnets, high in the air, a loud shout in the sweet language of our country will call out "A hundred thousand welcomes" to the most radiant and most lovely star in the Crown of Britain.

6: Speech by Niall Mac na h-Innse at Lochiel

The Reverend Dr. Niall Mac na h-Innse was a lecturer at the Presbyterian College of Montreal who was said to have taught courses there for some fifteen years on Gaelic language and literature.[38] He delivered the following speech in Lochiel, Ontario, in 1896 to commemorate the Highland pioneers of the settlement,[39] whom he defines primarily in terms of their language and their tradition of military service.

The early Gaelic settlers of Glengarry had fought as Loyalists during the American Revolutionary War. Glengarry regiments were later deployed during the Upper Canadian Rebellion of 1837. The king's representative sent a letter in early 1838 specifically to the settlers of this township, praising them for their obedience and dedication to the Crown: "Brave and loyal Highlanders of Lochiel ... I feel confident, if this unprincipled aggression should continue, that, in one body, you will advance to exterminate the perfidious invaders of our liberties, or, like Highlanders, perish with your backs to the field...."[40] Mac na h-Innse's text is similarly enthusiastic about presumed Highland martial virtues and royalism but seems deliberately archaistic, invoking the images of ancient Celtic warriors wielding swords and spears at a time when weaponry and battle tactics were changing rapidly.

The Gaelic immigrant communities in Glengarry County contained a mixture of Catholic and Protestant congregations although Lochiel itself was Presbyterian. Mac na h-Innse's text contains some subtle religious overtones, such as the implication that the Gaels of the past believed in obsolete superstitions. His statement that "cha do strìochd na Gàidheil riamh do dh'Ìmpirean uaibhreach na Ròimhe" (the Gaels never submitted to the haughty emperors of Rome) might be read as religious revisionism attempting to reimagine Scottish history through a Protestant lens that legitimated deference to the religious and political authority of the British Crown. This would have struck a chord in the contested religious environment of Canada, with its large numbers of Catholic Francophones. A militantly anti-Catholic religious identity was a crucial catalyst in the formation of the British Empire, as Linda Colley has argued:

> Time and time again, war with France brought Britons, whether they hailed from Wales, Scotland, or England, into confrontation with an obviously hostile Other and encouraged them to define themselves collectively against it. They defined themselves as

Protestants struggling for survival against the world's foremost Catholic power. They defined themselves against the French as they imagined them to be, superstitious, militarist, decadent and unfree.[41]

Mac na h-Innse's interests in Gaelic literature are exemplified by the extracts of traditional and contemporary song-poetry which are strewn throughout his text. He also intimates that he accepts James Macpherson's claim that the volumes of epic poetry he published in English (1760-1765) were translations of Gaelic poetry originally composed by Ossian. Although they were, in fact, loosely based on the characters and scenarios of medieval Gaelic literature, Macpherson adapted material creatively to appeal to the expectations and interests of an anglophone audience.[42] The name of the character who acts as the voice of the narrative itself, the poet Ossian, corresponds closely to the name of a corresponding figure in Gaelic literature ("Oisean"), but other names of many other people and places in Macpherson's compositions were much more contorted from their original forms or were entirely invented by him. The place name "Selma," for example, is a strange mutation of "Alma," the home base of the Fian (Fionn mac Cumhaill's warrior band).

Original Text

> B' àbhaist do bhàird no do dh'fhilidhean na Féinne anns na linntean a tha fad air chùl a bhith creidsinn anns an eòlas bheag air nithean spioradail a bh' aca, gun robh an sinnsirean 'nan ciar-thalla ann an ceò doilleir nan neul, a' sealltainn do ghnàth a-nuas orra is 'gam brosnachadh a bhith duineil, measail, sgiobalta anns gach gnìomh is gàbhadh is cunnart. Nach fhaod sinn a-nochd a bhith smuaineachadh gum bheil spioradan nan Gàidheal a rinn euchdan cho mór ann an Loch Iall anns na làithean a dh'aom ag amharc a-nuas oirnn le tlachd is le toileachas domhainn air a' chlach-chuimhne ealanta chuir an clann suas a chum meas is onair a thabhairt do chuimhne is do bhuaidhean lìonmhor nan Gàidheal a bha eudmhor, measail, sùrdail ann an Loch Iall.
>
> Tha an seanfhacal ag ràdh mu dheidhinn nan laoch is nan sonn a bha dìleas ann an strì nan lann, "Có nach cuireadh clach 'nan carn?" Their sinn uile, "có nach cuireadh clach ann an carnan

Ghàidheal dìcheallach dùrachdach toilichte a leag le neart an gàirdean craobhan garbha 's an àrd-bhaile seo, agus le iomadh Bee-Roiligidh a loisg le dragh nach robh suarach, le dealas a bha èasgaidh gach moch is gach an-moch, na craobhan tiugha, meurach agus a dheasaich ionadan-còmhnaidh agus teachd-an-tìr shubhailceach onarach dhaibh fhéin agus d'an cloinn?"

Tha briatharan tiamhaidh an Ollaimh MacLachainn, am bàrd milis, gleusta bhuineas do'r linn fhéin, freagarrach gu leòr mu dhéidhinn nan gleann is nan aonaichean anns an d' rugadh na Gàidheil a thàinig do Loch Iall:

A ghlinn ud shìos, a ghlinn ud shìos...

Agus ma bheir sinn géill do bhàrd Sheallama nam beusan ciùin is nan caomh-dhàn, creididh sinn gur e iarrtas dùrachdach nan Gàidheal a tha ann an suaimhneas a' bhàis anns a' bhaile seo, nam biodh comas aca air am beachdan is an comhairlean a chur an céill, gum biodh na Gàidheil a chuir an òrdugh a' chlach-chuimhne eireachdail seo, a' leantainn daonnan le cridheachan suilbhir treubha achdranach, ris gach nì as fhearr, as measarra, is as motha tlàths is buannachd ann an cliù is ann an stòldachd is an eachdraidh nan daoine geamnaidh gaisgeil bho'n tàinig iad.

Ged nach eil Canada ach òg ann an coimeas ri rìoghachdan uaibhreach làidir na Roinn-Eòrpa, b' éiginn di iomadh cunnart eagalach a sheasamh agus fuil a mic a dhòrtadh air son a còireachan is a saorsa 'dhìon bho'n nàmhaid fhuileachdach gharg. Dhearbh Gàidheil Ghlinn Garaidh, agus Gàidheil Loch Iall, maille ri càch, ann an cogadh no dhà, agus air iomadh blàr, gum bheil gàirdean nan Gàidheal anns an dùthaich seo fhathast foghainteach, neartmhor agus ealamh, agus gum bheil fìor-fhuil nan sonn a chìosnaich Bonaparte fhathast blàth is glan ann an cridheachan Gàidheil na siorramachd seo, Gàidheil a thug dearbhadh diongmhalta cheana gum bheil, agus gun urrainn dhaibh a bhith, gach àm mearganta mìleanta ann an strì nan lann air machair is faiche an àir.

Ma bhios feum air iomchair nan claidheamh is nan sleagh anns an aimsir a tha ri teachd, nochdaidh iad gun dèan iad ann an trusgan ciar na còmhraig, ann an àm leadairt nan lann is nan clogaidean, onair do na Gàidheil bho'n tàinig iad—Gàidheil a bha ciùin am feadh a bha sìth air gach sliabh is tràigh is aonach, agus a bha calma cosgarra an uair a thogadh an nàmhaid a ghuth gu dàna tàireil.

Agus a-nise, facal no dhà mu'n Ghàidhlig—mu'n chainnt aosmhor thapaidh a labhair laoich na h-Alba—laoich nach b' urrainn na Ròmanaich, leis gach feachd is feart anabarrach iomraiteach a bhuineadh dhaibh, riamh a chìosnachadh. Ged a thug iad buaidh aig blàr-cogaidh air Calgacus, an Gàidheal gagach, cha do strìochd na Gàidheil riamh do dh'Ìmpirean uaibhreach na Ròimhe.

A' cheud uair a bha mi anns a' bhaile seo, dh'innis cuideigin domh nach robh ach trì no ceithir de theaghlaichean ann an Loch Iall nach robh labhairt na Gàidhlig. Cha ruig sinn a leas nàire no rudhadh gruaidh a bhith oirnn mu dhéidhinn na Gàidhlig, oir bha i deas-labhrach, fileanta, agus còinneach liath m'a timcheall mun deachaidh tulgainn a dhèanamh air creathall Beurla no Fraingis. Tha na bàird Ghàidhealach le briathran dealbhach, fonnmhor a' dèanamh luaidh air meas is mórchuis na Gàidhlig. Tha Alasdair mac Mhaighstir Alasdair ag ràdh:

Gur i labhair Àdhamh ann am Parras fhéin...

Tha Donnchadh Bàn Mac an t-Saoir, bàrd oirdheirc aiginneach Ghlinn Urchaidh, ag ràdh le móran toileachais is cinnte, "Gur i 'Ghàidhlig an labhairt phrìseil chùramach a rinn cumhnanta ri Àdhamh." Tha gu cinnteach an sgeula nis sean is searbh—oir chaidh iomadh linn seachad on a thòisich e air a bhith air aithris—gun robh agus gum bheil a' Ghàidhlig ann am feasgar a treòir is a làithean; gum bheil i euslainteach agus aig ceann-uidhe a turais, agus gum feum i ann an ùine ghearr an deò deireannach a thoirt suas, is àite tostach a ghabhail ann an ciste nam marbh agus a bhith air a tasgaidh anns an ùir taobh ri taobh ris na Gàidheil a labhair i is a bha misneachail cliùiteach 'nan latha is 'nan inbhe fhéin.

Thàinig agus dh'fhalbh iomadh geamhradh agus samhradh, is sneachd is uisge, is fuachd is teas, is grian is gealach, on a thòisich luchd-mì-rùin air a bhith 'ga ràdh, gun robh a' Ghàidhlig breòite, truagh, agus gun robh i ag imeachd le ceum deireannach a dh'ionnsaigh na h-uaighe.

Ach tha a' Ghàidhlig beò beathail sunndach fhathast, ann an Loch Iall agus ann an iomadh àite is ceàrna eile. Tha freumh bunaiteach aice ann an tìr nan gleann is nam breacan. Tha iomadh comann air feadh na h-Alba ag altrum spéis bhlàth is dhomhainn dhi is a' dèanamh móran strì is tapaidh ás a leth. Tha i a' fàs 'na faillean fiùranach anns na h-Innsean, ann an Astràilia, ann an Aimearaga Tuath is Deas.

Is lìonmhor iadsan ann an Canada tha àrd is cumhachdach air feadh na dùthcha, a tha glé phròiseil gur Gàidheil a th' annta, agus gum bheil comas aca air cànain Oisein, bàrd Sheallama nam feart, a labhairt gu furasta, gu pongail, agus gu ceòlmhor. 'S ann da-rìreamh a tha a' Ghàidhlig aig an àm seo ag ath-nuadhachadh a h-òige is a' cur shobhraichean is neòineanan dreachmhor ann an suaicheantas a cinn is a maise. Ruithidh móran Ghàidheal an cuairt talmhaidh ann an Loch Iall mun téid an fhòd ghorm a chur gu bràth air uchd leathann làidir uasal na Gàidhlig. Is ro mhath, ma-tà, tha Niall MacLeòid, am Bàrd Sgitheanach, a' seinn:

Dùisg suas, a Ghàidhlig, is tog do ghuth...

Tha dòchas mór is deòthasach agam gun tig ás dachaidhean faoilidh Loch Iall anns na làithean nach fhaic sinne, iomadh Gàidheal a nì ainm mór is measail da fhéin ann am parlamaidean is oilthighean ar dùthcha. Tha dòchas làidir agam gum bi Gàidheil Loch Iall le móran sùird is eòlais a' cur gu buil ghasta mar thuathanaich nan achaidhean farsaing, còmhnard, beartach a chì mi air gach taobh dhìom.

'S e mo bheachd nach eil ann an Canada gu léir beatha as motha sonais is toil-inntinn as fhearr agus as fhallaine na beatha is saothair an tuathanaich. Tha dòchas mór is cinnteach agam, mar anns na làithean a bha is a dh'aom, gun éirich agus gum bi ann an Loch Iall anns na bliadhnaichean a tha ri teachd, iomadh nighean agus boireannach màlda, sèimh, sunndach, sgiamhach, a chumas suas ainm is cliù is beusan nam ban Gàidhealach anns gach linn is tìr.

Do gach seanair is seanmhair, do gach mac is nighean Gàidhealach ann am baile ainmeil Loch Iall, tha mi a' toirt mo mhìle beannachd, an latha chì is nach fhaic.⁴³

Translation

In times long since past, the poets and professional literati of the Fian used to believe in the little knowledge that they had of spiritual things, that their ancestors were in their shadowy hall in the dark mists of the clouds, constantly watching them from above and encouraging them to be brave, respectable, and neat in every action, risk and danger. Shouldn't we tonight think that the spirits of the Gaels who achieved great accomplishments in Lochiel in the past are looking down on us with delight and enjoyment at the elegant monument that their descendants erected in order to give honour and esteem to the memory and to the copious genius of the Gaels who were dedicated, esteemed and energetic in Lochiel?

The proverb states regarding the warriors and champions who were devout in the conflict of swords, "Who wouldn't place a stone on their cairn?" We can all say, "Who wouldn't place a stone on the cairns of the contented, diligent, well-intentioned Gaels who, with the strength of their arms, felled the rough trees in this city, and with many a community bee burnt the thick, well-branched trees with considerable effort and with zeal that was relentless, day and night, and who built habitations and gathered a virtuous and honourable income for themselves and for their children?"

The emotional words of Doctor MacLachainn, the melodious and adept poet who belongs to our own era, are sufficiently appropriate regarding the glens and peaks in which the Gaels who came to Lochiel were born:

O yonder glen below, o yonder glen below....

And if we take to heart the poet of Selma of the gentle manners and the tender songs, we will believe that it is the sincere desire of the Gaels who are in the serenity of Death in this township, if they had the ability to express their opinions and advice, that the [living] Gaels who have created this handsome monument should always follow with cheerful, brave, adventurous hearts every thing that is best, that is most prudent, that has the most kindness and profit in repute, in civility and in the history of the somber, heroic people from which they came.

Although Canada is yet young in comparison with the other strong and proud kingdoms of Europe, she has had to withstand many a terrible danger and spill the blood of her sons in order to defend her rights and her freedom from the violent and fierce enemy. The Gaels of Glengarry and the Gaels of Lochiel have proved, along with the others, in a war or two, and in many a battle, that the arms of the Gael in this country are still robust, strong and agile, and that the true blood of the heroes who defeated Bonaparte is still warm and pure in the hearts of the Gaels of this county, Gaels who have already provided firm proof that they are, and that they are capable of being, in all times brisk and soldier-like in the conflict of swords on the plains and fields of battle.

If there is a need for the brandishing of swords and spears in the time to come, they will demonstrate that they will, in the dusky shroud of the skirmish, at the time of the thrashing of the blades and the helmets, do honour to the Gaels from whom they come—Gaels who were tranquil as long as there was peace on every hillside and beach and summit, and who were brave and bellicose when the enemy boldly and tauntingly raised their voice.

And now, a word or two about Gaelic—about the ancient and accomplished language that the warriors of Scotland spoke—warriors that the Romans, with every exceedingly renowned troop and capacity that belonged to them, could never defeat. Although they triumphed on the battlefield against Calgacus, the armour-plated Gael, the Gaels never submitted to the haughty emperors of Rome.

The first time that I was in this township, someone told me that there were only three or four families in Lochiel who did not speak Gaelic. We do not need to suffer shame or the blushing of cheeks on account of Gaelic, for it is eloquent and articulate and was bedecked with grey moss before the cradles of English or French were ever rocked. The Highland poets with sagacious and melodious expressions make allusion to the esteem and magnificence of Gaelic. Alexander MacDonald says:

It is what Adam spoke in Paradise itself....

Duncan Ban Macintyre, the illustrious and high-spirited poet of Glenorchy, says with great pleasure and conviction, "Gaelic is the priceless and perceptive speech in which a covenant was made with Adam." The tale is certainly now old and worn out—for many an era has passed since it began to be told—that Gaelic was and is in the twilight of her days and her vigour; that she is sickly and at the end of her journey, and that she must in a short time expel her last breath and take a silent place in the coffin of the dead and be buried in the soil alongside the Gaels who spoke her and were courageous and renowned in their era and in their own rank.

Many a winter and summer have come and gone, with snow and rain, and cold and heat, and sun and moon, since the people of ill-will began saying it, that Gaelic is sickly and wretched and that she was departing with her last step toward the grave.

But Gaelic is still alive, vivacious and exuberant in Lochiel and in many other places and corners. She is firmly rooted in the land of the glens and the tartans. There are many organizations throughout Scotland that foster warm and deep affection for her and who are exerting themselves greatly on her behalf. She is growing fresh sprouts in the Indies, in Australia, and in North and South America.

There are many in Canada who are powerful and of high rank throughout the country who are very proud that they are Gaels and that they are capable of speaking the language of Ossian, the bard of virtuous Selma, with ease, precision and euphony. It is true that at this time Gaelic is renewing her youth and is adding primroses and daisies to her emblem and her beauty. Many Gaels will run their mortal course in Lochiel before the green sod is ever placed on the broad, strong and noble breast of Gaelic. Wonderfully, therefore, does Neil Macleod, the poet of Skye, sing:

Wake up, o Gaelic, and raise your voice....

I have great and fervent hope that in the days that we will not see, many Gaels will emerge from the hospitable homes of Lochiel who will make great and respectable names for themselves in the legislative assemblies and universities of our country. I have strong hope that the Gaels of Lochiel, with great zeal and erudition, will blossom to marvelous effect as farmers of the broad, level, fertile fields I see all around me.

It is my opinion that there is not in all of Canada a life that is more full of joy and pleasure, and healthier, than that of the life and occupation of the farmer. I have great and certain hope that, as in the days that were and have passed, many modest, gentle, cheerful and beautiful girls and women will arise and live in Lochiel in the years that are to come who will uphold the name, repute and virtues of Highland women in every age and in every land.

To every Gaelic grandfather and grandmother, to every Gaelic son and daughter in the illustrious township of Locheil, I give a thousand blessings, today and every day.

7: The Scots of Canada

The Reverend Dr. Alasdair MacGill-Eain Sinclair of Nova Scotia composed the following song-poem which was printed long after his death with the title "Albannaich Chanada" (The Scots of Canada, or Scottish-Canadians). His son stated that it was composed on June 6, 1911;[44] it appears to be the last poem that the accomplished Gaelic scholar ever composed.

Although the text is written in Gaelic, it presents a pan-Scottish identity to Canadians of Scottish ancestry unified by a common military inheritance and tartanistic iconography (lines 1-16). The account moves from Scotland to Canada, the latter of which is praised for its sublime landscape and virtuous people in much the same manner as the Highlands are in traditional verse. Gaels in Canada, however, do not suffer under tyrannical landlords (lines 19-20). The use of emphatic possessives in the text—"*My* people came from Scotland ... Canada is *our* country" (lines 1 and 17)—may indicate the desire to retain a trans-Atlantic link from the immigrant community to the ancestral homeland for the creation of a "hyphenated identity," such as the many that are popular today, but it may also suggest a triumphalist exclusion of other peoples from the spoils of the British conquest of North America.

Original Text

1 Bho Alba thàinig mo shluagh-sa
   Thar cuain do'n àirde an iar
   A chogadh air son Bhreatainn,
   Gu calma, seasmhach, dian.

5 Cha chualas riamh mu shàr-laoich
   A b' fior-fhuil am blàr nan lann
   Na luchd nam breacan uallach
   Is nam pìob a b' fhuaimneach srann.

   Nam bagradh nàimhdean guineach
10 Ar tìr a chur fo'[n] sàil
   Gach neach 's am bheil fuil Alba
   Bhiodh armaichte gun dàil.

   Bhiodh cuimhn' aca air an sinnsear
   'S an rìoghachd ri'n là;
15 Is dhòirteadh iad am fion-fhuil
   Mun strìochdadh iad do nàmh.

   'S e Canada ar dùthaich-ne,
   Tìr ùr na saorsa 's a bhìdh;
   Tìr mhath anns nach eil uachdarain
20 Gar fuadach ás na glinn.

   Tìr mhór nam beanntan craobhach
   Is nan raointean farsainn réidh;
   Tìr chaoin nan daoine sgairteil
   Is nam ban as taitniche beus.[45]

Translation

(1-4) My people came from Scotland across the ocean to the west to fight for Britain bravely, resolutely, keenly.

(5-8) No superheroes better in the battle of the blades were ever heard of than the people of the proud plaids and of the bagpipes of most thunderous droning.

(9-12) If malicious enemies would threaten to subdue our land, every person who has Scottish blood would immediately arm themselves.

(13-16) They would remember their ancestors in the kingdom at that time; they would spill their pure blood before they would yield to an enemy.

(17-20) Canada is our country, the new land of freedom and nourishment; a good land in which there are no landlords to expel us out of the glens.

(21-24) An enormous land of the forking mountains and of the smooth, wide plains; a gentle land of the hardy men and of the most virtuous women.

8: The Gaels of Nova Scotia

Alasdair MacÌosaig of St. Andrews Channel in Cape Breton composed this ode to the 85th Battalion of Nova Scotia, which fought in the First World War. He seems to have also provided the title. The 85th Battalion was among the Canadian forces who fought at the Battle of Vimy Ridge in 1917.

The chorus of this song immediately notifies us that it was modelled on the song by Iain MacGilleBhràth which started this chapter. The same set of conceits—fearlessness and indomitability—is applied to the Gaels here as elsewhere, but there is some ambiguity about their identity in relation to Britishness and lingering ethnic rivalries. While on the one hand, Alasdair asserts that the Gaels have outshone the English (line 14), he also subsumes them within British forces as a whole, praising them as the "people of the red coats" (lines 35-36). While he praises the service of Gaelic military forces and assures them that they will emerge victorious, he also acknowledges the high social costs that families paid (lines 17-28) in this tragic international conflict. It may be that he felt obliged, as a poet, to tell the story that so many other soldiers who died could not (line 28) and to justify the costs in terms of a positive political outcome (lines 19 and 39-40).

Original Text

<pre>
 1   Soraidh bhuam thar chuan air astar
        Gu fir shuaicheanta nam breacan:
        Dh'fhalbh iad uainn thar chuan air astar
        Gus an gleachd a bhuannachd.

 5   Gur e 'chuir mi 'n-diugh ri dànachd
        A thoirt iomradh air na Gàidheil,
        Na gaisgich a dh'fhalbh thar sàile
        Gus am blàr a bhuannachd.

        Chuireadh fios air Clann nan Gàidheal:
10   Riamh, cha do dh'aom ri aodann nàmhaid,
        Freumh de'n chraoibh as daoire dh'fhàs –
        Is iomadh blàr a fhuair iad.

        'Fhearaibh Albann Ùir, gun d' rinn sibh tapaidh:
        Fhuair sibh cliù os cionn fir Shasann –
15   Luchd mo rùin nach lùb le gealtachd
        Dol ri aodann cruadail.

        Is ged is duilich leam ri innse,
        Gum bheil móran dhiubh 'nan sìneadh,
        Thig an onair oirnn mar dhìleab
20   Ged is bochd 'gar dìth na tha uainn dhiubh.

        Is iomadh màthair a tha brònach
        Is a mac gaoil air aodann comhstrì,
        Agus [a] fear a tha fo'n fhòd
        A chaidh a leòn 's a' chruadal.

25   Is iomadh bean a tha dheth deurach
        Is a companach an déidh a tréigsinn
        Nach tig dhachaigh gu 'chéile
        'Thoirt dhi sgeul a chruadail.

        Gun robh an Gearmailteach cho foirmeil
30   Gus am Frangach 'chur an domail;
        Mur b' e Belgium bhith 'na choinneamh,
        Bhiodh gach fearann bhuaidhe.

        Is ged tha Gearmailtich cho làidir,
        Cumail cogaidh ri gach nàmhaid,
35   Gheibh na Breatannaich an àirde:
        Luchd nan còta ruadha.
</pre>

Théid an Caisear a dhìteadh;
Théid a chrochadh – siud tha 'dhìth oirnn –
Nì sinn réite anns gach rìoghachd
40   Agus sìth bhios buan dhuinn.⁴⁶

Translation

(1-4) Greetings from me far across the ocean to the distinguished men of the tartans who have departed from us a long distance across the ocean in order to win the conflict.

(5-8) I have been motivated today to compose poetry in order to comment on the Gaels, the heroes who have departed across the ocean in order to win the battle.

(9-12) The Gaelic people were called out [for war]: they never submitted before the face of an enemy; a branch of the most precious tree that ever grew; they had many a battle.

(13-16) O men of Nova Scotia, you have done smartly: you have earned repute above that of the men of England – the people beloved to me who will not yield from fright, going to face hardship.

(17-20) And although it is difficult for me to say, that many of you are laid out [dead], honour will be bestowed to us as a legacy, although those of us who remain are sorely in need of you.

(21-24) There is many a mother who is sad while her beloved son is on the field of conflict, and her husband who was wounded in the conflict lies beneath the sod.

(25-28) There is many a wife who is full of tears because of it after her companion has abandoned her and will not come home to his partner to tell her the tale of his hardship.

(29-32) The German was so pompous to cause the French such damage; if Belgium hadn't been across from him, he would not have been able to get territory.

(33-36) And although the Germans are strong, making war on every enemy, the British will get the upper hand: the people of the red coats.

(37-40) The Kaiser will be doomed; he will be hanged—that is what we need—we will create a smooth settlement in every kingdom and a peace that will be lasting for us.

4 – Migration

Soldiers and sailors who had fought in the North American theatre of the Seven Years' War (1756-1763) were eligible for land grants in British North America as rewards for their military service. Whether they happened to have found their foothold in the province of New York, Nova Scotia, or Quebec, these men actively encouraged their relations and friends to follow them. Migration from the Highlands is distinguished from that of other parts of Scotland by the durable bonds of community and kinship in Highland life that motivated Gaels to migrate and settle together in large groups. The strong sense of community solidarity sometimes led to consensual decisions about mass migration, such as when the MacDonald tenants of Cnòideart (Knoydart) decided to leave for Ontario in 1786:

> What is striking about this agreement is its egalitarian tone and, in particular, the communal commitment to emigration. In the face of socially and economically unacceptable losses, the tenants looked as a group for a solution to their problems and found it in communal emigration.[1]

Often times, however, smaller scale migration from a family or community stretched out over years or decades. Early emigrants wrote letters and sent messages back home, reassuring family and friends of their successes and encouraging others to follow them, a phenomenon often referred to as "chain migration." The channel of communication between the emigrant and his home community back in Scotland, however, could be very local and selective in its scope where emigration was concerned, as Thomas Douglas (Earl of Selkirk) noted in his 1805 treatise:

> The continued and repeated communication between these settlers, and their relations in Scotland, has given the people of every part of the Highlands a pretty accurate acquaintance with the circumstances of some particular colony; and the emigrants, though their ideas are often sanguine, are by no means so ignorant of the nature of the country they are going to, as some persons have supposed. But the information which any of the peasantry have of America, is all confined to one spot; to the peculiar circumstances of that place, they ascribe all those advantages which it has in common with other new settled countries. Of the other colonies they are perfectly ignorant, and have often very mistaken notions. Those, in particular, whose views are directed towards the southern states, have received very gloomy impressions of the climate of Canada, and of all the northern colonies. But to rectify these mistaken opinions, is by no means the greatest difficulty in bringing them to change their plans. The number of their friends or relations who have all gone to the same quarter, give it the attraction almost of another home.

Although some emigration from the Highlands continued to follow previous trails to the newly formed United States after the conclusion of the American Revolutionary War in 1783, it was much easier for Gaels to migrate northwards to the territories still controlled by the British Crown. Many colonists who had fought during the revolution as Loyalists relocated to British North America and formed new bridges for the continuing saga of emigration.

Until steamships began crossing the Atlantic in the 1860s, the voyage between Scotland and North America was long, dangerous and unpleasant. Many boats carried wood and other commodities from North American colonies and would have otherwise returned from Britain empty, but they were ill-suited for human occupation.[2] Besides the perils of the ocean voyage itself, people were ill-nourished and disease spread quickly and easily. A pipe-tune commemorating the departure of Highlanders for America was entitled "Tha an cuan a' cur eagal air Clann nan Gàidheal" (The Ocean Frightens the Gaelic People).[3] An account in English about the voyage of the ship *Hector* in

1773 to Pictou, Nova Scotia, depicts graphically the desperate state of the boat and the passengers:

> The ship was so rotten that the passengers could pick the wood out of her sides with their fingers. They met with a severe gale off the Newfoundland coast, and were driven back by it so far that it took them about fourteen days to get back to the point at which the storm met them. The accommodation was wretched, smallpox and dysentry broke out among the passengers. Eighteen of the children died. ... Their stock of provisions became almost exhausted, the water became scarce and bad; the remnant of provisions left consisted mainly of salt meat, which, from the scarcity of water, added greatly to their sufferings. The oatcake carried by them became mouldy, so that much of it had been thrown away before they dreamt of having such a long passage.[4]

The Rev. Donnchadh Blàrach wrote one of the few extended accounts in Gaelic of the Atlantic voyage in 1846 which portrays the tremendous forces of nature against which a ship, its crew and travellers had to battle in order to survive.

> Nuair a bha e a' dlùthachadh ri meadhan-oidhche, dh'at an fhairge suas 'na beanntaibh, agus thòisich an long ri luasgadh air bharraibh nan tonn. Bha an cuan a' slachdraich air taobhan na luinge, agus thàinig aon tonn aintheasach, gailbheach, agus bhuail e i air a deireadh. Thug e oirre breab a thoirt cosmhail ri each meanmnach; thilgeadh bun os cionn na cisteachan anns an robh mo leabhraichean agus m' aodach, maille ris gach nì a bha ann an seòmar na luinge, agus thaomadh a-mach gach nì a bha ann an ciste nan cungaidhean-leighis, a bhuineadh do'n Chaiptean, ionnas gu robh cuid de na soireachan-leighis air am bristeadh, agus gach nì a bha annta air chall. Shaoil leam gun do bhrist an tonn gailbheach seo a-staigh troimh chliathaich an t-soithich agus gum bitheamaid an grunnd a' chuain a thiota.

> As it approached midnight, the sea swelled up into mountainous proportions, and the ship began to roll on the top of the waves. The sea was battering the sides of the ship and one blustery, violent wave hit the stern. It made her give a kick like a prancing horse. The chests which held my books and clothes went topsyturvy, along with everything else in the ship's cabin. Everything

in the captain's medicine-chest poured out. Some of the medicine bottles were broken and their entire contents lost. I thought that the wild wave had broken in through the side of the ship and that we would soon be at the bottom of the ocean.[5]

Gaels were desperate enough, however, to leave the oppressions at home to risk the hazards of ocean travel to North America. The intricate weave of Highland society quickly unravelled. By the early 1800s, the old tacksmen class had essentially become extinct in the social structure of the Highlands.[6] Their descendants who desired to maintain their elevated social rank emigrated elsewhere, enlisted in the military, trained for the ministry or priesthood, or sought some official capacity in the landlord's new estate management scheme, becoming estranged from former kinsmen in the process:

> In the eighteenth century the role of the factor was usually assumed by one of the gentleman tacksmen. Records indicate that this official carried out his duties efficiently. He visited farms frequently, collected rents, observed the tenants at work, and encouraged their improvements. It is quite likely that, in addition to these duties, he was also baron-baillie, supervising and enforcing the tenants' duty to the laird. ... By the nineteenth century he was a very unpopular figure, if one is to judge by allusions in the songs of the emigrants.[7]

Some landlords encouraged tenants to remain on small plots of land called "crofts" on their estates, especially when the élite could exploit the servile workforce in the production of kelp. Being squeezed into small and marginal plots of land, however, made crofters increasingly reliant upon the potato as a foodstuff. The year 1846 is known in Gaelic as "a' bhliadhna a ghais am buntàta" (the year that the potato withered). This natural disaster which struck many regions of the North Atlantic for several years beginning in 1846 was only one of several factors accelerating massive depopulation in most parts of the Highlands in the 1840s and 1850s:

> In these two decades, the Scottish Highlands lost many more of their inhabitants than in any other similar period in the nineteenth century. The immediate cause was crop failure and, in particular, the potato blight, which devastated a vital subsistence crop of the region from the autumn of 1846. But such an explana-

tion, though commonplace in the literature, is hardly sufficient to account for the extraordinary volume of emigration. ... The crisis of these decades seems to have generated a widespread and, in some years, a desperate desire to get away which undermined for a time the traditional reluctance of the poorer peasant classes to surrender their lands. ... This social pattern was not simply a consequence of the ravages of famine on a peasant population. It was also the result of conscious design on the part of individual landowners and their agents.[8]

Landlords took advantage of nearly any opportunity to better themselves regardless of the impact on the tenantry, and having nearly unchecked powers on their estates they could bring pressures to bear on the peasantry to cause their expulsion. There was little political pressure to improve conditions as Highlanders were considered an inherently inferior race unworthy of special consideration and the universal right to vote was not granted to them (males, at any rate) until 1885.[9]

After Canadian Confederation in 1867, the first Prime Minister, John A. Macdonald, considered it one of his highest priorities to expand westward before the United States could claim the territory between British Columbia and Ontario. The construction of a railroad to connect Canadian centres of population and power, to carry goods and to aid in settlement, was therefore key to these plans.[10] The railroad had to be built and the Prairies needed to be occupied by loyal subjects; strenuous efforts were made to recruit Highlanders into these enterprises, often with less than equitable arrangements.

Word of mouth and letters received from relations and friends were reality checks against the exaggerations and embellishments made by emigration agents and settlement schemes. A very lively debate ensued in newspapers with a Gaelic readership in Scotland and Canada in the 1880s and 1890s, some contributors praising the virtues of their new homes and others casting aspersions on the land and the emigration agents who induced them to come over. It is also clear that Highlanders gave greater credence to materials printed in the Gaelic language than in English. A typical exchange occurred in the Gaelic column of *The Scottish Canadian* newspaper, printed in Toronto, in 1892. First came an enquiry from a correspondent only identified as "Tirisdeach" (a native of Tiree):

Tha sinn a' cluinntinn iomradh 's an eilean iomallach seo air mar a tha sibh a' seasamh còir nan Gàidheal an Canada agus mu'n oidheirp a tha sibh a' toirt a chum a' Ghàidhlig a chumail beò 's an dùthaich sin. ... Tha fios agaibh gum bheil àireamh mhór de mhuinntir an eilein seo thall an Canada agus cuid a' tagairt dol a-null fhathast. Cha do phill neach riamh air ais ás an t-saoghal ùr a thug fios cinnteach dhuinn mu chor nan càirdean a chaidh thairis, chan eil dearbhadh againn mu'n staid; oir ged a thig fear a-nall an-dràst' is a-rithist, a' moladh an àite, tha sinn fo amharas gum faod e bhith air a phàigheadh le luchd-riaghlaidh na dùthcha.

A-nis, on tha sibhse eòlach mu shuidheachadh ar luchd-dùthcha air gach taobh de'n linne, am bi sibh cho math is gun sgrìobh sibh féin no aon d'ur luchd-cuideachaidh litir a' toirt bhur beachd co-dhiubh as fearr do na Gàidheil, fuireach an tìr an dùthchais, no dol a dh'Aimearaga. Innsibh am bheil am fearann cho torrach is a tha an t-ainm, no am bheil am fuachd cho fuasach is gum bi daoine a' call am meuran is an òrdagan leis an reòthadh....[11]

We are hearing reports in this remote island about how you are defending the rights of the Gaels in Canada and about the efforts that you are making to keep the Gaelic language alive in that country. ... You will be aware that a great many of the natives of this island are over in Canada and some are still threatening to emigrate. Not a person ever returned from the New World to give us definitive information about the condition of the kinsfolk who went abroad, so we have no proof of their state; for although a man comes over now and again, extolling the place, we suspect that he may be paid by the [Canadian] government.

Now, since you are familiar with the situation of our compatriots on both sides of the ocean, would you be so good as to write—yourself, or one of your assistants—a letter giving your opinion about whether it is better for Gaels to stay in their native homeland or to go to North America. Tell us if the land is as fertile as reputed, or if the weather is so terribly cold that people lose their fingers and toes from the freezing....

The circulation of inexpensive print materials such as newspapers and periodicals meant that even remote islands like Tiree were no longer as isolated as they once were from communication and networks of information: the author of this letter could connect to a widely-dispersed web of correspondents who could help shape opinions and plans. A response to this enquiry, directed to the editor, was printed two weeks later by an anonymous correspondent identified only as "Canadach" (a Canadian).

> Air mo làimh, is math leam a bhith faicinn gum bheil bhur pàipear gleusta ag dol air faondradh gu eilean iomallach Thiriodh, agus, a-réir coltais, gum bheil naidheachdan ar dùthcha mar a tha iad air an cur sìos an-sin, air an leughadh leis na h-eileanaich. ... Tha fios aig muinntir Chanada gum bheil an dùthaich seo freagarrach air son thuathanach; gum bheil iad a' dèanadh gu math air an son féin is air son an teaghlaichean air feadh chòmhnardan Ontario, agus mór-fhearainn na h-Àird an Iar. Chan eil na h-uiread de chothrom aig luchd-ceaird—aig saoir, clachairean, goibhnean, luchd obair iarainn agus umha, is mar sin air adhart,—air airgead a chur ri chéile is beartas a dhèanamh. A' mhuinntir a tha math dheth ann an eilean Thiriodh, fanadh iad 's a' Ghàidhealtachd, a' toirt an aire air iasg a' chuain is air na geòidh a tha ri cuartag mu'n Dubh-Irtich; biodh iad toilichte taingeil le'n crannchur air oir a' chuain far am bheil fàs is fallaineachd 's an tràigh. ...[12]

> By my word, I'm glad to see that your excellent newspaper has found its way to the remote island of Tiree and, by all appearances, that the news of our country as it is reported there is being read by the islanders. ... The people of Canada know that this country is suitable for farmers; that they are doing well for themselves and for their families throughout the plains of Ontario, and the territories of the West. Craftsmen—carpenters, masons, smiths, iron-workers and coppersmiths, and so on—do not have so many opportunities to accumulate money and earn a good income. Those people who are well off on the island of Tiree should stay in the Highlands, giving particular heed to the fish of the ocean and the geese that circumnavigate the Dubh-Irtich; they should be content and grateful with their lot on the edge of

the ocean where there is sustenance and wholesomeness along the seashore. ...

The debate over the relative merits of unknown areas in the Canadian Prairies being opened for colonization was happening at the same time that Highland crofters in Scotland were organizing a political movement to assert their land rights. Effective new leaders, radical theology, civil disobedience and inspiration from Ireland gave Scottish Gaels new confidence that the day "to take control of their own destinies" had finally come. "The commercial landlordism introduced into the Highlands in the eighteenth century was at last on the retreat. Change was in the air. And for the first time in the nineteenth century, Gaelic poetry took on an optimistic tone."[13]

Emigration schemes had to try harder to pull potential emigrants from the Highlands. They responded to doubts and distrust by creating propagandist tracts in Gaelic, attempting to reassure potential emigrants in great detail that each of their concerns was legitimate but had been dealt with to the satisfaction of other settlers. In 1883, for example, the booklet *Dachaidhean Saora do na h-uile ann am Manitoba agus Canada an Iar-Thuath air Ruith Rathad-Iaruinn Chanada Pacific* (Free Homes to everybody in Manitoba and North-West Canada with the Operation of the Canadian Pacific Railway) was printed in Scotland. It begins with a letter, supposedly by a former tenant of Lady Emily Cathcart-Gordon in the Outer Hebrides, who relocated happily to Manitoba, that strains credibility beyond the breaking point. The supposed author of the letter, Dòmhnall MacDhiarmaid, praises his beloved noblewoman and the fine people of the Canadian Pacific Railway for all of their assistance helping him flourish far more than he ever could in Beinn nam Fadhla (Benbecula). He offers her his help in encouraging other tenants at home to join him and concludes with a warm blessing to her and her husband, Sir Reginald Archibald Edward Cathcart. Sir Reginald just happened to be on the board of a land company connected to the Canadian Pacific Railway.[14] The fact that the Cathcart-Gordons were profiting directly from both the draining of the population on their estates in Scotland and the relocation of those same people to Canada gives us reason to be suspicious of the authenticity of the letter attributed to MacDhiarmaid and the objectivity of the information in the booklet.

In the early 20th century, broken promises and the political obstacles erected by landlords compelled crofters to once again take direct action to assert their claims, including a long series of land raids across the Highlands and Islands in which men—often war veterans—reclaimed and occupied vacant properties. Although the First World War temporarily suspended a satisfactory resolution to these challenges, persistent pressure eventually resulted in the expansion and allocation of lands available to small-scale farmers in the Western Isles.[15] While these policy changes enshrined the security of tenure for many Gaels, economic hardship and inequality in Highland life have continued to present serious challenges to the native population to the present day. Nonetheless, the era of eviction and mass migration was finally over.

1: "That is the Way I Would Go"

According to oral history, Anna NicGill-Ìosa was among the five hundred people onboard the ship *McDonald* which left for Canada in 1786.[16] Although a later song-poem she composed about Upper Canada is full of praise for her adopted home,[17] this text suggests that she had mixed feelings about emigration before she left.

This ambivalence is reflected in the chorus of the song-poem itself: it is clear that the familiar roads that she would take were those of Clanranald territory, which she delineates in lines 5-8. Her identification with Clan Donald is shown in territorial terms as she extends her poem's geographical bounds to Cnòideart (Knoydart) and Lochaber (lines 21-24), and in symbolic terms as she enumerates the coat of arms of the Lords of the Isles (lines 37-40). The song thus expresses a tension between custom and attachment to home, on the one hand, and anticipation and uncertainty about the future, on the other.

Her text contains a brief allusion (line 14) to an old Gaelic cosmological idea about paradisal islands in the far west connected to beliefs in the Otherworld and the destination of the dead. "An t-Eilean Uaine" (The Green Island) is one of the more common names for this location in Gaelic oral narratives, and beliefs about such places may have well piqued the hopes of early emigrants. A Gaelic term indicating one of these Isles of the Blessed was taken up by the mariners of medieval Europe and copied onto nautical charts, and was eventually used as the name of the country of Brazil in South America.[18]

The depiction of nature in the Highlands in this song-poem is also very interesting, implying a healthy harmony between the rugged landscape and the human inhabitants. The deer herd (lines 25-28) seem to be guarding a natural spring—a common symbol for the source of life energy and wisdom—as their human counterparts once guarded territorial boundaries and hunting reserves.

Her text puts a positive spin on the emigration experience. Anna and her MacDonald kinsfolk were themselves the vanquished being driven away by escaping to British North America, even though she informs us that the Clan Donald is hardy and tenacious (line 34) and always drive off their opponents (line 35). Regardless, those in her situation would need to steel themselves with an optimistic and confident outlook to endure the many challenges before them.

Original Text

1   O, siud an taobh a ghabhainn
    E, siud an taobh a ghabhainn,
    'S gach aon taobh 'g am biodh an rathad,
    Ghabhainn e gu h-eòlach.

5   Gabhaidh sinn ar cead de Mhórar
    Àrasaig is Mùideart nam mór-bheann
    Eige is Canaidh ghorm nan ròiseal,
    Is Uibhist bhòidheach ghreannmhor.

    Falbhaidh sinn is cha dèan sinn fuireach
10 Fàgaidh sinn "slàn" agaibh uile;
    Seòlaidh sinn air bharr an tuinne,
    Dia 'chur turais oirnne.

    Falbhaidh sinn air bharr nan stuaidhean
    Ruigidh sinn an t-Eilean Uaine
15 Far am bi crodh-laoigh air bhuailtean
    Aig na fuarain bhòidheach.

    Tha na càirdean ann cho lìonmhor
    Thall 's a-bhos air feadh nan crìochan;
    Is ma dh'fhàgas mi 'h-aon diubh 'n dìochuimhn',
20 Is adhbhar mìothlachd dhomh-s' e.

    Cnòideart fhuar is Gleann Garadh,
    Far am bheil na fiùrain gheala;
    Uisge Ruaidh o'n Bhràighe thairis
    Gu Srath Inbhir Lòchaidh.

25   Chì mi na féidh air an fhuaran,
     A ghreidh fhéin 'nan treud mun cuairt air;
     'H-uile té is a sròn 's an fhuaradh
     Mun tig fuathas teann oirr'.

     Bu bhinn leam a' chaismeachd-mhaidne
30   An déidh dùsgadh ás mo chadal;
     Coileach dubh air barr gach meangain
     Fiadh 'na stad is e leòinte.

     Dòmhnallaich – 's ann daibh bu dual siud:
     Seasamh dìreach ri uchd cruadail,
35   Leanailteachd gu ruith na ruaige,
     Dìleas cruaidh gu dòrainn.

     Long is leòghann, craobh is caisteal,
     Fìreun an sròl ri croinn-bhratach,
     Làmh dhearg is eòlas a' bhradain
40   Is fraoch 's a' chaigeann còmhla riu.[19]

Translation

(1-4) Ó, that is the way that I would go, É, that is the way that I would go; any way the road would lead, I would take it with familiarity.

(5-8) We will take our leave of Morar, Arisaig and Moidart, Eigg and green Canna of the waves, and beautiful, lovely Uist.

(9-12) We will go away and we will not stay, we will leave you all with our blessings; we will sail on the crest of the wave, may God send us on our way.

(13-16) We will leave on the top of the sea pillars, we will reach the Green Isle where calves are in the folds near beautiful springs.

(17-20) The kinsfolk are so plentiful everywhere throughout these regions, and if I neglect to remember anyone, it will cause me displeasure.

(21-24) Cold Knoydart and Glengarry, home of the fair "saplings"; the River Roy from Brae Lochaber over to the strath of Inverlochy.

(25-28) I see the deer at the spring, its own herd is a warrior-band around it; every hind has her nose to the wind to warn her before danger comes near.

(29-32) The morning hike was melodious to me after I awoke from my slumber; a blackcock perched on each branch, a stag unmoving after being wounded.

(33-36) These are the hereditary customs of Clan Donald: to stand upright in the face of hardship, persistent in driving off the vanquished, and loyal and steadfast in danger.

(37-40) A galley and a lion, a tree and a castle, an eagle in a banner on a pole, a red hand and the salmon's wisdom, and heather in the pair along with them.

2: "It was on Sunday Morning"

Iain Liath MacDhòmhnaill composed the following song-poem about emigration in retrospect some years after his journey, when he had long been living in Glenroy, Charlottenburgh, Ontario. He was one of the Catholic Cnòideart MacDonalds, like Anna NicGill-Ìosa, author of the previous song, who left for Glengarry, Ontario, in 1786.[20] This text must have been meaningful to the people of the area, as it survived long enough in oral tradition to have been recorded by Professor Charles Dunn of Harvard University in 1960. It is an exemplary lament of exile.

Most details about the voyage are given as straightforward description. This song-poem is the most vivid eyewitness testimony of the early Glengarry migration. The movement away from the home community is likened to death: the beating of palms (line 13) was an expression of grief and one of the rituals of mourning. It is as if those who are on the ship are being carried away to an t-Eilean Uaine, the blessed island of the gods and the dead in the West. The rites of death were certainly in the author's consciousness, as they appear again at the end of the poem.

The initial elation of arriving in Canada (lines 37-40) is soon over. A series of contrasts follows between the author's old life in the Highlands and his new life in Canada, with the former being preferable to the latter. He associates the Highlands with health (lines 73-76), happiness (lines 38-39 and 77), companionship (lines 61-62), and prosperity (lines 59-60). His life in Canada, by contrast, is marred by excessive toil (lines 33-36), social rejection (lines 93-96, 105-106 and 113-119), physical deterioration (lines 81-104 and 109-112), and a startling consciousness of sin (lines 120-131). It is as though his dreams of an innocent Avalon have been rudely shattered.

As in the previous song-poem by Anna NicGill-Ìosa, nature figures prominently in expressing a sense of belonging to the homeland territory and the relationship of the human community to it. The rugged terrain ensured strength and longevity (lines 73-80), and the mountains provided clean air (line 52). Deer appear as the noble symbols of the hunt, but also as analogues of the well-ordered human community (lines 53-56). The description of nature in Canada (lines 41-48), by contrast, is negative in tone. The graves of ancestors were the focus of communal attachment to territory in Gaelic culture,[21] and the author laments not only that the emigrants have parted with the ancestors who rest in the soil (lines 31-32) but that that earth has now been taken over by a foreign people and the old Gaelic order has been totally extinguished (lines 65-72). This, he says, is what troubles him most.

The overriding theme of this text is death, not just the death of an individual but that of a community and culture.

Original Text

<pre>
 1   'S ann air madainn Di-Dòmhnaich,
      Rinn sinn seòladh bho thìr,
      Air long mhór nan trì crannag
      Is ar sagart parraiste leinn;
 5   Rinn e fhéin an àrd-ùrnaigh
      Rìgh nan Dùl 'gar dìon
      Is ris an aingeal naomh Ràfeal
      Ar cur sàbhailt gu tìr.

      Nuair a ghluais sinn bho chaladh,
10   Bha móran gail ann is caoidh –
      Iad a' falbh air gach bealach
      A' leigeal bheannachdan leinn;
      Bha iad a' bualadh am basan
      Gun dùil ri ar faicinn a-chaoidh;
15   Nuair a chuir i cùl ris an fhearann
      Is na siùil gheala ri croinn.

      Is gum bu bhòidheach an sealladh
      Nuair a chuir i cùl ris an tìr;
      Bha deagh chaiptein 'ga stiùireadh
20   Air a' chuan dubh-ghorm is na tuinn;
</pre>

Bha gach seòladair tapaidh
Air bharr gach slaite ri gnìomh,
Nuair chaidh na siùil àrda ri crannaibh
Is an cuan greannach 'na still.

25 A' cheud latha dhe'n fhoghar
'S ann a fhuair sinn fradharc bha gann;
'S ann a chunnaic sinn fearann
Ged bha sinn tamall air chall;
Rinn sinn móran toil-inntinn
30 A' dol air tìr anns an àm,
Ged a dh'fhàg sinn ar sinnsear
Anns na rìoghachdan thall.

Bhon a thàinig mi 'n taobh seo
Bha mi daonnan ri feum,
35 Dol a ghearradh na craoibhe
Le faobhar neo-gheur;
Ged a bhithinn fo airsneal
Cha bhiodh acaid 'nam chléibh:
'S ann a bhithinn cho aotrom
40 Is mi gun saothair fo'n ghréin.

Ach mìle marbhfhaisg air a' ghaoith
Tha i daonnan á tuath,
Is i cur neart anns na Faoillich
Gus na daoine bhith fuar;
45 Fad a' gheamhraidh is an earraich
Gum bi a' ghailleann cho buan
Is bidh a' chuileag as t-samhradh
A' cumail srann ri ar cluais.

Chan ionann is an t-àite
50 'S an d' fhuair mi m' àrach is mi òg:
Fo dhubhar nan àrd-bheann
Bu ghlan fàileadh fo ar sròn;
Far am biodh 'ghreigh mheangach
Is na laoigh bhallach air lòn
55 Ann an cois nan damh seanga
Bu bhòidheach sealladh fo chròic.

Fhuair mi greis dhe m' chleachdadh
An àite taitneach gu leòr:
'S an taigh mhór nach robh airce
60 Far am biodh pailteas air bòrd;
Far am biodh iomadh dìbhearsan

A' cluich air cairtean is air ceòl
Ann an comann nan àrmainn
Is gun dad an làthair dhiubh beò.

65 Gur e mheudaich mo mhulad
'N déidh na chunna mi ann
De shìol nan uachdaran prìseal
A bha dìleas 's gach àm;
Gun dh'fhalbh iad ás buileach
70 Is gun aon duine dhiubh thall,
Agus fearann ar sinnsear
Bhith fo chìobairean Gallt'.

Nuair a bha mi aig baile
Dhìrinn bealach is beinn;
75 Cha robh mùchadh air m' anail
No maille 'nam cheum
'S ann a bhithinn cho cridheil
Cur geall-ruith agus leum,
Is fhada chithinn bhuam sealladh
80 'N àm cromadh na gréin'.

'S ann a-nis tha mi smaointinn
Gun dh'fhalbh mo shaoghal gun fheum,
Bhon a lagaich an aois mi
Chuir i gaoid orm nach tréig;
85 Gun do leòn i mo phearsa
Gun lùths, gun tapachd, gun spéis;
Bidh mi daonnan a' gearain
Gur trom an t-eallach i fhéin.

Is bhon a rinn i mo leagadh,
90 Dh'fhalbh mo neart bhuam is mo threòir;
Tha mo ghruaidhean air seacadh
Dh'fhalbh gach maise bha 'm fheòil;
Ged a dh'éireadh iad uile
Is dèanamh ullamh gu falbh
95 'S ann bhios mise aig a' bhaile
'M bun na trealaich is mi balbh.

Nuair a théid mi air astar,
Bidh mo chasan cho trom
Is mi 'gan slaodadh a dh'aindeoin
100 Is mi 'nam chaman bochd crom;
Bidh mo làmh anns a' bhata
Cumail taice ri m' chom;

>   Is ri lughad an tuislidh
>   Nì mi tuiteam 's a' pholl.
>
> 105 Tha mo chuideachd an-dràsta
>   A' gabhail gràin orm is fuath;
>   Is bidh iad daonnan ag ràdhainn
>   Nach cum mi 'n fhàrdach dhaibh suas;
>   Bhon 's e duine gun spìod mi
> 110 Ach 'nam liobaid air sluagh,
>   Is truagh nach tugadh am bàs
>   Mo cheann bàn anns an uaigh.
>
>   Chuir siud trioblaid air m' inntinn
>   Nach dèan mi innseadh do chàich;
> 115 Is dh'fhàg mo chridhe cho ìosal
>   Is nach dèan e dìreadh gu bràth;
>   'S ann a ghabhas mi mulad
>   Ag éisteachd iullagaich chàich,
>   Is mi falbh dhe m' eòlas air m' aineol
>   Is an ùine 'teannadh air làimh.
>
> 120 Nuair a thàinig mi an taobh seo
>   Bha mi aotrom gun chéill;
>   Bu mhór am peacadh ri m' aodann
>   Is mi <'ga chiùrradh> dha réir;
>   Is mór an-diugh mo chùis eagail
> 125 'S na fhuair mi 'theagasg bhon chléir;
>   Bhith dol dh'ionnsaigh na cùirte
>   A' gabhail cunntas gu léir.
>
>   'S e siud deireadh gach duine
>   Nuair thig an cuireadh mun cuairt;
> 130 Chan urrainn dha fuireach
>   Nuair thig an sumanadh cruaidh;
>   Bidh a chàirdean 'ga ochanaich
>   Bhon 's e fasan an t-sluaigh
>   Nuair a théid a phasgadh
> 135 Anns a' chadal nach gluais.[22]

Translation

(1-8) It was on Sunday morning that we sailed away from the land on a large vessel with three masts and our parish priest along with us; he offered up a devout supplication for the King of the Elements [God] to protect us and for the archangel St. Raphael to deliver us safely to land.

(9-16) When we departed from the harbour, there was much crying and weeping as they followed along every path, leaving us with their blessings; they were striking their palms, never expecting to see us again; the ship turned her back to the land with her white sails up the mast.

(17-24) The sight was comely when she turned her back to the land; an excellent captain was steering her on the dark blue sea of waves; every sailor was adroit, busy aloft the masts; when the tall sails were hoisted and the bristly ocean was agitated.

(25-32) On the first day of the autumn, we caught a faint glimpse; indeed, we saw land, although we were lost for a while; we were greatly excited going to land at that time, even if we had left our [dead] ancestors in the far distant kingdoms.

(33-40) Since I have crossed over to this side [of the ocean], I have been constantly working; going to cut down the trees with a dull blade; even if I was fatigued [in Scotland], there would not be pain [of melancholy?] in my chest: I would be light-hearted, without any menial labour at all.

(41-48) A thousand curses on the wind, it is always coming out of the North, and it adds to the strength of the January squalls to make the people cold; throughout the winter and the spring, the storms are constant, and throughout the summer the mosquitoes buzz in our ears.

(49-56) This place is very different from where I was raised: in the shadow of the great mountains, the air was pure in our nostrils; there were antlered deer herds and speckled fawns grazing in the company of slender stags with great antlers who were beautiful to behold.

(57-64) For a while I was accustomed to a place that was pleasant enough: the great house that knew no scarcity, where there was plenty on the table; where there were many entertainments, playing cards and music in the company of the heroes, although none of them are now alive.

(65-72) What has increased my sorrow, after what I had seen of the descendants of the precious [Gaelic] nobles who were always faithful, is that they are now completely extinct, with not one left there, while the land of our ancestors is occupied by Lowland shepherds.

(73-80) When I was at home I would ascend mountain and gorge; I was not short of breath or slow of step; indeed, I was so happy-hearted, playing in running and leaping contests, and I could see far into the distance when the sun was sinking down.

(81-88) But now I am thinking that my life was misspent, since old age has weakened me and made me defective beyond repair; she has wounded my body, I am without vigour, speed or respect; I am constantly complaining that age is a heavy burden to bear.

(89-96) Since age has knocked me out, my strength and my energy have departed; my cheeks have withered and all of my physical attributes have waned; even if everyone else would arise and make ready to depart, I will be left at home at the bottom of the rubbish heap, mute.

(97-104) When I go a distance, my feet become so heavy, I struggle to drag them, I become a poor, bent shinty stick; I place my hand on the walking stick, giving support to my body, and with the slightest loss of balance, I will fall down in the mud.

(105-112) My family now detests and loathes me; they always say that I do not keep up the house for them; since I am slow and crippled, it is a pity that death has not taken my grey head to the grave.

(113-119) I do not talk to others about what has troubled my mind and left my heart so low that it will never recover; it causes me sorrow to listen to the amusement of others as I wander off in exile and the time comes close to hand.

(120-127) When I came to this country, I was light-hearted and foolish; the great sin was to my detriment and I was injured accordingly; but today I have great cause for fear with all I have been taught by the clergy, as I will be going before the [Heavenly] court and giving a complete account of myself.

(128-135) That is the conclusion of every person, when the invitation comes around; no one can stay behind when the severe summons arrives; his friends will keen him, as that is the common custom, when in inanimate slumber he is buried.

3: The Song of the Big Sheep

This next song-poem was composed by Iain Grannd, a native of Gleann Moireastain (Glenmoriston), in 1801 after the death of

Lieutenant-Colonel Iain Grannd, the tenth chieftain of the Grants. Radical changes were made to the running of his estate when the new landlord took control and as a result many of the natives migrated to Nova Scotia between 1801 and 1803.[23] Although the poet declares his intentions to leave immediately and rejoin his compatriots, he never actually left Scotland.

One of the most interesting things about this text is that two distinct versions of it were transcribed, one of them (A) in late-19th-century Scotland and the other (B) in early-20th-century Nova Scotia. This provides an instructive example of how items in oral tradition can be subtly moulded by the identities, experiences and contexts of the performers and audiences of these pieces.

One trivial difference between these versions concerns domestic architecture. The version in Scotland refers to the old-style door locks fashioned from wood (line 4 of version A), which were only used in exceptional circumstances. In this case, the implication is that the locks were fastened to keep the people from reoccupying their homes. While these domestic features would have remained familiar and in existence at the time in the Scottish Highlands, people in Nova Scotia over a century later may have lost memory of them. The Gaelic term "crann," which has a range of meanings, was instead reinterpreted by the descendants of emigrants to mean "plough" (line 20 of version B). Since people were being evicted from arable lands, often to barren sea-side areas (lines A 24 and B 28), such equipment is depicted as being cast aside.

The reference to battle-ready Gaels fighting the French in the version recorded in Scotland (lines 13-16 of version A) does not have any correlation in the version recorded in Nova Scotia. This allusion would still have relevance in the late-19th-century Highlands, given the frequent bursts of recruitment for British regiments in imperial enterprises. Not only was military recruitment less common in Nova Scotia, Gaelic communities were living alongside neighbouring Francophone communities and may not have wanted to rehearse such past conflicts.

Another interesting difference concerns the use of the term "gab-hail" which can mean "lease, feu, tenure" and, by extension, the lands granted by the lease to the tenant. These terms and practices were still the bane of the existence of the Highland tenantry in the 1880s, so it is no surprise that the word occurs twice in the variant of the song-poem recorded in Scotland (lines 2 and 20). The people in Nova Scotia, by contrast, had been freed from such oppressive policies; it was a detail of the text that they may have been glad to forget.

Original Text (A)

1   Deoch slàinte 'Choirneil nach maireann
    'S e chumadh seòl air a ghabhail;
    Nam biodh esan os ar cionn,
    Cha bhiodh na croinn air na sparran.

5   Bhiodh an tuath air an giullachd
    Is cha bhiodh gluasad air duine,
    Is cha bhiodh àrdan gun uaisl',
    Faighinn buaidh air a' chumant'.

    Tha gach uachdaran-fearainn
10 'S an taobh tuath air a mhealladh,
    'Bhith 'cur cùl ri'n cuid daoin'
    Air son caoraich na tearra.

    Bha sinn uair is bha sinn mìomhail
    Nuair bha Frangaich cho lìonmhor;
15 Ach ged thigeadh iad an-raoir,
    Cha do thoill sibh dhol sìos leo.

    Nam biodh aon rud ri tharraing,
    Bhiodh mo dhùil ri dhol thairis;
    On dh'fhalbh muinntir mo dhùthch',
20 Is beag mo shunnd ris a ghabhail.

    Bidh mi 'falbh is cha stad mi
    Is bidh mi trusadh mo bhagaist
    Is bidh mi còmhla ri càch
    Nach dèan m' fhàgail air cladach.

25 Ach a Rìgh air a' chathair
    Tha 'nad Bhuachaill is 'nad Athair –
    Bith 'nad fhasgaidh do'n treud
    Chaidh air reubadh na mara.

    Is a Chrìost' anns na Flaitheis,
30 Glac an stiùir 'nad làmhan
    Agus réitich an cuan
    Gus an sluagh leigeil thairis.[24]

Original Text (B)

1   Tha mi 'n dùil ri dhol thairis
    Mur dèan aon rud mo mhealladh;
    Bidh mi null air an luing
    Gabhail fuinn air mo leabaidh.

5   Ach a Rìgh anns na Flaitheis
    Glac an stiùir 'nad làmhan
    Agus réitich an cuan
    Gus an sluagh leigeil thairis.

    Rìgh nan Dùl air a' chathair
10 Tha 'nad Bhuachaill is 'nad Athair
    Cum do shùil air an treud
    Tha dol reubadh na mara.

    Tha gach uachdaran-fearainn
    'S an taobh tuath air a mhealladh –
15 Dol a thréigsinn nan daoin'
    Air son caoraich na tearra.

    Bàs a' Choirneil nach maireann
    Chuir an leòn seo air aigneadh;
    Fhad is a bha e air ar ceann
20 Cha robh crann air an fharadh.

    Bhiodh an tuath air an cumail
    Cha bhiodh gluasad air duine
    Is cha bhiodh àilgheas dhaoine uaisl'
    Faighinn buaidh air na curaidh.

25 Togaidh mi na bheil agam:
    Bidh mi 'falbh anns a' mhadainn
    Is bidh mi còmhla ri càch
    Nach dèan m' fhàgail air cladach.[25]

Translation (A)

(1-4) Here's a toast to the late Colonel, he would keep the estate in good order; if he were ruling over us, the doors [of houses] would not be bolted shut.

(5-8) The tenantry would be nurtured and people would not be unsettled; the arrogance of non-nobles would not triumph over the commoners.

(9-12) Every landlord in the north has been deluded, turning their backs on their people in preference for tar-smeared sheep.

(13-16) There was a time when we were aggressive, when the French were plentiful; but even if they came last night, you did not deserve to go to defeat with them.

(17-20) If I could choose one thing, I would want to emigrate; ever since the people of my country have left, I take little pleasure in the farm-lease.

(21-24) I will leave and I will not linger, and I will gather together my baggage, and I will be with the rest who will not abandon me on a seashore.

(25-28) O God in the heavens, you are a shepherd and a father; be a shelter to the flock who have been sundered by the sea.

(29-32) O Christ in heaven, take the rudder in your hands and calm the seas so that the host may travel across.

Translation (B)

(1-4) I expect to emigrate before anything deludes me; I will go over on the vessel, singing a tune on my bed.

(5-8) O God in the heavens, take the rudder in your hands and smooth the seas so that the host may travel across.

(9-12) O God of the elements on the heavenly throne, you are a shepherd and a father; keep your eye on the flock who is going to sunder the seas.

(13-16) Every landlord in the north has been deluded—going to abandon the people in preference for tar-smeared sheep.

(17-20) It is the death of the late Colonel that brought this wound to mind; for as long as he ruled over us, the plough was not laid [uselessly] in the loft.

(21-24) The tenantry was well kept and people were not unsettled, and the whims of the nobles did not triumph over the soldiers.

(25-28) I will gather all that I possess and I will leave in the morning; I will be with the rest who will not abandon me on a seashore.

4: Coming to America

Ailean "the Ridge" MacDhòmhnaill is supposed to have composed the following song while on the boat from Scotland to Nova Scotia in

1816 at the age of twenty-two. Ailean's song is based on a much older song by a fellow Lochaber poet, Dòmhnall Donn Bhoth-Fhionntainn, who flourished in the 17th century.[26] Ailean's emigration song makes clear allusions to some sections of the older song, such as these:

> Mi aig sàil Beinn MhicDhuibhe
> Is neo-shocrach mo shuidhe
> Is mi coimhead srath dubh-uisg' an eòin. ...
>
> Chì mi dùthaich nan Rothach
> Is fada bhuam i mu m' chomhair
> Is tric a thug mi na lothan air falbh.
>
> Agus machair nan Dubh-Ghall
> Dh'fhàg mi thall air mo chùlaibh
> 'S tric a mharcaich mi cùrs-each cruinn gorm.[27]

I am at the base of [the mountain] Ben Macdui, although I am unsettled as I look at the strath of the black water of the bird. ...

I see Munro territory which is far in front of me; I often took the colts away [from there].

I have left the Lowlands of the utter non-Gaels far behind, it is often that I rode the dark, firm-built courser [horse].

Ailean's song-poem can be categorized metrically as an "iorram," a metre and genre that was particularly associated with the discussion of politics and the praise of clans and chieftains.[28] The song can be divided into four sections according to time: Ailean first describes his current situation (lines 1-15); he then contemplates the challenges he expects to encounter once landing in North America (lines 16-21); he proceeds by recalling his friendships in Scotland in the past (lines 22-33); he concludes by expressing his hopes for the future (lines 34-37).

The first seven stanzas of this song-poem convey danger and anxiety: the boat is constantly confronting the forces of the ocean and wild weather which challenge her physical resilience (lines 3, 7, 9 and 11); the wild creatures of the deep add to the threats (lines 5-6). There are further dangers to overcome even if he reaches his destination on dry land: there are fierce and treacherous people (lines 16-17), as well as dark, dense, oppressive forests (lines 19-21) in which unknown wild animals lurk (lines 20-21). These are not literal descriptions of a place he had seen but rather the projections of his imagination and rhetorical devices meant to convey a particular message about migration.

Figure 4.1 – The first two generations of the "Ridge" MacDonalds, Ailean (Allan) and Alasdair (Alexander), both accomplished Gaelic poets. Portrait in possession of Isobel MacDonald and used with her permission.

Ailean was married to Catrìona NicMhuirich (or Nic a' Phearsain); her brothers Aonghus and Iain are named in this song as very close companions of the author. Once he begins to reminisce about them, he contrasts his current situation from that which he enjoyed in Scotland; while his friends traverse the familiar rugged hills (line 26), possibly to hunt, Ailean is only traversing the ocean. Ailean delighted in their company in the past and hopes that they will join him in the future.

There is little doubt that Ailean choose to model his song on the older text "Mi aig sàil Beinn MhicDhuibhe" in order to inflect his migration narrative with a sense of heroic achievement, rather than conceding to defeat or humiliation. The metre itself strengthens this argument. The message of this song is most effectively interpreted through this rhetorical lens: the way in which he depicts North America and the people and animals that he will encounter there heightens the potential danger and thus enhances his own achievements in overcoming them (at least his anticipation of doing so). As derogatory as his descriptions of exotic peoples may be to modern sensibilities, we should first consider their symbolic significance.

Reading the emigration song against the earlier model allows us to see more clearly how Ailean is turning the voyage to America into a valiant adventure by drawing parallels with familiar literary precedents. Like his predecessor Dòmhnall Donn, Ailean is seated (at the prow of a boat) but unsettled, facing the waters of a perilous journey (the ocean); instead of mountains to cross, he must cross the sea waves; instead of the cattle of the earlier poem, he and the other passengers are in awe of the enormous whales; like the older outlaw,

Ailean and his family were now on the run, seeking asylum from a country that had turned against them.

Why does Ailean characterize North America by the people who are, from his point of view, its most exotic inhabitants? Perhaps this reflects his anxiety in encountering the people most alien to him and about whom he must have heard various tales and rumours. These rhetorical figures probably play an oppositional role in his heroic narrative which parallel that of the Lowlander in Dòmhnall Donn's song. Warriors prove their prowess by defending their interests and conquering enemies. The concept of an essentialized polarization between Gael and non-Gael is an old one in Highland tradition, with the Lowlander in the role of the archetypal Other by the 15th century. The stereotype of the Gall (Lowlander) is commonly projected upon non-Gaels in North America in Gaelic texts, including this song. In fact, the same aural terminology "glòir nan Gall" (speech of the Lowlander, line 18) is used in a similarly derisive tone in a popular song from late-16th-century Lochaber.[29]

Ailean also characterizes alien peoples by their skin colours. The colour "buidhe" seems to be used to denote Indigenous Americans in his song.[30] The translation of Gaelic colour terms into English is problematic for many reasons. The term "buidhe" is used for a range of colours from "light yellow" to "grey" but it also has associations with luck and thankfulness, and hence may be a pun. This illustrates some of the perils of using translations rigidly without knowledge of Gaelic semantics.

This song illustrates a common strategy for turning the shame of dispossession into a narrative of self-determination and triumph, using the model offered by Dòmhnall Donn. It is surely significant, however, that Ailean projects the negative characteristics of Lowlanders upon people of colour, rather than traditional rivals such as Lowlanders and Englishmen. This song was composed on the boat and does not reflect any actual experiences in Nova Scotia, but it is indicative of the racial divisions that emerged in North America and foreshadows the efforts of numerous immigrant groups to improve their social status and access to privilege by distancing themselves from people of colour and affirming their inclusion in the white, Anglo-Saxon status quo.

Original Text

1   Mi an toiseach na luinge
      Is neo-shocrach mo shuidhe
      Is mi coimhead nan sruth tha 'tighinn oirnn;

      Chì mi thallad fo m' shùilean
5   A' mhuc-mhara 's i brùchdail
      Sruithean geala 'gan spùtadh bho sròin.

      Mi air barr nan tonn fiadhaich
      Falbh le luing air a fiaradh
      Is caithream gaoithe bho'n iar 's i 'na sròin.

10   I ri acain is ri dìosgail
      Sreap a-suas ris gach fiadh-bheann –
      B' fhearr nach fhaca mi riamh i fo seòl.

      Gura truagh leam a càradh,
      Dol a-suas ris na màmaibh
15   Cur nan cuartagan gàbhaidh fo tòin.

      Dol do thìr nam fear buidhe
      Is nan nìgearan dubha
      Is ann leam fhìn nach bu shùgach an glòir.

      Anns na doireachan dubha
20   Far nach goireadh a' chuthag
      Ach coille gun uighean gun eòin.

      Dh'fhàg mi deagh Mhac a' Phearsain
      Leam bu mhiann a bhith 'gad fhaicinn
      Is gum bu bhinn leam fhéin facail do bheòil.

25   Tha thusa dìreach mar b' àbhaist
      Air do sgrìob ris an Làirig[31]
      Is mise dìreadh ri barr an tuinn mhóir.

      Ach Aonghuis, a charaid,
      Is mi nach dìochuimhnich t' fharraid
30   Is nach iarradh an dealachdainn bheò.

      Ceud fàilte dhut, Iain
      Dh'éireadh fonn air mo chridhe
      Nuair a chithinn thu tighinn 'nam chòir.

      'S e mo ghuidhe 's mo dhùrachd
35   Gun tigeadh sibh 'n taobh seo
      Is gum faic mi le m' shùilean sibh beò.[32]

Translation

(1-3) I am in the prow of the boat, although I am unsettled as I look at the ocean currents that are coming over us.

(4-6) I see over yonder before my eyes the whale as it squirts water—white streams erupting from its snout.

(7-9) I am on the crest of the wild waves, travelling with a vessel that is pitched at an angle with a blast of wind from the west in her prow.

(10-12) She sighs and creaks, climbing up each wild mountain [of ocean-water]—better that I had never seen her under sail.

(13-15) Wretched to me is her condition, going up the summits of water, sending each dangerous eddy beneath her stern.

(16-18) Going to the land of the "yellow" men, and the black niggers, their speech does not sound pleasant to me.

(19-21) In the dark thickets where the cuckoo does not call; there are only forests without eggs or birds.

(22-24) I left good MacPherson; I wish that I could see you, as the words from your mouth are like music to me.

(25-27) You are just as usual on your ascent up the Làirig as I am ascending the crest of the great wave.

(28-30) But Angus, o friend, I would never forget your request and I would never want to part in life.

(31-33) A hundred welcomes to you, o Iain, my heart would sing when I would see you approaching.

(34-36) It is my wish and my sincere desire that you all would come over here so that I may see you alive with my eyes.

5: MacNiven and the People of Uist

Although landlords and the migrants themselves figure prominently in stories of the Scottish exodus, the emigration agent is easily overlooked. "Indeed, in the long-running, complex and often contentious saga of Scottish emigration, one of the most consistent, enigmatic and controversial characters has always been the emigration agent."[33] The agent alluded to in the following song only by his surname is doubtlessly Archibald MacNiven of Tobermory, Mull. By his own account, he estimated that he was responsible for the emigration of over 16,000

Gaels to North America between 1820 and 1840, over half of whom went to Cape Breton.[34] This song was composed by a native of Uist who was recruited by MacNiven's schemes and was clearly unhappy with the outcome.

The winters in Canada were more extreme than those that Gaels had experienced in Scotland, where simple deer-hide footgear (cuaran) sufficed for most purposes. Several Gaelic poets remark on the bulky and inconvenient boots that were necessary for winter travel in Canada (see lines 61-64 of text 4.10, for example) and there is likely something beyond their literal unwieldiness that is being alluded to. Not only does this footgear represent the awkward and alien accoutrement that Gaels had to adopt to survive,[35] but they probably also indicate the obstacles to mobility—geographical, economic and social—that Gaels faced in their new circumstances.

Original Text

1 Muinntir Uibhist 'rinn an eucoir
   Uile gu léir nuair a ghluais iad;
   Thug iad an cuid do MhacNaoimhein
   Gus an cur 'thìr an fhuachda;
5 Chan eil gnothach aig duin' aost' ann –
   Duine faoin, cha dèan e buannachd –
   Ach luchd airgid, is gillean òga:
   Is iad as dòcha dèanamh suas ann.

   Thug am Muileach an car buileach
10 Ás a h-uile gin a spùill e –
   Bha e fo'n aois bha air liathadh –
   Le 'bhreugan a' tighinn do'n dùthaich;
   Gur math a dh'fhaodadh am Bàillidh
   Fàbhar a dhèanamh dhuinne,
15 Mur biodh gun d' rinn iad suas ris
   Gus ar fuadach ás an dùthaich.

   Seo an geamhradh a tha fada –
   Is fhada dh'fhairich mi am bliadhn' e –
   Eadar Samhainn agus Bealtainn
20 Is a h-uile rud gann 'ga iarraidh;
   Is e bhith cruinneachadh bhuntàta,
   Nì a shàraich mi is a riaslaich:
   Seo an geamhradh a tha fada
   Dh'fhàg e mi gu falamh fiachach.

25   Is fhaide na sin fuachd na h-oidhche
'N àm ar sìnidh anns an leabaidh;
Ciamar a dh'fhaodas sinn bhith blàth ann
Is còig troighean a dh'àrd de shneachd ann;
Cha dèan aodach-uachdair feum ann
30   Is fheudar éirigh chun an teine;
Taobh mu seach sinn, fad na h-oidhche,
Bhith 'ga thionndadh ris an teallach.

Fhuair mis' ann an toiseach còmhdaich,
Mògaisean a chur mu m' chasan;
35   Chan eil duine 'chuir orm eòlas
Nach bu mhath an spòrs leis m' fhaicinn:
Casan móra fada pliadhach
Is iad 'gan riasladh feadh an t-sneachda,
Làn chloutan 'gan cur sìos annt'
40   'Gan druideadh le iallan craicinn.[36]

Translation

(1-8) It is the people of Uist who committed a misdeed when they migrated; they paid their money to MacNiven so that he could send them to the land of the cold; an old person has no business there—an idle man will not prosper—only the wealthy and young men are those most likely to do well there.

(9-16) The Mull-man—he was not yet at the age of greying—has totally deceived everyone he has plundered with his lies to come to this country; the magistrate might very well do us a favour, if it weren't for the fact that he conspired [with MacNiven] to expel us out of the country.

(17-24) This is the long winter—I certainly felt it long this year—between Hallowe'en and Beltane, and all scarcities are being sought out; it is the gathering of potatoes that has harassed and vexed me; this is the long winter that has left me empty-pocketed and in debt.

(25-32) Longer than that is the cold of the night-time, when we stretch out in bed; how can we be warm there when there are five feet of snow piled high? Bed clothes are useless and it is necessary to arise to light a fire; all night long we are rolling over, to alternate which side is warmed by the fire.

(33-40) I initially got coverings, moccasins to put around my feet; there was no one who came to know me who doesn't make sport in seeing me; large, long, splay-footed feet being dragged through the snow, stuffed with the rags shoved down in them, and closed shut with leather thongs.

6: Sailing to Prince Edward Island

Gaelic periodicals, and the newspaper *Mac-Talla* of Cape Breton in particular, were able to tap the memories of the early waves of emigrants before they were entirely gone. This memoir about a voyage that was meant to leave the Hebrides for Canada illustrates the difficulties of the weather as well as the frequent conflicts of leadership onboard emigrant vessels. Many contributors to newspapers used pseudonyms and the author of this piece was only identified as "Murchadh Cam" from Baile an Tobair (probably the township now called "Springton"[37]), Prince Edward Island.

Original Text

> Rinn Cona iomradh 's a' *Mhac-Talla* o chionn greis air ais air an ànradh a bha luchd-imrich a' faotainn a' tighinn ás an t-seann dùthaich anns na soithichean-seòlaidh, mun do thòisich na bàtaichean-toit air ruith, agus gu cinnteach 's ann da b' fhìor. Thàinig a trì dhe na tubaichean dona dh'ionnsaigh an eilein seo anns a' bhliadhna 1840. Thàinig mise ann an té dhiubh, agus ma thàinig, theab nach tigeadh! Bha sinn dà sheachdain an Loch Ùige, seachdain an Tobar Mhoire, agus trì latha an acarsaid Charlottetown, agus còig seachdain is trì latha gun fhearann 'fhaicinn. Agus mur biodh i gu mise thoirt air ais a-rithist do'n Eilean Sgitheanach, cha chuirinn-sa mo chas air a clàr tuilleadh.
>
> Ach 's ann a bha mi 'dol a sgrìobhadh beagan mu thé dhiubh, mu'n luing an-aobhach *Kingston*, Caiptin Mann. Chuir i staigh a luchd anns an Làraich, goirid o cheann a deas Rathasaidh. Thadhail i ann an Steòrnabhaigh. Sheòl i le luchd luachmhor – trì ceud is trì fichead 's a cóig de luchd-imrich, a thuilleadh air cloinn bhig. Bha a' ruith a cùrsa leis na ghiùlaineadh i [le] soirbheas fàbharach ás a déidh, fad trì latha gu leth. Agus ged a bha na daoine bochda air an cràdh air son gun do "dhealaich na càirdean ri chéile," bha iad an dòchas gun ruigeadh an long mhór Aimearaga leò.

Ach, mo thruaighe! cha d' ràinig! cha ruig! Dh'éirich stoirm ghàbhaidh 'nan aghaidh – an long 'ga tilgeadh suas is domhain sìos, is na tuinn a' dol thairis oirre; – agus, mo thruaighe! na bu mhiosa na sin uile, thòisich i air sgaoileadh; agus ged a bha an sgioba bochd air a' phump gus an robh iad a' toirt suas, 's ann a' sìor-dhìreadh a bha an t-uisge innte!

Mu mheadhan oidhche dh'éibh am mate ris an luchd-imrich iad a dhol suas dha'n cuideachadh, air neo gum biodh iad 's a' ghrunnd. Ghrad-leum ochd fir dheug a-suas – is b' e sin na gaisgich! Ach nuair a bha iad air an claoidh, thuig iad nach dèanadh taomadh an gnothach – nach ruigeadh i Aimearaga 'chaoidh!

Dh'éibh iad ris an sgiobair a cur timcheall is tilleadh, ach 's e nach tilleadh – an t-eucoireach! 'S ann a thuirt a' bhiast gun robh i leathach cuain is nach tilleadh ged a rachadh i fodha. Thuig iad gun robh na seòladairean deònach tilleadh agus gu fortanach, bha seòladair treun air bòrd: Johnston. Dh'éibh e ris a' mhate, is e breith air an stiùir, "Thoir thusa dhomhsa an cùrsa is bheir mis' air ais i, ma dh'fhanas i an uachdar." Thuirt e ris an sgiobair nan gluaiseadh e 'theanga gum biodh e ann an iarainn mun canadh e "theab."

Am feadh is a bha an ùpraid seo air bòrd, bha na truaghain a bha fo rùm an droch staid, a' faicinn an uisge 'tighinn a-staigh shìos is shuas. Bha aon duine bochd, is nuair a chunnaic e poca buntàta leis a' dol fodha, rug e air, 'ga chumail 'na uchd. Dh'éibh duine cneasta ris, "Coma leat dheth, a dhuine thruaigh! Chan fhada gus am bi thu fhéin is do phòca 's a' ghrunnd!"

Bha bean chòir – bean 'ic Coinnich – is aois thrì mìosan an leanabh aice; agus an uair bu chruaidhe 'chùis air fad, thilg i 'leanabh air leaba Mhurchaidh 'ic Mhannain is dh'éibh i ris, "O Mhurchaidh, thoir sin do nèamh!" Bha fios aig a h-uile neach gun robh Murchadh a' dol a nèamh; oir, ged nach robh aon lide foghlaim aige, bha móran dhe'n Fhìrinn aige air chuimhne is bha e cumail adhraidh moch is an-moch.

Ach gu sgeula fada 'dhèanamh goirid, thàinig fiath is chuir i h-aghaidh air an taigh, is cha robh de chridh' aig an sgiobair darra-bheig a thighinn ás a bheul; agus dh'oibrich an sgioba gu toileach gus an d' ràinig i Steòrnabhaigh, far an d' fhuair iad uile aiste sàbhailte. Lean na làmhan rithe uile ach Johnston. Ràinig i air éiginn Obar Dheadhain; cha d' ràinig i buileach an cidhe nuair a chaidh i sìos. Dh'fhan an luchd-imrich an Steòrnabhaigh gus an d' fhuair iad soitheach ùr làidir, *Heroine*, Caiptin Walker, duine math, a thug a-nall iad sàbhailte.[38]

Translation

In a recent issue of *Mac-Talla*, Cona mentioned the terrible storms faced by emigrants coming from the old country in the sailing ships before the steam ships began to operate and he was indeed correct. Three of those terrible tubs came to this island in the year 1840. I came in one of them, and although I did, I almost didn't! We spent two weeks in Loch Ùige, a week in Tobermory, three days in Charlottetown harbour, and five weeks and three days without seeing land. If she hadn't returned me back to the Isle of Skye, I would have never set foot onboard her again.

But I was going to write a little bit about one of them, about the luckless vessel *Kingston*, run by Captain Mann. She dropped her cargo at Làrach, close to the southern end of Raasay. Then she visited Stornoway. She sailed off with a valuable cargo—three hundred and sixty-five emigrants, as well as small children. She was making her way with all that she could carry with a favourable tailwind for three and a half days. And even though the poor people had suffered because they were parted from their kinsfolk, they were hopeful that the great vessel would reach America with them in it.

But, alas! It did not and would not! A dangerous storm arose against them – the vessel thrown up and deep down, and the waves crashing over her;—and, alas! worse than all of that, she began to come loose; and even though the poor crew was working the pump until they were giving up, the water was constantly filling up the boat!

About midnight, the mate shouted to the emigrants to go up to help them, or else they would sink to the bottom of the sea.

Eighteen men instantly leapt up—what heroes they were! When they were worn out, they realized that bailing out the water would never work—they would never reach America!

They shouted to the captain to turn her around and return, but he wouldn't—the criminal! Indeed, the beast said that she [the ship] was halfway across the ocean and he wouldn't turn her around even if she were going under. They realized that the sailors were willing to return and fortunately, there was a brave sailor on deck: Johnston. He shouted to the mate as he grabbed the helm, "Give me the route and I will take her back, if she stays above water." He said to the captain that if he made a peep that he would be in chains before he could say, "Almost."

All of the time that this mayhem was happening on deck, the pitiful creatures below deck were in a terrible state, seeing the water coming in from above and below. There was one poor man there who, when he saw a bag of potatoes that belonged to him going under the water, grabbed it and kept it close to his chest. A pious man shouted to him, "Never mind that, poor fellow! It won't be long until you yourself and your bag will be at the bottom of the sea!"

There was a goodly woman—Mrs. MacKenzie—who had a three-month-old baby; and when the situation looked the worst, she tossed her baby on the bed of Murdo Buchanan, and she shouted to him, "O Murdo, take that to Heaven!" Everybody knew that Murdo was going to Heaven; this was because, although he didn't have a lick of education, he had memorized a great deal of the Bible and he prayed in the morning and at night.

But to make the long story short, a calm came and she turned back homeward, and the captain didn't dare to let a peep come out of his mouth; and the crew worked gladly until she reached Stornoway, where everybody came out safely. All of the hands stayed with her except for Johnston. She reached Aberdeen with great difficulty; she had almost reached the pier when she sank. The emigrants stayed in Stornoway until they got a fresh, sturdy boat, *Heroine*, run by Captain Walker, a good man, who took them across safely.

7: From Kilmartin to Tiverton, Ontario

Alasdair Friseal collected the following anecdote from Seumas Mac-Caluim, who was living in Tiverton, Ontario, around the year 1903. It recalls his journey from Scotland in the year 1843. According to Friseal, Seumas spoke "Gàidhlig cho snasmhor coimhlionta 's ged a bhiodh i a' tighinn o bheul a sheanar nam bu bheò e" (Gaelic so perfect and eloquent that you'd think it was coming from his grandfather's mouth, if he were alive).

This narrative provides a full account of migration from sea voyage to settlement on land and illustrates the importance of community and kinship networks to emigrants: not only did MacCaluim's family apparently follow relations in chain migration from Scotland to Canada, but they helped each other out as they built their new lives and continued to follow each other's secondary migrations of a smaller scale through Ontario in later years.

Original Text

>B' e ainm m' athar Niall MacCaluim. Bha e a' còmhnaidh 's an t-seann-dùthaich aig Sloc a' Mhuilinn, faisg air Cille Mhàrtainn ann an Siorramachd Earra-Ghàidheal. Bha e pòsta ri Ceit Chaimbeul, a rugadh is a thogadh 's an àite cheudna. Bha mar theaghlach aca dithis mhac agus dithis nighean: Aonghus agus Seòras, Anna agus Peigi. Bha Anna pòsta ri Dòmhnall MacArtair, agus Peigi ri Seumas Dùghallach.
>
>Thàinig an teaghlach gu Canada 's a' bhliadhna ochd ceud deug dà fhichead is a trì – bliadhna dealachaidh na h-Eaglaise Saoire. Bha mi fichead bliadhna a dh'aois aig an àm, agus bha m' inntinn làn throm le bhith fàgail tìr mo bhreith is mo chàirdean. Ach bha mi òg, tapaidh agus solarach mu m' fhortan agus bha m' aodann air Canada mar gum b' ann air tìr bheartach far am faighinn cothrom air mo shuidheachadh a leasachadh. ...
>
>A thuilleadh air sin, bha càirdean thall romhainn agus bha sinn dol mar theaghlach, a sheasadh ri guailne a chéile. Bha sinn mu shé sheachdainean air a' chuan gu Cuibec bho Ghrianaig. B' e ainm an t-soithich air an do sheòl sinn an *Tay-of-Greenock*. Bu Ghàidheil a bha 's a' mhór-chuid de'n chuideachd a bha air bòrd, móran diubh o Chille Mhàrtainn, mar a bha sinn fhéin, cuid eile

o Thireadh, is o Shiorramachd Pheairt. Labhradh a' chuid a bu mhò dhiubh Gàidhlig.

Bha an turas-mara an eatarras math: bha stoirm is ciùin greis mu seach ann. Ach cha robh muir cho colgach is as àbhaist a bhith air Maol Chinn-Tìre againn ré fad ar turais. Bha cridhealachd nach bu bheag againn an-dràsta is a-rithist mar an ceudna. Bha feadhainn ann, òg agus sean, a bha math air òran a ghabhail, agus bha feadhainn a dh'innseadh sgeulachdan a chuireadh fiamh air gaisgich na Féinne, nam biodh iad 's an éisteachd.

Ach le sin uile, bha iomadh cridhe fìor mhuladach a chionn dealachadh ri càirdean is dàimhich nach fhaiceadh iad gu bràth tuille agus cha b'urrainn do na mnài na deòir a chumail air an ais nuair a chluicheadh am pìobaire "Cumha MhicCruimein." ...

Agus, cha robh sinn gun chothrom air adhradh fhollaiseach a mhealtainn air an luing; agus cha ruig mi leas a ràdh gun do mheas sinn uile 'na shochair mhór e. Cha robh cumhachd aig òran, no aig ceòl, ar tarraing air ar n-ais gu cuimhneachan ar seann dachaighean, mar a bha aig adhradh an Tighearna air a' chuan mhór. Air madainn là na Sàbaid, mar a thogadh sinn uile ar guthana gu foirmeala 's an t-seinn, a' ghaoth a-mhàin a' séideadh caithream leinn, b' éiginn duinn a bhith cuimhneachadh air Dia ar n-athraichean, agus air móralachd Iehòbhah. ...

Agus, aig crìoch ar turais, cha b' e ceòl na pìoba, no fonn nan òran a bhith lìonadh ar cridheachan gu mór ach moladh do'n Fhreastal chaoimhneil sin a threòraich gu sàbhailt sinn thar a' chuan. ...

Bho Chuibec thàinig sinn air an uisge, suas gu cridhe Chanada Uachdaraich. Sgaoil na Tiristich gu Brock, na Peartaich gu àitean eile air an t-slighe, ach chum a' chuid a bu mhò de na Màrtainnich còmhla gus an d' ràinig iad Port Stanley. Sgaoil iad o sin am measg bhailtean-dùthcha Yarmouth, Dunwick, agus Southwold. Air dhuinn tìr a chur fo'r casan aig Port Stanley, chaidh triùir no ceathar againn a lorgachadh a-mach air càirdean beagan mhìltean bho'n phort, agus thachair dithis chaileagan òga oirnn air an rathad mhór, a' giùlain cruinneag uisge.

Dh'fheòraich mi fhéin diubh c' ainm a bh' orra agus fhreagair iad gum bu Chaimbeulaich iad.

"Is c' ainm a bh' air ur màthair?" dh'fheòraich mi.

"Bha NicCaluim," fhreagair iad.

Ars mi fhéin do m' chompanaich, "Is mise a' cheud fhear againn fhuair a-mach dàimheach," oir dh'aithnich mi gu grad gum b' ann ri cloinn piuthar m' athar a bha sinn a' bruidhinn. Chaidh sinn leis na caileagan dha'n taigh agus dh'ith mi ann an-sin a' cheud ghreim bìdh a dh'ith mi air tìr ann an Canada – aran cruithneachd agus bainne, greim cho blasta biadhachail is a dh'ith mi riamh. B' ann da-rìreadh gu taigh mo chàirdean a thàinig sinn agus fhuair sinn aoidheachd eireachdail gu dearbh. Air an fheasgar sin fhéin, bha ar n-àirneis agus ar n-uile sheilbh air an tabhairt gu taigh ar caraid leis na daimh, agus dh'fhan sinn ann an-sin còmhla riutha mu dhà mhìos.

Ré na h-ùine seo, dh'fhiosraich sinn a-mach fearann air ar son fhéin agus dh'imich sinn agus ghabh sinn seilbh air. Bha e suidhichte faisg air abhainn Thames, air an dara concession do Shouthwold, dlùth air Fingal. A' cheud oidhche a chuir sinn seachad ann an-sin air an fhearann ùr, cha robh aig m' athair ach aona thastan Yorkach agus chaidh a thoirt seachad air an oidhche sin fhéin air son builinn arain.

Bha airgead gann ach bha càil is neart is spionnadh againn uile eadar dhaoine is mhnathan agus shoirbhich leinn. Dh'fhan mise beagan mhìosan air m' ais ag obair air an rathad mhór a bha iad a' cur sìos eadar Port Stanley agus Lunnain. B' e mo chuid-sa a bhith ag ullachadh fiodh air son ùrlar an rathaid. Bha am fiodh ceithir òirleach ann an tiughaid de'n ghiuthas a b' àlainn ann an Canada. Fhuair mi dusan dolair 's a' mhìos agus mo bhiadh mar dhuais.

Bha bràthair da m' athair a shuidhich anns a' cheàrn seo mun dh'fhàg sinne an t-seann dùthaich agus thog a chuid chloinne taigh air ar son air an fhearann a fhuair sinn. Bhuineadh am fearann do'n Cherry Reserves agus phàigh sinn dà dholar air gach acair,[39] a' pàigheadh fichead dolar sìos. Chuir sinn fhéin ùrlar de dh'fhiodh – darach sgoilte – agus ballachan-tarsaing de'n fhiodh cheudna, 's an taigh agus mur an robh e ro àilgheasach, bha e blàth tioram agus rinn e an gnothach.

Bha dragh mhór againn 's a' cheud dol a-mach. Cha robh àite-achadh sam bith air a dhèanamh. Bha againn ri mìn, buntàta, is goireasan eile a ghiùlain air ar guailne agus bu doirbh an obair e. Thòisich sinn an-sin air àiteachadh an fhearainn, a' réiteachadh, a' ruamhradh, a' tarraing ás nan stoc, is a' losgadh an fhiodha, gus an d' fhuair sinn beagan talmhainn ullamh air son sìl. A lìon beag is beag, fhuair sinn air ar n-adhart mar ar coimhearsnaich agus thuinich sinn air tìr ar gabhaltais.

Dh'fhan sinn aig Fingal mu dhà bhliadhna deug, agus an-sin thàinig sinn gu Kincardine. Chaochail m' athair aon gheamhradh an déidh sin, agus mo mhàthair bliadhna an déidh sin a-rithist. Thàinig mo phiuthair, a bha pòsta ri Dòmhnall MacArtair, còmhla rinn gu Kincardine agus mu dhà bhliadhna 'nar déidh-ne thàinig mo bhràthair, mar an ceudna, agus shuidhich e aig Lorne, faisg air Kincardine. Dh'fhan mo phiuthair, a bha pòsta ri Seumas Dùghallach, ann an Southwold gus an do chaochail a fear. Sin agad iomradh air teaghlach m' athar is mar a thàinig sinn gu Canada.

Mu mo theaghlach fhéin, chan eil móran agam ri ràdh, ach seo agad e, bheag no mhór a nì thu dheth. Bha mi pòsta dà uair. An déidh dhuinn tighinn gu Canada, phòs mi fhéin is Màiri Tuairnear, té a mhuinntir taobh Locha Fìne. ... Bha sinne am measg na ceud fheadhna a thàinig a-steach do'n ceàrn seo de Shiorramachd Bhruis, agus b' ann domhsa a thàinig a' cheud litir bho riaghladair nan sgoilean aig Kincardine, air son sgoil 'fhosgladh ann an Lorne. Tha mi a-nis a' dol a-steach do'n cheithir ficheadamh bliadhna dha m' aois ach tha mi slàn fallain, agus ann an cor cho goireasach is a bu mhath leam a bhith an déidh deagh chath a chur ris an t-saoghal.[40]

Translation

My father's name was Neal MacCallum. He lived in the old country at Sloc a' Mhuilinn, close to Kilmartin in Argyllshire.

He was married to Kate Campbell who was born and raised in the same place. They had a family that consisted of two sons and two daughters: Angus and George, Anna and Peggy. Anna was married to Donald MacArthur, and Peggy to James MacDougall.

The family came to Canada in the year eighteen hundred forty three—the year that the Free Church went out on its own. I was twenty years old at that time and my mind was very heavy from leaving the land of my birth and my kinsfolk. But I was young, capable and ambitious for my fortune and I had set my sights on Canada as though on a wealthy land where I would find the opportunity to improve my circumstances....

On top of that, there were relations out there before us and we were going as a family who would stick together. We were about six weeks at sea from Greenock to Quebec. The name of the vessel on which we sailed was *Tay-of-Greenock*. Most of the company onboard were Gaels, many of them from Kilmartin, as we were ourselves, others from Tiree and from Perthshire. The majority spoke Gaelic.

The sea voyage was tolerably good: there were alternating periods of storm and calm. But throughout our trip the sea was not as angry as it usually is around our end of the Mull of Kintyre. We enjoyed great merriment now and again as well. There were a number, both young and old, who were good at singing songs, and a few who could tell stories that would alarm the heroes of the Fian, if they were listening.

But for all of that, there was many a heart that was truly sorrowful because of parting with friends and relations they would never see again and the women could not hold the tears back when the bagpiper played "MacCrimmon's Lament." ...

And we enjoyed open public worship on the vessel; and I need not explain that we all considered it a great consolation. No song or music was as powerful at pulling us back to remember our old home as was the worship of the Lord on the great sea. On the morning of the Sabbath, as we all raised up our voices ceremoniously in song, with only the wind to accompany our voices, we had to remember the God of our forefathers and the greatness of Jehovah. ...

And, at the end of our journey, it was not the music of the bagpipes or the melodies of secular songs that filled our hearts to bursting, but the praise of that kind Providence that led us safely across the ocean. ...

From Quebec we came by boat right into the heart of Upper Canada. The Tiree people went their own way to Brock, the Perthshire people to other places on the way, but the majority of the Kilmartin people stayed together until they arrived at Port Stanley. From there they branched off among the rural townships of Yarmouth, Dunwick, and Southwold. After we put our feet down on dry land at Port Stanley, three or four of us went out to search for friends a few miles away from the port, and a couple of girls happened upon us on the main road, carrying pails of water.

I myself asked them what their names were and they answered that they were Campbells.

"And what was your mother's name?" I asked.

"It was MacCallum," they answered.

I said to my companions, "I am the first one of us to have found a relation," for I recognized instantly that it was to the children of my father's sister that we were speaking. We went with the girls to their house and I ate the first bite of food there that I ever ate on land in Canada—wheat bread and milk, a snack as tasty and nourishing as I had ever eaten. It was indeed to the house of my relations that we had come and we had truly splendid hospitality. That very afternoon, our furnishings and our every possession were taken to the house of our kin by the oxen, and we stayed there with them for about two months.

During this time, we found out about property for ourselves and we went there and we took possession of it. It was situated close to the river Thames, on the second concession of Southwold, close to Fingal. The first night we spent there on the new property, my father had no more than a single York shilling, and it was spent that very night for a loaf of bread.

Money was in short supply but we all had health, strength and energy, both men and women, and we prospered. I stayed back working for a few months on the main road that they were putting down between Port Stanley and London. It was my duty to prepare wood for the foundation of the road. The wood was the most beautiful pinewood in Canada, four inches in thickness. I received a dozen dollars a month and my meals as wages.

My father had a brother who settled in this area before we left the old country and his children built a house for us on the property that we got. The land belonged to the Cherry Reserves and we paid two dollars an acre, paying an initial deposit of twenty dollars. We laid down a wooden foundation of split oak and cross walls of the same timber in the house, and although it wasn't too extravagant, it was warm and dry and sufficed for our purposes.

We had a great deal of difficulty, initially. No cultivation had ever been done. We had to carry meal, potatoes, and other necessities on our shoulders and the work was difficult. Then we started to cultivate the land, clearing, digging, pulling out the stumps, and burning the wood, until we got a bit of soil ready for seed. Little by little, we progressed like our neighbours and we settled on our own titled land.

We stayed at Fingal for about twelve years, and then we came to Kincardine. My father died a winter after that, and my mother the year after that one. My sister, who was married to Donald MacArthur, came along with us to Kincardine and about two years after us my brother came likewise and he settled at Lorne, close to Kincardine. My sister, who was married to James MacDougall, stayed in Southwold until her husband died. There you have the account of my father's family and how we came to Canada.

About my own family, I don't have much to say, but here it is, whatever you might make of it. I was married twice. After we came to Canada, Mary Turner, a woman of the people of Loch

Fyne-side, and I married. ... We were among the first group who came in to this part of Bruce County, and it was to me that the first letter from the school magistrate at Kincardine came, in order to open a school in Lorne. I am now entering the eightieth year of my life, but I am whole and healthy, and in as fit a shape as I would wish to be after fighting a good fight with the world.

8: Gaelic Guidebook for the Emigrant

In the year 1841 Roibeart MacDhùghaill published the first complete guidebook in Gaelic for Scottish Highlanders hoping to relocate to North America, entitled *Ceann-Iùil an Fhir Imrich* (The Emigrant's Guide). It contains practical advice about many aspects of emigration not found in other Gaelic sources, including the detailed information given in the excerpt below. As MacDhùghaill explains, America had become the stuff of legend and speculation to the rural inhabitants of the Highlands, many of whom had often never been far from home. They could be easily defrauded or robbed in the big city, and they knew little of the challenges on the long voyage facing them on the boat as well as in North America itself once they reached land.

Increasing levels of literacy encouraged MacDhùghaill to publish a book in Gaelic to potential emigrants from the Highlands. MacDhùghaill, in fact, penned articles for the popular periodical *Cuairtear nan Gleann* (1840-1843) which was highly influential in the development of modern Gaelic prose. His writing style is very conversational and employs proverbs and quotes from songs to convey his message to readers, and to those listening to his text being read aloud.

Original Text

Fosgladh: Tha imrich nan Gàidheal do dh'Aimearaga mu thuath a-nis air tighinn gu bhith 'na cuspair-sgeòil, chan ann a-mhàin do luchd-àiteachaidh "nan gleann" (oir is cian fada o'n là a dh'fhàg "dealachadh nan treun" luaidh acasan air a' ghnothach seo), ach mar an ceudna do mhaithibh na tìre; ionnas gun do mheas àrd-chomhairle na Rìoghachd i airidh air am mion-rannsachadh fhéin o chionn ghoirid. Thog seo inntinn a' mhór-shluaigh gu léir, air chor is gun robh gach sean is òg a' feitheamh gu furachair ri "deireadh gach sgeòil an-asgaidh."

Ach cha robh am mosgladh seo ach a' cumail 'nan cuimhne "gur treise greim cailliche na tarraing laoich."

Tha na Gàidheil mar a bha iad roimhe: móran diubh gun chuid; agus an còmhnadh, mo thruaighe! chaidh 'dhiùltadh dhaibh, a dh'aindeoin dìcheall an luchd-tagraidh. Ach ged a chuir seo stad air an imrich ann an tomhas mór, cha do chuir e tost air am beòil o bhith bruidhinn uimpe; tha Aimearaga 'na seanchas cho ùr is a bha i riamh. Gach beag agus mór a' bith-labhairt mu'n dealbh a tha e 'tarraing 'na inntinn fhéin – mu'n nì nach fhac', agus gu mór as lugha na sin, nach do thuig e riamh.

Bhrosnaich seo mise, uair no dhà, gus oidheirp a thoirt air feòir-linn bheag a thilgeadh feadh thiodhlaca chàich; ach thug mi fainear gun robh an torr a bh' ann diubh cho farsaing-chòsach is gun sìoladh i sìos ann cho fad is nach toirte 'n aire dhi agus gum bitheadh "ceann-iùil" sgiobalta laghach de'n ghnè air am bheil mi nis a' tionnsgnadh móran na b' fheumaile.

Tha e fìor gum bheil iomadh leabhar sgrìobhte cheana mu'n nì seo; gidheadh, chan fhiosraich mi gum bheil aon leabhar air a sgrìobhadh mu'n nì seo a-mhàin fhathast, air son feuma muinntreach nan Garbh-Chrìoch:

Anns a' chànain do'n tug sinn ar gaol
Is nach tuigear a caochladh leinn.

Cha mhó na sin a shaoilear leam nach biodh rudeigin de'n t-seòrsa seo anabarrach feumail do'n "fhear-imrich" air iomadh seòl : – mar chomhairlich' an àm a bhith 'falbh – mar cheann-iùil fad na slighe – mar oid'-ionnsaich', agus mar chompanach 's an dùthaich ùir. Chan eil teagamh nach gnothach cudthromach teannadh ri innseadh do'n "fhear-imrich" ciamar a dh'fhalbhas, ciamar a ruigeas, agus ciod a nì e 'n-déidh ruigheachd; ach bu chòir dhomh-s' a bhith comasach air a chur 'na earalas mu seo, "oir is mise a bh' ann is a chunnaic e." ...

Ullachadh, &c: ... Gach fear a tha dol air an turas seo, ma-thà, thoireadh e leis, mas urrainn e, na nithean a leanas: am pailteas de dh'aodach cuim is leapach – osain – boineidean leathann gorma, an seòrsa ris an can na Tuathaich "sgrath," chan fhiù a' bhoineid bhiorach an t-aiseag 'fhaotainn – éideadh mór de dh'anart-cotain air son léintean – éideadh cùrainn air son pheiteinean bàna – éideadh plangaid air son bhriogaisean glùineach – éideadh de chainb chaoil air son thriubhsairean samhraidh. Bhiodh seo 'na ghoireas comharraicht' oir is beag nach eil na nitheannan seo dà phrìs ann an Canada.

Mar an ceudna, toraichean – gimleidean – caibe no dhà de'n t-seòrsa as treasa – beagan de thàirrnean iarainn, a bhios aige ri làimh air an t-slighe agus an déidh ruigheachd. Air son trealaich de dh'uidheam saorsaineach, mar tha locair, gilbean, agus mar sin, na biodh e 'ga thoirt leis. Chan fhaigh am fear-imrich ùine gus a bhith ri ciotaireachd mar sin an Canada. Ged a thòisicheadh e rithe, bhriseadh e an uidheam aig meud na cabhaig a bhiodh air gus a faotainn tro làimh agus bhiodh sin 'na chall mór an déidh an luach-aiseig a phàigheadh. Is fhearr do neach fear-ceàirde 'fhaotainn gu obair de'n ghnè seo; oir an-sin gheibh e i air a dèanamh [gu] ceart, gun e fhéin a bhith 'call ùine rithe. 'S e seo dòigh as saoire air a cheann mu dheireadh an Aimearaga.

A thaobh phoitean is uidheam-chòcaireachd, mas e am fear-imrich a tha gus a bhith 'deasachadh a bhìdh fhéin dol a-null air a' chuan, bidh e feumail dha roinn a thoirt leis; mur h-e, cha chomhairlichinn dha an ceannach a-bhos: ach ma thachras dhoibh a bhith aige cheana, seo math dha an cumail air son fheuma 's an dùthaich ùir. Cha dèan aghann-ròstaidh de'n t-seòrsa 'th' aca 's a' Ghàidhealtachd feum a chunna duine riamh thall. Tha na soithichean staoine ro dhaor ann is chan eil an seòrsa tha iad a' dèanamh ann math cuideachd: [cha?] mheasainn crìonnta do dhuine an toirt leis. Cha chòir tuagh idir a thoirt a-null oir chan aithne do ghaibhnibh Albannach gin a dhèanamh 's am bi feum.

Is còir do'n fhear-imrich gach nì bhios e 'toirt leis a chàramh gu cearmanta ann an cisteachaibh ceàrnach, gun bhith ro mhór, no am barailtibh, agus a bhith ro chùramach mu 'chuid an àm a bhith dol air bòrd luinge, gu sònraichte mas ann á baile mór a sheòlas e; oir is àbhaist do'n phràbar tionaladh mu leithid de ghnothach, agus gach corp dhiubh a bhith air bogadan gus rud sam bith air am faigh iad an crògan a thiolpadh leò.

Tha caochladh sheòrsaichean bìdh ro thaitneach agus ro fheumail cuideachd aig fairge; agus bu chòir do na h-uile neach a bheireadh an Tabh a Siar fo cheann a theann oidheirp 'thoirt air beagan de gach gnè lòin a ghabhadh cnuasachadh dha a thabhairt leis. Chan ann idir air son geòcairean a dhèanamh dhiubh tha mi a' comhairleachadh seo dhoibh. 'S ann tha mi 'gan cur 'nan earalas on tha fios agam gum bheil e feumail air son an slàinte agus on tha barail agam gum bheil an laimhrig fuasach anagoireasach ri luchd-imrich a bhios air an astar sin. Is còir do dhuine bhith furachair mu na goireasan seo, an déidh a dhol air bòrd cuideachd, oir "Chan ann am Bòid uile tha an t-olc"; bidh caora charrach 's an treud, eadhan an déidh 'dhol gu fairge, no is iongantach e.[41]

Translation

Foreword: Highland emigration to North America has now become a subject of discussion, not only for the inhabitants of "the glens" (for it has been quite a long time since the "departure of the heroes" caused them to talk about this matter), but likewise for the élite of the land; even to the point that the United Kingdom's executive council considered it appropriate to conduct their own thorough investigation a short while ago. This raised the hopes of the entire population, so that every person, young and old, was waiting diligently for the well-considered conclusions. But this excitement only reminded them that "the grip of an old crone is stronger than the pull of a champion."

The Gaels are as they were before: many of them own nothing; and alas! assistance has been denied to them, despite the best efforts of their advocates. But even though this slowed down emigration to a large degree, it has not silenced their mouths from speaking about it; America is as hot a topic as it ever was. People large and small are constantly talking about the depiction that it forms in their own minds—about the things that they've never seen, and at the very least, that they've never understood.

This inspired me, once or twice, to make an attempt to throw in my own two cents' worth, among the contributions of others; but I noticed that the many [books] that exist are so vague and full of holes that my own might disappear without being noticed and that a nice, systematic guidebook of the sort that I am now commencing would be much more useful.

It is true that there are already many books published about this topic: even so, I have not learned of one book that has been written specifically about this topic for the use of the people of the Highlands:

In the language to which we have given our affection
And we cannot understand any other.

Even more than that I thought that something of this sort would be extremely useful to the emigrant in many ways: as an advisor at the time of departure—as a guide throughout the journey—as a teacher, and as a companion in the new land. There is no doubt that it is an important matter to begin to explain to the emigrant how to depart, how to arrive, and what to do after arrival; and I ought to be capable of providing him with precautions, for I have been there and know myself.

Preparation, &c: ... Every man who is going on this journey, then, should take with him, if he is able, the following items: plenty of personal clothes and bedding—socks—wide, blue bonnets, the kind that the people of the North call "husk," pointed bonnets are not worth ordering—a large roll of cotton fabric for shirts—a roll of flannel for white undervests – a roll of plaiding for knee-high trousers—a roll of thin canvas for summer trousers. These would be excellent resources as they are nearly twice the price in Canada.

Likewise, augers—gimlets—a spade or two of the strongest sort—some iron nails, to have on hand on the journey and after arrival. As for an assortment of carpentry tools, such as a plane, chisel, and so on, he shouldn't take them with him. The emigrant won't have time to bother with the likes of that in Canada. Even if he were to start doing that kind of work, he would break the tool due to the great hurry he would be in to get it done and that would be a great loss after the cost of delivery was paid. It is better for a person to employ a craftsman to do this kind of work;

for he can get it done properly, without wasting his own time on it. In America, this is the least expensive method, all things considered.

Regarding pots and cooking equipment, if it is the emigrant who will be preparing his own food going across the ocean, it will be helpful for him to bring a variety with him; if he won't be, I would not advise him to buy them here [in Scotland]; but if he happens to own them already, it will be good for him to keep them for use in the new country. The roasting pans of the sort they have in the Highlands won't be of any use in the far country. Tin utensils are very expensive and the sort that they make now are not good either; I would [not?] consider it prudent for a man to take them with him. He definitely shouldn't take an axe over with him as I do not know any Scottish smiths who can make serviceable ones.

The emigrant should pack everything that he takes with him compactly in rectangular chests, without making it too large or putting things in barrels, and should be extremely watchful of his possessions when it is time to go aboard a ship, especially if he is sailing out of a large town; for it is a common custom for the riffraff to loiter around such activities, and every one of them to be bobbing around in order for them to steal away anything they can lay their paws on.

There is a variety of types of food that are very pleasant as well as beneficial at sea; each and every person who undertakes to travel the Western Ocean should do his very best to take with him a little of every kind of meal that can be nibbled. I am certainly not advising this in order to make gluttons of people. I am rather giving precautions as I know that it is useful for their health and as I am of the opinion that the harbour is extremely ill-suited for emigrants who have travelled a long distance. A person needs to be watchful of these necessary goods after he has gone onboard as well, since "Not all of the evil is on the isle of Bute"; it would be unusual if there was not always a mangy sheep in the flock, even after going to sea.

9: From the Isle of Lewis to Quebec

Although the exact circumstances of the departure of Iain Greumach in 1863 are somewhat unclear—there is debate as to whether his home community of Gabhsainn mu Thuath (North Galston) on the Isle of Lewis was cleared or not—poverty and economic hegemony were driving factors, according to his own testimony. He and his sister joined other natives of Lewis who had been settling the Eastern Townships of Quebec since at least the 1850s.[42]

The story remembered about this song—whether it reflects historical events accurately or not—is an interesting testimony to the perceived power of the poet in Gaelic society, his duty in expressing truth, and the fear that others had of that power, not least those who hoped to benefit from emigration:

> After John Graham wrote his poem describing the hardships they had suffered, he was summoned to Montreal to attend a court because of what he said. He had a smattering of English and, when he was asked to plead, he said he would plead guilty if they could point out any lies in his poem. Nobody could point out any lies, but they warned him that they would never get the country settled if he gave it a bad name.[43]

His text describes the treatment meted out to the vulnerable lower classes in Lewis in dehumanizing tones: emigrants are like flies let loose (line 32), and greedy merchants strip them bare like hens and leave them exposed to the harsh elements (lines 47-48). It was much to his disappointment that the same merciless forces of economic exploitation preyed on victims similarly in Quebec (lines 41-50) and his hopes for financial freedom in Canada seem to have been crushed (lines 51-58). His faith in the banks of Glasgow and Edinburgh to develop Lewis equitably and favourably for its population (lines 59-66) seems rather naive.[44]

Original Text

1   B' e siud bliadhna na h-éiginn:
     Shil na speuran na frasan,
     Bha an crodh air na stéillean
     Ri dol eug leis an acras;
5   Cha robh connadh ri fhaotainn
     Air gach taobh do'n bhaile,

Is chaidh gach bruthach agus garradh
Chur gu làr air son teine.

Dhiùilt na siameurlan sìol dhuinn
10 Air son biadh na sìol-cura;
Is rinn na ceannaichean cumhnant
Gun làn an dùirn 'thoirt do dhuine;
Mura pàigheadh sinn sìos e
Leis an iasg bho'n an dubhan,
15 No le crùna na Rìoghachd,
Cha deidheadh sgrìobag air duine.

'S ann bho Loch an Dùnain a sheòl sinn
Air ar fògradh á Alba;
Is iomadh neach a bha tùirseach
20 Nuair a chaill sinn Mùirneag 's an an-moch;
Am bàta-iarainn gu sunndach
Null leinn gu fairge
Dh'ionnsaigh Baile Doire an Éirinn
Far an d' fhuair sinn té'ile gu falbh leinn.

25 *Ealasaid* bhòidheach
Is i an òrdugh gu guanach,
Le cuid chroinn agus ròpan
Dol a sheòladh a' chuain leinn;
Dh'ionnsaigh fearann Cholumbuis
30 Air an turas bu luaithe dhi,
Far na sgap sinn uile
Mar bhucas chuileagan 'déidh 'fhuasgladh.

Bliadhna trì fichead is a trì –
Gur tric a bhios 'nam chuimhne –
35 Nuair fhuair Tòmas an t-earraid,
An cabhaig, a lùb sinn;
Ach leamsa gum bu shòlasach
A bhith seòladh gu Quebec
Ann am bàta gun cheanna-bheairt
40 Làn de gharbh-chlachan muille.

Tha dà cheannaiche làmh rium
Anns a' cheàrnaidh seo do'n talamh:
Fear ann an Lingwick tàmh dhiubh
Is fear a' fàs ann an Winslow;
45 Is cuimhnich ma thig thu
Bidh thu aca 'nan ìnean
Mar gun spìonadh tu 'chearc

	Is gun leigeadh tu i 's an Fhaoilleach;
	Chan eil rian agad dhol ás bhuapa
50	Gun a bhith air t' fhad anns an Legion.

    Ma chluinneas tu mo dhàn-sa,
    An àite tàimh anns am bheil thu,
    Thoir am muir agus an tràigh ort
    Mus tig thu dh'àiteach' na coille;
55 Chan eil saidhbhreas ri fhaotainn
    Air an taobh seo de'n Atlàntic
    Ach coille mhór do'n speur
    Fad 's as léir dhomh ri 'fhaicinn.

    'S e Eilean Leódhuis an t-eilean
60 Anns am bheil gach goireas tha feumail;
    Pailteas airgid an tasgadh
    Am banca Ghlaschu is Dhùn Éideann,
    Is trì bancannan eile
    Chùl air an sin ag éirigh:
65 Stìmearan snasail,
    Tarraing bho fhéillearan.[45]

Translation

(1-8) That was the year of extreme difficulty: rain showered down from the skies, cattle were carried on biers, dying from hunger; no fuel could be found anywhere around the village, and so every hillside and dyke was razed to feed the fires.

(9-16) The factors refused to give us seed in order to sow food crops and the merchants entered an agreement not to give a fistful of it to anyone; if we could not pay for it with the fish from the fishing-hook or with British crown coins, no one would have as much as a scratch.

(17-24) It was from Loch an Dùnain that we sailed, expelled out of Scotland; many a person was mournful when we lost sight of [the hill] Mùirneag in the twilight; the iron boat cheerily going over with us to sea toward Derry in Ireland, where we got another boat to leave with us.

(25-32) Lovely *Elizabeth*, giddily made ready with her masts and ropes, going to sail the ocean with us toward the land of Columbus, making the trip as quickly as she could, where we all parted ways like a box of flies after it is opened.

(33-40) I often recall the year 1863 when Thomas got the sheriff's order that hurriedly overpowered us; but I thought it gladdening to be sailing to Quebec in a boat without sailing gear, full of rough-hewn stones.

(41-48) There are two merchants next to me in this region of the country; one man lives in Lingwick and the other flourishes in Winslow; and remember if you come that they will have you in their grip; just as you would pluck the chicken and let it go in January, there is no way for you to escape from them without being fully involved in the Legion.

(49-58) If you hear my song in your current dwelling place, go to the sea and to the shoreside [of Scotland] before you come to farm the forest [in Canada]; there are no riches to be had on this side of the Atlantic, only an enormous forest reaching to the sky as far as I am able to see.

(59-66) Lewis is the island in which every advantageous resource can be found; there is plenty of money stored up in the banks of Glasgow and Edinburgh, and three other banks besides are being developed there; stylish steamers are hauling loads from merchants.

10: Dòmhnall's Testimony about Manitoba

The following song-poem was among the materials that appeared during the prolonged parley about migration to the Prairies in one of the radical Highland newspapers in Scotland. The text was introduced by the following note:

> If you think that "Teist Dhòmhnaill air Manitoba" is worthy of a place in the *Scottish Highlander*, please insert it. My motive for troubling you at the present time is to forewarn my friends and relations, the crofters, to be on their guard against the most ungodly trap which is prepared for them by land speculators at home and out here, and backed up by the British Government. Woe to the people when the rulers of the country combine with the rogues and land peddlers to deprive the hard-working, poor, industrious people of the fruit of their labour. Such is the case now, and has been since Canada bought the North West. A residence of forty-seven years in this country has made me pretty well acquainted with the result of mortgages, and I truly

believe that mortgages in Manitoba will never be redeemed, but after a few years of hard labour, and all the social discomforts in an arctic climate, the poor deluded crofters will lose all their improvements, or become tenants under landlords as bad as they left in Scotland, and that is enough to say. Now, sir, upon you as an independent journalist, and recognised defender of crofters, devolves the task of exposing, and if possible, frustrating this last dodge of the united villainy of Scottish Tory landlords and their fast friends, the boodlers, and blind shareholders in Canadian land companies. The crofter who is so infatuated as not to heed your warning richly deserves a taste of the Canadian Siberia.

The "Seòras" named in line 72 is Sir George Stephen, the first president of the Canadian Pacific Railway who profited enormously from the enterprise. The emigrants who cultivated lands in Manitoba as part of the colonization scheme fostered by the expansion of the railroads were to pay half of their annual crop: an extortionate proportion. Some were so irate about the rates that they fled to Dakota.[46] The "Emily" named in line 27 is Lady Emily Gordon-Cathcart, the landlady of Beinn nam Fadhla (Benbecula) and Cluainidh (Cluny in Badenoch).

Although the identity of the author is not certain, Dòmhnall Òg MacFhionghain, an immigrant to St. Andrew's, Manitoba, is a likely candidate. As a native of Beinn nam Fadhla, he would have been familiar with Lady Emily. His friend Dòmhnall Chaluim named in line 41 is probably Dòmhnall MacAonghuis, a native of Gearanais (Gerinish), South Uist, who also emigrated to Manitoba.[47] This song was modelled on an older love song, although the incongruity of the affections of the chorus and the disparaging topics of the verses may represent an ironic slight to Lady Emily.

Original Text

1   Hi ri rì ho rathaill ó,
    Rathaill ó, rathaill ó
    Hi ri rì ho rathaill ó
    Is i 'n nighean donn as bòidhche.

5   Is mór an sluagh a dh'fhàg na Bàigh
    Gu tighinn gu Manitoba chrainntidh;
    Nam b' e 'n-diugh an-dé do phàirt dhinn,
        Gum biodh dàil 'nar seòladh.

Dh'fhàg sinn dùthaich fhallain bhlàth
10   Bha tàchdarach an taic' an t-sàile
Ged bha na h-uachdarain 'nam plàigh
   Bha sinn air làr ar n-eòlais.

Chaidh sinn gu h-uachdarain charach
A reic sinn, colann agus anam,
15   Ri rathad-iarrainn gun bheannachd
   Is feannar sinn gu'r brògan.

Fhuair triùcairean an dùthaich rapach
Air sia sgillinn an t-acair –
Aig dà dholar chruinn is cairteal,
20   Nì am prasgan stòras.

Rinneadh plot le droch-bheairt suas
Air taobh bhos is thall a' chuain,
Chum gum mealladh iad an sluagh
   Gu tìr an fhuachd is an dòlais.

25 Tha Coileach-feucaig an Dùn Éideann
Leis nach truagh an tuath 'nan éiginn;
Nan iarradh Emily ar ceusadh
   Bhiodh an t-eun ud deònach.

Bha mìle breugair air son duais,
30   Le leabhraichean a' dol mun cuairt
A' moladh na h-Àirde 'n Iar Thuath
   Is gach buaidh bh' air Manitòba.

Cha robh beachd-sgeòil bu deòin le caillich,
Bho Bhun Leódhuis gu Ceann Bharraigh,
35   Nach deachaidh a leughadh mu'n fhearann
   Le geallanaibh gun sòradh.

Ràinig sinn "Fearann a' Gheallaidh":
Bha an reòthadh cho cruaidh ri stallaidh;
Corr is dà throigh dheug 's an talamh –
40   Cha bhiodh seangan beò ann.

Dh'fhaighnich mi de Dhòmhnall Chaluim
"Cuin thig an deidh ás an talamh?"
Thuirt e le tùirse rium, "A charaid,
   Fanaidh i ri d' bheò ann."

45   B' fhearr leam na 'bhò-laoigh a b' fhearr
Bha riamh aig bodaich Inbhir Àir
Nach do chreid mi 'bhreug bho'n ghràisg
   Mu fhàsach Mhanitòba.

MIGRATION

    Is iomadh allaban is cuaradh
50 Aig daoine anns an tìr gun tuar;
    Bidh gaoth á tuath le nuallan fuar
        A' toirt nan cluas is nan sròn dhinn.

    'Nar fàrdaich gun tuar am fuar-mhadainn,
    Bidh liath reòthadh air a' phlaide,
55 Bùrn agus lionn, meug no bainne
        Mar ghlainneachan reòite.

    Nuair bhios blizzard 's an tìr aognaidh
    Feumar béin gach béist mar aodach;
    Cha dèan cloth de chloimh ar saoradh
60   Bheir a' ghaoth an fheòil dhinn.

    An Albainn, am madainn Chéitinn,
    Rachainn cas-rùisgt' thun nan sléibhtean;
    Cha bhiodh feum air mogais éitigh
        Is cha bhiodh béin 'gar còmhdach.

65 Is sinn a rinn imrich gun àgh
    Gu boglaich Mhanitòba ghràinde;
    Chan iarrainn tuilleadh de dh'ànradh
        Dha m' nàmhaid na tha oirnne.

    Bidh sinn ag obair mar thràillean
70 Air fearann alcah bàite;
    Ged a thogamaid am barr,
        Bidh cus de'n ghràin aig Seòras.

    Bidh trian no corr dheth, dheòin no dh'aindeoin,
    Aig rathad-iarainn air son fàraidh;
75 Goill is Gàidheil air am mealladh
        Is am fearann fo mhòrtgage.

    Tha clann nan treun-fhear gleusta maiseach,
    Bu mhath gu feum air sléibh is air machair,
    An-diugh 'gan léireadh is béin 'gan seacadh
80   Is cuid de'n casan reòite.

    Mas beò mi gus an tig an t-Earrach
    Fàgaidh mi "Fearann a' Gheallaidh,"
    Ruigidh mi Dakota thall ud:
        Tha fearann agus òr ann.[48]

Translation

(1-4) ...She is the most lovely brunette.

(5-8) A huge crowd left the Bays [of Uist] to come to withering cold Manitoba; if today were yesterday for some of us, we would delay our expedition.

(9-12) We left a healthy, warm country that was well provisioned near the sea-water; although the landlords were a plague, we were on familiar ground.

(13-16) We went to wily landlords who sold us, body and soul, to the cursed railroad, and we will be flayed down to our shoes.

(17-20) Rogues got the filthy country for six pence an acre—at an even two and a quarter dollars, the scoundrels will make a fortune.

(21-24) A plot was concocted with evil intent on both sides of the ocean so that they could deceive the people to the land of the cold and the misery.

(25-28) There is a peacock in Edinburgh who has no compassion for the tenantry in their distress; if Emily asked for us to be crucified, that bird would be willing.

(29-32) A thousand liars wanted a payoff and were going around with books, extolling the North West and every virtue possessed by Manitoba.

(33-36) There wasn't an idea that an old woman fancied, from the Butt of Lewis to Barra Head, that wasn't declaimed from a book about the land with unconditional promises [of prosperity].

(37-40) We reached "the Promised Land": the freeze was as hard as rock; more than a dozen feet into the ground—not an ant could survive in it.

(41-44) I asked Donald Calum, "When will the land thaw out?" He said to me dejectedly, "My friend, it will stay like that for a lifetime."

(45-48) I wish even more than to have the best calf of the Lowland churls of Ayr that I had never believed the lie of the scoundrels about the wilderness of Manitoba.

(49-52) The people in this bleak land suffer many aberrations and hardships; the north wind comes with a cold howl to rip the ears and noses from us.

(53-56) In our bleak quarters in the cold morning, a grey frost covers the blanket; water and liquid, whey and milk are like frozen glasses.

(57-60) When a blizzard comes to the dreary land, the furs of every animal are needed as clothing; woolen clothing will not suffice as the wind rips the flesh off us.

(61-64) In Scotland, on a May morning, I would travel barefoot to the hills; there was no need for hideous moccasins and furs would not cover us.

(65-68) We certainly made an ill-fated migration to the swamps of grim Manitoba; I wouldn't wish more misfortune on my enemy than we ourselves suffer.

(69-72) We work like slaves on the land saturated with alkali; even if we produce the harvest, George gets an excess of the grain.

(73-76) No less than a third is taken by the railroad as the cost of freight, whether we like it or not; Gaels and non-Gaels have been deceived, while their land is under mortgage.

(77-80) The descendants of the handsome, adept champions who were of good use on hillside and plain are in agony today as they wither under furs, some of them with frozen feet.

(81-84) If I am still alive when spring comes, I will leave "the Promised Land"; I will arrive in yonder Dakota where there is land and gold.

11: In Praise of the Canadian Prairies

The Dominion of Canada printed a Gaelic booklet in 1907 entitled *Machraichean Móra Chanada* (The Great Prairies of Canada) with the aim of convincing Highlanders to settle in the Prairies. The booklet is 36 pages long and features photographs testifying to the agricultural bounty of the region and the comfortable living conditions there. In fact, the cover of the booklet contrasts a small, drab thatched house in the Highlands with a large and colourful two-story house on the Prairies. The author of the publication is listed on the title page as "Ailghinn La Bhruinn"; although this may be a Gaelicization of the (likely French) name of the actual author of an English text upon which this was based, Alasdair Friseal certainly wrote the Gaelic text.[49]

This propagandist tract employs several strategies to win over the confidence of its Gaelic readers. It directly refutes complaints about the region's harsh weather and conditions prominent in other texts (such as song 4.10), emphasizing the mildness of the climate, the fitness of the families living there and the material wealth that many have attained. It reassures us that any legitimate problems were investigated and resolved by a benevolent government. Rather than admitting to any deficiencies in the environment or economic arrangements, it instead pins the blame on the indolence of those who have raised complaints about their experiences. The otherwise foreign territory is made less intimidating by stressing the many long-standing Highland settlements in Canada as a whole and the social networks into which Gaels will be able to tap after they arrive. The depictions of the landscape which make comparison to places in Scotland, and even to tartan, help to make the unfamiliar familiar, at least in the imagination.

It is noteworthy that the Gaelic term "machair" used to signify "Prairie" in this text is also the conventional term used in reference to the Lowlands of Scotland. The tract commends the Canadian Prairies as an emigrant destination over the Scottish Lowlands, however, by highlighting the ability of Gaels to exercise their own cultural and linguistic freedoms in a new space which they can construct on their own terms, rather than having to assimilate to alien norms. This is interesting evidence that the author(s) expected that at least some Gaels valued the intrinsic worth of their language and culture enough to choose to pass it on to future generations given such opportunities.

Original Text

> Ré lethcheud bliadhna an déidh seo, dh'fhàg móran Ghàidheal tìr an athraichean. Chaidh cuid diubh gu Galltachd – do na bailtean móra, do na h-obraichean móra far an robh a' chuid bu mhò dhiubh air an slugadh suas am measg choigreach. Dh'fhàs, mar bu tric, an clann suas ann an aineolas air cànain, is air gnè nan Gàidheal agus, an-diugh, chan eil dad ri fhaotainn diubh ach na h-ainmean a chì neach thairis air dorsainn nam bùth air an t-sràid.
>
> Air an làimh eile, thàinig móran mhìltean de na Gàidheil do Chanada Uachdarach agus thog iad fearann. Shoirbhich gu math leò. Chan eil teagamh nach robh obair chruaidh aca ri

dèanamh 's na làithean ud. Bha na craobhan ri'n gearradh sìos; bha an talamh ri ruamhradh, bha taighean ri'n togail, bha cuid is rud ri chosnadh air son teaghlaichean òga, gun lùths gun chobhair, agus bha airgead cho gann ri sneachd an t-samhraidh. Ach bhuannaich iad gu dìcheallach agus thar gach éiginn agus bochdainn; dh'éirich iad gu comhfhurtachd, agus móran diubh gu àilgheas agus beartas. Chum iad 'nam badanan sluaigh ri chéile; chum iad beò cànain agus móran de chleachdaidhean an athraichean, agus gus an là an-diugh gheibhear daoine, mnathan agus clann, 's an dara, agus 's an tritheamh ginealach dhaibhsan a thàinig an toiseach, a labhras is a leughas Gàidhlig cho math ri gach dalach neach ann an aon sam bith de dh'eileanan siar na Gàidhealtachd. Sin agaibh coimeas eadar iadsan a dh'fhàg a' Ghàidhealtachd air son na Galltachd agus air son Canada dhà no thrì linntinn roimhe seo. Có dhe'n dithis a rinn an taghadh a b' fhearr? Tha mi fhéin a' creidsinn gun d' rinn iadsan a thàinig gu Canada. ...

Bho na briathran a sgrìobh mi cheana, bidh e soilleir do'n leughadair gum bheil na Gàidheil lìonmhor agus gu cubhaidh-seach ann an Canada. Tha muinntir Ghàidhealach ri'm faotainn bho chuan gu cuan, agus tha móran de sheann spioraid agus chàirdeas an athraichean air an cleachdadh 'nam measg. Tha fàilte chridheil air a toirt do gach aon neach a tha tighinn a-mach bho'n Ghàidhealtachd. Chan ann am measg choigreach a tha neach a' tuiteam nuair a ruigeas e a' cheann-uidhe aig aon de bhailtean beaga no móra Chanada an Iar. ...

Air an latha an-diugh tha a' Ghàidhlig air a cleachdadh anns na h-eaglaisean far am bheil na Gàidheil lìonmhor, agus tha na se-ann dòighean air an cumail suas. Bhiodh e cho buailteach dhuit a thighinn air searmon Ghàidhlig ann an Toronto, Winnipeg, Regina, no Edmonton, is a bhiodh e ann am Peairt, Struidhle, Obar Dheadhain, no gach dalach baile air machair na h-Alba; agus is taitneach an nì gum bheil na Gàidheil a dh'fhàg an da-chaighean fada as an déidh, cho cuimhneachail air teangaidh is air creideamh an sinnsear. Dh'fhaoidte móran tuille a ràdh mu'n Ghàidhlig ann an Canada – mu na comannan Gàidhlig a tha air chois anns na bailtean móra, mu na buidhnean a tha ag ionnsachadh na Gàidhlig ann an sgoiltean-oidhche, – is mar sin air adhart, ach tha móran fhathast ri innseadh mu chor na dùthcha. ...

Ré na h-ùine 's an robh mi ann am Manitoba, agus bha mi ann ri aimsir cho fuar is a dh'fhairicheadh an-sin bho aon cheann a' gheamhraidh gus a cheann eile, cha deachaidh éis no mì-ghoireas gus a chuid as lugha a chur orm le fuachd no le gailleann. Thadhail mi air móran Ghàidheal a shuidhich 's an àite, cuid diubh corr is fichead bliadhna roimhe sin. Am measg dusain no dhà theaghlach, cha robh a h-aon a bha a' gearan an cor, ach bha iad uile toilichte le'n staid. Cha robh a h-aon a dh'atharraicheadh a shuidheachadh, a rachadh gu àite eile, a reiceadh fhearainn mur faigheadh e a làn phrìs.

Bha cuid ann aig an robh tairgsean airson am fearainn – bho fhichead gu còig thar fhichead dolair an acair – is cha robh iad a' gabhail na tairgse. Cuimhnich gun d' fhuair iad sin an fhearainn an asgaidh agus gun robh iad a' dèanadh airgid air son iomadh bliadhna. Còig puinnd Shasannach an acair, – 's e sin ochd ceud puinnd Shasannach air son ochd fichead acair, meud an tuathanais chumanta. Bha e laghach da-rìreadh a bhith dol a-staigh do na taighean a dh'fhaicinn nan teaghlaichean. Ann an siud bha feadhainn òg cho smearail beòthail is a chitheadh tu ann an àite sam bith fo'n ghréin, gun bhruaillean a' cur dragh air an inntinn is gun smuain gun robh dùthaich eile ann cho tìorail, gasta ris an dùthaich 's an d' rugadh iad, –eadhon Manitoba. ...

Tha Machair mhór Chanada mìle de mhìltean air a fad agus ceudan de mhìltean air a leud. Is àlainn an tìr seo; taitneach do'n t-sùil, coibhneil do dhuine is do dh'ainmhidh. Tha am fonn torrach, na coilltean làn de dh'fhiodh air son feum an duine; na mèinneachan guail lìonmhor agus a' cur thairis le meud an lànachd a chum beatha is blàths a thoirt do na taighean-còmhnaidh; tha móran uisgeachan fuar, fionnar air am faotainn 's gach ceàrn; tha aibhnichean ann air am bheil na bàtaichean-smùid a' dol latha an déidh latha a' giùlan goireas de gach seòrsa o bhailtean na Roinn-Eòrpa agus a' toirt air an ais cruithneachd is cinneas eile na dùthcha; tha sruthan beaga a' claiseadh is a' taiseachadh an fhearainn cho lìonmhor is a tha na sreathan ann am breacan Gàidhealach; tha lochan beaga air aghaidh na tìre mar reultan air aghaidh na h-iarmailt air oidhche ghlan reòta gheamhraidh, os cionn Eilean Leódhuis; tha cnuic is beanntan a' briseadh fàire air cuairt iomallach na Machrach 'gar dìdean o ghaoith is o ghailleann. Tha an t-adhar fìor-ghlan tioram neartail agus fallain, ré na bliadhna air fad; tha an aimsir seasgair slàinteil, a' toirt gealltanais air slàinte bodhaig agus móran làithean do neach a ghnàthaicheas cùram 'na chaitheamh-beatha is 'na ghiùlan an ceann a dhleastanais. ...

Air a' bhliadhna mu dheireadh, thàinig móran Ghàidheal thairis a dhol a dh'obair air an rathad-iarainn ann an Canada fo fhastadh luchd an rathaid. Bha cuid de'n bheachd nach robh iad toilichte leis mar a bhuineadh riutha anns an dùthaich seo agus, air ball, ghabh uachdaranachd na tìre an cùis an làimh, agus thugadh a' chùis gu solas an latha. ...

Tha cuid de dhaoine ann do'n dual a bhith a-chaoidh ri cànran is a' gearan, is bhiodh iad mi-thoilichte ann an Gàradh Edein fhéin. Sin an fheadhainn a gheibh thu an-dràsta is a-rithist, a' gearan air Canada. Cha tugainn éisteachd sam bith dhaibh. Cha robh ràmh math, no cas-chrom mhath, no òrd math, no tuagh mhath, riamh aca 'nan làmhan. Dhaibhsan, bha na h-uile beart is inneal dona, gun fheum; cha robh nì no neach riamh ceart ach iadsan, nam b' fhìor iad fhéin; ach ann am beachd muinntir eile, cha b' e an t-òrd, no a' chas-chrom a bha cearr, ach na culaidh-thruaigh nach b' urrainn an làimhseachadh gu ceart.

Cha chuala mi riamh neach a' gearan air Canada a thàinig a dh'ionnsaigh na dùthcha le inntinn air a dèanamh suas gun robh e 'dol a shoirbheachadh. Neach sam bith aig am bheil slàinte agus a tha geur dìcheallach an dail obair sam bith a thig 'na rathad a dhèanamh cho math is as urrainn da ; – tha mi ag ràdh ann an seo, tha goireas, tha saidhbhreas, tha pailteas, roimhe anns an dùthaich seo, mur caith thu le struidheas anameasarra, am beò-shlàinte a tha an soirbheas a' cur thugad. Chan e seo mo bheachd-sa a-mhàin; 's e beachd gach neach aig am bheil cothrom beachd a thogail air cuid agus cuibhreann sluaigh nam Machraichean móra.[50]

Translation

During the following fifty years, many Gaels left the land of their fathers. Some of them went to the Lowlands—to the big cities, for substantial careers where the majority of them were swallowed up by a foreign people. Most often, their children grew up ignorant of the language and character of the Gaels, and today there is nothing left of them but the names you see over the doors of shops on the street.

On the other hand, many thousands of Gaels came to Upper Canada and they cultivated the land and prospered. There's no doubt that they had to do hard work in those days. The trees had to be cut down; the soil had to be broken up, houses had to be built, young families had to acquire assets, without outside assistance, and money was as scarce as snow in the summer. But they succeeded with great effort in the face of great hardship and poverty; they ascended to great contentment and many of them to privilege and wealth. They stuck together in clusters; they kept alive the language and customs of their forefathers, and until this day men, women and children of the second and third generations of the original settlers can be found who speak and read Gaelic as well as anybody in the Western Isles of Scotland. There you have the difference between those who left the Highlands for the Lowlands and for Canada two or three generations ago. Which of them made the better choice? I myself believe those who chose to come to Canada made the better one. ...

From the words that I have written previously, it will be clear to the reader that the Gaels are plentiful and comfortably situated in Canada. The Gaelic people can be found from sea to sea, and much of the old spirit and kinship of their forefathers is maintained among them. A warm welcome is given to everyone who comes out from the Highlands. It is not among strangers that a person finds himself when he reaches his destination at one of the settlements, large or small, in western Canada. ...

In the present day Gaelic is used in the churches where Gaels are plentiful, and the old traditions are kept up. You are as likely to come across a Gaelic sermon in Toronto, Winnipeg, Regina, or

Edmonton as you are in Perth, Stirling, Aberdeen or any other city in the Scottish Lowlands; and it is a wonderful thing that the Gaels who left their homes far behind them are so tenacious of the language and religion of their ancestors. Much more could be said about Gaelic in Canada—about the Gaelic societies that are established in the big cities, about the organizations that are teaching Gaelic in the night schools,—and so forth, but there is still much to say about the condition of the country....

Throughout the time that I was in Manitoba, and I was there while the weather was as cold as it can be experienced from one end of the winter to the other, I was not troubled with the slightest hindrance or inconvenience by the cold or storms. I visited many Gaels who settled in the area, some of them more than twenty years before that. Among a dozen or more families, not one of them was complaining about their condition, they were all contented with their condition. Not one of them would change his situation, or go somewhere else, or sell his land unless they got its full value.

There were some who had received offers for their land—from twenty to twenty-five dollars an acre and they were not accepting the offers. Remember that they got the land freely and they had been making money for many years. Five English pounds an acre,—that is eight hundred English pounds for one hundred and sixty acres, the common farm size. It was pleasant indeed to go into the houses to see the families. The youth there were as healthy and active as you can see anywhere in the world, without any distractions to trouble their minds, without any idea that any other land was as commodious and wonderful as the land in which they had been born, namely, Manitoba....

The great Canadian Prairie is a thousand miles in length and hundreds of miles in breadth. This land is beautiful; pleasant to the eye, kind to man and to beast. The soil is fertile, the forests are full of wood for human usage; the coal mines are plentiful and overflowing with abundance which can supply warmth and life to habitations; there are many cold, cool waters to be had in every corner; there are rivers on which steamboats travel day after day transporting supplies of every kind from the cities of Europe and returning wheat and other products of the country with them; the small streams that furrow and water the land are as numerous as the stripes in a Highland tartan; the little lakelets on the surface of the land are like stars in the heavens on a clear, cold winter's evening over the Isle of Lewis; the hills and mountains dot the horizon on the outskirts of the Prairies, protecting us from winds and storms. The air is pure, dry, strong, and wholesome throughout the entire year. The climate is comfortable and healthy, guaranteeing corporal well-being and a long life to anyone who is committed to exercising judiciousness in his lifestyle and in his behaviour. ...

Last year, many Gaels immigrated to work on the railroad in Canada, being employed by them. Some decided that they weren't happy with the way they were treated in this country, and the national authority immediately took the matter into their hands, and it was investigated. ...

There are people whose natural inclination it will always be to wail and complain, and they would be dissatisfied in the Garden of Eden itself. Those are the people you find, now and again, complaining about Canada. I wouldn't pay any attention to them. They never had a good oar, or a good spade, or a good hammer, or a good axe, in their hands. For them, every tool and machine is bad and useless; there was never a person or thing that was correct except themselves, if they are to be believed; but in other people's opinions, it was not the hammer or the spade that was faulty but the objects of pity who could not handle them correctly.

I have never heard anyone complaining about Canada who came to the country with his mind made up that he was going to succeed. Anyone who is healthy and who is sharp and industrious in any work that comes his way will do as well as is possible; what I am saying here is that there are resources, there is affluence, there is abundance to be found in this country; there is plentitude before you for a livelihood, if you do not squander it with excessive extravagance. This is not only my opinion; it is the opinion of every person who has the opportunity to offer his thoughts about the worldly goods and allotments of the people of the great Prairies.

5 – Settlement

The experiences of emigration—regardless of the degree of coercion—and immigration brought about an inevitable process of introspection on the cause and meaning of the tumultuous events of the 18th- and 19th-century Highlands. As Robert Dunbar has argued, the literary expressions of Canadian Gaelic poets were important to their audiences because there had been "no greater crisis than that brought on by the departure from the Old World and the challenge of rebuilding Gaelic communities in the New."[1] Although different communities faced different dilemmas, negotiated differing forces, and came to individual conclusions, they often resorted to similar traditional ideals and literary conventions to express their understandings of these processes and justify their opinions.

The wide variety of stances and sentiments evident in texts about the experiences of Gaels in Canada demonstrate that Highland immigrants were not all of one mind. The social status of the immigrant, his or her relationship to community and the state of development of the built environment encountered appear to have been overriding concerns. Those who came from the lower social orders along with their extended families and friends, and did not have major economic or practical obstacles to overcome to commence their livelihood, were the most likely to express satisfaction with immigration. Those who had been more economically comfortable in Scotland, who came by themselves or left many loved ones behind, or who arrived in harsh or hostile environments were most likely to bemoan their fate. Some people did reconsider perspectives over time, however, especially if they were joined later by relations or their conditions improved.

The songs that were composed about these experiences often made their way back to Scotland and could colour the expectations of potential migrants. Am Bàrd MacGill-Eain provides the classic example of the change of heart about migration: one of the last professional poets to enjoy any patronage from a chieftain, he was overwhelmed by the enormous scale of the challenges facing him when he landed in Nova Scotia. His song "A' Choille Ghruamach" (The Gloomy Forest), one of the best known texts about Gaelic emigration, is an expression of disappointment and regret. It quickly became so well established in the emigrant repertoire that it easily eclipses his later songs taking delight in the Gaelic communities in Nova Scotia and their prosperity.[2] Gaels themselves have long commented on the ambivalences of emigration, as illustrated by this excerpt from an early-20th-century article.

> An uair a bha na Gàidheil a' suidheachadh anns an dùthaich seo, bha iad a' fulang iomadh deuchainn, agus a' faighinn móran tàire ris nach robh dùil aca mun d' fhàg iad thall. Bha an crannchur 's an tìr seo cho aocoltach ri mar bha an cor anns an t-seann dùthaich is nach eil e iongantach ged bhiodh iad a' cur uimhireachd air an atharrachadh a thàinig air an t-saoghal daibh ri linn dachaigh an sinnsear fhàgail.

> Bha cuid diubh a bhiodh air uairibh a' call am misnich gu buileach; agus sgrìobh iad sin iomadh litir a-null a' dì-moladh na dùthcha seo gu mór, iadsan aig an robh a bheag no mhór de ghibht na bàrdachd, chuireadh iad an dì-moladh sin ann an cruth òrain.

> Chaidh an t-òran as ainmeile tha againn air a' chuspair seo a dhèanamh leis a' Bhàrd MacGill-Eain, bàrd neo-chumanta math, bliadhna no dhà an déidh dha àite thogail, mar a thuirt e fhéin, "am meadhan fàsaich air Abhainn Bhàrnaidh" an Siorramachd Phictou. Is aithne dhuinn uile an t-òran brèagha sin. Thatar ag innse gun deach "A' Choille Ghruamach," mar a theirte ris, a sheinn air banais ann an Tobar Mhoire am Muile, beagan mhìosan an déidh do'n bhàrd an t-òran a sgrìobhadh agus mun do sguir am fear-seinn, cha robh sùil thioram anns a' chuideachd.

Bha òrain eile air an dèanamh cuideachd, òrain nach fhaodar a choimeas ri saothair Iain MhicGill-Eain, a chionn gun d' rinneadh iad le daoine aig nach robh comas a' bhàird ann an tomhas cho mór is a bha aigesan. Tha a' chuid as motha dhiubh sin air a dhol á cuimhne.[3]

When the Gaels were settling in this country, they endured many tribulations and they encountered more difficulties than they had expected before they had emigrated. Their fate in this land was so unlike their conditions in the old country that it would not be surprising if they were shocked by the changes that came upon their lives on account of leaving the home of their ancestors.

At times some of them lost their courage altogether; and those people wrote many letters back home greatly disparaging this country, and those who had a greater or lesser gift of poetry would express that disparagement in the form of a song.

The most famous song that we have on this subject was composed by The Bard MacLean, an uncommonly good poet, a year or two after he had built a place, as he said himself, "in the middle of the wilderness on Barney's River" in Pictou County. We all know this beautiful song. It is said that "The Gloomy Forest," as it is called, was sung at a wedding in Tobermory on the island of Mull, a few months after the poet had written the song and that there was not a dry eye in the company by the time that the singer was finished.

There were many other songs that were also composed, songs that cannot be compared to the creations of John MacLean because they were made by people who did not have nearly as great a command of poetry as he had. The majority of those others have been forgotten.

Some of the many challenges encountered by immigrant Gaels settling in Canada are described by the texts in this chapter: draining swamps (5.1), learning about unfamiliar species (5.4), protecting themselves, their produce and their livestock from hostile predators (5.5, 5.6 and 5.12), surviving in harsh climates (5.10 and 5.14), managing with the lack of infrastructure (5.3, 5.7) and coping with a dominant anglophone majority culture that did not value other languages, especially Gaelic (5.11, 5.12 and 5.14).

The most pressing of all concerns for the early colonists, however, were the forests. Gaels referred to the North American continent with such kennings as "Dùthaich nan Craobh" (The Land of Trees) and Highland immigrants looked upon this vast expanse of trees with a mixture of admiration and anxiety. While woodlands were intuitively understood to represent vitality and primal integrity in Gaelic tradition, the inevitable consequence of sustaining themselves with the fruits of agriculture and pastoralism was that the forests had to be cleared. It was a task that was both heroic in scope and tragic in nature.[4] Texts in this chapter (5.1, 5.2, 5.12 and 5.13) and others remark on this herculean undertaking, but some also express affection for woodlands and regret for their loss (5.7 and 5.8).

Similar ambivalences and anxieties pervade Gaelic perceptions of and relations with First Nations. The desire of Gaels to create conceptual bridges to indigenous populations is apparent in many early encounters. In his *Ceann-Iùil an Fhir-Imrich* (The Emigrant's Guide), for example, Roibeart MacDhùghaill attempted to allay the fears of potential emigrants by relating information about the landscape, peoples, and languages to what they already knew in the Highlands, especially their own native language. He provides Gaelic etymologies for place names, personal names, and ordinary words in native languages, going so far as to state: "Tha cainnt shocrach, bhogar, grinn ac', dìreach meangan de'n Ghàidhlig agus nam biodh an dream a sgrìobh i an toiseach làn eòlach air a' Ghàidhlig, bhiodh an dà chainnt anabarrach coltach ri chéile" (They have an easy-going, soft and elegant language, just a branch of the Gaelic, and if the first people who recorded it had been fully acquainted with Gaelic, the two languages would look extremely similar to one another).[5] Such assertions imply some form of kinship. In fact, he draws a wide range of parallels between Highlanders and First Nations, including their clothing, carriage, and social structures.

These empathetic links were severely tried and often broken once colonization intensified and contention over land and resources increased. An account of the settlement of the parish of East Bay in Cape Breton, Nova Scotia, illustrates the nature of such conflicts:

The first Scotch settlers of East Bay were Donald Gillis and Duncan Currie, followed soon by Donald MacIsaac. This was in 1812. The following year a number of other Scotch families came from P[rince] E[dward] Island, namely MacEacherns, Macdonalds, MacGillivrays, ... The Indians were quite numerous here when the first Scotch settlements were made. The present glebe land was then occupied by the Indians. Bishop MacEachern, then Father MacEachern, on one of his first visits here, bought the land from one Tomma who was then chief of the tribe, granted to Bishop MacEachern in 1823. ...

The Indians at this early period, though received into the Church and instructed in the faith by the French Missionaries, were still only partly civilized and they acted as if they were lords and masters of the whole country. They were saucy and imposed in many ways on the few white people who first settled in the country. ... While they were strong and numerous they had their own way. They also took care to select the best lands adjacent to the best fishing places.[6]

Some Gaelic poets of the 18th century called the native people "Coilltich" (Forest-dwellers).[7] The numerous associations of forests in Gaelic tradition can help to shed light on what this term might have signified for Gaels. The most obvious way to interpret this ethnonym is that the native peoples were seen as inextricably connected to the territory they inhabited, which were dominated by the ubiquitous woods. In a number of Gaelic tales, immigrant Highlanders do indeed describe their first encounters with native peoples as happening at the edge of the forest or as a result of trying to fell it.[8]

A less generous interpretation of the name would be to see it as a Gaelic equivalent of "savage" or "salvage," English pejorative terms often used of native peoples ultimately derived from a Latin word denoting the woods and hence wilderness. It is certainly possible that this derogatory sense was originally intended, since Gaels coming to North America to fight in the Seven Years' War knew that most First Nations had allied themselves with their enemies, the French.

The forest was a place beyond the reach of human law and order, and therefore a refuge for fugitives and exiles. The Gaelic expression "fo'n choille," literally meaning "under cover of the forest," was used of outlaws and people who had moved themselves beyond social control. Native peoples seem to be associated with these traits in at least one early poem from North America.[9]

The irony in all of this is that Gaels had a very long and tenacious tradition of identifying with woods and of using tree terminology and metaphors to praise their own celebrities.[10] If Gaels are assigning this term to native peoples with ill intent and insinuating that woodlands had negative, or at least undesirable, implications, then this suggests that immigrants are distancing themselves from their supposedly "primitive" past in order to identify with the dominant anglophone hegemony and are projecting unwanted associations onto First Nations.[11] This pattern is manifest in one account in this chapter (text 5.14) where the author blames the "wild Indians" for hostilities in which the Gaels were equally involved. Such behaviours suggest that Gaels in both Scotland and North America felt strong pressure to identify with anglophones and to dissociate from others. As Gaels (along with other immigrants) were colonizing native lands, they themselves were being colonized by imperial values and ideologies. Gaels, all too often, succumbed to and participated in a hegemony resolved to claim absolute authority over native peoples and their territories under the guise of "civilization" and innate superiority.

1: "I Am Dejected in the Bog by Myself"

The following song was composed in the Glengarry settlement of Ontario, although the name of the author and time of its composition has not survived. It appears to reflect the conditions and challenges faced by the early settlers of the area, which suggests that it was composed in the late 18th century or early 19th century. The word "bruilidh" does not seem to appear in any other Gaelic text; it may be a borrowing from another language, clearly intended to mean "bog" or "swampland."

This poem attests to the difficulty of clearing the woods and draining swamps to make the soil suitable for agricultural activity. These tasks required the right tools—such as axes and horses—and summoned the collective contributions of the community. The men undertake their task as though engaged in a battle with nature, equipped with weaponry (lines 8, 18, 32, 45-46 and 54). The conviviality of the company, especially singing (line 51) and the sharing of food and drink (lines 58-60) after the work was done, served as the common reward.

There is a religious message at the end of the poem (lines 61-68) that earthly toils and rewards needed to be kept in their proper perspective. The conclusion reminds the audience not to get so caught up in their worldly pursuits, and comical antics, that they forget their spiritual duties. As this quatrain is slightly disjointed from the rest of the song, however, it is possible that it was a late addition.

Original Text

1   Ill ù ill ill ó ill ó ill ill ì
     Ill ù ill ill ó ill ó ill ill ì
     Ill ù ill ill ó agus ó hilin ì
     Tha mise fo mhulad 's a' bhruilidh leam fhìn.

5   'S ann dh'éirich am breamas
     Dha'n bhodach ghlas ruadh
     Nuair shanndaich e fearann
     Is gun e math air an tuaigh;
     Tha e nise gun ghearran
10   'Bheir maid' ás an t-suamp,
     Is gur mór a' chùis-mhagaidh,
     An t-amadan truagh.

     'S e am bruilidh dubh fiadhaich
     Chuir fiabhras 'nam cheann,
15   Le stumpaichean fiara
     Is le 'fhriamhaichean cam';
     Cha dèan mis' am bliadhna
     Reubadh le crann
     'S ann nì e mo liathadh
20   Cóig bliadhna ro'n àm.

     Tha 'm bruilidh nas cùrsa
     Na's urrainn domh inns',
     Le stumpaichean giubhais
     Is na h-uimhir dhiubh innt';
25   Cha dèan mise glanadh
     Gun chosgais dhomh fhìn,
     Is gur truagh mar a tha mi
     Is gun bharr a bhith innt'.

     Nam falbhadh an Dùbhlachd
30   Is gun tilleadh am blàths,

Is gum faighinn-sa gluasad
Spaid chruadhach 'nam làimh,
Gun dèanainn-s' i tioram
Ged is lùbach i 'n-dràst;
35 Leiginn sìos gu Iain Stiùbhart
A sùghadh a-bhàn.

'S ann labhair Iain Stiùbhart
Le 'ghnùis rium fhìn
"Chan eil do shùgh bhuamsa,
40 Tha suamp agam fhìn:
Leig seachad mun cuairt e
Gu Ruairidh 'na still;
Nì Alasdair Tàillear
Canàl nach bi clì."

45 Thig Aonghus is na gillean
Is bheir iad clig air an tuaigh;
Thig daoine dha m' chòmhnadh
Á Cnòideart a-nuas;
Théid na dùin 'chur an òrdugh
50 Le seòltachd an t-sluaigh,
Is bheir sinn greis air na h-òrain
Mar chleachd sinn thar 'chuain.

Nam faicinn-s' a' tighinn
An sgiob' ud le'n tuaigh
55 Gun éireadh mo chridhe,
Ged bhithinn fo ghruaim;
Rachainn suas do'n bhilleids
Leis a' phige bheag ruadh,
Is gheibhinn bho Chòsaidh
60 Gach seòrsa bhiodh bhuam.

A bhodaich, dèan faiceall
Is thoir an aire dhuit fhéin:
Bith cuimhneach air t' anam
Is leig seachad gach seud;
65 Ged tha thu 's a' bhruilidh,
Chan ann duit bhios a feum
Ma théid thu dha'n t-sìorr'achd
'S a' bhliadhna seo fhéin.[12]

Translation

(1-4) ...I am dejected in the bog by myself.

(5-12) The greying red-haired codger brought the mischief upon himself when he coveted land without being good with the axe; he now lacks a workhorse that will pull sticks out of the swamp; the pathetic idiot has made a big laughing-stock of himself.

(13-20) It is the dark, wild bog that has put a fever into my head, with its twisted stumps and its winding roots; I will not be able to tear it up this year with a plough, and it will cause me to turn grey five years too early.

(21-27) The bog is coarser than I can express, with many pine stumps in it; I will not be able to clean it up without considerable expense to myself, and I am in a wretched state, unable to grow produce in it.

(28-36) If the gloomy winter would leave, and the warmth would return, so that I was able to work a steel shovel in my hand, I would make it dry, even though it is currently marshy; I would release the drainage down to John Stewart.

(37-44) Indeed, John Stewart said, right in my face, "I don't need your drainage, I have my own swamp; let it go out and around in a torrent to Rory; Alasdair Taylor will make a sturdy canal."

(45-52) Angus and the lads will come and use the axe; people will come down from Knoydart to help me; the piles will be put in good order by the people's ingenuity, and then we will spend a while singing as we used to do on the other side of the ocean.

(53-60) If I were to see that crew coming with the axe, my heart would swell, even if I were gloomy; I would go down to the village with the little red jug and I would get every sort [of drink] that I want from Kosey.

(61-68) O codger, be watchful and look after yourself: be mindful of your soul and detach yourself from every [worldly] treasure; although you are in the bog, you are the one whom it will not serve if you go to eternity this very year.

2: Clearing the Forests

Alasdair Friseal wrote this brief description about the clearing of Canadian woods in his larger account of the Gaels of Canada. He met many of the early settlers in various communities in Ontario, and those who knew them, who related these anecdotes to him. Gaels had very similar experiences and strategies where they encountered forests, be they in Ontario or Nova Scotia.

Original Text

> Bha a' choille dòmhal, tiugh ri gearradh sìos leis na tuaghan, craobh an déidh craoibh, na muilleanan diubh; bha i an-sin air a losgadh eadar gheug is chrann, oir cha robh dòigh air móran di a reic; bha an sìol air a chur air feadh nan stoc agus barr air a thogail ás an luaithre, gun treabhadh no ruamhradh. Bliadhna an déidh bliadhna, bha seo a' dol air adhart, na h-uile bliadhna a' faicinn tuille fearainn air a réiteachadh, na taighean-còmhnaidh air an leasachadh, agus na saibhlean air an uidheamachadh gu goireasach. Bha seo uile a' cost ùine, saothair, agus neart an duine, 's ma thugadh an talamh fo smachd, b' ann, mar bu trice, aig prìs a bha tuille is daor air a shon.
>
> Na saoileamaid gun robh dùthaich fhialaidh shaidhbhir a' feitheamh air na Gàidheil a thàinig an toiseach gu Canada. B' ann le fallas an gruaidh is le neart am bodhaig a rinn iad tìr thabhairteach di, a' giùlain uallach trom ri teas an t-samhraidh agus ri fuachd guineach a' gheamhraidh, gus an d' fhàs iad 'nam mnathan is nan daoine breòite eucaileach, an spionnadh is an neart gu tur air an sgrios. Tha e air uairibh air a chumail a-mach le muinntir aineolach gum bheil na Gàidheil neo-sgoinneil, leisg, is gur e sin adhbhar am bochdainn 'nan tìr fhéin. Cha b' urrainn freagairt na bu dhearbhta a bhith air a toirt do'n bheachd mhearachdach seo na raointean farsaing Chanada, air an do bhuilich na Gàidheil saothair a bha da-rìreamh mìorbhaileach.[13]

Translation

> The forest was thick and dense to cut down with the axes, tree after tree, millions of them; then it was burnt, both branch and

trunk, for there was no way to sell much of it; the seed was scattered throughout the stumps and crops raised in the ashes, without needing to plough or delve. Year after year, this went on, each succeeding year seeing more land cleared, homesteads improved, and barns equipped richly. All of this took time, labour and human strength, and if the land was tamed, it was, more often than not, at too great of a cost.

Let us not think that a rich, hospitable country was waiting for the Gaels when they originally came to Canada. It was with the sweat of their brows and the strength of their bodies that they made a bountiful land of it, carrying a heavy load in the heat of the summer and in the biting cold of the winter, until they became infirm and broken women and men, their energy and vigour totally destroyed. It is sometimes claimed by ignorant people that the Gaels are feeble and lazy, and that that is the reason for their poverty in their own country. There can be no more verifiable proof against this erroneous claim than the broad fields of Canada, on which the Gaels completed efforts that were truly marvellous.

3: "I Am Vexed Today"

The author of this next song, Alasdair MacGilleMhaoil, was one of those settlers who was unsatisfied with the life that he found in North America—Glengarry, Ontario, to be exact—comparing it unfavourably with the life that he left behind in the Highlands.

As we saw in several texts in chapter 2, MacGilleMhaoil draws contrasts between Scotland and North America in terms of the associations he makes between places and states of mind and body. Since coming to North America, he has become full of negative feelings (lines 1-6); if he were to merely make contact with water from the Scottish Highlands (lines 13-14), he would become reinvigorated (lines 15-21). While in Scotland he enjoyed the privilege of hunting the deer (lines 9-10), but has literally fallen in stature since coming to British North America (lines 11-12).[14] He now ekes out a meagre and lowly existence that does not provide proper nourishment (lines 7-8). MacGilleMhaoil also claims that besides the necessary fundamentals of survival, the higher marks of civilization—clothing and education—are also lacking in his new home (lines 27-28). It is his nostalgia for the "normality" that he once knew in Scotland (line 4) that has left him disgruntled about his current condition.

Original Text

1   Gur bruailleanach mis' an-diugh
     Tha smuairein is mulad orm;
     Gur bruailleanach mis' an-diugh
     'S e 'n cumantas 'gam thàladh.

5   Bhon thàinig mi do'n rìoghachd seo
     Tha mulad mór is mì-ghean orm:
     Chan fhaigh mi fiù na sithne ann
     Bheir sgrìob do bhean no 'phàiste.

     Bu dùthchas dhomh bhith sònraichte
10   'Am shealgair fhiadh is bu chòir dhomh e;
     Ged tha mi anns na frògan seo
     Mar bhroc is a shròn 's na h-àilltean.

     Nam faighinn deoch á fuaran
     De'n dh'fhàg mi 's an tìr uain-neulaich,
15   Gum fàsainn lùthmhor luaineach
     Is bheirinn boc á cluain an fhàsaich.

     Gum fàsainn lùthmhor mireanach
     Gu h-anamadail, glé spioradail,
     A dhìreadh ris na firichean,
20   A shireadh fir na cràice.

     Gum fàsainn sunndach acfhainneach,
     A shiubhal bheann is aisirean;
     Nuair dh'fhàsainn sgìth d'an astar
     Gheobhainn cadal air an àrd-bheann.

25   Ge math an t-àit' Aimearaga
     Tha iomadh nì 'na dheireas ann:
     Dìth aodaich, is gun luchd-teagaisg ann,
     Is gun oilean air ar n-àlach.[15]

Translation

(1-4) I am vexed today, anxiety and grief trouble me; I am vexed today, it is ordinary life that is calling to me.

(5-8) Ever since I came to this country, I have been afflicted by great sorrow and discontent; I cannot even get enough venison here to satisfy a woman or child.

(9-12) It was my hereditary lot to be distinguished as a deer-hunter and it was my right; even though I am [now] in the marshes like a badger with his nose in the rocky banks.

(13-16) If I could get a drink from a spring of those that I left behind in the green-hued country, I would become strong and energized, and I would get a buck from the wilderness meadow.

(17-20) I would become strong and lively, high-spirited and excited, to climb up the high mountain grounds, to search out the antlered ones.

(21-24) I would become cheerful and prepared to traverse mountains and high passes; when the distance would make me tired, I would get sleep on the high mountain.

(25-28) Although America is a good place, many things are scarce here: a lack of clothing, teachers, and education for our offspring.

4: "I am Gloomy"

According to Alasdair Friseal, who transcribed this account from an oral informant in Ontario around the end of the 19th century, the following song was composed by a poet of the surname MacCuidhein (MacQueen) who left Aodann Bàn (Edinbane) in the Isle of Skye. The account explains that the poet MacCuidhein composed it in the voice of a drover who had been one of the other members of the emigration party. Although he had considered himself a well-travelled and worldly man, the drover was greatly mystified by the fire-flies of the swamps, which exemplify the alienness of the strange new world which they now inhabited.

> An déidh dha tighinn air imrich do Chanada, air dha a bhith aon latha maille ri cuideachd chridheil, theann am bàrd ri cuimhneachadh air tìr eòlais anns an robh e òg a' mire: 's e sin tìr nam beann 's nan gleann 's nan gaisgeach anns am minic a shuidh comann cridheil mu'n bhòrd ag òl an drama agus a' seinn nan òran; mar an ceudna air a' mhuinntir a bha tighinn maille ris agus air an tàire a fhuair iad agus air gach nì a bha a' cur mór-ioghnadh orra; agus mar an ceudna a bha a' cur eagal orra: oir bha an dròbhair maille ris.

Mar a chì sibh air a chur sìos anns an òran, [b' e] seann duine còir [e] a bha aosmhor liath a shiubhail Gàidhealtachd is Galltachd agus roinn mhór de Shasainn, gidheadh an uair a thàinig e do thìr choigreach air aineoil, do dhùthaich nan craobh, ghabh e eagal an uair a chunnaic e suampa dùmhail 'na theine an uair a bha iad a' tighinn an àirde suampa dubh a' Chatanaich. An uair a chunnaic e na cuileagan – teine a' lasadh air gach taobh dheth – shaoil leis gun robh an dùthaich 'na teine ach bha am bàrd 'ga chumail am misneachd, nach robh cunnart ann ach sùil dha'n tug am bàrd. Bha an dròbhair a' lasadh a phìob-thombàc ri té de na cuileagan-teine, ged a chumadh e fhathast i, cha lasadh i.

Ach coma co-dhiubh, lean iad air an adhart gus an tàinig iad a dh'ionnsaigh nan càirdean ann an Kenyon. Mar sin, dh'innseadh dha'n dròbhair nach robh cunnart sam bith 's na cuileagan uaine. Chunnaic an dròbhair gun robh an tìr taitneach do'n t-sùil agus math a chum bìdh. Mar sin, thug e cliù agus taing do'n Tì a ghiùlain leo thar a' chuain fharsaing thro gach gàbhadh a dh'ionnsaigh nan càirdean ann an Kenyon.

After he had immigrated to Canada, after he had been one day in the company of a merry band, the poet began to reminisce about his native land in which he played when he was young: that is, the land of the mountains and the glens and the warriors in which a happy group of people often sat around the table drinking a dram and singing the songs; likewise, he reminisced about the people who were coming along with him and about the difficulties they suffered and about everything that was amazing them; and likewise, that were frightening them: for the drover was along with them.

As you will see set down in the song, [the drover] was a goodly old man who was aged and grey, who had travelled the Highlands and the Lowlands and a large part of England, although when he came to the foreign land unknown to him, to "the land of trees," he became frightened when he saw a dense bog on fire when they were going in the direction of the black swamp of the Catanach. When he saw the flies—a fire burning on each of their ends—he thought that the land was on fire and the poet was reassuring him that there was no danger except what the poet expected. The drover was trying to light his tobacco pipe with one of the fire-flies, and although he kept trying it, it wouldn't light.

But in any case, they kept going until they came to their kinsfolk in Kenyon. The drover was told that the green flies did not pose any danger. The drover saw that the land was pleasing to the eye and good for [growing] food. Therefore, he gave praise and thanks to the One who conveyed him with them across the wide ocean through every peril to the kinsfolk in Kenyon.

The metre and refrain of this song is apparently based on an older song from southern Argyllshire.[16] More than one variant of this song circulated in Glengarry communities; the late Professor Charles Dunn collected a longer version of it in 1960 with very different words.[17]

Original Text

1 Ho ró, tha mi fo ghruaimean,
   Chan ioghnadh mi gluasad duilich;
   Is fada tha mi bho thìr mo chàirdean
   Far an d' rinn mi 'm fàgail uile,
5 Ho ró, tha mi fo ghruaimean.

   Ach nam fosgladh mo chàil dhomh
   Is gun dèanainn an dàn seo ullamh
   Gun innsinn mu chliù an àite
   Far am bheil mi a' cnàmh le mulad.

10 O'n latha thàinig mi do'n dùthaich
   Gur tric mo shùilean a' sileadh
   Is mi ri ionndrainn m' eòlais
   Far an robh mi òg a' mire.[18]

Translation

(1-5) *Ho ró*, I am gloomy; it is no surprise that my movement is difficult; I am far away from the land of my kinsfolk where I left them all behind; *Ho ró*, I am gloomy.

(6-9) But if my health were to be restored so that I could finish this song-poem, and I could relate praise of this place where I am wasting away with sorrow.

(10-13) From the day that I came to the land, my eyes have often teared up as I pine for my native land, where I played when I was young.

5: Curses on the Mice

When the following song-poem appeared in the March 1851 issue of *An Cuairtear Òg Gàidhealach*, the author was identified only by the initials "I. P." It is possible that this stands for "Iain am Pìobaire," which would most likely be a short-hand way of referring to Iain "am Pìobaire" MacGhilleBhràth.

From time to time, mice infested communities so badly that they had to get outside assistance to overcome the devastation of their food, as happened in the year 1815.

> In 1815 the country was ravaged by the plague of mice—the year of the mice—*bliadhna nan luch*. In the month of March immense numbers of large mice with thick bodies and short tails made their appearance. Nobody knows how or whence they came. So numerous were they that a fall of two or three inches of snow was packed down by their tracks. In the beginning the crops looked most promising, but by the time the wheat was headed out it was found to be cut off near the roots. ... A while after the appearance of the larger mice, a smaller kind appeared, and then a deadly feud arose among them which tended to diminish their numbers.[19]

Gaels believed poets and their verses had so much power that satires could drive vermin away and send them in another direction.[20] This text belongs to a long literary lineage that stretches far back into the medieval period. Like an enemy that must be intimidated and disarmed, the poet expresses the ill-will and dislike of the people in his area for mice (lines 9-16). He commands the mice to leave the town (line 25), insisting that they find a new home where they will be welcomed with a greater supply of food. The poet praises Caledonia, in the south-west corner of Nova Scotia, as their ultimate destination.

Original Text

1   Is iomadh creachadair an taobh-s'
      Am measg na tuathadh:
      Mathain, marsantan, is maoir,
      A' sìor-thoirt uatha;
5   Tha luchaidhean ann cho lìonmhor
      Is nach fhàg iad sìol air barr sguaibe;

     Is am beagan a théid fo dhìon deth
     Is bochd a' bhrìgh an àm a' bhualaidh.

     Mallachd bhuan o shluagh gach dùthcha
10   Laghdachadh cunntais an t-seòrs' ud;
     Neasgaidean, cait, clamhain, dùldachd,
     Bàs is fanntachadh 's gach dòigh dhuibh;
     Is leibh gamhlas uile shliochd Àdhaimh
     Is chan eil bàigh aig neach tha beò ribh;
15   Is duilich leam nach deach ur bàthadh
     Mun d'fhuair sibh 's an Àirc aig Nòa.

     Is lìonmhor neach bh' an dùil bhith glùtach,
     Càiseach, coirceach,
     Gruitheamach, lìth-bhusach, mucach,
20   Eòrnach, brotach;
     Tha 'mhàileid gu leòbach acrach
     Binnteach, gortach;
     Le pòr storach nan sròn smuilceach
     Is nan spòg loirceach.

25   Imichibh grad ás an dùthaich
     Is na faiceam aon sùil ri m' bheò dhibh;
     Togaibh an Iar-dheas air cùrsa
     Gu rathad ùr Chaledòni;
     Tuinichibh am measg nan Dùitseach
30   Agus muinntir Musquodòbit;
     Gheibh sibh coirce is eòrna is flùr ann
     Is cha bhi cùram a chionn lòin dhuibh.[21]

Translation

(1-8) There are many plunderers here among the farmers: bears, merchants and bureaucrats, constantly taking away from them; the mice are so plentiful that they will not leave a seed on the crop's sheaves; and the little of it that will be protected will be of poor quality when the time comes to thresh it.

(9-16) [May] everlasting curses from the people of every country decrease the numbers of that species [mice]; boils, cats, buzzards, winter weather, death and weakness in every way to them; you have the malice of all of Adam's offspring; no living person has any affection for you; I am sorry that you were not drowned before you got into Noah's Ark.

(17-24) There are many people who expected to have a big appetite, loaded with cheese, oats, and curd-butter, with grease on their lips, lots of pigs, barley and soup; [instead] the [food] storage is ragged, hungry, curdling, and miserly from the looting breed of the curled noses and the stubby paws.

(25-32) Quickly depart from the country, and so that not a single eye sees you for the rest of my life; set a course for the south-west, on the new road to Caledonia; settle among the Dutch and the people of Musquodoboit; you will get oats, barley, and flour there and you will have no reason to worry about food.

6: The Bear's Song

The following song-poem was composed by Dòmhnall Moireastan of Kenyon, Ontario, who was active in the first few decades of the 19th century. He composed it when a bear ran off with a neighbour's pig. Bears were dangerous pests to many of the early colonists.[22] Although they had been extinct in Scotland for about half a millennium before the Gaels arrived in North America, they immediately recognized them and used their native name for them. Many Gaelic compositions described encounters with bears in immigrant communities, often displaying a mixture of comedy and anxiety. The following verses could be categorized as mock heroic: despite being led to believe that heroic combat might ensue, the protagonist is talked out of an encounter with his animal opponent by a prudent woman (lines 33-36).

Original Text

1   Ho is hi rì o hó ro thall
          Ho is hi rì o hó ro thall
          Ho is hi rì o hó ro thall
          Is mairg tha fuireach gu bràth anns an àite 'tha ann.

5   Is leam is duilich mar thachair
        Do mhac Ruairidh bhuachaille;
        Bhon bha m' eòlas cho gast' air
        Is e fada mun cuairt dhomh:
        Duine foinneamh deas toirteil
10   De Chloinn Torcaill a' chruadail,
        Is nan robh aire air a' mhortair
        Cha d' rinn e 'mhuc a thoirt bhuaidhe.

Thàinig famhair 's an dorcha
Gu Tormad mac Ruairidh;
15 Cha robh an duine fo armachd
Cha robh farbhas mun cuairt da;
Na bithibh idir am barail
Gur h-i gealtachd a bhuail e:
Bha e fada bho dhaoine
20 Is bha e 'glaodhaich is cha chual' iad.

Bha e 'cluinntinn a <tar>tar
Is gu grad chuir e 'chluas ris;
Cha robh aire air a chadal
'S ann a b' fhada siud bhuaidhe,
25 'Cluinntinn sgreuchail na muice
Is theich na h-uirceanan bhuaipe;
Tha an dòlas air tighinn
Neo 'se 'n cuthach a bhuail i.

Dh'éirich e 'n àirde
30 Is chuir e làmh anns gach ursainn
Is bha cuid diubh gu sgàthach
A' cluinntinn àinich an trustair;
Thuirt màthair Iain Bhàin ris,
"Gabh mu thàmh is na can dìog ris –
35 Ma tharras e greim ort,
Bidh thu 'd bhloighean thiota."

Is truagh nach robh claidheamh
'Nad làimh anns an uair sin,
No musgaid mhath chinnteach
40 Air a lìonadh le luaidhe;
Do shùil dùinte air an amhairc
Is tu caitheamh air thuairmeas;
Is nan tugadh i sradan,
Bhiodh am mathan gun ghluasad.

45 Galair a' ghonaidh
Air an rogaire bhradach:
Mèirleach na feòla
An eòrna is a' choirce;
Chan fhaigh earraidean còir ort,
50 Chan eil dòigh air do ghlacadh;
Chan eil craobh anns an àite
Air a h-àirde nach streap thu.[23]

Translation

(1-4) ...woe to him who will live forever in this place.

(5-12) I am sorry about what happened to the son of Rory the cowherd, since I was so fond of him and he had been around me for a long time; [he is] a handsome, skillful and strong man of the hardy Clan Torquil, and if the murderer had been noticed, he wouldn't have taken the pig from him.

(13-20) A monster came in the dark to Norman the son of Rory; the man was not armed, he had no knowledge of the situation; do not allow yourself to believe that he was struck with cowardice: he [the bear] was far from people, he was bellowing and they didn't hear him.

(21-28) He [Norman] was hearing the commotion and he quickly concentrated his ear to it; he didn't think about sleep [then], that was far from his mind, hearing the screeching of the pig; the piglets fled away from her [the pig]; agony had come, or else it [i.e., the pig] was struck with madness.

(29-36) He arose and he put his hands on each pillar; some of them [the pigs] became frightened, hearing the heavy breathing of the brute; Fair John's mother said to him [Norman], "Get some rest and don't say anything to him—if he [the bear] gets a grip on you, he'll tear you to pieces in an instant."

(37-44) It is a pity that you didn't have a sword in your hand at that moment, or a good, trusty musket filled up with a lead ball, with your eye aimed on the target as you fired with your best aim; if [the hammer] were to strike [the gunpowder], the bear would be dead-still.

(45-52) May the thieving rogue suffer a cursed illness: the robber of meat, barley and oats; officers of the law will not be able to claim you [bear], there is no way to capture you; there is no tree, no matter how high, that you will not climb.

7: An Account of Prince Edward Island and Cape Breton

The following text is an extract of a much longer account by an author identified only as "Sgiathanach" (a person from the Isle of Skye) for a popular Gaelic newspaper in 1848. It was composed just as large-scale migration from the Scottish Highlands to Cape Breton was effectively coming to an end and shows that Gaels had thoroughly permeated both Cape Breton and Prince Edward Island. While this lengthy report seems to have been written to encourage migration to the Canadian Maritimes, it also contains many details about the geography and history of the region that indicate the curiosity of contemporary Gaelic readers about the wider world.

The writer demonstrates a great aesthetic appreciation for the natural beauty of the region, especially trees, for which he had a full vocabulary for all of the varieties that existed in Scotland. He also acknowledges their practical and utilitarian value, of course, especially given their scarcity in Scotland. The description of the hunting practices of First Nations suggests an admiration of their skills and their knowledge of the natural environment.

Original Text

> Tha gach àite am fagus do Mhurray Harbour air an àiteachadh le Gàidheil, agus gu sònraichte le Sgiathanaich chòire a bha dol air imrich á eilean am breith bho chionn móran bhliadhnaichean air ais. Chan eil taigh an-sin anns nach cluinnear a' Ghàidhlig 'ga labhairt, mar ann am Muile, Earra-Ghaidheal, no 's an Eilean Sgiathanach. Chan eil teagamh sam bith nach mór an toil-inntinn a bheir *Fear-Tathaich nam Beann* do na Gàidheil chliùiteach an uair a ruigeas e iad ann an Eilean Eòin. Agus tha e cinnteach gun dèan iad gàirdeachas ri caraid cho dìleas an uair a théid e d'an ionnsaigh leis gach sgeul fìrinneach agus taitneach air an toir e iomradh. Mo làmh-sa gum faigh e deagh chairtealan ann am Murray Harbour, agus mar an ceudna o gach Gàidheal aig Souris, Rollo Bay, Fortune Bay, Howe Bay, Broughton Bay – seadh, o gach Gàidheal ann an Eilean Eòin air fad. B' olc an airidh mur faigheadh! ...
>
> Tha an t-eilean seo [Ceap Breatainn] 'na laidhe ann an Geodha St. Lawrence, beagan an ear air Eilean Eòin, an ear-thuath air Nova Scotia, agus an iar-dheas air Newfoundland. Ann an cumachd tha e leth-char cosmhail ri bròig eich. Tha e mu dheich is còig fichead mìle ann am fad, agus eadar fichead agus ceithir fichead mìle ann an leud. Tha e air a dhealachadh o Nova Scotia le caolas Chanso, nach eil ach beagan mhìltean air leud, ach trid

am faod na longan as motha air an t-saoghal seòladh suas ann an tèarainteachd a dh'ionnsaigh St. Lawrence.

Eucosmhail ri Eilean Eòin, tha Ceap Breatainn 'na fhearann garbh, creagach, agus monadail. Tha sloc is cnoc is carraig cho lìonmhor ann is a gheibhear iad ann an àite air bith de Gharbh-Chrìochan na h-Alba. Air an taobh an iar gu léir, tha an tìr am fochar na mara anabarrach garbh agus cunnartach, gun ach gann fasgadh sam bith ann do shoitheachibh, gun gheodha, gun acarsaid tèarainte, agus gun dòchas idir do'n mharaiche ri h-ànradh cuain, ach dùil eagalach ri long-bhriseadh agus bàs. Goirid o thràigh, tha na creagan ag éirigh suas 'nam binneanaibh àrda, agus 'nan stùcan cho cas agus corrach is gum bheil iad ann an iomadh àite eagalach eadhan ri amharc orra. ...

Thugadh an t-ainm "Ceap Breatainn" an toiseach air an rudha as fhaide an ear 's an eilean agus uaidhe seo, thugadh ainm air an eilean uile. Rinn Frangaich á Nova Scotia agus á Newfoundland greim air an toiseach, agus anns a' bhliadhna 1713, ghabh àireamh bheag dhiubh còmhnaidh ann air son iasgaich. Thog iad taighean am fochar a' chladaich ann an àitean freagarrach air son tioramachadh an éisg. Ro'n bhliadhna seo, chan fhacas iomchaidh do na Frangaich suidheachadh no àiteachas sam bith a dhèanamh air an eilean, ach a-mhàin le beagan iasgairean ann am mìosan an t-samhraidh. Ach cha b' fhad gus an d' atharraich iad am baral a thaobh na cùise seo, agus chum daingneach làidir a dhèanamh aig beul na h-aibhne St. Lawrence, rùnaich iad sluaigh a chur air an eilean, agus Baile Louisburgh a thogail agus a dhìonadh.

Cha robh na gnothaichean, gidheadh, ach goirid air an dòigh seo. Ghlacadh am baile agus an t-eilean le chéile leis na feachdan Breatannach 's a' bhliadhna 1745, aig a' cheart àm anns an robh iomadh cath agus creach fhuilteach air feadh na h-Alba, a thaobh cùisean mì-shealbhach a' Phrionnsa Teàrlach. An déidh cruaidh-chath a mhair ré naoidh agus dà fhichead là, anns an do shònraich na Frangaich iad fhéin air son an euchd agus an cruadail, theannaicheadh Louisburgh, agus thugadh thairis do Bhreatann e, air an ochdamh là deug do mhìos-meadhanach an t-samhraidh. Ghlacadh aig an àm cheudna trì soithichean-cogaidh Frangach, a bha air am meas, maille ri stòras agus ceannachd a' bhaile, aig barrachd is muillean airgid!

Goirid o'n àm sin, fhuair Sasann còir mar an ceudna air Eilean Eòin, agus chuireadh an luchd-àiteachaidh ás an eilean air longaibh do'n Fhraing. Beagan an déidh seo, thugadh Ceap Breatainn do na Frangaich air ais, ann an iomlaid air son Mhadras anns na h-Innsibh an Ear. Cha b' fhad, gidheadh, an ùine a mheal iad, oir thugadh uatha e rithist le Sasainn 's a' bhliadhna 1758; agus o'n là sin gus an là an-diugh, tha uachdaranachd aig Sasainn air Ceap Breatainn. ...

'S e Sydney a-nis prìomh-bhaile an eilein, ach is eucosmhail e ri Louisburgh air sheòl sam bith. Tha e air a thogail air rudha beagan mhìltean deas air beul an locha ris an abrar "Bras d' Or." Tha dùthaich bhòidheach mun cuairt do'n bhaile; agus tha gach àite ro thaitneach le coilltean, creagan, uisgeachan, raointean, agus fearann-treabhaidh mu'n seach. Tha am baile gu riaghailteach air a chur a-mach, agus gàradh-lios dlùth-cheangailte ach beag ris gach taigh. Chan eil ro mhóran thaighean ann fhathast, ach 'nam measg tha gearastan, stòr-thaighean, taigh an uachdrain, eaglaisean, taigh-cùirt, agus mar sin sìos.

Tha uile ghnothaichean cudthromach an eilein air an socrachadh ann an Sydney, a-réir lagha Bhreatainn, agus chan eil am baile aig àm air bith gun bhuidheann shaighdear chum a dhìonadh. Ged tha deagh acarsaid agus iomadh cothrom is goireas eile am fochar a' bhaile, an déidh sin, chan eil e ach gu mall a' tighinn air aghaidh. Tha e deiseil ri iasgach, agus air a chuairteachadh le deagh fhearann air son tuathanachd. Tha fiodh de gach gné a' fàs gu teann air, agus tha na tuill-ghuail lìonmhor air gach taobh. Do thaobh a' ghuail fhéin, tha cothrom mór aig a' Cheap thar Eilean Eòin, far nach eil gual sam bith. Am fagus do'n bhaile, tha an luchd-àiteachaidh air an dèanamh suas de dh'Albannaich, Shasannaich, Ghàidheil, Éireannaich, agus sheann saighdeirean a fhuair fearann agus iad seo uile am measg a chéile. ...

Tha móran Ghàidheal a' còmhnaidh goirid o Phort Hood, a tha ri iasgach agus àiteachadh mu seach. Tha móran ola 'ga dhèanamh an-seo á gruthanaibh an éisg, a tha ro fheumail do mhuinntir na dùthcha. An iar air Port Hood tha Mabou, Broad Cove, Marguerite, agus Cheticamp, a tha air an àiteachadh le Albannaich, Frangaich, Americanaich, air feadh a chéile. ...

Tha am Bras d' Or fhéin air a dhealachadh 'na dhà mheur le eilean tarbhach ris an abrar Boulardrie, a tha fichead mìle air fad, agus dà mhìle am bitheantas air leud. Goirear am Bras d' Or Mór agus am Bras d' Or Beag ris na meòir seo. Tha uisgeachan nan loch seo 'gan sgaoileadh fhéin a-staigh do'n dùthaich 'nam meòir bheaga an-siud is an-seo, gus am bheil an Ceap air a bhreacadh le lochaibh sàile. Mar seo, gheibh soithichean a-staigh do bhroinn an eilein, agus tha cothrom mór aig luchd-malairt an gnothaichean a ghiùlan air aghaidh. Tha Boulardrie 'na eilean àillidh agus luachmhor, agus air àiteachadh ach beag le Gàidheil agus Éireannaich.

Tha an earrann as motha de na Gàidheil a chaidh air imrich do'n Cheap air an suidheachadh mu na lochaibh lìonmhor aig Bras d' Or, far am bheil deagh fhearann agus deagh iasgach aca ri'm faotainn. Tha lochan sàile, lochan uisge, aibhnichean, creagan, coilltean, achaidhean tarbhach, agus gach goireas nàdarra, a dh'iarradh duine ro lìonmhor agus pailt 's na ceàrnaibh seo. ...

Chan urrainn cainnt sam bith dearrsadh nan coilltean sin, aig an àm seo de'n bhliadhna, a chur an céill! Tha an deirge as soilleire, – an gorm-eutrom, an donn, am buidhe, an scàrlaid as deàlraiche, agus dathan eile gun àireamh, mar gum b' ann air an cothlamadh am measg a chéile, agus a' dearrsadh le soilleireachd do-chur an céill! Cha tuigear idir anns an dùthaich seo, an laise a chithear air barrach nan coill, an àm do'n duilleach a bhith crìonadh aig deireadh na bliadhna!

Do thaobh àireamh agus gné nan craobh, cha fhreagair e ach beagan a labhairt anns an àite seo. Cha lugha na ceithir seòrsa deug giubhais, còig seòrsa beithe, agus ceithir seòrsa daraich, a gheibhear anns a' cheart eilean seo. 'S e an giuthas buidhe as luachmhoire, oir chan e a-mhàin gum bheil e 'na dheagh fhiodh, ach tha e fàs gu meud anabarrach mór. Is minic a gheibhear craobhan de'n ghiuthas seo a thomhaiseas còig troighe deug mu'n bhun, sia fichead troigh ann an àirde, agus ceithir fichead troigh dhiubh sin, air nach faighear aon mheur no meanglan. Am measg nan seòrsa eugsamhla fiodha tha fàs 's a' Cheap, faodar na leanas ainmeachadh: giubhas, darach, aitinn, faighbhile, leamhan, uinseann, caoran, beithe, feàrna, maple (ás an dèanar an siùcar), critheann, agus mar sin sìos. A thuilleadh air gach fiodh dhiubh seo, tha iomadh seòrsa eile ann air nach eil Gàidhlig. ...

Chan eil teagamh sam bith nach taitneach an sealladh na coilltean seo gu léir do na Gàidheil a chaidh air imrich do dh'Aimearaga, á ceàrnaibh àraid de'n Ghàidhealtachd, agus ás na h-eileanaibh an iar, far nach robh a bheag sam bith de'n choille a' fàs, agus far am b' éiginn daibh dol gu minic air bàtaichean astar cheudan mìle a dh'iarraidh beagan mhaidean cama crotach air son cheangal agus chabar d'an taighibh. Bu mhath, da-rìreabh, anns an Eilean Sgitheanach fhéin agus anns an Eilean Fhada, o Rudha na Circe gu Barraigh, beagan de'n bharrachd fiodha a tha aig muinntir a' Cheap. Dhèanadh iad sòlas nach bu bheag ri nì a tha 'nan crìochaibh fhéin cho luachmhor agus cho gann. ...

Is ealanta da-rìreabh na h-Innseanaich chum bric, bradain, easganna, agus na h-uiread de dh'iasgan eile a ghlacadh mar a leanas, air na feasgair shamhraidh: Théid iad a-mach air sgoth eutrom le leus-sholasaibh a' lasadh. Tha na leòis seo air an dèanamh de rùsg na craoibhe-beithe. Gabhar maide còig no sia troighean ann am fad agus nithear sgoltadh 'na cheann. Sàthar an rùsg beithe 's an sgoltadh seo, cuirear teine ris, agus suidhichear am maide-solais seo aig toiseach an sgoth. Seasaidh an t-Innseanach goirid o'n t-solas le cas air beul-mór na sgotha air gach taobh; agus le sleagh, no morghath, fichead, no còig troighe fichead, ann am fad aige 'na làimh. Ged is ciogailteach an t-àite anns am bheil e, seasaidh e ann gu daingeann le 'shùil suidhichte gu geur air an uisge. Gluaisidh a' bhean an sgoth gu còmhnard mall le ràmh, agus aon uair is gum faic a companach an t-iasg, nì e cuimse air leis a' mhorghath, agus tha e cho ealanta geurshùileach is gur h-ainneamh leis aon bhuille iomrallachadh. Mar seo, dheònaich am Freastal uile-ghlic do'n eilean seo iomadh nì chum feum agus maith an duine. ...

Air do na Gàidheil a bhith cheana lìonmhor, an dà chuid 's a' Cheap agus ann an Eilean Eòin, agus air do dhùil a bhith aig móran, faodaidh e bhith, á Garbh-Chrìochan agus eileanan na h-Alba, dùthaich am breith 'fhàgail, agus dol air imrich do dh'Aimearaga maille ri'n càirdibh, tha e freagarrach beagan fiosrachaidh a thoirt seachad mu thimcheall fearann agus cosnaidh nan eilean seo, cho math is mu'n duais a gheibh an luchd-oibre, agus an luach air am faighear gach goireas a dh'fhaodas a bhith dhìth orra. Cha mhór nach eil fearann Eilein Eòin gu léir air a shuidheachadh cheana air uachdaranaibh móra, mar a tha Morairean Selkirk, Westmoreland, Queensberry, Melvelle, Townsend, agus na h-uiread eile. Air do Chrùn Bhreatann a bhith air dealachadh ris an fhearann, air an dòigh seo, 'na earrannan móra, chan eil a bheag ri fhaotainn deth ach air son màil, mur ceannaichear as ùr e o na h-uachdarain aig am bheil e. Ach anns a' Cheap, air an làimh eile, tha móran fearainn fhathast ann an làmhaibh a' Chrùin agus ri reiceadh. ...

Tha sinn an dòchas, o na dh'aithriseadh a-nis mu'n Cheap, gum faod deagh bheachd a bhith aig ar luchd-leughaidh mu nàdar agus mu mhaitheas an eilein sin. Ged is miann leinn an fhìrinn a chur an céill, a-réir ar fiosrachaidh, mu thimcheall Aimearaga, agus gach àite eile, tha sin a' fàgail ar luchd-dùthcha gu'm barail fhéin mu dhol air imrich d'an ionnsaigh. 'S i gun teagamh ar beachd fhéin gun soirbhicheadh teaghlaichean làidir nas fhearr thall na bhos, agus gum biodh an imrich chum mórbhuannachd, gu sònraichte d'an sliochd, ach an déidh sin uile, breithnicheadh iad air an son fhéin. Bheir sinn an déidh seo, ma chaomhainear sinn, beagan chomhairlean orrasan aig am bheil dùil ri dol a-null, agus leigidh sinn ris doibh nas aithne dhuinn mu gach deisealachd a bhith iomchaidh dhoibh a dèanamh. 'S e gun teagamh dùrachd ar cridhe gach fiosrachadh feumail a thoirt d'ar luchd-dùthcha agus gach dìcheall 'nar comas a dhèanamh air son an leas, a thaobh an dà chuid am maith aimsireil agus spioradail.[24]

Translation

Every place close to Murray Harbour has been settled by Gaels, and especially by goodly people from the Isle of Skye who migrated from the island of their birth many years ago. There is not a single house in which Gaelic is not heard being spoken, just as in Mull, Argyll or the Isle of Skye. There is no doubt at all that the [newspaper] *Fear-Tathaich nam Beann* will bring great joy to the renowned Gaels when it reaches them on Prince Edward Island. And it is certain that they will rejoice at such a loyal friend when he approaches them bearing with him every true and pleasant story about which he makes mention. I can assure you that he will find excellent quarters in Murray Harbour, and likewise from every Gael in Souris, Rollo Bay, Fortune Bay, Howe Bay, Broughton Bay—yes, from every Gael in Prince Edward Island altogether. It is ill-deserved if he does not! ...

This island [Cape Breton] is situated in the Gulf of St. Lawrence, a little to the east of Prince Edward Island, north-east of Nova Scotia, and south-west of Newfoundland. In shape, it is somewhat similar to a horseshoe. It is about 110 miles [177 km] long, and between 20 and 80 miles [32 and 129 km] in width. It is separated from Nova Scotia by the Strait of Canso, that is barely a few miles wide, but through which the largest vessels in the world can sail safely toward the St. Lawrence.

Unlike Prince Edward Island, Cape Breton is rough, craggy and mountainous terrain. Hollows, hills and cliffs are as plentiful here as they are in any part of the Highlands of Scotland. On the entire west coast, the land that is in proximity to the ocean is exceedingly rough and dangerous, with hardly any shelter at all for vessels, without a bay or safe harbour; when the ocean is rough the mariner can have no hope but can only expect a shipwreck and death. Close to the shore, the cliffs rise up to become tall pinnacles and peaks that are so steep and uneven that in many places it is frightening to even look at them. ...

The name "Cape Breton" was initially given to the promontory further to the east on the island and from that the name extended to the entire island. The French of Nova Scotia and Newfoundland took ahold of it at first, and in the year 1713, a small number of them took residence there for the fishing. They built houses close to the shore in places that were suitable for drying fish. Before this year, it was not seen to be appropriate for the French to settle or make any cultivation at all on the island, except for a few fishermen during the summer months. But it was not long until they changed their minds regarding this matter, and in order to construct a strong defense at the mouth of the St. Lawrence River, they determined to place a population on the island and to build the village of Louisbourg and defend it.

However, matters did not stay like this for long. Both the village and the island were seized by British troops in the year 1745, at the same time as there were many bloody battles and raids throughout Scotland, on account of the ill-fated Prince Charles. After a desperate siege that lasted forty-nine days, in which the French distinguished themselves for their battle-deeds and their hardiness, Louisbourg was captured and surrendered to Britain, on the eighteenth day of June. At the same time, three French warships were seized that, together with supplies and the merchandise of the village, were valued at more than a million pounds!

Close to that time, England likewise claimed the rights to Prince Edward Island, and the inhabitants were driven out of the island on ships to France. A little after this, Cape Breton was given back to the French, in exchange for the Madras in the East Indies. They did not enjoy that time for long, however, for it was taken from them by England again in the year 1758; and from that day until the present day, England has ruled over Cape Breton. ...

Sydney is now the capital of the island, and is unlike Louisbourg in every way. It has been built on a promontory a few miles south of the entrance of the lake which is called "Bras d' Or." The town is surrounded by beautiful land; and every place is very pleasant with forests, crags, waters, fields and agricultural land in turn. The town has been laid out in an orderly fashion, with a garden closely tied to nearly each house. There aren't too many houses there yet, but among them there is a fortress, stores, a governor's house, churches, court and so forth.

All of the important affairs of the island are settled in Sydney, according to the laws of Britain, and the town is at no time lacking a troop of soldiers to protect it. Although there is a good harbour and many other facilities and resources close to the town, other than that, it is progressing very slowly. It is equipped for fishing and surrounded by good land for farming. Trees of every variety grow close to it and coal mines are plentiful in every direction. Regarding the coal itself, Cape Breton has a greater potential than Prince Edward Island, where there is no coal at all. Close to the town, the residents are made up of Scots, English people, Gaels, Irish people, and veteran soldiers who got land, and they are all intermixed. ...

Many Gaels reside close to Port Hood who engage in fishing and agriculture in turn. A great deal of oil is made here out of the livers of the fish that is very beneficial for the people of the place. West of Port Hood is Mabou, Broad Cove, Marguerite, and Cheticamp, which have been settled by Scots, French people and Americans, all intermixed. ...

The Bras d' Or itself is divided into two branches by a fertile island that is called Boulardrie and is twenty miles long, and generally two miles wide. These branches are called the Big Bras d' Or and the Little Bras d' Or. The waters of this lake spread themselves inwards on the land into small branches here and there so that Cape Breton is speckled with salt-water lakes. Therefore, vessels can come to the interior of the island, and merchants have great opportunities to carry on their enterprises. Boulardrie is a beautiful and valuable island, settled almost entirely by Gaels and Irish people.

The majority of the Gaels who emigrated to Cape Breton have settled around the plentiful lakes of Bras d' Or, where they can have access to good land and good fishing. All of the salt-water lakes, fresh-water lakes, rivers, crags, forests, fertile fields, and every natural resource that a person could want are plentiful in these locales. ...

There is no language that can describe the colours of these forests at this time of the year! The brightest red—light green, brown, yellow, the shiniest scarlet, and countless other colours, as though they had been mixed with each other, and shining with inexpressible brightness! The intensity that is seen in the foliage of the forests when the leaves are dying at the end of the year cannot at all be comprehended in this country [Scotland]!

Regarding the number and species of trees, it is only suitable to say a little here. There are at least fourteen different species of pine, five species of birch, and four species of oak that are found in this same island. The yellow pine is the most valuable, because it is not only excellent timber, it grows to be exceedingly big. Very often trees of this species of pine are found that measure fifteen feet around the base and one hundred and twenty feet in height, and eighty feet of that height are free of branches and limbs. Among the different kinds of wood that grow in Cape Breton the following can be named: pine, oak, juniper, beech, elm, ash, rowan, birch, alder, maple (from which syrup is made), aspen, and so on. Besides each of these woods, there are many others for which there is no Gaelic term. ...

There is no doubt whatsoever that the Gaels who immigrated to North America from particular parts of the Highlands and from the Western Isles, where there was hardly any forest growing, and from which they often had to go on boats for distances of hundreds of miles in order to seek a few crooked and bent sticks for the couples and rafters of their homes, thoroughly enjoy the sight of these forests. It would be good, indeed, for some of the excess wood that the people of the Cape have [to be] on the Isle of Skye itself and in the Long Island from Point to Barra. They would greatly celebrate having something that is so valuable and rare in their own territory. ...

The Indians catch trout, salmon, eels and many other types of fish in a truly skillful way on the summer evenings in the following manner. They go out in a lightweight boat with torch-fires burning. These torches are made from the bark of the birch tree. A stick five or six feet in length is obtained and split at its end. The birch bark is inserted into this split, it is lit with fire, and the burning stick is placed at the front of the boat. The Indian stands close to the light with his foot on each side of the open width of the boat; and with a spear, or fishing-javelin, of fifteen or twenty feet in his hand. Although he is in a precarious situation, he will stand there firmly with an eye fixed sharply on the water. His wife will move the boat smoothly and evenly with an oar, and once her companion sees a fish, he will thrust at it with the spear, and he is so skilled and sharp-eyed that one blow seldom goes astray. Thus, all-knowing Providence has granted to this island many things that are to the benefit and good of people. ...

Since the Gaels have become numerous, both in Cape Breton and in Prince Edward Island, and since many from the Highlands and Islands of Scotland have come to expect that they would likely leave the land of their birth and emigrate to America along with their kinsfolk, it is appropriate to provide a little information regarding the land and employment of this island, as well as about the payment that workers get, and the price for each item that they might need. The land of Prince Edward Island is nearly all colonized by nobility, such as Lords Selkirk, Westmoreland, Queensberry, Melvelle, Townsend, and many others. Since the British Crown released the land in this manner as large parcels, hardly any of it can be had except for rent, if it cannot be purchased afresh from the nobles who own it. But in Cape Breton, on the other hand, there is still much land in the hands of the Crown available for purchase. ...

We hope, from what has been related now about Cape Breton, that our readers may have a positive opinion about the nature and virtues of that island. Although we desire to express the truth, to the best of our knowledge, regarding America and every other place, we leave our compatriots to their own opinions about emigrating to those places. It is indeed our own opinion that strong families would succeed better over yonder than here at home, and that their emigration would yield great rewards, especially to their descendants, but in the wake of all of that, let them decide for themselves. We will provide advice following this, if we are spared, to those who expect to travel over, and we will explain to them all that we know about all of the preparations that are appropriate for them to do. It is indeed the sincere wish of our hearts to provide all useful knowledge to our compatriots and to make every effort that is in our power for their benefit, in terms of both their secular and spiritual welfare.

8: The Song of the Fire

As the poet Lachlann MacMhuirich implies in the following song-poem, composed around the mid 19th century, the "war on the woods" sometimes got out of control. According to the lore that accompanied this poem in print, Aonghus Gobha was responsible for starting the conflagration in Cape Breton. He is not explicitly named in the poem, but everyone in the community would have known that he was to blame. By the early 20th century, other Gaelic commentators were also expressing regret about the loss of forests that happened in Canada as a result of European settlement:

> An uair a thainig ar seanairean do'n dùthaich seo, bha iad a' meas na coille mar nàmhaid. A bharrachd air bhith cumail an fhearainn uapa, bha i 'na h-àite còmhnaidh do bheathaichean-fiadhaich a bhiodh gu tric a' toirt air falbh pàirt de'n bheagan feudail a bhiodh aca. ... Tha call mór air a dhèanamh anns an dùthaich seo na h-uile bliadhna le losgadh na coille. ... A thuilleadh air sin, tha maise na dùthcha air a milleadh, nì a tha calg-dhìreach an aghaidh toil an Fhreastail.[25]

> When our ancestors came to this country, they considered the forest to be their enemy. On top of keeping the soil from them, it was a habitat for wild animals that were frequently taking away some of the little livestock that they had. ... Great damage is done to this land every year by the burning of woods. ... As well as all of that, the beauty of the land is ruined, something that is directly opposed to the will of Providence.

In the introduction accompanying this piece in the Gaelic column of the newspaper *The Casket*, the editor, Pàdraig MacNeacail, highlighted the ecological critique embedded in the humour of the song:

> Chuir am bàrd crìoch fìor mhath air an òran ged is ann le fealla-dhà a rinn e e. Nuair a ghabhas duine beachd air a' chall a tha teine dèanamh air coille, air eòin, is air beathaichean eile, eadhan ged shàbhaileas na daoine, chì e cho cùramach is as fheudar e bhith an àm losgadh droighnich no fuighealach sam bith.

> The poet brought the song to a very good conclusion even though he did so with humour. When someone takes consideration of the damage that fire inflicts on woods, on birds, and on other

creatures, even if it spares people, he will see how careful he must be when refuse timber or any debris at all is burnt.

The author implies nearly from the start that poetry has a social function in broadcasting disapproval of bad behaviour (line 8), such as this fire. The community which the poet defends in this piece seems to extend to the natural world, as he spends three stanzas depicting the injury done to animals, and not all of them are domesticated or friendly creatures.

Original Text

1 Nach nàr an sealladh e 's an Eilean:
   Smearsaid air feadh na beinne
   Pàirceannan chur 'nan teine
   Le coire chlann daoine.

5 'S tìm dhomh dol an òrdugh
   Is teannachadh ri òran
   Mu'n duine rinn an dò-bheart
   Bu chòir dhuinn aoireadh:
   Nuair leig e 'n teine air fògradh
10 A-mach air feadh nam frògaibh,
   Is nuair chaidh e feadh na còinnich
   Bha an ceò air feadh an t-saoghail.

   B' e turas na truaighe
   Nuair thug e 'n teine suas leis
15 'Ga chur 's a' mhosgan ruadh
   Gus na ghual e 'na chraoslach;
   Nuair fhuair an soirbheas greim air
   Is a chaidh e anns an droighnich,
   Chan fhaiceamaid ach soills'
20 Agus boillsgeach gach taobh dhuinn.

   Gur e Dòmhnall Raonaill
   An uair sin bha 'na éiginn,
   A' teicheadh ás a léine
   Ag éigheach is a' glaodhaich;
25 Anna is i fo ghruaimean,
   Ranaidh, an taobh shuas dhi,
   Is thug Alasdair ás ruaig
   Mar gum bualadh an caoch e.

   Sin far an robh smùid
30 Nuair a chaidh e 's an spruis dhlùth:

SETTLEMENT

      Ghabh e mach air feadh a' Chùil,
      Gur e an Grùdair a dhìoghail
      Nuair loisgeadh air a' phàirc
      Is a mhilleadh am buntàta;
35   Ged a theannadh iad ri bhàthadh,
      Cha b' fheàirrd' iad an saothair.

      'S ann feasgar Di-Dòmhnaich
      Bha nathraichean 'gam fògradh;
      Bha maighich air an ròsladh
40   Is eòin air an slaopadh;
      B' e siud an gnothach gràineil
      Dha'n fhear a chuir 'nan smàl iad:
      Cha ghearain sinn gu bràth air
      Bhon shàbhail[eadh] na daoine.

45   Is iomadh maigheach tarrghlas
      Bha ruith air feadh an àite;
      An glagaire 'gan tarstal
      Is e làn dhe'n cuid gaoisne;
      Gu'n coinneachadh 's gach àite
50   Is air feadh na pàirc-bhuntàta;
      Gun d' fhuair e 'n cur an sàs
      Ann am bàthach nan caorach.

      Is iomadh madadh-ruadh
      A bha ruith air feadh nam bruach;
55   An earball air an gualann
      Gu luath air feadh an aonaich;
      Na fithich is iad ag éigheach;
      Na ròcaisean 'nan éiginn;
      Na smeòraich iad fhéin,
60   Thug iad réic, is chan e 'n t-ioghnadh.

      Tha mi an dòchas
      Gun éist sibh ris an òran,
      A h-uile duine beò
      A tha còmhnaidh an taobh-sa;
65   Gun toir sibh 'n aire an còmhnaidh,
      Ur gnothaich a bhith dòigheil,
      Is gun teine 'chur ri eòin
      Gus am pòr a chur aog oirnn.[26]

Translation

(1-4) The sight is a disgrace in the island: smoke ash throughout the mountain and grazing fields set on fire through human wrongdoing.

(5-12) It is time for me to get ready and begin a song about the person who did the misdeed, we ought to condemn him; when he let the fire go wandering out throughout the hollows and when it went through the ferns, the smoke spread throughout the world.

(13-20) It was a wretched expedition when he brought the fire up with him, putting it in the ruddy, rotting wood until it was inflamed into an insatiable blaze; when the breeze caught hold of it and it went into the refuse timber, we couldn't see anything but light and glare in every direction around us.

(21-28) It was Donald son of Ronald who was in a crisis then, fleeing with nothing but his shirt, screaming and yelling; while Anna was surly and Ronny was above her, and Alexander took off as though he were suddenly struck with madness.

(29-36) That's where the smoke was, when [the fire] went into the dense spruce: it launched out into the Rear, and it cost the Brewer dearly when the grazing field was burnt and the potatoes were ruined; although they tried to quench it, they were none the better for their labour.

(37-44) It was Sunday afternoon that the snakes were sent into exile; the hares were roasted and the birds were parboiled; it was a disagreeable act for the man who extinguished them: we will never make complaint of him again, since the people were saved.

(45-52) There were many grey-bellied hares who were hurtling around the area, getting chomped by the wolf, who was full of their fur; encountering them at every turn and throughout the potato fields, until he captured them in the sheep byre.

(53-60) There were many foxes who were racing throughout the ridges; their tails on their shoulders, [moving] quickly throughout the hill; while the ravens were wailing and the crows were in crisis; the thrushes themselves howled, which is not surprising.

(61-68) I hope that you all will listen to the song, every living person who lives over here; that you will always be careful how you manage things and that you not set fire to the birds and cause their progeny to bring death upon us.

9: The Gaelic Communities of Megantic, Quebec

The author of the following account of the Eastern Townships of Quebec in 1890 is identified only as "MacÙisdein." He was clearly a Scottish Gael, possibly from the Western Isles, who lived elsewhere—most likely Montreal. His is one of the few contemporary testimonies in Gaelic of the life of the immigrant communities there before they were assimilated into Canada's two dominant linguistic majorities. The text confirms that the church played a strong unifying role in the community and was one of the few domains in which Gaelic played an important role.

Original Text

> Air mo thuras, an latha roimhe, chuir mi seachad an t-Sàbaid aig Baile Mhegantic, ann am Mór-Roinn Quebec. Tha an t-ionad seo de'n dùthaich creagach, àrd, le beanntan mór' air am bheil ceò na h-iarmailt gu tric ag aomadh, mar air fuar-bheanntan na Gàidhealtachd. Tha coille throm a' còmhdachadh na tìre agus tha iomadh sruth is caochan a' dèanadh torman air feadh nan doire is a' taomadh an uisgeachan anns na lochaibh a tha lìonmhor am measg nam beann. Air bruachan Loch Mhegantic thog móran Ghàidheal an àite còmhnaidh, bho Eilean an Fhraoich, bho "Leódhus bheag riabhach a bha riamh 's an taobh tuath."
>
> Tha iad fada bho Chuan Siar an eòlais, ach cha d' fhàg iad na h-uile nì a bhuineadh do'n Ghàidhealtachd 'nan déidh. Cha d' fhàg iad cliù an sinnsir no cridhe an athraichean agus cha do dhì-chuimhnich iad an cànain mhàthaireil, no an teagasg a fhuair iad ris a' ghlùin. Cluinnear a' Ghàidhlig gu fileanta, agus tha meas oirre dol am meud mar as mó a tha a' Bheurla is an Fhrangais a' dèanamh greim air an òigridh.
>
> Aig an àm seo, chan eil ministear suidhichte aig an t-sluagh agus tha searmonaiche òg bho Oilthigh Mhoirin,[27] a' saothrachadh 'nam measg. Chaidh mi leis do'n eaglais, a bha cóig mìle bho'n taigh-òsta, thar rathad garbh a bha doirbh a ghabhail ach bha

an acfhainn làidir, is an t-each toileach. Bha mu thuaiream air trì cheud pearsa an làthair agus thug an sealladh air ais cuimhneachan air Ùig, Carlabha is Tairbeart na h-Earadh.

Bha mnàthan le subagan a' còmhdach an cinn, bha seann daoine air an éideadh mar bu dual, bha an fheadhainn òg gu stòlda, stuama, ag éisteachd le aire do'n fhacal a bha air a labhairt. Ré dà uair a thìm chaidh an t-seirbheis air a h-adhart, ach cha d' fhàg neach air bith an taigh-adhraidh. Bha na Sailm air an seinn ris na seann fhuinn Ghàidhealach agus bu mhilis an ceòl an rinneadh leotha. Cha robh feum air inneal ciùil, bha an cridhe is am bilean air an gleusadh agus bha toirm an guth a' lìonadh na h-àitreibh le moladh do Dhia.

Bu dhrùidhteach an nì a bhith maille riutha, a bhith cluinntinn earail air a labhairt gu dìleas ann am briathran nam beann, a bhith cur suas an achanaich dhùrachdaich, agus a' togail guth buidheachais air son maitheis agus trocairean an Tighearna.

Gu ma fada a dh'imicheas iad anns na nithean seo, ann an ceuman daoine diadhaidh Eilein Leódhuis.[28]

Translation

On my journey, the other day, I spent the Sabbath in the town of Megantic, in the Province of Quebec. This part of the country is craggy and high, with great mountains upon which the mist of the heavens often descends, just like the cold mountains of the Highlands. There is a thick forest covering the land and there are many brooks and streamlets that make babbling noises throughout the groves and pour their waters into the lakes that are plentiful among the mountains. Many Gaels built their residences on the banks of Lake Megantic, from the "Island of Heather," from "little, dappled Lewis that was always in the north."

They are far away from the familiar Western Ocean, but they did not leave everything behind them that pertains to the Highlands. They did not leave the reputation of their ancestors or the spirit of their forefathers, and they have not forgotten their mother tongue, or the tutoring that they got on the knee [of their parents]. Fluent Gaelic is heard and esteem for the language is growing greater as the youth make a stronger hold on English and French.

At this time, the population do not have a settled minister and there is a young sermonizer from Collège Sainte-Marie, labouring among them. I went with him to the church, that was five miles from the inn, across a rough road that was difficult to travel but the rig was strong and the horse was willing. There were about three hundred people in attendance, and the sight brought back memories of Ùig, Carloway and Tarbert.

The women covered their heads with linen mutches, the old people were clothed according to tradition, the youth were self-controlled and solemn, listening attentively to the words that were spoken. During the two hours that the service progressed, not a single person left the house of worship. The psalms were sung to the old Highland melodies, and the music that was made with them was sweet. There was no need of musical instruments, their hearts and their lips were in tune and the resonance of their voices filled the edifice with the praise of God.

Being with them left a strong impression on me, to be hearing exhortations spoken faithfully in the language of the mountains, to be lifting up their sincere prayers, and to be giving a word of thanks for the mercy and the blessings of the Lord.

May they persist for a long time in these matters, in the footsteps of the pious people of the Island of Lewis.

10: Immigration to Saltcoats, Saskatchewan

Reverend Dòmhnall Dòmhnallach wrote the following account of the Highland settlement in Saltcoats, Saskatchewan, in 1937. Although the original immigrants had lived as fishermen in Scotland, they were expected to adapt quickly to farming on the Prairies in harsh, unfamiliar conditions on poor land with an underdeveloped infrastructure. It is not surprising that the original emigrants essentially deserted the settlements in less than two decades.[29]

Original Text

Thàinig dà fhichead teaghlach is a cóig a-nall á Leódhus, na h-Earradh agus Uibhist a Tuath 's a' bhliadhna 1889 agus dh'àitich iad mu'n sgìre mun cuairt air Saltcoats far an robh crìoch an rathaid-iarainn aig an àm. A' cheud trì bliadhna an déidh dhaibh suidheachadh air an fhearann, bha an tiormachd cho anabarrach trom agus nach robh móran cinneis air a' bharr. An-sin anns a' bhliadhna 1892 agus 1893 dhùin an geamhradh a-staigh mu'n 14mh latha de'n Dàmhair le sneachda, fuachd is gailleann, a' cumail roimhe gun móran dioclaidh fad a' gheamhraidh agus air an 15mh latha de'n Chéitean, 's e sléighichean a b' fheudar dhaibh a thoirt leo gu ruige Saltcoats.

Chaill a' chuid bu mhò de na tuathanaich am beagan stoc a shealbhaich iad agus bha iad air dhroch càradh. Chaill iad am misneach cho mór agus gun do dh'imrich iad air falbh gu ruige Manitoba is Ontario. Cha do dh'fhuirich ach àireamh bheag de'n cheud luchd-àiteachaidh. Bhon uair sin thàinig àireamh de'n càirdean a-nall agus shuidhich iad 's an sgìreachd anns an dh'fhalbh a' cheud bhuidheann a thàinig.

Tha a' Ghàidhlig, ged is duilich ri ràdh, air dol air ais seach mar a bha i an toiseach agus is cinnteach gum bheil sin 'na chall mór do na Gàidheil a tha còmhnaidh mu thimcheall an àite seo.

De na seann teaghlaichean Gàidhealach a shuidhich an-seo an 1889, chan eil an làthair an-diugh ach triùir sheann mhnathan. Thiodhlaic sinn an latha roimhe té dhiubh seo, bean Choinnich Nic̀Iomhair. Bha i ceithir fichead bliadhna is a h-aon deug a dh'aois. Chaochail a companach o chionn dà bhliadhna; bha e ceithir fichead bliadhna is a sia deug. Thàinig iad á Leódhus, Alba.

Tha iomadh sgeula neònach air aithris mu'n t-seann luchd-àiteachaidh. 'S e daimh a bh' aca a' dèanamh na h-oibreach àn àite each, a bha ainneamh 's an aimsir ud. Co-dhiubh, an àm an fhogharaidh, an déidh an cruithneachd a bhuain, dh'fhalbh cóignear thuathanach le lóid de'n chruithneachd do'n mhuileann a b' fhaisge orra, leth-cheud mìle air falbh am Manitoba.

An uair a ràinig iad an abhainn, bha 'bhruach cho cas agus cam is nach leigeadh an t-eagal leo na lóid 'thoirt sìos leis na daimh. 'S e rinn iad, na daimh 'fhuasgladh ás na carbadan rothach agus rug fear dhiubh air a' chrann a bha an ceangal ri acfhainn nan damh agus rug càch air ròpanan làidir a cheangail iad air cùl an lóid gus a chumail air ais.

Ach cha deachaidh iad fada air aghaidh nuair thàinig am fear aig an robh greim air a' chrann gu lùb a bh' anns an rathad, agus a dh'aindeoin a dhìchill, dh'fhairtlich air an carbad is a lód a tharraing a dh'ionnsaigh an rathaid, agus an carbad a thoirt ás a chéile 'na phìosan is a dhèanamh suas a-rithist. 'S ann an uair sin a thug iad fainear gun robh còir aca air na rothan a ghlasadh.

Chan eil an-seo ach faoineas an coimeas ris a h-uile ànradh is cruadal a dh'fhulaing an ceud luchd-àiteachaidh am fàsaichean móra Chanada. Is iomadh latha chuir iad feum air an gaisge, am misneach is an treubhantas.[30]

Translation

Forty-five families came over from Lewis, Harris and North Uist in the year 1889 and they colonized the area around Saltcoats where the railroad ended at that time. The first three years after they had been settled on the land, there was such a severe drought that there was not much of a harvest. Then in the years 1892 and 1893, the winter closed in around the fourteenth day of October with snow, frigidity and storms, staying like that without much respite throughout the winter, and on the fifteenth day of May, they had to take sleighs to Saltcoats.

The majority of the tenantry lost the little livestock that they possessed and they were in distress. They became so discouraged that they moved on to Manitoba and Ontario. Only a small number of the original settlers remained. Since that time, a number of their relations have come over and they have settled in the county from which the first group who came left.

Although it is sad to say, Gaelic is deteriorating compared to what it was initially and it is certain that that is a great loss to the Gaels who live around this area.

Of the old Highland families who settled here in 1889, only three old women remain today. The other day we buried one of them, the wife of Kenneth MacIver. She was ninety-one years of age. Her companion died two years ago; he was ninety-six years of age. They came from the Isle of Lewis, Scotland.

There are many unusual stories told about the old settlers. They had oxen to do the work rather than horses, which were scarce at that time. Anyway, at harvest time, after the wheat had been reaped, five farmers departed with a load of wheat to the mill that was closest to them, fifty miles away in Manitoba.

When they reached the river, the bank was so steep and twisty that they were afraid for the oxen to take the load downhill. What they did was to unfetter the oxen from the wheeled wagons and one of the men seized hold of the shaft that was connected to the yoke and the other men seized hold of strong ropes that they connected to the back end of the load to hold back its weight.

But they did not go far when the man who had hold of the shaft came to a bend that was in the road, and despite his best effort, he was unable to conduct the wagon and the load toward the road, and the wagon fell apart in pieces and had to be reassembled again. It was then that they realized that they needed to secure the wheels in place.

But this is trivial in comparison to all of the distresses and hardships that the first colonists of the great wildernesses of Canada endured. They had to make use of their heroism, courage and bravery on many days.

11: Gaelic Communities in Prince Edward Island

The following letter was written by "C. C." of Srath Alba (Strathalbyn), Prince Edward Island, on July 20, 1893 and sent to the newspaper *Mac-Talla*. As emigration often happened as chains of families and communities from the same source areas in Scotland, where religious affiliation was a defining feature of local identity, it is not surprising to see that denominational identity was a strong component of the reconstituted immigrant communities (even though people were often not as theologically committed as some might expect today). Language could be a unifying factor as well, especially when it was a source of pride rather than shame.

Original Text

Tha do charaid "Cabar Féidh" an Lunnainn ag iarraidh fios fhaotainn ciamar tha a' Ghàidhlig air a cumail suas an cèarnan fa leth de Chanada. Is còir freagradh thoirt do'n iarrtas sin. Nì mise mo dhìcheall air fios a thoirt mar tha a' chùis an Eilean a' Phrionnsa.

Anns an eilean seo, tha 109,000 sluaigh. Tha iad seo air an dèanamh suas de Shasannaich, Albannaich, Éireannaich, agus beagan Innseanach; ach 's e Albannaich is clann Albannach a' chuid is lìonmhoire de luchd-àitiche an Eilein seo. Agus dhiubh seo, buinidh a' chuid as pailte do Thìr nam Beann. Ann an aidmheil, tha iad air an roinn mar seo: 62,000 Protastanach agus 47,000 Pàpanach.

Anns an Eaglais Chléirich, tha 34,000 sluaigh, air an roinn 'nan deich co-thionalan fichead. Ann an deich dhiubh sin, tha Gàidhlig air a searmonachadh agus ann an trì no ceithir eile, bu chòir i bhith air a searmonachadh ach tha ministearan Gàidhlig gann agus ged tha Gàidhlig aig an t-sluagh, tuigidh iad Beurla.

Anns an Eaglais Phàpanaich, tha mu thimcheall 28 co-thional is mun cuairt air an àireamh sin de shagairt. Is Gàidheal ochd deug dhiubh, agus is Easbaig Gàidhealach th' air an ceann, an t-Urram. I. C. Dòmhnallach an Charlottetown.

Tha againn mar an ceudna 6,000 Baisteach, 7,000 de'n Eaglais Shasannaich, agus 13,000 Methodach, ach chan aithne dhomh gu bheil móran Gàidhlig 'nam measg sin.

Tha an seann mhuinntir glé mheasail air a' Ghàidhlig ach tha an òigridh cho fileanta anns a' Bheurla is gur i as deiseile le móran aca bhith labhairt. Is tha cuid againn, mar tha agaibh fhéin, 'fhir mo chridhe, a' call na Gàidhlig anns na Stàitean. Chan eil a' Ghàidhlig air a teagasg 's na sgoiltean is mar sin tha móran nach urrainn a leughadh. Ach, coma co-dhiubh, tha eòlas a' fàs agus mar sin, tuilleadh luach aig muinntir 'ga chur air a' Ghàidhlig mar chànain aosmhor agus bhlasta.

Slàn leat. Is math leam thu bhith fàs mór.[31]

Translation

Your friend "Cabar Féidh" in London is seeking information about how Gaelic is holding up in different corners of Canada. It is appropriate to provide a response to that request. I will do my very best to offer information about how the matter stands in Prince Edward Island.

In this island, there is a population of 109,000. They are made up of English people, Scots, Irish people, and a few Indians; but Scots and the descendants of Scots are the majority of the inhabitants of this island. And of those, the majority derive from the Highlands. Regarding religion, they are divided thusly: 62,000 Protestants and 47,000 Catholics.

In the Presbyterian Church, there is a population of 34,000, divided into thirty congregations. In ten of those, sermons are delivered in Gaelic and in three or four others, sermons should be delivered in Gaelic but Gaelic-speaking ministers are scarce and although the population speaks Gaelic, they can understand English.

In the Catholic Church, there are about twenty-eight congregations and about that same number of priests. Eighteen of them are Gaels and a Gaelic bishop is in charge of them, the Rev. J. C. MacDonald in Charlottetown.

We likewise have 6,000 Baptists, 7,000 Anglicans, and 13,000 Methodists, but I am not aware that there are many Gaels among them.

The old people are very fond of Gaelic but the youth are so fluent in English that it is the language that many of them are most likely to speak. And some of us, like some of you, dear reader, are losing the Gaelic language in the United States. Gaelic is not taught in the schools and therefore many people are unable to read it. But in any case, knowledge is increasing and as it does, people are placing greater value on Gaelic as a venerable and enjoyable language.

Farewell. I'm glad that you are growing strong.

12: The Gaels in Cape Breton

The editor of *Mac-Talla*, Eòin MacFhionghain, compiled and wrote the following account of the history of the communities of immigrants from the Scottish Highlands and Western Isles in Cape Breton in 1903. It is arguably the best essay written on the subject to the present. As a Gaelic speaker in regular communication with many other Gaels who shared his intense interest in the history and literature of his people, he was able to draw upon the memories of Highlanders who had emigrated from Scotland themselves or those who were passing on the traditions of immigrants who had witnessed and lived through these events.

Although MacFhionghain is aware of the causes of the disintegration of Gaelic society and the subsequent emigration of Highland communities, his critique becomes depoliticized right at the point that he begins to critique the aristocracy. This loss of courage to challenge social injustices is indicative of the resignation many Gaels felt about political and social matters after a long period of disenfranchisement. Religion offered an alternative outlet for their hopes and energies, reassuring them that God would deal with worldly misdeeds since none of the secular authorities seemed interested in doing so. MacFhionghain certainly overstates the harmony that he supposed to exist at that time between landlords and crofters on Highland estates. To the extent that there was any equilibrium, it was a hard-won result of the Land Agitation just a generation before—not some Divine judgement.

Nonetheless, MacFhionghain subtly expresses the ambivalences and tradeoffs that a people in transition—"undergoing development," as we might call it today—were facing and the regrets that at least some members of future generations would feel about losing their language and leaving self-sufficient and tightly-knit communities. He reassures Gaels that the challenges of assimilation that they face, while very real and pressing to them in their own lives, were global ones emerging in many regions. Like many other Gaelic intellectuals of his era, he was well-educated about world affairs and could understand the issues facing his people in a larger context.

Original Text

Am measg nan Gàidheal, anns gach dùthaich 's am bheil iad, is tric a chluinnear a bhith gearain air na fasanan Gallta. Tha iad a' tolladh a-staigh a lìon beagan is beagan, a' cur nan seann fhasanan Gàidhealach air chùl, agus chan urrainnear am bacadh. Tha an nì ceudna a' dol air adhart ann an dùthchannan eile, fasanan is cleachdaidhean nan dùthchannan beaga a' dol á sealladh is fasanan is cleachdaidhean nan dùthchannan móra a' gabhail an àite. Is dual do'n chùis leantainn mar sin, gus mu dheireadh thall am bi a' mhór-chuid de'n t-saoghal mar aon dùthaich agus mar aon shluagh, air neo gus an gabh muinntir gach dùthcha aithreachas is am pill iad gu gnàths an athraichean fhéin.

Cha mhór a smaoinicheadh gun dèanadh atharrachadh fasain sluagh treun, tìr-ghràdhach mar bha na Gàidheil a chur air imrich thar cuain, ach chan eil teagamh nach b' e an t-atharrachadh cleachdaidh a thàinig orra mar shluagh an déidh Bliadhna Theàrlaich as coireach gum bheil an eachdraidh ghoirid seo ri sgrìobhadh an-diugh. Gu ruige an àm sin, bha na Gàidheil air an roinn 'nam fineachan anns an robh gach ceann-feadhna mar athair teaghlaich móir agus an fhine uile mar chloinn dha. Anns na làithean sin, b' i toil a' chinn-fheadhna ann an tomhas mór toil na fine, agus b' e math na fine math a' chinn-fheadhna. An àm togail creiche no toirt a-mach tòrachd bha iad mar aon duine: an àm sìthe bha gach duine na 'thuathanach, agus an àm cogaidh bha gach duine na 'shaighdear.

Agus chan eil teagamh mur biodh Bliadhna Theàrlaich, nach biodh a' mhór chuid de na Gàidheil air fuireach an tìr nam beann, is nach biodh an sliochd an-sin an-diugh ag iasgach, a' sealg is a' dol air àiridh mar bu nòs ri linn Dhonnachaidh Bhàin. Ach cha b' e sin a bha an dàn dhaibh. Bha rompa sgapadh air feadh an t-saoghail, agus bha Blàr Chùil-Lodair agus na reachdan cruaidhe Sasannach a thàinig 'na dhéidh coireach ri obair an sgapaidh a thòiseachadh. Nan robh iad air am fàgail fo'n t-seann òrdugh, an saorsa nam beann, cha mhór dhiubh a ghluaiseadh gu bràth á duthaich an sinnsireachd, ach fo'n òrdugh ùr chuireadh éiginn orra. Bha an t-sìth ['g]a cumail o bhliadhna gu bliadhna, gun chothrom falbh is tighinn mar a chleachd iad, ro chuingeil leotha.

Bhristeadh na bannan dàimh is dìlseachd a bha roimhe sin a' ceangal nam fineachan ris na cinn-fheadhna. Chan fhaodadh an ceann-feadhna a shluagh a ghairm a-mach gu cogadh na b' fhaide, agus a lìon beagan is beagan, thàinig e gu bhith a' call a dhreuchd mar athair a shluaigh is gu bhith a' fàs 'na uachdaran fearainn, is iadsan 'nan tuath bhig is 'nan croitearan. Dh'fhadaidh seo an cridheachan an t-sluaigh spiorad an-fhois agus mun do ruith móran bhliadhnachan, thòisich buidhnean beaga dhiubh ri dhol air imrich thar cuain. Thòisich na cinn-fheadhna aig an àm cheudna ri barrachd dhe'n ùine 'chur seachad air a' Ghalltachd agus an-sin bha iad a' cur cùl ri cleachdaidhean na Gàidhealtachd, is a' call an eòlais air an luchd-cinnidh. Agus mar bha iad a' call an eòlais orra bha iad a' call am bàigh riutha is mar sin air an ullachadh air son na rinn iad an ceann tìme.

Ann am frithealadh nan cruinneachaidhean greadhnach is fleadhach anns na bailtean móra, rinn móran dhiubh ana-caitheamh air am maoin. Cha robh an sporanan ro throm, ach ged nach robh, dh'fheumadh iad ceum a chumail riuthasan aig an robh saidhbhreas. Bha iad mar sin bliadhna an déidh bliadhna a' dol anns na fiachan, agus air a cheann mu dheireadh b' fheudar do iomadh fear dealachadh ris an oighreachd a fhuair e o shinnsir is a bhuineadh air tùs do'n fhine cho math is a bhuineadh i do'n cheann-fheadhna.

Aig an àm a bha seo a' tachairt, bha prìs mhór air caoraich is air crodh, agus air son an crannchur a leasachadh, thòisich iad ri cumail spréidhe is chaorach. Agus nuair bha am fearann a' fàs gann, thòisich iad ri fògradh an t-sluaigh air son tuilleadh àite 'dhèanamh do na h-ainmhidhean. B' ann air am fògradh mar seo a bha móran dhiubhsan a shuidhich ann an Canada. Gun teagamh thàinig móran eile de shaorsa an toile fhéin, air dhaibh a bhith faotainn misnich uapasan a bha bhos rompa; ach faodar a bhith cinnteach mur biodh na ceud bhuidhnean a thàinig a-nall air an cur ann dh'an aindeoin, nach biodh ann an Canada an-diugh ach àireamh glé bheag de shliochd nan Gàidheal.

B' ann mu'n bhliadhna 1784 a thòisicheadh ri fògradh nan Gàidheal. Thatar a' cur air Diùc Athaill gum b' e theann ris an obair an-iochdmhor sin an toiseach, ach cha b' fhada bha e rithe nuair a ghabh cinn-fheadhna eile 'eisimpleir. Chaidh an sluagh fhògradh á Srath Ghlas, á Gleann Garaidh, á Cnòideart is á Loch Abar eadar 1784 is 1805. An déidh sin bha móran air an cur air falbh á Cataibh. Agus anns na h-Eileanan: bha eilean Ruim air fhàsachadh 's a' bhliadhna 1826, agus Eilean nam Muc an 1828. Á Uibhist a' Chinn a Tuath bha móran air am fògradh 's a' bhliadhna 1849, agus á Uibhist a' Chinn a Deas is á Barraigh an 1851. Bha seo uile air a dhèanamh a chum àite 'dhèanamh do chrodh is do chaoraich. Bha Galltachd na h-Alba agus Sasann freagarrach air son togail arbhair, ach beanntan àrda na Gàidhealtachd, bha iad na b' fhearr gu togail cruidh is chaorach; agus smaoinich sealbhadairean an fhearainn gum bu mhath an cothrom air saidhbhreas a chur ri chéile nam faigheadh iad an tuath dhùthchasach a chur air falbh agus na beanntan far am b' àbhaist crodh nan tuathanach a bhith air àiridh 's an t-samhradh a chur fo chrodh is fo chaoraich.

Chan eilear an seo a' dol a thoirt iomradh air gach fòirneart is ana-ceartas a dh'fhuiling an sluagh bochd seo a' fàgail an dùth-cha. Cha mhó a bheirear breith orrasan a bha ri obair an-ioch-dmhor an fhògraidh. Thugadh breith air a' mhór chuid dhiubh cheana le Breitheamh as àirde na breitheamhan na talmhainn. Tha cuid dhiubh air an dubhadh ás gu buileach, gun aon de'n sliochd beò air thalamh, agus cuid eile a dh'fhàg sliochd aig nach eil òirleach de dh'oighreachd an sinnsir. Faodaidh ana-ceartas is eucoir làmh-an-uachdar 'fhaotainn air ceart is còir, ach eadhon anns an t-saoghal seo, cha téid luchd na h-eucoir ás o pheanas.

Agus an-diugh is fìor ainneamh an oighreachd Ghàidhealach a tha an seilbh sliochd nam feadhnach a bu choireach ris an fhògradh. Bhiodh e ceart ainmeachadh an-seo gun robh móran de na cinn-fheadhna nach do chuir éiginn sam bith air an t-sluagh an oighreachdan 'fhàgail. Chuidich iad leothasan a bha deònach falbh, ach dhéilig iad gu caoimhneil, ceart riuthasan a dh'fhuirich; agus an-diugh tha sliochd nan ceann-feadhna sin is an sluagh a tha air an oighreachdan a' faighinn air adhart gu sìtheil càirdeil, gun aon taobh a' faotainn coire d'an taobh eile.

Anns an t-seann dùthaich cha robh crannchur ar n-athraichean ach car bochd a-réir ar barail-ne a tha air ar cleachdadh ri pailteas is goireasan an latha an-diugh. Bu tuathanach mór esan aig an robh deich no dusan acaire fearainn, deich no dusan mart, is treud beag chaorach. Bha iad a' còmhnaidh ann an taighean tughte anns nach robh bharr air dhà no trì sheòmraichean, cuid anns am biodh simileir is cuid anns nach biodh. Bha iad a dh'easbhuidh iomadh nì air am bheil an sliochd anns an dùthaich seo ag amharc mar nithean nach gabh dèanamh ás aonais, ach chan eil sin ag ràdh nach robh iad ann an tomhas mór sona. Mur robh aca gach goireas is grinneas air an cuir sinne feum, bha aca na b' fhearr, a bhith toilichte le'n staid. Mur robh iad beairteach, cha robh eòlas aca air agus mar sin, cha robh iad 'ga ionndrainn. Bha am pailteas bìdh is aodaich aca, bha slàinte is fallaineachd aca, agus bha iad a' mealtainn sìth is càirdeis am measg a chéile.

Rinn an dòigh seo air an robh iad a' tighinn beò anns an t-seann dùthaich an ullachadh air son am beòshlaint a dhèanamh anns an dùthaich ùir. Bha iad cleachdte ri siubhal fraoiche is ri dìreadh mhonaidhean, ri ruamhar is ri buain mòine, agus rinn an cleachdadh sin an cruadhachadh fa chomhair siubhail chnoc is ghleann, bàireadh sneachd, is gearradh coille na dùthcha seo. Bha iomadh deuchainn is cruadal rompa air an taobh seo dhe'n chuan mhór, agus chaidh an ullachadh air an son leis an Tì sin nach do chuir riamh uallach air druim nach robh comasach air a giùlain.

Thàinig iad a-nall 'nan grunnan beaga o bhliadhna gu bliadhna, luchd luinge am-bliadhna, dà luchd an ath-bhliadhna, agus luchd no dhà eile an treas bliadhna. Cha robh iomradh air soithichean-smùide 's na h-àmannan sin agus cha robh na soithichean-seòlaidh ach mall agus neo-chinnteach. Bha iomadh ànradh ri fhulang a bharrachd air an tinneas-mhara. Bha móran de na sgiobairean nach robh os cionn an cothrom a ghabhail air na daoine bochda a bha ag earbsa am beatha is an cuid riutha 's an imrich.

Cha b' ann air Ceap Breatainn a thug na Gàidheil an aghaidh an toiseach: b' e an t-àite mu dheireadh do'n do thòisich iad ri tighinn. Shuidhich móran diubh air Eilean a' Phrionnsa cho tràth ri 1769, agus ceithir bliadhna an déidh sin, ràinig a' cheud soitheach-imrich Pictou. Ach ged bha iad a' taomadh a-nall do'n dà àite sin gach bliadhna an déidh sin, cha tàinig aon do Cheap Breatainn gu ceann corr is fichead bliadhna. B' ann eadar 1791 is 1795 a thàinig àireamh dhiubhsan a bha air fearainn a thogail air tìr-mór thairis air Caol Chanso do Cheap Breatainn, agus a shuidhich iad air a' chladach an iar, cuid timcheall Shiùdaig is cuid eile mu Acarsaid Mhàbou. Beagan bhliadhnaichean an déidh sin, thòisich soithichean ri tighinn gu taobh an ear an eilein. Ràinig a' cheud tè Sidni 's a' bhliadhna 1802, air an t-siathamh latha deug de cheud mhìos an fhoghair. Bha oirre seo ceud is ceithir teaghlaichean, mu thrì cheud pearsa eadar shean is òg.

An déidh sin, bha na soithichean a' tighinn gu math tric, agus bha Ceap Breatainn lìonadh suas cho bras is a bha an t-Eilean is tìr-mór roimhe sin. An déidh na bliadhna 1828, cha robh na h-uiread dhiubh a' tighinn, agus anns a' bhliadhna 1843 thàinig an soitheach mu dheireadh, agus sguir imrich nan Gàidheal do Cheap Breatainn. "Is beag fios aig fear an tàimh air ànradh fear na mara." Tha seo fìor d'ar taobh-ne tha beò an Ceap Breatainn an-diugh agus nach fhaca is nach d' fhuiling gach cruaidh-chàs is cruadal is ànradh tro'n deachaidh ar n-athraichean.

Thàinig a' mhór chuid dhiubh a-nall gun aca air chùl an làimhe na chumadh beò gu ceann bliadhna iad, agus cha robh aca ach dol a ghleachd ris a' choille air son am beòshlaint. Anns a' cheud dol a-mach, bha iad a' togail bhothan anns an deasaicheadh iad biadh is anns an caidleadh iad gus am biodh 'nan comas taighean na b' fhearr a chur suas. An déidh seo mar gheibheadh iad ùine is cothrom ro thoiseach a' gheamhraidh, bha iad, le cuideachadh nan coimhearsnach, ma bha iad ann, cuideachadh nach deach a-riamh iarraidh gun fhaotainn, a' togail taighe b' fhearr, ged a shaoileadh àl an latha an-diugh nach robh am fearr ann. Bhiodh an taigh seo air a dhèanamh air logaichean air an càradh air a chéile, is na sgaran eadarra air an calcadh le còinnich, maidean snaidhte no bùird shàbhte mar ùrlar, agus am mullach air a thughadh le cairt nan craobh. Bhiodh simileir 's an darna ceann de'n bhothan seo, a' cumail blàiths is solais ris an teaghlach.

Bha a' choille pailt agus cha bhiodh dìth connaidh orra. B' e 'cheud bharr a chuireadh iad mar bu trice buntàta, agus 's e sin le annlan éisg is sìthne bu bhiadh dhaibh roinn mhór de'n bhliadhna. An ceann bliadhna no dhà, bhiodh iad a' cur coirce, cruithneachd is eòrna, agus thòisicheadh iad ri cumail beagan spréidhe is chaorach. Bha na h-eòin is beothaichean beaga na coille 'nan nàimhdean do'n bharr agus na fiadh-bheothaichean móra do na h-ainmhidhean; b' iomadh pàirce bheag shìl a chuireadh a dholaidh leis na feòragan; b' iomadh mart mhath is caora a rinn feist an gàraidh a' mhathain. Rè nam bliadhnachan a bha iad a' cìsneachadh na coille, cha robh iad gun an cuid fhéin de dheuchainnean an t-saoghail, deuchainnean is cruadalan air nach eil eòlas sam bith againne, agus ris nach bitheamaid deònach seasamh. Ach a dh'aindeoin sin, bha toileachas-inntinn 'nam measg air am bheil sinn mar an ceudna aineolach, agus ràinig àireamh nach bu bheag dhiubh aois mhór mun deach an gairm air falbh, aois nach ruig iadsan a tha 'tighinn beò ann am pailteas is an sògh ar latha-ne.

Mar a shiubhail na bliadhnachan, shiubhail a' choille mhór; dh'fhàs na h-àiteachan réitichte na bu mhotha, agus dhlùthaich iad ri chéile. A lìon fear is fear, chaidh na taighean-logaichean 'fhàsachadh, agus ghabh an sluagh còmhnaidh ann an taighean bu mhotha, bu shoilleire agus a b' fhearr. Dh'fhàs an spréidh is na caoraich na bu lìonmhoire, agus shoirbhich le làimh an dìcheallaich.

Dh'fhosgladh rathaidean air feadh na dùthcha, thogadh taighean-sgoile agus eaglaisean. Gun teagamh dh'fhaodadh iomadh adhartas tighinn air an dùthaich nach tàinig oirre; ach có an dùthaich mu nach faodar sin a ràdh? Agus chan i h-uile dùthaich mu'm faodar a ràdh gun do thionndaidh i, ri aon linn, o bhith 'na dùthaich choilltich fhàsail, gu bhith 'na dùthaich thoraich àitichte, anns am bheil móran a' dèanamh beairteis, agus anns nach eil ach glé bheag de dh'fhìor bhochdainn, mar a dh'fhaodar a ràdh le fìrinn mu Cheap Breatainn.

Bhiodh iad air barrachd adhartais a dhèanamh nan robh iad air leantainn ris an fhearann na b' fhearr na rinn iad. Ach tha iomadh bliadhna on thòisich an òigridh ri fàgail dùthaich an àraich mar a dh'fhàg an athraichean dùthaich an sinnsir. Tha bailtean nan Stàidean agus na tuarastail mhóra thatar a' pàigheadh an caochladh cheàrnan 'gan tarraing air falbh o'n dachaighean. Is àireamh glé bheag dhiubh aig nach eil dùil ri tilleadh an àm falbh agus tha móran a' dèanamh sin, ach 's ann an déidh dhaibh làithean an trèine is an spionnaidh a chur seachad ann an tìr chéin, agus tha na fearainn, a bha ré na h-ùine sin air am fàgail am freastal sheann daoine, air dol a dholaidh cho mór is gun gabh iad iomadh bliadhna de chruaidh-chosnadh mun toir iad beòshlainte cheart a-rithist.

Faodaidh e bhith gun atharraich seo fhathast is gun gabh iadsan a tha aig an àm seo a' dèanamh tàir air obair fearainn tlachd innte. Ged tha cuid dhe na dh'fhalbh air soirbheachadh gu math, tha a' chuid as motha nach do leasaich an crannchur idir, a tha 'nan luchd-gearraidh-fiodha is -tarraing-uisge do choigrich nuair dh'fhaodadh iad a bhith 'nan tighearnan air an cuid fearainn fhéin, gun dìth is gun deireas.

Ach a dh'aindeoin an fhalbh seo, a tha air a chuideachadh gu mór le spiorad na h-an-fhois a fhuair na Gàidheil òga mar dhìleab bho'n athraichean, chan eil na h-uiread a' fàgail is gum bheil an t-eilean a' sgur de bhith Gàidhealach. Ged tha na fearainn ann an iomadh àite air an dearmad, chan eil iad air an creic no a' tuiteam an làmhan mhuinntir eile. Mar seo tha gach àite bha air a thogail le Gàidheil an toiseach ann an seilbh Ghàidheal fhathast, agus bithidh gus an dealaich riutha an gràdh is an ceangal ri dachaigh na h-òige a bha riamh fuaighte ri nàdar a' Ghàidheil.

Thatar a' meas gun tàinig air imrich do Cheap Breatainn uile gu léir mu chóig mìle fichead de na Gàidheil. Tha a thrì uiread sin dhe'n sliochd ann an-diugh mur eil an corr, agus faodar a ràdh gun a dhol bharr na fìrinn gum bheil dà thrian dhiubh sin aig am bheil Gàidhlig. Tha ceàrnan dhe'n eilean anns am bheil an sluagh 'nan cainnt cho Gàidhealach is a gheibhear ann an ceàrna sam bith de Ghàidhealtachd na h-Alba. Tha iad air an dòighean atharrachadh, oir tha iad a' cur eòlais air goireasan air nach eil iadsan a dh'fhàgadh thall, ach 'nan cainnt is 'nan còmhradh tha iad fhathast cho Gàidhealach ri fàd mòine.

Gheibhear sgìreachdan anns am bheil an sluagh, sean is òg, comasach gu leòr air Beurla labhairt, ach eadarra fhéin agus ri fear-cuairt aig am bi i, cha chleachd iad am bitheantas ach a' Ghàidhlig. Ma tha Ghàidhlig a' dol a dh'fhaighinn bàs ann an Ceap Breatainn, chan ann air chabhaig. Tha an latha air siubhal anns am biodhte dèanamh tàire air an t-seana chainnt seo, eadhan le a càirdean. Àireamh bhliadhnachan air ais, nuair bha eòlas gann, agus am fear aig an robh beagan Beurla air a mheas 'na àrd-sgoilear, cha robh iad tearc a theireadh gum bu chòir cur ás do'n Ghàidhlig. Cha chluinnear daoine labhairt air a' mhodh sin an-diugh. Tha iad a' toirt fa-near, mar nach robh muinntir an àma sin, gum bheil cothrom aig fear dà chainnt nach eil aig fear na h-aon chainnt ann an toirt a-mach foghlaim; a bharr air sin gur i cainnt an sinnsir, anns am bheil móran de'n eachdraidh agus an t-iomlan de'n litreachas ri fhaotainn, agus gur cainnt i air am bheil àrd-fhoghlamaichean a' cur luach mór, agus mar sin fhéin, gum bu mhór am beud a leigeil bàs gun deagh adhbhar.

Gu leigeil fhaicinn cho fìor Ghàidhealach is a tha Ceap Breatainn, faodar iomradh a thoirt air àireamh nan àiteachan 's am bheil Gàidhlig air a searmonachadh is air a cleachdadh an co-cheangal ri nithean cràbhach. Buinidh na Gàidheil gu ìre bhig uile do dhà eaglais, an Eaglais Chléireach, agus an Eaglais Chaitligeach. Aig na Cléirich tha air an eilean naodh deug air fhichead eaglais is àite-searmonachaidh agus chan eil ach sia dhiubh sin anns nach eil Gàidhlig air a searmonachadh. Aig àm a bhith sgrìobhadh seo, tha cóig deug air fhichead minister suidhichte aca agus tha naoidh air fhichead dhiubh a' searmonachadh Gàidhlig.

Aig na Caitligich, tha seachd deug air fhichead parraist, agus chan eil ach sia dhiubh gun Ghàidhlig. Tha dà fhichead is aon sagart aca ann an seirbhis agus is luchd Gàidhlig a h-aon deug air fhichead dhiubh. Nan rachamaid gu luchd na Pàrlamaid, chitheamaid gur Gàidheil is luchd Gàidhlig ceathrar de'n chóignear a tha sinn a' cur do Àrd-Phàrlamaid Chanada, agus cóignear de'n ochdnar a tha 'dol do Phàrlamaid Nobha Scotia. Agus do thaobh nan comhairleach, de'm bheil ann an comhairlean nan ceithir siorrachdan, trì fichead is ochd deug – is có ghearaineadh air an gainnead? – is Gàidheil a bhruidhneas Gàidhlig leth cheud is a h-ochd. Agus cha bu chòir a leigeil á cuimhne gur ann an Sidni, ceann-bhaile an eilein, a tha an aon phàipear Gàidhlig a tha air uachdar an t-saoghail – am *Mac-Talla*.

Ann an caochladh cheàrnan de'n eilean tha na Gàidheil a thàinig ás na h-aon àiteachan air suidheachadh còmhladh. Ann am Mira, sgìreachd mhór a tha deas air Sidni, chan fhaighear ach Uibhistich; ann an St. Anns, an Siorrachd Bhictoria, agus aig na Caoil Bheaga, gheibhear muinntir Leódhuis is na h-Earadh; aig Grand River, is àiteachan eile timcheall air, gheibhear muinntir Ghearrloch is Loch Aills – tha grunn theaghlaichean á Gearrloch mar an ceudna air Beinn nan Gearrloch; tha àireamh de na Sgiathanaich timcheall Hogamah 's air cùl Bhaddeck; tha na Barraich air taobh deas Lochan a Bhras d' Or, is air an taobh tuath eadar Sidni is na Caoil Mhóra; tha Muilich, Collaich, Rumaich, Tiristich is Mucanaich an ceann a deas Siorrachd Inbhir Nis; agus Abraich, Móraraich, is Cnòideartaich an cois a' chladaich o Chaolas Chanso gu Margaree.

Gheibhear cuid de na h-àiteachan air an ainmeachadh air àiteachan anns an t-seann dùthaich: Beinn Leódhuis, Loch Uibhist, Gleann Bharra, Gleann is Beinn nan Sgiathanach, Beinn nan Gearrloch, an Abhainn Mhuileach, an Tairbeart, Solas, Baoghastal, Gleann Comhann, etc. Chan eil na h-ainmean Gàidhealach, co-dhiù, cho lìonmhor is a shaoileamaid a bhitheadh iad, gu seachd sònraichte on bha cuid de na h-àiteachan gus o chionn ghoirid a' dol fo ainmean cho mi-fhreagarrach ris "An Éiphit," "Sodom," "An Tuirc," is "Bengal," ged a b' fhearr iad sin fhéin na na h-ainmean àrd-fhuaimneach gun bhrìgh gun bhladh, a thugadh air iomadh àite o chionn beagan bhliadhnachan.

Chan urrainnear anns an eachdraidh ghoirid seo sgrìobhadh gu mionaideach mu gach car a chuir na Gàidheil dhiubh on dh'fhàg iad tìr nam beann gus an latha an-diugh, ach thugadh ionnsaigh air cunntas aithghearr agus fìrinneach a thoirt air an imrich – an càradh 's an dùthaich thall – na nithean a ghluais iad gu falbh aiste – na deuchainnean tro'n deachaidh iad a' dèanamh dhachaighean dhaibh fhéin 's an dùthaich seo – agus an soirbheachadh a chuir am Freastal orra fhéin is air an cloinn on shuidhich iad air tùs anns a' "Choille Ghruamaich."[32]

Translation

Complaints can often be heard among the Gaels, in every country in which they can be found, about foreign customs. They have been creeping in, bit by bit, displacing Highland customs and they cannot be stopped. The same thing is happening in other countries, the customs and practices of the little countries becoming eclipsed and the customs and practices of the large countries taking their place. It is natural for the matter to continue until eventually the majority of the world will become like a single country and a single society, or else until the populations of countries feel remorse and return to the habits of their own forefathers.

It could hardly be imagined that a change in custom could cause a brave, patriotic people, such as the Gaels were, to migrate across the ocean, but there is no doubt that the change in habits that came over them as a society after the Jacobite Rising of 1745 is the cause for this short history to be written today. Until that time, the Gaels were divided into clans in which each chieftain was like the father of a large family and the entire clan like his children. In those days, the will of the chieftain was, to a large extent, the will of the clan, and the good of the clan was the good of the chieftain. When the time came to host a cattle raid or to pursue enemies, they were as a single person: during peace time, every man was a farmer, and during war time, every man was a soldier.

And there is no doubt that if it weren't for the Jacobite Rising of 1745, the majority of the Gaels would have stayed in the

Highlands, and their descendants would be there today fishing, hunting and going to the sheiling as was the custom during the era of Duncan Ban. But that was not their fate. It was their lot to be scattered across the globe, and the Battle of Culloden and the harsh English legislation that came after it were responsible for initiating diaspora. If they had been left under the older system, in the freedom of the mountains, not many of them would have ever moved from the land of their ancestors, but under the new order they did so under duress. Peace was kept from year to year, but they felt confined by being kept from the privilege of coming and going as they once enjoyed.

The bonds of kinship and loyalty that previously connected the clans to the chieftains were broken. The chieftain could not call out his troops to battle any longer, and bit by bit, he came to be losing his role as the father of his people and to become a landlord, and they became his minor tenantry and crofters. This awoke a spirit of restlessness in the hearts of the people and before too many years had passed, small groups of them began to emigrate across the ocean. At the same time, the chieftains began to spend more of their time in the Lowlands and there they rejected the customs of the Highlands, and lost their intimacy with their kinsfolk. And as they lost their intimacy with them, they lost their sympathy for them and thereby were prepared for their future deeds.

Many of them spent their money prodigiously when participating in grand and festive social gatherings in the big cities. They did not have vast stores of money, but even though they did not, they had to keep up with those who were wealthy. Therefore, they went into debt year after year, until finally many of them had to relinquish the estates that they received from their ancestors and that originally belonged to the clan as much as they belonged to the chieftain.

At the time that this was happening, sheep and cattle were valued at high prices and in order to enhance their fortunes, they [the chieftains] began to raise sheep and livestock. When they began to run out of land, they started to evict the people in order to make room for the animals. Many of those who settled

SETTLEMENT

in Canada were exiled in this manner. Doubtlessly, many others came of their own free will, after they had been encouraged by those who came here before them; but it is certain that if the first groups had not been sent over against their will, there would be very few people of Gaelic ancestry in Canada today.

It was around the year 1784 that the Highland Clearances began. The Duke of Atholl is claimed to have been the first to begin this merciless work, but he was not long at it when the other chieftains followed his example. The population was cleared from Strathglass, from Glengarry, from Knoydart, and from Lochaber between 1784 and 1805. After that, many were sent out of Caithness. And in the islands: Rum was cleared in the year 1826, and Muck in 1828. Many were evicted out of North Uist in the year 1849 and from South Uist and Barra in the year 1851. All of this was done in order to make room for cattle and sheep. The Lowlands of Scotland and England are suitable for growing grains, but the tall mountains of the Highlands were better for raising cattle and sheep; and the possessors of the land thought that there was a good opportunity to put together a fortune if they could get rid of the indigenous population and to stock the mountains, where the farmers' cattle would be grazing in the summer, with [their own] sheep and cattle.

Mention will not here be made of every oppression and injustice that this poor population experienced who were leaving their country. Neither will a judgement be made on those who were engaged in the merciless work of eviction. Most of them have already been convicted by a judge greater than the earthly judges. Some of them have been blotted out entirely, without a single living member of their lineage on the face of the earth, and there are others who have left descendants who do not own an inch of the estates of their ancestors. Injustice and misdeeds may gain the upper hand over right and justice, but even in this world, the evil-doers cannot escape from punishment.

And today, there are extremely few Highland estates that are possessed by the descendants of those who were responsible for the Clearances. It would be proper to state here that there were many of the chieftains who did not put any pressure at all on the tenantry to leave their estates. They helped those who were willing to leave, but they dealt kindly and justly with those who stayed; and today, the descendants of those chieftains and the populations that are on their estates are getting along peacefully and amiably, without one side finding fault with the other.

In the old country, our forefathers' fortune was rather poor according to our own perceptions, who are used to modern comforts and plentitude. A man who had ten or twelve acres of land, ten to twelve milch-cows and a small herd of sheep was a large-scale farmer. They lived in thatched houses in which there were no more than two or three rooms, some of which would have a chimney and some of which would not. They lacked many things that their descendants in this country would look upon as things they could not live without, but that is not to say that they were not to a great degree happy. Although they did not have every convenience and luxury that we utilize, they had something better: being content with their circumstances. Although they were not wealthy, they were not conscious of it and therefore they did not miss it. They had plenty of food and clothing, they had health and well-being, and they enjoyed peace and kinship among each other.

The way of life that they had in the old country prepared them for sustaining themselves in the new world. They were accustomed to traversing the heather and climbing the moors, to cutting and harvesting peat, and those habits hardened them for the traversing of hills and glens, enduring snow, and felling the forests of this country. There were many challenges and difficulties that faced them on this side of the great ocean, and they were prepared for them by the One who never put a burden on a back that was not capable of carrying it.

They came over in small groups from year to year, one boat-load this year, two boat-loads the next year, and one or two more the third year. There was no such thing as steamboats in those times and the sailing ships were slow and unpredictable. They had to endure many difficulties besides seasickness. Many of the captains were not above taking advantage of the poor people who had entrusted their lives and possessions to them in the process of emigrating.

Gaels did not initially set their course for Cape Breton: it was the last place that they started to arrive. Many of them settled in Prince Edward Island as early as 1769, and four years after that, the first immigrant ship arrived at Pictou. Although they flooded in to those two places every year thereafter, not one came to Cape Breton until more than twenty years had passed. It was between 1791 and 1795 that a number of those who colonized the mainland at the Strait of Canso, across from Cape Breton, came [to the island] and they settled on the west coast, some around Judique and others around Mabou Harbour. A few years after that, ships began to come to the eastern side of the island. The first one arrived at Sydney in the year 1802, on the sixteenth day of the first month of autumn. There were more than 104 families onboard—about 300 people, both young and old.

After that, the ships came fairly frequently, and Cape Breton was filling up as quickly as Prince Edward Island and the mainland had before that. Not so many were coming after the year 1828, and in the year 1843, the last ship came and Highland emigration to Cape Breton stopped. "The man who stays settled has little understanding of the distresses of the seaman." This is true of those of us who are alive in Cape Breton today who did not see or endure all of the hardships and crises and distresses that our forefathers went through.

The majority of them came over without anything at hand that would sustain them to the end of a year, and they had no choice but to wrestle with the forest in order to survive. Initially, they constructed cabins in which they would prepare food and sleep until they were capable of erecting better homes. After that, as time and opportunities allowed before the onset of winter, they would, with the help of neighbours, if they had any, who would never be asked without a positive response, assist in constructing a better house, even though their offspring today wouldn't believe that there was any improvement. This house would be made from logs fitted into one another, with the gaps between them stuffed with moss, carved wood or sawed boards as a floor, and the roof thatched with tree bark. There would be a chimney in one end of this cabin, to keep the family warm and give them light.

The woods were plentiful and they had no lack of firewood. Potatoes would usually be the first crops that they planted, and for a great deal of the year their food consisted of that flavoured with fish and venison. After a year or two, they would plant oats, wheat and barley, and they would begin to raise some sheep and other livestock. The birds and small animals of the woods were the enemies of the crops and the large wild beasts were [enemies] to the animals; many fields of seed were ruined by the squirrels; many a good milch-cow and sheep provided a feast in the bear's den. During the years that they were conquering the forest they were not without their own earthly tribulations, tribulations and hardships about which we have no knowledge, and which we would not be able to withstand. But despite that, they shared much enjoyment among themselves about which we are also ignorant, and no small number of them reached a great old age before they were called away, an age that those who live in the luxury and plentitude of our day will not reach.

As the years passed, so did the great forest pass away; the leveled places became larger and grew closer together. One by one, the log-houses were abandoned and the population took habitation in houses that were larger, better and better lit. The sheep and livestock grew more numerous, and the diligent enjoyed success.

Roads opened up throughout the country, schools and churches were built. Undoubtedly, many advances could come to the country which have not; but is there a country about which this could not be said? And it's not every country about which it could be said that it was transformed, during the space of a single lifetime, from a forested wilderness to a fertile, cultivated land in which many people are enjoying prosperity and in which there is very little true poverty, as can be said truly about Cape Breton.

They would have made further advancement if they had stuck to the land better than they did. But it is many years since the young people began to leave the land of their youth as their forefathers had left the land of their ancestors. The cities of the United States and the high wages that are being paid in numerous areas are drawing them away from their homes. The number of them who do not expect to return when they leave is very small, and many are doing that, but it is only after they have spent the most productive days of their lives in a foreign country, and the properties, that were all of that time left in the hands of old people, have degenerated so badly that they will take many years of hard labour before they can provide a proper livelihood again.

It may be that this will change yet and that those people who at this point disparage working on the land will find satisfaction in it. Although some of those who left have fared well, the majority, who are the hewers of wood and drawers of water for strangers, have not increased their prosperity at all, when they could be lords on their own properties, without want or deprivation.

But despite this out-migration, that has greatly increased the restless spirit that the young Gaels inherited as the legacy of their ancestors, not so many are leaving as to de-Gaelicize the island. Although the lands in many places are neglected, they have not been sold and are not falling into the hands of other peoples. Thus, every place that was cultivated by Gaels initially is still in the possession of Gaels, and they will be until they [the owners] relinquish the devotion for and bond to the childhood home that was ever intrinsic to the Gaelic constitution.

It is estimated that altogether about 25,000 Gaels immigrated to Cape Breton. Three times that many of their descendants, if not more, are there today, and it can be said without deviating from the truth that two-thirds of them can speak Gaelic. There are pockets of the island in which the population is as Gaelic in their speech as can be found in any pocket of the Highlands of Scotland. They have adapted their customs, since they are gaining familiarity with conveniences that were unknown to those who were left behind [in Scotland], but in their speech and their conversation, they are still as Gaelic as a sod of peat.

Areas can be found in which the population, young and old, are capable enough of speaking English, but between themselves and to travellers who can speak it, they generally will not use anything but Gaelic. If Gaelic is going to die in Cape Breton, it is not in a hurry. The day has passed in which this ancient language was denigrated, even by its friends. A number of years back, when learning was scarce, and the man who had a little bit of English was considered a great scholar, there were many people who said that Gaelic ought to be stamped out. People are not heard speaking in that manner today. They are aware, as people of those past times were not, that a bilingual person has advantages that a monolingual person does not have in learning; and on top of that, that [Gaelic] is the speech of their ancestors in which there is a great deal of history and an abundance of literature to be had, and that it is a language in which high-ranking scholars place considerable value, and thus, that it would be a great loss if it was left to die without a good reason.

In order to show how truly Gaelic Cape Breton is, an account could be made of the number of places in which Gaelic is used for delivering sermons and for devotional purposes. The Gaels belong to a very large extent to two churches, the Presbyterian Church and the Catholic Church. The Presbyterians of the island have thirty-nine churches and places of worship, and there are only six of those at which Gaelic is not used for sermons. At the time that this has been written, there are thirty-five ministers settled among them and twenty-nine of them deliver sermons in Gaelic.

The Catholics have thirty-seven parishes and Gaelic is absent in only six of those. They have forty-one priests in service and thirty-one of them are Gaelic speakers. If we were to go to the members of Parliament, we would see that four of the five people that we send to the national Parliament of Canada are Gaels and Gaelic speakers, and five of the eight people who attend the General Assembly of Nova Scotia. And regarding councilors, who come from the councils of four counties, there are seventy-eight—and who can complain of their scarcity?—fifty-eight of them are Gaels who speak Gaelic. And we should not forget that

SETTLEMENT

Sydney, the capital of the island, is the home to the only Gaelic newspaper in the entire world—*Mac-Talla*.

In some pockets of the island, the Gaels who came from the same original locales are settled together. In Mira, a large region south of Sydney, only Uist-people can be found; in St. Ann's, in Victoria County, and in the Little Narrows, the people of Lewis and Harris are to be found; at Grand River, and other places around it, the people of Gairloch and Lochalsh are to be found—likewise, there are a few families from Gairloch at Gairloch Mountain; there is a number of Skye-people around Whycocomagh and the Rear of Baddeck; the people of Barra are on the south side of the Bras d' Or lakes and on the north shore between Sydney and the Big Narrows; there are people from Mull, Coll, Rum, Tiree and Muck in the south part of Inverness County; and people from Lochaber, Morar, and Knoydart along the shore from the Strait of Canso to Margaree.

Some of the places have been named after places in the old country: Lewis Mountain, Loch Uist, Barra Glen, Skye Glen, Skye Mountain, Gairloch Mountain, Mull River, Tarbert, Sollas, Boisdale, Glencoe, etc. The Gaelic names are not as plentiful as we would expect them to be, most especially since some of the places were until recently going under names as unsuitable as "Egypt," "Sodom," "Turkey," and "Bengal," even though those names themselves were better than the loud, meaningless, and vapid names that were given to many places a few years ago.

This short history cannot make a detailed exposition of every undertaking of the Gaels from the time they left the Highlands to the present, but an attempt has been made to provide a brief and truthful account about their migration—their circumstances in the old country—the things that motivated them to leave it—the tribulations through which they went building homes for themselves in this country—and the success that Providence has provided for them and their children who initially settled in "The Gloomy Forest."

13: The Song of Clandonald

The following song-poem was composed by Iain MacGilleFhaolain about the Highland settlement in Alberta that was christened "Clandonald." Being in praise of a place and the people living there, it is not surprising that the author modelled it on another Gaelic song of a similar nature, "Moladh na Lanndaidh," which is in praise of the island of Islay and its people.

The Clandonald colony was the most ambitious of the many emigration schemes undertaken by Father Anndra MacDhòmhnaill (R. Andrew MacDonell). In 1925 he purchased the 32,000 acres for the settlement from a Belgian corporation based in Winnipeg by negotiating for a loan of $100,000 with the president of the Canadian Pacific Railway, the Scottish Immigrant Aid Society and the British government. Father Dòmhnall Mac an t-Saoir (Donald Macintyre) of Barra (referred to in line 47) came to help with arrangements on the site. Although the Scottish Immigrant Aid Society was non-denominational in scope, Father Anndra was leveraging its resources to create settlements of a strongly Catholic nature. This was only one of many criticisms levelled against him and his numerous elaborate emigration schemes which ultimately spurred the Canadian government to revoke his credentials as an official agent in 1929.[33]

The letter accompanying the song-poem when it was printed in the Nova Scotian newspaper *The Casket* demonstrates an interest in maintaining social networks across Gaelic communities.

> Seo duanag a chaidh a dhèanamh an taobh an iar Chanada le aon de na Gàidheil a thàinig imrich ás na h-Eileanan o chionn beagan bhliadhnaichean. 'S mór an toileachadh a bheir e do Ghàidheil na h-Albann Nuaidh a chluinntinn gu bheil an luchd-dàimh an Alberta a' soirbheachadh cho gasta.

> Here is a little poem that was made in the west of Canada by one of the Gaels who emigrated from the islands a few years ago. It will give the Gaels of Nova Scotia great enjoyment to hear that their relations in Alberta are prospering so well.

The text itself reflects the separate but interrelated layers of identity, sometimes focusing specifically on the Hebridean origin of the settlers (lines 1 and 13), sometimes celebrating a pan-Gaelic identity in opposition to the non-Gaels (lines 6 and 21), and at other times declaiming their common kinship through Clan Donald, as embodied in the name of the settlement itself (lines 4, 12, 20, 28 and 51). The author's Catholic identity is evident in the references to churches established in the colony (lines 49-53). Religious affiliation was certainly a factor that drove migration from the Southern Hebrides to Canada, both in the sense that the major landholder in the islands at this time—Lady Emily (see poem 4.10)—was unsympathetic to her Catholic tenants and that Hebrideans preferred better options than relocating to the Scottish Lowlands where "to be a Catholic ... in the 1920s was to be a second-class citizen."[34]

This song-poem again demonstrates how Highland militarism, and symbols of militaristic triumphalism, offered a form of psychological compensation for the Gaels' experience of socio-economic marginalization. This paean to the Gaelic colony draws on a literary tradition of extolling the battle skills of warriors defending or winning "sword-land" in hard-fought conquest against enemies.[35] It also likens the clearing of forests to warfare fought against nature itself (lines 33-34 and 37-39) or the reaping of harvests (lines 35-36 and 40).

A family of renowned Gaelic storytellers were among those who went to Clandonald. In his celebrated collection of Gaelic oral narratives entitled *Popular Tales of the West Highlands* (1860), John F. Campbell described Dòmhnall Mac a' Phì of South Uist as one of the most impressive storytellers that he had met.[36] In 1979 Dr. Margaret Mackay recorded one of the older settlers of Clandonald with the same surname telling a Gaelic wonder tale that was very similar to ones recorded more than a century before by Campbell's fieldworkers in Dòmhnall Mac a' Phì's neighbourhood in the Hebrides.[37]

Original Text

1   Hó na h-Eileanaich, ho gù,
     Choisinn buaidh 's gach ceàrn do'n Chrùn;
     Tha 'bhuaidh sin ac' an-diugh, is cliù,
     Air fearann ùr Chlann Dòmhnaill.

5   Ge bu bhuan sibh fhéin 's ur clann,
     Gabhail seilbh am measg nan Gall,
     Is bochd an àireamh bhith cho gann
     Nach faighte a-nall an corr dhibh?

     Bheirte nall an corr gun dàil,
10   Is cha bhi orr' aithreachas gu bràth;

B' i mo dhùrachd iad bhith tàmh
'Nar nàbachd an Clann Dòmhnaill.

Sliochd nan Eileanan an Iar:
Có bheir buaidh orr' ann an gnìomh?
15 Is iomadh blàr 's na rinn iad dìol:
Bu leo riamh a' chòmhrag.

Clann nan laoch tha làidir treun
Air muir is air a dhèanadh feum –
Nàmhaid riamh, cha d' chuir ra-treut
20 Air do threud, Chlann Dòmhnaill.

Thug clann nan Gall dhuinn coinneamh chruaidh
Air son ainm a' bhail' 'thoirt bhuainn;
Ach chuir an leòghann orra ruaig –
Bu dual dhi bhith 'gan spòltadh.

25 An cnoc a b' àirde 's a' bhail' ùr,
Gun sgaoil sinn bratach clann mo rùin,
Is an leòghann chreuchdach air a cùl
Ag innse cliù Chlann Dòmhnaill.

O fhuair sinn gach goireas dh'ar miann
30 Is nì sinn tòiseachadh gu dian
Air an talamh 'bhristeadh sìos,
Gu dèan sinn biadh is stòras.

'Fhearaibh tapaidh, bithibh cruaidh!
Oibrichibh gu math an tuagh;
35 Bidh a' choille leibh a-nuas
Mar speal a' buain an eòrna.

Is ged tha i doirbh a' toirt á sàs
Na bheil fo'n talamh dhith a' fàs,
Siud na fir a bheir i barr
40 Gun dèan iad barr is beò-shlaint'.

Chì sibh iad a' falbh gun dàil,
Ann an carbad nach bi cearr,
Cuid dhiubh, fhuair iad mar tha
Is b' e àit' an àigh, Clann Dòmhnaill.

45 Bitheamaid taingeal 'Dhia nan dùl
Air son gach cothroim thug E dhuinn;
Maighstir Dòmhnall air ar cùl
'Gar stiùradh, is Maighstir Anndra.

> Th' an Eaglais Naomh-sa, 'Dhia nan Gràs,
> 50 A' sìor sgaoileadh anns gach ceàrn;
> Th' an Clann Dòmhnall an-diugh dhiubh dhà
> Is bidh gu bràth 'toirt glòir dhut.
>
> Bidh mi crìochnachadh mo dhàin
> Guidhe sonas dhuibh gu bràth:
> 55 Saoghal fada is cridhe slàn
> Is ur sporan làn an-còmhnaidh.[38]

Translation

(1-4) *Hó*, the Islanders, *ho gù*, who won victory in every region for the Crown; they enjoy that victory today, and renown, on the new land of Clandonald.

(5-8) Although you yourselves and your descendants had long enjoyed land-ownership among the non-Gaels, it is a shame that you are so small in number: should we not bring over the rest of you?

(9-12) Let the rest be brought over immediately and they will never regret it; it is my sincere wish for them to reside in our neighbourhood in Clandonald.

(13-16) The people of the Western Isles: who can outdo them? They meted out retribution in many wars and they always won the conflict.

(17-20) The descendants of the warriors who are strong and brave at sea and whatever was needed—an enemy never forced your tribe to retreat, o Clan Donald.

(21-24) The non-Gael has made a hard confrontation with us in order to take the name of the township away from us; but the lion forced them to flee—it is in her hereditary nature to hack them up!

(25-28) Let us unfurl the banner of my beloved clan on the highest hill in the new township, with the ferocious lion behind it proclaiming the renown of Clandonald.

(29-32) We received every resource that we desire and we shall zealously begin to break down the land until we can make food and wealth.

(33-36) O valiant lads, be hardy! Work the axe well; you will fell the forest like the scythe harvests the barley.

(37-40) And although it is difficult to pull out everything that is growing underground, those are the men who can wrest it up until they create crops and a livelihood.

(41-44) You will see them leaving immediately in a splendid wagon, they have already got some of them, and Clandonald is where prosperity can be found.

(45-48) Let us be thankful to God of the elements for all of the opportunities He has given to us; with Father Donald at our back, steering us, and Father Andrew.

(49-52) The Holy Church, o God of the Graces, is constantly spreading throughout every corner [of the world]; Clandonald has two of them today and they will eternally praise you.

(53-56) I will conclude my song-poem wishing happiness for you always; a long life and a healthy heart, and for your sporran to be full always.

14: The Gaels of Winnipeg

As the author of this text (identified only as "Neacail") reminds us, Scottish Gaels were among the earliest European explorers and colonizers of this part of Canada, drawn in by the fur trade. In 1811 the 5th Earl of Selkirk initiated the Red River Colony near Winnipeg. Highlanders cleared from Kildonan by the Countess of Caithness arrived in 1813, naming their new settlement "Kildonan" after their old home.[39]

Neacail's depiction of bloody conflict between European fur traders and "wild Indians" is a poor representation of the people actually involved in the Battle of Seven Oaks in 1816 and the reasons for their dispute. Gaels were, in fact, on both sides of the hostilities. Metis trappers, under the leadership of the half-Gaelic Cuthbert Grant, supplied the furs to the North West Company and were directly challenged by the establishment of Selkirk's colony. Selkirk had bought a controlling share in the Hudson Bay Company, which was in competition with the "Nor'Westers" for territory and control of resources. Tensions escalated between the two sides for months before a violent confrontation broke out. The Metis victory started the weakening of the North West Company that led to its merger with the HBC in 1821.[40]

SETTLEMENT

The fur trade attracted a small number of immigrants from many countries: Bibles were ordered in 1826 for the congregations of the Red River Valley in English, Gaelic, German, Danish, Italian and French. In 1831 the Hudson Bay Company began recruiting Gaels from the Isle of Lewis to work in the region, although the number of such Highland immigrants remained small until after the Dominion of Canada annexed the region as the province of Manitoba in 1870.[41]

There were enough Gaelic speakers in Winnipeg in 1925 to warrant a visit from Highland missionaries, and a correspondent writing from the city to *The Stornoway Gazette* (printed on the Isle of Lewis, Scotland) called for the establishment of a church and minister to serve the Gaelic-speaking population there.[42] The author of this letter expresses disappointment that so little had been done to aid in sustaining the Gaels as an ethnic group in and around Winnipeg.

Original Text

B' iad na Gàidheil a' cheud mhuinntir a stéidhich anns a' cheàrn seo de Chanada. Ann an 1799, bha mu thuaiream leth[43] malairt nam bian molach 'ga chur air n-adhart leis na Gàidheil. Roimhe seo, dh'fhoillsich Alasdair MacCoinnich roinn mhór de Chanada an Iar. Còmhla ris, bha Alasdair MacAoidh a rannsaich am fearann mu thimcheall steud-shruthan bras' Abhainn mhór MhicCoinnich, a tha air ainmeachadh air an duine uasal sin.

Gu misneachail treunmhor, gun eagal, gun fhiamh, chum iad an Iar (eadhain a' bhàis) oir aig an àm sin, bha an tìr làn de dh'Innseanaich fhiadhaich, gus mu dheireadh, an déidh naoidh mìosan de thìm, ràinig iad Cuan ciùin na h-Àird' an Iar. B' e Gàidheal misneachail eile, Mr. Sìm Friseal, a chaidh suas an Abhainn Friseal anns a' bhliadhna 1807.

Fad àireamh bhliadhnaichean, bha aimhreit agus comh-spairn fuilteach eadar na marsantan is na daoine malairt air an darna taobh, agus na h-Innseanaich fhiadhaich air an taobh eile. Anns na làithean dorcha muladach nuair a bha iad a' fuadach nan Catach á seilbh an fhearainn air a' Ghàidhealtachd, thàinig àireamh dhiubh bho'n t-siorramachd sin agus rinn iad àiteachas an-seo, mu thimcheall Kildonan.

Bha pailteas Gàidhlig 'ga labhairt anns an dùthaich seo aig an àm sin, agus mar an ceudna, misneach agus treubhantas. "Is coma leam cogadh no sìth," theireadh iad, agus rinn na marsantan móran buannachd leotha.

Bha seann duine 'nar measg, MacGill-Ìosa, aig an robh cuimhne nuair a bha iad a' fuadach nam Frangach á baile mór Winnipeg, agus a chunnaic iad a' snàmh thairis air an abhainn, a' teicheadh air falbh. Aig àm cruinneachadh nan Gàidheal anns a' gheamhradh, sheinneadh iad uile an t-òran Gàidhlig, "Hé 'n clò dubh, och o ró seinn," a' bualadh an dòrn air a' bhòrd a' cumail tìm, agus le pailteas de'n uisge-bheatha mun cuairt. "Chuireadh e blàths air a' chridhe nuair bhiodh e fuar."

Ach 's e atharrachadh iongantach a tha ri fhaicinn a-nis. Dh'fhàs fàsaichean an Iar làn de shluagh a thàinig ás gach tìr de'n Roinn Eòrpa, agus tha iad uile cumail suas an cànain dùthchasaich le pàipearan-naidheachd agus leabhraichean agus a' co-oibreachadh mar seo, tha iad a' cinntinn air adhart gu math.

Air an latha an-diugh, tha na Gàidheil air an sgapadh gu h-iomlan anns gach ceàrn agus chan eil móran dhiubh an aon àite sam bith mar sin. Chaill cuid dhiubh an cànain agus cleachdainnean an sinnsreadh. Bha mi am bùth leabhraichean as motha a th' anns a' bhaile seo o chionn ghoirid agus cha robh leabhar sam bith an Gàidhlig 'ga chumail ann. Cha robh eadhan *Eachdraidh na h-Albann*. Am bheil e iongantach, ma-tà, gun robh na ceudan fhear a thàinig o'n Ghàidhealtachd gu'n obair ann an Canada an Iar, agus a' mhór-chuid dhiubh ag obair air son am bòrd? Nam biodh na seann Ghàidheil air a chéile leanailt nuair a thàinig iad do'n dùthaich ùir seo, cha bhiodh a' chùis mar seo. Bha a h-uile cinneadh eile a' dèanamh sin agus tha iad nas làidire a-nis an àireamh. Tha a' mhór-chuid de na h-Eileanaich a thàinig a-mach an-seo mu thimcheall Féidh Ruaidh. Bha mi an-sin fad mìos an 1910 agus chan fhaca mi fiadh fad is a bha mi ann. Tha an ceàrn sin glé àrd, ceithir mìle troigh nas àirde na a' mhuir.

Chunnaic mi na h-Eileanaich fad is a bha iad a' fantainn am Winnipeg air an turas an Iar. Bha roinn dhiubh a thàinig anns a' Chogadh Mhór, gaisgich threun agus eireachdail. Bha pailteas cloinne agus seann daoine 'nam measg. Cheannaich na gillean ubhlan agus òr-mheasan eile, agus fhuair gach bodach agus leanabh criomag mar bu ghnàth leis na Gàidheil. Cha chuir gu bàs le goirt no fuachd na feumaich, fad is a bhios Gàidheal beò. Cha robh sgàil sannt féineil an t-saoghail an-seo, bha na pàistean neo-dhàna, gun chomas ruigheachd air an toradh bhrosnachail.

Chuir mi pàipear a dh'ionnsaigh fear dhiubh, balachan tapaidh a bha air luinge an àm a' chogaidh, agus fhuair mi fios air n-ais ag aithris gun robh e fad Latha Nollaig a' leughadh an *Oban Times*, am pàipear a chuir mi ga ionnsaigh, agus gum b' e a' cheud phàipear a chunnaic e anns an dùthaich seo. Thuirt e nach robh an dòigh a bh' aca ag àiteach a' còrdadh ri feadhainn dhiubh. Bha e ag ràdhainn, ged a tha na h-Eileanaich freagarrach cruadalach, gidheadh, bha na tuathanaich choigreach fòirneartach. Chan eil fhios ro mhath agam mu thimcheall nan gnothaichean sin, ach tha deagh bharail agam air fulangas nan daoine bochda anns an dùthaich chruaidh a tha seo.

Bha mi an Alberta anns an t-samhradh 1919, agus aig an àm sin, bha teas anabarrach anns an dùthaich. Bha na treudan a' bàsachadh le cion an fheòir a bha loisgte agus leis a' phàthadh. Bha connadh agus guail cho gann is gum b' éiginn do chuid de theaghlaichean an àirneis a losgadh anns a' gheamhradh fhuar.

Tha na taighean-sgoile gann agus fada air leth. Air uairibh, bidh am buntàta 'ga reòthadh anns an talamh agus an-dràsta is a-rithist, marbhaidh an reòthadh-samhraidh na meanglan. Gu ainmig agus gu tearc, chì na Gàidheil fògradh pàipear-naidheachd dhachaigh, mar nach biodh caraid còir aca anns an t-seann dùthaich. Gheibh iad naidheachdan an t-saoghail air son còig seantachan, ach cha leasaich sin an deagh bheusan. Thàinig na daoine bochda seo fo'n bharail gun robh a' Ghàidhealtachd ro lìonta de shluagh (gidheadh, tha talamh treabhachail gu leòr an-sin fhathast) agus gun robh na cruaidh-chàsan aca seachad nuair thàinig iad do'n dùthaich seo. Tha mi duilich air son iad a bhith 'nam fir-fhearainn agus leis a' ghort agus cìsean troma, chaill iad na h-uile.

Is iomadh Gàidheal ionraic òg a tha air a mhealladh le fiosan mearachdach, le companaich chealgach. Air son gum bheil fìor Ghàidheal 'na dhuine uasal, cha chuir e amharas air neach sam bith eile. Air an taobh eile, tha an dùthaich seo slàinteil, grianail agus gu tric sìolmhor. Tha àitean anns an Iar far an urrainn beathachadh taitneach a bhith aig fear, ach chan eil iad a' gairm móran mu na h-àiteachan sin.[44]

Translation

The Gaels were the first people who were established in this corner of Canada. In 1799, the Gaels were involved in conducting the fur trade. Before this, Alexander Mackenzie discovered a great deal of the west of Canada. Along with him, Alexander MacKay investigated the land around the rough rapids of the great MacKenzie River that are named after that noble man.

Courageous and brave, fearless and undaunted, they kept going westward (even to death), for at that time, the land was full of wild Indians, until finally, after nine months, they arrived at the Pacific Ocean in the West. It was another courageous Gael, Mr. Simon Fraser, who went up the Fraser River in the year 1807.

For a number of years, there was contention and bloody conflict between the merchants and the traders, on the one side, and the wild Indians on the other side. In those dark and sad days, when they were expelling the people of Caithness from the land they occupied in the Highlands, a number of them came from that region and they settled here, around Kildonan.

Plenty of Gaelic was being spoken in this area at that time, and likewise, there was courage and bravery. "It matters not to me whether there is peace or war," they would say, and the merchants profited greatly from them.

There was an old man among us, Gillies, who could remember when the French were expelled from the great city of Winnipeg, and saw them swimming across the river, fleeing. When the Gaels would gather together in the winter, they would all sing the Gaelic song, "*Hé*, the black cloth, *och o ró* sing," beating their fists on the table to keep time, with plenty of whiskey around. "It would keep the heart warm when it was cold."

But the change that is visible now is incredible. The wildernesses of the west are full of people who have come from every country in Europe, and they all maintain their native languages with newspapers and books, and cooperating thusly, they are progressing well.

Today, the Gaels are totally scattered in every direction and there are not many of them at all in any single place. Some of them have lost their language and the customs of their ancestors. I was in the largest bookshop that there is in the city a short while ago and they did not have a single book in Gaelic, not even *The History of Scotland*. Is it surprising, then, that hundreds of men came from the Highlands for their work in Western Canada and the majority of them worked for lodgings? If the older Gaels had stuck together when they came to the new world, the situation would not be like this. Every other ethnic group did that and they are stronger in numbers. The majority of the Islanders who came out here are around Red Deer. I was there for a month in 1910 and I didn't see a single deer for as long as I was there. That area is very high in altitude, four thousand feet above sea level.

I saw the Islanders when they stayed in Winnipeg on their journey westwards. There were some of them who came in the Great War, brave and handsome soldiers. There were plenty of children and old people among them. The young men bought apples and other citrus fruits, and every old man and child got a share, as is the Gaelic custom. The needy will never die from hunger or cold, for as long as a Gael is alive. The pall of the selfish greed of this world was not in evidence, and the children were well-behaved and were prevented from reaching a state of defiance.

I sent a newspaper to one of them, a fine young man who was on the ship during the war, and I got word back saying that he spent all of Christmas Day reading *The Oban Times*, the newspaper that I sent him, and that it was the first newspaper that he saw in this country. He said that the way that they were farming did not appeal to some of them. He said that although the Islanders were suitable and hardy, nonetheless, the foreign farmers were overbearing. I don't know too much about those matters, but I have a strong opinion about the suffering of the poor people in this grueling country.

I was in Alberta in the summer of 1919 and at that time, there was extreme heat in the country. The herds were dying from the shortage of grass that was scorched and from thirst. Firewood and coal was so scarce that some families had to burn their furniture in the cold winter.

The schoolhouses are few and far apart. Sometimes, potatoes freeze in the ground and now and again the summer frost kills the roots. Very infrequently, Gaels will see a stray newspaper from home, as though they didn't have a close friend in the old country. They can get the news of the world for five cents, but that will not improve their excellent virtues. These poor people came to believe that the Highlands were overcrowded with people (although there is still plenty of arable land there) and that their troubles were over when they came to this country. I am sorry that they are landowners, since with famine and heavy taxes, they lost everything.

There are many upstanding young Gaels who are deceived by faulty information and by dishonest companions. Because the true Gael is a gentleman, he does not harbour suspicions about other people. On the other hand, this country is healthy, sunny and often fertile. There are places in the west where a man can have a pleasant livelihood, but they are not inviting many people to those places.

15: The Song of the Reaper

The following song-poem was composed by Murchadh D. MacDhòmhnaill, whose family had left the Isle of Lewis when he was very young to settle in the Eastern Townships of Quebec. Like many others of his era, he travelled annually to the Prairies to work during harvest time.[45] It is perhaps not surprising that a man who lived such a restless life would write one of the most direct statements about a sense of place to be found in the Gaelic poetry of North American immigrant communities.

The opening stanza of the song is a reference to a humourous Gaelic saying: "Steòrnabhagh mór a' chaisteil, am baile as motha air an t-saoghal" (Great Stornoway of the castle, the largest city in the world). This saying pokes fun at the rustics from remote villages who were awed by the relative size of the largest urban settlement in the Outer Hebrides, although the specific target of this humour depends upon the person delivering it. The allusion to this saying in the song is appropriate, however, given that it could refer to both the original Steòrnabhagh in Lewis and the new Stornoway in Quebec.

Place names are at the very core of the message of the poem: these names commemorate the origins of the settlers and the ties between them and those that they had left behind. With the assimilation of immigrant communities, these place names have indeed proven to be one of the most enduring legacies of Highland migration, even if they are translated or transliterated into English.

The sense of loss incurred by emigration is certainly tangible in the text, especially in terms of the breaking of families and communities (lines 12-16 and 20). Like many other immigrant songs, the poet draws sharp contrasts between features of the old country and the new (lines 29-40), but in this particular text these comparisons do not carry overtly negative overtones.

Original Text

1 Chan e Steòrnabhagh Saskatchewan –
Baile as motha th' air an t-saoghal –
Ach ged bhiodh a mheudachd ainmeil,
Is ann do'n ainm thug mise gaol.

5 Chaidh a thogail air a' phràiridh
Leis na Gàidheil a thàinig nall,
Is thug iad ainm á tìr nan laoch air,
Baile caomh 's an robh iad thall.

Is toigh leam faicinn luchd na Gàidhlig
10 Anns gach ceàrnaidh de'n t-saoghal
Cumail ainm nam bailtean gràdhach
Far an dh'fhàg iad luchd an gaoil.

Dh'fhàg cuid piuthar, dh'fhàg cuid bràthair,
Dh'fhàg cuid athair is màthair chaomh;

15 Dh'fhàg cuid eile Sìne is Màiri –
    Gruagaich bhlàth d' an tug iad gaol.

    Dh'fhàg iad eilean caomh na h-Alba
    'S an robh gaisgich chalm' o thùs,
    Is sheòl iad thar a' chuain do'n fhàsach
20 Is leig iad slàn le càirdean dlùth'.

    Thog iad bailtean is thug iad ainm orr',
    Fad air falbh an dùthaich chéin:
    "Steòrnabhagh" is "Baile Bharabhais" –
    Bailtean ás an dh'fhalbh iad fhéin.

25 Chì thu cuid ann ás na h-Earadh
    'S an robh maraichean o thùs;
    Far am faighear sluagh a' chàirdeis
    Is coibhneas-gràidh a ghnàth 'nan gnùis.

    Chan fhaic thu sgadan no lìon ann
30 Is chan eil bàtan-iasgaich ann;
    Ach tha coirc' is eòrna biadht' ann
    Is cruithneachd diasach nach eil gann.

    Chan fhaic thu cruinneachadh ghruagach
    Is duanag aca luadh a' chlò;
35 Ach chì thu marcachd air eich luatha iad
    Siubhal suas am monadh mór.

    Chan fhaic thu crodh-laoigh air àirigh
    'Gan àrach le gruagach dhonn;
    Ach 'gan ruith le marcaich shiubhlach
40 Gu lùthmhor air pràiridh lom.

    Ach ma gheibh sinn sèasan seachad
    Is gum bi Freastal gu math dhuinn,
    Théid sinn dhachaigh gu'r càirdean
    'S iad a bhios bàigheil rinn.

45 Nuair a ruigeas sinne Marston,
    Nì sinn gàirdeachas nach gann;
    Gheibh sinn coibhneas o na càirdean,
    Luchd ar gaoil a dh'fhàg sinn ann.

    Beannachd leibh a-nis, a chàirdean,
50 Luchd na Gàidhlig, beannachd leibh;
    Guidheam sìth is slàint' is sòlas
    Dhuibh an Steòrnabhagh a chaoidh.[46]

Translation

(1-4) Saskatchewan is not Stornoway—the largest city in the world—and although its size may be renowned, it is its name with which I have fallen in love.

(5-8) It was built on the prairie by the Gaels who immigrated and they gave it a name from the land of heroes, a dear town in which they lived over yonder.

(9-12) I enjoy seeing Gaelic speakers in every corner of the world keeping alive the names of their beloved towns where they left their loved ones behind.

(13-16) Some left a sister, some left a brother, some left a father and a dear mother; others left Jean and Mary—warm-hearted women with whom they fell in love.

(17-20) They left the dear island of Scotland, original home of the daring warriors, and they sailed across the ocean to the wilderness and they gave their farewell to close friends.

(21-24) They built towns and they named them, far away in a foreign land: "Stornoway" and "Barvas"—towns from which they themselves had emigrated.

(25-28) You will see some [people] from Harris, original home of the sailors; where the folk of goodwill are found with loving kindness always in their countenance.

(29-32) You will not see herring or fishing-nets there and there are no fishing-boats; but there are oats and barley for eating there, and crops of wheat in plenty.

(33-36) You will not find a gathering of girls singing a song as they full the woolen cloth; but you will see them riding fast horses, travelling up the great heights.

(37-40) You will not see cattle being raised by brown-haired women at the sheiling, but rather being driven vigorously by speedy cowboys on the bare prairie.

(41-44) But if we get past another season and Providence is good to us, we will go home to our kinsfolk, they are the ones who will show us affection.

(45-48) When we arrive at Marston, we will rejoice greatly; we will receive kindness from the kinsfolk, our beloved ones whom we left behind.

(49-52) Goodbye for now, o kinsfolk, Gaelic speakers, goodbye for now; I pray that you will have peace, health, and contentment always in Stornoway.

6 – Love and Death

It is in the praise (and dispraise) of family members, friends, and leaders of the community that we can see the greatest continuity in the functions, genres and conventions of Gaelic literature, connecting the cultural expressions of Canadian Gaels to precedents in medieval Scotland. These compositions provide the clearest demonstration of the vitality and longevity of tradition brought by immigrants with them from the Highlands to Canada: symbols, images, styles, values and practices that derive directly from medieval Gaeldom that manifest particular ways of being in the world, understanding the human community and expressing relationships between people and culture.

Gaelic song-poetry commemorates the memorable events in the community and the special achievements of its members: births, weddings, the raising of buildings, humourous misadventures, natural catastrophes, and so on. As elsewhere, poetry was a compelling vehicle for expressing and sharing emotions, not least of which was romantic love. We can expect poetic license to be exercised and hyperbole to appear in the creation of verse meant to flatter and woo the object of the bard's affections.

As already intimated in the chapter 1, however, the Gaelic literary tradition developed with the praise of social leaders as its main purpose and focus. It is in song-poems derived from this practice that we can see the most sophisticated forms of verbal expression, especially when delivered in musical performance.

The role of the warrior, protector of the *fine* and *tuath*, great in body, with immense physical strength, is both centre and apex. Through epithets, references to battles, ancestry, physical strength, weapons, loyalty, and so on, and taking these in all their direct and oblique references, and in all possible permutations, the bards produce a glorification of the warrior that permeates the poems of a brief, late manifestation of an heroic age.[1]

As this chapter demonstrates, however, poets were able to adapt literary conventions to new settings, subjects and occasions, whether by extending established practices or creating new ones.

In the New World, Gaels had title to their land, and the world of chiefs and landlords became a thing of the past, and a similar transformation in the nature of praise poetry took place. The poets of the emigrant generation, like their counterparts in Scotland, redeployed the rich Gaelic panegyric tradition in the service of new subjects, and these were the leaders and builders of New World Gaelic communities. ... [T]he poets of the emigrant generation keenly devoted themselves to the task of redeploying the panegyric tradition in the support of local leaders. Of particular prominence were the clergy. Also important were exemplars of community values, either tradition bearers or those skilled in the Gaelic arts, or persons who exhibited great loyalty to deeply held community values.[2]

Gaelic song-poetry had particular importance, and assumed heightenaed emotional expression, when the social order faced a serious crisis, such as the loss of leadership through death. It was in such circumstances that audiences needed the continuity and stability of communal values to be asserted and confirmed by the spokespeople of tradition.

The diction is codified in sets of conventional images, mostly densely concentrated in the heroic elegy composed at the point of crisis brought about by the death of a leader—in other words, when it was most necessary to reaffirm the traditional values of the community.[3]

The function of the elegy was not just to present the actual qualities and features of the subject, but to present to the community and the subject's potential successor the ideals to which they were expected to aspire. While many individuals may have been fully deserving of the praise they were given, the hyperbole inherent in the genre must be seen not as idle flattery but as archetypal depictions of the qualities and characteristics most cherished by Gaels.

> Though the bards were quick to ridicule the living in their satires, they were always willing to eulogize the dead in their elegies. If we make allowance for the exaggeration inherent in both, the two genres, apparently so antithetical, when considered in conjunction actually provide a fairly coherent portrait of the private lives of the pioneers.[4]

Gaelic poets usually begin their elegies with some description about their location, their emotional state, the time of death or when they heard about it, and a statement about the social role or capacity filled by the deceased.[5] It is also conventional for the poet to dwell on and relate details about the corpse, the carrying of the body to the grave, the placement of the remains into the coffin, and the interring of the deceased into the grave. While these details may intensify the grief of survivors and give them a focus for that grief, they also serve as a verbal record that the dead have been properly dealt with according to the time-honoured procedures and protocols of tradition.[6] Elegies also provide an occasion for poets to contemplate the human predicament and the Christian message of salvation (and damnation).

1: Elegy to Tòmas Friseal

The following song-poem was composed in 1813 by the Rev. Seumas MacGriogair, then residing in Pictou County, Nova Scotia, on the death of his close friend, Tòmas Friseal. It is thus one of the earliest surviving Scottish Gaelic elegies in Canada. It was modelled on a celebrated lament to a leader of the MacGregors of Ruadhshruth (Roro) who died early in the 17th century,[7] thus adding to the weight and formality of the emotions conveyed.

Tòmas Friseal left Scotland in 1783. He and his wife Maighread carved out a farm where New Glasgow is today.[8] MacGriogair was relieved to find someone who was qualified to assist in administering to a growing population, a man who actually had many mutual friends in Scotland.

> Ever since I accepted the Synod's appointment, I had been concerned lest I should find no elders in Pictou, and thus not have

a regular session. It was, therefore, a great happiness to me, that I now heard of three on the East River, who had been ordained in Scotland, viz., Thomas Fraser, and Simon Fraser, who had officiated in the parish of Kirkhill with my late respected and dear friend, the Rev. Alexander Fraser.[9]

As his biographer notes, Friseal and MacGriogair struck up a fast friendship: "Thomas Fraser was one of his closest companions and firmest supporters almost till his death."[10] He acquired the nickname "Deacon Thomas" on account of his duties in the church.

This elegy illustrates how the rhetoric developed by the Gaelic literati for the praise of chieftains and battle champions was transformed to pay tribute to the spiritual "warriors" of the church and the values and beliefs that they advanced. The affection between the two men is immediately conveyed from the start (lines 1-10), an intimacy that parallels that of the Highland chieftain and Gaelic poet of old. The qualities attributed by MacGriogair to his friend are much the same as those glorified in warriors: courage and intrepidity (line 17), strength (line 18), nobility (line 21), zealousness (line 22), and so on. These virtues are intentionally cultivated through individual discipline (lines 15, 18, 20, 25-28 and 38) and utilized to defend the church (lines 24). Gaelic poets of old often depicted a clan leader's hand as dispensing food and drink to his dependents or as wielding weapons; Friseal's hand is said by MacGriogair (lines 29-32) to wield the Psalms which enables him to deliver flawless songs of worship.

The same kennings used to extol the power and skills of warriors are harnessed to applaud Friseal's religious deeds and roles. He is the "ursainn-chatha" (battle-pillar) of the church, protecting it from enemies (lines 35-36). Although he leaves his antagonists wounded, these are injuries of morality inflicted through righteous living and a godly attitude (lines 37-40). Keeping up the good fight required endurance and stamina (line 46), but during times of peace, hospitality and neighbourly kindness were cardinal virtues (lines 49-52). The moral compass expected of the chieftain is manifest in Friseal's handling of his civic responsibilities (lines 53-56).

Even though it is acknowledged that the community, especially the descendants who have survived him, are aggrieved, his example is said to provide a glorious inheritance for them in guiding their lives (lines 57-60). The example of his life and the way that it is to be understood is, of course, provided by this poem itself.

Original Text

   1   Lìon mulad ro mhór mi,
        Cha tog ceòl e o m' inntinn:
        Chuireadh caidreach mo shòlais
        Fo na fòidibh gu h-ìosail.

   5   Bha do chridhe ro bhlàth dhomh,
        'S e mo chràdh thu bhith dhìth orm;
        Có a lìonas dhomh t' àite
        Measg na dh'fhàg thu 's an tìr seo?

        Bu tric 'nar n-uaigneas an seòmar
  10   Is bhiodh ar còmhradh gun mhì-thlachd;
        Cha bhiodh sgannal no sgleò ann
        Is bhiodh an-còmhnaidh gràdh Chrìost ann.

        Bha thu measail mu'n reachd ud
        Chuireas peacaich fo dhìteadh;
  15   Is cha b' ain-fhios dhut an cleachdadh
        Chuireas dreach air a' Chrìostaidh.

        Bha thu misneachail dàna,
        Bha thu làidir 'nad inntinn;
        Cha bu toil leat an t-àrdan,
  20   Is cha b' àill leat e 'chinntinn.

        Bha thu uasal 'nad bheusaibh,
        Bha thu eudmhor mu'n Fhìrinn;
        Bha thu foghainteach treubhach
        Nuair a dh'éireadh an strìth aic'.

  25   B' e do ghnàth mun do theast thu
        Bhith ri d' dhleastanas sìnte;
        Anns gach dreuchd 's an do sheas thu
        Bha thu freastalach cinnteach.

        Làmh 'thogail nan Salm thu,
  30   An taigh-searmoin na sgìre,
        Chuireadh mach iad gu dealbhach
        Gun chearbaich, gun dìobradh.

        Ann an cléir is an séisean
        Is tric a sheas thu droch shìde;
  35   Ursainn-chatha na h-eaglais;
        'N aghaidh beag-nàir' luchd-mìoruin.

　　　　Is tric a dh'fhuiling thu 'n cùl-chainnt
　　　　Dh'fhàg do ghiùlan fo bhinn iad;
　　　　Dh'fhàg do chaithris is t' ùmhlachd
40　　　Goirt' ciùrrte 'n cridh' iad.

　　　　Fàs do theaghlaich, bu mhiann leat
　　　　Anns an diadhachd nach dìobair;
　　　　Chleachd thu adhradh 'n àm fianais
　　　　Gun a shianadh gu dìomhair.

45　　　Is iomadh Sàbaid thug teist ort
　　　　Nach robh leisge no sgìos ort
　　　　Ann an teagasg dhaibh cheistean
　　　　Is an leas ás a' Bhìoball.

　　　　Bha thu caoimhneil ri d' nàbaidh,
50　　　Thoill thu 'ghràdh is a shìochaint;
　　　　Bha thu fialaidh mu t' fhàrdaich
　　　　Bu mhath phàirteachadh bìdh thu.

　　　　Sheas thu gnothach na dùthcha
　　　　Le làn-chùram is le dìcheall;
55　　　Mas ann air breith no air jury
　　　　B' e do rùn a bhith dìleas.

　　　　Nam biodh do shliochd a bha cràiteach
　　　　An là dh'fhàg iad 's a' chill thu
　　　　Leantainn t' eiseamplar àlainn
60　　　'S e a b' fhearr dhaibh na mìltean.[11]

Translation

(1-4) Sadness has filled me greatly, music will not relieve my mind; my delightful companion has been put down under the sod.

(5-8) Your heart was very warm to me, it pains me to be without you; who will fill your place for me among all those that you left in this land?

(9-12) We were often on our own in a room and our conversation was always agreeable; there was never any gossip or pretence and there was always the love of Christ.

(13-16) You were mindful about that ordinance that condemns sinners; you were not ignorant of the practices that suit a Christian.

(17-20) You were courageous and bold; you were strong-minded; you did not like arrogance and it was not your ambition to foster it.

(21-24) You were noble in your manners, you were passionate about the Truth; you were formidable and brave when it [the Truth] was challenged.

(25-28) Before you died it was your habit to meet your responsibilities fully; you were attentive and reliable in every role that you ever took.

(29-32) Yours was a hand that held the Psalms in the county's house of worship; they would be delivered sagaciously, without rough edges or fault.

(33-36) In the Presbytery and in the Kirk Session you often withstood difficult times; [you were] the battle-pillar of the church who endured the impudence of enemies.

(37-40) You often experienced their back-biting but your behaviour left them condemned; your watchfulness and humility left them sore and wounded in their hearts.

(41-44) Your desire was to nurture your family in constantly faithful godliness; you practiced worship when it was time to bear witness without concealing it in secrecy.

(45-48) It was testified on many Sabbaths that you bear no sign of laziness or fatigue in teaching them the Catechism and its rationale from the Bible.

(49-52) You were kind to your neighbour, you earned his affection and his peace; you were generous around your household, you were good at sharing food.

(53-56) You defended the affairs of the country with great conscientiousness and effort; whether you deliberated a judgment or were on a jury, it was your desire to be upstanding.

(57-60) Even though your descendants were afflicted on the day that they left you in the grave, following your exquisite example would be better for them than secular matters.

2: Elegy to Bishop Uilleam Friseal

Uilleam Friseal was born in Gleann Canaich, Scotland, in 1779. He was sent to attend the Royal Scots College at Valladolid, Spain in 1794 at the age of fifteen and completed his training in 1804.[12] He was sent to Nova Scotia in 1822 and was consecrated as bishop in the Antigonish church in 1827.[13] This elegy to him was composed after his death in 1851 by Iain Boid.

Oral tradition about Bishop Friseal, as well as the contents of this song-poem itself, attest to the continuity of Gaelic secular culture in Catholic communities: whereas most traditional ideals had become mere metaphors or analogies for Presbyterians, they still retained their literal significance for Catholic Gaels of this era. Friseal was renowned as a man of prodigious strength: Gaelic folktales about his ability to throw the shot-put and to surpass the brawn of blacksmiths have been told virtually to the present in Nova Scotia. He was also said to be a consummate Gaelic singer and a devotee of bagpipe music.[14]

Friseal is praised as a "ceannard" of the people (line 15, a term usually reserved for chieftains), and is deemed noble (line 16). Indeed, the poet spends an entire stanza (lines 41-48) describing the three means by which Friseal has earned noble status: through his religious office, through both his paternal and maternal ancestry, and from his close kinship to the Fraser chieftains.[15] There is little to suggest that his social significance was narrowed by religious denomination: the people under his charge and affected by his death are the Gaels as a whole (lines 29 and 93-96) who are bereaved and bewildered without his leadership (lines 27-28). Just as an effective chieftain of old was able to attract and retain important allies, so is Friseal able to make a positive impression in many countries and earn the respect of powerful magnates (lines 49-56).

The praise of Friseal's strength and bodily capacities (lines 33-40) can be understood as literal statements. He is described as guiding his flock like a shepherd (lines 57-58) and his moral judgement and counsel (lines 59-63 and 65-68) were as much assets for a bishop as Highland leaders of the past. Although the chieftains of old had to be able to resort to aggression and force, only when necessary (line 81-82), intelligence and reason had much greater importance and wider application (lines 69-72 and 83-88). Generosity, especially to the poor, had long been a responsibility expected of the Gaelic elite and its literary representation was easily transferred to a religious context and office using the same symbolism (lines 73-80 and 107-108).

Original Text

1 An deicheamh mìosa de'n bhliadhna
　Ochd ceud deug h-aon is leth-cheud,
　An ceithreamh latha de'n mhìos sin,
　An àm ciaradh do'n fheasgar,
5 Fhuair mi sgeul ás a' bhaile
　A chuir car 'nam bhreislich:
　Sgeul ro dhubhach do dhaoine
　Gun do chaochail an t-Easbaig.

　O, gur fada luinneag is gur fada
10 Is bliadhn' air fad leam gach lò,
　Bhon a chàireadh, gu h-ìosal,
　Do chorp prìseal fo'n fhòid;
　Tha mo chridhe-sa brùite
　Is bidh mi tùrsach ri m' bheò
15 Bhon a dh'fhalbh ceannard an t-sluaigh seo:
　An t-Easbaig uasal gun phròis.

　Fhuair sinn sealladh bha goirt dhuinn
　A thug osnaichean cléibh dhuinn,
　Coimhead aodann an abstoil
20 Bha 'na chorp air an déilidh;
　Shil ar sùilean gu frasach
　Is thàinig smal air ar léirsinn;
　Is neul an aoig air ar gruaidhean,
　Chaidh ar buaireadh is ar léireadh.

25 Is beag an t-ioghnadh do chàirdean
　A bhith cràiteach ['gad] iargain
　Mar uain earraich gun mhàthair,
　Is iad a' méilich 'ga h-iarraidh;
　Tha gach Gàidheal a bharr orr'
30 Anns an àit' an-diugh cianail;
　A' caoidh is a' tuireadh an àrmainn
　Thug am Bàs bhuainn do'n t-Sìorraidheachd.

　Bha thu àlainn 'ad phearsa
　Is bha thu neartmhor thar mhìltean;
35 Bha thu fulangach sgairteil
　Làidir spracail coilionta;
　Cha robh uasal cho tlachdmhor

Riut, no faisg air, 'ad sgìreachd;
Fear do choltais, chan fhaicteadh
40   Ann an astar 's an rìoghachd.

Bha thu uasal an toiseach
Bho'n àrd-oifig a lìon thu;
Bha thu uasal an ath-uair
Bho d' dheagh athair is bho shinnsre;
45   Bha thu uasal bho d' mhàthair
Thog is dh'àraich air chìch thu;
Is bha thu àrd bho d' cheann-cinnidh:
Sàr Mhac-Shimidh gun mhì-chliù.

Bu mhór t' urram an Albainn
50   Is bha thu ainmeil an Éirinn;
Bha thu cliùmhor an Sasainn:
Thugadh seachad ort sgeul anns
Gach ceàrn de'n taobh tuath seo;
Thug na h-uachdarain spéis dhut;

55   Is ge mór Iarla Dundonald
Thug e onar e fhéin dhut.
Bu tu 'm buachaille b' àirde
Bha 's a' cheàrn seo a' riaghladh;
Bha do chomhairlean sàr-mhath
60   Anns gach càs 's an robh deuchainn;
Chuir thu iomadh olc gràineil
Ás an àite le d' riaghladh;
Is iomadh math th' air do thàillibh,
Is gann gun àireamh mi trian dhiubh.

65   Bha thu déidheil air ceartas;
Bha thu smachdail air eucoir;
Bha do chomhairlean fallain
Bho'n deas theanga bu ghéire;
Nuair a dh'fhosgladh tu 'm Bìoball,
70   Bheirteadh mìneachadh réidh leat;
Is gheibhteadh seòladh le peacaich
Gu bhith gleachd ri 'n droch bheusan.

Bha thu daonnan a' lasadh
Le fìor charthannachd bhràith'reil;
75   Bu tu cobhair nam bochdan
Nuair a chitheadh tu 'm fàillinn;
Bhiodh do dhorsan dhaibh fosgailt'

Nuair a ghlaisteadh le càch iad;
Is làmhan sgaoilte na fialachd
80   A' co-lìonadh nan àithntean.

Bha thu ciùin mar an leanaban,
Is bha thu garg nuair a dh'fheumteadh;
Is tu bu mhath air an t-searmon
Cha bu chearbach o d' bheul e;
85   Thigeadh fuasgladh gach facail
Ann an ealamhachd réidh dhut;
Is le feabhas do bhriathran
Leam bu mhiann bhith ['gad] éisteachd.

Bu tu reula na h-iùil dhuinn,
90   Ar sgiath-chùil is ar geàrd daingeann;
Bha gach seòrsa fo d' chùram
Is do shùil orra thairis;
Leat-s' cha robh e gu mùthadh
Cia 'n dùthaich no 'n aidmheil;
95   Bha do chridh' air clann-daoine
Is e le gaol a' cur thairis.

Bha do bheatha is do ghluasad
Ré do chuairt dhuinn mar sgàthan;
Riamh, chan fhacas is cha chualas
100   Is cha d' fhuaradh ort fàillinn;
Cha robh subhailc bha luachmhor
Nach robh fuaighte ri d' nàdar;
Bha thu glan mar an daoimean
Is gun fhoill mar am pàiste.

105   Is tu nach togadh an deachamh
Ged is ceart do na cléir e;
Is cha chumadh tu tastan
Gun a sgapadh air feumaich;
Chuir thu cùil ris a' bheartas
110   Bhon a sheachain Mac Dhé e
Is rinn thu roghainn de'n bhochdainn
Mar rinn abstol na ceud linn.

Nis bhon chrìochnaich thu t' ùine
Is do chùrs' air an talamh,
115   Is bhon chàireadh 's an ùir thu
An ciste dhùinte 's an anart,
Is mór mo dhòchas is mo dhùrachd

    Gun do ghiùlaineadh t' anam
    Leis na h-aingil air sgiathaibh
120 Gu tìr ghrianaich nam beannachd.[16]

Translation

(1-8) In the tenth month of the year eighteen hundred fifty-one, on the fourth day of that month, when the afternoon was becoming dusky, I heard news from the town that stunned me: very sad news for people, that the Bishop had died.

(9-16) It is a long, long refrain, and every day feels as fully long as a year to me since your precious body was placed down below the sod; my heart is broken and I will be mournful all my life since the leader of the people has gone: the noble and unpretentious Bishop.

(17-24) We caught a sight that was sore for us, that brought sighs to our chests, looking upon the face of the apostle, a corpse on the death bier; our eyes shed showers of tears and our vision was obscured; a look of dread was on our faces, we were vexed and destroyed.

(25-32) It is no surprise for your friends to be miserable bewailing your loss like motherless lambs in the spring, as they bleat seeking her out; over and besides them, every Gael in this place is melancholy today; lamenting and keening the champion who Death took from us to Eternity.

(33-40) You had a magnificent appearance and you were exceptionally strong; you were hardy, energetic, powerful, commanding, and accomplished; there was not a nobleman in your diocese as pleasant as you, or even close to it; no man like you could be seen at any distance in the kingdom.

(41-48) You were noble firstly from the high office you filled; you were noble additionally from your goodly father and ancestry; you were noble from your mother who raised and nurtured you on her breast; you were eminent on account of your chieftain: excellent Fraser of Lovat, who had no infamy.

(49-56) Your honour was great in Scotland and you were famous in Ireland; you were renowned in England: you were spoken about in every corner of this northern land; the aristocrats were fond of you; although the Earl of Dundonald is eminent, he himself honoured you.

LOVE AND DEATH

(57-64) You were the most supreme pastor who was governing in this area; your counsel was excellent in every difficult distress; you purged the place of many odious evils with your governance; you are responsible for many good things and I can hardly enumerate a third of them.

(65-72) You were keen on justice; you brought discipline to impropriety; your sound counsels came from the sharpest, most elegant tongue; when you would open the Bible, you would offer a clear exposition; sinners received guidance to struggle with their vices.

(73-80) You were constantly shining with true brotherly charity; you were the salvation of the poor when you saw them in their need; your doors were always open for them when others had locked theirs; with outstretched hands of generosity, [you were] fulfilling the commandments.

(81-88) You were calm, like a little child, and you were fierce when necessary; you were good at the sermon, it did not come out awkwardly from your mouth; you were well suited to offer the explanation of every word in smooth sagacity; it was my desire to listen to you because of the high caliber of your oratory.

(89-96) You were the guiding star for us, our rear shield and our fortified guard; every type of person was under your protection, your eye upon them; it was of no consequence to you what country or denomination they belonged to; your heart was given to all of humanity and overflowed with love.

(97-104) Your life and your conduct was like a mirror to us throughout your life's journey; no failure of yours was ever seen, heard or found; there was no valued virtue that was not attached to your character; you were pure, like a diamond, and guileless like a child.

(105-112) You would not exact the tithing [for yourself], even though it is right for the clergy to do so; you would never keep a shilling without distributing it to the needy; you turned your back on affluence, since the Son of God shunned it and you made poverty a conscious choice like the apostles of the first generation did.

(113-120) Now, since you have completed your time and your journey on the earth, and since you have been placed into the soil in a closed coffin and linen, it is my great hope and sincere wish that your soul will be carried by the winged angels to the sunny land of blessings.

3: Ontario Love Song

The author of this love song-poem is identified only as "Loch Abar nam Bó" (Lochaber of the Cattle) in the newspaper *Cuairtear nan Coillte* (The Traveller of the Forests) from Kingston, Ontario, which printed it. This pen name probably indicates the place of the author's family origins in Scotland. The text suggests that he hopes to buy land in Quebec where he can start a family with the woman with whom he has fallen in love, a woman surnamed Nic an t-Saoir (Macintyre) who was raised on the Isle of Mull.

Although this text follows many of the conventions of love songs in Gaelic tradition, it also makes some unusual departures. The final line of the chorus (line 4) demonstrates an unusual degree of reserve for a Highlander in love, which may signal some unease or hesitation on the part of the composer. The contrast between Canada and the Scottish Highlands is exemplified by the forest and the heather (lines 6 and 8). Some gender-specific tropes in this text are reversed from their normal usages: it is usually the infatuated female who says that she will joyfully run barefoot to see her sweetheart (lines 19-20), just as it is usually the woman who attempts to convey the message that she is healthy through an intermediate agent[17] (lines 23-24). It is hard to know the reason for these irregularities in this text: perhaps both author and sweetheart are women? In any case, it is clear that experimentation with Gaelic literary forms was well underway.

Original Text

1   Ho a ho ró mo chailin
        Ho a ho ró mo chailin
        Huill a ho ró mo chuachag
        Cha b' e m' fhuath-sa bhith ri d' thaobh.

5   Rìgh, gur mise tha fo mhulad,
        An-seo fo dhubhar nan craobh,
        Is mi cuimhneach air a' chailin
        Is tric bha maille rium 's an fhraoch.

        Is tric mi 'bruadar 'nam chadal
10   A bhith mar ri bean mo ghaoil;

>   Is nuair a dhùisgeas mi 's a' mhadainn,
>   Chan eil ann ach faileas faoin.
>
>   Bheir mi sgrìob a-sìos do Chuibeac
>   Dh'fhaotainn còir air fearann saor,
> 15 Dh'fheuchainn 'n tàinig muinntir Mhuile
>   No 'm bheil guth air Nic an t-Saoir.
>
>   Rìgh, nan tigeadh tu dha'n dùthaich,
>   Bhiodh mo chùram dh'aon taobh –
>   'S mi gun siubhladh air mo bhonnaibh
> 20 Dhèanadh coinneamh riut, a ghaoil.
>
>   Fhir a shiubhlas is gaoth an iar leat
>   Thoir mo bhriathran-sa gu mo ghaol
>   Is innis dhi gum bheil mi fallain
>   Is gum bheil fadal orm dha taobh.[18]

Translation

(1-4) *Ho a ho ró*, my girl ... *Huill a ho ró*, my cuckoo, I wouldn't abhor being by your side.

(5-8) God, it is me who is sad, here under the shade of the trees, as I recall the girl who was often with me in the heather.

(9-12) I often dream in my sleep that I am together with the woman I love; when I awake in the morning, it is just an empty illusion.

(13-16) I will take a trip down to Quebec to get the rights to free land and to see if the people of Mull have come, or if there is any word of Ms. Macintyre.

(17-20) If you would come to the country, my anxiety would be over—I would run bare-footed to greet you, o beloved.

(21-24) O man who travels with the west wind, take my message to my beloved and tell her that I am well and that I long to be at her side.

4: Elegy to Iain MacGilleBhràth

The following elegy was composed to the celebrated musician-scholar Iain MacGilleBhràth "am Pìobaire Mór" (the Great Bagpiper) on his death on April 19, 1860, in Nova Scotia by an unnamed brother. It is sung to the tune of "Cumha Chlann Dòmhnaill" (The Lament of

Clan Donald),[19] which is appropriate given his kinship and cultural affiliations. This song gives us a parting glimpse of the last vestiges of the aristocratic Highland order: MacGilleBhràth was one of the last Gaelic poets and musicians to enjoy professional patronage in Scotland, and as this text relates, he had revelled in the company of others of similar station on the famous yacht the Dubh-Ghleannach before he left for Nova Scotia.[20] After settling in Antigonish County he changed his career to schoolteacher (lines 37-40).

The high social rank and personal attainments of both Iain himself and the family in general are strongly emphasized (lines 9-12). The stress on manners and gentility (lines 11, 31 and 40) is interesting in light of the book entitled *Companach an Òganaich* (The Youth's Companion) written by MacGilleBhràth's son Alasdair in 1836 in Gaelic to provide advice about morality and etiquette to those aspiring to upward mobility.[21] MacGilleBhràth had received considerable formal education (lines 33-35, 45 and 49) and was deeply immersed in the history, literature and music of his people, having been trained by a hereditary piping instructor on the Isle of Skye (lines 54-56). His pre-eminence on the instrument is described in some detail in the poem (lines 57-65), which makes allusion (line 67) to one of the celebrated Gaelic poets of the early-19th-century Highlands, Alasdair MacFhionghain of Morar, who praised MacGilleBhràth's musical skills in one of his own compositions. MacGilleBhràth is praised for his great intellectual capacities, enabled by remarkable powers of memory (lines 51-52), and for his work recovering Gaelic poetry that was later printed in *An Cuairtear Òg Gàidhealach*[22] (lines 73-78). One of his original compositions was a religious hymn about the crucifixion (described in lines 81-88).[23]

Original Text

1   Seo an saoghal neo-chinnteach
      Dhomh fhìn gur tric carach e;
      Dhomh a b' fhaoin a thoil-inntinn
      Is anns gach nì, tha e mearachdach;
5   Duinn daonnan a dh'innseadh
      A bhith sìth ris gur h-amaideachd
      Seach a' mhaoin a tha brìgheil
      Is nach dìobair ach maireannach.

      Dh'fhalbh taghadh mo theaghlaich
10   Is deagh loinn bha ri amharc orr':

LOVE AND DEATH

    Is bha roghainn 'nan giùlain
    Anns gach puing anns an gabhainn iad;
    'S e mhill mo mheomhair is mo chuimhne
    Bhith 'gan ionndrainn is nach faighear iad;
15 A Rìgh 'gan glèidheadh 'na chaoimhneas
    Is a thoirt roinn dhoibh 'na Fhlaitheanas.

    A-nis, dhuinn nochdadh a' bhliadhna
    A thug deuchainn do dh'iomadh aon:
    An trì fichead is ochd ceudan
20 Is na deich ceudna ann a bhuineas dhi;
    A chuir gu dhachaigh na sìorr'achd –
    Is b' e ar miann iad bhith fuireach leinn –
    Iomadh pearsa dheagh ìomhaigh
    Is té bhrèagha thar cumantas.

25 Tha m' fhulangas air dùbladh
    Ged is iomadh ciùrradh a dh'fhairich mi;
    Tha mo mhulad air dùsgadh
    Le cneadh ùir 'chuir ri m' an-shocair;
    Is mi duilich mu'n diùbhail
30 A rinn an ùir a-nis 'fhalach orm;
    Chaill mi bràthair deagh ghiùlain,
    Cha b' e 'n-diugh measg nam fearaibh e.

    A bha deas ann am foghlam
    Is a bha 'chòmhradh glé amasach;
35 Fiosrach, aithneach an reusan
    Is bha 'chléir an deagh bharail air;
    Is iomadh aon 'rinn e sheòladh
    Le sgoil dhòigheil mar b' aithne dha;
    Ged bha saoghal toirt éis dha,
40 B' ionraic beus dha gun charachadh.

    Nuair bha thu 'd dhuine òg ann,
    Bha thu stòlda suidhichte
    Is do chleachdadh neo-phròiseil
    Anns gach còisreadh an suidheadh tu;
45 Dh'innsteadh eachdraidh Roinn-Eòrpa dhoibh
    Leis gach eòlas ro uidheamach;
    Is gach neach bhiodh an tòir
    Air do chòmhradh deagh liubhairte.

    Fhuair thu foghlam gun fhòtas,
50 Bhiodh tu 'n còmhradh nan Tighearnan;
    Fhuair thu meomhair an corr

Thug siud eòlas is deagh rian dhut;
An Triath Gleannach, le bàigh riut,
'Chuir gu MacAoidh thu 'n tìr Sgitheanach;
55 Thug e dhut ceòl nan Gàidheal
Is cha bu chearr bhuat a-rithist e.

Bhiodh a màladh is lùb air
Is na duis 'cur lùths ris a' cheileireadh;
Ceòl toilichte cliùiteach
60 Is meòir dhùbailte ri mion-bhualadh;
Crunn-lùth glan-phronnadh siùbhlach
An déidh an ùrlair ro eireachdail
Agus caithream bho'n t-sionnsair
'Cur séis-chiùil ri puirt ealanta.

65 Do mheòir ghrinn 'bheireadh caismeachd,
Ghabhadh tlachd is thugadh moladh dhoibh
Le MacFhionghain nam baidal
Thug dhuinn eachdraidh nan ealan orr'
Air bòrd 's an Dubh-Ghleannach
70 Seinn gu caithreamach sgalanta;
Bha fir mhórail ann mar riut
Is do cheannard Gleannach, deagh Alasdair.

Is tric a shaoraich thu duanaibh
Is cha bu shuarach toirt aire dhoibh;
75 Is iomadh aon dhiubh tha clò-bhuailte
Snasail suairc-fhaclach annasach;
Cha robh 's an dùthaich mun cuairt duinn
Na bheireadh buaidh ort 's na ceannaibh sin;
Bha 'Cheòlraidh dhut fuasgailt',
80 Cha bhiodh cruaidh-cheist 'na eallach ort.

Dheilbh thu soilleir m'ar Slànaighear
Anns gach pàirt bha de dh'fhulangas
An robh an coireach toirt tàir dha
Mar ri cràdh 'bha ro mhuladach;
85 Bhon a ghluais e do'n Ghàradh
Is fallus fola a' sruthadh dheth,
Gus na bhuadhaich le Bàs e
'S an d' fhuair e sàthadh 'n t-sleagh ghuinideich.

Is trom cràdh-bhròn do chéilidh
90 Leis an Eug tha sibh dealaichte;
'S an àm 'theann sibh ri chéile
Bha i stéidheil mar leannan dhut;

Rinn i càirdean a thréigsinn
Is anns gach ceum, gun do lean i thu;
95 Is bha 'gnàths mar ri 'beusan
Flath[ail] réidh-bheartach ceanalta.

Thug i mic dhut bha dealbhach,
Bu trom feara-ghreimeach pearsant' iad;
Cha bu pheasanta meanbh iad
100 Ach mar dhearbh-ghaisgich sgairteil iad;
'S iad nach casadh gu feargach
Air aon aing'nadh a thachradh riuth';
Is on a thugadh air falbh iad,
Thug siud marbhadh dha d' phearsain-sa.

105 Is gun ann a-nis ach an aon fhear
Is la[dh] eutrom ri fhaicinn dhiubh;
Tha mi meas dha gu maoth e
Gu 'mhàthair chaomh, bhith 'na thaic dhi;
'S iad na pàrantan 'shaothraich
110 Bu chòir gaol a thoirt snasail dhoibh;
Thug Dia àithnt' is cha chlaon e
Is caillear aoibh rinn mur tachair sin.

Tha mo chuimhn' ann am fàillinn
Le iomadh ànradh tha casadh orm;
115 Chan eil sgoinn ann am thàlaint'
Gu cur Gàidhlig an snasadh bhuam
Ann am chom a bhios làthail
Trom-thàladh le acfhainnean;
On tha thu teann air do chàradh
120 An taigh caol clàraibh nach fhaicear thu.

Guidheam, Athair na Sìorraidheachd,
E bhith miadhail mu t' anam-sa
Is am Mac a fhuair riasladh
Le phiantan a cheannaich thu
125 Agus Spiorad na sìochaibh
E 'thoirt ìocadh o d' mhearachd dhut;
On 's iad an aon Trianaid
Gu luthaig dìon measg nan Aingeal dhut.[24]

Translation

(1-8) This world is uncertain, it is often deceiving to me; it would be vain for me to take pleasure in it and every thing that is imperfect; we are often told that it is foolish to be at peace with it [the world] rather than the treasure that is of consequence and does not vanish but is everlasting.

(9-16) The paragon of my family has departed, a fine brightness to be gazing at them: there was excellence in their comportment, in every aspect of whatever I assessed about them; it ruins my remembrance and memory to long for them and yet not have them; o God, protect them in your mercy and take some of them to Heaven.

(17-24) Now, we have been presented with a year that has been a trial for many of us: the year eighteen-hundred and sixty, with the same ten that belong to it; many people of good appearance, and an uncommonly beautiful woman, were sent to their eternal home who we wanted to stay with us.

(25-32) Although I have experienced many wounds, my suffering is doubled; my sadness has awoken with a fresh hurt that has added to my unease; I am grieved about the loss that the soil has now hidden from me; I have lost the well-mannered brother, he was not among the men today.

(33-40) He was well educated and his conversation was eloquent; knowledgable and well-reasoned, the clergy had a high opinion of him; he gave many people guidance with systematic education as he knew it; although the world held him back, his morals were unwaveringly upright.

(41-48) When you were a young man, you were somber and sedate and your manner was humble in every company you settled yourself; you told the history of Europe to them with every well-furnished fact and everyone sought you out for your intelligent conversation.

(49-56) You received a flawless education, you engaged in conversation with lords; you were endowed with prodigious memory and that provided you with knowledge and structure; the chieftain of Glenaladale, with affection for you, sent you to MacKay in the land of Skye; he gave you the music of the Gaels and you learned it properly.

(57-64) The curved airbag and the drones would energize the revelry; merry, renowned music with doubled fingers making delicate blows; a cleanly-cut, nimble quick measure after an exquisite melody-air, and a blast from the chanter adding forceful notes to artful tunes.

(65-72) Your elegant fingers would deliver a march, playing triumphantly and loudly; MacKinnon of the battles, who related their history to us on-board the Dubh-Ghleannach, appreciated them and praised them; the magnificent men were with you, and your chieftain of Glenaladale, excellent Alexander.

(73-80) Often did you set free poems and they are worthy of attention; many of them have been published and are elegant, kind-worded and interesting; there was no one in the region around us who could outdo you in such pursuits; the Muses were unleashed for you, no intellectual challenge could defeat you.

(81-88) You created a clear depiction of our Saviour in every aspect of his crucifixion when the sinner taunted him, along with the pain that was exceedingly wretched; from the point that he left the Garden, with streams of blood pouring from him, until he triumphed with Death and received a thrust from the poisoned spear.

(89-96) It is a sad agony for your spouse that Death has parted you; at the time that you joined together, she was unwavering as your sweetheart; she left her kin behind and she followed you at every step; and her habits along with her morals were noble, congruous and gentle.

(97-104) She gave you sons who were handsome, they were burly, manly-gripping, and statuesque; they were not peasant-like or stunted but were truly warrior-like and energetic; they were not ones who would explode angrily from any maliciousness that happened upon them; and your person was given mortal blows since they were taken away.

(105-112) And now there is only one, it is a delight to see him; I am delicately suggesting to him that he go to his gentle mother, to be her support; it is proper to give fastidious affection to the parents who laboured [for us]; God gave a commandment that was quite correct, and if it is not followed, we will lose favour.

(113-120) The many tragedies that are befalling me are causing my memory to fail me; my talents are not substantial enough for my mundane self, distracted by secular machinery, to express myself eloquently in Gaelic, since you are close to being positioned in a slender house of timbers [i.e., the grave] where you will not be seen.

(121-128) I now pray, o Father of Eternity, that he will be respectful about your soul—and the Son you redeemed with pain and the Spirit of peace—that He will redeem you from your shortcomings; since they are the singular Trinity, may protection among the Angels be granted to you.

5: Seònaid's Lullaby

Alasdair Ruadh MacCoinnich of McGillivray Township, Middlesex County, Ontario, wrote the following song to a young girl named Seònaid. MacCoinnich expresses his deep affection for her in verse by praying for her spiritual well-being, hoping in particular that she will be cared for by his religious community (described in greater detail in text 7.5). MacCoinnich depicts the bond between himself and the girl in terms of poetic expression: he hopes that they will complement each other's creative expression (lines 2-4).

Like many other pious poets, MacCoinnich alludes to an anecdote from the Bible to help him express his message. The tale in 2 Kings 5:1-19 relates the story of Naaman, a war-leader who was plagued with leprosy. Naaman's wife had been given a girl who had been captured in Israel as her servant and this girl told Naaman that he could be cured by a prophet in Samaria. Naaman went into the river Jordan and was healed. This suggests that the girl named in this poem, Seònaid, was not a family member; perhaps she was a child rescued from slavery or was adopted from the Wilberforce Colored Colony, established near Lucan in Middlesex County in the 1830s.[25] This would explain the further Biblical reference to Ruth and Naomi, since Ruth came to accept Naomi's people, the Israelites, as her own, even though she was a Moabite by birth. MacCoinnich wishes for Seònaid to be baptized in the Sauble River, which is the westernmost boundary of McGillivray Township.

Original Text

1   A Sheònaid bheag bhrònach:
    Ma dh'éireas ort òran
    Tha mi am barail is an dòchas
    Gun dèan mi an corr dhut mu'm bàs dhomh.

5   Mas deòin Dhasan tha riaghladh
    Is mi gun guidheadh is gun iarradh

LOVE AND DEATH

    Bhith 'gad fhaicinn 's an fhìon-lios
    A[g òl] á cìochan na lànachd.

    Mar bha caileag bheag Naamain
10 Sìor-innseadh mu'n fhàidhe
    A thug esan do'n tìr
    'S an d' fhuair e innseadh mu'n t-slàinte.

    Is mis' tha cinnteach nuair phill e
    Gur i bha leis prìseil
15 Is nach robh móran 's an tìr
    Dhèanadh nì dha 'na h-àite.

    Nuair a shuidheadh iad còmhla
    Bu ro mhilis an còmhradh;
    Cha b' e an saoghal bu cheòl dhoibh
20 Ged bu mhór a chuid gàraich.

    O, nach baist sibh mo Sheònaid,
    Is gur e nì e réir òrduigh,
    Is ma bhios am ministear deònach:
    Tha uisge gu leòr ann an Sauble.

25 Is nuair théid an t-uisge ort a thaomadh,
    Bidh sinn a' guidhe gu daoineil
    Gun tigeadh spiorad an aonaidh
    Air do mhaoth-chridhe, ge bàth thu.

    Bidh Alasdair Cléireach
30 Dèanamh suas dheth nì feumail;
    Bidh Dòmhnall Friseal da-réir sin
    Is cha bheag an teud anns a' bhannd e.

    Ma gheibh mi mo dhùrachd
    Bidh Maighstir Lachlainn 's a' chùbaid,
35 Is bidh e guidhe le dùrachd
    Gum bi driùchd tighinn o'n Àird ort.

    'S e nì do stiùradh gu h-òrdail
    Dh'ionnsaigh slighe na còrach,
    Is bheir e 'n cumantas lòn dhut
40 Is an deas as bòidhche chaidh 'ràdha.

    Ged a cheannaicheadh daor i
    Nithear dhutsa cho saor i
    Is chan iarrair ach t' aonta
    Gun toir thu daonnan do ghràdh dhi.

45 O, gun canadh thu, Sheònaid,
    Mar thuirt Ruth ri Naòmi,
    "'S e do shluagh-sa mo shòlas,
    Leam bu deòin bhith de'n àireamh."

    Bidh mi nise co-dhùnadh –
50 Cha toir mi thairis mo dhùil dhiot
    Nach bi thu fhathast le dùrachd
    A' toirt ùmhlachd do àitheantan.[26]

Translation

(1-4) O little, sad Janet: if a song rises in you, I expect and hope that I will complete it before I die.

(5-8) If it is the will of Him who rules, I hope and pray that I will see you in the vineyard drinking from engorged breasts.

(9-12) Just as Naaman's little maid was always telling about the prophet who took him to the country in which he was told about [healing his] health.

(13-16) I am sure that when he returned that he valued her and that there weren't many in the land who could do anything for him in her stead.

(17-20) When they sat down together, their conversation was very sweet; the world did not provide music for them, even though it roared loudly [for their attention].

(21-24) Oh, will you not baptize my Janet? The minister will do it properly, if he is willing: there is plenty of water in Sauble.

(25-28) When the water is poured over you, we will be charitably praying that the spirit of unity will come into your tender heart, even though you are child-like.

(29-32) Alasdair Clark will be preparing something useful; Donald Fraser will act accordingly and he will not be a small string in that band.

(33-36) If I am granted my wish, Master Lachlainn will be in the pulpit, and he will be praying sincerely that dew will come from the Heavens on you.

(37-40) He is the one who will steer you in an orderly manner toward the path of righteousness, and he will always provide for you and offer the most splendid kind of life that has ever been imagined.

(41-44) Although it cost dearly, it will be given to you freely if you only agree to always love it.

(45-48) Oh, may you say, Janet, as Ruth said to Naomi, "Your people are my joy, I long to be in their number."

(49-52) I will now conclude: I will not overstate my expectations for you, that you will in the future sincerely honour the commandments.

6: "The Great Hearts of Generosity"

The following song-poem is a tribute to the early Highland settlers of Antigonish County, composed by Dùghall "the Old Squire" Mac-GilleBhràth. Only two verses survive to testify to the pride felt about the achievements of the Gaelic immigrant generation and the decline that was beginning to affect the rural settlements of Nova Scotia in the late 19th century.

Original Text

```
 1   Cridheachan móra na fialachd
     Anns an robh an gnìomh is a' chiall;
     Cha robh sgrubaireachd 'nan nàdar
     Anns gach àit' a bhiodh gu feum;
 5   A' togail eaglaisean is 'gam pàigheadh;
     Dh'fhàg iad pàtaran 'nan déidh,
     Is ma théid an leanailt le càch
     Cha bhi fàillinn ann an nì.

     Seallaibh an-diugh air an dùthaich
10   A rinn na daoine tùrail treun':
     An liuthad àite 'chaidh rùsgadh
     O'n choille bu dlùth gu léir;
     Tha iad fhéin a' cnàmh 's an talamh
     Is feadhainn eile 'gabhail feum:
15   Siud mar tha cùisean nàdair
     Anns gach àite tha fo'n ghréin.[27]
```

Translation

(1-8) Action and good sense belonged to the great hearts of generosity; they had no incivility in their character but were available wherever they were needed; building churches

Figure 6.1 – Plaque commemorating the settlement of Gaels at Àrasaig (Arisaig), Nova Scotia. Photograph taken by Michael Newton.

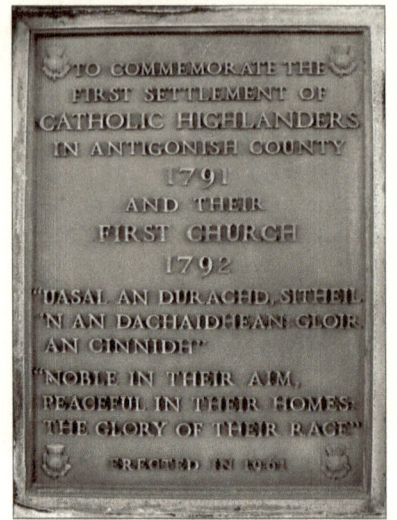

and paying for them; they left precedents and if others follow them, nothing will be inadequate.

(9-16) Look today at the land that the sensible and strong people worked: many places had been carved out from the very densest forest; they themselves decay in the earth while a few others are [still] in service; that is the nature of things everywhere in the world.

7: Lament for Edith and Dòmhnall

Fionnlagh MacRisnidh from Red Mountain, Quebec, composed the following elegy in 1882 to his first daughter Edith and a family member, Dòmhnall, who died of smallpox in Arizona while serving in the American military.[28] Although the poet laments them individually, most of the poem is a long meditation on Death, who is personified as a cruel and inexorable foe.

Original Text

1   Tha fear a' siubhail 's gach àite ris an canar "am Bàs"
    Is cha toir duine gu bràth cìs dheth;
    'S e thug uamsa mo ghràdh, bha mar lili a' fàs
    Is cha dèan briathran mo chràidh innse.

5   Càit' am faic mi air chuairt, an àit' measg sluaigh,
    [Sian] cho maiseach ri gruaidh m' Edith?
    Ach cha robh t' aghaidh bheag buan, rinn am Bàs do thoirt bhuam,
    'S e mo chreach 'chuir d'an uaigh sìnte thu.

    Thug thu màthair uam òg, nuair bha mi gun treòir,
10 Is dh'fhàg siud mi tighinn beò éiginneach;

Is thig thu dh'aithghearr gu seòlt' le do ghath air mo
    thòir-s',
Chan eil neach tha beò théid uat.

Bheir thu leat iad 's gach àit', bho'n rìgh chun tràill,
An duine bochd is fear an àrd-shaidhbhreis;
15 Is tu fear rannsaich gach cùil, eadar bhothan is chùirt,
Is cha robh riamh 'nad rùn caoimhneas.

Ach nach tusa bha cruaidh, mo leanabh gaoil 'thoirt uam,
Is nach dèan teanga mo thruaighe innse;
Is cha dèan aighear no ceòl cridh' subhach thoirt dhomhsa
20 Gus an laigh mi 's na fòid sìnte.

Ach ged tha mi ri bròn, agad fhéin air mo leòn,
Is duilich leam thu bhith 'n tòir chàirdean;
Is tu thug Dòmhnall MacLeòid, fear bu treun de na seòid,
Bho'n mhàthair rinn òg àrach.

25 Siud an gasan bha grinn, gille bàn Mhurchaidh dhuinn,
Is lean thu mach e gu beinn Arizòna;
Is rinn thu leabaidh ri craoibh, bho chasan bhiast siubhail
    oidhche
Is tha 'chàirdean ri caoidh throim air.

Is nach bu chianail dh'an triùir, rinn rath-thiodhlaic as ùr
30 Gus a companach dlùth 'fhàgail,
Cha bu duine e ach brùid, nach biodh deur air an t-sùil,
'Gad thasgadh an dùthaich fhàsail.

Anns an àite seo fhéin, is tric tha thu cur an céill
Gur tu 'n gadaiche as tréine gàirdean;
35 Is chan eil ceàrnaidh bho'n ghréin air an cuala sinn sgeul
Nach do sgap thu o chéile càirdean.

Bha mi uairean fo thùirse, is thigeadh deòir air mo shùil
A' call luchd dàimh agus dlùth chàirdean;
Ach seo 'bhuille bha ciùirrte, lot gu bràth bhios ùr,
40 Seo pian na saighde a rinn m' àmhghar.

Nuas o thoiseach an t-saoghail, eadar òg agus aosta,
Is iomadh pearsa gun ghaoid a fhuair thu;
Is iomadh leannan ro chaomh bhrist thu 'n <còrdadh a'
    gaoil>
Is iomadh neach, 'nam shaoghal, bhuail thu.

45 Is riamh cha d' fhuair thu gu leòr, is cha mhò dh'fhàgas tu
    corr,
Cha dol ás gun do chòrsa 'fhaotainn;

Chan eil lighiche beò bheir do phuinnsinn á feòl,
Nì thu casaid is cha chlòdh aon thu.

Bu tu 'n teachdaire cruaidh, is tu gun tàmh air a ruaig,
50   Is cha dèan ruith an <t-searraich> luath t' fhàgail;
Dearg nàmhaid gach sluaigh, is iomadh làmh 'rinn thu fuar,
On chuir thu do'n uaigh Àbel.[29]

Translation

(1-4) There is one who travels everywhere who is called "Death" and no one will ever defeat him; he is the one who took my beloved from me, who was growing like a lily, and no words can express my agony.

(5-8) Where will I see, anywhere among people, anything as lovely as the cheek of my Edith? But your little face did not last, Death took you from me, it destroys me to lay you down into the grave.

(9-12) You took a mother from me when I was young and vulnerable, that left me struggling to stay alive; and soon you will come after me cunningly with your spear, no person can escape alive from you.

(13-16) You take them away with you from every place, from the king to the slave, the poor man and the man of great wealth; you are the one who ransacks every corner, both peasant cabin and royal court, and kindness was never in your intentions.

(17-20) Weren't you cruel, to take my beloved child from me, and no tongue can express my anguish; no mirth or music can give a happy heart to me until I lie down stretched out under the sod.

(21-24) But even though I am mourning, wounded by you, I am sorry that you are in pursuit of kin; you are the one who took Donald MacLeod, the bravest hero of them all, from his mother who had nurtured him since his youth.

(25-28) He was the stripling who was handsome, the blond son of brown-haired Murdo; you followed him out to a mountain in Arizona; you made his bed next to a tree, away from the reach of beasts that move in the night, and his relations weep heavily for him.

(29-32) And was it not sad for the three people who made a fresh burial to leave their close companion; it is not a person but a brute who would not shed a tear interring you in a wilderness.

(33-36) In this place itself, you often declare that you are the thief with the strongest biceps; and there is no corner of the world about which we've ever heard where you did not part relations from one another.

(37-40) I have been dejected at times, and tears have come to my eyes, losing kin and close friends; but this is the blow that was agonizing, a wound that will be constantly fresh, this is the pain of the arrow that brought my affliction.

(41-44) Down through time, since the beginning of the world, you have had both young and old, and many flawless people; you have broken many exceedingly tender sweethearts in the bonds of love; you have struck many people in my life.

(45-48) And you never got enough, and you will hardly leave anything, there is no escape without taking your course; there is no doctor alive who can remove your poison from flesh; you will pronounce doom and no one can defeat you.

(49-52) You are the harsh messenger, and in ceaseless pursuit, and no galloping colt can outpace you; the utter enemy of every people, you have made many hands cold ever since you sent Abel to the grave.

8: Elegy for Father Niall MacLeòid

The following elegy was composed by Lachlann MacMhuirich upon the death of Monsignor Niall MacLeòid in 1891. It presents a fascinating study of Gaelic traditional values and literary conventions, such as the choice to use the metre and tune of an elegy composed ca.1715 for Ailean Dearg of Clanranald[30] as the basis of this song-poem.

Niall MacLeòid was born in Knoydart, Nova Scotia, in 1807. He and Cailean MacFhionghain (see text 7.3) were cousins and they went together in 1828 to receive their training in Rome. MacLeòid was settled as priest in East Bay, at the south of the Bras d' Or Lake of Cape Breton, in 1838 and remained there until he passed away.[31] Like Bishop Friseal (text 6.2), MacLeòid is depicted as a towering leader and protector of his people, like an earthwork wall that protects land (lines 21-22). He has the requisite qualities of a Highland chieftain: he supports the vulnerable (lines 31-32), displays warrior prowess and hardiness (line 33) and governs with kindness (lines 35-36) and intelligence (lines 51-52).

Indeed, MacLeòid is brought into the fold of the champions of old by emphasizing his capacities for defending his people against enemies, conjuring up the age-old conflict between Highlanders and their rivals. MacLeòid is bold and unflinching in the face of hostility, especially when he is called upon to protect his fellow Gaels (lines 59-60). He has, in return, earned the admiration and loyalty of men who would take vengeance for any slight done to him (lines 67-76), a devotion which is compared to that of Highlanders for Prince Charles Edward Stewart during the 1745 Jacobite Rising (line 77-78).

The priest is further praised according to tradition specific to his MacLeòid lineage. The poet refers to the fairy flag of Dunvegan (line 81) which, according to received belief, the MacLeòid chieftains could use up to three times to guarantee their success in battle.[32] Although several Gaelic kindreds are known historically to have had a significant admixture of Norse ancestry, the MacLeòid chieftains and poets were the only ones not to obscure their Scandinavian origins and to indeed commemorate them (as seen in line 88). Regardless of this acknowledgement of their ethnic pedigree, what was important to this poet and most others was their duty to protect the Gaelic community from anti-Gaelic antagonism (lines 83-84). The kin group is praised using traditional tree symbolism (lines 85-87) and the poet immediately and self-consciously assures us of the truth of his words (lines 89-90).

Original Text

1 Gur e naidheachd Di-Ciadaoin
Rinn mo ghluasad gu liathadh –
Dhrùidh e trom air na crìochan,
Gun thréig Maighstir Niall sinn –
5   Is iomadh aon leis an deuchainn is tùrs' e
    Is iomadh aon leis an deuchainn is tùrs' e.

Bha do chàirdean mun cuairt ort
Is anns gach àite, nuair chual' iad,
Air an cràdh is air an gualadh;
10 'N àm do thogail air ghuaillean
    Bha na deòir air an gruaidhean a' sruthladh
    Bha na deòir air an gruaidhean a' sruthladh.

Bha do pharaiste brònach
Anns a' mhadainn Di-Dòmhnaich
15 Thu bhith 'n tasgadh fo bhòrdaibh
Gun astar, gun chòmhradh,
    Is do bheul meachair bu bhòidhch' air a dhùnadh
    Is do bheul meachair bu bhòidhch' air a dhùnadh.

'Fhir nan tàlantan trice
20 Bha gun fhàillinn 'nad mhisnich;
Gur e 'n gàradh a bhristeadh
Thug an tearnadh 'nar misnich
    Bhon a chàireadh fo lic anns an ùir thu
    Bhon a chàireadh fo lic anns an ùir thu.

25 Ged tha uasal 'nad ionad
Nach eil fuathach aig duine;
Fear 'nad àite, chan urrainn
Tighinn 's an làraich ud tuilleadh
    Théid nas àirde ann an iomadach biùthas
30   Théid nas àirde ann an iomadach biùthas.

Ann an iochd is ann am fuasgladh
Ann am bàigh ris na truaghain;
Ann an gaisge is an cruadal;
Ann an diadhachd gun bhruaillean;
35   Ann an rianalachd suairce neo-bhrùideil
    Ann an rianalachd suairce neo-bhrùideil.

Gun tàir 'thoirt dha d' sheòrsa:
Fear a b' fhearr na 'm MacLeòid ud
Cha do chuir e air cleòca
40 Dol do'n eaglais Di-Dòmhnaich
    Is cha do sheas e 'na bhrògan air ùrlar
    Is cha do sheas e 'na bhrògan air ùrlar.

Leth-cheud bliadhn' agus corr
A-nis bhon chleachd thu na bòidean
45 Fo lagh Eaglais na Ròimhe –
Chan fhacas do mhórchuis
    'Fhir a shneachnadh am bòst, is seadh, ro'n
        ùmhlachd
    'Fhir a shneachnadh am bòst, is seadh, ro'n
        ùmhlachd.

Beul na fìrinn bu bheusach
50 Aig do Bhìoball gu leughadh,

　　　　'Gan robh tuigs' agus reusan
　　　　Agus gliocas dha réir sin
　　　　　　Ged a bhuannaich an t-Eug bhuainn a-null e
　　　　　　Ged a bhuannaich an t-Eug bhuainn a-null e.

55　　Bha gach luaidh a' co-fhàs riut,
　　　　Bha thu buan air an làraich,
　　　　Is tu gu misneachail dàna
　　　　'Fhir nach clisgeadh ro nàmhaid
　　　　　　'Fhir nach fhaiceadh na Gàidheil fo mhùiseig
60　　　　'Fhir nach fhaiceadh na Gàidheil fo mhùiseig.

　　　　Cha robh cron ort ri àireamh
　　　　Bho do mhullach gu d' shàilean
　　　　Troigh chuimir air sràid thu
　　　　Fo chom cumadail dàicheil
65　　　　'Gan robh slinnein is gàirdean an diùlnaich
　　　　　　'Gan robh slinnein is gàirdean an diùlnaich.

　　　　Is nam b' e fear-tòireachd no fuadain
　　　　No luchd-fòirneirt thug bhuainn thu
　　　　Is iomadh òganach a ghluaiseadh
70　　Dol gu deònach 's an tuasaid
　　　　　　Is fuil a dhòirteadh 'na stuadh feadh na dùthcha
　　　　　　Is fuil a dhòirteadh 'na stuadh feadh na dùthcha.

　　　　Is iomadh treun-fhear dhe d' chinneadh
　　　　Dhèanadh éirigh gun teine,
75　　Dol gu reubadh is gu milleadh
　　　　Mar bu bheus dha na gillean,
　　　　　　Chuir le chéil' ann an iomairt a' Phrionnsa
　　　　　　Chuir le chéil' ann an iomairt a' Phrionnsa.

　　　　Bha thu d' fhine nan uaislean
80　　Rinn na batail a bhuannachd
　　　　Fo na brataichean buadhach:
　　　　Is iomadh eachdraidh 's an cualas
　　　　　　Gun do sgap is gun do ruaig iad na Dubh-Ghoill
　　　　　　Gun do sgap is gun do ruaig iad na Dubh-Ghoill.

85　　Cha chraobh chrìonaich is cha mhosgan
　　　　Bhon a fhreumhaich thu 'n toiseach
　　　　Ach coille lìonmhor an fhortain
　　　　De dh'fhuil dhìreach Rìgh Lochlann,
　　　　　　Is chan eil breugan no brosgal 'nam chunntas
90　　　　Is chan eil breugan no brosgal 'nam chunntas.

Ach dé feum dhomh bhith 'g iomradh
Air bheag leughaidh no seanchais
Mu bheus nam fear ainmeil,
Bhon tha 'n t-Eug gu bhith sealg orm
95   Is math leinn uile gum falaichear fo'n ùir sinn
    Is math leinn uile gum falaichear fo'n ùir sinn.

Ach 's e reusan mo bhàrdachd
Am fear a tha mi 'g àireamh
Rinn mo bhaisteadh 'nam phàiste
100 Is air na chleachd mi bhith dàna –
    Is cha b' e 'fhasan no àbhaist mo dhiùltadh
    Is cha b' e 'fhasan no àbhaist mo dhiùltadh.

Leis an tlachd a bh' aig Dia dhe,
Chuir e cuireadh gu iarraidh
105 E dhol dhachaigh gu sìorraidh,
Is dh'fhàg sinne bochd cianail
    Bhon a thugadh bho fhianais ar sùl e
    Bhon a thugadh bho fhianais ar sùl e.

'S E 'n Tì phrìseil thug bhuainn e
110 Null dha'n Rìoghachd as buaine;
Guidheam Crìosta 'chur buaidhean
Ann an ciall is ann an stuamachd
    Air an fhear tha 'na bhuachaill' as ùr oirnn
    Air an fhear tha 'na bhuachaill' as ùr oirnn.

115 Ged a leanainn gu bràth air
Dh'fhaodainn tuilleadh a ràdha
Mu urram an àrmainn;
Dh'fhaighte coire dha m' Ghàidhlig
    Is còir dhomh sgur is a bhith sàmhach is co-dhùnadh
120   Is còir dhomh sgur is a bhith sàmhach is co-dhùnadh.[33]

Translation

(1-6) It was Wednesday's news that hastened my hair turning gray—it created a great impression throughout the land, that Father Neil has left us—there are many for whom this is the most sorrowful tribulation.

(7-12) Your friends around you and everywhere were agonized and tormented when they heard [the news]; when they raised you up on their shoulders, the tears on their cheeks were streaming.

(13-18) Your parish was sorrowful on Sunday morning that you were encased beneath boards, stiff and silent, after your most lovely and tender mouth had been closed.

(19-24) O man of the frequent talents who was unfailing in courage, it was the breaking of the dyke that caused our spirits to decline, since you have been placed under a gravestone in the ground.

(25-30) Although there is a gentleman in your position that no one dislikes, no man can ever take your place in that role who will surpass you in many capacities of renown.

(31-36) In assistance to and in affection and compassion for the wretched; in heroism and in hardiness; in non-fanatical godliness; in kind and civil governance.

(37-42) Without intending any insult to your kind [let me say]: no man ever wore a cloak going to church on Sunday, or stood on two feet on the floor, who was better than that MacLeod.

(43-48) It is more than fifty years since you took the vows under the rules of the Church of Rome–your arrogance was never seen, o man who would indeed refrain from boasting in preference for meekness.

(49-54) [You had] the most virtuous mouth of truth for reading from your Bible; you had comprehension, reason and wisdom because of that, even though Death has taken you away from us by force.

(55-60) Every cause for praise matured equally in you; you were perpetually on the battle-field; you were the one who was courageous and bold, o man who would not flinch before an enemy, o man who would not tolerate the Gaels being mistreated.

(61-66) You had no flaws to name from the top of your head to the soles of your feet; you were an elegant foot on a street under a shapely and handsome trunk which had the shoulders and biceps of a warrior.

(67-72) If it were a rival, a stranger or an oppressor who had taken you from us, many young men would prepare to go willingly into the combat and spill spates of blood throughout the land.

(73-78) There was many a brave warrior of your clan who would arise without fire, going to hack and destroy, as was the custom of the lads who strove together in the Prince's campaign.

(79-84) You were of the clan of the aristocrats who won the battles under the magical banners: many historical accounts relate that they scattered and routed the non-Gaels.

(85-90) You did not originally spring from withered or rotten wood but rather the fecund forest of good fortune of the pure blood of the King of Scandinavia; there are no lies or flattery in my account.

(91-96) But what use is it for me to refer to the morals of famous men with inadequate reference to texts or historical lore, since Death will be hunting me down: we all think it is best that we will be hidden under the soil [of the grave].

(97-102) But the reason for my poetry is the man that I am describing, who baptized me as a child and to whom I used to be ill-behaved—it was not his habit or practice to drive me away.

(103-106) God took so much delight in him that he sent him an invitation to come home for eternity, and left us wretched and longing since he was taken from the sight of our eyes.

(107-112) It was the precious One who took him from us over to the everlasting Kingdom; I pray that Christ shall bestow capacities of judgement and moderation to the man who will be our new shepherd.

(113-120) If I could go on forever, I could say more about the dignity of this champion; fault will be found with my Gaelic and I ought to cease, be quiet and conclude.

9: "My Heart is Agonized"

The following song-poem was printed in the 1890s in Orillia, Ontario. No author's name has survived, but it was clearly composed by a husband calling desperately upon God to restore the health of the mother of his children. Most of the Scottish settlers in Orillia had come from the Southern Hebrides, particularly Islay,[34] which were securely within the Presbyterian orbit of Argyllshire. The multiple allusions in the song to Biblical anecdotes and precedents—raising Lazarus from the dead (line 18), saving Isaac from being his father's sacrificial offering (line 21), infant Jesus escaping King Herod's wrath (line 23), Daniel escaping from the lion's den (line 26)—are strongly redolent of Protestant literary practice. The poet seems to be asking God to show His mercy to his wife just as He had to others through miracles in the past. In return, she will make her children devout Christians (line 39).

Original Text

1 Mo chridhe cràiteach, cha tig dhomh gàire;
Mo chom air fàilneadh, gun stàth mar sgleò:
Ag \<amharc\> phàistean as easbhuidh màthar,
A Rìgh nan Gràsan, siud fàth mo leòin.

5 Is gur truagh leam càramh na mnà thug gràdh dhomh
Mo chreach is mo léir mar dh'éirich dhi:
I 'n teasaich ghàbhaidh le neart gu sàrach';
O, Dhé, 's e t' fhàbhar bho'n bhàs, bheir i.

Is gur tric mi ag ùrnaigh le cridhe làn dùrachd
10 "A Rìgh nan Dùl, gum bi 'chùis nas fheàrr;
Is gun dèan i éirigh bho'n teasaich bhéisteil
Mar bhoillsgeadh gréine gun seud uimpe cearr.

"Is gun dèan thu fàbhar ri mo phàistean
Nach dèan thu ['m] fàgail gun taic gun treòir;
15 Is gun tog thu slàn i bho'n teasaich ghràineil
Le d' chumhachd, O Àrd-Rìgh, mas dàn dhut deòin.

"Is gun tog thu suas i bho'n teasaich uamhainn
Mar thog thu 'n t-uaigheach a-nuas làn deò;
Is air àm ro àraid a rinn thu fàbhar
20 Is thug thu 'm bàsach dha 'mhàthair beò.

"Mar shàbhail Ìosaig air beinne na h-ìobairt
Is chuir thu dlighe air gach nì dha d' ghlòir;
Mar shaoir thu Slànaighear bho làimh Rìgh Herod
Nuair bha geur-leanmhainn \<teann\> m'a thòir.

25 "Mar shaoir na leanaban bho theas nan àmhainnean
Is gheàrd thu Daniel an crò nan leòghann:
O, deòinich euchd do gach uile creutair
A tha fo éislean gu deurach breòite.

"Is deòinich cluas do gach truailleach
30 Tha ag iarraidh buaidh air gach buaireas feòl';
Is deòinich sìth do gach àireach dìleas
Tha \<dèanamh\> strì air an t-slighe nach meall.

>   "O, éist ri m' iarrtas, ged as neo-fhiachail mi –
>   Cruimheag chrìonach neo-riaghailteach dhall –
> 35   Bhon dh'fhuiling Crìosta is a phàigh na fiachan
>   Na leig dhomh, 'Thighearna, 'n t-Sìth shìorraidh 'chall.
>
>   "O, fàg am màthair do m' chlann an-dràsta
>   Gu'n togail àraid air ràth is còir,
>   Gu'n togail Crìostail làn creideimh is diadhachd;
> 40   Do thoil-sa biodh dèanta, o Dhia na glòir."³⁵

Translation

(1-4) My heart is agonized, a smile does not suit me; my body has failed me, it is as useless as a wraith; looking upon children who have no mother, o God of the Graces, that is the reason for my agony.

(5-8) The condition of the woman who loved me makes me feel wretched, what has befallen her is my ruination and my destruction; she is in a dangerous fever that has the strength to vex her; o God, it is your favour that will save her from death.

(9-12) I am often praying with a heart full of sincerity, "O God of the Elements, may the matter improve; and may she arise from the beastly fever like the shining of the sun, with nothing amiss about her.

(13-16) "And grant a favour to my children that you will not leave them without support or oversight; and raise her up whole from this terrible fever with your power, o God, if you are destined to will it.

(17-20) "And that you will raise her up from the dreadful fever, as you raised up the man from the grave, full of vitality; and at an appointed time you performed a miracle and presented the dead man to his mother alive.

(21-24) "Just as Isaac was saved on the mountain of sacrifice, and you ordained everything, for your glory; as you spared the Saviour from the hand of King Herod, when those in pursuit were getting close to him.

(25-28) "Just as you spared the infants from the heat of the furnaces and you protected Daniel in the lions' den; oh, grant a favour to every single creature that is afflicted, full of tears and infirm.

(29-32) "And lend an ear to every unworthy person who seeks victory over every temptation of the flesh; and grant peace to every faithful cattle-herder who is striving on the path of truth.

(33-36) "Oh, listen to my petition, even though I am unworthy—a small, unruly, blind maggot—since Christ has suffered and paid the debt, do not allow me, o Lord, to lose eternal Peace.

(37-40) "Oh, leave their mother to my children for now to raise them carefully in a virtuous house, to give them a Christian upbringing full of faith and godliness; your will be done, o God of glory."

10: Lament for Gilleasbaig MacEalair

Gilleasbaig MacEalair (Archibald McKellar) was born in 1816 in Gleann Siora, Argyllshire, Scotland, but his family migrated to Aldborough, Ontario, when he was twenty months old. He was initially sent to school there but he did so well that he was soon sent to grammar school in Niagara and then later to a prestigious academy in Geneva, New York. His family migrated again to another farm close to the river Thames near Chatham township, where he worked until 1849 in the timber trade.

After proving himself as a businessman, he became involved in matters of government. "Nuair a dh'éirich Uilleam L. MacCoinnich 's a' bhliadhna 1837, an aghaidh droch riaghladh na tìre, bha MacEalair 'na dhuine òg, sgairteil agus chaidh e a-mach le cuideachd de dhaoine air taobh a' Chrùin" (When William L. MacKenzie rebelled in the year 1837, against the ill governance of the country,

Figure 6.2 – Gilleasbaig MacEalair (Archibald MacKellar). Portrait from Friseal (1897), Leabhar nan Sonn.

MacEalair was an energetic young man and he went out with a body of men on the side of the [British] Crown).[36] He went into politics in Kent County in 1841 and served in the Legislative Assembly of Ontario and the Canadian Parliament for many years.

MacEalair was the President of the Gaelic Society of Hamilton when he died in 1894. He was said to be very fond of his native language ("duine aig an robh meas mór air a chainnt mhàtharail") and was literate in Gaelic.[37] The following elegy to him was composed by the association's official poet, Uilleam Moireach, specifically for publication in the periodical *Mac-Talla* (Echo). It lays heavy emphasis on MacEalair's military services to defeat the Upper Canada Rebellion, thus giving Moireach reason to deploy Gaelic literary conventions relating to the warrior tradition (especially lines 22-24). Even more central to the poem is the idea of reputation that outlasts the life of the hero through the memory of deeds enshrined in the words of poets. Orality abounds in the elegy in references to voices, sounds, words, names, verbal exchanges and social occasions which were held in order for songs to be sung (especially lines 2-4, 7-8, 15, 19, 25, 28 and 32).

The elegy is also interesting for how it melds MacEalair's Gaelic origins and his Canadian upbringing. His devotion to the Highlands is repeatedly stated and encoded in symbols of its landscape and plant life (lines 16-18 and 29-30). Although Beinn Mhór is a common place name (simply meaning "Large Mountain") that recurs in many parts of the Highlands, the particular location referred to must be that between Loch Eck and Loch Fyne in Argyllshire, not far from Inverary. Canada, in contrast, is not imagined in terms of the physical landscape but of the human community. This representational asymmetry reflects the loss

Figure 6.3 – Uilleam Moireach (William Murray), official poet of Comunn Gàidhlig Hamilton (the Gaelic Society of Hamilton). Portrait from Clark, Selections from Scottish Canadian Poets.

of the Gaelic population to British North America, leaving an empty and idyllic Highland landscape. The Canadian community itself is depicted as being made up of Gaels and anglophones (line 19) who perpetually hold him in honour for securing Canadian sovereignty (lines 25-27 and 31-32). This exclusionary depiction of the constitution of Canadian society, of course, reveals Gaelic deference to the dominant anglophone majority.

Original Text

1   Soraidh leat, a ghaisgich aosta a bu charaid do'n t-sluagh sin
Nach deach an ainm' riamh le eas-onair, no le mì-chliù a thruailleadh;
Cha chluinn sinne tuilleadh 'nar talla do ghuth a bu toigh leinn,
Nach deach riamh a thogail ach gu moladh as aoibhinn.

5   Gu bràth leis an aoibhneas a nì na Gàidheil 'chur am follais
Nuair fo gheasaibh aig ceannard le[is am] miann an solas,
Sinne thug gu minig àrd-mholadh do d' chomas;
Tuilleadh, cha mheal sinn do luach aig cuirm no aig coinneimh.

Ach ged a-nis mar na laoich a bh' an Albainn o shean,
10   No na rìghrean air tìr Phalestine a choinnich an-sin,
Tha do phearsa a bha òirdheirc a' strìochdadh is a' crìonadh
Tha do spiorad an-diugh, le misneach 'gar lìonadh.

Ach ged dubhach tha sinne, air cruinneachadh mun cuairt
Air a' chiste seo, dh'fheumas a bhith air a càradh 's an uaigh,
15   Bidh ainm MhicEalair 'nar cridheachan air chuimhne
Gach bliadhna air ath-nuadhach mar ùr-fhraoch nam beann.

Bha 'ghràdh cho làidir is cho buan do dhùthaich nam beann
Ris na monaidhean tha sealltainn sìos air Loch Long
Is a chliù, bidh maireann measg Shasannach is Ghàidheal
20   Gus an caochail duinealachd is an trèig gaisge an t-àl.

Coltach ris na laoich aig Oisean, ann an làithean òig',
Chuir e an ruaig air gach nàmhaid bha dian air a thòir;
'Na sheann aois, mar each cogaidh mu sgaoil air an raon,
Bu shunndach leis tilleadh gu cruaidh-chath nan laoch.

25 An Canada, ni clann nach do rugadh fhathast sgeul air
Mar chuir MacEalair neo-sgàthach an ruaig air a nàmhaid,
Is iad 'sealbhachadh toradh an t-sìl a chuir e le rath
Is bheir am *Mac-Talla* an fhreagairt d'ar n-iollach "Glé mhath!"

Cho fad is a nì 'Bheinn Mhór, a tha uasal, suidhe air a bunait
30 Is a chinneas fraoch air bruach nan caochan tha nuas aiste sruthadh,
Cho fad is a nì Canada mairsinn is onair aice 'na làimh,
Bidh ainm agus cliù MhicEalair air chumail air chui mhne.[38]

Translation

(1-4) Farewell to you, o aged warrior who was a friend to that people who were never spoken of disrespectfully or stained by scandal; we will not hear in our hall any longer your voice, that we loved, that was never raised except to make most joyous praise.

(5-8) With the joy that the Gaels will always exhibit when they are charmed by a leader whose desire is the light, we often gave high praise to your ability; we will never again enjoy your worth at a feast or a gathering.

(9-12) But now even though like the heroes of old in Scotland, or like the kings over Palestine who met there, your body, which was illustrious, is surrendering and withering, [although] your spirit is today filling us with inspiration.

(13-16) But even though we, who are gathered around this coffin that must be placed into the grave, are mournful, McKellar's name will be remembered in our hearts every year anew like the fresh heather of the mountains.

(17-20) His love of the Highlands was as strong and enduring as the moors that look down over Loch Long, and his fame will endure among English people and Gaels until manliness comes to an end and heroism forsakes the young.

(21-24) Like the heroes of Ossian in the days of his youth, he chased off every enemy who was pursuing him hotly; in his old age, like a war-horse set free on the field, he was happy to return to the hard fight of the heroes.

(25-28) Children yet unborn will speak about him in Canada, about how fearless McKellar scattered his enemy, as they claim the fruit of the seed that he planted with good fortune, and [the newspaper] *Echo* will second our cry of, "Well done!"

(29-32) For as long as Benmore, that is noble, sits on its foundation and heather grows on the banks of the streamlets that flow down from it, for as long as Canada endures and holds honour in her hand, the name and fame of McKellar will be retained in memory.

11: Eulogy to a Horse

The following song-poem was composed by Dr. Dòmhnall D. MacDhòmhnaill in praise of his horse, "Alasdair," probably in the latter part of the 19th century. In an age before motor vehicles, a speedy and reliable horse was the only way for a doctor to get to his patients when they needed his urgent care (as seen in lines 25-28). MacDhòmhnaill doesn't just describe his horse as a valuable asset: the poem speaks directly and affectionately to Alasdair as a beloved companion whom he will protect and never abandon or betray (lines 33-35). The poet draws upon the conventions of Gaelic panegyric in likening his equestrian friend to a warrior (lines 3 and 10) and king (line 10) who has many of the same qualities that a Highland hero would personify. At the same time, MacDhòmhnaill also delineates Alasdair's physical features in a more realistic manner (particularly lines 5-20).

The only place names mentioned are ones that originate in Scottish Gaeldom. "Garbh-Chrìochan" (Rough-Bounds, line 22) is a term used in general sense for the geographical Highlands as a whole, or in more restricted sense to a particular region of the Western Highlands from Cnòideart (Knoydart) to Mùideart (Moidart).[39] The latter is an area from which the majority of the population of Glengarry County, Ontario, hailed. The place name "Ailbheinn" (also line 22) may be an allusion to an area of Assynt named for a large rocky outcrop, anglicized as "Elphin." On the other hand, this toponym more likely alludes to the headquarters of the Fian, "Almhain" (in modern Gaelic), a name that is generally rendered "the Hill of Allen" in English. Even if these places can be interpreted as having real onomastic counterparts in Ontario,[40] the doctor is certainly also drawing upon the literary associations of these toponyms to reimagine the Canadian landscape with the heroic potential of Gaelic tradition, thus casting himself and his horse as protagonists conducting praiseworthy acts of gallantry.

Original Text

1   Ho ró is tu m' òigeach aigeannach luath
       Nach dèan orm tréigsinn dol a dh'fhaicinn an t-sluaigh,
       Is chan fhaca mi caochladh laoch thug ort buaidh
       Ged is iomadh each smiorail a tharraing riut suas.

5   Is glan do ghiùlain an acfhainn no 'n dìollaid fo mhar-
          caich;
       Is tu sgiansgar gasta nach tòisich am bruaich;
       Is ged is lìonmhor each sgairteil a shìn riut air astar,
       Làn tùchain is acain, gun chaisg e 's an ruaig.

       Do chasan cho dìreach, do bhrògan cho fìnealta,
10   Is tu 'n gaisgeach glan prìseil, is tu rìgh nan each cuanta:
       Do chluasan cho biorach, do shùilean gun tiomadh
       Do ghualainn tiugh diongmhalt, bròg sgiobalt dhubh
          chruaidh.

       Is earball trom gàbhaidh, cùl sleistean làidir,
       Druim goirid, deagh àirnean, com àlainn gun truaill,
15   Ceum fìnealta bòidheach is amhach chrom fheòlmhor,
       Muing fhada fo d' sgòrnan, trom òrach 'na duail.

       Ri gailleann no gaoithean, ri samhradh is Faoilteach,
       Thu deiseil dhomh daonnan gun saobhan gun ghruaim;
       Is ged shiubhladh tu mìltean tro fhrògan is fhrìthean,
20   Gun mhasladh, gun mhì-ghean, gun till thu air chuairt.

       Is tric a dh'fhalbh sinn gu foirmeil ri oidhche dhorch
          stoirmeil
       A shiubhal nan Garbh-Chrìoch mu'n Ailbheinn gu tuath;
       Air allaban an-moch, air aineol gun armachd,
       Tro fhrògan droch rathaidean is aith-bhealach fuar.

25   Is tric a ràinig bean-ghlùine an oisinn 'na crùban,
       Ri aslaich is ri ùrnaigh, gun dlùthaich'maid luath;
       Ag ùrnaigh le briathran làn dùrachd is diadhachd
       Nach dèanamaid dì-chuimhne le ìoc 'thighinn mun
          cuairt.

Is bho chionn corr is dusan bliadhna, bhon tharraing mi srian ort,
30 Bha thu dìleas gun diomb a dhèanamh gnìomh anns gach uair;
Cha dealaich gu bràth sinn mur dealaich am bàs sinn;
Fhad is maireann domh làrach, bidh stàth dhuts' ann buan.

Alasdair cheutaich, cha dèan mi do thréigsinn,
Cha reic mi ri béist thu no eucorach cruaidh;
35 Is cha leig le fear idir do mhasladh no do mhilleadh,
Bheir mi coirce dhut r'a itheadh is gach nì a bhios fial.[41]

Translation

(1-4) *Ho ró*, you are my high-spirited, fast stallion that will never let me down, going to see people; I never saw a handful of other young ones who would surpass you, even though many energetic horses have competed with you.

(5-8) You are well behaved when taken out for a ride with a saddle or gear; you are an excellent charger who will not startle on an embankment; although there are many energetic horses who can keep up with your pace, breathing hoarsely and sighing, you will subdue them in the pursuit.

(9-12) Your legs are straight, your shoes of high quality, you are the pure, precious warrior, you are the king of the showy horses: your ears are sharp, your eyes are fearless, your shoulder is thick and firm, with a tidy, black, hard shoe.

(13-16) A heavy, impressive tail, the back of your quarters are strong, a short back, good kidneys, a beautiful and unblemished trunk; an elegant, lovely step and a fleshy, curved neck, a long, heavy, golden, plaited mane around your throat.

(17-20) You are always ready for me, without going astray or becoming surly, whether in storm or wind, summer or winter; and even if you travel for miles through marshes and moors, you will come back around with no reproach or displeasure.

(21-24) We often left briskly during a dark and stormy night to travel the Highlands around Allen/Elphin to the north; late and wandering lost, in a strange place and unarmed, through the mires of bad roads and cold byways.

(25-28) Often did a midwife reach the corner hunkered down, pleading and praying that we would come quick; praying with supplications full of sincerity and godliness that we would not forget to come around with medicine.

(29-32) For more than a dozen years, since I put reins on you, you have been loyal, not showing displeasure in the deeds you have done at every turn; we will never part unless death parts us; for as long as I remain here, you will always have a good use.

(33-36) O handsome Alasdair, I will not abandon you, I will not sell you to a brute or a hardened criminal; and I will not allow any man to disrespect or ruin you, I will give you oats to eat and everything that is generous.

12: The Macdonalds of Bailey's Brook

The following song-poem was composed by an anonymous poet from Dùn Mac Glais, Pictou County, Nova Scotia in 1900 to the patriarch Dòmhnall D. MacDhòmhnaill and his family in Bailey's Brook. When MacDhòmhnaill died in 1906, he was one of the wealthiest men in eastern Nova Scotia, an entrepreneur who owned and operated a farm, general store, boat harbour, shipping business, ship-building enterprise and more. Macdonald partnered with J. W. Carmichael of New Glasgow in some of these operations.[42] Although engaged in very modern and mercantile activities, the poet harkens back to the literary conventions used to compliment Highland chieftains: the song begins with a customary toast (line 1), he is declaimed to be the son of a nobleman (line 5), his wife (Mary Elizabeth Chisholm) is asserted to descend from a warrior lineage (line 8), and he has procured fame (line 30). His wife Mary did in fact take care of the children of her brother Joseph who had lost his wife,[43] which enables the poet to demonstrate that she personified the Highland virtue of generosity (line 21).

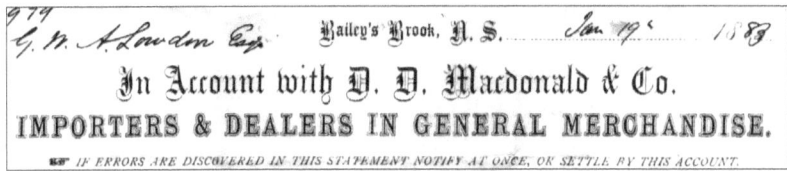

Figure 6.4 – The masthead of the business of Dòmhnall MacDhòmhnaill (Donald Macdonald) of Bailey's Brook, Nova Scotia. Image used with permission of the Antigonish Heritage Museum.

Their daughter Margaret (born in 1873) was to become the matron-in-chief of Canada's military nurses during the First World War. At the time that this poem was composed she was stationed in South Africa to tend to British soldiers fighting in the Second Boer War under the leadership of Lord Roberts. The poet is quick to congratulate her for her brush with titled gentry (line 40), but while Roberts had reliable ancestral qualifications, his military strategy in the war had the detrimental effect of undermining the health of soldiers and medical staff.[44]

Clara Dennis, travelling around Nova Scotia in the 1930s, attested to the enduring Gaelic character of the immigrant settlement at Bailey's Brook:

> "In Bailey's Brook you first meet with the Gaelic as you journey east from New Glasgow," said my host. In the home in the evenings the people speak the old language, and floating on the evening air you may hear the old pastoral songs in the Gaelic or a mother lulling her babe to sleep crooning Gaelic lullabies. Later, in a cotter's little home on the mountain-side, I heard the Gaelic sung. A father, a mother and their little girl sang old Gaelic songs: sang 'mid the hills and dales of New Scotland, of the mountains and glens of the old Scotland that their fathers left.[45]

Original Text

1   Deoch-slàinte 'Ghàidheil mhór-chridhich
      Tha sònraichte 's an àite:
      Seadh, Dòmhnall "Daniel" Dòmhnallach
      Tha còmhnaidh 'n Allt a' Bhàillidh;
5   Is mac e 'n fhìor dhuin' uasail
      Do'm bu dual bhith fearail làidir,
      Is do'n mhnaoi ghast' a bhuaineadh
      Bho'n deagh shluagh a bhuaileadh claidhmh'ean.

      Is ainneamh fear 's a' mharsantachd
10   Nì malairt ris cho sàbhailt';
      Bu mhath dha 'n latha dh'amais e
      Air an ainnir tha ris tàthte;
      Is na bannan caoine beannaichte
      A theannaicheadh gu làidir;
15   An ceanglaichean cho daingeann
      Is nach dealaich ach am bàs iad.

       'S i Màiri a bhean fhìnealta
       Is gur sìobhalt' i 'na nàdar;
       'Na beusaibh uile, chithear leinn
20   Sàr ghliocas agus àilleachd
       Is i sealltainn ris na dìlleachdain
       A tha air dhìth am màthar;
       Chan eòl dhomh gin 's an sgìreachd seo
       Da-rìreadh a bheir buaidh oirr'.

25   'S e Dòmhnall am fear piseachail,
       Tha sliochd aige tha bàigheil;
       Tha 'nigheanan is a ghillean
       Làn de dh'fhiosrachadh is de thàlann;
       Thug cùram is gliocas airgead dha,
30   Tha ainm dheth anns gach àite;
       Is malairt le 'chuid toitichean
       Tha ruith gun fhois air sàile.

       Tha nighean dha 'na ban-altraim
       An Africa nan cràdh-lot,
35   A' cuideachadh le caoimhnealas
       Ri saighdearaibh na Ban-rìghinn;
       A' frithealadh 's an ospadal
       Is a' dotaireachd gun phàigheadh;
       Ach cunntaidh sinn i fortanach
40   Lord Roberts a chur fàilt' oirr'.[46]

Translation

(1-8) [Here's] a toast to the great-hearted Gael who is distinguished in this place: Donald "Daniel" Macdonald who lives in Bailey's Brook; he is the son of the truly noble man whose ancestral custom was to be masculine and strong, and of the excellent woman who was descended from the splendid swordsmen.

(9-16) There are few merchants who are so successful at their business; the day that he happened upon the woman to whom he is attached was a good one, with the tender, blessed bonds that clasped so strongly; their relationship is so secure that nothing but death can separate them.

(17-24) Mary is his refined wife and she is civil in her nature; we can see in all of her manners superb wisdom and beauty as she looks after the orphans who lack their mother; I truly do not know anyone in this region who outshines her.

(25-32) Donald is the lucky man, he has warm-hearted progeny; his daughters and his sons are well educated and talented; discretion and wisdom have granted him money, he is renowned everywhere, as his steamships carry merchandise that travels ceaselessly on the sea.

(33-40) He has a daughter who is a nurse in Africa of the sore wounds, assisting the Queen's soldiers with kindness; attending in the hospital, and practicing medicine without monetary reward; but we will count her fortunate, since Lord Roberts has saluted her.

13: "The Journey that I Took from the Town"

The following song-poem was composed by Cailean MacÌomhair while he was still living in the Eastern Townships of Quebec about a visit he made to the nearby town of Lennoxville. He seems to have titled the song himself from the first line of the first stanza, although the chorus and melody are based on an older song which was composed to a woman who emigrated to Canada from the Isle of Skye.[47]

This song depicts a man in the throes of infatuation, riding a streetcar while singing his heart out in Gaelic. A poet such as MacÌomhair was very aware of the power of words to praise (line 15) and woo (lines 39, 43, and 45-48), but he is also self-conscious of the marginal status of the language in which he sings. He chooses the most remote seat on the streetcar (line 14), and although he professes to be unfazed by those who can hear him (lines 19-20), he also relays the impression that fellow passengers thought his language was strange and exotic (lines 21-24).

Original Text

1 Càit' an caidil an nigheanag a-nochd?
   Càit' an caidil an nigheanag?
   Och, ge b' e àit' an laigh mo luaidh
   Gur truagh nach robh mi fhìn ann.

5 An turas thug mi bho'n bhaile
   Is leam nach b' aithreach céilidh:
   Ged a bha mi dhìth a chadal
   B' aigeannach mo cheum leis.

LOVE AND DEATH

  Nuair ràinig mi steach Lennoxville
10 Air m' aire, cha robh mo chàirdean;
  Bha m' inntinn daingeann smuaintinn
  [Gur] truagh 'ghruagach, bhith 'ga fàgail.

  Shuidh mi steach air bòrd nan cars,
  Thagh mi 'n t-àit' a b' uaignich';
15 Sheinn mi suas air cliù mo leannain,
  A' bhanarach neo-ghruamach.

  Sheinn mi suas oirr' anns a' Ghàidhlig,
  Cainnt mo mhàthar, fuaim oirr',
  Ho rì, gur beag a bha de m' dhiù
20 De'n bha gach taobh de dh'uaislibh.

  Thigeadh iad an-siud is an-seo
  A dh'éisteachd fuaim na Gàidhlig,
  Is theireadh iad, "Có chuala riamh,
  An saoghal Dhia, do chànain?"

25 Is truagh, a Rìgh, nach mi bha 'n-dràst'
  Is mo dhà làimh mu do ghuaillibh;
  B' fhearr leam e na 'm pàigheadh-mìos'
  A b' fhearr a-riamh a fhuair mi.

  Thug mi gean dhut, thug mi toil dhut,
30 Thug mi mo làmh is mo chridh' dhut;
  Och, is cruaidh am beud mur faigh mi còir ort
  Le lagh stòld' a' Bhìobaill.

  Is gile leam do chruth na 'n canach
  No 'n eala air na cuaintean;
35 Is milse leam do phòg na meal
  Nan seilleanan beaga ruadha.

  Is buidhe do dh'fhear a gheibh mo leannan,
  Bean nam basan mìne;
  Nach buidhe dhomh ma gheibh mi 'n guth
40 Gum bheil thu 'n urras fìor dhomh.

  Nuair a théid mi do'n bhaile
  Far am bi gach nigheanag,
  Cha chan mi guth le cridhe glan:
  Tha m' aigne-sa do'n aon té.

45 Bidh mi minig rithe bruidhinn,
  'Ga mealladh is a' strìth rith' –
  Saoilidh cuid gum bi mo chridhe
  Bruidhinn rithe fìrinn.[48]

Translation

(1-4) Where will the lassie sleep tonight? Where will the lassie sleep? Och, wherever my darling may lay herself down, it is a pity that I am not there myself.

(5-8) The journey that I took from the town, I have no regrets about the visit; even though I was short of sleep, my step was high-spirited.

(9-12) When I arrived in Lennoxville, my friends were not on my mind; my brain was firmly thinking that it was a pity to leave the girl behind.

(13-16) I sat down inside onboard the cars, I chose the most isolated place; I sang aloud about the glory of my sweetheart, the happy-natured maiden.

(17-20) I sang aloud about her in Gaelic, my mother tongue, resounding "*ho rì*," and I cared very little about [the opinions of] the good people around me.

(21-24) They would come here and there to listen to the sound of Gaelic, and they would say, "Who on God's green earth ever heard your language?"

(25-28) It is a pity, o God, that I do not now have both of my hands around your shoulders; I would prefer that over the best month's pay that I ever earned.

(29-32) I have fallen in love with you, I have given my hand and my heart to you; och, it will be a terrible blow if I do not get permission to have you under the staid law of the Bible.

(33-36) Your semblance is fairer to me than the cottongrass, or the swan on the waters; your kiss is sweeter to me than the honey of the little ruddy bees.

(37-40) Lucky the man who will have my darling, woman of the dainty hands; I certainly will be lucky if I get word that you are really true to me.

(41-44) When I go to the town where all the girls are, I cannot say anything [to flatter them] with a pure heart; my soul belongs to one woman.

(45-48) I often talk to her, flirting with her and teasing her—some people think that my heart speaks the truth to her.

14: Elegy for Iain Alasdair MacLachlainn

Dr. Dòmhnall D. MacDhòmhnaill composed the following elegy to his friend Iain Alasdair MacLachlainn (John A. McLachlan) of Glen Nevis, Ontario, after his death on August 18, 1908, at the age of thirty-six. MacDhòmhnaill chose a metre[49] for this elegy which was strongly associated with the praise of clans and clan leaders but which had become increasingly obsolete during the 19th century, lending an archaic air to this piece. MacLachlainn was himself a poet known by the nickname "the Bard of Glengarry" and was literate in Gaelic (see also poem 9.6).

As we might expect from an elegy in this metre, MacLachlainn is praised as embodying the finest virtues with archaistic literary conventions. The newspaper that printed this text insisted that he was worthy of this tribute as he exhibited "those moral and intellectual qualities which endeared him to all who had the pleasure of his acquaintance." The song, we are told, "bears testimony to the excellent virtues of the deceased, and to the esteem in which he was held by his Glengarry friends." MacDhòmhnaill enumerates these attributes and aligns them with traditional values: cheerfulness, generosity, honour, humility, sex appeal and so on (lines 10-21 and 30).

MacLachlainn is commended as a "true Gael" who remained loyal to his language and people (lines 15 and 28-29). MacDhòmhnaill brings attention to the intellectual and artistic gifts (line 22) that were the basis of his talents as a musician (lines 24 and 27), a singer (lines 48 and 54) and a poet (lines 4, 18, 24 and 39). Just as poets were expected to validate the chieftain in terms of his lineage, MacLachlainn's life is placed within the larger ancestral matrix of origins and traits (lines 34-39), revealing that his grandfather had been a native of Cnòideart (Knoydart), Scotland (line 36).

Despite the rhetoric derived from the praise of lofty leaders elsewhere in the poem, MacDhòmhnaill sometimes represents the more mundane work life and responsibilities of his friend, working in the field (line 31), herding cattle (line 45) and milking them (line 47). Although his friends and relations mourn his passing, his talents are now said to be exercised in Heaven for the glory of God (line 54).

Original Text

1   O! gur muladach a tha mi
    Bhon a fhuair mi ['n] sgeul bàis seo
    Is bidh mi tuilleadh is mi cràiteach fo bhròn.

    Dh'eug MacLachainn am bàrd òg
5   Moch 's a' mhadainn Di-Màirt oirnn
    Is gun aon phiuthair gun bhràthair 'na chòir.

    Air dha cadal 'na shlàinte,
    Thàinig teachdair' bho'n Bhàs air
    Is tha e 'n-dràst' air a chàradh fo'n fhòid.

10 Dh'eug an t-òigear glan uasal
    A bha fearail 'na ghluasad
    Is a bha stuama is suairc anns gach dòigh.

    Fear fial furanach nàrach,
    Mùirneach iriosal càirdeil;
15 B' e sàr charaid na Gàidhlig mar bu chòir.

    A' ghnùis a b' àillidh ri sireadh,
    An t-sùil bu bhlàithe gun tioma,
    Is teanga bhlasta ri innse gach sgeòil.

    Chaill sinn ùr-ròs a' ghlinne
20 A dh'fhalbh is gun dùil ri e 'thilleadh;
    Is lìonmhor maighdean tha sileadh nan deòir.

    Is mór na buaidhean a fhuair e –
    Fear a choimeis, is tearc a chualas,
    Air deas-chainnt, air duanachd, is air ceòl.

25 Ann an comann fìor-chridheil
    Gum biodh fonn air gach cridhe
    Nuair a ghlacadh e 'n fhidheall 'na dhòrn.

    Mar bu dual dha'n fhìor Ghàidheal
    Chum e suas a dheagh chànain
30 Is bha e carthannach pàirteach mu'n bhòrd.

    B' e sàr chosnach 's an achadh,
    B' e clach-oisinn an taighe,
    A thug athair mar dhachaigh dha òg.

    Thriall a sheanair 'na òige
35 Ás a sheann àite-còmhnaidh
    'S a' Ghlas Choille ann an Cnòideart nan seòid.

       Do Chlann Dòmhnaill bha 'mhàthair
       Is do Niall Bàn bha e càirdeach
       Dha'm bu dùthchasach bàrdachd is treòir.

40   Tha 'luchd-eòlais is a chàirdean
       Is iad gun mhireadh gun mhànran
       Ri sìor chràbhadh is ri fàsgadh nan dòrn.

       Chaoidh, cha bhi e ag éirigh
       Air an òg-mhadainn Chéitinn
45   Is e ag iomain na spréidh bho na lòin.

       Is cha téid e do'n bhuaile
       A bhleoghann a' chruidh ghuaillfhinn
       Is e a' gabhail dhaibh duanag nam bò.

       Feast, chan fhaicear e 'n còmhlann
50   Anns a' chlachan Di-Dòmhnaich
       Is cha mhò chluinnear deas-chòmhradh a bheòil.

       Ach le gràsan an Àird-Rìgh
       Tha e 'n-dràst' aig a Shlànair
       Seinn cliù Dhé ann am Parras na glòir.⁵⁰

Translation

(1-3) Oh! Sad I am since I got this death notice, and I will always be agonized and mournful.

(4-6) McLachlan the young poet has died, to our loss, early on Tuesday morning without a sister or brother nearby.

(7-9) After he had fallen asleep in full health, a messenger from Death came to him and he is now placed under the sod.

(10-12) The pure, noble young man has died, who was manly in his carriage and who was temperate and good-natured in every way.

(13-15) A generous, welcoming, modest man, joyful, humble and friendly; he was a true friend of Gaelic, as he should have been.

(16-18) The most comely countenance to be found, the warmest steady eye, and an eloquent tongue for recounting every story.

(19-21) We have lost the fresh rose of the glen who has departed with no expectation of returning; many maidens are shedding tears.

(22-24) He was endowed with great abilities—it is seldom one hears about a man who equalled him for articulateness, for poetic skills, and for musical ability.

(25-27) In a truly merry company, every heart would swell when he would grasp the fiddle in his grip.

(28-30) As is the ancestral inheritance of the true Gael, he kept up his excellent language and he was charitable and generous at the table.

(31-33) He was an excellent worker in the field, he was the cornerstone of the house that his father gave him as a home when he was young.

(34-36) His grandfather emigrated in his youth from his former home in Glas-Choille in Knoydart of the champions.

(37-39) His mother belonged to Clan Donald and he was related to Fair Neil who was born with the gifts of poetry and leadership.

(40-42) His acquaintances and relations have lost their playfulness and festive mood, and are constantly praying and wringing their hands.

(43-45) He will never arise again on an early May morning and drive the cattle from the fields.

(46-48) He will never go to the cattle fold to milk the white-shouldered cattle as he sings a milking-lilt to them.

(49-51) He will never be seen in a crowd in the village on Sunday, neither will the excellent conversation of his mouth be heard.

(52-54) But by the grace of God, he is now with his Saviour, singing God's praise in glorious Paradise.

7 – Religion

Religion had a profound influence on the processes of colonization and the experiences of immigrants in the Americas during this era. Of course, religion was so deeply intertwined with every other aspect of culture and society that it cannot be neatly extracted from economic practices, political ideologies, literary activity, moral standards, ethnic identity, collective narratives of destiny and so on. This was as true of migration and colonization from the British Isles as it was of any other region of Europe.

> More than any other cultural practice, religion had a far-reaching impact on the very process of colonization and the world that resulted. Religion fueled expansion, justifying conquest and the authority that was established in the wake of those conquests. To a great extent, it sorted people into migrant streams....[1]

Religion had been a determining factor in the development of European culture and was embedded in the identities of European colonists. Before the development of racial ideology in the 18th century, the supposed superiorities of European civilization, as opposed to the barbarism of the indigenous peoples of the Americas, was often expressed in religious terms.[2]

Vestiges of this faith-based hierarchy are visible in Gaelic poetry about emigration in the 19th century. When Dòmhnall Mac a' Ghobhainn on the Isle of Lewis laments the absence of his brother in Canada, he portrays a stark theological dichotomy between the two environments. At home his brother was guided by the church,

Far an cluinneadh tu briathran o bheul nach fiaradh an Fhìrinn
'S tu an-diugh measg fhineachan fiadhaich nach cuala diadhachd o'n sinnsear.³

Where you would hear words from a mouth that would not twist the Truth, but today you are among wild tribes who have not heard godliness from their ancestors.

This depiction of a pious and god-fearing population adhering closely to the Scriptures in the Hebrides is, of course, not only a gross simplification, it is sadly ironic. Once Protestant fervour took hold in the Lowlands, the Highlands and the Hebrides in particular were portrayed as heathen zones that need to be converted and reformed. King James VI of Scotland (1566-1625) planned and partially attempted colonization schemes in the Gàidhealtachd.⁴ In 1598 he granted Lowlanders the right to "root out" the "barbarous inhabitants" of the Isle of Lewis, who were said to be "void of all religion and humanity," equating them with "Turks and Infidels."⁵

Other initiatives were less violent but no less assured of their righteous mission to civilize the "apostate" Gaels. The Society in Scotland for the Propagation of Christian Knowledge (often referred to with the acronym SSPCK) was founded in London with royal endorsement in 1709 to promote "Christian knowledge and increase of piety and virtue within Scotland, especially in the Highlands, Islands and remote places thereof, where error, idolatry, superstition and ignorance do mostly abound ..."⁶

These efforts to correct the supposed heresies and recalcitrance of the Highlanders had limited impact until the late 18th century, however, when Gaelic secular culture had been dealt a fatal blow and people looked desperately for a new faith to fill the void left by their native leaders and intelligentsia.⁷ Political impotence and cultural marginalization fostered the embrace of a "recluse religion ... [that sought] at the same time to dominate ordinary, open society"⁸ whose members were willing to reject and repudiate their former selves in order to be redeemed. "Psychologically, the price the Gaels paid for this world view was that they came to regard the Gàidhealtachd itself as a heathen mission-field."⁹ Regardless, some Highland communities remained doggedly Catholic and eventually emigrated to Canada in high numbers due to the pressures exerted on them in Scotland.

The Scottish, and later British, Crown had thus used a forceful mixture of religion, colonization and violence within the Gàidhealtachd itself well before Highlanders emigrated to join the streams of other settlers in the Americas. Christianity provided a theological rationale for the civilizing mission of European empires and Protestantism gave an even sharper edge to British imperial ambitions launched across the Atlantic in competition against "papist" rivals. Scotland's participation in the British imperial experience cannot have but reinforced common ideological assumptions and cultural conceits.

> From the seventeenth century, the English-speaking peoples on both continents defined themselves by wars that upheld, at least for a while, a guiding political culture of a Low Church, Calvinistic Protestantism, commercially adept, militantly expansionist, and highly convinced, in the Old World, New World, or both, that it represented a chosen people and a manifest destiny. ... The Protestant religion was at the core of English nationalism, and the Catholicism of France and Spain menaced both. Thus the triangle of religion, war, and politics.[10]

The religious conquest of the Highlands was part of the larger imperial enterprise and missionary efforts that helped to build the infrastructure and train the personnel who went further afield. Some SSPCK missionaries in North America, for example, served both among emigrant Gaels and Native Americans.[11] The success of the Protestant undertaking in the Gàidhealtachd seemed to offer proof that it could be effective in other colonial outposts.

> Missionary enterprise in the Highlands shaped strategy at home in Scotland and abroad. It helped to support the wider cause of mission, but it also laid down some markers for the ways in which native cultures and indigenous languages were approached by missionary bodies operating beyond the Highlands in what can be termed broadly "foreign" contexts. The Highlands were also invoked from time to time as a shining example of the pacification of "wild" peoples and the eradication of "barbarism" by means of the Gospel. This held out the hope that other "barbarians" could be tamed in like manner.[12]

Religion was one of the primary lenses through which Highland culture and history was viewed in the 19th century. While the region was (and is) still assumed to be a backwater of superstition and primitive customs, it was commonly asserted—not least by native converts themselves—that the Protestant mission had tamed the people and brought them into the fold of modernity. Such colonial ideologies are reflected in a range of sources, such as the opening of this popular account of the evangelization of Highland Ross-shire, later reprinted in Canada:

> Wild and uncultivated, as their native hills, were the people of the north, when already, in some parts of the Lowlands, the desert was beginning to "rejoice and blossom as the rose." The winter of the north had lasted long, and dark and dreary had it been throughout. ... His ignorance and superstition made the rude Highlander all the more manageable in the hands of the clergy, and they therefore carefully kept him a heathen. ... Savage heathen could everywhere be found, trained Papists in very few places, when the light of the gospel first shone on the north.[13]

It is little wonder that people who accepted such a fundamentally self-deprecatory view of their own history as a people could be co-opted into the expansion of that crusade of reformation to other "heathen."

Theological conformity was enabled by the use of texts via universal literacy. Religious texts provided counsel and encouragement to European colonists not just in the daily challenges of their personal lives but as statements about the larger meaning of imperial enterprises. Colonists could find ready parallels and analogies in the book of Exodus, in particular,[14] but all manner of spiritual literature could be drawn from.

> Quite aside from its ideological and organizational prowess, religion provided a discursive map of opportunities and perils that guided the post-Reformation state and its various agents in their overseas endeavors. By "narratives" we mean more than the storylines found in the Christian canon, though these were obviously crucial sources of inspiration and guidance for New World migrants: we also mean the more elusive if no less potent schemas that framed the private and public quests for spiritual perfection of Reformation-era Christians.[15]

We have already seen how ancient motifs about island paradises, surviving in Gaelic oral narrative, may have conditioned Highlanders' expectations about emigration (songs 4.1 and 4.2). Elements of Gaelic hagiography, from oral and written sources, acquired new significance to some Highlanders in immigrant communities. Some Gaelic ministers seem to have understood their role to be similar to that of the early Celtic saints of Scotland and Ireland, working in a spiritual and literal wilderness where the heathen had to be converted. The Rev. Donnchadh Blàrach wrote Gaelic essays for the Nova Scotia newspaper *Mac-Talla* about ancient Gaelic history that suggest not only how men of his station comprehended the past but also how that imagined past provided precedent and legitimation for the contemporary "civilizing mission" of church and empire. He and his fellow ministers would have instinctively understood the parallels between their own circumstances and those of the medieval pioneers of Scottish Christianity, as demonstrated in his essay published in 1899:

> Bha taobh tuath na Gàidhealtachd còmhdaichte le tiugh dhorchadas an iodhal-aoraidh, agus aineolach air Rathad na Slàinte troimh Chrìosd gus an d' thàinig Calum-cille. ...
>
> Aig an àm sin bha an t-slighe garbh, deacair ri siubhal, le beanntaibh agus le aibhnichibh, maille ri caolasan-mara 'n uair nach robh rathaidean-móra sam bith ann, no bàtaichean-aisig ach gann. ...
>
> Bha na ceud theachdairean soisgeulach so 'nan daoine foghlaimte, diadhaidh, saoithreachail agus thriall iad a bhos agus thall air feadh na Gàidhealtachd agus Eileanan na h-Alba a' cur an céill sgeul aoibhneach na slàinte do'n luchd-àitich borb agus aineolach.
>
> The north of the Highlands were cloaked in the deep darkness of idolatry, and unaware of the Road of Salvation through Christ until Columba came. ...
>
> At that time the route was rough, difficult to travel, with hills and rivers, as well as channels when there were no roads, and ferry boats were hard to find. ...
>
> These first Christian missionaries were learned, godly, hardworking men who travelled far and wide through the Highlands and Islands of Scotland declaring the happy tale of salvation to uncivilized and uninformed natives.[16]

The conditions of the early stages of settlement of Gaels in Canada were so difficult as to force greater co-operation, and less rancour, between rival branches of Christianity than was often the case in the British Isles.

> When the clergy first came out to the New World, their territory was so tremendous and the difficulties of travelling so desperate that they could reach only a small part of the people desiring their ministrations. ... The few clergymen who came to Canada from Scotland in the first part of the nineteenth century were quite insufficient to cope with the great population they had to serve. Sectarian differences had to be forgotten. When they could reach no minister, Presbyterians had their children baptized by itinerant Catholic priests. And even in the later part of the century many communities were still supplied only irregularly.[17]

Early Gaelic immigrant society was not as susceptible to religious factionalism as churchmen may have wished: not only were many early emigrants fairly indifferent about religion, there are many cases of Gaelic cultural allegiances triumphing over narrow theological differences.[18] Many people changed denominations, especially when marrying or integrating into a new community.

An anecdote from the Rev. Seumas MacGriogair, Protestant minister of Pictou County, shows the inherent cultural affinity of Gaels regardless of denomination and the efforts of churchmen to control and divide them. When Catholic Gaels arrived too late in the year in 1791 to establish their own homesteads, MacGriogair asked members of his own congregation to billet them until the winter was over. The local Protestant Gaels treated them kindly, although Bishop Aonghus MacEachairn admonished his Catholic flock not to be swayed by the rival faith and "threatened them with excommunication if they would come to hear [MacGriogair's] preaching." MacGriogair himself came to regret his intervention after their departure, for

> they were more dangerous guests in the congregation than I was aware of; not from the strength of their arguments for Popish doctrines, but from the powerful influence of their profane conversation. Much of their time was spent in naughty diversions. ... The minds of the Protestant Highlanders, being partly tinctured with these superstitions before the arrival of the Roman Catholics, were less prepared to resist their influences than the

minds of more reasoning and sceptical Christians. ... To this day we have not got wholly over these bad lessons.[19]

There were, to be sure, increasing tensions and conflicting loyalties between people's allegiance to a common Gaelic identity, on the one hand, and the demands of religion, on the other. Priests and ministers were charged with maintaining and converting adherents to their own faith, rather than protecting ethnic distinctions across denominational divides. Religious institutions tended to retrench their dogmas during the course of the 19th century and this must have further fragmented Gaelic immigrant communities.

> About [the year] 1815 religious questions began to disturb the community, principally denominational questions. The original inhabitants were originally from the Highlands of Scotland and belonged to the Established Church. Very little was known at that time here of sectarian distinctions which were then beginning to obtain from Scotland. ... No man knew scarcely what to do, or whom to place confidence in or ask for advice. Old ties of friendship were broken up; the peace of families was destroyed; and strife and bad blood were rife and near.[20]

The size and number of Gaelic-speaking congregations during the early part of the 19th century forced clergy and church of Catholic and Protestant branches to accommodate the language, especially for the older generations who tended to be monoglot Gaelic speakers unlikely to acquire sufficient fluency in English. Two services—one in Gaelic, the other in English—were held in many churches as the younger generations assimilated to dominant anglophone norms. Even at the end of the century, however, there was sufficient demand for Gaelic-speaking clergy in the Presbyterian congregations alone in Canada to justify the funding of scholarships for training them formally in the use of the language at the Montreal Presbyterian College. "The ministers of one hundred and twenty congregations of our Church still require Gaelic for the efficient discharge of their duties."[21]

Religion is a complex and multifaceted, even self-contradictory, realm. Folklore collectors working among the Gaelic-speaking communities of Canada, for example, collected many humorous and satirical jokes about religion, religious figures and religious beliefs by informants who were themselves priests, ministers and active church members. "Such lighthearted anecdotes provide welcome comic release in a community where strict adherence to religious doctrine might produce religiously motivated repression and inhibition."[22] Other materials collected from such informants also testify to the survival of much older "supernatural" beliefs that are at variance with orthodox Christianity. Whatever else can be said about it in political, cultural or military terms, the texts in this chapter also testify to the degree to which religion is a profoundly personal, social and spiritual dimension of the human experience that provided comfort and sustenance during the many challenges of immigrant life.

1: Odes to Assist the Faith of the Gaels

The following short, self-titled poem appears at the end of a book of hymns composed by the Rev. Seumas MacGriogair and published in the year 1819. He explained the way in which he composed these pieces, and why, in a letter that he wrote in 1817: "I composed these poems in part travelling through the dreary wilderness of America, hoping that they might do some good, but seeing little prospect of it."[23]

This compact text exemplifies the criticism of secular culture that ministers such as MacGriogair expressed. The potential reader is addressed as a person who appreciates music (line 1), but the poet hopes to direct those musical interests toward heavenly rather than worldly priorities. Unlike typical Gaelic poets of that era, MacGriogair does not indulge in the praise of powerful leaders (line 5), in the celebration of alcohol (line 6) or the romantic follies of youth (line 7), all presumably vain pursuits that cause people to lose their chance for eternal salvation (line 8). His words, it is claimed, guide the reader instead toward truth, justice, safety and peace (lines 9-12). It is perhaps ironic that many of the tunes for these hymns, as well as the poetic forms that were used to convey these messages, were the products of the highly sophisticated secular culture that is being censured.

Original Text

1   'Fhir tha suigeartach ceòlmhor,
    Ceannaich-sa mo leabhar-òran:
    Theag' gun dèan e feum ri d' bheò dhut,
    Ged nach mór a phrìs.

5   Chan eil adhradh air duine còir ann,
    Chan eil moladh air an òl ann,

No air sùgradh baoth na h-òige
Bheir bròn ort aig do chrìch.

Ach tha fìrinnean gun sgleò ann
10 Is comhairlean na còrach
Gu d' theasairginn o dhò-bheart
Is gu d' sheòladh chum na sìth.²⁴

Translation

(1-4) O man, who is light-hearted and musical, purchase my book of songs: perhaps it will be useful to you throughout your life, even though it is not expensive.

(5-8) No goodly person is adored in it, there is no praise of drinking or of the foolish playfulness of youth in it that will bring sorrow upon you at the end of your life.

(9-12) But it does have unambiguous truths in it and virtuous advice to save you from evil deeds and to direct you toward peace.

2: The Dissemination of the Scriptures

The following song-poem, entitled by the Rev. Seumas MacGriogair "Craobh-Sgaoileadh a' Bhìobaill agus an t-Soisgeil" (The Dissemination of the Bible and the Gospel),²⁵ appeared in his 1819 volume of hymns along with the previous text. It shares the metre and tune of an earlier popular song by Donnchadh Bàn Mac an t-Saoir (Duncan Ban Macintyre), "Fhuair mi naidheachd as ùr" (I Have Just Got the Latest News),²⁶ celebrating and disseminating the news about the 1782 repeal of the *Disarming Act* of 1746. This legislation overturned the punitive measures enacted after Culloden and thus enabled Highland men to reclaim their traditional clothing. MacGriogair's song is certainly pushing against the message in Donnchadh Bàn's text, exercising the semantic range of Gaelic "naidheachd" (news, message, story) and contrasting it with the Gospel (whose name in Gaelic, as in English, means "good news"). MacGriogair asserts that the glorious message that he has to offer is more gladdening and important than the secular news in the poetry of Donnchadh Bàn and other popular poets because it deals not with earthly vanities that ebb and flow (lines 1-2) but with the eternal truths of Christian salvation. MacGriogair thus presents a self-conscious rejection of the secular function of Gaelic panegyric—and of secular Gaelic culture as a whole—and retargets these resources toward spiritual goals with dreams of a Protestant imperium.

The first three stanzas enumerate, and then snub, the typical ingredients of Gaelic secular praise poetry: comparisons to legendary figures, such as the Fian (lines 5-6), references to noble pursuits, such as hunting (lines 7-8) and the raiding of Lowland rivals (lines 9-10), descriptions of resplendent clothing and personal appearance (lines 11-12), and accolades for the martial prowess of the Gaels as a people (lines 13-16). The third stanza rebuffs the centrality of "tribal" consciousness in Gaelic literature, his own clan (Clan Gregor) being the first of three distinguished kin-groups named (line 19).

MacGriogair then celebrates the global expansion of the Protestant crusade. The Gaelic terminology and idiom of warfare found in traditional panegyric is retained but conquests are framed in spiritual, psychological, cultural and geographical terms and a new authority and system of control imposed on outer as well as inner affairs. The civil-barbaric duality is used to portray those who are not within the bounds of Christendom in the negative: they are ignorant, blind, savage, wretched, deviant, deficient, unloving, evil and unattractive. Missionaries are capable and willing to bring them the "good news" in their own languages, however (lines 41-44), going northward (lines 45-48), southward into Africa (lines 65-72), westward to Native Americans and Pacific Ocean islanders (lines 73-76) and eastward to the Jewish and Muslim world (lines 93-95). Even the Catholics will belatedly join the Reformation (line 91). MacGriogair has thus internalized, and produced a Gaelic form of, the self-aggrandizing religious vision of the British Empire.

He extols the work of two societies in particular for their role in these efforts. The first (lines 113-36) is the Society in Scotland for Propagating Christian Knowledge, which sponsored a translation of Old and New Testaments into vernacular Scottish Gaelic. Much of this scholarly work was completed by the father and son team of Revs. Seumas and Iain Stiùbhart (lines 117-20), men who shared their surname with Scottish kings and lords. MacGriogair also pays tribute to the Society for the Support of Gaelic Schools, founded in Edinburgh in 1810 to promote Gaelic literacy in the Highlands (lines 137-52).[27]

RELIGION

Now that proper materials and structures have been put into place, he maintains, the Gaels can follow the example of the Lowlanders and emerge out of their (supposed) rut of stubborn primitiveness. In glorifying the education then made available in religious schools (lines 169-76), he is, of course, ignoring the centuries of Gaelic institutions of learning before the destruction of native culture (as discussed in chapter 1). His view of secular Highland culture in the past in general is overly pessimistic and his expectations of the benefits of integration of the region into the mainstream of British society are overly optimistic (lines 181-84). Perhaps he did not concern himself too much with the long-term prospects of socio-economic developments, as his final stanza suggests that he saw the dissemination of the Gospels into the far-flung corners of the world as a sign of the end-times.[28]

Original Text

<pre>
 1   Tha aoibhneas ag lìonadh mo chrì,
     Is cha tràghadh do shìth mo chuim:
     Tha naidheachd nas taitnich' 's an tìr
     Na chualas ri linn mo chuimhn':
 5   Cha naidheachd air Oisean nam Fian
     No gaisgeach 'bha riamh am feachd:
     Cha naidheachd air sealgaireachd fhiadh
     No giùlain am bian gu teach.

     Cha naidheachd air creachadh nan Gall
10   Le ceatharn nan gleann is nan stùc
     No idir air siubhal nam beann
     An éideadh nach ceangladh glùn;
     Cha naidheachd air tapadh nan Gàidheal
     No treubhantas àrd an lann
15   A' leagadh an nàimhdean gu làr
     No sgoltadh an cnàmh is an ceann.

     Cha naidheachd air fineachaibh treun'
     A chogadh is nach géilleadh beò:
     Clann Ghriogair a bha aineolach gleust'
20   Is nach tric a bha réidh ri còir;
     Clann Dòmhnaill le'm b' aiteas làmh dheargh;
     Clann Chamshroin bha calm' gun chéill;
     Is mar sin gach clann eil' a b' fhearr ainm
     Is gach ceannard bu ghairg' na 'chéil'.
</pre>

325

25 Ach naidheachd air Soisgeul nan gràs
    Bhith sgaoileadh 's gach àird mun cuairt,
    Is am Bìoball le facal na slàint'
    Bhith ruigheachd gach àit' le buaidh;
    'Toirt caochladh air inntinn an t-sluaigh,
30 'Gan ciùineach' mar uain gu sìth,
    A' claoidheach gach àrdain is uaill
    Is a' cur gach droch bhuaidh fo chìs.

    Tha 'm Freastal ag obair le buaidh:
    Le carthannachd, ghluais an tìr
35 Chum cost air an t-Soisgeul 'chur suas
    Anns gach àit' am bheil sluagh 'na dhìth;
    Bidh teachdairean eudmhor nach mall
    A' siubhal 's gach ball gun chlos,
    A' nochdadh do thruaghanaibh dall
40 Na slighe nach cam gu fois.

    Càirear Bìobaill am pailteas an clò
    An cainntibh nan slògh gu léir:
    Cainntean coimheach a dh'iomadach seòrs'
    Mu nach cuala sinn sgleò, no sgeul;
45 Théid an Sgriobtar gu grad do'n Taobh Tuath
    Gu Ruiseanaich ghruamach bhorb',
    Gu Lochlannaich is Lapanaich fhuar
    Is Tartaraich luath gu colg.

    Ni 'n Fhìrinn iad callta gun dàil
50 Is lìonar le gràs an crìdh';
    Cha mhair iad 'nan coimhich air gràdh
    No cleachdainnibh blàth na sìth':
    Oir tréigidh iad buirbeachd an gnè
    Is leanaidh iad sèamhachd Chrìost';
55 Thig creideamh 'gan ionnsaigh o nèamh
    Chuireas mais' air am mèinn gu sìor.

    Ge farsaing ta Àisia Mhór,
    Ge lìonmhor a slògh thar meas,
    Ge h-iomadh an cànain, is an dòigh,
60 Is ge pailt tha gach sògh 'nam measg,
    Ge daingeann ta ceangal an crìdh'
    Ri adhradh nan ìodhal balbh
    Ruigidh 'n Sgriobtar gach ceàrna d'an tìr
    Is bheir e leis iad le sgrìob air falbh.

65   Daoin' odhar is dubh' an Taobh Deas
       An Afraic fo theas na gréin':
       Ged bha iad 'nan tràillibh is 'nan creich
       Aig muinntir gun seirc gun chéill,
       Ni 'm Bìoball is an Soisgeul iad saor
70   Is bidh iad 'nan laoich aig Crìost;
       Gabhaidh 'n anam r'a Fhìrinn is r'a ghaol
       Is bheir a spiorad dhoibh naomhachd fhìor.

       Théid an Soisgeul le 'sholas mar ghrian
       A dh'ionnsaigh an Iar mun cuairt
75   Aimearaga is Innseanaich fhiadht'
       Is Eileanaich cian a' chuain;
       Tàid aineolach allaidh gun chiall!
       Tàid buaireasach fiadhaich coirbt'!
       Tàid dìorrasach dìoghaltach dian
80   Bras àrdanach iargalt' borb.

       Sàr chothrom do Shoisgeul na slàint'
       Is do chumhachd nan gràs aig Crìost'
       Bheir maitheanas saor dhoibh gun dàil
       Is creideamh bhios làidir fìor
85   A ghlanas an crìdhe gun chàird
       O'n truailleachd ghràineil bhreun;
       A cho-chumas ri Dia iad le gràdh
       Is le naomhachd 'nan càil is 'nan gleus.

       Bidh gach aidmheil is creideamh 'nan aon
90   Gun seachran gun aomadh clì;
       Thig na Pàpanaich thugainn gu saor
       An ceanglaichibh gaoil is sìth;
       Thig Arabaich is Turcaich le chéil'
       Is théid Mahomet éigheach sìos;
95   Thig na h-Iùdhaich le dùrachd 'nan déidh
       Thoirt ùmhlachd is géill do Chrìost'.

       Cha bhi dùthaich no rìoghachd fo'n ghréin,
       No fine, no treubh, no clann,
       Air nach soillsich an Soisgeul gu réidh
100 Mun dìobair an fhéill a th' ann;
       Nach aoibhinn an obair do dhaoin'
       Am Bìoball a sgaoileadh an céin!
       Bhith gnàthach' an dìchill is am maoin
       'Chur innleachdan gaoil an céill!

105 Cia cliùiteach na cuideachdan còir'
    As seirceil is òirdheirc gnè,
    Ghabh Freastal 'na làimh 'chur air dòigh
    A' ghnothaich ud as bòidhche sgèimh!
    Tàid dùsgadh an t-sluaigh gu bhith fial
110 'Thoirt mhìltean is chiadan seach;
    Tàid 'caitheadh gach peighinn le ciall
    'Chur a' Bhìobaill an iar is an ear.

    Guma sona do'n cheud chuideachd chaoin
    A dh'ullaich le'n saothair e dhuinn,
115 Anns a' chànain d'an tug sinn ar gaol
    Is nach tuigteadh a caochladh leinn;
    B' iad Stiubhartaibh fine an àigh:
    Is math choisinn iad gràdh gach linn
    A ghnàthaich an ionnsachadh àrd
120 'Ga thionndadh gu Gàidhlig ghrinn.

    Guma maireann do'n chuideachd as uaisl'
    Fhuair urram is buaidh thar chàch
    Bhios cruinn an Lunainn an t-sluaigh
    'N àm tighinn mun cuairt do'n Mhàigh;
125 Siud cuideachd a dh'éirich 'nar n-airc
    'Chur Bhìoball am pailteas nall
    Na dhìolas ar bochdan air fad
    Is na lìonas gach srath is gach gleann.

    Tha 'chuideachd ud 'sìor-dhol am meud,
130 Gun laigse d'an eud no sgìos;
    Tha 'n obair a' sgaoileadh an céin
    Air fad, is air leud gach tìr;
    Rìgh! Gur iomadach mìl', is deich mìl'
    Da'n tug iad am Bìoball seach;
135 'S e m' earbsa nach teirig dhoibh cìs
    Fhad is a bhios e dhìth air neach.

    Bidh 'chuideachd ud eile 'am sgeul
    Tha 'm Baile Dhùn Éideann cruinn,
    Tha tarraing gach inneal is teud
140 A dh'ionnsachadh leughaidh dhuinn;
    Tàid cruinneachadh airgid is òir
    O dhaoinibh ta còir is stuam
    Is 'ga chaitheamh le cùram ro mhór
    'Chur sgoilean gu òrdail suas.

145 Los gum faighear, le sean is le h-òg,
    Deagh theagasg is foghlam suairc
    Is gun leugh iad na comhairlean còir'
    Thug Dia dhuinn gar seòladh suas;
    Oir ged a bhiodh Bìobaill gu leòr
150 Aig big is aig móir an t-sluaigh,
    Mur b' aithne dhoibh an leughadh air chòir,
    Chan fhaigheadh iad eòlas uath'.

    Bha na Gàidheil ro aineolach dhall:
    Bha ionnsachadh gann 'nam measg;
155 Bha 'n eòlas cho tana is cho mall
    Is nach b' aithne dhoibh 'n call a mheas';
    Cha chreideadh iad buannachd no stàth
    Bhith 'n sgoilearachd àrd d'an cloinn,
    Ged fheudadh iad 'fhaicinn gach là
160 Gur i thog o'n làr na Goill.

    Ach b' annsa leo 'n t-airgead is an t-òr
    A chaitheamh gu gòrach truagh
    Ri amaideachd, òranaibh is òl,
    Ri bainnsibh is ri ceòl da'n cluais;
165 Chan ioghnadh ged bha iad gun chàil
    De fhocal na slàint' aig Dia;
    Ged choisinn an nàmhaid an gràdh
    Is ged bha iad toirt da 'mhiann.

    Ach théid aineolas nis ás an tìr,
170 Is gach cleachdadh neo-dhìreach crom;
    Is mealaidh sinn sonas is sìth
    Gun fharmad no strì 'nar fonn;
    Théid sgoilean 'chur suas anns gach ceàrn;
    Bidh leabhraichean Gàidhlig pailt;
175 Bidh eòlas is diadhachd a' fàs;
    Thig gach duine gu stàth is gu rath.

    Nis togaidh na Gàidheil an ceann
    Is cha bhi iad am fang nas mò;
    Bidh aca àrd fhoghlam nan Gall,
180 Is tuigse neo-mhall 'na chòir;
    Théid innleachdan is oibrean air bonn
    Chuireas saidhbhreas 'nar fonn gu pailt;
    Bidh 'n dìblidh cho làidir ri sonn
    Is am bochd, cha bhi lom le airc.

185 Thig na linntean gu cinnteach mun cuairt,
    Tha 'n Sgrìobtar a' luaidh, thig oirnn
    'S an téid Sàtan a cheangal gu cruaidh
    Is nach meall e an sluagh le sgleò;
    Bidh fìrinn is sìochaint is gaol
190 A' ceangal chloinn-daoin' ri chéil';
    Chan fhaicear fear dona mì-naomh,
    Théid olc ás an t-saoghal is beud.[29]

Translation

(1-8) Joy is filling my heart and the peace of my body cannot be drained; there is more pleasing news in the land than was ever heard in living memory; it is not a story about Ossian of the Fian, or any warrior that was ever in a war band; it is not a story about a deer hunt or the carrying of their hides to a house.

(9-16) It is not a story about raids on the Lowlanders by the caterans of the glens and peaks, or at all [a story] about travelling the mountains in clothing that does not encumber the knees; it is not a story about the manliness of the Gaels or the great bravery of their blades striking their enemies to the ground, or splitting their bones and skulls.

(17-24) It is not a story about brave clans who would fight and would not surrender as long as they lived: Clan Gregor who were unlearned and cunning, and often at odds with justice; Clan Donald who rejoiced in the Red Hand; Clan Cameron, who were daring but foolhardy; and so on, with all of the best respected clans, with each chieftain more fierce than the rest.

(25-32) But rather a tale about the "Good News" [the Gospel] of grace that is spreading around in every direction; the Bible with its message of salvation is reaching everywhere with success, causing people to change their mindsets and pacifying them to tranquility like lambs, subduing every arrogance and source of pride, and subjugating all evil influences.

(33-40) Providence is working with good success: it has moved the [Christian] land with charitable love to increase the spending on the Gospel on behalf of the population who lack it; zealous and swift missionaries will be ceaselessly travelling every area, guiding blind wretches to the straight and unerring road to peace.

(41-48) Plentiful Bibles will be printed in the languages of all peoples, foreign tongues of every sort about which we have not heard any information; the Scriptures will be immediately sent to the North, to dour, barbaric Russians, to cold Scandinavians and Laplanders, and to Tartars who are quick to anger.

(49-56) The Truth will tame them immediately and their hearts will be filled with grace; they will not remain as strangers to love or the warm habits of peace: for they will forsake the barbarism of their nature and they will follow the gentleness of Christ; faith will come to them from heaven that will forever adorn their mien.

(57-64) Although great Asia is expansive, and although its people are innumerable beyond measure, although their languages and customs are many, and although they indulge in many decadences, although their hearts are strongly fettered to the worship of mute idols, the Scriptures will reach every corner of their land and it will sweep all of those things away.

(65-72) The dark and swarthy people of the South, under the sun's heat in Africa: although they were taken as slaves by cruel and unenlightened people, the Bible and the Scriptures will set them free and they will become Christ's warriors; their souls will accept his Truth and his love and his spirit will grant them true divinity.

(73-80) The Gospel with its enlightenment will go forth like the sun toward the West around America and the wild "Indians" and the distant Islanders of the ocean; they are ignorant, savage, irrational! They are fierce, wild and immoral! They are recalcitrant, vindictive and violent, impulsive, arrogant, hostile, and barbaric.

(81-88) It is an excellent opportunity for the Gospel of salvation, and for the power of Christ's grace, to offer them immediate forgiveness and a faith that will be strong and true, that will, without discretion, purify their hearts of odious, putrid contamination; and which will bond them to God with love and with sanctity in their beings and in their manners.

(89-96) Every denomination and faith will be united, without divergence or the squandering of energy; the Papists will come to us of their own free will in ties of affection and peace; both Arabs and Turks will come and Mohammed will be denounced; the Jews will come after them in sincerity to pay obeisance, and submit, to Christ.

(97-104) There will not be a country or kingdom in the world, or a kindred, tribe, or clan, on which the Gospel will not shine clearly before this celebration is over; is it not joyous work for people to disseminate the Bible far and wide? To exercise their efforts and their prosperity in setting up the instruments of endearment!

(105-112) How renowned are the goodly organizations, of the most charitable and illustrious nature, which Providence has taken by the hand to establish that most decorous line of work! They are inspiring people to be generous, to donate hundreds and thousands; they are spending every penny sensibly to send the Bible east and west.

(113-120) Here's a salute to the first kind organization who, with their efforts, prepared it [the Bible] for us in the language that we love, for we cannot understand any other; they were Stewarts, the prosperous kindred; they have well earned the affection of every generation, putting their great learning to use in translating it into elegant Gaelic.

(121-128) May the most noble organization enjoy a long life, which has received honour and success above all others; they gather together in the populous city of London when May-time comes around; that is an organization that emerged during our troubles to send Bibles in plenty over to supply all of our poor people and fill up every strath and glen.

(129-136) That organization is constantly expanding without any deficiency in their fervour or energy; their work is spreading far abroad and throughout every land; O God! they have donated the Bible to many thousands and tens of thousands; I am confident their funds will not run out as long as anyone needs one [a Bible].

(137-144) I must also give news of that other organization that is assembled in Edinburgh, that marshals every strategy and device to teach us to read; they are collecting silver and gold from people who are virtuous and meek, and spend it with extreme care to establish schools in an organized manner.

(145-152) In order that young and old can get a fine and genteel education and will be able to read the goodly counsels that God has given us to lead us upwards; for even if all of the young and old of the population possessed a Bible, if they were not able to read properly, they would not get wisdom from it.

(153-160) The Gaels were very ignorant and blind: learning was scarce among them; their knowledge was so superficial and stagnant that they had no way to understand what they were missing; they would not believe that lofty learning had any benefit or purpose for their children, even though they could see every day that it was responsible for elevating the Lowlanders from uncouthness.

(161-168) But they preferred to spend silver and gold witlessly and pitifully on foolishness, songs and drink, on weddings and on music for their ears; it is little wonder that they were not predisposed to God's message of salvation, or that the enemy [Satan] secured their devotion and that they granted him his wish.

(169-176) Ignorance will now be banished from the land, as well as every warped and deformed habit; and we will enjoy happiness and peace, with no jealousy or conflict on our ground; schools will be erected in every corner; Gaelic books will be plentiful; knowledge and godliness will increase; every person will be put to good purpose and succeed.

(177-184) Now the Gaels will raise their heads and they will no longer be impeded; they will have the lofty learning of the Lowlanders and lively intellect along with it; inventions and industries will be founded that will greatly enrich our land; the downtrodden will be as strong as the champion and the pauper will no longer be destitute because of poverty.

(185-192) Certainly, the time will come about that the Scriptures tell us will come, and Satan will be firmly tied and he will not deceive people with his deviousness; truth, peace and love will bind humanity together; the wicked and unholy will be seen no more, sin and trauma will leave the world.

3: A Song to Bishop Cailean MacFhionghain

Cailean F. MacFhionghain (Colin F. MacKinnon) was born in 1810 at Williams Point, Antigonish County, Nova Scotia. He was sent to Rome for his religious training in 1829, earning a Doctor of Divinity as well as all three of the major orders before returning to Nova Scotia in 1837. Soon after his return MacFhionghain was made the first resident pastor of the newly created St. Andrews parish in Antigonish County. He became a close friend of Bishop Uilleam Friseal (see text 6.2) and was said to have "exerted a strong influence" on his superior. In 1851, not long after the death of Bishop Friseal (line 45), MacFhionghain was appointed to be the second Bishop of the Diocese of Arichat.[30] It was attested in later years that the arc of his career had been predicted by a female seer in much the same manner as prophecies made about the heroes of Gaelic folk legend:

Figure 7.1 – A statue of Bishop Cailean MacFhionghain (Colin MacKinnon) on the grounds of Saint Francis Xavier University. Photograph by Michael Newton.

> Nuair a bha an t-Easbaig MacFhionghain 'na ghille òg, dh'fhalbh e fhéin agus triùir no ceathrar de ghillean eile do'n Ròimh. Dh'fhalbh leo sgioba is bàta ás a' Bhàgh an Ear air an ceum gu Arichat far an robh iad a' dol a ghabhail luinge a dhol do'n Ròimh. Thadhail iad anns an Linne Mhóir agus chaidh iad a-staigh do thaigh seann bhean bhochd a b' aithne dhaibh. Thug na gillean rudeigin á cùl-an-dùirn do'n t-seann bhean. Is dòcha leam gun robh MacFhionghain air cùlaibh chàich. Thug esan, a-réir coltais, bonn bu mhotha na thug gin de chàch dhi. Dh'amharc i air agus dhùr-bheachdnaich i. Thug i beannachd air agus thuirt i ris, "Bithidh là ann nuair a bhios tusa 'nad cheannard air càch"; agus b' ann mar b' fhìor.[31]

When Bishop MacKinnon was a young lad, he and three or four other boys went off to Rome. A crew and boat from East Bay went along with them on their way to Arichat where they were going to board a vessel bound for Rome. They stopped for a visit in Port Royal and they went inside of the house of an old, poor woman whom they knew. The boys gave the old woman something that they held in their fists. It seems that MacKinnon was behind the others. He gave her, apparently, a larger coin than the others had given her. She looked at him and studied him very carefully. She gave him her blessing and she said to him, "There will come a day when you will become the leader of the others"; and indeed, it came true.

MacFhionghain's parishioners were clearly very fond of him: two different Gaelic odes were composed to him by poets in St. Andrews when he was transferred to Arichat, grieving his loss as though he had died.

The name of the author of this piece has not survived. It is modelled on an older song of exile from Loch Aillse (close to the Isle of Skye in Scotland), probably from the late 18th century.[32] In this case, however, it is not the poet but the subject of his address, the newly appointed bishop, who is departing. MacFhionghain is praised similarly to the many paragons celebrated in the poems of chapter 6 for his leadership (lines 11 and 13), intelligence (lines 8, 23 and 26), eloquence (lines 12, 14, 18, 21-24, 27 and 47), handsome appearance (lines 25, 27 and 29), affable personality (lines 11 and 29-30) and for his spiritual power from which his parishioners hoped to benefit (lines 16, 33-36 and 51-52). The poet also places special emphasis on his identity as a Gael, petitioning church leaders to be loyal to the immigrant community's native language and to help maintain prestige for it (lines 41-44 and 47).

Original Text

1 Ó-chóin, a Rìgh! gur mi tha muladach,
O, is trom tha m' inntinn, cha till na chunnaic mi:
Tha fòid dha'n cuibhreadh 'na chlaoidh do iomadh aon;
'S e as còir duinn suim 'chur 's an roinn nach diombuan dhuinn.

5 O, 's miste an t-àite seo, 'n tràth-s' na dhealaich ris
Is easbhuidh làthail, nach d' fhàgadh Cailean dhuinn;
Ùr an t-Easbaig àghmhor, is gràdh gach parraist' air,
Is teist ro àrd air, is a thàlainn barraichte.

Tha sinn fo smuairean, ged tha e maireann ann,
10 On rinn e gluasad gu tàmh a dh'Arichat;
Is e dhuinn mar bhuachaill, cur blàths 's gach anam leis,
Is nach cluinn sinn fuaim bho 'ghuth àghmhor amasach.

[Le comain uachdaran][33] anns an fhearann seo
Gu soillseach luaidheachd an uain a cheannaich dhuinn

15   An oighreachd uasal as buaine a leanas rinn
Gu'r roinn dhi buannachd is air duais bhith maireann innte.

Tha eaglais greunach, le stìopall adharach,
Le altair bhoisgeill, bu bhinn a labhairt bhuaithe;
A ghuth, cha chluinn sinn, o'n fhìrinn fhlathasach,
20   Is e measg nam Frangach, am fear cinnteach maitheasach.

Nuair ghlacte 'm Bìoball, bu phrìseil liubhairt dhuinn
Gach facal mìnicht', am brìgh ro uidheamach;
Gach car on dh'inntrig, a chinnt a shuidheachadh,
Cho math dha-rìreabh is a dh'innseadh bruidhinn dhuinn.

25   A phearsa mhòdhar, gur còmhnard cuimir i,
Ge deas 'fhoghlum, gun phròis, gun iongantas;
Cruth maiseach ro ghlan, a ròs-bhil binn-fhaclach
Ri seirbheas Dhòmhnaich, bu ghlòir 'na ionad e.

B' e siud an déideag, tha ceutach, carthannach,
30   Le tlachd is ùmhlachd is ciùineachd fharasta;
Chan eil an éiginn, na "Éigneig" ghreannach ann,
Ach "Inbhir Aoidh" ann, mar dh'fhaoiltich Alasdair.

Is trom ur n-iomagain, ['ga] leanmhainn tuille rinn;
Is mór ur [meanmna],[34] gu sealbh a thuinidh dhuinn;
35   A dheagh MhicFhionghain, tha ionmhainn uile leinn,
'S gach seòl a dhearbh dhuinn, do sheirbheis urramach.

Bu ghnothach stàthail e, is aoibhneas spioradail
A bha do'n charaid, on d' rinn thu cinneachadh;
Gun d' fhuair iad làithean, is do choibhneas thilleadh dhoibh
40   Gu ìobairt àrd 'chur 'nam pàirt mun d' imich iad.

On tha na Gàidheil 's a' cheàrn-s' air tuineachadh
Gur mór an t-àgh dhuinn, is am blàths mu chumair rinn:
Ur cànain mhàthrail, 's gach càs, bidh urram dhi,
Is a' chléir 'na ghnàths sin, bhith tàmh leinn bunailteach.

45   On thug am bàs bhuam na dh'fhàillinn 'fhulangas
Is a tha mo chàileachd air fàs ro uireasbhach,
Is nach cuir mi Gàidhlig an tàth mar bhuineadh dhut,
'S e beart as fhearr dhomh, bhith sàmhach buileach dhe.

Mo dhùrachd làidir, do shlàint' bhith maireann dhut
50   Is Rìgh nan gràsan a ghnàth bhith maille riut;

Cur guth an àrd ris, gu stàth dha m' anam-sa
On gheibh thu fàbhar is 'nar càs gur barant' thu.³⁵

Translation

(1-4) Woe is me, o God! I am the one who is struck by sorrow; oh, my mind is heavy, as that which I saw will never return: the encumbering earth is an affliction to many [people]; we ought to prioritize that which will not be fleeting for us.

(5-8) Oh, this place has suffered since he has been separated from us, it is a daily loss that Colin has not been left to us; the favoured Bishop was wonderful and every parish loved him, he had an excellent reputation and his talents were superb.

(9-12) Although he is alive, we have been dejected ever since he moved to reside in Arichat; he was like a shepherd to us, keeping every soul warm; we will never hear another sound from his favoured and eloquent voice.

(13-16) With the favour of the nobles in this land, to praise the lamb brightly who bought the exalted inheritance for us that will follow us eternally so that we can take a portion of it for our benefit, for a reward that will endure.

(17-20) His church is splendid, with its tall steeple and its shining altar from which he spoke melodiously; we will never hear his voice from the heavenly truth while he remains among the French, the dependable and virtuous man.

(21-24) When he gripped the Bible, he explained every word to us in a cherished manner, their meaning being well elaborated; he established the certainty of every event [since Creation] just as well, indeed, as anything can be told to us.

(25-28) His gentle appearance was smooth and tidy; although his learning was polished, it had no arrogance or uncanniness; his handsome form was pure, his rosy lips were musical during the Sunday service, he was a glory in his dwelling place.

(29-32) He was the darling who is stately and charitable, with delight, humility and easy gentility; there is no distress, or gloomy "Éigneig", but only "Inbhir Aoidh," as Alexander was called.³⁶

(33-36) Your concerns are serious and always follow us; your ambition that prosperity will abide with us is great; o great MacKinnon, beloved to all of us, who has demonstrated honourable service to us in every way.

(37-40) It was an advantageous matter, and a spiritual delight, for your relation[s] from whom you grew; they lived long, and your kindness was returned to them by making a great sacrifice for them before they passed on.

(41-44) Since the Gaels have settled in this region, we have enjoyed much prosperity and we have enjoyed kindness; your mother tongue will be honoured in every circumstance and the clergy remain steadfast with us in that custom.

(45-48) Since death has taken from me he whose suffering [finally] came to an end, and my constitution has become very frail, my use of Gaelic does not cohere, like it did for you, so the best thing for me to do is to be completely silent.

(49-52) I sincerely wish for your good health to persist and for the King of graces to always be with you; raise your voice on high for the benefit of my soul, since you find favour and you are a surety of our interests.

4: A Morning Hymn

The poet Iain Òg MacGilleBhràth probably provided the title "Laoidh Maidne" himself for the following song-poem. It is a hymn intended to aid the supplicant in starting each day fully prepared and conscious of the spiritual perils that await the unwary. The enemy mentioned in line 29 is probably the Devil. The last two stanzas bear some resemblance to the so-called "breastplate" or "lorica" genre of prayers and charms, calling on divine powers (particularly the Christian God) for protection and safekeeping.

Original Text

1   M' anam, fosgail suas do shùilean!
     Tha là ùr an-diugh 'nad thairgse;
     Criosaich thu fhéin le deagh rùintean
     Is leasaich gach tùrn am bheil dearmad;
5   Tha do nàimhdean lìonmhor dlùth dhut,
     Le saighdean puinnseant' a' sealg ort,
     Is théid do lot, mur gabh thu cùram,
     'S ann 'ad dhùsgadh fo d' chuid armaibh.

     Cuimhnich do leannanan peacaidh
10   Tha 'gad thàladh le'n cuid brìodail:
     Dh'fhàg iad do nàdar cho gealtach

RELIGION

    Is gun smachdaich iad thu le smìdeadh;
    Ged a thionndaidheas tu ascaoin
    Bheir do chleachdainnean dhut mìobhadh;
15 Ach fa dheòidh, ma bhios tu buadhmhor,
    'S ann as àirde duais do strìth.

    Ach chì thu fhathast gu brònach
    Do ghòraiche is ceann nan smaointean,
    Bhith 'n dùil gun dèan e gu leòr dhut,
20 A' ruith dhòighean chlann-daoine;
    Ma tha thus' an dùil ri tròcair,
    Biodh do dheòthas ionnsaigh an aon rud;
    Cum do cheum a-réir an òrduigh
    Is cur an neònaidh pròis an t-saoghail.

25 Ach tòisich an-diugh le misnich
    Agus sgrios na tha cur fiamh ort;
    Dèan deagh fheum de'n tìm tha làthair
    Is gun a-màireach ann do'n Chrìostaidh;
    Brist thro chuibhrichean do nàmhaid
30 Tha 'gad thàladh anns na lìonaibh
    Dh'fheuch am meall e gu uchd bàis thu
    Gus do nàrachadh 's an t-sìorraidheachd.

    Och, a Chrìost' a rinn mo cheannach
    Le d' chuid fal' air crann na Pàise:
35 Neartaich mo dhùrachd gu d' leanailt
    Is thoir dhomh aithreachas mu'n fhàillinn;
    Biodh do chumhachd dhomh mar chleòca
    Gu m' dhìon ás gach seòrsa gàbhaidh,
    Is 'nad reul-iùil domh an-seo air fògradh
40 Gu m' stiùireadh 's a' cheò tro'n fhàsach.[37]

Translation

(1-8) O my soul, open your eyes! There is a new day at hand today; gird yourself with good intentions and improve every effort in which may be negligence; your numerous enemies are close to you, hunting you with poisonous arrows, and if you do not take care, you will be wounded; be awake in your armour.

(9-16) Remember the wooers of vice who tempt you with their sweet words; they have left your nature so weak that they can sway you with a mere nudge; even if you turn a new leaf, your habits will bring you woe; but ultimately, if you are victorious, you will receive the highest rewards for your efforts.

(17-24) But you will yet sadly see your foolishness and the end result of those thoughts, to expect that it will suffice for you to pursue secular interests; if you expect mercy, let your enthusiasm be directed toward a single thing; keep yourself in proper step and reduce your worldly pride to nil.

(25-32) But start today with high spirits and disregard what causes you fear; make good use of the time you have, since no man is promised tomorrow; break through the chains of your enemy who draws you into his snares, to try to dupe you to the point of death and humiliate you for eternity.

(33-40) O Christ, who paid for me with your blood on the cross of suffering: strengthen my resolve to follow you and forgive me for failures; let your power be a cloak for me, to protect me from every manner of danger, and be a polestar for me here in exile, to steer me in the mist through the desert.

5: A Song about the Presbyterian Church of Canada

The following song-poem was composed by Alasdair Ruadh MacCoinnich in Middlesex, Ontario, probably about the year 1875. This was when the Presbyterian Church in Canada was established through the consolidation of many congregations that had previously been independent, a process referred to by MacCoinnich as "an t-Aonadh" (the Union). The church that MacCoinnich attended in East Williams had been led by the Rev. Lachlainn Mac a' Phearsain (Lachlan McPherson, 1814-1886), known to his Gaelic congregants as "Maighstir Lachlainn," since 1849.

> In person he was smaller than the others, but in qualities of head and heart he was the peer of all. He labored as a student with much acceptance in the newly settled districts of Huron and Bruce, sowing the seed that has since ripened into many flourishing congregations. ...For several years he was the only minister in the township [of East Williams].[38]
>
> There was nothing trifling or frivolous about him, and yet he was perfectly free from everything like affectation in his manners. He had that dignity that so befits the servant of Christ, and yet he answered to a remarkable degree Paul's description of a Christian minister, "gentle, apt to teach, patient, meek." ...He

was a patient, conscientious student; and every week wrote out in full two long sermons, one in Gaelic and the other in English, but the manuscript was never brought into the pulpit. ...

And when the Free Church and United Presbyterian Church were united in 1861, Lachlan McPherson and his devoted people testified against the union, and refused to enter it. ... Afterwards, however, Mr. McPherson and his people came into the united church, only to leave it forever, along with his life-long friend, John Ross of Brucefield, and their two elders, when the larger union of 1875 was consummated. ... Strange that a man of such mild and gentle spirit should yet, Athanasius-like, stand out alone against the action of all the ministers of his church. But such a man was Lachlan McPherson. He combined the lion and the lamb. To him conscience was supreme, and its behests he always obeyed at whatever cost.[39]

Maighstir Lachlainn was clearly opposed to the threat to the autonomy of local congregations through this incorporation. Many other Presbyterians in Huron and Bruce Counties whom he had served earlier seem to have shared his concerns (lines 105-12). Maighstir Lachlainn's local congregation was known by the nickname "the McPherson Church" after they left the union in 1875. When he retired from his post in 1883, however, the congregation began to reconcile itself to the national body.[40]

The poet expresses his disapproval of these church politics, stressing the discord they had sown where there once was harmony (lines 3-8 and 57-64), by declaring his faith in Maighstir Lachlainn's righteousness (lines 9-24 and 73-116), and by attributing the motivation of the national church to avarice and self-aggrandizement (lines 25-32, 49-56, 65-72 and 133-36). His rhetoric is peppered with Biblical analogies, likening the Presbyterian Church in Canada to Babylon (line 28) and the traitor Judas (line 49), and its behaviour to the hypocritical idolatry of Naamon in 2 Kings 5 (lines 35-40). Maighstir Lachlainn is compared to Noah (line 77) and those who have abandoned him are said to have committed a betrayal like the brothers of Gehazi, also in 2 Kings 5 (line 48). The poet's use of English loanwords is interesting in that they seem to emphasize foreign and unassimilated concepts and practices that he wishes to keep at some distance: "petition" (line 31), "pass" (line 32), "portion" (line 134) and "smuggle" (line 135).

Original Text

1   Is bochd an t-Aonadh a fhuair sinne,
      Is goirt a' bhuaidh thug e mach dhuinn:
      Thog e roinnean measg chàirdean,
      Nì tha gràineil ri fhaicinn;
5   Chan e an tionail ri chéile
      No dad de'n fheum tha 'nam beachd dhuinn:
      Seall mar tha sinn air faontradh
      Mach o'n aonachd a chleachd sinn.

      Is bochd nach b' urra sinn luaidh
10   Air cuid de bhuaidhean Mhaighstir Lachlainn
      Tha 'na theachdaire dìleas
      Air son sinn 'thoirt gu fasgadh:
      Ged tha cuid ris an diombadh
      Nach do lùb e le 'm beachdan,
15   'S ann air seasmhachd na Fìrinn',
      Rinn e inntinn a chleachdadh.

      Is iomadh trioblaid a fhuair e
      Agus buaireadh a ghleac ris
      Dh'fheuch am faighte ann an sàs e
20   No an tàradh a ghlacadh;
      Ach bha esan cho treubhach
      Is bha a cheum cho neo-lapach
      Leis a' mhais' a chuir gràs air,
      Cha do thàr iad a-steach e.

25   Nach e 'n t-Aonadh bha gàbhail,
      Feuch có a thàras a ghlacadh?
      Ged a bhiodh tu cho gràineil
      Ri Bàbilon mhaslach,
      Thig a-steach mar a tha thu!
30   Chan eil càil gu do bhacadh:
      Tha 'm petition cho làidir
      Is gun tug a' Phàrlamaid pass dhut.

      Tha cuid is an cogais 'gan càineadh
      Ged a thàr iad a-steach ann;
35   Their iad maille ri Naaman,
      Mar bu ghnàthach a chleachdadh,
      "Nuair a théid mi 'thaigh Remon
      Is a leigeas esan a thaic rium,
      Thoir dhomh maitheanas bàigheil
40   Ged tha fàillinn 's a' chleachdadh."

Tha cuid ann a tha gleusta:
Tha iad geur agus sgaiteach;
Is ged a dh'fheudas iad cainnt
A chur le samhla an cleachdadh,
45 Ge b' e nì 'their càch riuth',
'S e do chàradh <'dh'fhàg> mais' oirr';
'S e mo bheachd, is chan àicheadh,
Gur iad bràithrean Gehàsi.

Ged bha sporan aig Iùdas
50 Cha do chum e o'n pheacadh;
Bha e 'n-còmhnaidh 'ga iarraidh
Bhith 'ga lìonadh gu gasta;
Cha bu bheag leis an rògair
Gun dòrlach 'na achlais,
55 Leis cho mór is a thug 'shannt dha
Chuir e 'mhaighstir a-steach ann.

Is bochd am feum rinn e dhomhsa,
'S e fìor bhròn thug e steach dhomh;
Thug e uainn de na càirdean,
60 Roinn cho blàth is a bha agam;
Tha iomadh aon anns an tìr dhiubh
Nach gabh innse an ceartuair;
Ach sgrìob e buileach uam Sìne,
Ar leam nach dìobradh 's a' ghleacadh.

65 Biodh a' Chléir a-nis ciallach
Agus riaraichte 'nan aignidh
On a fhuair iad na dh'iarr iad
An cuid cheud 'chur am farsaing;
Cha b' e lìonadh am pòca
70 A bha seòladh nan Abstol
Ach acrach is ìotmhor
Rùisgt' 'nan cinn agus cas-rùisgt'.

A Mhaighstir Lachlainn, le d' dhìlseachd,
Is mór an nì tha ri fhaicinn
75 Mar a sheas thu cho dìleas
Ri Fìrinn an t-Soisgeil;
Tha thu nis mar bha Noah
'Nad aonar 's a' ghleacadh;
Ach air bhith dhut anns an Àirc
80 Gheibh thu sàbhailte dhachaigh.

Ach ma philleas tu sàbhailte,
'S i do làmh théid a ghlacadh;
Nuair a thig thu gur n-ionnsaigh
'S iad a lùbas a-steach riut
85 Is a thogas an fhianais
Gur thu a bhiadhadh na h-acraich;
Do na doill, bu cheann-iùil thu,
Thoirt dhaibh sùilean ri fhaicinn.

Cha b' e seann aran liath
90 Gheibhte riamh 'nad bhascaid
Ach na buileannan àlainn
De'n mhàna 'fhras ort;
Dh'fhàg siud thu cho ungta
Agus cumta 'nad bheachdan;
95 Nuair shileas an driùchd ort
Bidh na h-ubhlan 'gan sgapadh.

Ach 's e adhbhar do shòlais
Gum bheil do chòir air a deachdadh,
Gum bheil na gàirdeannan glòrmhor
100 An-còmhnaidh 'nan taic dhut;
'S e do cheann e is t' fhear-pòsta
Bheir e lòn dhut an-asgaidh;
'S e do shagart is do rìgh e
T' fhàidh prìseal 'chuir maise ort.

105 Is iomadh aon a th' ag ùrnaigh
Gum biodh gach cùis a' dol leatsa,
Is gun cluinnte do chliù
Am measg nan dùthchannan farsaing;
Tha luchd-àideachaidh Huron
110 Air an glùn anns a' ghleacadh;
Muinntir Ashfield cho cianail
Sìor-mhiannachadh t' fhaicinn.

Ach on nach urrainn mi cainnt
Chur gu band ann an cleachdadh
115 Mu thimcheall nam buadhan
Tha fuaighte ri d' mhaise,
'S ann a dh'fhanas mi sàmhach
Ach a' cànran is ag athchuinge;
Is bidh sinn an-còmhnaidh ag ùrnaigh
120 Gum biodh gach cùis a' dol leatsa.

Ged a tha mi ri òran
Mar as gnàth leam a chleachdadh
Cha mhór a thig gu mo chòmhnadh
Na sheòladh mo bheachdan;
125 Is mise a dh'fhaodadh a ràdh
Gur e mo bhràithrean bha lapach
Is mur b' e an gobha bhith làimh rium
Cha mhór nach fàgadh mo neart mi.

Their iad fhéin iad bhith òrdail
130 Anns an eòlas a chleachd iad
Is gum bheil an ceumannan còmhnard
Is nach eil seòl ri cur ás dhaibh;
Ach mas e 'n Fhìrinn a sheòl iad
Chum a' phortion a ghlacadh
Car-son a smugglaig iad uainne,
136 An nì bu chruaidh leinn a ghlacadh.[41]

Translation

(1-8) This Union that we have got is a wretched one, sore is the effect it has had on us; it has divided friends from each other, a thing that is horrid to see; they do not intend to create a united congregation or anything that is of use to us; look at how we have foundered from the unity that we once enjoyed.

(9-16) It is a pity that we could not call on some of the virtues of pastor Lachlainn, who is a faithful messenger, to bring us to shelter: although some are displeased with him, as they could not sway him to their opinions, he used his intellect to defend the Truth.

(17-24) He encountered many troubles, and he wrestled with many temptations that tried to ensnare him or tar him with disgrace; but he was so valorous and his step so unfaltering through the adornment that grace gave him, that they were never able to draw him in.

(25-32) Wasn't the Union tyrannical, trying to see who it could seize? Even if you are as horrid as ignominious Babylon, come on inside as you are! There is nothing to stop you: the petition was so persuasive that Parliament has given you a free pass.

(33-40) There are some whose conscience is nagging them, even if they have joined in; they will say along with Naaman, as was his custom, "When I go to the temple of Rimmon, and he shows me his favour, please forgive me, even if the custom is flawed."

(41-48) There are some who are cunning: they are barb-tongued and vicious; although they can use rhetoric effectively, whatever anyone else says to them, it was your efforts that adorned it [the Church?]; it is my opinion, and it cannot be denied, that they are the brethren of Gehazi.

(49-56) Although Judas had a wallet, it did not keep him from sin; he was constantly seeking it [sin] out in order to fill it [the wallet] up nicely; the rogue did not like to be without a load on his person; given his penchant for greed, he put his master in it.

(57-64) It [the Presbyterian Church in Canada] has done little good for me, it has caused me true sorrow; it has taken friends away from us, a group as warm-hearted as any I ever had; there are many of them in this land who cannot be named at this time, but it tore Jean away from me entirely, whom I reckoned would not give up the fight.

(65-72) Let the Presbytery be sensible now and satisfied in their minds, since they got what they wanted: to spread out their first hundred; the apostles were not driven by the desire to fill their pockets, they were hungry and thirsty, bareheaded and barefooted.

(73-80) O pastor Lachlainn, with your devotion, it is a great thing to see how you stood as faithfully as the Truth of the Gospel; you are now like Noah, alone in the struggle; but after you have been in the Ark, you will get home safely.

(81-88) But if you do return safely, it is your hand that will be taken; when you come to meet them, they are the ones who will submit to you and will testify that you are the one who fed the hungry; you were a polestar to the blind who gave them eyes with which to see.

(89-96) It is not old, mouldy bread that was ever found in your basket, but beautiful loaves of mana that showered down on you that left you so anointed and set in your opinions; when the dew trickles on you, the apples are spread out.

(97-104) But the reason for your solace is that your claim has been committed to writing, that the illustrious arms are always supporting you; he [God] is your chief and your spouse, he will give you free sustenance; he is your priest and your king, your precious prophet who has adorned you.

(105-112) Many people are praying that everything would go your way, and that your good name would be heard in far-flung lands; the communicants of Huron are on their knees in the struggle; the people of Ashfield are filled with longing, constantly desiring to see you.

(113-120) But since I cannot find language to express effectively those virtues that are connected to you, I will remain silent, except to murmur and supplicate; and we will always be praying that everything will go your way.

(121-128) Although I am engaged in song, as is my wont, hardly anything is coming to my aid that will direct my ideas; I can say that it is my brethren who were faltering, and if the smith hadn't been next to me, my strength would have nearly left me.

(129-136) They [Presbyterian Church in Canada] will say themselves that they are orthodox in the wisdom that they practice and that their steps are on the level and there is no way to avoid them; but if it is the Truth that has inspired them, in order to seize the portion, why would they smuggle away from us that thing that was hard for us to catch?

6: The Farmer's Thanksgiving Hymn

The following hymn was composed and titled by Gilleasbaig MacFhilip to celebrate the bounty of the earth as bestowed by God upon those who labour on the land. Lest we become too distracted by the earthly pleasures so vividly illustrated in his verses, however, Gilleasbaig concludes by reminding us that much greater rewards await us in Heaven (line 28).

Original Text

1   'S e an t-Earrach an t-àm, le grian is le frasan
       A chuir crann agus gearran am feum
       Chum is nach bi teanntachd ann no gainnead
       Ri àm na gaillinn is na gaoithe;
5   Th' an geamhradh tighinn dlùth le sneachd is le reòthadh
       Is bidh lòn an sabhal is fo'n làr;
       Is le pailteas 'nar làimh is le taing 'nar cridhe
       Gach dùil a bhith sona is sàmhach.

       Àrd-mholadh is cliù do'n Tì thug spionnadh
10   Is comas air cur agus buain:
       Gach gnìomh d' ar làimh is E fhéin a bheannaich
       Nuair dhòirt E 'mhaitheas a-nuas;

>   Le uisge nan speur is le blàths is le solas
>   O'n ghréin a chruthaich E fhéin;
> 15 Is le driùchd anns an oidhche is e ùr gach madainn
>   A' toirt fàs air fochann is feur.
>
>   'S e Dàibhidh a sgrìobh 's a' Bhìoball dhuinne
>   Àrd-mholadh is cliù do'n Triath;
>   Is is motha gu mór as fiosrach sinne
> 20 Nach d' fhàilnich 'fhacal e riamh;
>   Bidh geamhradh is samhradh ann is earrach
>   Is fogharadh fo m' chomhair gach ré;
>   Is gach gealladh riamh a labhradh leis-san
>   Tha fìor is cho maireann ris fhéin.
>
> 25 Mar sin, bheir sinn cliù do Dhia ar n-Athair
>   Is do dh'Ìosa Crìosta gach uair
>   Air son maitheis gach là agus gràs air thalamh
>   Is nas fhearr nuair ruigeas sinn shuas.[42]

Translation

(1-8) The Spring is the time, with sunshine and showers, that put the plough and work-horse to use so that there will not be crisis or dearth during the storms and windy times; the winter approaches with snow and freezing cold, and provisions will be in the barn and under the ground; and with plentitude in our hands, and thanksgiving in our hearts, we have every expectation of being happy and content.

(9-16) Great praise and esteem to Him who gave strength and capacity to sow and reap: He himself has blessed every deed for our hands when He poured down bounty from above; with the rain of the skies, and with warmth, and with light from the sun that He himself created; and with night-time dew which is fresh every morning, bringing growth to tender shoots and grass.

(17-24) It was David who wrote great praise and esteem to the Lord for us in the Bible; and even much greater is our knowledge that his word has never failed; I encounter winter and summer, spring and autumn, each in turn; and every promise that he has ever spoken has been as true and eternal as He is Himself.

(25-28) Therefore, we will give praise constantly to God our Father and to Jesus Christ, for the bounty of every day and grace on the earth, and even better when we arrive up above.

7: "That is the Drink I Would Imbibe"

The following hymn was composed by Donnchadh Mitseall, among a number that he wrote in the 1870s. It is modelled closely on a well-known secular song of the "roll call of the allies" variety, where each clan is invited to come share the drink of warrior-companionship with a Cameron leader:

>Siud agaibh an deoch a dh'òlainn,
>Deoch-slàint' a' Chamshronaich bhòidhich,
>Siud agaibh an deoch a dh'òlainn.
>Dh'òlainn deoch-slàinte 'n fhir ruaidh
>Chaidh thar a' ghualainn Di-Dòmhnaich...[43]

>That is the drink that I would imbibe,
>The toast to the handsome Cameron-man,
>That is the drink that I would imbibe.
>I would imbibe a toast to the red-haired man
>Who departed across the ridge on Sunday...

Instead of the alcoholic toast of military alliance in the original song, however, this hymn celebrates the metaphorical drink of the acceptance of Christian salvation, drawing on the symbolism of communion wine. This text provides an excellent example of how Gaelic songs in the popular repertoire could provide a framework for religious poets who could adapt the familiar imagery and literary devices to carry a spiritual message. The poem affirms the Gaelic penchant for songs and singing but redirects these energies in service of God (lines 13 and 63).

Original Text

1 Siud agaibh an deoch a dh'òlainn,
   Deoch-slàint' an anama o'n dòrainn,
   Siud agaibh an deoch a dh'òlainn.

   Deoch gràidh sìorraidh Dhé, an Athar,
5 Do gach anam 'chuir ann dòchas.

   'S mise dh'òladh i le h-aighear
   Ach thus', Athair, 'ga thoirt dhomhsa.

   An deoch thug réite dhuinn o'n chartas
   A bha bacadh dol gu glòir dhuinn.

10 An deoch ud a rinn slàinte do mhìltean
   Nuair 's a' phrìosan bha iad leòinte.

SEANCHAIDH NA COILLE

Seadh, gun òlainn dhith le h-aoibhneas
Anns an oidhche is gun seinninn òrain.

An deoch a cheannaich Crìosta 's an latha ud
15 Mach o'n Athair air son mhóran.

Nuair a dhòirt E 'mach fuil anam
Anns an latha ud a bha dòbhaidh.

An deoch a fhuair e dhuinn 's an latha ud
Nuair a chathaich E ris an leòghann.

20 An deoch a fhuair E air crann ceusaidh
Fuil na réite air an dòigh sin.

An latha fhuair E 'mach an ìocshlaint
A thug sìochaint air gach dòigh dhuinn.

Thug E buaidh a-mach 's an latha ud
25 Is chaidh E dhachaigh dh'ionnsaigh glòire.

Is tha E 'n-diugh an làthair an Athar
Air a' chathair ann am mórachd.

Siud an deoch a nì do shàsachd
Anns an fhàsaich fhad as beò thu.

30 Is tha i 'n-diugh gu saor 's an fhacal
Is i an-asgaidh do na dh'òlas.

Is ma dh'òlas tusa dhith anam
Cha bhi pathadh chaoidh ri d' bheò ort.

Seadh, ma dh'òl thu dhith gu caoimhneil
35 Rinneadh aoibhneas a bha mór leat.

Ach do shoitheach bochd eu-dìonach
Feumaidh Crìosta a chur an òrdugh.

An eadh, cha mhór a nì e 'chumail
Ged is duilich leam an còmhradh.

40 Ach mór d' òl thu idir fhathast
Is motha is fad a bha thu 'ad chòmhnaidh.

Thig a-nis le t' uile anam
Is rach gu t' Athair ann am mórachd.

Agus iarr air air son Chrìosta
45 E bhith sìth riut anns an lò seo.

Iarr air do pheacain a mhaitheadh
Fhad is tha agad latha tròcair.

RELIGION

    Nis on a tha mi gu co-dhùnadh
    Bidh mi 'n dùil gun dèan thu òl dhith.

50 Is gun dì-chuimhnich thu do bhochdainn
    Is gach dosgainn bha an tòir ort.

    Is nì thu aoibhneas 'n-sin thar labhairt
    Is do thaic bhith air an-còmhnaidh.

    Nì E lòchrann do d' chasan
55 Is bheir E sanas air an ròd dhuit.

    Nì E solas do d' cheumadh
    A nì treubhach fhad is beò thu.

    Nì E lorg dhuit anns an abhainn
    A' dol thairis air bruach Iòrdain.

60 Gus fa dheóidh an tig thu dhachaigh
    Gu bhith maille ris an-còmhnaidh.

    Gus an coinnich riut na h-ainglean
    Is an seinn thu 'n-sin gu ceòlmhor.

    Nuair a chòmhlaicheas na bràithrean
65 Ann am Parras, nì iad òl dhith.

    Mar as trice a rinn 'nan latha
    Nuair air thalamh bha an còmhnaidh.

    An dream a dh'fhalbh dhiubh ás a' chadal
    Tha iad maille ris an-còmhnaidh.

70 Is òlaidh iad gu saor de'n abhainn
    A' ruith a-mach o'n chathair thròcair.[44]

Translation

(1-3) That is the drink that I would imbibe, the toast of the soul freed from torment, that is the drink that I would imbibe.

(4-5) The drink of eternal love of God the Father for every soul that has placed faith in him.

(6-7) I would drink it with cheer if you, Father, would only give it to me.

(8-9) The drink that freed us from debt that was preventing us from going to glory.

(10-11) That drink that renewed the health of thousands when they were in prison, wounded.

(12-13) Yes, I would drink of it with joy in the night and I would sing songs.

(14-15) The drink that Christ bought that day from the Father for multitudes.

(16-17) When He spilled his life's blood on that day that was dreadful.

(18-19) The drink that He got for us that day when He battled with the lion.

(20-21) The drink that He got on the Cross, the blood of atonement [won] in that manner.

(22-23) The day that He secured the remedy that brought peace to us in every way.

(24-25) He secured victory on that day and He went home to glory.

(26-27) He is today in the presence of the Father on the throne in majesty.

(28-29) That is the drink that will satisfy you in the desert for as long as you live.

(30-31) Today it is free to ask for and it is free to those who drink it.

(32-33) And if you drink of it, you will never be thirsty as long as you live.

(34-35) Yes, if you drank of it kindly, it gave you joy that you felt was great.

(36-37) If your poor vessel is leaky, Christ must set it right.

(38-39) If so, it will not hold much, even if it is hard for me to discuss.

(40-41) If you drank a great deal of it yet, your life would be the longer.

(42-43) Come now with your whole soul and go to your Father in majesty.

(44-45) And ask him for Christ to be at peace with you on this day.

(46-47) Ask him to forgive your sins while you have a day of mercy.

(48-49) Now that I am about to conclude, I expect that you will drink of it.

RELIGION

(50-51) And that you will forget your hardship and every misfortune that was pursuing you.

(52-52) And that you rejoice there beyond words and that he will always be your support.

(53-54) He will provide a lantern for your feet and He will show you signs on the way.

(55-56) He will make a light for your steps that will keep you straight for as along as you live.

(57-58) He will make a staff for you in the river going over the banks of the Jordan.

(60-61) Until at last you come home to be with Him always.

(62-63) Until you meet the angels and you sing there musically.

(64-65) When the brethren come together in Paradise, they will drink of it.

(66-67) As they often did in their era when they were living on earth.

(68-69) Those of them who departed from this sleep are with Him always.

(70-71) And they drink freely of the river that flows out of the throne of mercy.

8: The Bible

The following song-poem was composed by Aonghus MacFhionghain in 1914, when he was living near Vancouver. It is a paean to the Bible that borrows elements of the Gaelic panegyric code to exalt its subject, despite the Bible being an inanimate object rather than a human being. The poet looks to the Bible for defense and sustenance (lines 7-8), for example, just as was expected of clan chieftains of old. The Bible is the top-most book (line 9), just as the chieftain or king was expected to outshine others. It has withstood attack from enemies (lines 11, 13 and 54), earned fame and renown (lines 20, 50 and 65-66), and attracts dependents looking for the guidance, shelter and nourishment it can offer (lines 5-6, 21-23, 29-32 and 61-64).

As a physical object, the Gaelic Bible is a cherished token of his ancestral homeland, written in his beloved native language (lines 33-53). As the foundation of authority for a hegemonic institution,

MacFhionghain expects that the Bible will eventually reign supreme among all peoples, whom he categorizes by skin colours into racial groups (lines 69-72).

Original Text

1   Thàinig thugam thar a' chuan
    Leabhar luachmhor an deagh sgéil:
    Air breith is àrach is bàs an Uain
    Is iomadh buain air moladh Dhé.

5   Nì mi lòchran dhiot is fear-iùil
    Is inneal-stiùiridh do mo cheum:
    Gheibh mi beatha, neart, is lùths
    Aig crùbadh dhomh fo sgàil do sgéith.

    Chan eil leabhar ann bheir barr ort:
10 Dheachdadh thu bho làthair Dhé,
    Is cha toir claidheamh buille bàis dhuit:
    Is ionann thu is Immanuel fhéin.

    Is iomadh ionnsaigh guineach garg
    Thug iad ort bho'n aimsir chéin
15 Ach tha do ghlòir an-diugh gun chearb;
    'S e as ainm dhuit "Facal Dhé."

    Théid muir is talamh bun os cionn,
    Théid air chùl an Cruinne-Cé,
    Ach maireannach bidh tusa chaoidh,
20 Do dhàn is do chliù air feadh gach ré.

    Ged tha mi aineolach 'ad chùirtibh
    Bheir mi ùmhlachd dhuit is spéis;
    Iarraidh mi an solas-iùil ud
    Is gheibh mi dlùth do'n ìobairt réit'.

25 'Nad dhìomhaireachd, cha ghrunnaich nàdar
    Mur sil an gràs a-nuas o Nèamh;
    Is nam bitheadh déidh agam do phàirt riut
    Gheibhinn e 'ad lànachd féin.

    Gheibh am bochd is an deòiridh dìon bhuat
30 Is tu fear biadhachaidh an treud;
    Air do chluaintean nì thu feurach,
    Siabaidh tu bho 'n sùil an deur.

    Thàinig thu air astar buan
    Thar a' chuan á tìr mo ghràidh;

35   'S e mo bhràthair a chuir thu bhuaidh
Is cha toir duais thu ás mo làimh.

Thàinig thu á tìr mo dhùthcha,
Anns a' chainnt rinn ùr do sgeul:
Gàidhlig chùbhraidh tìr an fhraoich,
40   Is caoimh' leam i na ceòl nan teud.

Tìr nam bodach 'dhèanadh ùrnaigh
Bheireadh an driùchd a-nuas o Nèamh,
Bheireadh neart do'n chuilc bhrùite
Is chuireadh an caol smùid am meud.

45   'S ann ro aonaranach a bha mi
Bho nach robh thu làthair liùm;
Ach o'n rinn thu tighinn sàbhailt
Gléidhidh mi thu ghnàth le mùirn.

Cuiridh mi fàilt' ort is furan,
50   Bheir mi urram dhuit is géill;
Leughaidh mi ri gréin is coinneal
Cuibhrionn dhiot gu ceann mo réis.

Thàinig thu gu dùthaich choimheach
A bheir toibheum dhuit is beum;
55   Ach Ifrinn shìos, ged dhlùthadh 'na tarraing,
Cha téid thairis Facal Dhé.

Ach iarmad bheag tha fhathast ann
Measg gach dath is teang' is treubh
Le'n ionmhainn thu is nach leig air chall
60   Rann air bith tha annad fhéin.

Dèan éifeachdach do theachd a-nall;
Tha m' anam fann a' cur ort feum;
Dèan dìreach dhomh gach nì tha cam
Is an t-ionad garbh 'na chòmhnard réidh.

65   Thigeadh beannachd leat is buaidh
Is foillseachadh air luach do sgéil;
Glaodhaidh sean is òg riut suas
Mar an sluagh bha aig an fhéill.

Biodh dubh is buidhe, geal is ruadh,
70   Dèanamh luaidh air fuil na réit';
Coimhlion dhuinn do ghealladh buan
Is glòraicht' bidh an t-Uan d'a réir.[45]

Translation

(1-4) A precious book of the good story came to me from across the ocean about the birth and upbringing and death of the Lamb, and the many fruits of the praise of God.

(5-8) I will make a lantern and a guide of you, and a compass for my steps: I will get life, strength and energy by crouching under the shadow of your shield.

(9-12) There is no book that can excel you: you were recorded in the presence of God and no sword can strike you dead: you are equivalent to Immanuel himself.

(13-16) They have made many vicious and rough assaults on you since ancient times, but today your glory is unharmed; your name is "the Word of God."

(17-20) The sea and earth will be turned upside down, the Earth will come to an end, but you will last forever, your destiny and your renown throughout all time.

(21-24) Although I am unknown in your courts, I give you obeisance and devotion; I will seek out that guiding light and I will become close to that sacrifice of atonement.

(25-28) Human nature cannot fathom your mysteries unless grace showers down from Heaven; and if I desired a portion of it from you, I would get it in your own fullness.

(29-32) The pauper and the exile get protection from you, you are the food-giver of the masses; you provide grazing in your meadows, you wipe the tear from their eyes.

(33-36) You came across a long expanse of the ocean from the land that I love; it was my brother who sent you, and no amount of money will make me give you up.

(37-40) You came from my native land, in the language that has refreshed your story: fragrant Gaelic from the land of heather, more beloved to me than the music of [harp] strings.

(41-44) The land of the old men who would offer prayer that could bring the dew down from Heaven, that would give strength to the broken reed and would enliven the wick's thin smoke.

(45-48) I was exceedingly lonely because you were not with me; but now that you have come safely, I will keep you always with joy.

(49-52) I will welcome you heartily, I will honour you and obey you; I will read an excerpt from you by sunlight and by candlelight to the end of my life.

(53-56) You came to an alien land that will insult and taunt you; even if Hell below were to draw itself close, it would not overpower the Word of God.

(57-60) There is still a small remnant that still exists among every colour and language and race who cherish you and will not allow any verse that is in you to be lost.

(61-64) Let your journey over be efficacious; my weak soul is making good avail of you; make straight for me each thing that is crooked, and make the rough place into a smooth plain for me.

(65-68) Let blessings and victory come with you and a revelation of the worth of your story; young and old will be called up to you like the crowd that was at the feast.

(69-72) Let black and yellow, white and red, declaim the Blood of the atonement; fulfill for us your eternal promise and the Lamb will be glorified accordingly.

9: The Missionary on Lake Winnipeg

The following tale about a Presbyterian missionary on Lake Winnipeg was printed without an attribution to a source or information about the time when it was supposed to have happened. Although it is almost certainly based on an actual event, it is more significant for what it reveals in symbolic terms about the perceptions and beliefs of early-20th-century Presbyterian Gaels in Canada, especially regarding their role in proselytizing First Nations communities, than any historical data it might contain.

The tale suggests that the author believed that a positive and symbiotic relationship could result from missionary work. It was the stubborn insistence of the outsider that the native boatmen take dangerous short-cuts which forced them to land on the island: the natives had superior knowledge of the geography and climate, and were able to extract resources effectively (catching the fish that fed them). The missionary, however, through the (presumably) superior cultural achievement of mathematics finds the optimal solution for distributing the food and treats the natives much more humanely than the fur traders they had dealt with before. This ultimately wins their trust and they choose of their own free will to come to the missionary, integrate into his community and accept his religion.

Original Text

Bha fear de theachdairean an t-Soisgeil a' siubhal ann an àirde tuath Chanada. Bha e ann an cabhaig, agus dh'iarr e air na h-Innseanaich a bha 'ga aiseag ann an canoe a dhol dìreach o rudha gu rudha an àite bhith dèanamh an turais fada le bhith cumail faisg air a' chladach. Bha sin 'na nì cunnartach, gu sònraichte o nach robh aca ach eathar a bha air a dèanamh le beillig. Tha Loch Winnipeg 'na muir stoirmeil, agus tha baghannan farsaing air.

Eadar dà rubha, astar mór o thìr, rug an soirbheas orra agus cha robh nì ri dhèanamh ach a dhol an taobh a chuireadh a' ghaoth is na tuinn iad. Gu fortanach, dh'amais iad air eilean beag anns an loch, agus fhuair iad fasgadh, ach bha còignear Innseanach rompa, air an aon chàradh riutha fhéin, ach gun ghreim bìdh aca. Riaraich an soisgeulaiche orra am beagan a bh' aige fhéin, uiread is uiread do gach aon.

Bha dòchas aige nach biodh am fuireach air an eilean fada. Ach lean an stoirm roimpe, agus air a' cheathramh latha b' fheudar dhaibh uile bhith teannachadh nan crios; bha am biadh air teirgsinn.

Chaill a' chuid mhór de na h-Innseanaich am misneach gu tur, ach bha aon fhear 'nam measg a thug ionnsaigh air iasgach. Lùb e priona air chumadh dubhain, fhuair e pìos de ròpan tearra, agus bìdeag de dh'aodach dearg mar bhiadh. Leis an uidheam-iasgaich sin, chaidh aige air aon iasg nach robh ro mhór a thoirt gu tìr.

Rinn iad teine ann an cabhaig, agus chuireadh an t-iasg ann an coire ga bhruich, ach mun robh an t-uisge air deagh ghoil, chaidh a thoirt barr an teine, agus bha na daoine acrach a' dol mu ithe. Chuir iad an treas cuid de'n iasg fo chomhair an t-soisgeulaiche, ag ràdh ris gum b' e siud a chuid-san.

Bu mhath a thaitinn am fialaidheachd ris, ach chan aontaicheadh e leis an roinn idir. "Chan e sin an dòigh as fhearr air a roinn," ars esan.

Chuir e an t-iasg cuideachd, na bha iad a' toirt dhasan agus na bha iad a' cumail dhaibh fhéin. An-sin dh'fhosgail e a sgian agus chunnt e na daoine, "a h-aon, a dha, a trì, a ceithir, a còig, a sia, a seachd, a h-ochd," agus ghearr e an t-iasg 'na ochd mìrean de'n aon mheudachd agus thug e mìr do gach fear, a' cumail mìr dha fhéin cuideachd.

"Bidh an aon uiread againn uile," ars esan.

An là 'r na- mhàireach, dh'fhàs an t-sìde na b' fhearr agus fhuair an dà chuideachd falbh an taobh a bha iad a' dol. Ach bha an gnìomh neo-fhéineil a rinn an soisgeulaiche air drùdhadh iongantach a dhèanamh air na daoine fiadhaich. Bha e ri fhoghlam gun robh a dhèanadas gu bhith cho tarbhach ri theagasg.

Àireamh mhìosan an déidh sin, ràinig còignear Innseanach am baile beag anns an robh a chòmhnaidh, iad fhéin is an teaghlaichean, agus dh'iarr iad cead an dachaigh a dhèanamh faisg air agus iad toigheach air an dòigh ùr ionnsachadh.

Cha robh an teachdaire 'gan aithneachadh. "Car-son a tha sibh ag iarraidh sin?" dh'fheòraich e. "Chan fhaca mi duine dhibh anns na coinneamhan."

"Is sinne na fir air an do roinn sibh an t-iasg," arsa fear dhiubh, a' toirt ga chuimhne mar thachair air Loch Winnipeg. "Nam bu cheannaiche-béin a bhiodh 'nur n-àite, ghabhadh e na bheireamaid dha, agus is dòcha gun iarradh e tuilleadh. Ach an uair a chunnaic sinn mar a rinn sibhse, dh'aithnich sinn gum bu duine math a bh' annaibh, agus tha sinn a-nis an-seo ag iarraidh gun ionnsaich sibh dhuinn an dòigh ùr."[46]

Translation

A missionary was once travelling in the north of Canada. He was in a hurry, and he asked the Indians who were transporting him in a canoe to go directly from headland to headland rather than making the trip long by keeping close to the shore. That was dangerous, especially since they only had a vessel that was made with tree bark. Lake Winnipeg is a stormy body of water and it contains expansive bays.

Between two headlands, a great distance from land, a storm hit them and there was nothing to do but to go the direction that the wind and waves took them. Fortunately, they happened upon a small island in the lake, and they found shelter, but there were five Indians there before them in the same situation as themselves and they didn't have any food. The missionary shared the little he had with them, an equal share with each one.

He hoped that they would not stay on the island for long. But the storm continued on, and on the fourth day they all had to tighten their belts; all of the food had run out.

Most of the Indians had completely given up hope, but there was one man among them who tried to fish. He bent a pin into the shape of a hook, he got a piece of tarred rope, and a little bit of red cloth as bait. With that fishing tackle, he was able to bring to land one fish that was not too big.

They made a fire hurriedly and the fish was put into a pot to boil, but before the water was brought to a full boil, it was taken from the fire and the hungry people made ready to eat it. They put a third of the fish in front of the missionary, telling him that that was his share.

He greatly appreciated their generosity, but he did not at all agree with the division. "That is not the best way to divide it," he said.

He put the fish back together, the part that they gave him together with what they were keeping for themselves. Then he opened his knife and he counted the people, "one, two, three, four, five, six, seven, eight," and he cut the fish into eight pieces of equal size and he gave a piece to each man, keeping a piece for himself as well.

"We will all have the same amount," he said.

The next day the weather improved and the two companies were able to travel on their way. But the selfless act that the missionary did left a marvellous impression on the wild people. He was to learn that his conduct was as productive as his teaching.

A number of months after that, five Indians arrived in the little village in which he was living, themselves and their families, and they asked permission to make their home close to him as they were keen to learn the new way.

The missionary did not recognize them. "Why do you want to do that?" he asked. "I have not seen any of you in the meetings."

"We are the men for whom you divided the fish," said one of them, reminding him of what had happened on Lake Winnipeg. "If a fur trader had been in your place, he would have taken what we gave him, and he probably would have asked for more. But when we saw what you did, we realized that you were a good man, and now we are here wanting you to teach us the new way."

10: About the United Church of Canada

The process of uniting individual congregations into a larger religious institution continued apace and culminated in the creation of a national Protestant church in 1925, the United Church of Canada. Just as seen in song-poem 7.5 about the 1875 merger, the proposition divided many Gaelic congregations. The Gaelic journal *An Solus Iùil* (The Guiding Light) was established at the same time to assist Highland congregations in negotiating these momentous transformations of direction and leadership. The first official issue declares its purpose and calls for reconciliation after congregations voted on the contentious issue:

> Bidh e leis an Eaglais Aonaichte, ach cha bhi e ri connsachadh gun fheum aig àm sam bith, agus cha dèan e càineadh air muinntir sam bith nach bi 'ga dheagh thoillltinn. Feuchaidh e ri bhith ceart agus coibhneil anns gach nì agus air gach dòigh. ...
>
> Tha an cath seachad. Roghnaich an sluagh mu'n chùis a bha fo'n comhair a-réir an eòlais. Chaidh a' mhór chuid leis an Eaglais

Aonaichte, ach tha cuideachd nach beag a dhiùlt a dhol leatha, a' cur rompa fuireach air leth. Is ainneamh àite anns nach eil daoine air an roinn 'nam barail; air fad 's air leud na dùthcha gheibhear co-thionalan, sgìreachdan agus eadhon teaghlaichean air an roinn, air chor is gum faighear an-diugh muinntir a bha agus a tha 'nan dlùth-chàirdean ag adhradh air falbh o chéile.[47]

It [the newspaper] will be on the side of the United Church, but it will not engage in any unnecessary quarrelling at any time, and it will not disparage any people who do not truly deserve it. It will try to be correct and kind in every matter and in every respect. ...

The battle is now over. The people have voted about the matter that was before them according to their knowledge. The majority joined the United Church, but there is no small number who refused to join it, resolving to remain independent. There is hardly a place where people are not divided in their opinions; throughout the length and breadth of the country, there can be found congregations, counties and even families that are divided, to the point that today people can be found who were and are close relations worshipping separate from each other.

It was not long before many Gaelic congregations felt the negative impacts of the resulting divisions which further weakened those aspects of Highland Presbyterianism that differed from anglophone practice, including the language used for worship.[48]

I was told many times in 1932 and 1937 that the formation of the United Church of Canada had been a severe setback to Gaelic, as Gaelic congregations had joined and were then without Gaelic ministers, while Gaelic ministers had refused to join and were left without congregations.[49]

The following song-poem was composed by Murchadh Moireasdain to protest the formation of the United Church and convince his local congregants to remain as an independent entity. The "Rosach" (Ross) of line 128 is Dòmhnall Ros who ministered to the Gaelic congregations around Mira Bay, Cape Breton, between 1840 and 1870.[50] The "Muillear" of line 115 is the Rev. E. D. Millar of Yarmouth, then the Moderator of the Synod of the Maritime Provinces.

RELIGION

Like the protest song by MacCoinnich against amalgamation (song-poem 7.5), Moireasdain contrasts the peaceful fellowship and wise leadership of the past with the present dissension caused by unification. Loyalty to Gaelic in private and public spheres is a laudable trait of the old worthies (lines 47-50 and 133-34). The poet attributes greed and a will to power as motivating those behind unification (lines 66, 83-84 and 115-122). He proclaims that the United Church of Canada will eventually fail and his own church succeed, because God is on his side (lines 71-82 and 87-90).

Original Text

<pre>
1   O, nach fhan sibh
        'S an eaglais 's am bu chòir dhuibh?
        An eaglais a th' againn
        Tha i brèagh' ri faicinn;
5   Is gun d' chum sinn gu glan i
        Le barrachd de bhòta.

        Is ioma ministear beannaicht'
        Th' an-diugh fo'n talamh
        A bha riamh 'ga leantainn
10   Is an anam aig tròcair.

        Bha éildearan againn
        A' riaghladh nam beannachd,
        An-diugh le'n cinn ghlasa:
        Chan fhan duine dhiubh còmhl' rinn.

15   An Union a th' againn,
        Cha mhór sheall i 'bheannachd:
        'S ann bhrist i gach parraist'
        A bh' againne còrdte.

        Mhill i na càirdean
20   An-diugh anns gach àite
        Gu ruige nam bràithrean
        A b' àbhaist bhith còrdte.

        A dh'aindeoin an dìcheill
        Gun d' ghléidh sinn na trì dhiubh;
25   Bha 'n Cruithear leinn,
        Tha E dìleas d' ar seòrsa.

        Ged a rinn sibh a fàgail
        Mar uan bhiodh gun mhàthair,
</pre>

Chan eil i gun chàirdean
30 Nì làidir gu leòr i.

An taigh th' air a riaghladh
Le beannachd is le diadhachd,
Bidh gràine de 'shìol ann:
'S e Dia chumas beò e.

35 Mur biodh gun do thachair
An Judge a bhith againn,
Bha Caorstaidh is Anna
Air tighinn dhachaigh gun bhòtadh.

Siud am fear a bha dìleas
40 Le briathran na Fìrinn',
Is cha b' urrainn dhaibh 'dhìteadh
Le nì de'n cuid eòlais.

Is fhad is a bha e againn
A' riaghladh air thalamh,
45 'S e dhèanadh an ceartas
Cha leanadh e neo-ghloin'.

Cha robh diobhar dé 'n t-àite –
Aig a thaigh no air sràid e –
Bha a chridhe cho blàth:
50 Bha 'Ghàidhlig aige 'n-còmhnaidh.

Gun d' fhalbh e bho dhachaigh
Air thuras do'n bhaile;
Is gun choinnich e 'n Teachdair'
Thug dhachaigh gu glòir e.

55 Siud am fear a bha dìreach
Le briathran na Fìrinn';
Cha b' ann air na mìltean
Bhiodh 'inntinn an-còmhnaidh.

Tha a chàirdean 'ga ionndrainn
60 On chàradh fo'n ùir e;
'S ann aige bha 'n cliù
Anns gach dùthaich de 'eòlas.

Nuair bha Crìost' air an talamh
'S i 'n àithn' thug e seachad
65 An soisgeul a sgapadh
Gun dad ach aon chòta.

Cha mhór tha de'n nì sin
An-diugh air an inntinn;
'S ann tha iad a' strì
70 Ris na mìltean is corr dheth.

Ach chì sibh le'r sùilean .
Am beagan de ùine
Gum bi 'n eaglais ùr
Aig a' ghrunn nach eil mór dhiubh.

75 Ach an là théid sibh innte
Rannsaichibh am Bìoball
Ach am faigh sibh aon nì ann
Nì sibh nas cinntich' á tròcair.

Nuair thig stranger do'n àite
80 Is a chì e na dhà dhiubh
Bidh e a' foighneachd de Shammy,
"Am bheil Pàpanaich còmhl' ribh?"

An eaglais tha thall ud,
Tha i brèagha 'nam shealladh;
85 Gun cumadh i barrachd
Is am parraiste còmhla.

An Dia a bh' againn,
Gur E a th' an-diugh againn;
Is nì Esan an ceartas –
90 Bidh na h-amadain gòrach.

An duine tha beannaicht'
'Na ghiùlan air thalamh,
'S ann aige th' an gealladh
Aig cathair na tròcair.

95 Bha éildearan againn
Bha measail 's a' pharraist'
A dh'fhalbh 'nam bharail-s'
An ceathrar dhiubh còmhla.

Chan eil mi 'gur càineadh,
100 Chan eil e 'nam nàdar;
Tha mi duilich an-dràsta
Gun na càirdean bhith còmhla.

Na dèanaibh mo dhìteadh
Ged dh'innsinn an fhìrinn;
105 Tha dragh ann air m' inntinn
An nì th' ann 'nur seòrsa.

        Tha dithis 's an àite,
        'S e an cridhe tha blàth dhi;
        Gun d' shìn iad an làmh dhi
110   Is b' fheairrde gu leòr e.

        Ur pàrantan dìleas
        A thog i le dìcheall:
        Gu dé bhuail 'nur n-inntinn
        Toirt dìmeas d'a seòrsa.

115   Th' am Muillear ag ràitinn
        On chaidh e mar chaidh e,
        "Nì mis' dhaibh an sàbhadh
        Cha charge mi aon ghròt orr'."

        Ged dhèanadh tu 'shàbhadh,
120   Gach bior a th' air t' àite,
        Ma tha do chridhe gun ghràs ann,
        Chan fheairrd' thu móran.

        Ach, Aonghuis, a charaid
        An do chuimhnich thu t' athair?
125   Bha e riamh 'ga leantainn
        Gu'n deachaidh am fòd air.

        Nuair bha mi 'nam bhalach,
        'S e 'n Rosach a bh' againn
        Le searmonan glana
130   'G[an t]oirt seachad an-còmhnaidh.

        Nuair thigeadh an t-Sàbaid
        Bhiodh searmon no dhà ann;
        B' e 'n toiseach a' Ghàidhlig,
        'S i b' fhearr le mo sheòrsa.

135   Fhad is a bha e air thalamh
        Gu'n d' rinn e ar leantainn,
        Gus 'n tàinig an Teachdair'
        Thug dhachaigh gu glòir e.

        Nuair a rinn e ar fàgail
140   Thàinig Gordon 'na àite;
        Tha fear 'ainm anns an àite
        Ge b' có dha thug e 'bhòta.[51]

Translation

(1-6) Oh, won't you stay in the church where you ought to be? The church we have is beautiful to behold; and we have kept her pure with a surplus of votes.

(7-10) There are many blessed ministers who are under the soil today, who followed her always and their souls are at peace.

(11-14) We had elders who oversaw the blessings [but] today none of them, with their grey heads, will stay with us.

(15-18) This Union that we have, it won't show us any blessing: indeed, it has broken every parish that we had harmonized.

(19-22) It has ruined the friends today everywhere, even the brethren that used to be in harmony.

(23-26) Despite their best attempts, we have preserved three of them; the Creator was on our side, he is faithful to our sort.

(27-30) Although you have left it [the church], like a motherless lamb, it is not without friends who will make it strong enough.

(31-34) The house that is ruled with blessings and godliness will have a grain of seed: it is God who will keep it alive.

(35-38) If it weren't that we happened to have the Judge, Kirsty and Anna would have come home without voting.

(39-42) There you have the man who was loyal with the words of Truth, and they could not denounce him with any of their own knowledge.

(43-46) For as long as we had him governing in this world, he would do justice and he would not follow corruption.

(47-50) The place didn't matter—whether he was at home or on the street—his heart was warm; he always spoke Gaelic.

(51-54) He left home on a journey to the town and he encountered the Messenger who took him home to glory.

(55-58) That is the man who was plainspoken with the words of the Truth; it was not on secular matters that his mind was constantly occupied.

(59-62) His friends miss him since he was placed in the soil; he is the one who was esteemed in every land that he was known.

(63-66) When Christ was on earth, the commandment that he made was to disseminate the Gospel, owning nothing but a single coat.

(67-70) There is not much of that today on their minds; indeed, they are striving with the thousands, and more.

(71-74) But you will see with your own eyes in a short time that the new church will sink to the bottom.

(75-78) But on the day in which you go in, search through the Bible until you find one thing in it that will make you the surer of mercy.

(79-82) When a stranger comes to the place and he sees the two of them [the two different churches], he will ask Sammy, "Are there Papists here with you?"

(83-86) That church over yonder, it is pretty looking; it would hold more than the combined parish.

(87-90) The God that we knew, he is still with us today; He is the one who will do justice—the fools will remain foolish.

(91-94) The man who is blessed in his earthly conduct, he is the one who has the promise of the throne of mercy.

(95-98) We had elders who were esteemed in the parish who diverged in their opinions, the four of them together.

(99-102) I am not disparaging you, it is not in my nature; I am sorry at present that those friends are not together.

(103-106) Do not condemn me for speaking the truth: my mind is troubled by the makeup of your sort.

(107-10) There are two people in the place and their hearts are friendly to it [the church]; they have reached out to her and it is the better for it.

(111-14) Your faithful parents who built it with great effort: what caused your mind to disrespect its kind?

(115-18) The Miller says, given the way that things went, "I will do the sawing for them, and I won't charge a single groat."

(119-122) Even if you do the sawing, every single mote that is in your spot, if you heart lacks grace you won't get much benefit.

(123-26) But, o Angus, friend, did you remember your father? He always followed it [the church] up until the sod was placed on him.

(127-30) When I was a boy, we had Ross, who always delivered excellent sermons.

RELIGION

(131-34) When the Sabbath would come, there would be a sermon or two; first came the Gaelic, and it was preferred by my sort.

(135-38) For as long as he was on the earth, he followed us, up until the Messenger came who took him away home to glory.

(139-42) When he left us, Gordon came to replace him; a man of his name is in place, regardless of who he voted for.

11: National Hymn

The following song-poem was composed and titled by Eòin Mac-Fhionghain. It is an inclusive prayer for divine favour on behalf of urban as well as rural populations (lines 11-12), for Canadians as well as all people of the world (lines 1-2). Besides its religious message, this hymn also makes a strong statement about a sense of belonging to Canada, which could now be considered "our own native land" (line 4), rather than the original homeland in Scotland. The graves of ancestors rooted Gaelic communities to the soil[52] (line 5) and the descendants of those who had emigrated from Scotland could now boast that they could live where they chose to live (lines 8 and 16).

Original Text

1   A Dhia, nuair théid ar n-ùrnaigh suas
    Air son gach sluaigh fo'n ghréin,
    Do bheannachd, iarramaid le dùil,
    Do thìr ar dùthchais fhéin.

5   Ar sinnsir tha an-seo fo'n fhòid
    Is ar càirdean còir' a' tàmh,
    An-seo tha fàs [an àlaich òig]:
    Seo tìr ar deòin is ar gràidh.

    O, dìon ar crìochan o gach nàmh!
10 Biodh sìth ar n-àrois buan;
    Thoir soirbheachadh do'n bhaile mhór,
    Cuir saidhbhreas lòin air cluan.

    Le eòlas, fìrinn agus gràdh,
    Thoir dhuinn bhith ghnàth mar aon;
15 Ar cnuic is ar glinn gu caithream gluais
    Le òrain sluaigh tha saor.

> Gun earb sinn riut, a Dhia nan Dùl
> Ar dùthaich anns gach càs;
> Bi fhéin mar thearmann dhi is mar iùil
20   Is 'ad charaid dlùth gu bràth.[53]

Translation

(1-4) O God, when our supplication goes upwards on behalf of every people in the world, let us ask for your blessing with hope for our own native land.

(5-8) Our ancestors are here under the sod, and our goodly friends are resident here, and the young generation is growing up here: this is the land of our choice and our affection.

(9-12) Oh, protect our territory from every enemy! Let the peace of our habitation last; bring prosperity to the big city, infuse the meadow with fruitfulness.

(13-16) With wisdom, truth and love, let us always be as one; inspire our hills and glens to rejoice with the songs of a people who are free.

(17-20) We entrust to you, o God of the Elements, our land in every circumstance; be as a sanctuary and a counselor to her, and a close friend always.

8 – Language and Literature

No question has persisted to occupy and concern poets as much and for so long as that of the survival of their language. As Gaelic literary expressions composed since the beginning of the 18th century demonstrate,[1] poets were keenly aware of the instrumental role of language in expressing, transmitting, embodying and engaging with Highland culture and identity. Iain Crichton Mac a' Ghobhainn, one of the outstanding Gaelic poets of the 20th century, explores how the treatment of Gaelic has constituted an assault on the Gàidhealtachd and its integrity as a living entity:

> The problem of language is, one supposes, the most important one that faces the person who analyses his own experience in the islands, for it is in many ways central to an island experience. As I have already said, for the islander to lose his language utterly would be to lose, to a great extent, the meaning of his life, and to become a member of a sordid colony on the edge of an imperialist world. ...
>
> There is no question that a language holds a community together in its various manifestations, and that to have to learn a new language in order to be educated at all is a dangerous and potentially fatal attack on that community and those who form part of it. For the imperialist language is imperiously and contemptuously degrading the native one. ...
>
> The Gaelic speaker feels himself to be inferior, and his language inferior.[2]

Despite the acquiescence of many, the Gaelic language in Canada has always had a loyal and vocal following by people who have struggled for its survival and expressed their aspirations in literary form. What has been eloquently observed about the role of the Welsh language and literary tradition in upholding and enriching Wales as a distinct ethnic community and associated identity is also relevant for understanding the importance of Gaelic.

> Languages are very delicate networks of historically accumulated associations, and a thought in Welsh has innumerable and untraceable connections with the thought of past centuries, with the environment, with the scenery even, with one's mother and father, with their mothers and fathers, with the moral and emotional terms in which the community has discussed its differences. ... The language is, of course, the vehicle of the literature. Literature in fact is language used at its highest level. Welsh literature is both the expression of this life under hatches and the escape from it. ... Welsh literature tells the Welshman that his language is not inferior and that he has a princely inheritance.[3]

Thomas Douglas (Earl of Selkirk) had proposed in 1805 that ethnic enclaves which spoke languages other than English could act as buffer zones to protect British North America from the radical, revolutionary spirit of the United States. Both Irish and Scottish Gaels, he knew, would relish the freedom to maintain and develop their linguistic inheritance.

> A national settlement, speaking their original and favourite dialect will be particularly attractive to the Irish as to the Highlanders; and it will be of use to preserve among the Settlers, those national customs and peculiarities, which are associated in their minds, with the traditions of the ancient greatness of their race.[4]

The mass migration of families from the Scottish Highlands, many of which spoke nothing but Gaelic, established the language in virtually every pocket of settlement in British North America in the 19th century, from Newfoundland to Vancouver. This made it, for a time, the third-most-spoken European language at the time of Canadian confederation, as census figures testify.

A comparison of the 1901 and 1931 figures illustrates the extent to which Gaelic was truly a Canadian language at the turn of the century, with robust communities across the country. Conversely, it also shows how rapidly the language went into decline in the intervening three decades.[5]

Settlement in self-sufficient communities allowed Gaelic to be transmitted across several generations, sometimes with less interference and disruption than in Scotland itself. An account of Prince Edward Island in 1828 claims:

> I have observed, that wherever the Highlanders form distinct settlements, their habits, their system of husbandry, disregard for comfort in their houses, their ancient hospitable customs and their language, undergo no sensible change. They frequently pass their winter evenings reciting traditionary poems, in Gaelic, which have been transmitted to them by their forefathers; and I have known many who might with more propriety be called genuine counterparts of the Highlanders who fought at Culloden, than can now, from the changes which have during the last fifty years taken place, be found in any part of Scotland.[6]

A Scottish traveler in Cornwall, Ontario, in 1879 was impressed with the amount of Gaelic that he found and declared that it was

> the most Highland place I have been in yet. The second and third generation speak Gaelic; but the young who are now growing are not likely to know any. Almost everyone I have seen is of Knoydart stock. Nearly all are MacDonalds. ... All of these, and Mr. George MacDonald, the post-master, speak Gaelic, as they do all over Glengarry, with the most perfect accent, and with scarcely any, if any, admixture of English. Indeed, I have no hesitation in saying that the Gaelic of this Glengarry is much better than that of the old Glengarry.[7]

An inhabitant of Dunvegan, Glengarry, Ontario, concurred with the resilience of Gaelic culture there in the late 19th century and compared the state of the language and customs unfavourably with the Scottish Gàidhealtachd due to domination and assimilative pressures of anglophones in Britain:

> Agus is iongantach agus bochd ri innseadh gum bheil na Gàidheil a' fàs coltach ris na Goill anns a' cheum seo. Tha sinn

ann an cunnart gun caill sinn ar dùthchasachd gu léir mur amhairc sinn romhainn. Tha e 'na nì iongantach r'a innseadh gun coinnich neach an-diugh ris an tuilleadh de dhuinealas ann a bhith a' cumail ri dòigh nan athraichean ann an Canada na ann an Gàidhealtachd na h-Albann. Tha ann an cuid de cheàrnaibh de Chanada muinntir a chaidh a bhreith is àrach air an taobh seo dhe'n chuan agus chuireadh iad nàire air an càirdean air Alba air son gloine an Gàidhlig, an cùram mu chumail suas beul-aithris agus gnàth-fhacail an sinnsearachd, agus air son mar tha iad a' taisbeanadh nan déiligeadh ri aon a chéile, gum bheil a' ruith 'nan cuislean fuil bhlàth a rinn Gàidhealtachd na h-Albann 's na linntibh a dh'fhalbh ainmeil air son a caoimhneis agus a cathrannais. Bha mi gu mór air mo ghoirteachadh air mo thuras do'n Ghàidhealtachd o chionn dà bhliadhna a bhith coinneachadh ris an spiorad spìocach a tha gu mór a' tarmachadh ann am broilleach nan Gall a' riaghladh ann an cuid de cheàrnaibh na Gàidhealtachd. Ma tha neach air son coinneachadh ri fìor Ghàidheil an latha an-diugh, feumaidh e amharc air an son 's na tìrean céine.[8]

And it is strange and sad to say that the Gaels are becoming similar to the Lowlanders [or non-Gaels] in this sense. We are in danger of losing our culture entirely if we do not watch where we are going. It is a strange thing to say that someone can today encounter greater valour in maintaining the ancestral traditions in Canada than in the Highlands of Scotland. There are people in certain corners of Canada who were born and raised on this side of the ocean who would shame their relations in Scotland for the purity of their Gaelic and the attention that they pay in keeping the oral traditions and idioms of their ancestors alive, and for how they deal with one another; the warm blood runs in their veins that the Gàidhealtachd of Scotland made illustrious for kindliness and charity in the days of old. I was greatly upset on my trip to the Highlands two years ago to encounter a sense of miserliness that accumulates thickly in the hearts of the Lowlanders [or non-Gaels] governing some of the parts of the Highlands. If someone wants to meet real Gaels in the present day, he must look for them in foreign countries.

The strength of the language in larger settlements also meant that people of other ethnic origins had to learn to speak Gaelic in order to interact with the community and integrate into it fully. Many Gaels who urged their peers to stay faithful to their language and not accept negative stereotypes about it liked to point out people from other ethnic groups who were capable and proud Gaelic speakers, as did the Rev. Tormad MacDhòmhnaill in 1933:

> Ged is duilich leinn aideachadh, 'se na Gàidheil féin nàimhdean as motha tha aig a' Ghàidhlig an-diugh. Coltach ris an amadan bhochd aig nach robh tuigse air fiach airgid, tha aineolas air a luach a' toirt orra a' cur air chùl air son nì nach eil idir ri bhith air a choimeas rithe. Bha uair ann, is gur e na Goill bu mhotha mì-rùn agus fuath dhi. ... Thachair gu leòr oirnn ann an Canada anns nach eil boinne de dh'fhuil a' Ghàidheil, a thàinig 'nan cloinn a-nall á Sasainn agus a thog a' Ghàidhlig gun saothair anns na taighean agus a labhras an-diugh i cho fileanta ciatach ri Gàidheal sam bith nach do dh'fhàg Alba riamh. Chan e sin a-mhàin, ach chunnaic sinn daoine de gach dath agus cinneadh ann an Canada a labhras i gu eireachdail.[9]

> Although it is difficult for us to admit, the Gaels themselves are the worst enemies that Gaelic has today. Like the poor fool who does not understand the value of money, the ignorance of its value causes them to turn their backs on it for something that cannot at all be compared to it. There was a time when it was the Lowlanders who had the greatest aversion and hatred for it. ... We have met plenty of people in Canada who do not have a single drop of Gaelic blood, who migrated over from England as children and picked up Gaelic effortlessly at home and who speak it today as fluently and beautifully as any Gael who never left Scotland. Not only that, but we have seen people of every colour and race in Canada who speak it elegantly.

Gaels in the United States recognized that their ancestral inheritance connected them to geographically disparate communities that crossed artificially created boundaries of nation-states but that their compatriots in Canada were enjoying more success in sustaining their language and culture. At a céilidh in New York in 1905, for example,

Mr. Donald Currie paid a glowing tribute to the Canadian Gaelic-speaking Highlanders, who were keeping alive the language, poetry and customs of their forefathers. The present meeting reminded him of a genuine Highland céilidh. Whether we be born on this side of the Atlantic or in Tìr nam Beann, he said, let us never forget that we are Gaels, speaking the same language, and in a measure possessed of the same characteristics as our forefathers. Before dispersing, the company joined in singing "Gabhaidh sinn an rathad mór" and wishing Mr and Mrs McLean h-uile latha sona dhoibh.[10]

We have already seen many comments about issues of language in previous texts: people have asserted their love for Gaelic (texts 2.5, 3.6, 5.11, 5.15 and 7.8), people have been praised for their loyalty to the language (texts 6.14, 7.3 and 7.10), emigration to Canada has been portrayed as the most effective means of preserving the language and culture (text 4.11), Gaels have acknowledged the stigmas which have been created for their language by anglophones (texts 3.6 and 5.12), and some Canadian Gaels have been castigated for abandoning their native tongue (text 3.2). Unlike immigrant groups from beyond the British Isles, Scottish Gaels (like the Irish and Welsh) had a long-standing history of conflict with the anglophone world and had been represented as the "primitive Other" in the venerated canon of anglophone literature and historiography. The dominance of Anglocentric perspectives in Canada as well as in the national institutions of their own homeland presented an extra dimension of difficulty for Gaels to maintain their language and culture.

There were a number of strategies that Gaels who were resolute in their dedication to their language pursued in order to defend the language and encourage others to maintain and develop it: the composition of Gaelic literature, especially oral song-poetry, exalting the language and calling for linguistic solidarity among immigrants; the creation of print media to connect individuals across Canada and the wider world into an "imagined" Gàidhealtachd that negotiated the terms of modernity; the establishment of Gaelic organizations to use the language in social settings and engage in political issues (discussed further in the next chapter).

Most of the rhetorical devices and arguments used to promote allegiance to Gaelic were first employed in two foundational poems,

"Air teachd on Spáin, do shliochd an Gháoidheil ghlais" (When the Descendants of Gaoidheal Glas Came from Spain), written by Maighstir Seathan MacGill-Eain and printed in 1707, and "Moladh an ùghdair don t-seann chànain Ghàidhlig" (The Author's Praise of the Ancient Gaelic Language) written by Alasdair mac Mhaighstir Alasdair and printed in his 1751 poetry anthology. These poems depict Gaelic as the original language of the Scots, a noble tongue spoken by the national founding figures and heroes of the past, capable of forming great literature and articulating serious intellectual content. They portray Gaelic as a language under attack by anglophone enemies who threaten the well-being of Gaeldom and are turning Highlanders against their own ancestral inheritance. Mac Mhaighstir Alasdair's poem established as a common literary motif the notion that Gaelic was humankind's first language, spoken by Adam in the Garden of Eden, a claim made earlier by Rev. David Malcolm in 1738.[11]

Nearly all of the texts in this volume that attempt to elevate Gaelic echo the conceit that it was spoken by Adam and by great luminaries in Scottish history, and used to great effect by respected poets. Most also stress the role of language in forming and nurturing the social bonds of family and community, and the betrayal to the intimacy and trust of those relationships represented by abandoning Gaelic in favour of English.

The emergence of Gaelic newspapers, and Gaelic columns in anglophone newspapers, was always marked by song-poems praising the efforts of the editor, the contributors and the subscribers in maintaining the language and literary tradition. Dozens of such odes survive from poets from all over North America celebrating these verbal manifestations of the continuity of their cultural heritage on the continent, virtually none of which have ever been discussed or integrated into the mainstream histories of the legacy of Scottish immigrants in Canada. Murchadh D. MacDhòmhnaill, writing in 1929 from Spring Hill (now "Nantes"), Quebec, composed a concise example of the genre to pay tribute to the newspaper *Fear na Céilidh*, printed in Cape Breton but enjoying subscribers all over Canada:

> Cumaibh suas i, cainnt nan uaislean,
> Suas le uaill is cliù dhi;
> Suas gu h-àrd i, na leig bàs leath',
> Cainnt ar màthar, rùn dhi;
> Chan eil a' Ghàidhlig fhathast marbh,

Ar nàmhaid dhearg ged lùigeadh;
Chan eil i ach 'na cadal balbh,
Is chan eil i doirbh ri dùsgadh.[12]

Keep it alive, the language of the noble people,
Alive with pride and renown;
Strongly alive, do not allow it to die,
Our mother tongue, [show] love for it;
Gaelic is not yet dead,
Even though our bitter enemy would wish it;
It is only silently sleeping,
And it is not difficult to waken.

Newspapers were able to connect literate Gaels all over the globe to communication networks so that they could share common interests, not least their linguistic and literary heritage. Such periodicals allowed not only the collection and preservation of items circulating in oral tradition but experimentation with new forms and genres of literature, such as short stories and novellas, some of them original and some of them translated from English.[13] A letter to *Mac-Talla* in 1903 from a correspondent identified only as "Calum Dubh" in Ottawa expressed the pride of the Gaelic community in these literary ventures and its hopes that they would thrive.

Tha mór-spéis agam dha na seann-òrain bhlasda, bhinn tha sibh a' cur an clò, 's dha na litrichean pongail tha an-dràsda 's a-rithist ann, gu sònraichte litrichean Iain Rothaich, a tha toirt cunntais air an t-seann mhuinntir a dh'fhàg St Anns beagan bhliadhnaichean mu'n d' rugadh mi ach air an cuala mi iomadh iomradh cliùiteach agus tréibhdhìreach. Chan eil mi dèanamh mì-bhuil de na seanfhacail a tha mi [a'] leughadh ann bho àm gu àm, 's tha cruinneachadh math agam dhiubh, ged tha 'chuid nach deach fhathast an clò nas brìghmhoire na tha iad dreachmhor.

Tha mi toilichte bhith faicinn gum bheil e 'nur comas a bhith toirt seachad duaisean air son litrichean Gàidhlig ged tha mi dhe'n bheachd gur ann bu chòir dha na h-uile fear anns am bheil smior na Gàidhlig bhith toirt dhuibhse duais air son na tha sibh a' dèanadh chum an cànain aosta bhlasta thàinig a-nuas troimh linntibh thar chunntas a chumail suas. Gun teagamh nam biodh an luchd-leughaidh dìleas agus duineil bhiodh an comas sin agaibh. Chan eil agamsa air ach mar a thuirt a' chailleach a bha air mhisg, "Is math ma mhaireas."

Chan eil Gàidheil lìonmhor 's a' bhaile seo ach am beagan a th' ann, tha iad glé mheasail air a' chànain a dh'fhàg an sinnsir aca mar dhìleab, 's tha iad uile guidhe gun soirbhich gu math le ur pàipear grinn.[14]

I am hugely fond of the delicious and melodious traditional songs that you are printing, and of the concise letters that appear now and again, especially the letters of John Munro, that provide an account of the old population who left St. Anns a few years before I was born but about whom I have heard many positive and upstanding descriptions. I am making some use of the proverbs that I read from time to time, and I have a large collection of them myself, although those that have not yet been printed are more useful than they are decorous.

I am glad to see that it is in your capacity to give prizes for Gaelic letters although I am of the opinion that every person who has the spark of Gaelic in him ought to be giving an award to you for what you are doing to keep alive the ancient, eloquent language that has come down through innumerable ages. Without a doubt, if the readership was as loyal and manly [as you are], you would be able to do that. I do not have anything to add to that except what the old woman who was drunk said: "It's good if it lasts."

Gaels are not plentiful in this city but those who are here greatly esteem the language that their ancestors left them as a legacy, and they are all praying that your polished newspaper will prosper.

Gaelic newspapers began in Canada as early as 1840, although most were short-lived and overly dependent upon reprinting materials from Scottish sources.[15] The longest-running Gaelic newspaper, *Mac-Talla* of Nova Scotia (1892-1904), had subscribers and contributors not only all over Canada but all over the world and printed a wide spectrum of genres and materials. These print materials could only be effective to the degree that people were able to read them but formal education seldom made allowances for literacy in Gaelic. Insecurity and shame about the inability to read and write is sometimes revealed in the letters from readers and contributors to Gaelic periodicals.[16]

Figure 8.1 – Advertising for Mac-Talla *on its own pages. The central logo of a Highlander echoes that of Cuairtear nan Gleann. On either side are two traditional sayings: "Guma fada beò a' Ghàidhlig" (May Gaelic live long) and "Lean gu dlùth ri cliù do shinnsir" (Follow the renown of your ancestors closely). On the bottom line the reader is entreated "Cha bu chòir do Ghàidheal sam bith a bhith ás aonais" (No Gael should be without it). Image from copy of the newspaper in Michael Newton's private collection.*

The long-standing habits of mind produced by the oral-dominant nature of Gaelic song-poetry is reflected even in the odes written in praise of newspapers and newspaper columns. Advocates of literacy and published media intuitively harkened back to the deeply-rooted notions of orality and the aural transmission of tradition. The name of the newspaper *Mac-Talla* itself means "echo" and is probably an allusion to a 17th-century song-poem about the waning of support for the traditional arts among some of its last patrons, the MacLeods of Dunvegan.[17]

Poets who wished to praise, or more generally discuss, books and newspapers in Gaelic could do so by personifying their inanimate subject and then applying the conventions of the panegyric code to it. This rhetorical strategy was actually pioneered no later than 1567 in a dedicatory poem opening the Gaelic adaptation of the *Book of Common Order*, exhorting it to venture forth and convert the Gaels of both Scotland and Ireland.[18] Similar poems were composed in the following decades by Irish Gaelic poets to their own manuscripts and books. Whether the Bàrd MacGill-Eain—who was literate and highly knowledgeable about Gaelic literary tradition—consciously invoked a literary device with which he was already familiar (see text 8.2) or reinvented it through an organic extension of existing metaphorical resources, it is suggestive of the significant continuities that connect Canadian Gaelic literature to the expressions of much earlier times.

Gaels dedicated to the preservation of their language and literature began to establish events and organizations with this express purpose in mind, often inspired by the foundation of An Comunn Gàidhealach in Scotland in 1892 and the Irish Revival movement of the late 19th century. Correspondents scattered across North America proposed in letters to *The Scottish American* newspaper in 1902 that an annual celebration of Gaelic literature and music be established on the model of the Royal Scottish Mòd. Donald MacVicar, of Portage La Prairie, Manitoba, was among those who wrote in to support the idea:

> It seems to me that there is no better method of conserving all that is noblest in Gaelic literature, or fostering the loving spirit of clanship, than by such an institution; and I trust that our Highland societies throughout the continent may give Mrs. Campbell's proposal their early and earnest support, that we may soon welcome its accomplishment.[19]

Although this institution was not established at a North American level at that time, smaller regional efforts did emerge over the next few decades, such as the Vancouver Mòd in 1934. A group of the Gaelic worthies of Glengarry with similar concerns initiated a literary society in 1909.

> A Gaelic revival is in prospect in the County of Glengarry, Ontario. In many portions of Canada the Gaelic has been rapidly disappearing, together with many of the customs which were common among the early settlers. Some of the leading men are banded together to change the present tendency and restore the former order of things. Amongst them are Senator McMillan, Mr John F. MacGregor, Dr D. D. McDonald, Mr Angus McDonald, Mr Norman McRae, Mr D. N. McLeod and Mr Angus Cameron.[20]

The Gaelic language needed to be nurtured, extended and developed to deal with the demands of urban "modernity" and in fact Gaels all over Canada have been doing just this since the late 19th century: Comunn Gàidhlig Thoronto (the Gaelic Society of Toronto) began as a debating club discussing the political and social controversies of the day, all in Gaelic (see chapter 9); *Mac-Talla* coined and used many neologisms to discuss contemporary news and innovations;[21] *Mosgladh* printed terminology specific to the politics of commerce in the interests of the growing co-operative movement in the 1930s;[22] a Gaelic booklet intended for students and printed in Sydney, Cape Breton, in 1939 included a glossary of useful terms of this sort.[23] It was no fault of their own, or inherent shortcoming of the language itself, that stalled such efforts but rather the undermining of the linguistic community by the Anglocentric prejudices that held sway throughout the British Empire. Anglophone privilege was built into imperial institutions, whether in Britain or abroad, and any concessions to other languages were hard-won when they were accommodated at all. In assessing the position of Gaelic in the discourse of multiculturalism within Canadian history, for example, Robert Dunbar notes:

> Until well into the 20th century, the dominant approach to the existence of cultural and linguistic diversity in almost all of those territories that now form the Canadian federation was one which has been described as "Anglo-conformity." This approach to diversity was essentially assimilationist: cultural and linguistic difference should be replaced by a common identity based on a shared language—English—and shared cultural values—broadly speaking, "British" ones. This approach to diversity was based on assumptions about the supposed superiority of anglophone British culture, and the belief that "lesser" peoples would benefit from participation in a supposedly "higher" civilization.[24]

There are many reasons why members of a community may change their linguistic allegiances, not least the reality of gradual accommodation to the dominant language of the social environment in which they live. The common pattern in North America when immigrants enter into highly interconnected, urban settings is that the ancestral language is lost within three generations.[25] This does not explain why or how the shift from Gaelic to English happened in the more substantial and cohesive rural settlements, such as in the Maritimes, however. Dòmhnall MacGill-Eain Sinclair, writing in 1950, described deliberate attempts to eradicate Gaelic in Nova Scotia through coercion.

> ...in Scotland it has suffered greatly by restrictive laws. In the Highlands, children whose mother tongue it was, were forbidden to speak it in school, and if caught speaking it, were punished. This strange idea came over to Nova Scotia. Dr. Chisholm of Bridgeville, Pictou County, told me that in his early days children who spoke Gaelic were accompanied home from school by others who were to report to the teacher if they heard Gaelic spoken. If caught they were punished, just as in Scotland. Thus in about one generation Gaelic was killed in Pictou County.

Many of the older folk reserved it as a sort of secret code to be used when children were about.[26]

Gaelic commentators remark on the trauma inflicted on people through the stigmatization of their language and the internalization of contemptuous attitudes cast on the community by anglophones. Efforts to provide symbolic or substantial recognition for Gaelic in any official capacity in Canada have typically met intractable resistance.[27] Some of that resistance has come from the upper ranks of Gaelic immigrant society itself, men who were often the first converts to the rewards available through Anglo-conformity.

> One of the most pernicious effects of the exclusion of Gaelic from the elite domains of society is that it was generally the most prosperous districts of Gaelic regions and almost always the natural leadership of the community that received the earliest and most thorough exposure to these anglicizing institutions. The very regions that should have acted as the engines for the culture's continued adaptation and prosperity encouraged its stagnation and decline; and the very people who became best placed to consolidate the language's strengths and ensure its healthy evolution and continued development were, by the very mechanism that placed them in their positions of authority, educated to do exactly the opposite.[28]

Organizations in Nova Scotia have made repeated efforts spanning decades to secure a place for Gaelic, alongside English and French, in the formal educational institutions of the province. Concerted attempts carried out by an alliance of groups through political channels in the 1920s is described in the first issue of the bilingual journal *Mosgladh* (Awakening):

> Cha d' fhuair a' Ghàidhlig agus clann nan Gàidheal an ceartas còireach sin. 'S e dì-meas agus mearachd glé mhór a tha ri fhaicinn 's a' chùis, agus leis gach ànradh agus sàrachadh a fhuair iad, 's ann a tha creideas glé charanach ri thoirt dhaibh air son a bhith, idir, air bonn cho mall 's a tha iad. Agus a-réir mar a tha iad air bonn, 's coltach e, gun teagamh, gur ann a' tighinn beò nas làidire tha 'Ghàidhlig. Bheir an timcheallachadh beag seo a-nis mo luchd-leughaidh a dh'ionnsaigh a' ghnothaich mun do thòisich mi: A' Ghàidhlig anns na sgoiltean.

Mu thrì bliadhna air ais, chuir Comunn Gàidhlig Shidnidh guth-iarrtais, le suas ri deich mìle ainm cudthromach, gu pàrlamaid Ùr-Albainn, a' guidh orra a' Ghàidhlig a chur 'na ionad anns na sgoilean 's a' Mhór-Roinn seo. 'S còir taing clann nan Gàidheal gu dìlinn a bhith ri comain oifigich Comunn Gàidhlig Shidnidh air son a saothair bhuadhail. ...

Ach is iomadh cnap-starra fhathast ri dhìreadh leis a' bhrataich mun urrainnear "buaidh ullamh" a ghairm. ...[29]

The Gaelic language and the Gaelic people did not get that proper justice. Outright disrespect and injustice is what can be seen in the matter, and with every calamity and oppression that they experienced, indeed one has to give them credit for being established at all, however delayed they are. And given how they are established, it seems, doubtlessly, that Gaelic survives all the stronger. This little tangent will now take my readers back toward the matter about which I began: Gaelic in the schools.

About three years ago, the Sydney Gaelic Society sent a petition, with up to ten thousand important names, to the Nova Scotia Assembly, beseeching them to put Gaelic in place in the schools of this province. The Gaelic people ought to be eternally indebted to the officers of the Sydney Gaelic Society for their successful efforts. ...

But there are many obstacles still to overcome with the war-banner [in hand] before "complete victory" can be declared. ...

A frustrated Nova Scotian activist commented in 1939 on the ongoing struggle and humiliation:

Strange to say, although French, German and Greek were placed on the school curriculum of Nova Scotia, no effort was made to have Gaelic taught to the thousands of our stalwart Scottish youth, whose ancestors played so prominent a part in the building of the country. Why German and Greek should be preferred to the ancient and expressive Gaelic I do not know. ... [30]

Lori Cox's research in Cape Breton, published in 1994, describes the downward spiral of collapse as Gaelic was excluded from domains that would have developed it and added to its prestige and social functions in communities where it had been dominant:

> Gaelic in the Cape Breton schools has been discouraged on three different levels: exclusion of the language as a medium of communication; exclusion from the curriculum of both the language and the culture which it embodied; and, in taking these actions, transmission of negative attitudes concerning the value and usefulness of the language and culture to the community at large. Without doubt, negative attitudes like these have been entirely responsible for the shift to English in the last fifty or sixty years.[31]

Similar causes and results were noted as effective in Glengarry by the third quarter of the 19th century, as reflected in these comments in 1884:

> During the lifetime of the first immigrants the Gaelic language was much in use, so much that knowledge of it was considered a necessary qualification for the Presbyterian pulpit. The common school, however, has brought the new generation to use the English tongue, and a Gaelic sermon is now rarely heard, though in some isolated sections the Gaelic language is in some measure of use.[32]

Canadians of Scottish Highland origin who accepted the inferior status of their ancestral language and culture could be easily persuaded to deny rights and status to others as well. When it was proposed in 1877 that an agricultural report be translated into French in New Brunswick, for example, Archibald McKenzie[33] (a member of the province's Legislative Assembly) decried the motion and insisted that the French follow the Highlanders' precedent of deference to Anglo-conformity.

> ...looking back over the vista of the years, we remember when Britain was of small account and that she became "Great" only when Scotland joined her. Wherever the English tongue prevails a Scotch name is found to honor the head of the administration. ... The manifest destiny of the English is that they shall predominate, because of their association with the Scotch, and if any language is to be particularly fostered it is that of those who gave and preserved these colonies to the British Crown. We, as Scotsmen, however, do not ask for legislative enactments, nor do

we beg for subsidies to maintain our language, for it is a gem to be displayed only on great occasions, and it is fitting only for the expression of great things. The English language is destined to be the language of the world—the language of commerce—and where there is a Frenchman who aspires to honor and enlightenment, though he may not attain to Gaelic, he will learn English. I was surprised a while ago to hear an hon[ourable] Member say the Scotch [Gaelic] was no language. It was a language before the French or English was ever thought of, and that gentleman, himself a Celt, should feel no pride in arguing against the language of his remote forefathers in favor of another and an alien tongue. To the victors belong the spoils. The British were the victors in this country, and those who accepted the conquerors' protection, and the free citizenship they now enjoy under the British flag, should also accept the English language.[34]

The validation offered by militaristic triumphalism under the "British" banner thus serves, for McKenzie and others of the same disposition, as a substitute for the cultural sovereignty and linguistic distinctiveness for which the French as a community were willing to press. In some cases, however, more conciliatory narratives were created to console those resigned to the obsolescence of Gaelic and the inevitable results of Anglo-conformity. A particularly interesting example of this from Bruce County, Ontario, explicitly tries to reconcile a younger generation with the loss of their ancestors' language.

Around the turn of the [20th] century a story was current regarding a settler newly arrived from England who found himself living among Gaelic speakers. This man became quite angry with some children who were laughing at their parents' mistakes in English.

"I don't laugh at them," he said, "but regard their efforts to talk with me as a high honour. English is not their native language—and they love dearly their Gaelic—and yet they will sacrifice all to talk with us and to build an English-speaking country."[35]

The English settler personifies the external assimilative forces of the English language pressing on the community but gives them a kind and compassionate face. The listener is meant to believe that the anglophone world was complimented by the efforts of Gaelic Canadians to communicate and collaborate with them. The tale readily admits the natural affection that people have for their mother tongue, but assumes that the process of nation-building was only possible on the linguistic terms dictated by anglophones. This bargain is presented as a predestined and mutually beneficial one.

There is little better proof of the colonization of Gaelic minds than the adoption of anti-Gaelic prejudices by Highland immigrants and their descendants and the conscious rejection of the norms of their ancestral community, especially in terms of language loyalty. Like flora and fauna, languages and cultures have evolved and declined throughout human history, but they are going extinct at an unprecedented rate in the present, particularly in areas that have been compromised through imperial-colonial relations.

> The Celtic languages were systematically undermined in an attempt to bring their speakers into cultural and political compliance. When this process was frustrated the metropolitan élites were quite prepared to forcibly remove them and replace them with an amenable work force ... it seems that while the speakers of Celtic languages, when faced with the conscious or subconscious choice between the metropolitan language and peripheral language, did often favor the metropolitan, this can hardly be called a free or benign choice.[36]

1: New Year's Eve near Lake Huron

The following description of the aftermath of a New Year's Eve céilidh in Bruce County, Ontario, in the mid 19th century was recorded by Alasdair Friseal. The elderly woman discussed in the tale, Cuarag, was poor, feeble and lived on the charity of others, but people valued her presence at céilidhs because of her ability to contribute her musical skills and her enthusiasm to do so. This anecdote thus demonstrates how the sharing of oral tradition promoted intergenerational ties and social cohesion.

Original Text

> Air Oidhche Challainn àraidh, mu dhà fhichead bliadhna roimhe seo, bha cruinneachadh de'n t-seòrsa seo ann an Siorramachd Bhruis, ri taobh Locha Huron. Bha grunn ghillean

òga agus chailean an làthair, agus bha sùgradh nach bu bheag air a' chuideachd. Ri àm dol dhachaigh, chaidh buidheann de na gillean seachad air taigh beag a bha ri taobh an rathaid, àite-còmhnaidh seana bhoireannaich air an robh am frith-ainm "Cuarag." B' aon de na seann bhoireannaich i aig nach robh dìlsean no luchd-dàimh anns an tìr seo, ach a bha 'tighinn beò air toirbheartas an luchd-dùthcha. Bha min-choirce is -chruithneachd, buntàta is measan eile, pailt anns an dùthaich, agus de na nithean sin, cha bhiodh uireasbhaidh air na cailleachan.

Cha bhiodh cuirm am measg nan coimhearsnach aig nach biodh Cuarag; bha i 'na deagh bhan-sgeulaiche, agus b' urrainn di fonn a chur air seann òran luaidh cho math ris an dara té. Cha robh i aig a' chruinneachadh àraidh air am bheil mi a' dèanadh aithris, agus bu mhór iongantas na cuideachd nach robh i an làthair. Shaoil cuid gun robh i tinn, oir 'nam beachd, cha chumadh nì eile air falbh i; bha cuid de'n bheachd gun robh i ann an éiginn, oir bha an geamhradh cruaidh air a' bhliadhna sin; is mar sin, bha cor Cuaraig air a cnuasachadh.[37]

Translation

On a particular New Year's Eve, about forty years ago, there was a gathering of this sort [a céilidh] in Bruce County, near Lake Huron. There was a group of boys and girls there, and the company was enjoying themselves greatly. When the time came to go home, a group of the boys went by a small house that was at the side of the road, the residence of an old woman who was known by the nickname "Cuarag." She was one of the old women who had no close friends or kin in that area, living on the charity of neighbours. Oatmeal, wheat flour, potatoes and other crops were plentiful in the area, and so the old women did not lack any of those things.

There was never a feast in the community at which Cuarag did not appear; she was an excellent storyteller and she could sing an old waulking song as well as any other woman. She was not at the particular gathering that I have related and the company was greatly surprised that she was not present. Some thought that she was sick, as in their opinion nothing else could keep her away; some believed that she had some emergency, as the winter had been severe that year; and so, Cuarag's well-being was being deliberated.

2: A Song to the *Traveller*

The following ode in praise of the newspaper *Cuairtear nan Gleann* (The Traveller of the Glens) was composed by Iain MacGill-Eain (Am Bàrd MacGill-Eain) in about 1842. This newspaper was printed in Scotland and written entirely in Scottish Gaelic, largely the work of the Rev. Dr. Tormod MacLeòid, better known by his nickname "Caraid nan Gàidheal" (the Friend of the Gaels). His previous periodical, *An Teachdaire Gaelach* (The Highland Messenger) ran from 1829 to 1831, and this one ran from 1840 to 1843. Both of them were highly influential in the development of vernacular Gaelic expository prose and enjoyed contributions from, and readers in, locations all over globe, including Nova Scotia.

Figure 8.2 – The masthead of the Scottish newspaper Cuairtear nan Gleann. *The slogan "An là a chì 's nach fhaic" comes from a traditional toast wishing people well every day, whether or not they see them. Image courtesy of Dr. Sheila Kidd, University of Glasgow.*

By exercising poetic license to personify a newspaper, MacGill-Eain can draw liberally from the elements of the Gaelic panegyric code. Just as a migrant or any other traveller might do, the newspaper traverses the mountains and sails the seas (lines 1-2) and its arrival is greeted with a toast (line 4). Just as a Highlander on a journey would need to be well clothed, the newspaper has arrived in a durable package ornamented with shipping information (line 17-36). The newspaper is likened to an old character of the neighbourhood, Iain Muilleir (lines 37-44), who is described elsewhere:

The "Iain Muilleir" referred to was a native of Sutherland; and he was commonly known as Bodach an Fhéilidh [the Old Man of the Kilt]. He was driven to this country when an old man by the Sutherland clearings. He wore the kilt in winter and summer; probably he never had a pair of trousers on. He was like his countryman, Rob Donn, a noted deer-hunter. He lived to the patriarchal age of one hundred and seven years.[38]

Like a person, the periodical has a lineage and ancestral inheritance: the *Traveller* is described as being the heir of its predecessor, *An Teachdaire Gaelach* (lines 51 and 54). Like the ideal Highland laddie, both its physical appearance (symbolized by the belted plaid) and its charm (manifest in its verbal dexterity and ability to entertain) make the *Traveller* a very popular figure, not least among the ladies (lines 9, 13 and 48-49). His fellow Gaels have a natural affinity for him as the most eloquent orator of their native tongue (lines 6-7, 46 and 49-50) and admire him for defying their common adversaries and quislings who threaten their linguistic and cultural inheritance (lines 36, 49-50, 55-56, 69-70 and 84).

This song-poem is an early example of the discussion of print media in vernacular Gaelic poetry and, perhaps ironically, a demonstration of the remarkable tenacity of the notion of orality. The *Traveller* relays information by speaking to an assembled audience, such as at céilidhs (line 7). The importance of periodicals to circulate Gaelic texts is mentioned in the song (lines 14-16), as is the common practice of reading aloud from them during céilidhs (line 11). Immigrant Gaels keep their speech alive in exile through the performance of song-poetry (line 71). MacGill-Eain will perform this song in praise of the Traveller when he joins friends in the tavern (lines 81-84). While printed media may temporarily capture and convey text, its ultimate value and function can only be realized, we might surmise from this text, when it is brought alive by the presence of both singer and audience.

Original Text

1   Deoch slàinte 'Chuairteir a ghluais á Albainn,
     Bho thìr nam mór-bheann, is a sheòl an fhairge
     Do'n dùthaich choilltich a thoirt dhuinn a sheanchais
     Is am fear nach òl i, biodh móran feirg ris!

5   Nuair thig an *Cuairtear* ud uair 's a' mhìos
     Gum bi na h-òganaich le toil-inntinn

A' tionail eòlais bho 'chòmhradh sìobhalt
Is bidh naidheachd ùr aig' air cliù an sinnsribh.

Gur lìonmhor maighdean tha ann an déidh air
10   Is a bhios le caoimhneas a' faighneachd sgéil de;
Le solas choinnlean a bhios 'ga leughadh
Is bidh eachdraidh-ghaoil aige do gach té dhiubh.

Chan iongnadh òigridh thoirt móran spéis da
Nuair tha na seann daoin' tha 'call an léirsinn,
15   Is an cinn air liathadh, cho dian an déidh air,
Is nach dèan iad 'fhaicinn mur cleachd iad speuclair.

'S e 'n *Cuairtear* Gàidh'lach an t-àrmann dealbhach
Le 'phearsa bhòidhich an còmhdach balla-breac,
Mar chleachd a shinnsribh gu dìreadh gharbhlach:
20   Is e fearail gleusta gu feum le armaibh.

Nuair thig e 'n tìr seo mu thìm na Samhna,
Bidh féileadh cuaiche mu 'chruachainn theannta
Is a bhreacan guaille gu h-uallach greannmhor
Is cha lagaich fuachd e no gruaim a' gheamhraidh.

25   Bidh boineid ghorm agus gearra-chòt ùr air,
Bidh osain dhealbhach mu 'chalpaibh dùmhail;
Bidh gartan stiallach thar fiar-bhréid cùil air
Is a bhrògain-éille, is b' e 'n t-éideadh dùthchais.

Bidh lann gheur stàillinn an crios 'bhràiste airgid air
30   Is biodag dhualach de chruaidh na Gearmailt;
Is dag air ghleusadh nach leum le cearbaich
Le sporan iallach de bhian an t-seanna bhruic.

'S e sin an t-éideadh tha eutrom uallach
Gu siubhal bheann agus ghleann is chruachan;
35   Is gu seasamh làraich an làthair cruadail:
Bu tric an nàmhaid an càs air ruaig leis.

Nuair a chì mi 'n *Cuairtear* tha uasal rìoghail,
Bidh mi 'ga shamhlachadh ri Iain Muilleir:
Tha fichead geamhradh bhon tha e 's an tìr seo
40   Is cha d' chuir e riamh air a shliasaid cuibhreach.

Tha corr is ceud bhon tha ciall is cuimhn' aig':
Is tric a shealg e damh dearg 's na frìthean
Air slios Beinn Àrmainn a b' àrd ri dìreadh;
Is an déidh an t-seòrs' ud, b' e 'n còmhlann fiachail.

45 Is a *Chuairteir* àlainn, tha tàmh 's na gleanntaibh,
    'Ga bheil a' Ghàidhlig is as fhearr a labhras i;
    Is nach gabh tàmailt ge b' e nì sealltainn riut:
    Is mór de chàirdean tha 'n-dràst an geall ort.

    Gun d' ghabh iad tlachd dhiot le beachd nach tréig iad
50 Bhon is Gàidheal gast' thu, tha sgairteil gleusta;
    Is tu oighr' an *Teachdaire* 'chleachd bhith beusach,
    Is cha d' fhàgadh masl' air a mhac 'na dhéidh leis.

    Is a *Chuairteir* ghràdhaich, cha tugainn fuath dhut,
    Gun robh do chàirdeas ri sàr dhaoin'-uasal;
55 Ged a rinn pàirt dhiubh do chàradh suarach
    A chaill a' Ghàidhlig, is na b' fhearr cha d' fhuair iad.

    'S i 'Ghàidhlig bhrìoghmhor bh' aig suinn na Féinne
    Is bu daoine calma 'nan aimsir féin iad;
    Is rinn Oisein dànachd daibh a-réir sin
60 Is gur h-ì bh' aig Pàdraig a bheannaich Éirinn.

    Gur mór na fiachan fo bheil na Gàidheil
    Do'n fhear a dh'inntrich air leabhar nàdair,
    Is a dhearbh le fìrinn gur h-ì bh' aig Àdhamh:
    'S e bainne-cìch a lìon gach cànain!

65 Bu lus bha prìseil i chinn 's a' Ghàradh
    Bha 'n stoc gun chrìonadh am brìgh is an àilleachd
    Is cha robh ann siantan a mhill a blàithean:
    Bu ghlan gun truailleadh a fuaim an là sin.

    A *Chuairteir* éibhinn, na tréig gu bràth i,
70 Is na leig air dìochuimhn' ri linn an àil-s' i!
    Bidh sinn 'ga seinn anns na coilltibh fàsaich
    Mar bha clann Israel a' seinn am Bàb'lon.

    Is a *Chuairteir* shìobhalt, ma nì thu m' iarrtas,
    Is gun cuir thu 'n t-òran seo 'n clò nan iarann
75 'Ad chaoimhneas, giùlain do'n chùrsa 'n iar e
    Do'n eilean ìosal, an tìr o'n thriall mi.

    Am baile gaolach a' Chaolais àillidh
    'S an robh mi 'còmhnaidh 'nam òige, fàg e
    Aig Cnoc MhicDhùghaill mu'n dlùth mo chàirdean
80 Is thoir fios gu'n ionnsaigh gum bheil mi 'm shlàinte.

    Nuair a bhios mi còmhla ri comann càirdeil,
    'Nar suidhe còmhnard mu bhòrd taigh-thàirne,
    Gun gabh mi 'n t-òran, gun òl, is gum pàigh mi
    Deoch-slàinte '*Chuairteir* le buaidh do'n Ghàidhlig.[39]

Translation

(1-4) [Here is] a toast to the *Traveller* who left Scotland, the land of great mountains, and who sailed the sea for the forested country to give us his news, and the man who does not drink it [the toast], let him be shown anger!

(5-8) When that *Traveller* comes once a month, the youths will gather information with pleasure from his civil speech and he will bear fresh news about the renown of their ancestors.

(9-12) There are many maidens who are infatuated with him and who ask him his news with kindness; he will be reading by candle light and he has a beloved historical account for each one of them.

(13-16) It's not surprising for the youth to show him such affection when the old people with grey heads, who are losing their sight, are so keenly after him although they cannot see him unless they use spectacles.

(17-20) The Highland *Traveller* is the handsome warrior, with his beautiful body in ornamented coverings, just as his ancestors did in order to ascend the rough territory: he is manly and adept, equipped for deployment with weaponry.

(21-24) When he comes to this country at about Hallowe'en time, he has a belted plaid around his svelte waist; the tartan around his shoulder is proud and elegant, and neither the cold nor the gloom of the winter can weaken him.

(25-28) He will wear a blue bonnet and a fresh waistcoat, well-cut hose around his muscular calves; a striped garter across the sash on his back, along with laced shoes: that was the native uniform.

(29-32) He will wear a sharp, steel blade in a belt with silver buckle and an ornamented dagger of German iron; with a well-tempered pistol that will not accidentally fire, and a sporran with thongs made of the skin of an old badger.

(33-36) That is the uniform that is light and proud for travelling mountains, glens and hills and for standing one's ground in the face of hardship: often was the hard-pressed enemy forced to flee because of it.

(37-40) When I see the *Traveller* who is noble and royal, I liken him to John Miller: he has been in this country for twenty winters and he has never put binders [i.e., trousers] on his thighs.

(41-44) He has more than a hundred [years] of sense and memory: often did he stalk the red deer in the hunting forests on the side of Beinn Àrmainn that was high to climb, [going] after those sorts [of creatures], it was a worthy group.

(45-48) O handsome *Traveller*, who resides in the glens, who has the best Gaelic of any who speak it and who will not be mortified, regardless of who sees you: there are many friends who are now in love with you.

(49-52) They have taken pleasure in you with the opinion that they will not desert you, as you are a splendid Gael who is vivacious and expert; you are the heir of the *Messenger* who used to be virtuous and he did not leave any disgrace for his son after him.

(53-56) O beloved *Traveller*, I would not show you hatred, you are related to superb nobility; although some of them have left you in an abysmal state and lost their Gaelic, but they did not find anything better.

(57-60) The substantial Gaelic was the language of the Fian warriors and they were valorous men in their own day; Ossian composed poetry to them accordingly, and it [Gaelic] was the language of Patrick who blessed Ireland.

(61-64) The Gaels are greatly indebted to the man who initiated the study of natural history and who demonstrated truthfully that Adam spoke it [Gaelic]: it is the breast-milk that has suffused every language!

(65-68) It was a precious flower that grew in the Garden [of Eden] from the trunk that was impeccable in essence and beauty; there were no elements to destroy her blossoms: her tones were pure and undefiled on that day.

(69-72) O joyous *Traveller*, never forsake it [Gaelic] and do not allow her to be forgotten during the lifetime of this generation! We will sing it in the wilderness forests just as the children of Israel sang in Babylon.

(73-76) O civil *Traveller*, if you fulfill my request and you print this song in iron type, carry it to the west coast in your kindness to the low-lying island, the land from which I departed.

(77-80) The beloved town of the lovely strait in which I resided in my youth, leave it [the newspaper] at MacDougall's Hill—my kin are densely populated around it—and send word to them that I am healthy.

(81-84) When I am together with a friendly group, sitting level around the table of a tavern, I will sing a song, drink and pay for a toast to the prosperity of Gaelic.

3: In Praise of the *Young Highland Traveller*

The following song-poem was composed by an author only named as "Iain mac Alasdair" in the Gaelic newspaper *An Cuairtear Òg Gàidhealach* (The Young Highland Traveller) in which it was printed and which is the subject of its praise. This all-Gaelic monthly publication was started by Iain Boid in Antigonish, Nova Scotia, in 1851 and ran for about a year. It carried a range of materials, some reprinted from Scottish sources and some gathered from oral tradition in Nova Scotia.[40] The following introductory text that prefaced the ode below urges the periodical to be a means of preserving the lore surviving among some of the members of the community:

Figure 8.3 – Portrait (believed to be) of Iain Boid (John Boyd), founder of Nova Scotia's first Gaelic newspaper. Portrait in possession of the Antigonish Heritage Museum and used with their permission.

> Fhuair mi h-aon no dhà de na *Cuairtearan Òga*, agus ged a tha e fhathast ann an aois a leanabachd, tha 'n oidheirp gealltaineach, tha dòchas ri àrach, ma gheibh an *Cuairtear* misneach mhath bho luchd dùthcha, gun gabhair an tuille[adh] saothair, gus a dhèanamh nas luachmhoire fhathast, bheir seillein saothraicheil mil ás gach lus. Tha móran de sheann seanchas air chuimhne am measg cuid de na Gàidheil a fhreagradh gu

math 's a' *Chuairtear*. Bheirinn comhairle air a leithid seo do dh'fheadhainn, an grad sgrìobhadh, is an cur air adhart. Mur urrainn iad fhéin seo a dhèanamh, rachadh iad gu aon a tha comasach. Tha mi an dòchas nach diùlt neach air bith seo gus an *Cuairtear* a dhèanamh cho luachmhor dha luchd-leughaidh is a dh'fhaodar – Cluinneadh <tu?> an-dràst' agus a-rithist bho d' charaid, Iain mac Alasdair.

I received one or two of the *Young Travellers*, and even though he is still in his infancy, the effort [he has made] is promising; there is hope of developing it, if the *Traveller* gets strong encouragement from his compatriots; further effort can be undertaken to make it even more valuable; industrious bees can extract honey from every flower. There is a great deal of traditional lore in the memories of some of the Gaels that would be very suitable for the *Traveller*. I would offer advice to these sort of people to record it quickly and to send it on. If they themselves cannot do it, they should go to someone who is able. I hope that nobody will decline this [idea] to make the *Traveller* as valuable as possible to its readers—you will hear from your friend, Iain mac Alasdair, now and again.

The ode to the newspaper follows the precedent of personifying a subject in order to draw on the literary resources developed for the praise of humans, particularly of the "here's a toast to..." genre. Like any hero, the *Young Highland Traveller* is expected to have a distinguished pedigree. We might infer that the previous two generations in his lineage (lines 6-7) refer to *Cuairtear nan Gleann* and *An Teachdaire Gaelach*, also mentioned in the previous poem (text 8.2).

Echoing the message of the accompanying prose, the poem expresses hope that the newspaper will develop and realize its full potential in committing to print, and thus to long-term storage, the memories of the community (lines 8-11). A collective effort will be necessary in order for this to happen, of course, so the poet attempts to rally the audience to this cause. He reminds them of their common identity as Gaels, invoking images of the martial tradition, and spurs them on to defeat their ancient rivals, the Lowlanders (lines 12-15). He also uses familial analogies, comparing the mother tongue, Gaelic, to a biological mother and appeals to the Biblical commandment to honour one's parents (lines 16-17). He concludes by praising the publisher of the newspaper, reassuring him that he will receive the necessary assistance needed to make his enterprise successful (lines 20-23). Printing this song in the newspaper itself, and thus circulating it through the community, was intended to spur readers and listeners into action on his behalf.

Original Text

1 Thogainn fonn an àrmainn smiorail,
 Ann an tìr nan craobh air aineol,
 Thogainn fonn an àrmainn smiorail

 Fàilt' ort, a *Chuairteir Ghàidhealaich*
5 Is mi 'dh'òladh do dheoch-slàinte:
 Mhic an fhir bu ro mhath Gàidhlig
 Is i gun fhàillinn aig do sheanair.

 Is ged tha ortsa smachd na h-òige,
 Tha mi fhéin ro fhad an dòchas
10 Gum bi fhathast cnàimh is feòil ort,
 Cuimhne dhomhail throm 'ad phearsa.

 Ma bhios Gàidheil mar bu dual daibh
 Nì iad cruinneachadh mun cuairt dhut;
 Togaidh iad a' bhratach shuaicheant'
15 A gheibh buaidh air clann nan Gallaibh.

 Theirinn ribh, a Chlann nan Gàidheal,
 Bithibh measail air ur màthair:
 Gabhaibh treis de'n *Chuairtear* Ghàidhlig!
 Is mór mo bhàigh ris, gheibh mi fear dhiubh.

20 Guma slàn do'n fhear a thòisich
 Air a' *Chuairtear* 'chur an òrdugh;
 Gabh air t' adhart, gheibh thu còmhnadh
 Na chumas de chlò air a bheannaibh.[41]

Translation

(1-3) I would raise a tune to the doughty warrior in exile in the land of trees, I would raise a tune to the doughty warrior.

(4-7) Welcome to you, o *Highland Traveller*, it is I who would drink a toast to you: the son of the man who had excellent Gaelic, and your grandfather spoke it flawlessly.

(8-11) Although you are under the influence of youth, I myself have high hopes that your flesh and bones will grow, and that you will develop a deep and excellent memory.

(12-15) If Gaels follow their ancestral precedent, they will gather around you; they will lift up the unmistakable banner that will secure victory over the non-Gaels.

(16-19) I would say to you, o Gaelic people, be respectful of your mother: subscribe for a while to the Gaelic *Traveller*! I am greatly fond of it, I will take one of them.

(20-23) Good health to the man who established the *Traveller*; proceed forward, you will get enough help to keep the paper on the racks [of the printing press].

4: In Praise of Gaelic in Hamilton, Ontario

The following ode was composed by Eóghann Siosal in Hamilton, Ontario, in praise of Gaelic and the organization in Toronto charged with sustaining and enriching it in the city (discussed further in the next chapter). Many other poems express antagonism toward the English language and the anglophone rivals of the Gaels,[42] but in this text Siosal seems to advocate a complementary relationship between Gaelic and English. While English has its place and value in utilitarian domains, Gaelic should be esteemed and nurtured by those for whom it is an ancestral inheritance.

He states that it is unnatural and shameful for those who have names of Gaelic derivation to be unable to speak it (lines 13-16). His own devotion to Gaelic was fostered within the family setting, particularly by his mother (line 18). Siosal emphasizes the reciprocal relationship between language and society, for when addressing the language later in the poem he affirms that it is Gaelic itself that has fostered poets and their craft (lines 41-42).

He spends five stanzas legitimating Gaelic by enumerating poets whose literary achievements were expressed through the medium of the language. The first eight of these lived their lives entirely in Scotland, between the mid 17th century and the mid 18th century. One of them, however, Eóghann MacColla (see texts 8.5 and 8.6 below), was a celebrated poet who was born in Scotland but lived most of his life in Canada. His collection of original Gaelic poetry, *Clàrsach nam Beann* (The Harp of the Mountains), was extremely popular, enjoying five editions. He thus embodies the continuity of Gaelic literary production, forming a bridge across time and space that connects the immigrant community in Ontario to the more distant past in the Highlands.

Original Text

    1   Tha Beurla agus Gàidhlig agam,
            Tha Beurla agus Gàidhlig agam,
            Is ged tha Beurla dhomh ro fheumail
            Gur i 'Ghàidhlig m' fheudail chaidreach.

    5   Mo bheannachd-sa do'n chomann chliùiteach
            Chuir *an t-Albannach* do m' ionnsaigh;
            Is cuid dhe sgrìobht' an cainnt mo dhùthcha
            Do'n d'thug mis' an ùidh 'bhios maireann.

            Is mo bheannachd do'n chomann ghràdhach
   10   Tha ann an Toronto tàmhachd
            Is tha 'g ath-bheòthachadh na Gàidhlig
            Tha 'n impis dol bàs 'chion cleachdaidh.

            An saoil sibh féin nach mór an tàmailt
            Daoin' tha giùlain ainmean Ghàidheal
   15   Mar tha Camshronaich is Clann Phàrlain
            Bhith gun Ghàidhlig air an teangaidh.

            Is mi nach dì-chuimhnich a' chànain
            Dh'ionnsaich mi air glùn mo mhàthar:
            A' chainnt bhlasta, thaitneach, àghmhor,
   20   Nach eil nas fhearr air an talamh.

            A' chainnt thaitneach sgairteil shùghmhor
            Anns an do dh'fheuch na bàird an dùrachd;
            Is mis' a-chaoidh nach cuir mo chùl rith'
            Gus an dùin mo shùil 's a' chadal.

   25   A' chainnt taitneach gun dad meang oirr'
            Anns an do dh'fheuch na bàird bha greannmhor:
            Uilleam Ros is Iain Manndach,
            Ailean Dall nan rann is MacLachlainn.

            Sheinn an Dòmhnallach cliù Theàrlaich;
   30   Mac an t-Saoir, sheinn cliù nan àrd-bheann;
            Sheinn Rob Donn gu fonnmhor àlainn
            Is sheinn Iain Lom mu bhlàir is mu bhatail.

            Ach theirgeadh ùine dhomh bhith 'g àireamh
            Na sheinn de bhàird bhinn 's a' Ghàidhlig;
   35   Agus sguiridh mi dhiubh an-dràsta
            Le ainm aoin tha làthair fhathast.

　　　　Sheinn MacColla air a' Chlàrsaich
　　　　'S ann da féin bu mhath a thàinig;
　　　　Gu cinnteach, 's e rìgh nam bàrd e
40　　Le 'dhà chànain 's an aon teangaidh.

　　　　Is naing-mhuime altraim nam bàrd thu;
　　　　Is iomadh aon dhiubh rinn thu àrach
　　　　O'n là labhradh thu 's a' Ghàradh
　　　　Nuair bha Àdhamh ann 'na bhalach.

45　　An uair thàinig Eubh 'na làthair
　　　　Làn de chliù, de mhùirn, is de àilleachd,
　　　　Thuirt e, "'Fheudail, ciamar tha thu?
　　　　Air mo làimh, gur tu mo leannan!"⁴³

Translation

(1-4) I speak English and Gaelic ... and although English is very useful to me, Gaelic is my amiable darling.

(5-8) My blessings to the renowned group who sent *The [Canadian] Scotsman* to me; some of it is written in the language of my native land, in which I have invested interest that will last.

(9-12) And my blessings to the beloved group that resides in Toronto and is reviving the Gaelic that is close to dying due to a lack of use.

(13-16) Do you think yourself that it is a great insult that people who carry the names of Gaels, such as Cameron and MacFarlane, do not have Gaelic on their tongues?

(17-20) I am the one who will not forget the language that I learned on my mother's knee: the delicious, pleasant, magnificent language, there is not a better one on the earth.

(21-24) The enjoyable, vigorous, intelligent language in which the poets expressed their feelings; I am the one who will never turn his back on it, until my eye shuts in sleep.

(25-28) The enjoyable language that has no blemish, in which the poets who were lively strived: William Ross and Stammering Iain, Blind Allan [MacDougall] of the verses and [Ewan?] MacLachlan.

(29-32) [Alexander] MacDonald sang the renown of [Prince] Charles; [Duncan Ban] Macintyre sang the renown of the high mountains; Rob Donn sang musically and beautifully, and Iain Lom [MacDonald] sang about conflicts and battles.

(33-36) But the time would run out on my enumerating all that the euphonious poets sang; and I will decease from that now, with the name of one who is still present.

(37-40) [Evan] MacColl sang on the *Harp*, and it suited him well; surely, he is the king of the poets with his two languages in one tongue.

(41-44) You [Gaelic] are the grand-foster-parent of the poets, you have nurtured many of them since the day that you were spoken in the Garden [of Eden], when Adam was a boy there.

(45-48) When Eve came into his presence, full of renown, cheer and beauty, he said, "O darling, how are you? By my word, you are my sweetheart!"

5: A Portrait of Eóghann MacColla

The following is an extract from a longer account about Gaelic poet Eóghann MacColla, written and published in 1897, a year before he died, by Alasdair Friseal. It depicts MacColla as embodying the literary practices and cultural knowledge that was transferred from the Scottish Highlands to Canada along with the immigrants themselves.

Original Text

De na bàird ainmeil d'an tugadh àite ann an *Sàr Obair nam Bàrd Gaidhealach*, tha Eóghann MacColla a-mhàin beò. Bha a chliù cheana am beul a luchd-dùthcha trì fichead bliadhna roimhe seo, deich bliadhna mus deachaidh

Figure 8.4 – *Eóghann MacColla (Evan MacColl), Gaelic poet and official bard of several Scottish organizations in Ontario. Portrait from Fraser (1897),* Leabhar nan Sonn.

leabhar MhicCoinnich a chur a-mach. Chan e a-mhàin gun do mhair a chliù mar bhàrd ré an àm fhada seo, ach dh'fhàs e na bu shoilleire mar a bha an ùine a' dol seachad. Tha spéis mhór aig Gàidheil Chanada do'n fhilidh aosta a tha fhathast comasach air a' Cheòlraidh a thàladh gu "còmhradh binn" ann am feasgar a làithean. ...

Nan tachradh air neach geur-bheachdach a bhith an làthair aig aon do choinneamhan Comuinn Gàidhlig Thoronto, bu dualach dha duine fhaicinn an-sin 'na shuidhe air taobh deas fear na cathrach, a thogadh aire car tamaill. Tha e ag éisteachd gu fura-char ri briathran an fhir-labhairt, theagamh gum bheil a làmh ri chluais, oir a tha 'chlaisneachd a' fàilneachadh. Duine ìosail e, mu chòig troighean agus sia òirleach ann an àirde, seang ann am pearsa, ach cuimseach, sultmhor 'na dhreach agus smiorail, ealamh 'na ghluasad. ... 'Na cheithear fichead bliadhna 's a còig, 's e seo Eóghann MacColla. Ma tharlas dha labhairt air gnothach sam bith a dh'fhaodas a bhith fo chomhair na coinneimh, ach cha tric leis sin a dhèanamh, cluinnear briathran tarbhach a théid calg-dhìreach gu smior na cùise. Cha chanadh tu gun robh e deas-briathrach, ach theireadh tu gun robh e da-rìreamh drùidhteach. ...

Chaidh a shuidheachadh gun dàil ann an Taigh-Cìse Baile an Rìgh, Ontario, agus dh'fhan e an-sin gus a' bhliadhna 1880, nuair a thug e thairis obair a dhreuchd 'na shean aois, làn de làithean agus de dh'urram. ... Ré dà fhichead bliadhna a-nis tha ainm MhicCholla aithnichte agus air a mheas ro urramach am measg Ghaidheal is Ghall bho chuan gu cuan is bho dheas gu tuath ann an Aimearaga. Aig a dhachaigh ann am Baile an Rìgh, bha e 'na cheann-uidhe fialaidh; bha doras a thaigh fosgailte agus aoidheachd cridheil d'a luchd-eòlais is d'a luchd-dùthcha leis am bu mhath eòlas a chur air. Bha gach neach, bho'n deirceach bhreòite, leis am bu bhuidhe greim-bìdh fhaotainn, gus an duine saidhbhir a thigeadh a chum aon do bhàird ainmeil Chanada fhaicinn, bho'n duine òg an geall air eòlas aig Oilthigh Bhaile an Rìgh, a bhiodh gu tric aig taobh a chagailt, gu daoine a bha cheana iomraiteach ann an ealain dhiongmhalta nan sgoil, di-beathta aig fàrdach a' bhàird. Do neach aig an robh spéis do bhàrdachd na Gàidhealtachd, no do litreachas Bheurla, bhiodh céilidh ann an taigh MhicCholla ro thaitneach. ...

Bha e 'na sheanchaidh barraichte. Bha min-eòlas aige air obair nam bàrd, agus air eachdraidh am beatha. B' urrainn da sreath an déidh sreath is rann an déidh rainn a ràdh de sheann òrain nach fhaca sùil riamh air taobh duilleig leabhair, agus bha fiosrachadh iongantach aige air ainmean dhaoine is àitean a tha tachairt rinn ann an òrain Ghàidhlig. Air oidhche gheamhraidh, nuair a chruinnicheadh a theaghlach is dithis no triùir luchd-tadhail mun cuairt air a ghealbhan, bu dual do'n t-seanchaidh tionndadh air na fineachan Gàidhealach, air an eachdraidh, an cleachdaidhean, is am bàrdachd. Dh'fhosgladh cridhe a' bhàird agus tharraingeadh e a-mach ás a storais nithean nuadh agus sean air son toil-inntinn na cuideachd. ...

Bha e 'na bhall de'n Chomunn Oiseanach, agus rinn e a chuibhrionn fhéin de'n obair a bha r'a dèanadh anns a' chomann. Do'n chomann seo, bha is tha e 'na bhàrd. Tha e 'na nì ceudna do Chomunn Gàidhlig Thoronto; 'na bhall urramach de Chomunn Ceilteach Mhontreal, is de Chomunn Albannach Chicago, is de Chomunn Albannach Dhubusque, Iowa; agus tha e 'na bhall de Chomunn Rìoghail Chanada, a chaidh a chur air bonn leis a' Mharcus Lathurnach nuair a bha e 'na àrd-uachdaran air Canada.[44]

Translation

Of the renowned poets who were given a place in *Masterpieces of the Highland Poets*, only Evan MacColl is still alive. His fame was already on the tongues of his compatriots sixty years ago, ten years before MacKenzie's book was published. It is not only the case that his fame as a poet has endured throughout this long period, but it has become brighter as the time has passed. The Gaels of Canada have great affection for the aged poet, who is still capable of courting the Muses to "melodious conversation" in the afternoon of his lifetime. ...

If a very observant person happened to be present at one of the meetings of the Gaelic Society of Toronto, he would usually see a man there sitting on the right side of the chairman who would hold his attention for a spell. He is listening carefully to the words of the speaker, probably with his hand to his ear, since his hearing is failing. He is a short man, about five feet and six inches in height, with a trim physique, but steady and meaty in his appearance and lively and brisk in his movement. ... This is Evan MacColl in his eighty-fifth year. If he happens to speak about anything that may come up before the meeting, although he doesn't believe that it happens often, a substantial remark will be heard going straight to the heart of the matter. You might not say that he was eloquent, but you would say that he is indeed impressive. ...

He was stationed immediately in the Customs House in Kingston, Ontario, and he stayed there until the year 1880, when he retired from his position in his old age, full of days and of honour. ... For forty years now, the name of MacColl has been recognized and respected honorably among the Gaels and non-Gaels, from sea to sea and from north to south in North America. At his home in Kingston, he was a generous host; the door of his home was open and cheerful hospitality [was offered] to his acquaintances and to his compatriots who wished to get to know him. Every person, from the feeble beggar, who hoped to get a small meal of food, to the wealthy man who came to see one of the famous poets of Canada, from the young man in search of knowledge at Kingston University, who was often at the hearthside, to the people who were already renowned in the established fields of the academy, was welcome at the poet's residence. For the individual who revered the poetry of the Highlands, or English literature, a céilidh in the home of MacColl was extremely enjoyable. ...

He was a pre-eminent tradition bearer. He was intimately informed about the work of the poets and about the history of their lives. He was able to recite line after line, and verse after verse, of old songs that have never been seen on the page of a book, and he had an amazing knowledge of the names of people and places that we encounter in Gaelic songs. On a winter's night, when the family and two or three visitors would gather together around the hearth, it was customary for the tradition bearer to turn to the Highland clans, to their history, customs and poetry. The heart of the poet would open up and he would pull out of his repertoire new and old items for the entertainment of the company. ...

He was a member of the Ossianic Society and he did his own share of the work that had to be done in the organization. He is and was a poet for this society. He is likewise for the Gaelic Society of Toronto; he is a honorary member of the Celtic Society of Montreal and of the Scottish Society of Chicago, and of the Scottish Society of Dubusque, Iowa; and he is a member of the Royal Society of Canada, that was founded by the Marquis of Lorne when he was the Governor General of Canada.

6: Salutations to Eóghann MacColla

The following ode to Eóghann MacColla was composed by Iain Mac a' Phearsain and rejoices in their friendship that had been forged long before—in 1836—when MacColla came to stay with Mac a' Phearsain's family in Kintyre, Scotland. Although MacColla has been largely forgotten in Canada today, he was clearly a very popular figure at the time, so much so that Mac a' Phearsain expects him to enjoy perpetual celebrity among Highland descendants (lines 19-20).

Original Text

1   Sonas buan do'n duanair ghasta
Dh'fhalbh Di-Luain fad' uainn air astar:
Guma slàn a thilleadh dhachaigh
Gu 'dheagh bhean am Bail' an Rìgh!

5   Mo rùn-charaid cridheil caoimhneil,
Is òg a thug mi spéis gun thoill dhut:
Is tric thug uair de d' chomann soillseach
Móran aoibhneis do mo chrìdh'.

    Riamh o'n oidhche laigh mi làmh riut
10   An taigh m' athar, cian bho'n àird seo –
Ged bu ghiullan beag mi 'n tràth ud –
Thug mi gràdh dhuit chaoidh nach crìon.

    Taing dhut air son tighinn gu m' fheòraich;
Taing dhuit cuideachd air son t' òrain,

15   Is iad cho maiseach milis òrdail
     Anns gach dòigh, air an cur sìos.

     Chan eil beann no gleann 'nar dùthaich
     Nach d' fhàg thu le d' ranndachd cliùiteach;
     Is bidh gach òigh is òigear cùirteil
20   A' toirt cliù ort feadh gach linn![45]

Translation

(1-4) Long-lasting happiness to the excellent poet who departed on a long journey from us on Monday: may he return home healthy to his good wife in Kingston!

(5-8) My cheery, kind dear friend, I was young when I bestowed affection on you that you deserved: often did an hour of your splendid companionship bring great joy to my heart.

(9-12) Ever since the night that I slept next to you[46] in my father's house, far away from this location—although I was only a young lad at the time—I have felt a bond of affection for you that will never fade away.

(13-16) Thank you for coming to ask for me; thank you also for your songs that are arranged so beautifully, sweetly and elegantly in every way.

(17-20) There is no mountain or glen in our native land that you did not make renowned with your versification; every maiden and courteous lad will sing your praises throughout every generation!

7: In Praise of Gaelic and of *Mac-Talla*

The following paean in praise of the Gaelic language and of the newspaper *Mac-Talla* (Echo) was printed in that periodical, having been contributed by someone using the pen-name "Gille-coma-leat-dheth" (The lad best ignored). It likely that this pen name refers to the detractors of Gaelic rather than to the person who transcribed and contributed the text, which included this accompanying introduction: "Tha e diombach de'n mhuinntir a tha dèanamh tàir air a' Ghàidhlig, agus tha e an-seo a' toirt ruith de'n teangaidh dhaibh; 's mo thogair aca. Chan eil annt' ach na blaomastairean." (He is peeved by the people who disparage Gaelic and he is here giving them a tongue lashing; I couldn't care less about them. They are nothing but dolts.)

Figure 8.5 – The masthead of the newspaper Mac-Talla. *The slogan "An nì nach cluinn mi an-diugh, chan aithris mi màireach" (that which I do not hear today I will not speak tomorrow) demonstrates the continued dominance of orality in Gaelic literary tradition, even in a printed periodical. Image from copy of the newspaper in Michael Newton's private collection.*

It is likely that the author latterly resided in St. Ann's, Cape Breton (line 48), although he was born in Scotland (lines 27 and 40). The poem must have been composed in the year 1893, when the World's Fair was held in Chicago (line 52). The international extravaganza featured a replica of an entire rural Irish village and a number of symbols of the Gaelic past that attracted a great deal of attention in North America. This exposition helped to coalesce a particular image of "ancient Ireland" which has remained dominant to the present.[47] The common ancestry of Scottish Gaelic and Irish seems to have been understood and taken for granted by the author.

The text acknowledges the contempt shown to the language and the stigmas that it accordingly suffers. While the chorus repeatedly asserts "I love Gaelic," the declaration that "I have never been ashamed of it" (line 12) alerts us to the fact that some people do in fact feel that shame or humiliate those who speak it. The numerous slanderers of Gaelic are denounced as "despicable blockheads" (line 19), but the poet is particularly disturbed by those who denigrate the language despite having a Gaelic background (lines 21-36). He also comments on the common phenomenon of native Gaelic speakers spending time in the United States and returning home claiming to have lost their mother tongue (lines 33-36).[48]

In the face of these forces, he highlights the emotional bonds formed with family in the language (lines 4, 9-10 and 56), the many respectable and celebrated figures who spoke the language to good effect (line 18), the upbeat attributes of Gaelic's homeland (lines 38-39), and its distribution around the world (lines 49-52). The author alludes to the nobility and great age of the language (lines 43-44 and 47) and praises Gaelic in terms of its musicality, given that it animates both song and instrumental music (lines 6 and 13-16). This helps to connect the text back thematically to the meaning of the name of the newspaper, *Mac-Talla* (Echo).

Original Text

1   Hó, gur toil leam, hé, gur toil leam,
        Hó, gur toil leam fhìn a' Ghàidhlig:
        Is mór an toileachadh gu cinnteach
        A bhith cluinntinn cainnt mo mhàthar.

5   Nuair thàinig *Mac-Tall*' 'am ionnsaigh,
        Is e cho fonnmhor ann an Gàidhlig,
        Thug e toileachadh do m' inntinn
        Is, ó, gu cinnteach, chuir mi fàilt' air.

        'Chainnt 's an d' fhuair mi toiseach m' eòlais
10   Agus treòrachadh mo mhàthar;
        Is ged a tha mi nis air liathadh,
        Cha do ghabh mi riamh dhi nàire.

        Cainnt tha binn am beul gach còisir
        Gu seinn òran, shailm is dhànaibh;
15   Is nuair a chluichear i le fìdhlear,
        Teichidh gach mì-ghean mar sgàile.

        Is lìonmhor urramach is uasal
        A thug buaidh an iomadh càs leath';
        Ged tha iomadh burraidh suarach
20   Dèanamh luaidh oirre le tàire.

        Cluinnidh tu iad siud ri 'stialladh
        Is ri 'riasladh, gun smid gràmair;
        Cainnt eile, ged tha i ciatach,
        Té nach cual' iad riamh o'm màthair.

25   Is nì tha duilich leam ri 'chunntas
        Is a' cur diombadh air mo nàdar,
        Gum bheil cuid an-diugh á m' dhùthaich
        Leis nach diù mar chainnt a' Ghàidhlig.

        Tha e amaideach is neònach,
30   Is cha bu chòir e bhith ri ràdha,
        Gum bheil clann nan Gàidheal còire
        Le'n cuid pròis a' dèanamh tàir oirr'.

        Ma théid cuid dhiubh null gan cosnadh,
        Measg nan Geangach beagan ràidhean,

35   Nuair a philleas iad do'n tìr seo,
"Chaill" na mì-shealbhaich an Gàidhlig!

'Chainnt a tha is a bhios snasmhor
An tìr ghasta nam ban àlainn:
Tìr nam beann, nan gleann is nan gaisgeach
40   Far an d' fhuair mi tacan m' àraich.

Ach nach mis' an duine gòrach
A bhith còmhradh mar a tha mi
Mu'n chainnt tha 'n-diugh cho uasal
Is an là chualas i aig Àdhamh.

45   Ged a shiubhladh neach na cuantan,
Deas is tuath air feadh gach ceàrna,
Càit' an cluinn e cainnt as uaisle
Na chluinnear aig sluagh Shaint Anns?

Tha i nise 'ga craobh-sgaoileadh
50   Feadh an t-saoghail, anns gach àite:
Tha i pailt an Carolìna
Is tha i 'm bliadhna ac' an Chicàgo.

Thig mi nise gu co-dhùnadh
Mun coisinn mi diombadh pàirt dhibh:
55   Ach tha 'Ghàidhlig leamsa cùbhraidh –
Chuir mi ùidh innte 'nam phàiste.

Mìle beannachd gu *Mac-Talla*!
Guma fada fallain slàn e!
Gun robh bliadhnaichean air thalamh
60   Mar a' ghaineamh nach gabh àireamh.[49]

Translation

(1-4) *Hó*, I love, *hé*, I love, *hó*, I myself love the Gaelic: it is surely a great joy to hear my mother's language.

(5-8) When *Echo* came my way, in such melodious Gaelic, it brought great delight to my mind and, oh, I certainly welcomed it.

(9-12) [Gaelic is] the language in which I received the foundation of my knowledge and the guidance of my mother; and although I have now turned grey, I have never been ashamed of it.

(13-16) The language that is melodious in the mouths of every choir for singing songs, psalms and ballads; and when it is played by a fiddler, all worry vanishes like a shadow.

(17-20) Many honourable and noble people have succeeded with its help in many difficult situations; although there are many despicable blockheads who speak of it with contempt.

(21-24) You can hear them scourging and mutilating it, with not an iota of grammar; any other language may be lovely, [but] they never heard it from their mothers.

(25-28) The thing that is difficult for me to reconcile and that vexes my disposition is that today there are some [people] from my native land who do not esteem Gaelic as a language.

(29-32) It is idiotic and strange, and it should not be the fact, that descendants of the goodly Gaels show it contempt in their arrogance.

(33-36) If some emigrate for employment among the Yankees for a few seasons, when they return to this land the unfortunate ones have "lost" their Gaelic!

(37-40) The language that is and will be polished in the lovely land of the beautiful women; the land of the mountains, the glens and the heroes, where I had a little of my upbringing.

(41-44) But am I not the foolish man to be speaking as I am about the language that is as noble today as it was the day that Adam was heard speaking it?

(45-48) Even if a person were to sail the seas, north and south throughout every region, where will he hear a language as noble as is heard from the population of St. Anns?

(49-52) It is now being disseminated throughout the world, in every place: it is plentiful in the Carolinas and they have it this year in Chicago.

(53-56) I will now come to a conclusion before I offend some of you: but I believe that Gaelic is fragrant—I bonded with it when I was a child.

(57-60) A thousand blessings to *Echo*! May it long be hale and healthy! May its years on the earth be as many as the grains of sand that cannot be counted.

8: "A Toast to the Gaelic Mothers"

The following song-poem by Coinneach A. MacFhearghuis celebrates the people largely responsible for the transmission and vitality of language: mothers. While the importance of the mother-child bond appears in other Gaelic songs, as does the echo of the term "mother tongue," which itself acknowledges this connection, this is the only Gaelic song entirely devoted to praising these unsung heroes of Gaelic cultural maintenance. It does so with the familiar "here's a toast to..." structure.

The chorus calls on the wider community to defend and sustain Gaelic and to never surrender to anglophone adversaries, with an emphasis on literacy in this long-term campaign (line 3). It is orality, however, rather than literacy that provides the frame of reference in the verses: mothers speak to their children to give them advice (lines 7 and 34) and to soothe them to sleep (lines 9 and 12); the virtues of the language itself endowed the speech of their ancestors with musicality and animated their songs and stories (lines 25-28); it is the best medium for communication with God (line 36); the reverberations of these speech acts from the past persist in the memory of those living (lines 31-32).

Original Text

>   1   Buaidh le cuideachd mo ghaoil
>   A sheasas ar cànain le bàigh,
>   'Ga labhairt, 'ga sgriobhadh is 'ga leughadh,
>   Is nach géill do'n Bheurla gu bràth.
>
>   5   Deoch-slàinte nam màthraichean Gàidhealach
>   Tha teagasg an cànain d'an clann
>   Is nach dearmad a labhairt gu'n seòladh
>   Is gu'n tàladh le còmhradh is rann:
>   An àm dhaibh bhith seasgair 's an iùbhraich
>   10   Tha 'gan giùlan gu cala na suain,
>   Có 'chainnt a bheir barr air a' Ghàidhlig
>   Gu crònan is mànran 'nan cluais?
>
>   Deoch-slàinte nam màthraichean Gàidhealach
>   Tha fhathast a' tàmh anns an tìr,
>   15   Bheir caochan á tobar na Gàidhlig
>   D'am pàistean le bainne na cìch';

A sheallas le truas air an dream sin
Tha toirt nithean Gallta d'an cloinn
Bhios mar fhlùr a nì cinntinn fo sgàil
20   Is a dh'fhàgas teas-gréine gun loinn.

Deoch-slàinte nam màthraichean Gàidhealach
A ghràdhaich an dìleab a fhuair;
A lasas teas-ghràdh is a bheir saorsa
D'an anaman tha 'n daorsa fo fhuachd;
25   A' chainnt anns an do labhair ar sinnsir
Gu binn anns na linntinn a thréig –
Bu chàirdeil a bhiodh iad 'nan còmhradh,
Bu bhrìoghmhor an òran is an sgeul.

Deoch-slàinte nam màthraichean Gàidhealach
30   Tha beò – agus sìth do na dh'fhalbh;
Tha fuaim an cuid luinneagan ceòlmhor
'Nam chluais, ged tha 'm beòil a-nis balbh;
Có 'chainnt sin as milse na 'Ghàidhlig
Gu labhairt ri pàiste le céill?
35   Có 'chainnt a bheir barr air ar cànain
Gu earbsa ri fàbharan Dhé?[50]

Translation

(1-4) Success to the crowd that I love who defend our language with affection, speaking it, writing it and reading it, and who will never yield to the English language.

(5-12) [Here's] a toast to the Gaelic mothers who teach their language to their children and will not neglect to speak it, in order to give them guidance and to lull them to sleep with talk and rhymes: when it is time for them [the children] to be comfortably situated in the yew-boat [cradle] that carries them to the harbour of slumber, what language can excel the Gaelic for crooning and making soothing talk in their ears?

(13-20) [Here's] a toast to the Gaelic mothers who still live in the land, who will bear a streamlet from the well of Gaelic to their children along with the milk of their breast; who look with pity on that sort who give foreign things to their children who will grow like a flower under a shadow and will not benefit from the warmth of the sun.

(21-28) [Here's] a toast to the Gaelic mothers who take delight in the heritage that they received; who ignite warm affection and will give freedom to the souls who are oppressed in the cold; the language which their ancestors spoke melodiously in past eras—they were friendly in their discourse, their songs and stories were full of significance.

(29-36) [Here's] a toast to the Gaelic mothers who are living—and peace to those who have departed; the sound of their musical choral songs are in my ear, even though their mouths are now mute; what language is sweeter than Gaelic for speaking with good sense to a child? What language could be better entrusted for finding favour with God?

9: Silenced Voices in Saskatchewan

The following song-poem is an elegy to the Gaelic colony of Moosomin, Saskatchewan, composed by Seumas MacFhionghain in 1925. Communities in marginal areas with small populations were more vulnerable to external developments and economic shifts than more cohesive and stable settlements such as those in Nova Scotia. Seumas had clearly been contemplating the history of his community and the factors that compromised their cultural and linguistic vitality for some time, for in 1921 he published a short memoir of the settlement that comments on the same issues and mentions characters which appear in his poem.

> On the 24th day of April, 1884, the good ship "Buenos-Ayrean" of the famous "Allan Line"—and, if I am not mistaken, the first all-steel steamship to cross the Atlantic—left Glasgow en route for Canada, carrying among her passengers the second and largest number of our pioneers, numbering in all 240 souls.
>
> All arrived at Moosomin, Saskatchewan (then the "North-West Territories") safe and sound, late in May, and after camping there for a couple of weeks, getting equipped and dodging the long horns of the motive power of those days, they were finally guided further west to their respective homesteads, and there left to wrestle with the obstinate oxen and the no less obstinate little breaker with the long wooden beam, the short, almost upright handles, and the screeching gauge-wheel, to break up the virgin prairie. ...

Another mistake—whoever was responsible for it—was the broadcast scattering of the people in various sections, instead of being in one good compact, wholesome Highland settlement, where the good old customs, language and traditions of the Gael could be cultivated to live for generations. If they were so settled they could also work together for the common good of the community, for means to a good end, as well as to a bad, can only be attained on the good old principle of "strength in numbers." ...

"[Eóghann] Beag agus Màiri an Eilein"— ...Ewan was a jolly soul, fond of the old Highland traditions, and many a long winter's night he helped to shorten by his entertaining tales of long ago. ...

"An Gobha Ruadh"—Ronald MacPhee of Ìochdar, S. Uist, widower, was 48 years old. ... Ronald was a blacksmith by trade and quite a character in his way. His vivid imagination, if cultivated by education in his youth, would have made him a great romancer, as he could spin yarns by the yard at short notice and keep it up indefinitely. ...

I may also mention, a source of great regret to all lovers of the Gaelic language, that the younger generation did not prove as true and faithful to their beautiful mother tongue, as for instance our Nova Scotian brethren, who, true to the language, faith and traditions of their fathers, have produced and are producing a big percentage of the smartest men in Canada.[51]

The chorus of his song repeatedly strikes the plaintive note of nostalgia that permeates his composition, which is full of contrasts between the past and the present. The homeland in Scotland is idealized as a land of heroes (line 6) and domineering mountains (line 10), although the poverty of the people there is clearly acknowledged (line 8). The plucky and bullish settlers wrested a living from the soil, with some cost to their physical condition (line 14), but were entertained and ennobled by the oral traditions that they brought with them and developed in communal céilidhs.

The poet's contemporary reality has diverged greatly from that initial state of affairs in the settlement and is the cause of his disappointment. The vitality of tradition once created and provided by living members of the community has been replaced by machinery and outsourced to specialists from remote locations: phonographs (lines 25-26), carrying the voices of Enrico Caruso and Harry Lauder (line 31), have displaced the folk narratives and song-poems borne by people intimately known by and related to céilidh-goers (lines 27-30); commercially-baked bread has replaced the ceremonial strùan Mhìcheil bannock which formed the centerpiece of one of the most popular holy-days on the ritual calendar of Hebridean Gaels[52] (lines 21-24).

While modern technology brings things at which to marvel—airplanes (line 34) and wireless communications (lines 37-38)—Seumas asserts that he prefers the familiar and local to the fantastic and exotic (lines 35 and 40). Among the cultural elements lost in the shuffle is the language beloved to him and his ancestors (lines 28 and 39). With the loss of those of allied cultural allegiances, however, the voices that enacted tradition have been replaced by silence and remain only in his memory (lines 41-44).

Original Text

1   Thàinig caochladh mór o'n là sin,
     Thàinig caochladh mór 's an t-saoghal,
     Cuid dhiubh is tùrsach leam an àireamh
     Thàinig caochladh mór o'n là sin.

5   B' ann dà fhichead bliadhn' an-uiridh
     Chuir sinn cùl ri tìr nan curaidh;
     Thog sinn siùil is ar cùrs o Uibhist
     Far am b' uireasbhach ar càirdean.

     Na suinn uaibhreach, sheòl le dòchas,
10   Tigh'nn a-nall á tìr nam mór-bheann
     Gu Saskatchewan gun stòras
     Dhèanamh beò-shlàint' anns an fhàsach.

     Bha sinn toilicht' air a' phràiridh,
     Obair chruaidh is slàint' a-réir sin;
15   Air an oidhche tric air chéilidh,
     'G innse sgeulachdan is bàrdachd.

     Cha robh innleachdan 'nar seòmar
     Mar tha 'n-diugh 's an tìr gu pròiseil
     Ach bha coibhneas rian gach lòin ann
20   Air bheag stròidhealachd no àilgheas.

     B' fhearr leam bonnach cailleach Mhìcheil –
     Ged bhiodh leth-òirleach de'n ìm air –

       Na gach aran grinn as mìlse
       Bhios le rìomhadh aig an àl seo.

25   Guth nam marbh an-diugh 'nar seòmar
       Le gob snàthaid seinn dhuinn òrain;
       B' fhearr an Gobha Ruadh le ròlaist
       Dèanamh spòrs dhuinn anns a' Ghàidhlig.

       B' fhearr leam Dòmhnall Òg le 'Cheòlraidh
30   Is Eóghann Beag ag innse stòiridh
       Na Carusa is Lauder còmhla ris:
       Siud na seòid nach teòidh mo nàdar.

       An-diugh tha daoine falbh 's na speuran
       Mar na h-eòin le inneal gleusta;
35   B' fhearr leam an damh ruadh 's a' phràiridh
       Is mi 's an t-sléigh ag éigheach, "Hà!" ris.

       Gheibh sinn radiogram á Cuba
       Is cluinnidh sinn, gun sreang, na Duitsich;
       Cainnt nan sonn is roinn de'n dìlsean:
40   Siud an dìleab nach do thàr iad.

       Chaochail is dh'fhalbh na daoine còire,
       Iain MacCormaic, lean an corr dhiubh;
       Air an cuimhne, is tric mi meòrach',
       Sinn a' còmhradh anns an t-sàmhchair.[53]

Translation

(1-4) A great change has come since that day, a great change has come on the world, a number of them make me sad, a great change has come since that day.

(5-8) It was forty years ago last year that we turned our backs to the land of the heroes; we hoisted the sail and set our course to leave Uist where our kin folk were destitute.

(9-12) The proud heroes who sailed with hope, coming across from the land of great mountains to Saskatchewan without any money to make a living in the wilderness.

(13-16) We were happy on the prairie, it was hard work and our health [was affected] accordingly; we held céilidhs frequently, telling stories and reciting poetry.

(17-20) There were no devices in our room like those that exist ostentatiously in the land today but kindness sharing every meal, with little waste or fussiness.

LANGUAGE AND LITERATURE

(21-24) I would prefer a Michaelmas bannock made by an old woman—even if it had a half-inch of butter on it—than the sweetest, refined bread that is valued by the people of today.

(25-28) The voices of the dead are in our room now, singing songs to us with a beaked needle; the Red Smith and his tall-tale entertaining us in Gaelic were better.

(29-32) I would prefer Young Donald with his Muses and Little Hugh telling a story over both Carusa and Lauder combined: those [latter men] are stars that do not ignite my passions.

(33-36) Today, people are travelling through the air like birds with an ingenious machine; I would prefer the red ox on the prairie with me on the sleigh shouting "Ha!" to it.

(37-40) We can get a radiogram from Cuba and we can hear the Dutch without a wire; [but] the language of the heroes and a portion of their allies: that is the heritage that they have not matched [in excellence].

(41-44) The goodly people have passed away and departed, such as John McCormick, and the rest have followed; I frequently recollect them in my mind, holding a dialogue with them in the silence.

10: News of *Awakening*

The following song-poem to the Gaelic periodical *Mosgladh* (Awakening) was composed by Dòmhnall MacPhàrlain during the winter of 1932, when it experienced a longer hiatus than usual

Figure 8.6 – The cover of the periodical Mosgladh, *incorporating iconography of both Scotland and Canada. The central X of the logo is an intentional visual pun on the Scottish saltire and the "X" of Xavier. Many Catholic priests trained at Saint Francis Xavier University. Photo taken by Michael Newton from the collection in the Angus L. Macdonald Library, St. Francis Xavier University.*

in its irregular publishing schedule. A total of 27 issues were printed between 1922 and 1933 under the auspices of Comunn Gàidhealach Caitligeach Chanada (The Scottish Catholic Society of Canada).

This text follows the common precedent of previous poems in personifying the periodical, whose ability to provide entertainment and good cheer was especially missed during the gloom of the Great Depression (lines 13-15). *Mosgladh* is depicted as a tradition-bearer faithful to the literary inheritance of Scottish Gaeldom, keeping alive tales of the distant past, such as those of the Fian (lines 21-24), the Scottish aristocracy (lines 25-32) and more conventional folk tale genres (lines 33-34), as well as songs (line 35). As usual, the transmission of these materials is described primarily in oral terms (lines 36-37), rather than in terms of literacy.

As the opening page of the last issue (in which this poem was printed) made explicit, the periodical struggled to find the financial resources to continue operating: "*Mosgladh*, like many a more pretentious venture, has fallen upon trying times, and the attempt to continue its publication has become increasingly difficult." MacPhàrlain exhorts the Gaels to stand together and to support the necessary costs of producing the publication (lines 41-48).

Original Text

1   An d' fhidir, no 'n d' fhairich
        No 'n cuala sibh,
        Dé dh'éirich do'n phàipear
        Bha luachmhor leinn?
5   Am mìosachan moltach
        Gum b' ainm da am *Mosgladh*:
        Gum bheil sinn fo sprochd dhe
        Nach d' fhuair sinn e.

        Tha corr is trì mìosan
10   Nach d' fhuair sinne sgeul air;
        Ma thréig e na crìochan-s'
         Gur truagh sinn dhe;
        Gach nì mar bu mhath leinn
        Nuair bha esan mar rinn
15   Is cha robh an Depression
        Cur gruaimean oirnn.

        Bha esan glé dhìleas
        Do dhùthaich ar sinnsear;

                    Bu tric rinn e innseadh
20   Gach buaidh a bh' oirre
            Is a' tabhairt dhuinn sgeula
            Mu eachdraidh na Féinne
            Is gach tapadh is euchdan
              Bha dualach dhaibh.

25   Gun tug e dhuinn cunntas
            Air eachdraidh nan Stiùbhart
            Màiri is am Prionnsa
              Is an cruaidh-chàsan;
            Flòiri NicDhòmhnaill
30   Is na gaisgich bha còmhl' rith'
            Toirt fasgadh do'n fhògarrach
              Uasal ud.

            Na sgeulachdan fiachail
            Is na h-ùirsgeulan ciatach;
35   Na h-òrain bu bhrèagha
              Leinn cluas 'thoirt dhaibh;
            Cha chluinn sinn iad tuilleadh
            Ma theirig an curaidh
            A dh'fhògradh gach mulad
40   As truaighe bhuainn.

            Ma thilleas e an taobh seo
            Gum pàigh sinn a shaothair;
            Gun dèan sinn ris faoilte
              Gach uair thig e;
45   Cha bhi e am fàillinn
            Ma sheasas na Gàidheil
            Gu curanta càirdeil
              Ri 'ghualainn-san.[54]

Translation

(1-8) Were you aware of, did you notice, or did you hear what happened to the newspaper that we found most valuable? The praiseworthy monthly that was called *Awakening*: it makes us very sad that we didn't receive it/him.

(9-16) It is more than three months since we heard anything about it/him; if it/he has fled this territory, we will be wretched; everything was as we wanted when it/he was with us and the Depression did not make us gloomy.

(17-24) It/he was very faithful to the native land of our ancestors; often did he describe all of its virtues and offered tales about the history of the Fian and all of the achievements and adventures that were natural for them.

(25-32) It/he gave us an account about the history of the Stewart [kings], Mary and Prince [Charles] and their predicaments; Flora MacDonald and the warriors that were along with her giving shelter to that noble refugee.

(33-40) The worthy narratives and the lovely romances; the songs we found most beautiful to which to give an ear; we will no longer hear them if the champion who could banish all of our worst sorrows has departed.

(41-48) If he returns our way we will reward his labour; we will rejoice in him every time he comes; he will not fail if the Gaels stand valorously and kindly at his shoulder.

9 – Identity and Associations

The establishment of organizations concerned with celebrating and sustaining ethnic identity is by definition something not likely to happen until a people leave their original home and enter into a new social context where they encounter dissimilar cultures and languages. They suddenly become more aware of their differences and may be concerned about maintaining them. Most Gaelic-speaking immigrants who came to Canada had been born and raised in homogeneous, rural communities where their language, culture and identity were largely taken for granted.

As we've already seen expressed in many previous Gaelic texts, the identity of Scottish Highlanders was (and remains) distinct from that of Lowlanders.[1] This sense of difference has persisted in immigrant contexts wherever Gaelic has remained a living language of the community.[2] Take, for example, the unapologetic acknowledgement of long-standing enmity described in an article on the history of religion in Scotland that appeared in the Presbyterian newspaper *An Solus Iùil*, printed in Sydney, Cape Breton, in 1926:

> Bha na Gàidheil agus na Goill anns an aon eaglais, ged bha iad fada, fada o bhith 'nan càirdean. Bha iad air bhith 'nan nàimhdean riamh o linn Chaluim a' Chinn Mhóir, an rìgh Gàidhealach a phòs ban-phrionnsa Shasannach. ... Riamh o'n latha sin bha na Goill, a lìon beagan is beagan, a' spùinneadh nan Gàidheal ... cha robh e 'nan comas riamh na machraichean torach a bhuineadh d'an sinnsir a chosnadh air ais o na Goill.[3]

The Gaels and the Lowlanders were in the same church, even though they were far, far from being friends. They had been enemies ever since the era of Malcolm Canmore, the Gaelic king who married an English princess. ... Ever since that day the Lowlanders, constantly, bit by bit, were dispossessing the Gaels ... They were never able to regain from the Lowlanders the fertile plains that had belonged to their ancestors.

A booklet printed in Cape Breton to provide lessons for Gaelic learners and school pupils in 1939 cannot help but include a joke which demonstrates how very foreign and incomprehensible the Lowlanders are to the Highlanders:

> Bha seana Ghàidheal a chuir seachad greis a dh'ùine air Galldachd ag ràdh an déidh tilleadh d'a dhùthaich féin, nach fhaca e amadain daoine riamh ach na Goill. Nuair thachras iad riut, cha chuir iad fàilt' sam bith ort ach, "Good day, Sir," ged a b'e an cur 's an cathadh bhiodh ann.[4]

> There was an old Gael who spent some time in the Lowlands who said after he had returned to his own native land that he had never seen a people as foolish as the Lowlanders. When they encounter you, they do not offer you any welcome but, "Good day, Sir," even if it is snowing hard.

On the other hand, we've also seen texts, particularly in chapter 3, in which Gaels eager to gain respectability among the dominant anglophone ascendancy were able and willing to project an artificially unified Scottish identity highlighting tartanism, militarism and loyalty to the British Crown. The contest of loyalties between local identity and imperial aspirations, ancestral Gaelic heritage and the Anglocentric orientation of the dominant institutions of the empire, were expressed and negotiated by Highland immigrants and their descendants in different ways in different contexts.

The first Gaelic organizations were established in urban areas outside of the Highlands where new economic opportunities attracted Gaels: the Highland Society of Glasgow in 1727,[5] the Gaelic Society of London in 1778, the Gaelic Club of Gentlemen (Glasgow) in 1780,[6] and so on. These early organizations had a strong influence on the ones that followed both within Scotland and outside of it. Most based their constitutions on that of the London association, which stated that its aims were to preserve "the Martial Spirit, Language, Dress, Music and Antiquities of the Ancient Caledonians," aid in the recovery of Gaelic literature, establish and support Gaelic schools, provide charity for poor Highlanders who had emigrated to other parts of the empire, and promote the improvement and general welfare of the Highlands.[7]

The conflicts over how to negotiate between the Gaelic cultural norms initially enshrined in these constitutions and the all-pervasive pressures of Anglo-conformity have replayed many times throughout the history of Gaelic associations and social contexts.[8] Indeed, the leaders of early Gaelic and Highland Societies were concerned with how they could integrate the Highlands into the mainstream of British society and its evolving social, economic and political norms without completely losing control over these processes and their consequences.

> The clubs were part of an emerging "civil society" in urban Britain typically composed of members of the professional classes, as well as petty gentry, and if members of the aristocracy joined they usually acted as patrons. ... Many of the [Highland Society of London]'s members were Highland landowners who were concerned about the fate of the Highlands and Islands in a time of accelerated economic and social change. They did not, however, wish to reverse this change; rather, they sought to direct it on their own terms. ... The progress towards modernity, or economic improvement, did not mean that elements of Highland culture had to be sacrificed because improvement, as conceived of by the HSL, combined progress with preservation.[9]

On the other hand, when considering how associations were directing developments on "their own terms," we need to remember that the members of these organizations were generally the Highland élite and their priorities and interests could differ considerably from the tenantry living on the soil.

The dominance of the élite members and their increasing adherence to Anglocentric norms, and their corresponding alienation from Gaelic ones, caused the linguistic and cultural objectives of these organizations to be demoted in a short time. Symbolic forms of ethnicity, particularly tartanism, took their place.[10] In 1782, for example, only four years after the Gaelic Society of London was formed, non-Gaelic-speaking Lowland soldiers returning from the American Revolution flooded the association's membership. Gaelic then ceased being the working language of the organization, whose name was changed to "the Highland Society of London." Members turned their attention instead to collecting tartans.[11] The Falkirk Tryst, an annual competition instituted by the Gaelic Society of London in 1781, initially included prizes for bagpipe performances and the recitation of an original Gaelic poem.[12] The 1783 event ended with protests against the "arrogant tradesmen" who were put in charge of competitions;[13] prizes for Gaelic poetry were discontinued then or shortly thereafter.[14] Recent research by bagpipe scholars validates the idea that the aristocrats who controlled pìobaireachd competitions had the effect of entirely reshaping and reinventing the musical tradition which they were entrusted to "preserve" by imposing urban, Anglocentric aesthetics.[15]

Nonetheless, the Highland Society brand proved popular. The Highland Society of Canada was the first branch to open in Canada, established in St. Raphael's, Glengarry County, Ontario, in 1818 after a commission to form a franchise of the Highland Society of London was obtained from the Duke of York. Simon MacGillivray, a vice-president of the London society, presided over the inaugural meeting.[16] In 1838 further branches were founded in Prince Edward Island and Halifax, Nova Scotia.[17] In 1843 the Society printed a booklet with the organization's aims and rules, listing the current branches, the leadership and members. Branches had by then been formed in Montreal, Toronto, Niagara, Hamilton, Amherstburg, Bytown (later "Ottawa"), Goderich and Johnstown District.[18] While most of the leaders (called "Vice Presidents") of each branch appear to have been native Highlanders, the chief of the Society was Sir Charles Bagot, Governor General of Canada, an Englishman with no ties to the Highlands.

The first surviving literary text from any of these associations comes from Toronto, apparently in 1858 (text 9.1).[19] This song-poem depicts a group strongly devoted to their native tongue and music, even while it indulges in some of the clichés of Highlandism prevailing at the time. Gaelic Societies have enjoyed a long life in Toronto. One was established in 1878 and modelled after the Gaelic debating societies then common in Scottish universities. Records indicate that it discussed many of the political issues and controversies of its time. In early 1881, for example, it released a strong and lengthy condemnation of the treatment of crofters in Scotland, probably the results of one of its debates. It begins:

IDENTITY AND ASSOCIATIONS

Gum bheil sinne, Comunn Gàidhealach Thoronto, fo dhoilgheas agus a' togail fianuis an aghaidh na h-eucoir 's an ainneart leis am bheil àireamh mhór d'ar luchd-dùthcha (air nach tugadh barr riamh air son treunadais agus gaisge) air am fòirneadh ás am fearann, agus air am fuadachadh ás a' Ghàidhealtachd, do bhailtibh móra Bhreatann is do thìribh céin...[20]

We, the Gaelic Society of Toronto, are troubled and bear witness against the injustice and the oppression with which a large number of our compatriots (who have never been excelled for their bravery or heroism) are forced out of their lands and cleared out of the Highlands to the large cities of Britain and to foreign lands...

By the early 20th century Gaelic organizations could be found in many parts of Canada. Comunn Gàidhealach Uinnipeg (The Highland Society of Winnipeg) was established in 1909 and still had more than fifty members in its rolls in 1942. The president of the organization, Seumas MacGilleMhìcheil, expressed the faith of its members that the foundation of the Gaelic College in Cape Breton in 1939 would aid in the survival of Gaelic in Canada: "'S e ar dòchas ... gun tog sibh gu h-àrd bratach na Gàidhlig. Tha sinn an dòchas gun dèan Gàidheil na dùthcha air fad spàirn chruaidh gu bhith a' cumail suas ar cànain..." (It is our hope ... that you will raise up high the Gaelic banner. We hope that all of the Gaels of the country will exert themselves vigorously to keep our language alive...).[21] Shortly before this, another resident of Winnipeg described the difficulties of the task, given the inferiority complex about the language that descendants of Highland immigrants had inherited from their treatment at the hands of anglophones:

Cha do rinn Gaidheil riamh fìor uaill ás an cànain fhéin gus an robh iad air an sgapadh am measg choimheach. Chaidh ar n-athraichean, cuid mhór dhiubh, fhògradh air falbh á Tìr an Gaoil air son àite a dhèanamh do na féidh is do na caoraich mhóra. ... Feumaidh ar cànain a bhith 'ga sìor sgrìobhadh agus 'ga leughadh ma tha fad saoghail air a dheònachadh dhi.[22]

The Gaels never took real pride in their own language until they had been dispersed among strangers. Our forefathers, the majority of them, were exiled out of the land that they loved in order to make room for deer and Border sheep. ... Our language must be constantly written and read if it is to be granted a full life.

Comunn Gàidhlig Bhancùbhar (The Vancouver Gaelic Society) was founded in 1908 by twenty members but within a year had several hundred. Its constitution seems to acknowledge that a lack of formal support for Gaelic had a negative effect on knowledge of and pride in the language and literary tradition and that the organization had to compensate for such shortcomings.

> This Society has for its objects the promotion of all matters of interest to the Celtic race, more especially to the Gaelic race, such as the diffusion of a wider knowledge of the Gaelic language among the descendants of the Gael, and the cultivation of a more general knowledge of its literature and music, the instilling in its members patriotism for the land that gave them birth; the perpetuation of the wearing of the national garb; the fostering of social intercourse among persons of Celtic or Gaelic birth residing in Vancouver; Scotsmen and Scotswomen coming to Vancouver, whether to settle there or on a visit, will be heartily welcomed by the worthy Chief or other members of the Society at all its regular meetings.[23]

Tartanism and socialising seem to have assumed an undue amount of the organization's attention, for within two years a rival society more directly focused on Gaelic's linguistic and literary heritage was formed from a portion of the previous society's membership.

> A strong new Gaelic society has been formed in Vancouver. It is to be known as the Vancouver Gaelic Literary Society. ... Thirty members signed the roll and paid their admission fee. ... At the meeting on Saturday evening last there were some regretful features owing to the interruptions from members of the old Gaelic society who took it upon themselves to oppose the organisation of a new society. The chairman of the newly formed society happened to have been junior chieftain of the old one and he dealt with the interruptionists in a way that showed them that the new society had a good reason for its existence, but that it had no wish to have a quarrel with the old one.[24]

The pressure that this splinter group exerted may have resulted in a renewed commitment to the aims of the original association in promoting and sustaining Gaelic, for in 1934 it began to hold an annual celebration of Gaelic song and literature. This event was modelled on the Royal National Mòd that was founded in 1892 in Scotland. The Vancouver Mòd included competitions for original compositions, the recital of Gaelic texts and the singing of Gaelic songs and was open to all North Americans.[25] It was held annually until 2007.

A resident of Cape Breton wrote to the newspaper *Mac-Talla* in 1893 to note with disappointment that despite the existence of such organizations in places such as Toronto,

> Is duilich leam r'a thuigsinn nach eil aon chomann de'n t-seòrsa sin againn an Ceap Breatainn no an àite sam bith eile fagus duinn, ged is ioma Gàidheal is mac Gàidheil a th'ann. Chan eil teagamh sam bith nach eil an "teud nàdarra 'na dùsgadh" am measg móran diubh fhathast, ged nach eil iad 'ga dhearbhadh an dòigh fhollaiseach.[26]

> It is sad for me to think that there isn't one single organization of this sort in Cape Breton or in any place that's near to us, even though there are many Gaels and Gaelic descendants here. There's no doubt at all that the "native harp-strings are aroused" among many of them still, although they aren't demonstrating it in a prominent manner.

Associations did spring up in Nova Scotia by the second quarter of the 20th century, however, especially with the mass movement of Gaels to urban areas within the province. At least two odes were composed to Comunn Gàidhlig Inbhir Nis (The Gaelic Society of Inverness, Nova Scotia) which was active in the 1920s, one of which expresses formulaic disdain for Highlanders' ancestral rivals:

> 'S i 'Ghàidhlig ghlan réidh, nach dìobair mi fhéin,
> Is gur taitneach o bheul nan nighean i.
> O, faodaidh na Goill bhith laighe 's a' choill
> Mun toir mise oidhche còmhla riu.[27]

> It's the eloquent and pure Gaelic that I will never abandon, it is pleasant from the mouths of maidens.

> O, the Lowlanders [or non-Gaels] can drop dead in the woods before I ever spend an evening with them.

Most odes to Gaelic societies in Nova Scotia depict members speaking their mother tongue to one another and enjoying their ancestral songs, music and dance together. They seldom demonstrate the need to earn the approval of the dominant anglophone majority by playing up Highlandism, militarism or a Protestant identity, themes that are palpable in songs from other areas of Canada. A song by Dòmhnall MacPhàrlain implies that Comunn Gàidhlig Inbhir Nis legitimated Gaelic's value by restoring its proper place in Scottish history and its association with people of worth, including the Fian. This was a strategy taken by many Scottish poets as well.[28]

> Gheibh sinn eòlas bhios cinnteach
> Mu eachdraidh ar sinnsear
> Is mu'n chainnt sin bha prìseil
> Am measg rìghrean is bhàrdaibh.
>
> Gheibh sinn sgeulachdan éibhinn
> Mu laochraidh na Féinne,
> Is iomadh gaisgeach glan ceutach
> Rinn euchdan 's na blàraibh.[29]

We get reliable knowledge about the history of our ancestors and about that language that was prized among the kings and poets.

We get inspiring stories about the heroes of the Fian and many a pure handsome hero who achieved great feats in battles.

All too often, however, especially in urban centres, the élite who established and ran Highland Societies were committed to little more than ensuring the loyalty of Gaels to the British Empire and validating their own positions of privilege by orchestrating the symbols of tartanism and the conceits of militarism. Rusty Bitterman illustrates this phenomenon through a reading of Roderick MacDonald's 1843 *Sketches of Highlanders: With an Account of Their Early Arrival in North America*:

> The focus is primarily on the courage and loyalty of Highlanders in the Jacobite rebellions, but he includes as well discussions of their loyalty to the British crown during the American Revolution, the War of 1812 and the Rebellions of 1837. ... Considerable emphasis is placed on the persistence of traditional loyalties to their betters that were to be found among the Highland population of the Maritimes. ... The timing of the establishment of Highland societies in the Maritimes, and elsewhere in British North

America, suggests their role in reconciling the lower classes to their place in the new order...[30]

There are many factors that would have influenced the degree to which Highland Societies, in their many forms, across Canada used and supported the Gaelic language: the origins, experiences and background of the organization's leadership; the autonomy (or dependence) of the local community with regard to anglophone institutions; the linguistic consciousness of members; the availability of sufficient numbers of fluent speakers; and so on. While Comunn Gàidhlig Thoronto began as an all-Gaelic debating society, it was reformed in 1887 with new rules that stated that

> while the Gaelic language should have preference in the conducting of the work of the Society, the use of English would not be excluded, thus widening the basis of membership, which, under the original Constitution practically debarred the admission of non-Gaelic speaking nominees.[31]

This compromise did not immediately dispel Gaelic: besides featuring Gaelic songs and other content in their monthly meetings, they sponsored and organized a Gaelic reading class, a Gaelic Bible class, a Gaelic choir and Gaelic concerts over a number of years.[32] Comunn Gàidhlig Hamilton (The Gaelic Society of Hamilton) drew up its constitution in Gaelic in 1894, stating explicitly "gum bi a' Ghàidhlig air a labhairt agus air a cuir an cleachdadh aig na h-uile coinneamh" (that Gaelic will be spoken and put to use at every meeting). Members of Comunn Gàidhlig Leòdhuis (The Lewis Gaelic Society), in 1920s Vancouver, read Gaelic newspapers aloud between Gaelic songs and dances, and wrote and performed their own Gaelic plays.[33]

It is frequently apparent, however, that those who valued the Gaelic language on its own terms, for its distinctive literary heritage and cultural expressions, felt marginalized within many organizations and criticized them as ineffective and misguided. Consider, for example, the letter in *Mac-Talla* from a correspondent in London (England) identified only as "L.L." who complains that Gaelic organizations cater to the interests of the aristocracy and military to the detriment of the language and culture they are meant to serve.

> Gun teagamh tha cor na Gàidhlig aig an àm so 'na chùis tàireil, mar aon do na Comunnan Gàidhlig agus do na Gàidheil anns

gach cearn. Tha mòran Chomunnan Gàidhlig air an sgaoileadh air feadh an t-saoghail, agus ma tha, ciod am feum a rinn iad riamh airson na Gàidhlig? Gu dearbh, is i an fhìrinn gun do rinn iad móran lochd di. Is ainmig a chluinneas neach fuaim ceòlmhor na Gàidhlig aig an coinneamhan, agus ma chuireas iad iomradh a-mach, mu an gnothaichean, is i a' Bheurla anns am bi e air a chlò-bhualadh. Chan e sin an dòigh airson a' Ghàidhlig a chumail suas. Is e dleasnas gach ball de Chomunn Gàidhlig gach nì a tha 'na chomas a dhèanamh gu eòlas air a' Ghàidhlig a sgaoileadh am fad agus am fagus, ach tha e coltach gum beil a chuid as mò diubh cho déidheil air dèanamh sodain ris na h-uaislean agus gur i a' Ghàidhlig bhochd an rud deireannach air an toir iad smuain. ... Tha cuid de na Comunnan so a' dèanamh an dìcholl a dh'fheuchainn am faigh iad na gillean Gàidhealach a ghabhail anns an Arm Dheirg, ged nach eil e soilleir ciod a tha aig sin ri dhèanamh ri Comunn Gàidhlig. ... Tha fear deasachaidh *Mhic-Talla* agus fear-deasachaidh *An Naidheachd Ghàidhealach*, ann an Albainn, a' deanamh tuilleadh air son na Gàidhlig na rinn na Comunnan Gàidhlig uile a tha air thalamh.[34]

Without a doubt, the current state of Gaelic is a cause for shame, and likewise for the Gaelic Societies and the Gaels everywhere. There are many Gaelic Societies distributed around the world, and yet, what use have they ever been to Gaelic? Indeed, it is the truth that they have done much damage to it. Seldom is the musical sound of Gaelic heard at their meetings, and if they issue any reports, they are printed in English. That is not the way to keep Gaelic alive. It is the responsibility of every Gaelic Society member to do everything in his power in order to spread the knowledge of Gaelic far and wide, but it seems that the majority of people are so eager to fawn over the nobility that poor Gaelic is the last thing that they think about. ... Some of these Societies are doing their very best to try to recruit the young Highland men into the British military, although it is not at all clear what this has to do with a Gaelic Society. ... The editor of *Mac-Talla* and the editor of *The Highland News* in Scotland, are doing more for Gaelic than all of the Gaelic Societies combined on the planet.

In an ideal world, these organizations would have helped to secure the rights of Gaelic speakers in Canadian society and aided in the survival of the language for future generations. For this to be possible, it would have been necessary to conceptualize Gaelic as a cultural cornerstone in its own right that transcended the ownership of any particular community that spoke it; linguistic devotion would have needed to be developed into political consciousness and activism. Instead, Gaelic had already been effectively stigmatized and Highlanders were too overawed by the triumphs of the anglophone world to defy its supremacy. Although early emigrants strongly identified with their original regional communities and Gaelic culture, these forms of identity had to compete with those promoted by institutions that enjoyed greater cultural prestige and wielded greater socio-economic power: the British State, the Dominion of Canada, whiteness, religious denominations, Highlandism (in its tartanistic form), and so on. It is hardly surprising that these newer formations gained at the expense of Gaelic, even though Gaelic identity has survived to varying degrees to the present.

1: An Ode to the Gaelic Society of Toronto

The following song-poem was composed by Eóghann MacColla in 1858. While he keeps his emphasis on the primary functions of the organization—maintaining the linguistic and literary heritage of the Highlands—he inevitably falls into some of the tartanistic stereotypes explored in chapter 3, such as the praise of the kilt (lines 5-6) and of the might of the presumably unconquerable Highland soldiers (lines 21-24). Highland societies were typically involved in the administration of Highland Games, the activities of which MacColla describes proudly as cultivating strength and health (lines 25-29). He also alludes to the dominant Protestant identity of Scotland and the contention that it held a monopoly on truth (line 36).

Regardless, the Gaelic language features strongly in MacColla's ode as the main focus of the organization and the central characteristic of Highland identity (lines 3 and 15-16). He touches on the claim that Gaelic was spoken in the Garden of Eden (line 4) and portrays Scotland as an inherently poetic nation, alluding to the long lineage of renowned bards from Oisean/Ossian to Donnchadh Bàn (lines 9-14). Like many poets before him,[35] MacColla integrates the bagpipe into this rhetoric of literary excellence by equating its instrumental melodies with song (line 19). He even extends his literary symbolism to the battlefield, where the rows of troops can be read like a book ("leughadh" on line 24 literally means "read" but also implies "understand, interpret"). He shows his awareness of his own social role as poet in his allusion to his duty to wish the members of the society well (line 8) and clearly relishes the prestige conferred upon poets (lines 13-14).

Original Text

1   Ceud fàilte air comann nan àrmann deas foinnidh
    Nì dùthchas an ath'raichean 'chumail suas:
    Seann dùthchas nan Gàidheal, an cliù is an cànain –
    A' chainnt sin a thàinig bho Àdhamh a-nuas –
5   Mar siud is an t-éideadh, air sràid no air sléibhte,
    Tha uallach deas eutrom – grinn, greadhnach an snuadh;
    Sàr-chomann mo chridhe! Chan iongnadh ged bhithinn
    An-seo, mar is dligheach, a' guidhe leò buaidh.

    Mo ghaol na fir ùra nach cuireadh an cùlaibh
10 Ri Ceòlraidh an dùthcha – fìor dhùthaich nam bàrd;
    Bho mhac Rìgh na Féinne gu Donnchadh Bàn geur-bhinn,
    Có 'n tìr sin fo'n ghréin air a h-aos-dàin bheir barr?
    Có 'n neach leis nach sòlas bhith 'n cuideachd luchd òrain?
    Deagh iomradh 'nan còmhradh, mo stòr agus m' àgh;
15 Bidh sibhse nis dìleas do chleachdainn cho rìoghail
    Is a-chaoidh cha téid dìth air cainnt ghrinn nam beann-àrd.

    Chan eòl domh toil-inntinn nas mó na bhith cluinntinn
    Pìob mhór nan dos cnàimh-gheal as fonnmhoire fuaim;
    Nuair théid i gu còmhradh air faiche no 'n seòmar,
20 B' e 'n ceòl thar gach ceòl leam a torman 'nam chluais;
    'N àm lannan a rùsgadh is na h-àrmainn do'n rùn i
    Air nàimhdean a' brùchdadh le gnùisean gun ghruaim;
    Suas "Gillean an Fhéilidh" air pìoban deagh ghleusach
    Is cha duilich ri leughadh có 'n taobh a gheibh buaidh.

25 Is iad cleachdainn nach miosa gu neartachadh chriosa
    Bhith tilgeadh nan cabar is a' cur na cloich-neirt;
    'S e siud a rinn làidir ar n-athraichean tà'chdach –
    Mo thruaigh iad 'thig cearr orr' a' stàilinn nan glac!
    Am fear leis an suarach bhith 'g altrum no luaidh air

30   Gach lùth-chleas grinn uasal tha 'n uair seo 'nur beachd:
Cha dèanainn a chàineadh, ged is cinnteach a tha mi
Gur sìochaire grannd e de dh'àl air bheag tlachd.

Ged is mithich nis dhomhsa bhith crìochnachadh m'
    òrain
Tha tuille gu leòr a bu mhiann leam a ràdh
35   Mu dheidhinn na tìr sin tha daonnan air m' inntinn:
Seann Albainn do-chìosnaicht' do'n Fhìrinn thug gràdh;
Ceud soraidh thar chuan bhuam 'ga h-ionnsaigh, mo
    chruadal
Bhith 'n taobh seo mar eun fuadain fad uaip' – ach ged
    tha –
Mun téid ás mo smuaintean tìr àlainn nan cruach-bheann
40   Bidh 'n cridhe seo fuar anns an luaithre a' cnàmh.[36]

Translation

(1-8) A hundred welcomes to the association of the skillful, handsome warriors who keep alive the culture of their forefathers; the ancient culture of the Gaels, their renown and their language—that language that has come down from Adam—and likewise the tartan plaid that is proud, dapper and light-weight, on the street or on a hill-side; elegant and cheerful is their appearance; my beloved, noble association! It is no surprise that I am here, as is dutiful, wishing them success.

(9-16) Beloved to me are the vibrant men who would never turn their backs to the Muse of their homeland—the true native land of the poets; from the son of the king of the Fian [i.e., Ossian] to sharply-melodic Duncan Ban, is there another country in the world whose artists can outdo her? Is there a person who does not find it joyful to be in the company of songsters? There are good statements in their conversation, that is my joy and delight; you will now be loyal to very royal customs and the elegant language of the Highlands will never be lost.

(17-24) I know of no greater pleasure than to listen to the great bagpipe of the white-boned drones which are most melodious in sound; when it [the bagpipe] begins to talk on a field or in a room, that music which I believe excels all others will be murmuring in my ear; when the blades are unsheathed and the heroes who love it [the bagpipe] have burst upon enemies with undisturbed countenances, "The Lads of the Plaids" will be played on well-tuned bagpipes and it won't be hard to understand which side will be victorious.

(25-32) Tossing the caber and throwing the shot-put are customs that are not bad for strengthening the abdominal muscles; they are what made our enterprising forefathers strong—I pity those who misspeak about them, anticipating encountering them! The man who thinks it below his dignity to practice or speak of all of the elegant and noble sports that we are now discussing: I would not condemn him although I am sure that he is an ugly runt of the most unpleasant sort.

(33-40) Although it is now time for me to be concluding my song, I have plenty more that I would like to say about that land that is always on my mind: ancient, invincible Scotland that has pledged its love to the Truth; a hundred greetings to her across the ocean from me, it is my misfortune to be on this side like a bird gone astray, far away from her—and although I am—this heart will be cold and decomposing in the dust before the beautiful land of the curvaceous mountains leaves my thoughts.

2: A Song to the Glengarry Highland Society

The following song-poem was composed by Dòmhnall Òg Grannd (a resident of the South Branch of the Raisin River) after a St. Andrew's Dinner in Alexandria in the year 1870. The text is modelled very closely upon the structure that John MacInnes has designated the "roll-call of the allies."[37] Rather than being summoned to warfare, prominent individuals and groups of people—some named by clan affiliation and others by regional origin—are praised for their participation in this event celebrating their national and linguistic identity.

"Craig" (line 75) is James Craig (1823-1874), a member of the Legislative Assembly of Ontario representing Glengarry County as a Conservative. Dòmhnall Sandfield (also line 75) is the Hon. Donald Alexander "Sandfield" MacDonald (1817-1896), who was then a Member of Parliament and later the Lieutenant-Governor of Ontario (1875-1880). Owen Quigley (1818-1878, mentioned on line 35) was a wealthy businessman in Lochiel, Ontario.

An aspiring leader in the old Highlands had to show his ability to command subordinates, to organize social functions, and to access critical financial resources. Feasts were an important means through which chieftains demonstrated these skills and acquired new followers; dispensing food and alcohol was understood as symbolizing the power and rule of a leader over his dependents and clients and their acceptance of his patronage.[38] There are certainly echoes of those ideas in this text.

The final four stanzas of this poem are dedicated to the importance of the Gaelic language to the identity of the members of the society and the community as a whole. The antiquity and virtues of the language are asserted, especially through the conventional conceit that it was spoken by Adam in the Garden of Eden (lines 84-88). It is depicted as particularly suited for literary and emotional expression (lines 81-82), which suggests an internalization of the Othering of the Celts common in anglophone discourse.[39] The poet concludes by exercising his social role in criticizing objectionable behaviour, attempting to shame those who have not passed the language on to their children.

Original Text

1   Gu baile mór na sgìreachd seo
     Gun d' iarr iad gu mo dhinnear mi:
     'S ann an-sin bha 'n comann sìobhalta
     Bha grinn 's a h-uile dòigh.

5   Mo bheannachd do'n phàirtidh ud
     Chaidh cruinn aig Alexandria
     Thoirt onair do na Gàidheil
     Is do Naomh Aindrea mar bu chòir.

     Bha fineachan na dùthcha ac' ann:
10   Bha Dòmhnallaich is Dùghallaich ann;
     Bha Granndaich agus Stiùbhartaich ann;
     Is Clann Fhionghain mhór an t-Srath.

     Bha Mac a' Phearsain Chluainidh ann;
     Bha Caimbeulaich is Clann Ualraig ann;
15   Bha Griogaraich o Ruadh-Shruth ann;
     Is daoine uaisle o Chlann MhicRath.

     Bha Siosalaich Shrath Ghlas aca;
     Gun robh MacLeòid is MacArtair ann;
     Clann GhilleMhaoil is an Catanach;
20   Is na h-Ailpinich bho shean.

     Bha Frisealaich na h-Àirde aca;
     Is MacCoinnich mór Chinn Tàile ac' ann;
     Shuidh MacGilleFhaolain làmh ris
     Is MacGilleBhràth is iad sin.

25　Bha Camshronaich o Lòchaidh ann;
　　Is bha ClannGhilleÌosa á Mórar ann;
　　MacAoidh is Mac an Tòisich ann;
　　Is MacNeacail mór is a mhac.

　　Bha Mac an t-Saoir is MacLachlainn ann;
30　MacRuairidh is MacBheathain ann;
　　Bha Fearghusanaich pailteas ann;
　　Is MacLabhrainn is Mac an Ab'.

　　Bha Urchadanaich is Guinnich ann
　　Is bha Moireastanaich cuide riutha
35　Clann Chormaic is Owen Quigley;
　　Is Leathanaich bho shean.

　　Bha Clann a' Phì is am Maighstir ann;
　　Is MacNéill bho thùs á Barraigh ann;
　　MacPhàil, Clann Diarmaid taice riutha;
40　MacCruimein is Lamont.

　　Is gann a tha de thìm agam
　　Na fineachan uile innse dhuibh;
　　Ach bruidhnidh sinn mu'n dinnear
　　Is mu'n a h-uile nì a bh' ac'.

45　Nam faiceadh sibhs' am bòrd a bh' ann!
　　Bha turkies air an ròstadh ann,
　　Bha muilt-fheòil agus geòidh ac',
　　Is gu leòr a dh'fheòil a' mhàirt.

　　Bha cearcan air an còcaireachd,
50　Bha haggis ann bha sònraichte;
　　Is bha miasan beaga bòidheach ann
　　De sheòrsachan nic nax.

　　Bha coffee agus tea ac',
　　Is bha siùcair geal 'na mhill innte;
55　Is bha mnathan òga 's nighneagan
　　'Ga shìneadh gu gach fear.

　　'S e Mac a' Phì, an Colbhasach,
　　A rinn an dinnear ainmeil ud;
　　Is ged chosg i móran airgid dha,
60　Gu dearbha bha i math.

　　Is an fheadhainn rinn a' chòcaireachd,
　　Guma fada beò bhios iad!
　　Gum foghnadh i do'n Ghòbhairnear,
　　Do Rìgh Deòrs no d'a mhac.

IDENTITY AND ASSOCIATIONS

65 Nis bruidhnidh sinn mu'n òl a bh'ann:
    Bha branndaidh is rum is beòr aca;
    Bha fìon is gin bho'n Òlaind ac',
    Is bròinean "Mac na Bracha."

    'S e pìobaireachd 'n ceòl a bh' ann,
70 Bha tòstaichean is bha òranan;
    Bha 'm president toirt òrdugh dhoibh,
    "Hurro! come fill your glass."

    Bha deoch air slàinte na Ban-rìgh ann
    Is air na prionnsaichean a thàinig uaip';
75 Air Craig is air Dòmhnall Sandfield
    Is air a' Phàrlamaid fa leth.[40]

    Ach sguiridh mi dhe'n dàn seo
    Is bruidhinidh mi mu'n Ghàidhlig ribh;
    Is innsidh mi mar thàinig i
80 Bho'n tìm a bh' ann o shean.

    A thaobh 's i cainnt as nàdaraich'
    Gu òrain is gu mànranachd;
    Gur h-i bh' anns an Àirc ac'
    Is aig Àdhamh is aig a bhean.

85 A' cheud fhacal a thuirt Àdhamh rithe,
    Nuair chunnaic e 's a' Ghàradh i:
    Chaidh e is rug e air làimh oirre
    "An tu th' ann, a ghràidh nam bean?"

    Is mór 'n t-adhbhar nàire dhaibh
90 Do phàirt de dhaoine an àite seo
    Nach ionnsaich iad a' Ghàidhlig
    Do'n cuid phàistean is do'n cuid mhac.[41]

Translation

(1-4) To the great city of this county, they asked me to come for my dinner: and that's where there was a polite organization that was elegant in every way.

(5-8) My blessings to that party gathered together at Alexandria to show honour to the Gaels and to St. Andrew, as they ought to.

(9-12) The clans of their native land were there: there were MacDonalds and MacDougalls; there were Grants and Stewarts; and great MacKinnons of Strath.

(13-16) MacPherson of Cluny was there; there were Campbells and Kennedys; there were MacGregors from Roro; and nobles of the MacRaes.

(17-20) The Chisholms of Strathglass were there; MacLeod and MacArthur were there; the MacMillans and the Cattanach and the MacAlpines from long ago.

(21-24) They had the Frasers of Aird; and they had great MacKenzie of Kintail there; MacLellan sat next to him and MacGillivray and the like.

(25-28) The Camerons of Lochy were there; the Gillises of Morar were there; MacKay and Macintosh were there; and great Nicholson and his son.

(29-32) Macintyre and MacLachlann were there; MacRury and MacBean were there; there were plenty of Fergussons there; and MacLauren and Macnab.

(33-36) People from Glen Urquhart and the Gunns were there; people from Glenmoriston were with them; MacCormicks and Owen Quigley and MacLeans from long ago.

(37-40) MacPhees and their priest were there; and MacNeil who was originally from Barra was there; MacPhail along with the MacDiarmids; MacCrimmon and Lamont.

(41-44) I hardly have enough time to relate all of the clans to you; but we will speak about the dinner and about everything that they had.

(45-48) If you could only see the table that was there! There were roasted turkeys there, mutton and goose-meat, and plenty of beef.

(49-52) They had cooked chicken, there was haggis that was exceptional; they had lovely little platters of various kinds of nicknacks.

(53-56) They had coffee and tea, they had a mound of white sugar; and young women and girls were offering them to every man.

(57-60) It was MacPhee, the Colonsay man, who put on this famous dinner; even though it cost him lots of money, it was indeed good.

(61-64) And those who did the cooking, may they live long! It would have been good enough for the Governor, for King George or his son.

(65-68) Now, we will speak about the drinking there: they had brandy and rum and beer; they had wine and gin from Holland, and drams of whiskey.

(69-72) Piobrach was the music, there were toasts and songs; the president gave them an order, "Hurro! come fill your glass."

(73-76) There was a toast to the health of the Queen and to the princes who were born to her; to Craig and to Donald Sandfield [MacDonald] and to the Parliament, one by one.

(77-80) But I will desist from this poem and I will speak to you about Gaelic; and I will discuss how it has come from the olden times.

(81-84) Regarding how it is the most natural language for songs and for entertainment; they spoke it in Noah's Ark, and Adam and his wife spoke it.

(85-88) The first word that Adam spoke to her when he saw her in the Garden: he went and grabbed her by the hand [and said], "Is it you, o beloved of women?"

(89-92) It is a great cause of shame for some of the people of this area that they they do not teach Gaelic to their daughters and to their sons.

3: An Ode to the Celtic Society of Montreal

The following ode to the Celtic Society of Montreal was composed by the association's official poet, Gilleasbaig MacFhilip, and delivered by him to members on December 6, 1883. Gaelic organizations that had "Ceilteach" (Celtic) and "Oiseanach" (Ossianic) in their titles had been established at Scottish universities since the late 18th century[42] and this group proclaimed its scholarly disposition by incorporating both terms: its Gaelic title was "Comunn Oiseanach a' Chnoic Rìoghail" (the Ossianic Society of Montreal). The constitution of the association begins with the following statements:

(1) The object of the Society shall be the promotion of the study of the Celtic Languages and Literature.
(2) Its members shall be confined to the following classes:
    a. Gentlemen and Ladies who by authorship, public addresses, or otherwise, have given evidence of their interest or eminence in Celtic Studies.
    b. Corresponding, Honorary, and Life-Members.

The founding members were aware that scholars in France and Germany had been advancing the study of Celtic literatures and that they could advocate for the same to be done in Canada. The association encouraged research in all Celtic literatures, but the majority of members had Scottish Gaelic ancestry and were most interested in studying that branch of the Celtic legacy. Regardless of linguistic allegiances and literary pursuits, they accepted the racial definition of Celticity in common currency during that era:

> ...it becomes us to ... draw together more strongly and sincerely the bonds of literary consanguinity which unite the Celts of Canada. If we are successful in deserving and obtaining the co-operation of the Celtic scholars of Canada, we can in all fairness hope to do something towards ornamenting, at least, the trees and fences of our common inheritance ... out of the material treasures which their industry and their sagacity have enabled them to accumulate in Canada, they will so aid us that we can procure for ourselves copies of the literary treasures of our common race.[43]

The ode itself begins by underlining the association's scholarly intentions and tools, including literacy in Gaelic (lines 1-3). Teachers of English are portrayed as the greatest threats to Gaelic (line 5), thus reflecting the negative impact of the formal institutions of learning. The organization, it is stated, hopes to vindicate the importance and value of Gaelic by calling attention to its presumed ancestral qualifications as the source of other esteemed languages of learning (line 11), which harkens back to the notion that Gaelic was spoken in the Garden of Eden (lines 4 and 14). The literary heritage of the Gaels is also represented by the figure of Oisean/Ossian (line 16), although this as much an allusion to the Ossianic Societies operating in Scottish universities as it is to the Gaelic literary character. The ode concludes by hoping that these intellectual endeavours will enhance the status of the Gaelic language and thereby encourage its survival in Montreal (lines 25-28) whose inhabitants will thus be worthy descendants of their forebears (line 8).

Original Text

1   Ann am Baile a' Chnoic Rìoghail, tha Gàidheil ro dhìleas,
     A' dèanamh an dìcheill, le eòlas nach gann;

A' cantainn, is a' leughadh, is a' sgrìobhadh na cànain
A labhradh an Eden: 's e a' Ghàidhlig a bh' ann.

5 A luchd-teagaisg na Beurla, bithibh tostach le chéile:
Tha comann air éirigh 's an t-saoghal seo mu thuath;
Comunn Oiseanach àlainn, a' teagasg na Gàidhlig,
Is iad fìor chlann nan Gàidheal a chumas i suas.

Nach seall sibh mun cuairt air àrd-sgoilearan uasal
10 Is a' Ghàidhlig 'na buannachd a thuigsinn gach cainnt –
A dh'ionnsachadh Greigis, Eabhra, Laidinn, is Beurla –
A chionn gur i freumh do gach cànain a th' ann.

Biodh an t-aineolach tàireil, mar as minic a bha iad,
Théid a' chainnt a bh' am Parras a chumail an àird;
15 Anns an dùthaich a dh'fhàg sinn, tha móran d' ar bràithrean
A' seinn, anns a' Ghàidhlig, cliù Oisein am bàrd.

Biodh an Comunn seo dìleas is làidir is lìonmhor
Is bidh móran r'a innseadh le fìrinn is r'a luadh
Mu na beachdan a sgaoil sinn a' lìonadh an t-saoghail seo
20 Le Gàidhlig ro fheumail is le eòlas bhios buan.

Agus cluinneadh na h-àiltean a thig 'nar déidh-ne
Mar a sgrìobh is mar a leugh sinn a' chànain as fhearr;
Is nuair a chuireas sinn crìoch air gach dleastanas a nì sinn
Innsidh eachdraidh fhìrinneach cuin agus càit.

25 Le "Ceud mìle fàilt'" do gach aon a tha làthair
A chum onair na Gàidhlig a mhaireas gach ré;
Biodh Baile a' Chnoic Rìoghail 'na bheannachd do mhìltean
Agus cànain nan Gàidheal cho maireann riuth' fhéin.[44]

Translation

(1-4) In the city of Montreal, Gaels are extremely loyal, doing their very best, with considerable knowledge; speaking and reading and writing the language that was spoken in Eden: it was Gaelic.

(5-8) O teachers of English, be silent, all of you: an organization has arisen in this northerly realm; a beautiful Ossianic association, teaching Gaelic and they are the true children of the Gael who keep it alive.

(9-12) Won't you look around at the noble, high-ranking scholars [who assert that] Gaelic is of benefit for understanding every language—for learning Greek, Hebrew, Latin and English—because it is the root of every language that exists.

(13-16) Let the ignorant person be contemptuous, as they have often been: the language that was in Paradise will be kept alive; in the country that we left, many of our brothers are singing, in Gaelic, the fame of the poet Ossian.

(17-20) May this Society be loyal and strong and numerous, and there will be much to say in truth, and to mention, about the ideas that we spread, filling this world with very beneficial Gaelic and with knowledge that will endure.

(21-24) And may the generations that come after us hear about how we wrote and read in the best language; when we complete every duty that we undertake, truthful history will relate the when and where of it.

(25-28) With a "Hundred Thousand Welcomes" to each one present who has maintained the honour of Gaelic that shall survive forever; may the city of Montreal be a blessing to thousands and the language of the Gaels be as enduring as they are themselves.

4: A Letter from Glengarry

The following letter was sent to the Gaelic newspaper *Mac-Talla* in 1893 by Aonghus MacGilleMhaoil in Laggan, Glengarry, Ontario.[45] This short text indicates that at least some Gaels had an intuitive understanding of the multiple dimensions of identity—ethnic origin, religious affiliation, mother tongue, occupation and national citizenship, for example—and how each of these dimensions could have multiple layers or contexts. It also exemplifies the loyalty that many Gaels had for their language and the efforts made by individuals to form networks across Canada to maintain communication and a sense of Gaelic identity.

Original Text

Thachair dhomh le tuiteamas aon dhe na pàipearan-naidheachd Gàidhlig (*Mac-Talla*) a tha thu a' clò-bhualadh 'fhaicinn is a leughadh. 'S e àireamh a' cheud latha dhe'n Ghiblean 1893 a

IDENTITY AND ASSOCIATIONS

chunnaic mi is ged is ann an Canada a rugadh is a dh'àraicheadh mi, gidheadh cha bu toil leam a' cheud chlach na clach idir a thilgeil air cainnt no air dùthaich m' athraichean. Tha móran Ghàidheal anns an t-siorramachd seo.

Mar charaid is mar fhear-dùthcha, tha mi ann an seo a' cur prìs bhliadhnail a' phàipeir 'gad ionnsaigh an dòchas gun gabh thu gu caoimhneil bho m' làimh e. Is gum bi do thoileachadh agam am pàipear 'fhaighinn an ùine ghoirid. Tha mi leth-char sean air son dol astar fada a dh'iarraidh fàbhar gabhail air do phàipear. Tha mi trì fichead bliadhna is a h-aon deug a dh'aois. Ach ma dh'fhaoidte gun amais mi air neach-eigin òg a ghabhas ri dol mun cuairt air son a' phàipeir.

Thainig mo phàrantan do'n àite seo á Loch Abar an Albainn 's a' bhliadhna 1802. Mar sin is Canadach mise a thaobh breith is àraich. A thaobh teachd-an-tìr, is tuathanach mi. Is a thaobh aidmheil, do dh'Eaglais Shaor na h-Alba. Nan robh thu cho teann orm is a tha thu cho fada ás, rachainn uair-eigin air chéilidh ort. Beannachd leat aig an àm seo.[46]

Translation

I accidentally happened upon one of the Gaelic newspapers (*Echo*) that you are publishing, and saw and read it. It was the edition of the first of April 1893 that I saw and although I was born and raised in Canada, nevertheless, I would not like to cast the first stone, or any stone at all, at the language of my forefathers or at their country. There are many Gaels in this county.

As a friend and compatriot, I am now sending the annual payment for the newspaper to you in the hope that you will take it kindly from my hand. And that I will have your permission to receive the newspaper in a short while. I am a little old to travel long distances in order to seek out subscribers for your newspaper. I am seventy-one years of age. But perhaps I will come across a young person who will be willing to go around on behalf of the newspaper.

My parents came to this place from Lochaber in Scotland in the year 1802. Therefore, I am a Canadian in terms of birth and upbringing. Regarding employment, I am a farmer. Regarding religion, I belong to the Free Church of Scotland. If you were as close to me as you are far away, I would come some time to visit you. Farewell for now.

5: An Ode to the Antigonish Highland Society

Alasdair MacGill-Eain Sinclair composed the following song-poem and delivered it on November 30, 1899 to the Antigonish Highland Society when they celebrated St. Andrew's Day. His own interests and priorities as a scholar are evident in how he validates Gaelic, although he also makes assertions that are unusual for a 19th-century churchman.

The overriding message of the text is the need to sustain the Gaelic language. The song begins with a toast (line 5), a common enough motif in clan songs of old, but it is a tribute to the Gaels in general rather than an address to a specific person. He attempts to goad his audience into rejecting the negative stigmas that obviously surrounded Gaelic at the time by proactively praising them for their loyalty to their ancestral language and the virtues with which they have been endowed as a result of it. Sinclair counters the stereotypes of Highlanders as crude barbarians by expressing admiration for their "civilized" virtues: intelligence, mannerliness, courteousness, and so on (lines 59-68). Some of the compliments that he pays to his audience allude to the clichés of tartanism and militarism: machismo (line 8), bravado (lines 10 and 12),

Figure 9.1 – Alasdair MacGill-Eain Sinclair (Alexander MacLean Sinclair), Gaelic scholar and poet. Portrait from The Celtic Monthly, *July 1907 (No. 10 Vol XV).*

hardiness (line 57), nobility (line 59) and so on. Sinclair asserts that the violence the enemies of Gaelic hope to inflict is ultimately aimed at Gaelic speakers and their ancestors: they should respond in kind by defending and cherishing this heritage (lines 35-44).

On the one hand, Sinclair employs an intellectually-oriented argument to validate the importance of Gaelic, appealing to the good sense and judgement of the audience (lines 11, 19, 21, 34 and 63). He refers to the research in Celtic philology then being conducted particularly by German scholars, who at that time led the field (lines 45-48). Their work was part of the larger field of Indo-European studies, which claimed that a family of languages had come to dominate a large extent of Europe and Asia because of the cultural and military superiority of the people who spoke them (lines 51-52). This narrative of empowered champions dovetailed neatly for Sinclair's purposes into the much later story of Highland emigration (lines 57-60), despite the obvious discontinuities. His esteem for Gaelic literature in both oral (lines 20, 22, 25, 87, 91 and 99) and written (lines 77-78, 85 and 99) form is evident in the song, and his inclusiveness of the Irish into the Gaelic fold (line 98) is unusual for his time.

On the other hand, Sinclair pleads on some very anti-intellectual grounds. The affection that Gaels should feel for their language is at least in part due to the familial piety that they are expected to share (lines 14, 24 and 41-44). He implies that Gaelic civility and graciousness (lines 59-68) contrasts with the profanity and godlessness of the non-Gaelic world, in part by parodying the theory of evolution (lines 69-72) of which he was a harsh critic.[47] Unlike the opposition of churchmen to what they considered "superstitions" and the excessive attention given to the secular literature of the Fian earlier in the 19th century (see text 7.1), Sinclair exhorts his audience to maintain their interest in traditional folktales and beliefs, even those regarding "supernatural" beings (lines 73-88). His portrayal of the Gaelic social order, in which women are charged with a majority of the manual labour (lines 25-32), is disturbingly paternalistic but it reflects the high degree of out-migration of women leaving the Canadian Maritimes to work as domestic servants in New England.[48]

Original Text

1 Cumaibh suas, a suas, a suas i,
Cumaibh suas, a suas, a suas i,

Cumaibh suas, a suas, a suas i,
Cumaibh suas a' Ghàidhlig.

5   Deoch-slàint' nan daoine furanach –
Na Gàidheil rìoghail urramach –
Tha cruinn a-nochd mar bhuineadh dhaibh:
De dhuinealas, gur làn iad.

Bidh fuil nan seann laoch Albannach
10   A' gluasad suas gu calma annta;
Is iad fhéin bhios sunndach seanchasach
Is gur mairg a thairgeadh tàir dhaibh.

Cha seall iad sìos gu dìmeasach
Air cleachdainnean an sinnsirean:
15   Na gaisgich throma, mhìleanta
Bh' an tìr nam fraoch-bheann àrda.

Bidh taigeis air a' bhòrd aca
Is a' phìob a' seinn na mòralachd;
Is bidh daoine fiosrach foghlaimte
20   Toirt òraidean le àgh dhaibh.

Cha mheas iad gur e gòraiche
Bhith seinn nan òran bòidheach sin
A chual' iad is a dh'fhoghlaim iad
Bho bheòil nan saoidh a dh'fhàg sinn.

25   Is taitneach leo na duanagan
A dh'éist iad bho na gruagaichibh
A bhleoghnadh bó le uallachas
Is a luaidheadh clò gu làidir.

Cha b' ionnan iad is na brònagan
30   Nach urrainn biadh a chòcaireachd;
Mu sguabadh tha gun eòlas ac'
Is gun cheòl annt' ach an cànran.

Na fir th' a-nochd 's an talla seo
Tha tùr a-staigh fo'm malaichean;
35   Is chan éist iad ris na balaich sin
Nì talach air ar cànain.

Chan éist iad ris na burraidhean
Th' ag ràdh mu'n Ghàidhlig urramaich
Gur còir bhith rithe fuileachdach
40   Is a cur gu tur fo shàiltibh.

Có e a bhiodh cho fuar-chridheach
Is gun sealladh e le suarachas
Air cainnt na màthar suairce sin
A thog a-suas 'na phàist' e?

45 Na cainntearan as neo-chearbaiche
Th' an-diugh am measg nan Gearmailteach:
Th' a' Ghàidhlig measail ainmeil ac'
Is cha mharbhadh iad gu bràth i.

Is cainnt tha brìoghail feumail i
50 A mhìneachadh gu h-éifeachdach
Mar sgaoil na h-Eòrpaich threun-làmhach
Bho chéile do gach ceàrna.

'S i a labhradh leis na daoine sin
A sheòl do'n dùthaich chraobhaich seo
55 A dh'fhaotainn bàigh is saors' innte
Is gun mhaoin ac' ach an t-slàinte.

Na daoine calma, cruadalach
A leag a' choille ghruamach dhuinn:
Bu churaidhean is daoine uasal iad
60 'Nan gluasad is 'nan nàdar.

Bu daoine modhail cùirteil iad;
Bu daoine suilbheir sunndach iad;
Bu daoine fiosrach tùrail iad;
Bu chliù do thìr nan sàr iad.

65 Cha tug iad spéis do shlaightearachd,
Is cùl-chàineadh, bu nì oillteill leò;
Bha iochd is gràdh a' soillseachadh
Gu boillsgeanta gach là annt'.

Biodh bodaich Ghallt' gu dìcheallach
70 A' seinn mu'n làthaich innleachdaich
A dh'fhàs na cuirp is na h-inntinnean –
Ma chinn iad fhéin o mhàgain.

Ach creididh sinne 'n spioradan
A labhras cainnt gu fileanta,
75 A chluicheas ceòl air innealan
Is le'm milis bhith neo-bhàsmhor.

Is leughaidh sinn na h-eachdraidhean
Tha sgrìobht' 's a' Ghàidhlig bhlast' againn:
Mu bhòcain is mu ghlaistigean
80 Is mu ghaisgeantachd 's na blàraibh.

Ri sìthichibh nan tulaichean,
Cha chuirear cùl gu buileach leinn:
Is iomadh Gàidheal urranta
Fhuair cuireadh bhuap' gu'n àros.

85 Mu Fhionn mac Cumhaill, leughaidh sinn!
Mu Dhiarmaid Donn na geur-shleagha;
Mu Oisein binn nan réidh-bhilean
Is gach treun mu'n d' rinneadh dàn leis.

Á'r sealladh, biodh na beadagain
90 Th' an dùil gur gnothach leibideach
A' Ghàidhlig fhonnmhor eagarach
A theagasg d'an cuid phàistean.

Ach beannachdan air bheannachdan
A chum nan daoine ceanalta
95 Le'm miann a faicinn maireannach
Is daingeann 's gach seann làraich.

A chum nan daoine léirsinneach
Measg Albannach is Éireannach
A labhras i is a leughas i
100 Is a tha toirt spéis d'a bàrdachd.[49]

Translation

(1-4) Keep it alive ... keep the Gaelic alive.

(5-8) [Here's] a toast to the hospitable people—the royal, noble Gaels—who are gathered together tonight as they ought to be: they are full of manliness.

(9-12) The blood of the ancient Scottish champions moves bravely in them; they are the ones who are cheerful and full of ancient lore; pity the one who shows them contempt.

(13-16) They will not look down disrespectfully on the customs of their ancestors: the hefty, bellicose warriors who were in the land of the high, heathery mountains.

(17-20) They will have haggis on the table and the bagpipes will sing majestically; knowledgeable and educated people will deliver talks to them joyfully.

(21-24) They will not consider it foolishness to be singing those beautiful songs that they heard and that they learned from the mouths of the wise people who have left us.

(25-28) They enjoy the ditties that they heard from the girls who would milk the cows with gaiety and would full the cloth with strength.

(29-32) They are unlike the sad women who cannot cook food; who are unacquainted with sweeping and have no music in them but grumbling.

(33-36) The men who are in this hall tonight have good sense in their heads; they will not listen to those ruffians who reproach our language.

(37-40) They will not listen to the blockheads who say about the honourable Gaelic that it is proper to be violent to it and to stamp it out entirely.

(41-44) Who could be so cold-hearted that he would look with indifference on the language of that gentle mother who raised him when he was child?

(45-48) The most exacting linguists are today among the Germans: Gaelic is worthy and illustrious in their estimation and they would never kill it.

(49-52) It is a language that is useful and full of substance to explain effectively how the strong-armed Indo-Europeans dispersed from one another into every corner [of the world].

(53-56) It is the language that those people spoke who sailed to this tree-filled country to find goodwill and freedom but who had no assets but their health.

(57-60) The brave, hardy people who felled the gloomy forest for us: they were champions and noble people in their behaviour and in their nature.

(61-64) They were mannerly, courteous people; they were cheerful, happy people; they were knowledgeable, sensible people; they were a credit to the land of the heroes.

(65-68) They felt no fondness for villainy and they considered backbiting a horrible thing; compassion and affection shone brightly in them every day.

(69-72) Let the non-Gaelic wretches dutifully sing about the ingenious bioplasm that caused the evolution of bodies and minds—if they themselves have evolved above crawling.

(73-76) But we will believe in spirits who can speak eloquently and can play music on instruments and relish being immortal.

(77-80) And we will read the accounts that we have written in lovely Gaelic about spectres and dryads, and about heroism in the battlefields.

(81-84) We will never totally turn our backs to the fairies of the knolls; many intrepid Gaels received an invitation from them to their abodes.

(85-88) We will read about Fionn mac Cumhaill! and about brown-haired Diarmaid of the sharp spear, about melodious Ossian of the harmonious lips and about every warrior about whom he composed a ballad.

(89-92) Get the rogues out of our sight who think that it is a scornful matter to teach the melodious and well-ordered Gaelic to their children.

(93-96) But blessings on top of blessings to the genteel people who wish to see it enduring and secure in its old locations.

(97-100) [Blessings] to the discerning people among the Scots and Irish who can speak and read it and who appreciate its poetry.

6: The Scotch Gathering of Alexandria

The following song-poem was composed by Dr. Dòmhnall Donnchadh MacDhòmhnaill on the occasion of the Scotch Gathering in Alexandria on September 2, 1905, held by an organization called "Sons of Scotland Benevolent Association." Although there are some technical faults in the poetry (inexact rhymes, inconsistent noun declensions and syllable length), the text is interesting for what it tells us about the perceptions of heritage among Glengarrians of the time and the ways in which they celebrated it. Among other things, it reveals that the organized "pilgrimage" back to the Highland homeland was already something of a heritage industry among members of this diasporic community.

The text opens with the depiction of a grand parade on the streets of Alexandria commemorating the Highland heritage of the area, replete with the tokens of tartanism: kilts, bagpipes, plaid and bonny lads and lasses who are said to epitomize gender-specific ideals (lines 5-32). The touchstones for these notions in the community by this time were no doubt a synthesis of the inherited Gaelic oral repertoire and the Highlandism of romantic anglophone literature, which was already being absorbed in the Glengarry region by the middle of the 19th century through the medium of Gaelic itself (as demonstrated in text 3.2).

The stereotypes give way to comments about the Gaelic language and specific individuals once the older generation appears in view (lines 33-34). Dr. MacDhòmhnaill describes his friend, the popular poet Iain MacLachlainn (see song-poem 6.14), of whom he was clearly very fond. He praises his ancestral credentials, including his kinship to an accomplished Gaelic poet and scholar (lines 42-44).[50] Another friend, John J. MacDonald of Glen Nevis, appears; he is not only decked out in his finest plaid but is said to be a Gaelic speaker. MacDhòmhnaill brings them into a more intimate, personal space where they share a highly cultivated Gaelic song which gives the doctor comfort (lines 57-64). A spatial reading of the text suggests that Gaelic is being removed from the public sphere of the common community and is becoming restricted to smaller social circles and personal friendships, even though the language's best literary practitioners can still compose elaborate poetry (lines 63-64).

MacDhòmhnaill discloses his desire to bring his closest Gaelic-speaking companions on a journey back to the "Old Country" with him: not Scotland in general but the Highlands in particular (lines 65-66). He expects to witness—or at least he ornaments his song with the hope of seeing—the idyllic scenes described in Gaelic poetry of gallant aristocrats hunting the deer in spectacular scenery that features vigorous and musical wildlife (lines 67-76). This pilgrimage would not be complete without visiting the specific locales of the Western Highlands from which the majority of the original immigrants had come (lines 77-82). The geographical catchment area of the pilgrimage then expands in scope to the outer rings of the Gàidhealtachd (lines 83-84), thence to the Lowlands (line 85), and finally to Ireland and England (line 86). MacDhòmhnaill expects a grand adventure with his companions, one that they will be able to relate in narrative form for the entertainment of people back home (lines 89-90 and 93-96). MacLachlainn will refine it further into the form of a song-poem (lines 91-92).

This text reveals the growing dominance of the tartanism in the community's self-conception of Scottish identity. The linguistic and literary inheritance of the Highland immigrants is rapidly receding to the confines of the elderly and even to the imagination itself.

Original Text

   1   Ill ù, ill ò ro hò
           Ill ù, ill ò ro hò
           Ill ù, ill ò ro hò
           Hillin ò ho ro hì.

   5   Am Baile Mhuilinn Chlann Dòmhnaill
          Bha là mór aig na seòid ann
          Le damhs', aighear is òrain
          Is le ceòl a bha binn.

          B' e là Comunn nan Gàidheal
 10   Is bha sluagh ás gach àite
          Is iad a' gabhail na sràide
          Ri ceòl àlainn nam pìob.

          Bha na brataich a' srannaich
          Ri barran nan crannaibh
 15   Is bha an t-sràid mhór le sròl flannach
          Is le anart fo dhìon.

          Bha gach gruagach cho banail
          Is ri guaillibh a leannain
          Is a bràighe caomh mar mhaothan eala
 20   Is gàirdean canach fo shìod'.

          Is gum bu ghuanach na h-òighean
          Cridheil suairce 'nan dòighean
          Is an gruaidhean mar na ròsan
          Is iad cho bòidheach is cho mìn.

 25   Bha luchd breacan an fhéilidh
          Tighinn dha'n Chomunn 'nan éididh,
          Gaisgich fhulangach threubhach
          Nach géilleadh 's an t-srì.

          'S ann an-sin bha na daoine uasal
 30   Is iad fearail 'nan gluasad
          Sheasadh làidir 's an tuasaid
          Is iad gu cruadalach clì.

          Gheibhte seann daoin' a' labhairt
          Anns a' Ghàidhlig cho ealamh
 35   Is mnathan còire Ghlinn Garadh
          Is iad fallain gun ghiamh.

Bha MacLachlainn am bàrd ann
Is e cho éibhinn is cho càirdeil;
Thàinig esan is fiamh a' ghàir' air
40   Is chuir e blàths air mo chrìdh'.

Do Niall Bàn tha e càirdeach
Is do MacLachlainn an sàr-bhàrd:
Sgoilear Gàidhlig a b' fhearr
A bha 'n Albainn ri 'thìm.

45   Thàinig Mac Iain a Chaiptein
Duin' uasal cho tlachdmhor,
Is fear Gàidhlig cho gasta
Is a tha 'n dràst' anns an tìr.

Ann am féileadh nan cuacha
50   Is sporan fialadh air uachdar
Breacan rìomhach mu ghualainn
Dhèanadh suaineach do rìgh.

Is ma gheibh mi mo dhùrachd
Théid na daoine seo null leam
55   Thar bharr nan tonn dubh-ghorm
Gu dùthaich nan suinn.

Thug mi staigh iad dha'n t-seòmar
Far am bheil mi a' còmhnaidh
Is ghabh MacLachlainn dhomh òran
60   A thug sòlas dhomh fhìn.

Is an t-òran a rinn e
Ann am briathran deas caoimhneil,
'S e bàrdachd cho toinnte
Is a rinneadh ri m' linn.

65   Nuair a théid sinn a dh'Albainn
Théid sinn mach air a' Gharbh-Chrìoch
Far am bi uaislean le'n armachd
A' sealg anns na frìth'.

Far am bi 'chuthaig is an smeòrach
70   Gabhail òran gu ceòlmhor
Is daimh sheangach na cròice
Ri crònan 's an t-sliabh.

Chì sinn lùthchleas a' bhradain
Leum gu sunndach 's a' mhadainn
75   Is sinn ag iasgach an sgadain
Ann am Bràighe Loch Fìn'.

Théid sinn thro Ghleann Garadh
Gu Cnòideart a' bharraich
Dha'n Ghlas Choille is Ruigh an Daraich
80 Gu Baile Inbhir Rìgh.⁵¹

Nuair a dh'fhàgas sinn Cnòideart
Chì sinn Mùideart is Mórar
Is gach àit' eadar Dòrnach
Is sròn àrd Chinn Tìr.

85 Sin mun cuairt a Dhùn Éideann
Is do Sasann is do dh'Éirinn;
Is thig sinn dhachaigh gu gleusta
Thar eudann nan tuinn.

'S ann an-sin bhios an stòiridh
90 Is gheibh MacLachlainn e 'n òrdugh
Is gun dèan e dheth òran
Le seòltachd ro ghrinn.

Théid na facail cho réidh dha
An eagain a chéile
95 Is gun cluinn sibh bhuaidhe sgeul
A bhios éibhinn ri innse.⁵²

Translation

(5-8) The lads had a grand day in Alexandria, with dancing, merriment and songs, and with music that was melodious.

(9-12) It was a day for the Gaelic Society and there were people from everywhere, marching down the street to the beautiful music of the bagpipes.

(13-16) The banners were fluttering against the tops of the poles and the great street was lined with purple flags and white cloths.

(17-20) Every woman was comely, next to her darling, with her tender bosom like the breast of a swan and her fair upper arms covered with silk.

(21-24) The maidens were giddy, cheerful and genteel in their manners, and their cheeks were like roses, so soft and beautiful.

(25-28) The people of the kilted tartan were coming to the Society in their uniforms, hardy and brave warriors who would never yield in the struggle.

IDENTITY AND ASSOCIATIONS

(29-32) [That is where] the noble people could be found who were manly in their carriage, who would stand steadfast in the conflict and who were vigorous and strong.

(33-36) Old people could be found speaking fluently in Gaelic, and the goodly women of Glengarry who were robust and without defect.

(37-40) The poet McLachlan was there, high-spirited and friendly; he came with a smile on his face and he warmed my heart.

(41-44) He is related to Fair Neil and to McLachlan the superb poet: the best Gaelic scholar who lived in Scotland in his day.

(45-48) [Mr. John J. MacDonald] his captain came, a gentleman who is most pleasant and as good a Gaelic speaker as any now alive in the land.

(49-52) In a pleated kilt with a generous sporran over it, a lovely tartan around his shoulder that would make a sash for a king.

(53-56) And if I am granted my wish, these men will go over with me across the dark blue waves to the land of heroes.

(57-60) I brought them into the chamber in which I live and McLachlan sang a song for me that gave me great solace.

(61-64) And the song that he composed in elegant and kind words is poetry as complex as any made in my lifetime.

(65-68) When we go to Scotland, we will go out to the Highlands where the nobles with their weapons hunt in the deer forests.

(69-72) Where the cuckoo and the thrush sing songs melodiously and the slender, antlered stags croon on the moor.

(73-76) We will see the salmon's athleticism, leaping merrily in the morning as we fish for the herring on the Braes of Loch Fyne.

(77-80) We will go through Glengarry to Knoydart of the branches, to Glaschoille and Ruigh an Daraich to the settlement of Inveree.

(81-84) When we leave Knoydart, we will see Moidart and Morar, and every place between Dornach and the high point of Kintyre.

(85-88) And thence around Edinburgh and to England and Ireland; and we will return home refreshed across the tops of the waves.

(89-92) Then we will have a story and McLachlan will get it prepared and he will make a song of it with refined intelligence.

(93-96) The words will come so smoothly to him, arranged together, that you will hear a narrative from him that will be exciting to recount.

7: A Song to the Gaels of Vancouver

The following song-poem was composed by Dòmhnall MacLeòid when he lived in Vancouver among thousands of fellow Gaels, as well as other ethnic groups. Two versions of this song were recorded from Gaelic speakers in California probably not more than a decade after it was composed that contained a stanza comparing the Gaels unfavourably with the Chinese (lines 65-72), given that the latter showed far more devotion to their ancestral language and traditions. When I interviewed the poet's son Niall in 2004, he related anecdotes about a Mongolian working for a Hebridean immigrant in Vancouver who had learned Gaelic![53] I have, therefore, restored this verse to the song, even though it was omitted from the version that was initially printed.

Figure 9.2 – Dòmhnall MacLeòid on left (holding baby) in Flat, Alaska. Portrait in possession of Dòmhnall's grandson Malcolm and used with his permission.

This song's structure and air is based on "Moladh Cabar-Féidh," composed by a Kintail poet about the 1715 Jacobite Rising. The surviving text of that song has heroic and satirical components which may be the result of the amalgamation of different authors and the result is now difficult to disentangle.[54] This song from Vancouver echoes that mixture of praise and dispraise. Although MacLeòid clearly expresses his disapproval of the attitudes and behaviours of many Gaels, he suggests that even harsher judgements may be forthcoming if the audience does not take corrective steps to guard and nurture their native language (lines 40, 48, 98 and 104). The poet shames them for betraying their mothers who sang Gaelic to them as children (lines 49-56), and goes so far as to compare those who prefer English to Judas Iscariot (line 80), selling out Gaelic to those who would persecute and utterly destroy it (lines 77-78). He also gives praise to those who deserve it (line 89).

Dòmhnall contrasts the current vulnerability of Gaelic to an earlier age when it was fostered by scholars and intellectuals (lines 13-16) and defended vigilantly as an integral part of Highland life and freedom (lines 25-32). The contemporary lack of cultivation of the language by its natural heirs is likened to seed that is carelessly sown in thin soil or left to be scattered by the elements (lines 17-24). Negative perceptions of Gaelic were intensified by experiences in the city, where many Highland immigrants attempt to free themselves of the "burden" of the language and assimilate to anglophone life (lines 33-38 and 41-44).

There were many dangers and uncertainties in the big urban centres of North America for those who came from small, rural communities and Dòmhnall attempts to persuade them that maintaining the grounding of their Gaelic roots will be useful to them in difficult times (lines 57-64). Gaelic poet Iain Crichton Mac a' Ghobhainn similarly observes the difficulties that some Highlanders faced when leaving the familiar, tightly-knit, kin-rooted communities of their youth for unknown urban areas:

> For the islander to enter the city was to enter a totally new kind of world which in many cases caused "culture shock," not so much because of the demands that the city made, but because of its impersonality, because one was no longer sustained by communal force. ... The city would have been the most terrifying place of all to a person brought up in a community and whose name was known to everybody.[55]

Dòmhnall praises the people of Cape Breton for providing a positive example of Gaelic loyalty, despite their economic disadvantages (line 86), since they are willing to make public use of their mother tongue (lines 93-96). He suggests that immigrants from Scotland brought a lack of confidence and inferiority complex with them to Canada and that the problem must therefore be addressed in "Tìr an

Fhraoich" (The Land of Heather)—Scotland—itself (lines 105-110). This is certainly one of the most insightful and compelling Canadian Gaelic songs about language loyalty.

Original Text

1   Mo chàirdean is mo luchd-dùthcha
    Teann dlùth is nì mi aithris dhuibh
    An nì a rinn mo mhù[t]hadh
    Is na cùisean a bhuineas dha:
5   Gàidheil chòire Bhancùbhair
    'Ga mùchadh is cha mhath leam sin,
    Iad uile 'call na Gàidhlig
    Bhon thàr iad do Chanada.

    Sìol nan daoine fearail
10 Smiorail sìmplidh geanail cothromach;
    Sìol nan daoine còire
    Làidir coibhneil bàigheil onarach
    A choisinn cliù dhaibh fhéin 's gach ceàrn
    Is do'n àite bhuineadh iad
15 Is a ghreimich riamh ri'n Gàidhlig
    Ged a b' àrd iad ann an sgoilearachd.

    Ach an-diugh gur ann tha 'n sìol-san
    'Ga chliathadh air tanalach
    Far nach gabh a freumhach
20 Ach siaban 's na sgoran i;
    Seargaidh i le tiormachd
    Is gu h-iomlan gu'n caillear i,
    Is cha toir blàths na gréine
    Oirr' éirigh 's an talamh sin.

25 A' chànain bhinn tha blasta grinn
    Bha ann bho linn ar seanairean:
    Is a dh'earb iad rinn a cumail cruinn
    Is gu'n dùin mo chill, gun lean i rium;
    'S i bh' aig na suinn a dh'àraich sinn
30 Is cha dèanadh prìs a ceannach bhuap';
    'S e gnothach nàire is calltachd
    'S an àm seo i 'thanachadh.

    An dèan thu innse dhomhsa
    An e pròis e no aineolas
35 Tha toirt air an òigridh
    Tha seòladh do Chanada

IDENTITY AND ASSOCIATIONS

  Gun caill iad uile a' Ghàidhlig
  Is nas fhearr, is truagh, chan aithne dhaibh;
  Is a' bharail bhios aig càch orr'
40 'S an dàn seo, chan aithris mi.

  'S ann their iad rium le sgallais treun
  Nach dèan e feum 's a' bhaile seo;
  Gun innte ach sac gun móran taic,
  Tha móran aca gearain rium;
45 Leisgeul leibideach, gun diù!
  Co-dhiù, 's e sin mo bharail-sa;
  Ach am breitheamh, nì mi 'fhàgail
  Aig càch chum a bhreithneachadh.

  A' chailleach chòir, do mhàthair,
50 A thàlaidh 's a' chreathall thu
  Le òrain bhlasta Ghàidhlig
  Nuair bha thu 'nad leanaban:
  Is gann nach fàg e tinn i
  Is le cinnt, bidh i eangarra,
55 Ma chluinneas i gun do chaill thu
  Do chainnt le d' chuid amaideis.

  Am foghlam a fhuair thu òg –
  'S ann ris bu chòir dhut greimeachadh;
  Na leig seachad e le d' dheòin
60 Ach gabh ann pròis is duinealas;
  Is cha bhi meòir aig neach tha beò
  A stiùireadh ort le leiteachas;
  Gun seall thu 'n clàr an aodainn
  Na dh'fhaodas tu a choinneachadh.

65 Nach seall thu air an t-Sìneach,
  Ged is ìseal 'nad shealladh e –
  Neach nach creid am Bìoball
  No 'n Fhìrinn, ged chanainn e;
  Tha e daingeann dìleas
70 Do rìoghachd is do sheanairean
  Gu cumail suas a chànain
  Ged bhiodh càch uile fanaid air.

  Bu chòir sin fhéin do chur air ghleus
  Gu seasamh treun bho amadain
75 Aig nach eil dhi tlachd no spéis
  Is gur beag am beud, ma chaillear i;
  Bu mhiann leò a reubadh

SEANCHAIDH NA COILLE

  Is a ceusadh 's a' bhaile seo;
  Tha cuid mhór dhiubh an-diugh
80 Air tionndadh 'nan Iùdas Iscariot.

  Rùisgidh mi mo cheann a-nis,
  Gun ghamhlas is gu fearanta,
  Do shìol nan daoine greannmhor
  Chum teann cliù ar seanairean:
85 Ceap Breatannaich ghlan' uasal
  Nach d' fhuair a leth de chothrom rinn –
  Chum iad suas a' Ghàidhlig
  Is a bàrdachd glé onarach.

  Cuidich leamsa seinn an cliù
90 Tha mi 'n dùil a bhuineas dhaibh,
  A lean cho dlùth 'nan taic 's gach cùis
  A' cumail grunnd ar seanairean;
  An uair a thachras mi air sràid
  Ri fear no dhà dhiubh as aithne dhomh,
95 Gur ann anns a' Ghàidhlig
  Théid fàilte chur gu geanail orm.

  Gur bochd a-nis a' chùis,
  An déidh mo dhùrachd is m' earail dhut,
  Mur dèan thu tionndadh
100 Is do chùl a chur ri amaideas;
  Chan eil i trom ri giùlain
  Is cha chum i gun chadal thu,
  Ach ma leigeas tu air chall i
  'S e bhios ann ach cùis-mhagaidh dhut.

105 A chlann mo ghaoil, an tìr an fhraoich,
  Mo Ghàidheil chaoimh, bith cabhagach!
  Is tog do ghlaodh an àird ri m' thaobh
  An dùthaich chraobhach Chanada;
  Air sgàth nan daoine còir' tha thall,
110 Dèan seasamh teann is neo-chàraichte
  Is na leig leis a' Ghàidhlig
  Dol bàs fad 's as maireann thu.[56]

Translation

(1-8) My friends and compatriots, come close and I will explain to you what has caused my injury and all that relates to it: the good Highlanders of Vancouver are extinguishing it [Gaelic]

IDENTITY AND ASSOCIATIONS

and I disapprove of that, they are all losing their Gaelic since they have come to Canada.

(9-16) The descendants of the manly, vigorous, friendly and fair-minded men; the descendants of the upright, strong, kind, affectionate and honourable people who earned fame for themselves in every corner [of the world] and for the place to which they belonged and who always held fast to their Gaelic even if they were accomplished in scholarship.

(17-24) But today their descendants are furrowing it in shallow ground where it cannot take root, like flotsam in the scores of rocks; it will wither with thirst entirely until it will be lost and the warmth of the sun will not cause it to rise in that soil.

(25-32) The melodious language that is tasty and elegant, that has been around since the age of our ancestors; they entrusted us to keep it intact and until my grave closes around me, it will stick to me; it is what the heroes who raised us spoke and no price could buy it from them; it is a matter of shame and loss that it is now thinning out.

(33-40) Will you tell me, is it pride or ignorance that is causing the youth who are sailing to Canada to completely lose their Gaelic for they don't know any better—what a pity! I will not relate in this poem the opinion that others have of them.

(41-48) Indeed, they [the youth] tell me with bold derision that it is of no use in this city; many of them complain to me that it is a burden that does not offer much support; it is a worthless and baseless excuse, at least that is my opinion; but I will leave the judgement for others to decide.

(49-56) That good old woman, your mother, who lulled you to sleep in the cradle with tasteful Gaelic songs when you were an infant: it will practically make her sick, and certainly she will be angry, if she hears that you have lost your language with your foolishness.

(57-64) You ought to hold tight to the tutelage that you received when you were young; do not willingly let it slip away but take pride in it and affection; [if you do,] no living person will be able to steer you with partiality and you will be able to stare in the face any challenge that you may encounter.

(65-72) Why don't you look at the Chinese person even if you think him low—a person, I must admit, who does not believe in the Bible or Scripture; he is steadfast and loyal to his country and to his ancestors in keeping his language alive, even if everyone else mocks him.

(73-80) That itself ought to inspire you to make a strong stand against fools who have no enjoyment of or love for it [Gaelic] and who think that there is no harm if it is lost; they would like to shred it up and crucify it in this city; a great many of them today have turned into Judas Iscariots.

(81-88) I will now bare my head, with good will and gallantly, to the descendants of the wonderful people who have carefully preserved the reputation of our forefathers: the pure and noble people of Cape Breton who haven't had half of the opportunities that we have—they have kept Gaelic alive and maintained its poetry honorably.

(89-96) Join me in singing the praises that I think they've earned, they who have diligently kept up their support in all matters to hold the ground of our grandfathers; when I encounter one or two of them that I know on the street, it is in Gaelic that they greet me warmheartedly.

(97-104) It will be a sad thing now, if after my benevolence and counsel to you, you do not change your direction and turn your back on foolishness; it [Gaelic] is not heavy to carry and will not keep you from sleep, but if you allow it to become lost, it will only be a reason to mock you.

(105-112) O beloved people in the land of heather, my dear Gaels, make haste! And raise your cry up alongside mine in the tree-filled land of Canada; on behalf of the good people over yonder, take a firm and unwavering stand and don't let Gaelic die as long as you live.

10 – Politics

The political systems and practices of government in North American colonies were largely derived from those of the empires that spawned them, although they could also be more liberal or more restrictive in particular times and places. The right to vote in British North America began in a highly discriminatory manner, restricting participation in democracy by gender (male only), wealth (only those who owned property or a particular minimum amount of assets), and religion (Protestants only). In addition, elections were initially administered in such a way as to lead inevitably to inequalities of participation: votes were taken orally, which meant that not only was it possible to influence or intimidate citizens, but that linguistic barriers could create obstacles to full participation.[1]

The beachheads of responsible government in the provinces were the legislative assemblies established in Nova Scotia (1758), Prince Edward Island (1773), New Brunswick (1785), Lower Canada (now Quebec, 1792) and Upper Canada (now Ontario, 1792). The popularly-appointed members of these chambers were, however, easily overpowered by the members of executive councils appointed by colonial governors (frictions that appear in text 10.1).

Many Gaels were able to settle in British North America on favourable terms and became land owners in a short time so they were often able to vote generations before they would have had they stayed at home in the Scottish Highlands.[2] This also meant that they had to learn unfamiliar concepts and habits of citizenship and government. An account of the Highland settlement in Middlesex County, Ontario, would have doubtlessly been applicable to many others:

In the early years there was practically no politics among the Highland settlers. For this there were several reasons. The franchise was to them an entirely new privilege, which they had never before enjoyed, and it took some time rightly to estimate its value, and realize its responsibility. The fight with the literal wolf and the wolf of hunger, the overshadowing influences of friendship and fraternity, and the yet higher claims of religion, so fully occupied their attention that politics had little or no place on their horizon. Besides, for a good while, no newspapers circulated, no electioneering stump orator visited them, and they had not the knowledge on which alone intelligent political opinion could be based. But a change began in 1837-8.[3]

Candidates and their supporters often attempted to cajole or entice voters by supplying them with alcohol, available in copious amounts during elections. Two of the Gaelic poems in this chapter (10.3 and 10.7) complain about "boodle" bribery used to try to buy votes. Highland settlers in Zorra, as elsewhere, were subject to the intoxicating effects of campaigning:

For some years after the first settlement, the Zorra pioneers took little interest in politics. What with the clearing the forest, "ploughing, sowing, reaping and mowing," they had hard work to provide food and clothes for themselves and their children. ... [T]he election lasted for five days, and feeling ran high. During the election, free meals and liquor were supplied by each candidate to his friends. Barrels of whiskey were placed near the polling booth; pails, dippers and little tin cups were supplied in abundance, and as may be easily imagined, the consequent scenes were far from edifying. The wonder is that under such circumstances the consequences were not even more serious.[4]

Most political Gaelic songs construct an analogy between campaigning and warfare: leaders (politicians) need to rally soldiers (boosters and voters) to join and support their objectives. In both cases, rulers needed to have effective spin doctors to extol their qualifications, promote their causes, and celebrate their victories. The earliest Gaelic poets made some attempt to align political and ethnic solidarity. Probably the most forceful surviving example of this comes from the 1851 election for one of the seats of Sydney County (now

Antigonish County) in Nova Scotia, which then consisted of a majority of Highland immigrants and their descendants. The poet, Alasdair Ailein Mhóir, Bàrd na Ceapaich, declares the importance of electing Iain MacFhionghain (John McKinnon, born 1808) rather than Power, his anglophone opponent, as the former could understand and represent Gaelic interests:

> Na th'againn de chlanna nan Gàidheal:
> Seasaibh ar làrach fhéin! ...
>
> Is gu cinnteach nam bi'maid cho gann
> Ri clanna nan Gall as tìr
> Is iadsan bhith bitheant' 's gach gleann
> Gur beag de chommand bhiodh leinn; ...
>
> Is tha sinn an guaillibh a chéile
> Gabhail gu léir mun cuairt;
> Cha lean sinn luchd-labhairt na Beurla,
> Nì sinn an tréigsinn buan ...[5]

All of us who are children of the Gael: let us defend our own ground!

And indeed if we were as sparse as the non-Gaels in the land and they were plentiful in the glens, we would have little power.

We are all standing shoulder to shoulder, all on the march together; we will not follow anglophones, we will forsake them forever...

In general the reality was that political parties and interests did not correspond to ethnic blocs. Gaelic poets were obviously aware of this and were able to exploit and extend Gaelic literary resources to reflect more complex circumstances. A song-poem composed by Maoileas MacGilleMhaoil of Finch (now North Stormont), Ontario, in praise of John "Sandfield" Macdonald, first premier of Ontario (1867-1871), promises the leader that his loyal kinsmen will at least answer his call to protect him from enemies when he needs assistance.

> Is nan tigeadh strì no euslan ort,
> Gun éireadh iad gu deònach leat:
> Na Gàidheil bidh gu léir agad
> Is gach treubh tha dhe na Dòmhnallaich;
> Ge b' e chuireadh eucoir ort
> Na dh'fheuchadh streup no còmhstri riut,

Is cinnteach mi gum feumadh e
Bhith ag iarraidh réite is còrdadh riut.

Dh'éireadh iad gu sunndach leat
Cha diùltadh iad an t-òrdugh bhuat;
Na Garanaich air thùs agad
Mar sin is na fiùrain Stormontach ...[6]

And if conflict or illness were to ever afflict you, they would rise willingly with you: all of the Gaels will join you, and every branch of the Clan Donald; whomever might cause you suffering or attempt to cause trouble or conflict, I am sure that he would have to seek peace and terms with you.

The following would rise cheerfully with you and would not refuse an order from you: in the vanguard you would have the people of Glengarry, and likewise the scions of Stormont....

Aonghus Y. MacGill-Fhaolain of Cape Breton composed the song-poem "An Sgiobair Ùr" (The New Skipper) to celebrate the election of Angus L. Macdonald as premiere of Nova Scotia in 1933. It was modelled on an anonymous waulking song dating to the mid 17th century in praise of Mac Mhic Ailein (Captain of Clanranald). Like many songs of its kind, it conveys his suitability as a leader by depicting him in charge of a Hebridean galley.[7] Although the underlying analogy of the ship of state has certainly been implicit in this literary device for centuries, the Cape Breton poet extends this conceit as the organizing principle of the entire text to describe the duties of a modern politician:

Sgiobair ùr air luing na Mór-roinn
Deagh MacDhòmhnaill th' air an stiùir.

Chuireas oirre gleus gu astar
Le deagh acfhainn agus criù.

Chumas i gu seasgair tioram
Anns an iomairt air an lunn. ...[8]

A new captain on the ship of the province, goodly MacDonald who is at the helm.

Who will get her moving with good equipment and crew.

Who will keep her comfortable and dry in the enterprise on the waves. ...

The "multiethnic" strands of Macdonald's ancestry are teased apart and highlighted to suggest that he is capable of representing the interests of Nova Scotia's diverse communities:

Cha lean mi do shloinneadh mórail
Foghnaidh gur e MacDhòmhnaill thu. ...

Fuil na Frainge mar an ceudna
Glan a' sìoladh 'nad ghnùis.

Cha tuirt mi, nan leanainn céin thu
Nach tug thu á Éirinn driùchd. ...

I will not trace your noble lineage, it will suffice that you are a MacDonald.

French blood likewise flows clean through your visage.

I wouldn't swear that I couldn't find Irish drops if I were to trace you far back.

Electing candidates to participate in political institutions was one thing, making those institutions actually work on behalf of Gaelic interests was another. Gestures made by Canadian Gaels in the political arena to press for any degree of linguistic rights exposed not just their naiveté about the nature of British imperialism but also their inability to challenge contemporary convictions about the nature of language in nation-states. They generally followed a consistent pattern of deferring to the supremacy of the dominant anglophone hegemony and were quick to provoke the ire of French-speaking rivals when the latter appeared to exercise or campaign for their own linguistic liberties. Take, for example, the following anecdote about Gilleasbaig MacEalair (described in text 6.10):

Tha e air aithris air gun robh e aon latha 'na shuidhe an taigh na Pàrlamaid nuair a dh'éirich Frangach is a thòisich e air labhairt 's a' chainnt aige fhéin air a' cheist a bha fo chomhair an taighe. Cha bu luaithe shuidh e na dh'éirich MacEalair is thug e dhaibh òraid eireachdail ann an Gàidhlig, mar sin a' dèanadh spòrs mór dhaibh-san a thuigeadh e is a' cur fearg is dorran air an Fhrangach, nach robh 'ga thuigsinn.[9]

It has been stated about him that one day he was sitting in the House of Parliament when a Francophone arose and began to speak in his own language about the matter that was before the house. No sooner had he sat down than McKellar arose and he delivered a brilliant oration in Gaelic, thus providing great entertainment for those who could understand him and causing great anger and offense to the Francophone, who didn't understand him.

MacEalair appears to be mocking the francophone challenge to Anglo-conformity by highlighting the real differences between ethnic communities and the contested role of language in the exercise of power and the representation of constituencies in the operation and structure of government. He does so, however, not in an attempt to foster mutual respect between equals but rather to legitimate the status quo of Anglocentric domination, which is presented as preferable to presumed tribalism.

It is an assumption of those Gaelic-speaking politicians who addressed the Nova Scotia Assembly (text 10.2) and Canadian Parliament (text 10.4) to affirm the legitimacy of the use of Gaelic that they could assert their rights in Canada on the basis of extending their rights as British citizens on British territory. The reality was that the Gaelic language did not even enjoy any status or protection in Scotland itself: the British Empire by its nature had been defined by the imposition of the cultural and linguistic standards of England.

> The English language was a weapon long before its reach became the stuff of silicon chips and satellites. From the fifteenth century to the millennium—from London's statutes governing late Cornwall, Wales and Ireland to the latter-day wizardries of computer software—the English language (spoken, written, and then electronic) has been not just a symbol of political hegemony but a powerful weapon in achieving and upholding it.[10]

For all of the British rhetoric about freedom and fair-play, despite all of the Scottish bombast about Wallace and Bannockburn, Scottish Gaels were too cowed and ill-equipped to press for their linguistic and cultural rights as a community. Those among them who thought that they had earned some sort of special favour by sacrificing themselves in the expansion of British hegemony—thus enabling the conquest of other peoples and territories—were sadly mistaken. They were in fact a subjugated people and were to be treated as such whenever their interests differed from those of anglophones.[11]

1: Election Rally of Pictou

The following song-poem was composed by Iain MacGill-Eain (Am Bàrd MacGill-Eain) in late September of 1830 in response to events that occurred during a week-long election held in Pictou for the Nova Scotia Assembly. This election played out the tensions between two major provincial bodies, the popularly-elected Colonial Assembly and the Crown-appointed Council. Both of these governmental groups had been dominated by a small élite group consisting of settlers from England and anglophone Loyalists who had relocated to Nova Scotia in the aftermath of the American Revolutionary War.[12] As his grandson, Alasdair MacGill-Eain Sinclair, comments in the notes to the song, the ethnic slurs against Gaels that emerged during the campaign galvanized MacGill-Eain into exercising the social role of the poet to call for political and ethnic solidarity.

> He took no special interest in the election, until he was told that one of the Liberal candidates had made some insulting reference to the Highlanders. He then went to work and composed this song. He spent the greater part of the night at it. He sang it [the] next day. Thousands were present. It had a most exciting effect. It is a real brosnachadh-catha [battle incitement].

One of the Liberal candidates had stated, possibly as a reaction to a scene of violence that had occurred in the course of the week of politicking, that the Gaels needed sulphur to relieve them of the mange (a skin disease causing itching) that plagued them:[13] this was a euphemistic way of claiming that they were a dirty and unsanitary people and hence uncivilized. MacGill-Eain counters this insult and attempts to uplift Gaelic self-esteem by drawing heavily from the rhetoric of tartanism and militarism discussed in chapter 3. The chorus is a formulaic toast to the Gaels, identifying them through the familiar metonymy of their tartan clothing (line 1). The sharing of alcohol (lines 1-3) was a very old ritual that bonded war leaders with their followers and could be easily transferred to the setting in Pictou, given that "Both parties kept open houses, and liquor flowed freely."

MacGill-Eain wastes no time in urging Gaels to unite under political leaders, recalling the martial victories of previous generations. They will bring shame upon themselves if they submit to those who have insulted them (lines 13-16). He alludes to two ancient rivalries that had become clichés in Lowland literature: the Caledonian confrontation with Roman troops and Robert the Bruce's victory over English forces at Bannockburn (lines 37-44). The fact that he skips forward in time and then chooses to mention the Battle of Fontenoy against French forces in 1745 (line 45) is very significant: MacGill-Eain hereby underscores his commitment to the empire and the loyalty of the Gaels by ignoring the Jacobite Risings and emphasizing their adherence to the British Crown in the same period instead. In fact, he says that the Black Watch earned a special distinction in this battle that they wore on their regimental uniform (lines 46-48). He continues the list of military engagements with other battles against the French (lines 49-56), harkening back to the ideological forces and military enterprises that underpinned a pan-British identity.

Although acknowledging their participation in British affairs, MacGill-Eain sustains the distinctiveness of the Gaels as a specific ethnic group, using the ethnonym "Gàidheal" four times (lines 9, 20, 57 and 83). He goads them into action by forcing them to confront the insult that they have been given as members of a specific ethnic community (line 74). On the other hand, he blurs the distinctions between a narrow Gaelic identity and a broader Scottish identity through allusions to national Scottish battles and to the thistle as a symbol of Scotland as a whole (line 76).

This song-poem and the anecdotes surrounding it offer an ideal illustration of the role of the poet to inspire people to action in real life. MacGill-Eain promises in the text itself to carry on in his literary duties by commemorating their political victory publicly in poetic form, should they triumph (lines 79-80).

Original Text

1 Deoch-slàinte luchd nam breacanan,
   Is a cur mun cuairt a b' aite leinn;
   Is gun òlamaid gu sgairteil i
   Air lasgairean a' chruadail.

5 Tha naidheachd ùr an-dràst' againn
   Air a' chùirt a th' aig a' Phàrlamaid;
   Is gach taobh a' cruinneachadh chàirdean,
   Dh'fheuch có as fhearr aca nì buannachd.

   Is a Ghàidhealaibh, bithibh ceannsgalach
10 Is cuimhnichibh ur ceannardan:

Is tric thug buaidh 's na campaichean
Ag iomairt lann le cruadal.

Gur mór an t-adhbhar nàire dhuibh
Ma ghéilleas sibh do'n Làsonach,
15   Do Dheòrsa no do dh'Àrchibald,
Is an tàir a thug na h-uaislean.

'S ann thubhairt iad gu mì-chiatach
Gur pronnasg a bha dhìth orra,
Is gun glanadh siud an sgrìobach
20   De na Gàidheil mhiodhair shuarach.

Ma dhearbh sibh riamh ur duinealas,
'S e seo an t-àm dhuibh cruinneachadh,
Is fheuchainn dhaibh gur h-urrainn sibh
An t-urram a thoirt bhuatha.

25   Cha chualas riamh aon tàmailt
Aig an t-sinnsearachd bhon tàinig sibh;
An àm dol sìos 's na blàraibh
Bu neo-sgàthach gu cur ruaig iad.

Nuair rùisgeadh iad am brataichean,
30   Is a sheinnt' a' phìob gu tartarach,
Bhiodh cliù air luchd nam breacan
Anns gach baiteal, mar a chualas.

B' e siud an còmhdach cleachdte dhaibh:
An t-osan grinn is na gartanan,
35   An còta gearr is am breacan
Air a phasgadh thar an guala.

Le'n clàidhmhnean, dhìon na sàr fhearaibh
Gach beinn is gleann a dh'àitich iad
Bho fheachd na Ròimhe àilleasaich
40   Gu calma, dàna, buadhach.

Aig Allt a' Bhonnaich, b' fheumail iad;
Bu ghuineach fuileach treubhach iad,
'Cur ás gu bras le'n geur-lannaibh
D'an nàimhdean féineil uaibhreach.

45   'S an là bha Fontenòi ann
Gun d'rinn iad gnìomh mar leòghannaibh;
Chuir sin an gorm ri'n còtaichean
Is tha còir ac' air o'n uair sin.

Bu lasgarra 's an Éipheit iad;
50   Bu sgairteil neartmhor creuchdach iad;
Thuig Bonaparte an tréinead
A tha 'n luchd nam féileadh cuaiche.

Is aig Waterloo, gum b' ainmeil iad:
Rinn iad an gaisge dhearbhadh ann;
55   Is gum bheil e sgrìobht' an airgead
Air an ceanna-bheirt mar a ghluais iad.

Cha robh na Gàidheil fàilinneach:
B' e 'm beus bhith seasmhach tàbhachdach;
Bhith beachdail reachdmhor àrdanach
60   Bhith dàn a' dol 's an tuasaid.

Bu teòm' air gnìomh na fairge iad;
Cha mhiosa 'shiubhal garbhlaich iad;
Bu mhiann leotha bhith sealgaireachd
Air earbachan 's na bruachan.

65   Ged is iomadh tìr a dh'ast'raich iad,
Cha chualas riamh fo mhasladh iad;
Gach beus a b' fhearr bha 'n taice riuth';
Bha 'n cleachdadh daonnan uasal.

A shliochd nan laoch a b' ainmeile,
70   Na leigibh dhibh le dearmadachd
Na daoin' tha 'n-diugh ag earbs' àsaibh:
Gun dearbh sibh mar bu dual dhuibh!

A' mhuinntir ud 'bha 'g ràitinn ribh
Nach b' fhiach sibh féin no 'Ghàidhealtachd:
75   Biodh cuimhn' agaibh an-dràst' orra
Is àrdaichibh an cluaran.

Ma nì sibh gnìomh gu h-eireachdail,
Is gun toir sibh cùis mu dheireadh dhiubh,
Gun dèan mi òran eile dhuibh
80   Is cha cheil mi air an t-sluagh e.

Bithibh dìleas ann am bràithreachas,
Is gach cridh' gun lùb, gun fhàilinn ann;
Ho ró air son nan Gàidheal,
Is an deoch-slàinte: cuir mun cuairt i![14]

POLITICS

Translation

(1-4) [Here's] a toast to the people of the plaids, we delight in sending it around; and let us drink it vigorously to the hardy heroes.

(5-8) We have fresh news now about the assembly being held by the Parliament; each side gathers friends to see which of them will be victorious.

(9-12) O Gaels, be assertive and remember your leaders: often were they victorious in the fields of battle wielding their swords with hardiness.

(13-16) It will be a great cause for shame if you submit to Lawson, to George or to Archibald, given the contempt these gentlemen have given.

(17-20) Indeed, they said indecently that sulphur is what they need and that that would cleanse the itch from the contemptible, worthless Gaels.

(21-24) If you ever demonstrated your manliness, this is the time for you to gather together to show them that you can take the honour [of victory] from them.

(25-28) No disgrace was ever heard about the ancestors from whom you descend; when it was time to go to engage in battle, they were fearless in scattering enemies.

(29-32) When they unfurled their banners and the bagpipes were played thunderously, the plaided people would enjoy renown in every battle, as has been heard.

(33-36) This was their habitual clothing: elegant hose and garters, the kilt jacket and the plaid, folded across their shoulder.

(37-40) With their swords these super-men protected every mountain and glen that they inhabited from the troops of haughty Rome resolutely, bravely and successfully.

(41-44) They were instrumental at Bannockburn; they were vicious, violent and gallant, dealing death with their sharp blades to their selfish and proud enemies.

(45-48) On the day of [the Battle of] Fontenoy, they performed like lions; that added the blue [distinction] to their coats and they have the right to it ever since.

(49-52) They were fiery in Egypt; they were vigorous, powerful, and destructive; Bonaparte understood the strength that is in the people of the folded plaids.

(53-56) They were illustrious at Waterloo: they proved their warriorhood there; their behaviour is inscribed in silver on their head-gear.

(57-60) The Gaels did not come short: it is their virtue to be durable and effective; to be attentive, robust, proud; to be bold going into the fray.

(61-64) They were expert at sea; they are no worse at travelling rough territory; they longed to be hunting the roe deer on the ridges.

(65-68) Although they have travelled many lands, it was never said that they brought disgrace on themselves; they kept company with all of the best virtues; their behaviour was always noble.

(69-72) O descendants of the most renowned warriors, do not let down through your neglect those people who are depending on you today: demonstrate your inheritance!

(73-76) Yonder folk who were telling you that you yourselves and all of Gaeldom is worthless: may you now remember them and raise up the thistle!

(77-80) If your deed is successful and you win the final round over them, I will compose another song for you and I will not keep it from the public.

(81-84) Be loyal in brotherhood, with every heart unyielding and steadfast; hurrah for the Gaels – send around the toast!

2: Gaelic in the Nova Scotia Assembly

The following address was delivered by Iain Moireasdan (John A. Morrison of Victoria County) in 1879 to the Nova Scotia Assembly to support the motion that Gaelic should be taught in the province's public schools.

> In 1879, Mr. MacGillivray of Antigonish addressed the issue of language and education in the House of Assembly. Responding to the concerns of members representing French-speaking districts, he outlined his hope that better provision for French-

speaking teachers in French districts would be made in the near future. Referring to his own experience as a Gaelic speaker, he highlighted the importance of learning in the mother tongue and stressed how necessary it was for teachers to be competent in the vernacular of the community. Mr. LeBlanc of Richmond County, enthusiastically supported his assessment of the situation, while another member of the House, Dr. Campbell, agreed that the matter should receive serious attention. However, when a third member, Mr. McCurdy, urged that any such bonus for French teachers in French districts also be made available for Gaelic teachers in the far more extensive Gaelic districts of the province, consensus quickly evaporated.

Mr. LeBlanc dismissed the suggestion, claiming that there were no Gaelic teachers and that there were not likely to be any in the future. LeBlanc's assertion led another member, John A. Morrison of Victoria County, to rise and give an angry speech in Gaelic praising the value inherent in the Gaelic language and outlining its importance. Morrison's Gaelic speech prompted a reply in French from Mr. LeBlanc, who backpedaled somewhat from his earlier position by stating he was not arguing against Gaelic provision.[15]

This political oration repeats the claim that Gaelic is the oldest of human languages, having been spoken in the Garden of Eden. This allusion demonstrates that its recurrence in Gaelic literature gave it wide currency and credence in the Gaelic community, even if it could not be validated by linguistics and carried little weight outside Gaelic circles. Moireasdan's derogatory comments about French, and less than flattering insinuations about English, underline the ethnic tensions of the province among the subaltern populations and the difficulties of securing the rights of minoritized groups in that period. It is also somewhat ironic that he recommends Gaelic as a means of gaining a better mastery of English.

Original Text

Fhir labhairt agus a dhaoine-uaisle urramach: air dhomh a bhith toirt fainear gu bheil oidheirpean móra air an cur air chois agus mór-aontainn air a thabhairt dhaibh le pairt de cheannardan urramach an-seo, agus an àiteachan eile, a chum a' chainnt Fhrangach a chur air chois anns an earrann seo de'n Uachdaranachd le tuilleadh pàighidh a bhith air a thabhairt do mhaighstearan-sgoile, a theagaisgeas do'n chlann Fhrangaich a' chànain Fhrangach, is fheudar dhomhsa labhairt.

Ach tha mise de'n bharail gum bheil a' Ghàidhlig urramach cho prìseil agus cho feumail a bhith air a teagasg ri cainnt sam bith eile. Gu fìrinneach, 's i a' Ghàidhlig a' chainnt as sine agus a' chainnt as fhearr a tha an-diugh air uachdar an t-saoghail. Tha dùil aig luchd labhairt na Beurla gum bheil a' chainnt sin nas dlighiche air urram na a' Ghàidhlig ach tha iadsan gòrach, agus tha mise cinnteach nach faighear an-diugh aon duine a bhruidhinneas a' Bheurla gu ceart ach an duine aig am bheil a' Ghàidhlig.

'S i a' Ghàidhlig a' cheud chainnt bha air an talamh agus nuair nach bi a' chainnt sin ann, cha bhi feum air cainnt sam bith eile. Mar sin, ma bhitheas ullachadh air a dhèanamh air son cainnt nam Frangach a theagasg, gu cinnteach feumar ullachadh a dhèanamh air son na Gàidhlig.

Tha na sgoilearan móra anns an t-seann dùthaich ag innseadh dhuinn gur i a' Ghàidhlig rìgh gach cainnte, gum bheil i beartach, deiseal, ealanta, binn-fhoclach, briatharach, agus glé mhath air son adhraidh agus gach nì math eile. 'S i a' Ghàidhlig a' chainnt a bha aig Àdhamh anns a' Ghàradh; 'S i a' chainnt a bha aig na bàird agus aig na seanchaidhean, agus feumar a cumail suas. Chan eil anns an Fhraingis ach plubartaich bhochd an taca rithe, agus chan eil pàirt de'n Bheurla móran nas fhearr.

Mar sin, tha mise ag ràdh "Suas leis a' Ghàidhlig," anns an sgoil agus ás an sgoil, agus ma bhitheas tastan air fhaotainn air son cainnt phràbach leibideach nam Frangach a chumail suas, bitheadh deich tastain air son na Gàidhlig mór-urramaiche, cainnt ar sinnsear. An cluinn sibh sin?[16]

Translation

Dear speaker and honourable members: after observing that serious efforts have been established and strong consensus given to them by some of the honourable representatives here, and in other places, in order to maintain the French language in this region of the Dominion by offering supplemental remuneration to school masters who will teach the French language to French children, I am impelled to speak.

I am of the opinion that it is as valuable and useful to teach the honourable Gaelic as any other language. In truth, Gaelic is the oldest language and best language on the planet today. English-speakers believe that that language is more deserving of honour than Gaelic but they are foolish and I am sure that not one person can be found today who speaks English properly who is not a Gaelic speaker.

Gaelic was the first language on the earth and when that language no longer exists, there will be no need for any other language at all. Therefore, if preparation is to be made to teach the language of the French, preparation must certainly be made for Gaelic.

The great scholars in the old country tell us that Gaelic is the king of all languages, that it is well stocked, mature, aesthetically pleasing, musical, full of idiomatic richness and excellent for worship and every other goodly purpose. Gaelic was the language spoken by Adam in the Garden. It is the language that was spoken by the poets and the tradition-bearers, and it must be kept alive. French is nothing but lamentable babble in comparison to it and a lot of English is not much better.

Therefore, I say, "[Let us] raise up the Gaelic," in school and out of school, and if a shilling is found to keep alive the slovenly and trifling language of the French, let there be ten shillings for the highly honourable Gaelic, the language of our ancestors. Do you hear that?

3: The Election of John Thompson

Alasdair "the Ridge" MacDhòmhnaill composed the following song-poem in 1885 during an election between John Sparrow David Thompson (Liberal-Conservative) and Dr. Alexander McIntosh (Independent Conservative). Thompson was from Halifax and did well in politics despite being a Catholic. The federal government needed a minister from Nova Scotia at that time who could be appointed to Sir John A. Macdonald's cabinet. Thompson had rejected the invitation to federal politics several times but a settlement was eventually reached that would allow him to assume the position of minister in the Department of Justice: the current Member of Parliament for the Antigonish electoral district, Angus MacIsaac, would be granted his wish to be a county court judge and Thompson would run for his vacant seat in the strongly Catholic constituency.[17]

Thompson actually had to win the vote, however, and this song-poem memorializes his victory over McIntosh that allowed him to join the federal cabinet. It is based on the melody and chorus from a Jacobite song by Alasdair mac Mhaighstir Alasdair rejoicing in the landing of Prince Charles Edward Stewart in 1745 in Clanranald territory (it even recycles the first couplet of the original).[18] That Thompson faced opposition from some people in the district is clear from the text: some antipathy seems to have come from non-Catholics voicing anti-Catholic sentiments (line 13), but the poet also implies that some Catholics are betraying one of their own (line 10).[19] McIntosh's supporters, like other influence peddlers of the age, attempted to sway voters with alcohol (line 12). MacDhòmhnaill claims that Thompson's sudden and rapid ascendancy signalled a successor to Sir John A. Macdonald's legacy (lines 25-26).

Original Text

1 Thug hó o là ill ho ó
   Thug ó ho ró nàill leibh
   Thug hó o là ill ho ó
   Seinn ó hó nàill leibh.

5 Moch 's a' mhadainn is mi dùsgadh
   Is mór mo shunnd is mo cheòl-gàire

   Bhon chaidh Thompson a chrùnadh
   Dh'aindeoin fùdar a nàmhaid

   Tha e 'n uachdar na cùise
10 'Dh'aindeoin "Iùdhaich" an àite

   'Cheart aindeoin an Dotair,
   Ged tha 'n grog 'na stuth làidir

   'Cheart aindeoin nam bigots
   Is gum bu mhios' iad na ['n] Sàtan

15   'Cheart aindeoin Chlann Ìosaig,
     Théid thu dìreach da'n chàibineat

     Is tha 'Phàrlamaid measail
     Is cha bhrist iad an-dràst' i

     Nuair bha dùil ac' a mùthadh
20   'S ann a dhlùth i gu làidir

     'S e Sior John a' chlach-mhullaich
     Is chan eil duin' ann bheir barr air

     Is chan fhaic sibh MacÌosaig
     Gu dìlinn 'na àite

25   Ach nuair dh'eugas Sior Iain
     Théid Sior Iain 'na làraich.[20]

Translation

(5-6) It is early in the morning as I awake and enjoy great delight and musical laughter.

(7-8) Since Thompson has been crowned despite the [gun] powder of his enemy.

(9-10) He is on top of the matter despite the "Jews" of the place.

(11-12) In direct opposition to the Doctor even though grog is strong stuff.

(13-14) In direct opposition to the bigots, and they are worse than Satan.

(15-16) In direct opposition to the MacIsaacs, you will go straight into the cabinet.

(17-18) And Parliament will have their confidence and they will not dismiss it yet.

(19-20) Although they expected to change it, it cohered strongly instead.

(21-22) Sir John [A. Macdonald] is the copestone and there is no one who can surpass him.

(23-24) And you will never see MacIsaac in his place.

(25-26) But when Sir John [A. Macdonald] dies, Sir John [Sparrow David Thompson] will take his place.

4: The Death of the Repeal of Canadian Federation

Many people in Nova Scotia felt that the province's fortunes had declined significantly after Confederation in 1867. This popular dissatisfaction led to the victory of the Liberal party in the provincial election of June 15, 1886 under William Stevens Fielding, who promised to repeal the province's membership in the Dominion of Canada. The *Morning Chronicle* newspaper of Halifax was a supporter of repeal although others, such as the *Eastern Chronicle* of Pictou (line 40), were against the measure. A number of Nova Scotia businessmen were strong supporters of the repeal, such as Iain MacGilleMhaoil (line 47), a successful merchant who operated in Antigonish.[21]

"Cribben" was the family nickname of a branch of the Clann MhicGilleBhràth (MacGillivrays) to which Aonghus MacGilleBhràth of Allt a' Bhàillidh (Bailey's Brook) belonged. He and Cailean F. MacÌosaig had won the two seats representing Antigonish County in the 1886 provincial election as Liberal candidates. The Liberals won twenty-nine seats in Nova Scotia during that election—five more than in 1882—but party members were not entirely united in their support for repeal.

Fielding proposed creating a new federation, the Maritime Union, consisting of Nova Scotia, New Brunswick and Prince Edward Island. The Liberals needed strong support in the federal election on April 22, 1887 in order to bring these plans to fruition. The other provinces showed little enthusiasm for Fielding's proposal, however, and the public proclamation made by William Gladstone, Prime Minister of the United Kingdom, a week before the election implying that the Empire would resist any breakup further eroded support. The Nova Scotia Liberals themselves grew increasingly tepid about the idea as the federal election approached and only won seven of the province's twenty-one seats. The repeal of Confederation died as a political cause in the province thereafter.[22]

Alasdair "the Ridge" MacDhòmhnaill composed the following song-poem in the aftermath of the Liberal defeat. This composition is a rare example of the use of allegory as a structural device in Gaelic literature. The bill for repeal is humorously personified as a baby who was killed after experiencing precocious growth while under the fosterage of his Liberal caretakers.

Original Text

1   Leanabh mór na h-ùpraid
     Rugadh 's a' mhìos June e,
     Is nam faigheadh e greis ùine
     Bha sùrd air gu fàs;
5   Is bha moganaich gun sùilean
     An dùil gun cuirte crùn air,
     Is gun riaghladh e gu lùthmhor
     An dùthaich gu bràth.

     Bha Cribben air bheag céille
10   'Na sheasamh air gach déile:
     Na h-òraidean 'gan leughadh
     Le beucadaich àrd;
     Na dotairean cho gleusta
     Gun bhaist' iad e gun chléireach;
15   Is gur h-e "repeal" a dh'eubh iad
     Air bàby an àigh.

     'S e 'chuis[l'] a bha 'gan lìonadh,
     Nuair bha e 'na sheachd mìosan,
     Gur h-ann a bha 'chuid fhiaclan
20   Ro chiatach a' fàs;
     Is gum faiceadh iad an fheusag
     A' tighinn a-mach gu lìonmhor;
     B' e siud an leanabh brèagha
     Bha miadhail 's an àm.

25   Ach gur mór an tàmailt
     A thàinig air a chàirdean,
     Na fir a bha 'ga àrach
     Is iad làidir 'na chùis;
     An àite a chur an àirde
30   Is a sparradh thar an nàbaidh,
     Gur h-ann a chaidh a bhàthadh
     Is a chàradh 's an ùir.

     Air oidhche dhorcha Dhòmhnaich
     Is mi ag imeachd ann am ònar,
35   Gun thachair orm an torradh
     Is bu deònach siud lium;
     Leanabh mór na comh-strì
     'Ga tharraing aig a' chòmhlan
     Is e 'n déidh a phasgadh dòigheil
40   'S a' *Chronicle Ùr.*

Nuair choimhead mi 'nan aodann
Gun d' aithnich mi na daoine:
Is gur h-ann a bha gach aon diubh
Gun aoibh air a ghnùis;
45 Na fir a bha cho saothrach
A' cogadh anns a' chaonnaig;
Gun robh MacGilleMhaoil ann
Is e caoineadh gu dlùth.

Bha Cribben ann is e leòinte,
50 Is e 'n déidh a chur air fògradh;
Bha an Dotair Mac an Tòisich
Is na deòir air a shùil;
Bha Cailean ann is e brònach
A' caoidh an leanaibh òig ud
55 A choisinn dha na vòtaichean
Mór' ann an June.

B' iad siud na daoine truagha
Bha buileach air an cuaradh:
A h-uile fear, is gruaim air,
60 Gun luaidheachd air sunnd
Mu'n leanabh mhór a fhuair iad
Is a bh' aca chum na tuasaid;
Bhon chàireadh anns an uaigh e
Cha bhuannaich iad cùis.

65 'S ann a nì na Tòries
An cur air cùl na còmhla,
Is an cumail mar as deònach
Ri'm beò ann an cùil;
Is bidh Iain Donn MacDhòmhnaill
70 'Na shuidhe mar as còir dha
Aig toiseach a chuid chonnspann
Gu seòlta anns a' chùirt.

'S e Cribben nach robh dìleas,
Ged gheall e cho ro chinnteach
75 Gum faigheadh e repeal dhuinn,
'S ann dhìobair e 'ghrunnd:
Nuair thàinig e gu mì-mhodhail
Is nach d' fhuair na bha 'dhìth air,
Gun thill e ri 'chuid dìobhairt
80 Cho dìblidh ri cù.

'S e Cribben bha gun nàir' aige
Tighinn a-mach an tràth ud
'Chur trioblaid air an àrmann
Tha 'n dràst' air ur ceann;
85 Ach thill sinn e le tàmailt
A chum an nid a dh'fhàg e,
Is bidh inisg air a chàirdean
Gu bràth e 'dhol ann.

'S e Cribben a bha truagh dhe
90 Nuair 'tharraing iad air chluais e;
Is ged 'phriob iad e gu tuasaid
Cha d' fhuair e ach tàir;
Is bhon nach d' éirich buaidh leis
B' fhearr dha nach do ghluais e
95 Is gun d' fhuirich e 's a' chuachain
Bha shuas air an sparr.[23]

Translation

(1-8) The big baby of commotion was born in the month of June and if he could get a bit more time, he was excited about getting bigger; ragged and visionless people expected that he would be crowned and that he would govern their country vigorously forever.

(9-16) Cribben had little sense, standing on every platform: speeches were read with loud bellowing; the doctors were so clever that they will baptize him without a clergyman; and "repeal" is what they called the providential baby.

(17-24) His blood vessels were filling up when he was seven months old, his teeth were maturing beautifully; and they could see a full beard materializing; that was the lovely baby who was in great demand at that time.

(25-32) But great was the humiliation that fell on his friends, those men who were nurturing him and were greatly committed to the matter; rather than raising him on high and driving him to surpass his peer, he was drowned and put into the grave.

(33-40) On a dark Sunday night as I was travelling on my own, I came across the burial [party] and I was well disposed to it; the great baby of the struggle being pulled by the company after being well swaddled in the new *Chronicle*.

(41-48) When I looked into their faces I recognized the people: indeed not a single one of them had any joy on his face; the men who had been so industrious, fighting in the battle; MacMillan was there, very distraught.

(49-56) Cribben was there, and was wounded and had been sent into exile; Doctor McIntosh had tears streaming from his eyes; Colin was there and was sad, keening that young infant who had earned him a majority of votes in June.

(57-64) Those were wretched people who were suffering terribly: every man was gloomy and made no mention of merriment regarding the great baby that they had found and possessed for the purposes of the dispute; they cannot triumph in the matter since he was arranged in the grave.

(65-72) Indeed, the Tories will put them [the Liberals] behind the door and keep them as they please in a corner for as long as they live; and "Brown" John Macdonald will sit skillfully in the front of his troops, as he has the right to do, in the court.

(73-80) It was Cribben who was not loyal even though he pledged so confidently that he would pass a repeal for us; indeed, he did not stand his ground: when he came rudely and he did not get what he wanted, he returned to his own vomit as dastardly as a dog.

(81-88) It was Cribben who was shameless coming out at that time to make trouble for the champion who is still now leading us; but we returned him with reproach back to the nest that he had left, and his friends will be embarrassed if he ever goes there.

(89-96) It was Cribben who suffered for it when they drew him by the ear; although they provoked him to brawl he got nothing but reproach; and since he did not triumph, it would have been better for him if he had never budged but had stayed in the nest that is up on the roof's cross-beam.

5: A Letter from the Gaelic Society of Bruce County

The executive committee of Comunn Gàidhealach Siorramachd Bhruis (the Gaelic Society of Bruce County, Ontario) penned the following letter on January 27, 1890 to Tòmas R. MacAonghuis in support of the Gaelic bill he presented to the Senate later that year (discussed in text 10.6 below). MacAonghuis seems to have sought endorsement of his proposal from numerous Gaelic communities, for he states that this "is a fair specimen of the letters and addresses that I have received from various parts of the Dominion, from Cape Breton to Vancouver."

While the letter corroborates the idea that Gaelic speakers are to be found in abundance in Canada, it also reveals the apprehension and tentativeness that they felt in making public declarations that would challenge the status quo privilege of the English language. The organization's message instead emphasizes that Gaels have been obsequiously loyal to the Crown and do not act in protest against the exclusionary hegemony enjoyed by English in official institutions, in contrast, we can infer, to the French.

Original Text

A Charaid Chaoimh : –

Is mór a' chomain a tha sibh a' cur air ur luchd-dùthcha bho cheann gu ceann na tìre seo, oir gu cinnteach, tha mór aoibhneas air Clann nan Gàidheal an-diugh nuair tha fios aca gum bheil, mar a thuirt an seanfhacal e, "Caraid anns a' chùirt a thagras an cùis is an còir." Ged nach eil sinne, mar Chomann, ag iarraidh no a' creidsinn gum bu chòir ach aon chànain a bhith air a cumail suas air costas na dùthcha, gidheadh, ma tha barrachd agus aon ri bhith air a cumail suas, cha b' i a' Ghàidhlig bu chòir a bhith air dheireadh.

Cha ruig sinne leas a chur 'nur cuimhne gum bheil mìltean de Chlann nan Gàidheal 's an dùthaich seo a tha dìleas do'n tìr is do'n Chrùn, agus ged nach robh an cànain air a cleachdadh an cùirt no am Pàrlamaid, cha chualas i riamh an dragh no an iorghaill.

Agus anns a' chearn sin de'n dùthaich ris an abrar an Àird an Iar Thuath, tha móran anns na bliadhnaichean seo ['gan] suidheachadh, is iad sin ás a' Ghàidhealtachd, agus gu sònraichte ás na h-Eileanan an Iar, nach tuig a bheag de chànain sam bith eile ach a' Ghàidhlig a dh'fhoghlaim iad bho am màthair ann an Tìr nam Beann.

Agus ma dh'fheumas tuilleadh agus aon chainnt a bhith againn an cùirt no am Pàrlamaid, gu dé a' chainnt as mutha còir air an urram sin 'fhaotainn na cainnt nan treun-laoch a sheas guala ri guala[inn] air Sliabh Abraham, am pìobairean a' seinn binncheòl na h-Alba, is an claidheamh mór a' dearrsadh an grian na h-òg-mhaidne, an latha a chaidh an dùthaich 'chosnadh do Chrùn Bhreatann.

Tha dòchas againn gun seas sibh gu dìleas duineil air cùl na teanga blasta binne 's an d' fhuair sinn ar n-altram is gum faic luchd-àiteachaidh na tìre gu léir, ged a dh'fhàg sinn Tìr nam Beann ri linn ar n-òige, nach eil sinn a' dìochuimhneachadh ar cànain no an dùthaich 's an deach ar n-àrach.

— Seumas MacIain, Riaghladair; Ealair MacAlasdair, Ionmhasair; Earais MacDhòmhnaill, Sgrìobhadair.[24]

Translation

Dear Friend : –

Your compatriots from ocean to ocean in this land are greatly indebted to you, for surely the Gaelic people are greatly delighted today when they know that they have, as the proverb says, "A friend in the court who will plead their rights and claims." Although we do not, as a Society, want or believe that anything other than one language should be maintained at the expense of the country, nevertheless, if more than one is to be maintained, Gaelic is not the language that should be left in last place.

We do not need to remind you that there are thousands of Gaelic descendants in this country who are loyal to the country and to the Crown, and even though their language has not been fostered in courts or in the Parliament, it was never heard to cause agitation or discord.

In that part of the country which is called the North-West, many people are settling in recent years who are from the Highlands, and especially from the Western Isles, and who do not understand much of any other language except the Gaelic that they learned from their mothers in the Highlands.

And if we must have more than one language in the courts or in Parliament, what language has a greater right to have that privilege than the language of the champions who stood shoulder to shoulder on the Plains of Abraham, their bagpipers playing the melodious music of Scotland, and their claymores shining in the morning sun, the day that the country was won for the British Crown.

We hope that you will stand loyally and bravely behind the dulcet, melodious language in which we received our upbringing and that the inhabitants of this entire land will see that although we left the Highlands in our youth, we are not forgetting our language or the country in which we were raised.

James Johnston, President; E. Alexander, Treasurer; E. McDonell, Secretary.

6: A Speech about Gaelic in the Canadian Senate

Tòmas R. MacAonghuis (Thomas Robert McInnes, 1840-1904) was born in Lake Ainslie, Cape Breton, to Gaelic-speaking parents who had emigrated from Inverness, Scotland. He served as senator for Ashcroft, British Columbia, from 1881 to 1897 and then as Lieutenant Governor of British Columbia from 1897 to 1900. He delivered a speech to the Senate of the Canadian Parliament on March 18, 1890 proposing to make Scottish Gaelic an official language of Canada, citing the figures from the 1881 census in support of his proposal. The number of people indicated as Scottish and Irish came to a total of 1,657,266, much larger than the number of those indicated as French (1,298,929) or English (881,301). Although he did not claim that all of those marked ethnically as Scots or Irish spoke a form of Gaelic, he asserted that a sizable number did and that that justified some measure of official recognition. His motion met with resistance and derision from several fellow members of the Senate.

> MacInnes's bill was treated as a time-wasting prank. The comments of several Senators were explicit: "I am sure we would not like to indulge in Gaelic as an official language. I do not know how to treat this matter—as a joke, or how. I cannot say anything

seriously about it, for it is evidently a joke." (Hon. Mr. Kaulbach) "...this Bill appears to me like a sort of far-fetched joke..." (Hon. Mr. Abbott).

Senator Kaulbach of Nova Scotia, who claimed to be a Gaelic learner himself, took particular exception to the bill. Resorting to familiar prejudices and stereotypes, he claimed that Gaelic was well suited to poetry and fairy tales but otherwise useless: ... "I am afraid that in any department of business in this country his language would be entirely useless—even in the part of the country [Scotland] from where these people come Gaelic is not used as an official language, and is it reasonable that privileges should be asked for Highland Scotchmen in this House that are not asked for in their own country?" ...

Senator Kaulbach argued, for instance, that the people of Lunenburg County, Nova Scotia, did not really begin to get on in the world until they eliminated German in their schools some two decades earlier. ... His fierce opposition to the Gaelic bill came from his belief that it would slow this English cultural manifest destiny and, thus, progress itself.[25]

Some of MacAonghuis's dialogue with members of the Senate in English appeals to a surprising degree to notions of the equality of peoples:[26] he acknowledges that Canada has many immigrant ethnic communities and declares that Gaelic is no less deserving than the languages of other groups. He states that he recognizes the validity of French claims and merely wishes to give Gaelic a similar status in the Dominion:

> I am not one of those who object to the perpetuation of the French language in this Parliament, providing Gaelic is put on the same footing. Every right and privilege accorded to the French Canadian people when they came under the British Crown should be most scrupulously guarded, and the minority should be treated in the most liberal spirit. ... I have no desire to decry the French; such an idea is foreign to me; I gladly acknowledge the invaluable services rendered by them as the explorers and pioneers of Canada. ... if there is one act of oppression more than another which would come home to a man's breast it is to

deprive him of the consolation of hearing, using and reading the language that his mother taught him.

His Gaelic text is not quite so generous, however, as he invokes British triumphalism over the previous French dominance in Canada and celebrates the participation of Irish and Scottish Gaels in British imperial efforts. Despite pressing for official recognition of Gaelic in Canada, portions of MacAonghuis's English text concede the dominant political ideology of the age that empires and nation-states have the right to impose a single, uniform language upon their citizens and that the forces of Anglocentric assimilation were inexorable:

> Notwithstanding that the [Gaelic] language was taught in the royal household to the royal family—that Gaelic chairs are endowed in the universities of Edinburgh, Oxford and Berlin (blessings brighten as they take their flight), I am fully conscious of the fact that it is passing away. I regret exceedingly that the most forcible and expressive of all languages is falling into disuse and being replaced by the great commercial language of the world. You need not fear that in recognizing Gaelic you are prolonging its life. You will not do that, for the trend of events points inevitably to one language and one nation; but you will be showing what is deserved—and what will be appreciated as much as it is deserved—gratitude to the Highlanders for the great part they have taken in the upbuilding of our nation. Neither the French nor the Gaelic languages will ever gain ascendency in the Dominion—of that we may be sure. They are passing away. They must eventually disappear: but till they do, let us recognize them. We owe it as a tribute of respect to those whose mother tongues they are. Let us not forget that it was the French that made Canada worth taking, and that it was the Highlanders who took it, and together they were the pioneers of the civilization that follow in their wake.

His Gaelic text more urgently exhorts fellow Gaelic-speaking senators to seize the opportunity to elevate the status of their native tongue. MacAonghuis thus nuances his rhetoric according to the audience he is addressing in each language. Nonetheless, his argument in English opens a vulnerability that Senator Kaulbach recognizes and attacks: if Canada is an extension of British territory and Gaels are to be treated accordingly, then their language is not entitled to any recognition or status. This demonstrates once again how the Gaelic community's deference and subservience to the British Empire ultimately undermined its cultural self-determination and its ability to maintain its ethnolinguistic distinctiveness.

Original Text

A cheannaird nan Seanairean agus a dhaoine-uaisle an t-Seanadh: Tha mi toilichte agus taingeil gum bheil anns an taigh urramach uasal seo móran de dhaoine caoimhneil còir a thuigeas agus a labhras an cànan eireachdail a tha mi a' bruidhinn.

Anns an dùthaich ùr fharsainn thoraich anns na chuir am Freastal caomh sinn a chòmhnaidh, dùthaich anns am bheil sluagh ás gach earrann is rìoghachd de'n t-saoghal a' cruinneachadh, is còir do'n luchd-riaghlaidh gum bi iad glic cùramach ceart agus onarach.

Feumaidh na Gàidheil an iarraidh mhath a thoirt doibh fhéin agus do riaghladh na dùthcha. Tha mi am barail gur ann orrasan a thig an t-uallach mór seo a ghiùlain gu bràth.

'S iad na h-Albannaich agus na h-Éireannaich cnàimh-droma na dùthcha againn, is iad a neart bho chuan gu cuan. Car-son, matà, nach faod sinne an cànan a dh'ionnsaich ar màthair duinn a chleachdadh cho math is a tha cinnich eile a' cleachdadh an cainnt dhùthchasaich fhéin? Car-son nach eil e cho ceart gum biodh Gàidhlig ri bruidhinn agus air a sgrìobhadh anns an taigh agus anns an t-seòmair seo, ri Fraingis?

Cha bhuin an dùthaich seo do'n Fhraing, 's e tha an-seo tìr Bhreatannach. Tha còir aig Gàidheil is aig Gàidhlig anns an dùthaich nach eil idir aig Frangaich no aig Fraingis. Is daor a cheannaich na Gàidheil an còir le fuil dheirg an cridhe. Is ann le làimh dheis a' chlaidheimh a fhuair iad cead suidhe ann am Pàrlamaid shaor a' bhaile mhóir seo. Is iomadh gaisgeach calma dhiubh a chaill a bheatha air Sliabh Abrahaim.

Car-son nach biodh sinne cho dàimheil do'n dùthaich ás an tàinig sinn fhéin agus ar sinnsir, agus do'n chànan ris na

Frangaich? Car-son nach toir sinne fhéin uibhir cheartais agus [a tha sinn a' toirt] dhaibhsan? Ma tha e ceart corr agus aon chànan a labhairt anns an t-seòmar seo, chan i a' Ghàidhlig bu chòir a bhith air dheireadh. 'S i cànan nan Gàidheal bu chòir a bhith air thoiseach 's an dùthaich seo. 'S e seo an t-àm seasamh dìleas "guaillibh ri guaillibh."

Bitheadh cànan Albann agus Éireann air a meas anns an dùthaich Bhreatannaich seo, cho math ri teanga na Frainge, nach cànan [a th'] ann ach brochan de gach seòrsa cainnt.

Faicibh a-nise am bheil na Frangaich toileach dèanamh ribhse mar tha sibhse dèanamh riuthasan. Bithibh duineil agus dìleas mu'm bi e ro an-moch. Chan eil sùil no cluas mac Gàidheil eadar Ceap Breatainn agus Bhancùbhar nach eil a' coimhead oirbh agus ag éisteachd ribh. Tha na Gàidheil agus na h-Éireannaich pailt: thoiribh ceartas daibh.

Mur am bheil rùm aig a' Ghàidhlig an Canada, car-son a bhios sinn ri cosgaisean a chumail suas Fraingis nach d' fhuair sinne—air nach eil eòlas againn is air nach eil sinn ag iarraidh eòlas. Ma bhios sinn dìleas dhuinn fhéin, bheir ur sliochd, bheir an dùthaich onair agus urram duinn: bitheadh meas aig an t-sluagh oirnn. Feumaidh sinn earalas fhaighinn agus a thabhairt. Cha tug nàmhaid buaidh riamh air na Gàidheil, cha robh Alba riamh fo chìs, agus car-son a-nise bhiodh ar cànan ann an éis urraim anns a' Phàrlamaid seo?[27]

Translation

Leader of the Senate and gentlemen of the Senate: I am pleased and grateful that there are many genteel and goodly people in this honourable and noble house who understand and who speak the wonderful language that I am speaking.

In this new, expansive and fertile country in which kind Providence has put us to reside, a country in which people from every corner and kingdom are gathering, it is proper for our politicians to be wise, careful, correct and honourable.

The Gaels must make a strong petition for themselves and for the governance of the country. I am of the opinion that this great responsibility will fall upon them to carry forever.

The Scots and the Irish are the backbone of our country, and they are her strength from ocean to ocean. Why then can we not use the language that our mother taught us just as other ethnic groups use their own native languages? Why is it not as proper for Gaelic to be spoken and written in this house, and in this room, as French?

This country does not belong to France; what this is is British territory. The Gaels and the Gaelic language have a right in this country that the French people and language do not have at all. The Gaels dearly paid for that right with the red blood of their hearts. It is with the right hand of the sword that they obtained the entitlement to sit in the noble Parliament of this great city. Many of their brave soldiers lost their lives on the Plains of Abraham.

Why would we not be as attached to the country from which we ourselves and our ancestors came, and to their language, as the French? Why can we not give ourselves the same justice as we give to them? If it is correct to speak more than one language in this room, Gaelic should not be left in last place. The language of the Gael ought to be out in front in this country. This is the time, therefore, to stand loyally "shoulder to shoulder."

Let the language of Scotland and of Ireland be respected in this British territory, at least as well as the language of France, that is not a real language but a mongrel of many different languages.

Now see if the French are willing to treat you as you treat them. Be brave and loyal before it is too late. There is not a Gael between Cape Breton and Vancouver whose eyes and ears are not watching you and listening to you. The Gaels and the Irish are plentiful: give them justice.

If there is no space for Gaelic in Canada, why are we sparing expenses to keep French alive that we did not receive? [French is a language] of which we do not have any knowledge and which we do not seek to know. If we are loyal to ourselves, our descendants and this country will give us honor and esteem: let the population respect us. We must exercise caution and foresight. No enemy ever triumphed over the Gaels, Scotland was never conquered, so why should our language be deprived of respect in this Parliament?

7: A Song about the Glengarry Election

An anonymous poet composed the following song to Uilleam Donnchadh MacLeòid (William Duncan McLeod, 1852-1908) after a gathering in Alexandria, Ontario, on May 29, 1902, the day that he won the election to represent Glengarry County in the Legislative Assembly of Ontario. MacLeòid was a Tory running against David M. McPherson, a Liberal, but both men were successful entrepreneurs in the cheese business (the latter was given the nickname "the Cheese King").[28]

The chorus of the song celebrates MacLeòid's political ascendancy as well as his membership in the Gaelic community (line 2). The song is structured like a summons to a clan gathering or military engagement, calling people together with the sound of bagpipes and drums (lines 5-6). The social exchanges of the evening are described in aural terms: conversations, speeches, and songs (lines 9 and 14-15). Unlike many other political occasions, however, a Temperance-inspired environment seems to have prevailed and held the flow of alcohol in check (whisky was called by the nick name "Mac an Tòisich" in Gaelic, line 16).

The poet proceeds with the "roll-call of allies," acknowledging all of those who played a part in the victory. Many Scottish Gaels named are categorized by the specific geographical region in the Highlands from which their ancestors had departed (lines 17-24), suggesting strong lines of continuity in the reconstituted communities in Glengarry. After naming supporters of Highland descent, he includes French, England and Irish supporters (lines 25-28). His remark that the religion of the Irish had not caused them to betray MacLeòid (line 27) exposes tensions in British-Irish relations in Canada. The poet returns to a belief in the pan-Gaelic unity behind MacLeòid (line 34), expressing pride in the candidate's membership in the community (lines 37-38) and trust in his ability to work on behalf of their interests (lines 39-40). Altogether this is an effective articulation of the concepts of representative democracy through a Gaelic lens.

Original Text

1   Hó! Gur toil leinn, Hé! Gur toil leinn
    Hó! Gur toil leinn fonn nan Gàidheal
    Is toil leinn fhéin, an sàr dhuine uasal
    A th' ag éirigh suas le àrdan.

5   Fuaim an druma, is ceòl na fideig,
    Rinn mo ghreasad thun an àite,
    Far an d' fhuair mi daoine seasmhach –
    Ghlaodh iad gun robh Ros a' fàillinn.

    Fhuair mi naidheachd air an roghainn,
10 Thug e misneach dhomh is càileachd:
    Choisinn MacLeòid dhuinn an latha
    Is dh'fhàg e Mac a' Phearsain cràiteach.

    'S ann an-sin a bha an oidhche chridheil,
    Ag òraideachd is a' gabhail òran;
15 Làn de chaoimhneas blàth is bruidhinn,
    Ged bha glas air Mac an Tòisich.

    Bha na Cnòideartaich is Eigich,
    Garanaich is Ealganaich làidir;
    Clann a' Phì bho thaobh Loch Airceig
20 Is Ceanadaich nach uilleagaich àicheadh.

    Camshronaich bho thìr nan Abrach;
    Clann an Linnein bho Chinn Tàile;
    Clann MhicGilleMhaoil, na gaisgich
    Nach eil tais, a dh'aindeoin tàire.

25 Chaidh leis Frangaich agus Sasannaich,
    Éireannaich bho Eilean Phàdraig;
    Foilleill cha robh an aidmheil:
    Chuidich iad a chur an àirde.

    Dh'fheuch iad boodle gus ar mealladh,
30 Dh'fheuch iad gach innleachd aig Sàtan;
    Dhùin iad suas sinn cruaidh, gu h-ealamh,
    'S ann a rinn e 'bheàrn a càradh.

    A-nis bhon chaidh MacLeòid a roghainn
    Leis gach fine am measg nan Gàidheal,

35   Caitheadh e 'n cleòc gun smàl air
     Is chan eadh fear eile 'na àite.

     'S an t-Siorramachd aig Gleann Garadh
     A chaidh a thogail is àrach:
     Duine a chum le cliù an càsan
40   Anns gach àit' an deach an càradh.²⁹

Translation

(1-4) *Hó!* We love, *hé!* we love, *hó!* We love the tune of the Gaels, we ourselves love the fine gentleman who is rising with pride.

(5-8) The sound of the drum and the music of the chanter, has quickened me to the place where I found steadfast men—they announced that Ross was losing.

(9-12) I received news about the election that gave me encouragement and strength: McLeod won the day for us and he left MacPherson damaged.

(13-16) That is where we had the cheery evening, giving speeches and singing songs; full of warm kindness and conversation, even though "Macintosh" was locked up.

(17-20) The people of Knoydart, Eigg, Glengarry and Glenelg were strong; MacPhees from Loch Arkaig-side and Kennedys who would not allow themselves to be denied.

(21-24) Camerons from the land of Lochaber; MacLennans from Kintail; MacMillans, the warriors who are not soft, despite ill-will [of enemies].

(25-28) The French people and English people joined him, and Irish people from Patrick's isle; their denomination was not traitorous; they helped to elect him.

(29-32) They [the opposition] tried [to use] boodle to deceive us; they tried every device available to Satan; they caused us to unite together, quickly and firmly, indeed it filled up the ranks.

(33-36) Now, since McLeod has been chosen by every clan among the Gaels, let him wear the untainted cloak and no one else other than him.

(37-40) He was raised and nurtured in Glengarry County: a man with good character who has upheld their interests everywhere they have been negotiated.

8: Scorn for the Bolsheviks

The large number of Canadian soldiers returning home at the end of the Great War expedited the eruption of unresolved social tensions that had been suppressed during the international conflict. Working classes who had been promised a better Canada were impatient for improvements in wages and labour practices, and discharged soldiers were competing for the first time with the women and recent immigrants who had entered the work force during their absence. The Russian Revolution led by the Bolsheviks in 1917 inspired labour leaders in industrialized nations to organize work forces into new forms of political power, adding to the sense of urgency and crisis in Canada.[30]

> Early in 1918, government and police officials began to express concern about the growth of the radical left. The Royal Northwest Mounted Police reported that the Industrial Workers of the World were gaining ground and launched an investigation. The Chief Press Censor noted an increase in the volume of radical literature published ...[31]

The government in Ottawa expressed strong suspicion of organized labour and the exploitation of "foreign" languages to convey information beyond its control. Legislation codified as Order-in-Council PC 2384, passed on September 25, 1918, restricted freedom of association, assembly, and speech.[32] It is particularly in the light of the distrust of alien tongues and influences that we can understand why Gaels, such as the author of the following song-poem, might feel compelled to make a public display of allegiance to the existing political order and to distance themselves from the radicalism of Bolsheviks and communists. After all, not even Britain was beyond Russian influence: John Maclean had been appointed as the first Bolshevik Consul in Scotland in 1917 and was arrested for sedition not long thereafter.[33]

The following song-poem was composed in 1919 by Dòmhnall MacDhòmhnaill, a native of the Isle of Tiree who was then living in Ottawa. His poem claims that his habits of frugality and "Protestant work ethic" were inherited from his grandmother (line 4), which may imply that he hoped to relieve Gaels (or perhaps Scots more widely) of any allegation of communist leanings on the basis of the presumed essential qualities of their character. Notwithstanding the valorization of individualistic capitalism asserted by his text, Highland society, especially during his own lifetime, had a strong communal ethos and greatly esteemed generosity, hospitality, charity, and cooperative economic production.

The last line of the poem is particularly interesting in how it exhibits consciousness of and draws attention to a feature of the Gaelic language with conceptual ramifications. Two different propositions are used to distinguish the possession of an object—which may be an impermanent condition—from belonging: "aig" in opposition to "le," respectively. He insists on the equation of possession and ownership, contrary to Gaelic norms, and declares the right to own what he possesses through capitalist production. He was originally raised on a small, rural island and in his youth he no doubt carried out the manual labour he mentions, but as an adult he made his career first as an artisan and then as a building contractor.[34] His song-poem demonstrates how Gaelic literature and cultural resources could be exploited creatively and selectively to express solidarity with the anglophone status quo and detachment from the ancestral past.

Original Text

1   Le dìcheall math o latha gu latha
    Ag obair tràth is an-moch
    Is a' cur mu seach gach peighinn bhàn:
    An àithne dh'fhàg mo sheanmhair;
5   An uair bhiodh càch a' pasgadh làmh
    Is a' cànran taobh a' ghealbhain,
    Bha mise dèanadach a ghnàth
    Is shàbhail mi suim airgid.

    Nuair bhiodh geòcairean ri pòit
10 An taighean-òst' is air margadh,
    A' cur an cuid an éirig stòp
    Is a' bòilich mu na chaill iad,
    Bha mis' air luing a' cosnadh stòrais,
    Toirt mo lòin thar fairge;
15 Is uidh air n-uidh, le cùram mór,
    Gun d' rinn mi dòrlach saidhbhreis.

    Thig fear feusagach le aoibh
    Is faighnichidh e 'n dràst' mi,
    Ag iarraidh orm mo chuid a roinn
20 Is leth a' chrùin 'thoirt dhasan;
    Innsidh e dhomh mar bu chòir

Mo stòras 'chur a phàigheadh
Gach ainfhiach tha air daoine bochd
A tha gun chosnadh làitheil.

25 'S e 'chreud an-diugh tha aig gu leòr
Bhith 'n tòir air cuid an nàbaidh;
Gach leisgean nach do rinn car riamh
Tha 'g iarraidh a bhith 'm pàirt rium;
Ach abaireadh gach neach a thoil
30 Mu'n lòn tha anns a' ghràisg ud –
Chan abair mise ris na coin
Ach "robairean" is "mèirlich."

Rinn mi treabhadh air cùl seisrich
Is leasaich mi buntàta;
35 Chuir mi seagal, coirc' is eòrna
Is rinn mi móran àitich;
Chuir mi na cearcan air ghur
A chuideachadh a' mhàil dhomh;
Is iarrar orm mo chuid a roinn
40 Ri slaightearan gun nàire?

Cho fad is a dh'fhanas daoine glic
Bidh meas air fear an dìcheill
Is bidh an leisgean daonnan falamh
Bochd, gun rath, gun dìreadh;
45 Faodaidh am Bolshevick stad
D'a chànran is d'a mhì-mhodh:
Choisinn mi mo chuid gu ceart
Is na th' agamsa: is leam fhìn e.[35]

Translation

(1-8) With the best efforts from day to day, working from dawn to dusk, and setting aside every spare penny: that is the commandment that my grandmother left to me; when others were wringing their hands and grumbling at the hearth-side, I was always industrious and I saved a good sum of money.

(9-16) When the spendthrifts were getting drunk in taverns and at markets, spending their money on tankards and bragging about how much they lost, I was on an ocean vessel earning a salary, bringing my sustenance across the sea; and little by little, with great care, I made a tidy profit.

(17-24) A jolly bearded man will come and query me, asking me to share my wealth, and to give half a crown to him; he will tell me how my wealth ought to be spent to pay off all of the debts of poor people who are unemployed.

(25-32) The creed that plenty of people follow today is to pursue the wealth of their neighbour; every lazy person who never did a bit of work is wanting to share with me; people can say what they want about the daily bread of that rabble—I will only call the dogs "robbers" and "thieves."

(33-40) I have done ploughing behind a team of horses and I have grown potatoes; I have sown rye, oats and barley and I have done a great deal of agriculture; I have set the hens to lay eggs in order to supplement my rent; and I am asked to share my wealth with the shameless bums?

(41-48) As long as people stay wise, the diligent man will be respected and the lazy man will always be destitute, poor, unlucky and defeated; the Bolshevik can quit his grumbling and his insolence; I have earned my wealth honestly and that which is in my possession: I own it.

9: A Song about the Nova Scotian Election

The following song-poem was composed by Calum MacGill-Ìosa in support of Ìosag MacDhùghaill (Isaac MacDougall, 1897-1969) when he ran as a Progressive candidate in the 1921 federal election to represent Inverness County, Cape Breton. Although MacDhùghaill was defeated, he ran again in 1925 as a member of the Conservative party and was successful in his bid.

The poet gives the candidate the same kinds of qualifications needed by a prospective Highland leader: proper ancestral qualifications (lines 5 and 15), reliability (lines 6-7), high social standing (lines 8 and 11), bravery in conflict

Figure 10.1 – Calum MacGill-Ìosa (Malcolm Gillis), poet and musician of Margaree, Cape Breton. The frontispiece portrait from MacDhùghaill (1939), Smeòrach nan Cnoc 's nan Gleann.

(line 16), and so on. After mentioning MacDhùghaill's campaign trail, MacGill-Ìosa begins to list communities in Inverness County that he asserts will support his candidate (lines 21-24, 29-32 and 44). He also brings attention to important demographic segments of the population: the French (lines 25-28), miners (line 33), farmers (line 36), and women (lines 37-40). As in earlier clan panegyric, this inventory is more of a rhetorical stance meant to goad support from the people named as doing so than an attempt to provide an accurate poll of voters.

Original Text

1 Ho hi rì 's na hi u ó
   Ho hi rì 's na hi u ó
   Hi ri rì 's na hi u ó
   Gheibh an Dùgh'llach mo bhót.

5 Mac an fhir 's an robh 'n tàlann
   Is nach biodh foilleill 'na nàdar,
   Is mi gun earbadh mo chàs ris:
   Thug e barr aig a' mhòd.

   Tha mo rùn-s' air an fhiùran
10 Is e ro uasal 'na ghiùlan;
   Is iomadh gin tha 'toirt cliù dhut,
   Toirt na h-ionnsaigh cho òg.

   Tha thu coibhneil 'nad nàdar,
   Ann ad chom, chan eil fàillinn;
15 Is tu 'shìol nam fear làidir
   Rachadh dàna 's an tòir.

   Bhon a chaidh thu tro'n dùthaich
   A thoirt foillseachadh ùr dhuinn,
   Is iomadh aon nach robh dùil ris
20 A thionndaidh a chòt!

   Muinntir Sheistico is Mhàbu
   Agus Shiudaic ag ràitinn
   Gur ann dìleas do'n àrmann
   Bhios an àireamh as mò.

25 Tha na Frangaich air tionndadh
   On dh'fhosgail an sùilean;
   Bidh iad leinn is chan eil cùram
   Nach bi 'chùis mar as còir.

Bidh fir Hogama chaomh leis;
30 Bidh an Léig air gach taobh leis;
Bidh Marg'rì leis is chan fhaoin siud,
Àite gaolach nam bò.

Bidh gach mèinneadair guail leis;
Bidh gach aon tha mun cuairt leis;
35 Bidh iad, deas agus tuath, leis,
Na tuathanaich chòir'.

Bidh na boireannaich dìleas
Anns gach àit' aig am bi iad,
Ma' ri gruagaichean rìomhach,
40 Trì mìl' agus corr!

Théid a' chrois air a' phàipear
Mu choinneimh ainm "Isaac";
'S mi tha cinnteach nach caill sinn
Daoine dàimheil Ghlen-cò.

45 Latha daingneachadh cùise,
Bidh sinn aighearach sunndach,
Is ceòl na pìoba cur sùrd oirnn
Seachad lùban Strath Lòrn.

Ma gheibh sinn ar dùrachd
50 Is gun téid esan do'n lùchairt,
Cha ruig gnothach na dùthcha
Leas cùram 'chur oirnn.[36]

Translation

(1-4) ...MacDougald will get my vote.

(5-8) The son of the man who was gifted and of an honest nature, I would entrust my interests to him: he excelled at the assembly.

(9-12) I favour the gallant who is very noble in his behaviour; many people acclaim him, running for office while still so young.

(13-16) You are kind by nature, there is no flaw in your body; you are a descendant of the strong men who would go boldly into the chase [of an attack].

(17-20) Since you went through the country to make a new appearance, many people whom we might not have expected have turned their coats [i.e., switched their allegiance to MacDougald]!

(21-24) The people of Chestico and Mabou and Judique are saying that the majority will be loyal to the hero.

(25-28) The French have changed their minds since their eyes opened; they will be on our side and there is no worry that the matter will not turn out properly.

(29-32) The men of kind Whycocomagh will be on his side; both sides of the Lake will be on his side; Margaree, the beloved place of the cattle, will be on his side and that's no idle boast.

(33-36) Every coal-miner will be on his side; everyone around will be on his side; the goodly farmers, north and south, will be on his side.

(37-40) The women will be loyal everywhere that they will be found, along with lovely maidens, over three thousand [of them]!

(41-44) The mark will go on the paper next to the name "Isaac"; I am convinced that we will not lose the benevolent people of Glencoe.

(45-48) We will be joyful and excited on election day, with the music of the bagpipes enlivening us going past the bends of Strathlorne.

(49-52) If we get our wish and he goes to the house of government, the realm's affairs will no longer cause us worry.

10: A Song about the General Election

Coinneach MacFhearghuis of the L' Àrdoise Highlands, Cape Breton, composed the following song-poem in the run up to the federal elections for the House of Commons on October 29, 1925. Unlike the exuberance and naive optimism of previous political poems, this text exudes skepticism and distrust. This reveals the dissatisfaction in the Maritimes with the existing political parties, whose interests and economic policies were focused on central and western Canada. MacFhearghuis's cynicism also indicates an awareness of the bitter rows and divisions erupting in and between political parties in Parliament at that time.[37]

Original Text

1　Tha daoine dripeil, bhos is thall,
　　Is tha bilean briathrachail neo-mhall,
　　A' cur an céill air feadh nan sgìrean
　　Nithean air bheag suim de'n fhìrinn.

　　Ciod ach gum bheil glaodh tro'n dùthaich
5　A tha dùsgadh suas nan diùlnach:
　　Pairtidhean a' strì le dìorras
　　Anns a' ghleachd seo, togail fiabhrais.

　　A nì sgaoileadh feadh na tìre,
　　Móran bhreug is beagan fìrinn:
10　Glaodh a chuireas sgàil air aodainn,
　　Reachdan agus feartan saorsa.

　　Grits, Progressives, agus Tóries
　　Strì có 'n dream dhiubh bhios le mór-ghuth
　　Buannachdail 's an taghadh ùr
15　A tha 'ga ghlaodhaich feadh ar dùthcha.[38]

Translation

(1-4) People are bustling, here and there, and quick blathering lips are declaring things throughout the ridings that have very little to do with the truth.

(5-8) What is it but a proclamation through the country that is arousing the warriors: [political] parties striving vehemently in this conflict, raising it to a fever pitch.

(9-12) What is spreading throughout the land is a lot of lies and little truth: a declaration that casts a shadow on faces, legislation and the attributes of freedom.

(13-16) Grits, Progressives, and Tories striving to see which one of them will be successful with the majority in the new election that is being called throughout the land.

Conclusions

This volume brings together and explores a selection of the many voices that survive from the extensive Scottish Gaelic immigrant communities that could once be found across Canada. It demonstrates that the emigrant generation had a keen sense of their distinctive identity and culture, and strong opinions about their personal experiences as well as their collective history as an ethnic group. These perceptions and traditions were sustained in some communities across multiple generations, and persist most strongly to the present in the Maritime provinces.

Immigrants from the Scottish Highlands and their descendants in Canada produced a significant branch of Gaelic literature that carried forward the cultural signifiers and artistic expressions with a very long lineage. Poets who had been born and raised in widely dispersed areas of Canada and Scotland—including locales in the Highlands where Gaelic has become extinct, such as southern Argyllshire and Perthshire—contributed their talents in a loosely-coupled social network to adapt and extend their literary inheritance to express their opinions, feelings and aspirations, and to commemorate their experiences in a new environment and rapidly changing world. Their compositions give us direct and intimate contact with them in a way that surpasses most anglophone texts, especially where matters of their culture, identity and world view are concerned. This sophisticated literary tradition was largely responsible for sustaining a value system, historical memory and set of cultural signifiers distinctive to the Gaelic community more essential and consequential than the superficial tokenism of tartanism.

CONCLUSIONS

There are numerous examples of Canadian Gaelic poets who wrestled with modern issues and looked with hopeful expectation at developments that they expected would benefit Gaeldom. Their literary productions demonstrate that Gaelic contained ample linguistic, literary and intellectual resources to deal with the contemporary world, even if the community lacked the confidence and infrastructure to realize these possibilities. In a survey of 20th-century Gaelic literature, for example, Ronald Black has noted of Cape Breton author Aonghus Y. MacGill-Fhaolain, "He was a gifted poet, musician and raconteur whose published stories may be said to mark the stirrings—regrettably still-born—of a modern Gaelic literature in Cape Breton."[1] That such a fundamental aspect of Gaelic heritage can be commonly ignored is an indication of the extent to which Gaeldom has been buried and obscured by the romantic but ultimately disempowering stereotypes created by the anglophone world.

Despite the millions of Canadians living today with ancestry that connects them to these Highland exiles—Canadians with the power and privilege to influence educational institutions and social attitudes—the legacy of their ancestors, especially as expressed in their own native tongue, has been largely forgotten. Apart from the occasional nod to the symbols of Highlandism, the imaginations and aspirations of the descendants of Gaelic emigrants have been occupied by ideas and values derived from English Canada. The only Canadians of Scottish descent worth celebrating, it is commonly implied, are those who achieved social, political and financial success by accommodating themselves to the anglophone order. This rapid assimilation to Anglo-conformity can be most effectively explained by considering it within the wider context of British imperialism.

As I write the conclusions to this collection of literature chronicling the experiences of Scottish Gaels in Canada, events are underway to commemorate the two-hundredth anniversary of the birth of John A. Macdonald. Prime Minister Stephen Harper, reflecting on the legacy of the Father of Confederation, waxes proudly about his continuation of the British enterprise in North America, with some anticipation of the 150th anniversary of the creation of the Dominion of Canada.

> Of the greatest importance for all of us, perhaps, was that Macdonald appropriated from the British constitution its conception of freedom, of "ordered liberty," of the balancing of

popular rule and minority rights, of (in the terms of the era) equality before the law and governments responsible through the legislature to the voters. ...

"In all countries the rights of the majority take care of themselves," Macdonald declared, "but it is only in countries like England, enjoying constitutional liberty, and safe from the tyranny of a single despot, or of an unbridled democracy, that the rights of minorities are regarded." The constitution Macdonald negotiated thus secured protection for Canadians against arbitrary interference by the state. It established, in his words, "absolute equality, having equal rights of every kind—of language, of religion, of property and of person."[2]

A group of international scholars met in Glasgow, Scotland, where Macdonald was born, to investigate the early story of his life more fully during the anniversary. Scotland, looking to assert its own cultural identity and place in world affairs, often looks beyond the British Isles to find exemplars of Scottish "success" and "triumph," with Canada being a favourite hunting ground. Tricia Marwick, Presiding Officer of the Scottish Parliament, attended celebrations of Macdonald's birthday in Kingston, Ontario, and remarked: "I think what is important is that we recognise famous Scots, people who've gone abroad and done wonderful things."[3]

Such glowing admiration can only be expressed by those who have benefited from the privileges selectively bestowed by British imperialism and are willing to overlook the profound injustices and inequalities that it produced and perpetuated. It is highly doubtful that Canada's first prime minister would be characterized as a nice man who did "wonderful things" by the native peoples whom he displaced and starved to death,[4] or by the insurgents of the 1869 Red River Resistance whom Macdonald called "impulsive half breeds." He was, at the least, complicit in colonial policies that were devastating to native peoples and profoundly unfair to non-European immigrants.[5]

Despite his Scottish birth, Macdonald always spoke of England as the mother country in the political arena. The fact that his parents were native Gaelic speakers from the Highlands did not predispose him to lift a finger to defend their language or even acknowledge its existence publicly. John A.'s behaviour in these matters was the rule rather than the exception.

The notion that Macdonald worked for the equality "of language, of religion, of property and of person" for all people in Canada, as Harper claims, is a convenient myth that turns a blind eye to the suffering, exploitation, dispossession and discrimination suffered by indigenous and racialized peoples in colonial territories. It even ignores the prejudices faced by members of his own ancestral ethnicity—Scottish Gaels—when they attempted to maintain, develop, and assert the legitimacy of their own language and culture. Macdonald's rhetoric of the racial, moral, social and cultural superiority of Britishness mark him out as an effective champion of extending the long legacy of Anglocentric hegemony into North America, one whose negative consequences have yet to be fully unravelled and acknowledged.

> The late nineteenth-century British Empire was a more modern institution, but it was not the benevolent force for good that imperial partisans recall it to be. Empires are, by definition, a form of permanent authoritarian rule that consigns a defeated community in perpetual subjecthood, most often for the purposes of exploitation and extraction. Empire builders justified this inequitable relationship by portraying subject peoples as inherently primitive and backward, and their promises to reform and uplift them were just empty rhetoric. Imperial rulers were fundamentally guilty of disguising hypocrisy in implying that they exploited their subjects for their own good.
>
> Empires were never humane, and imperial subjecthood was always demeaning and intolerable. The current romanticization of the British and French empires of the last century as stable, omnipotent, and benevolent rests on anachronistic nostalgia, willful historical ignorance, and the intentional racist denigration and exoticization of non-western peoples.[6]

A number of factors contributed to the accelerating success of English power during the early modern era in the British Isles and beyond: the concentration of power and authority in the south-east, a dominant language (English), a religious ideology purporting the manifest destiny of Protestants, the fluidity of social rank based on commercial profit, and the co-option of elites who projected centralized control onto local lands and populations. John Brewer famously characterized this system as the "fiscal-military state."[7] As territories were seized, the maximum economic potential was realized by minimizing the resident population needed to extract resources, dispossessing the "excess" and moving them to urban centres or to colonial outposts where the processes of colonization, conquest and dispossession were reiterated. Expropriation and dislocation were not accidental aftermaths of English imperial expansion but intrinsic to it.

> Of all Europe's major nations, England and then England-dominated Britain were the most inclined to use forms of emigration—indentured service, transportation of rebels and criminals, and a large-scale exodus of Celtic peasants from Ireland and the Scottish Highlands—to clear its territory of the ethnically, politically, and socially undesirable. Statistics that show eighteenth- and nineteenth-century Britons emigrating in much higher ratios than French or even Germans—almost 11 million left between 1750 and 1900—are weighted by a two-thirds Celtic departure that helped to make Britain lopsidedly English.[8]

The Highland elite were increasingly integrated into British affairs from the 17th century onward through a mixture of force and reward. Any remnants of an independent social order were swept out from under Scottish Gaeldom in the aftermath of the 1745 Jacobite Rising. The British Empire emerged as the world's most powerful political entity in the 19th century. Those who were willing to identify with its triumphant brand of imperialism were often able to reap the significant rewards of power and wealth that being a member of a dominant and privileged group entailed, but at the cost of relinquishing their own ancestral culture and aiding in the subjugation and colonization of others. Gaels compensated for presumed developmental shortcomings by recourse to their much vaunted military tradition, but given that this was in the service of expanding British imperial interests, they were ultimately underscoring their commitment to Anglocentric hegemony and undermining their own cultural sovereignty.

Many texts in this volume attest to the degree to which Gaels were eager to make a public display of their political and social alignment with the interests of the ruling anglophone elite, even though this required contradicting and violating their own historical experience and cultural norms. These convulsions are well illustrated by relations with the French. Scotland initiated an official alliance with

France against their common enemy, England, in 1295 but dissolved it in 1560 due to growing ties with England. Regardless, close ties between France and many parts of the Highlands, especially those of Catholic and Jacobite persuasion, persisted into the 18th century. There are Gaelic poems proudly acclaiming French connections right up to the 1745 Jacobite Rising.[9] According to oral tradition, fluency in the French language was a key asset exploited by the Highland troops at the Battle of the Plains of Abraham.[10] A common British identity, as Linda Colley has argued,[11] was defined in opposition to the French Empire. Many Gaelic poets in Canada sought validation of their British credentials by enumerating the battles they had fought on behalf of the British Empire against French enemies. Gaels commonly exhibited antagonism toward the French when political debates surfaced about the rights of linguistic communities in Canada.

These recurring patterns demonstrate the subordination of Gaeldom to the Anglocentric imperial order. If Gaels wanted access to power and privilege, they had to conform to anglophone norms, rather than being seen as a threat or challenge to them. Militarism was the passport to entry and tartanism the facade that hid the profound disruptions and costs to Gaeldom as a whole. Too many of the standard histories about the immigration of Scots in Canada simply celebrate their ability to assimilate and do not recognize the losses incurred by these processes and the conditions under which they occurred.

Leaders who should have helped develop the Gaelic language and culture according to its own norms and traditions were generally too concerned to ingratiate themselves to the dominant anglophone hegemony to negotiate the complexities of Gaeldom's transition into modernity on its own terms. While not always explicitly advocating for the elimination of the Gaelic language, relegating it to a mere symbol of an obsolete past—associated with "pre-modern" sentiments and traditions—left it bereft of political authority and cultural import. Some Gaels were less than enthusiastic about being conscripted into imperial enterprises or embracing secular materialism, and some did critique these activities, but on the whole the Highland elite were too deeply invested in Anglo-British imperialism to promote alternatives to Anglo-conformity and resistance was muted. Accidents of geography and biology made it possible for people of Gaelic ancestry to assume the role of honorary Anglo-Saxons.[12] Those willing to be convinced of the inferiority of their own ancestral culture and the necessity of assimilation to anglophone norms had few reservations about subjecting other peoples to the same treatment.

Outside of formal organs of the state, Gaelic communities sublimated much of their energy into religion as a result and reflection of their subjugation in the cultural sphere and their impotence in the political domain. While the degree to which this happened varied according to time and place, this redirection of interests gave Gaels control of a domain of their own which did not have to contend with the dominant powers. This had the unfortunate side-effect, however, of restricting their ability to build and develop structures and resources in the secular realm that may have enabled the maintenance of their culture and identity for the long term.

Emigration from the Highlands was sometimes voluntary to some degree, but it betokened cultural vulnerability and economic dependency. It was no guaranteed panacea for individual or community.

> It is not right that a whole culture should have been treated in this way, that like the Red Indians and the aborigines so many of our people should have had to leave their homes to inherit the worst aspects of a so-called superior civilisation. ...
>
> I think of them in Canada hacking down the dark tall trees, clearing away spruce so that they could plant. I recall both the successful and the unsuccessful, the latter who never wrote home because there was nothing to write about. I recall the broken ones who returned. And it is as if a terrible anger seizes me when I think of the many dead, the waste.[13]

Canadian Gaels express the expectation in many texts that they will be remembered for their legacy in North America. They would be disappointed, to say the least, that today they are generally lumped together with their long-time rivals, Lowland Scots, and even more often tossed into the "British" or "English-speaking" divide of Canadian ethnicity, as though they were indistinguishable from the people with whom they fought for centuries for their identity and cultural sovereignty. Many other immigrant groups can look back to homelands where their culture has been valorized and enshrined by national institutions that foster the development of its traditions of learning and literature. Until very recently Scottish Gaels, to the contrary, could only look back at their conquest and domination by rivals whom they had long deprecated and who gained the power to dictate educational and political policies and institutions that inferiorized Gaelic and attempted to replace it with English.

This volume contains only a small sampling of the sources available in books, periodicals, manuscripts and archives to tell the story of Canadian Gaelic communities in their own words. Despite a modest show of interest in Scottish Studies in North America, very little effort is being made to address and explore the Gaelic immigrant experience in the universities of either Canada or the United States. In fact, anglophone scholars and mainstream historians have all too often conspired to keep Gaelic voices obscured and peripheral. Take, for example, an essay published in 2014 about Scottish cultural organizations in the global diaspora in which two organizations originally formed by emigrants in Australia are extolled because they

> invited membership from across the multi-ethnic communities in which they operated from the outset. Additionally, both were careful to counter that inherently insular Gaelic language objective with a more accessible and inclusive expression of Highland culture, namely the staging of an annual Highland Games for the whole community.[14]

This is to entirely misunderstand the basis of culture in any community and to misrepresent the legitimate aspirations of those who established Gaelic-centred organizations. Language and literature provide the deepest and most significant strains of continuity in the Highland immigrant experience and the most effective means of accessing and transmitting cultural values, beliefs and practices. Gaelic is as legitimate a linguistic medium for inter-ethnic interchange as is English, French or Mohawk and acted as such in many Canadian locales. Although exotic clothing and ritualized ceremonies may add excitement and pageantry to social gatherings, they become mere tokens of ethnic origins pointing in the direction of Highland ancestry but empty of substantial content once the ability to access linguistic and literary expressions is lost. Canadian Gaels have been saying this for generations. The first issue of *Mosgladh* in 1922, for example, urged readers to focus on language as the foundation of their identity: "Highland games, Scottish concerts, bagpipe music, Highland dancing, are all popular but they scarcely help to perpetuate the Gaelic language."[15]

Popular histories of the colonization of North America commonly depict the confrontations of hostile hegemonies: "red" men versus "white" men, natives versus Europeans, British forces versus French forces, and so on. Ethnic labels like "British," "French" and even "native" and "indigenous" hide the diverse origins of those who were engaged in these encounters, the complex ways that they conceived of their own identities, and the perceptions that they had of the forces and events around them as they transpired. Although Chief Thayendanegea (Joseph Brant) and Iain "am Pìobaire" MacGilleBhràth (John MacGillivray) may have called themselves "British" in some contexts, they were members of communities with much deeper roots and more local and personal attachments. That these communities would be crushed and made virtually invisible by the empire of their political loyalty was probably beyond their comprehension and certainly beyond their control.

After over half of a millennium of domination and exploitation, the modern imperial era has left us a legacy of social injustice, cultural subordination, genocide, linguicide, and environmental crisis. It is only in the second half of the 20th century that the pretensions of empires—that they were inherently superior and worthy of supremacy over others—have given way to an understanding that, like all human beings, all cultures and languages have intrinsic value and dignity and are deserving of rights and protections.

It is only in the 21st century, after generations of campaigning, that Scottish Gaelic has been given any measure of official recognition in Canada. The only vestiges left of the Gaelic-speaking communities that were widely scattered across Canada at the time of Confederation are now to be found in Nova Scotia where Oifis Iomairtean na Gàidhlig (the Office of Gaelic Affairs) was established in 2006 to help "Nova Scotians reclaim their Gaelic language and identity as a basis for cultural, community, spiritual and economic renewal." The cultivation of the seeds remaining in Nova Scotia may help to restore some vitality to this heritage in the region, in the country, and perhaps in Scotland itself. Close to the end of his life in Nova Scotia, the Rev. Donnchadh Blàrach prophesied as much in his 1887 song-poem "Aiseirigh na Gàidhealtachd" (The Resurrection of the Highlands):

Gàidheil Aimeireaga thall
Is a' chlann a thàinig 'nan déidh

> Cuidichibh leotha 's an àm
> Mar chàirdibh nach meall is nach tréig;
> Togaidh seo 'm misneach o'n làr
> Is nì iad co-spàirn le chéil'
> A chum gum faigh iad air ais
> Gach còir a bh' aca bho chéin.
>
> Gaels across in America
> And the children who succeeded them,
> Help them at this time
> As friends who will not deceive or abandon;
> They will raise their courage from the ground
> And they will strive together
> In order to get back
> Every right that they had of old.[16]

The reparations due to Gaeldom are due to many other peoples as well. History is never over and the conquerors do not have to have the last word. Even now, after generations of conflict and marginalization, First Nations in Canada are asserting their sovereignty, pressing for their treaty rights and reinvigorating their languages, just as Gaels in Scotland continue to strive for land reform and to revitalize their disenfranchised native tongue.

Like so many other aspects of the human experience, history is socially constructed. Without the ability to detect and understand the records produced by people about their experiences as members of a particular social community, we cannot properly comprehend the meaning of the past from their own collective point of view or even realize that interpretations that differ from our own are possible.

> The negation of indigenous views of history was a critical part of asserting colonial ideology, partly because such views were regarded as clearly "primitive" and "incorrect" and mostly because they challenged and resisted the mission of colonization. ... [H]istory is mostly about power. It is the story of the powerful and how they became powerful, and then how they use their power to keep them in positions in which they can continue to dominate others. It is because of this relationship with power that we have been excluded, marginalized and "Othered." ... To hold alternative histories is to hold alternative knowledges.[17]

While the descendants of Highland immigrants may not endorse all of the exploits and attitudes of their ancestors, and may not wish to reclaim and revive all of the aspects of their culture, they at least have the right to know what they were and to understand their significance to people at that time. Gaels in Scotland and Canada can act as allies, partners and collaborators in the necessary tasks of decolonization by disavowing and helping to deconstruct the oppressive ideologies of imperialism that legitimated the conquest and domination of their own homeland and those of other subordinated peoples. Recovery from past injustices can only begin when all voices can be heard, acknowledged, and affirmed on their own terms. I hope that the echoes of Gaels in the land of trees released by the texts in this volume help to foster that long-awaited dialogue.

Biographies

The following biographical entries offer brief descriptions of the authors and collectors of the texts in this volume. I have not created entries for people about whom I could not find any substantial or reliable information. I have only provided references for information that is found in sources outside those used for the texts themselves. Entries are listed by the original Gaelic name of the author; any Gaelic nickname or patronymic follows in parentheses; the English transliteration of their names appear in double-quotation marks within the parentheses.

BLÀRACH, DONNCHADH ("REVEREND DUNCAN BLAIR"): Born in Srath Chura (Strachur), Cowal, Scotland in 1815 and trained for the ministry in Edinburgh. He came initially to Canada in 1846 but returned to Scotland in 1850. He was married in Scotland and relocated permanently to Nova Scotia in 1851. Passed away in 1893.[1]

BOID, IAIN ("JOHN BOYD"): Born in Àrasaig (Arisaig), Scotland, in 1797. His family emigrated to South River, Antigonish County in 1801. He published a book to teach Gaelic literacy in 1848 and published a Gaelic newspaper *An Cuairtear Òg Gàidhealach* from 1851 to 1852 (see text 8.3). He established the bilingual newspaper *The Casket* in 1852. He passed away in 1871 in Antigonish.[2] He composed song-poem 6.2.

FRISEAL, ALASDAIR ("ALEXANDER FRASER"): Born in Cill Taraghlain (Kiltarlity), Scotland, in 1860. He emigrated to Toronto in 1886 to work as a journalist with *The Toronto Mail*. He was elected to be the president of Comunn Gàidhlig Thoronto (the Gaelic Society of Toronto) in 1894. He took up the position of provincial archivist for the province of Ontario in 1903 and filled that role until 1935. He produced a great deal of work about the history and literature of Gaelic Canada and founded Comunn Gàidhlig Chanada (the Gaelic Society of Canada). He passed away in 1936.[3] He wrote texts 4.11, 5.2 and 8.5 and gathered texts 4.7, 5.4 and 8.1 from oral tradition.

Grannd, Iain (Iain mac Ghilleasbaig, "John Grant"): His father, Gilleasbaig, was a celebrated poet who was closely connected to the Grants of Glenmoriston. He joined the army in 1772 and earned the rank of sergeant before retiring. He returned to Glenmoriston before passing away.[4] He composed song-poem 4.3.

Greumach, Iain ("John Graham"): Born in 1815 in Gabhsainn mu Thuath (North Galson), Isle of Lewis, Scotland, to Michael Graham and Mary Paterson. He and his sister Ann "Bothan" migrated to Marston, Quebec in the year 1863. He was said to have died of loneliness in Scotstown, Quebec in the year 1876.[5] He composed song-poem 4.9.

Mac a' Phearsain, Iain ("John MacPherson"): A native of Cùr (Cour), Kintyre, Scotland, he emigrated at some date after 1836 to Canada. He occupied a small farm near London, Ontario. He composed song-poem 8.6.

MacCodruim, Iain (Iain mac Fhearchair, "John MacCodrum"): Born in 1693 and lived his entire life on the Isle of North Uist, Scotland. His reputation as a seanchaidh and poet was such that Alasdair mac Mhaighstir Alasdair and James "Ossian" Macpherson sought him out. Sir James MacDonald of Sleat appointed him to be his official bard. Died in 1779. He composed song-poem 2.2.

MacCoinnich, Alasdair Ruadh ("Red Alexander MacKenzie"): Born in North Uist. Emigrated to McGillivray Township ("North Middlesex" today), Middlesex County, Ontario in about the 1830s. He passed away when he was 96 years of age.[6] He composed song-poems 6.5 and 7.5.

BIOGRAPHIES

MacCoinnich, Coinneach ("Kenneth MacKenzie"): Born in 1758 at Caisteal Leathoir (Castle Leather), near Inverness, Scotland. He earned a living as a sailor and writer (he was literate in Gaelic). He passed away about the year 1837 in Ireland.[7] He composed song-poem 2.3.

MacColla, Eóghann (Bàrd Loch Fìne, "Evan MacColl"): Born in 1808 on Lochfyneside, Argyll, Scotland. He migrated to Liverpool, England, in 1839 and from there to Kingston, Ontario, in 1850. He was very active in Gaelic circles in Toronto, where he passed away in 1898. He composed song 9.1 and is described in text 8.5 and song-poem 8.6.

MacDhòmhnaill, Ailean ("Allan MacDonald," "Allan 'the Ridge'"): Born at Allt an t-Srathain in Brae Lochaber, Scotland, in 1794. He was descended from the MacDonalds of Both-Fhionntainn (Bohuntin), a family known as "Sliochd an Taighe." His family migrated in 1816 to Nova Scotia, initially settling in South-West Ridge, Mabou. In 1847 the family relocated again to Upper South River, Antigonish County, Nova Scotia. He passed away in 1868.[8] He composed song-poem 4.4.

MacDhòmhnaill, Alasdair ("Alexander MacDonald," "Alexander 'The Ridge'"): The son of Ailean above. Born in 1823 at South-West Ridge, Mabou, Nova Scotia, but relocated with his family in 1847 to Upper South River, Antigonish County. He passed away in 1904. He composed song-poems 10.3 and 10.4.

MacDhòmhnaill, Dòmhnall ("Donald MacDonald"): Born in Caolas, Isle of Tiree, Scotland, in 1858. He moved to Glasgow, Scotland, at the age of fifteen and, after several other relocations, in 1889 he moved to Toronto. He was active in Gaelic circles and was a noted singer. He moved to New York and after only a few months founded the New York Celtic Society. After a stint of work back in his native Tiree he relocated to Ottawa (no later than 1912) and died there in 1919.[9] He composed song-poem 10.8.

MacDhòmhnaill, Dòmhnall Donnchadh ("Doctor Donald Duncan MacDonald"): Born in 1858 in Alexandria, Ontario. He earned a living as a doctor but composed numerous Gaelic song-poems, including 6.11, 6.14 and 9.6. He passed away in 1927.

MacDhòmhnaill, Iain (Iain mac Dhòmhnuill mhic Aonghuis, Iain Liath, "John MacDonald"): A native of Cnòideart (Knoydart), Scotland. He emigrated in 1786 and shortly thereafter came to reside at Glenroy (now South Glengarry), Ontario, Canada. He composed song-poem 4.2.

MacDhòmhnaill, Murchadh D. ("Murdo MacDonald"): Born at Tolastadh bho Thuath (North Tolsta), Isle of Lewis, Scotland, in 1870. His family migrated to Quebec (probably the town of Spring Hill, now called "Nantes") when he was three years of age. He spent time working in Saskatchewan and California. He was still alive after the Second World War.[10] He composed song-poem 5.15.

MacDhùghaill, Roibeart ("Robert MacDougall"): Born in Fartairchill (Fortingall), Perthshire, Scotland in 1813. He emigrated to Goderich Township, Huron Tract, in 1836 with his father where his two brothers had already spent three years. He returned to Scotland in 1839 and worked as a journalist for the Gaelic newspaper *Cuairtear nan Gleann*. He relocated to Australia in 1841, where he passed away in 1887.[11] He wrote text 4.8.

MacFhearghuis, Coinneach A. ("Kenneth Fergusson"): Born in the L' Àrdoise Highlands, Richmond County, Cape Breton in 1870. He is said to have composed close to fifty songs, although many of them have been lost. He passed away in 1928.[12] He composed song-poems 8.8 and 10.10.

MacFhilip, Gilleasbaig (Bàrd Dall Mhegantic, "Archibald MacKillop"): Born at Loch Raonasa (Lochranza), Isle of Arran, Scotland, in 1824. His father, also named Gilleasbaig, was a factor for the Duke of Hamilton and in 1829 arranged for a vessel (the *Caledonia*) to transport migrants to Canada, including his own family. They initially settled in Inverness, Quebec. Gilleasbaig (the son) and his brother Calum attended the University of Toronto, but his eye was injured as a student, causing him to become blind.[13] Gilleasbaig was the official poet of Comunn Gàidhlig Mhontreal between 1883 and 1894.[14] He went to reside among the Gaels of Glengarry later in life and passed away in 1905. He composed song-poems 3.3, 7.6 and 9.3.

MacFhionghain, Aonghus ("Angus MacKinnon"): Origins uncertain. He was at the Presbyterian Church of Kitsilano (close to Vancouver), British Columbia, in 1916 and settled as the minister there in about 1923.[15] He composed song-poem 7.8.

MacFhionghain, Dòmhnall Òg ("Donald MacKinnon"): Born in 1825 on the Isle of Benbecula, Scotland. He earned his living as a stonemason but was renowned as a poet. He emigrated with his family to St. Andrews, Manitoba, in the year 1884. He passed away in 1912.[16] He is likely to have composed song-poem 4.10.

MacFhionghain, Eòin ("Jonathon G. MacKinnon"): Born in Whycocomagh, Cape Breton, in 1869. He was the editor and publisher of Gaelic newspapers *Mac-Talla* 1892-1904 and *Fear na Céilidh* 1928-1929, and edited the Gaelic column "Cùil na Gàidhlig" in *The Sydney Record*. He was the vice-president of the Gaelic Foundation and the first Dean at the Gaelic College in Cape Breton, where he taught Gaelic. He passed away in 1944.[17] He wrote text 5.12 and song-poem 7.11.

MacFhionghain, Seumas ("James MacKinnon"): Born in 1871 in Baile a' Mhanaich (Balivanich), Isle of Benbecula, Scotland, son of Dòmhnall Òg MacFhionghain above. His family emigrated to St. Andrews, Manitoba, in 1884. He worked as a civil servant in Moosomin and was literate in Gaelic. He passed away in 1946.[18] He composed song-poem 8.9.

MacGill-Eain, Iain (Bàrd Thighearna Chola, Am Bàrd MacGill-Eain, "John MacLean"): Born at Caolas, Isle of Tiree, Scotland, in 1787. He began work as a cobbler at sixteen years of age but poetry was his true calling. He was literate in Gaelic, conducted fieldwork to collect poetry from oral tradition, and published an anthology in 1818 consisting of twenty-two of his own poems and thirty-four by other poets. Shortly after this he decided to emigrate to British North

America. He and his family arrived in Pictou, Nova Scotia, about October of 1819. He eventually settled at Barney's River on a farmstead he named "Baile 'Chnoic." He relocated again in 1830 in a settlement named "Gleann a' Bhàird," in Antigonish County. He passed away in 1848.[19] He composed song-poems 8.2 and 10.1.

MacGilleBhràth, Dùghall ("Dougald MacGillivray," "The Old Squire"): Born in 1802, the first child born to Gaelic emigrants in Antigonish County, Nova Scotia. He lived in South River, Antigonish County, until he died in 1896. He composed song-poem 6.6.

MacGilleBhràth, Iain (Iain am Pìobaire, "John MacGillivray"): Born about the year 1784 in Àrasaig (Arisaig), Scotland. He was for a time under the employ of Alexander MacDonald of Glenalladale (Alasdair Ruadh †1815) as his poet and bagpiper. He emigrated to Nova Scotia in 1818 and settled at Highfield, Antigonish County. He initially tried his hand at farming but began teaching formally in 1840. He passed away in 1862.[20] He composed song-poem 3.1 and probably 5.5, and is the subject of song-poem 6.4.

MacGilleBhràth, Iain Òg ("John MacGillivray"): Born in 1830 in Highfield, Antigonish County, Nova Scotia (son of Iain am Pìobaire above). He received formal instruction on the bagpipe from his father. He set up his own residence in Maryvale where he lived until he died in 1901. He composed song-poem 7.4.

MacGilleMhaoil, Alasdair (Alasdair mac Eóghainn mhic Ghilleasbaig mhic Dhòmhnaill Duinn, "Alexander MacMillan"): Born in Reisibeal in Suaineart (Sunart), Scotland, in 1764. His family belonged to a branch of the MacMillans known as "Clann Iain Léith na Coille"; his mother (Eamhair nighean Ghilleasbaig mhic Eóghainn mhic Dhòmhnaill Mhóir) was a native of Suaineart (Sunart). He was raised in Lochaber and emigrated to Glengarry, Ontario, in 1802. He passed away in 1853 at his home in Kenyon Township (now North Glengarry). He composed song-poem 5.3.

MacGill-Ìosa, Calum ("Malcolm Gillis," "The Margaree Bard"): Born in 1856 in Upper Margaree, Cape Breton. He worked as a teacher but was celebrated in his community as a poet, fiddler, bagpiper and singer. He passed away in 1929.²¹ He composed song-poem 10.9.

MacGriogair, Seumas ("Reverend James MacGregor"): Born in 1759 in Port Mór (now "St. Fillans"), Perthshire, Scotland. He emigrated to Nova Scotia in 1786 and was the first Gaelic-speaking Protestant minister in the province. He published a book of Gaelic hymns in 1819. He passed away in 1830. He composed song-poems 6.1, 7.1 and 7.2.

MacÌomhair, Cailean ("Colin MacIver"): Born in Barbhas (Barvas), Isle of Lewis, Scotland in 1833. His family emigrated to Milan, Quebec, when he was young. Mac-Talla Publishing published a booklet of his songs in 1902. He passed away in 1918 in Seattle.²² He composed song-poem 6.13.

MacLeòid, Dòmhnall ("Donald MacLeod"): Born on the Isle of Berneray, Scotland, in 1882. He emigrated to Canada as a young man, initially to the Yukon but eventually settling in Vancouver, where he died in 1949. He composed a number of songs and recorded at least a couple of them for Beltona Records. He composed song-poem 9.7.

MacMhuirich, Lachlann (Am Bàrd Ruadh, "Lachlann Currie"): Lachlann's family was descended from the renowned dynasty of professional Gaelic literati who worked for Clanranald. He was born in 1852 in Upper Grand Mira, Cape Breton, and worked in a copper mine close to Gillies Lake. He passed away in 1926.²³ He composed song-poems 5.8 and 6.8.

Mac na h-Innse, Niall ("Reverend Neil McNish"): A native of Argyllshire, Scotland, who graduated from Edinburgh University in 1869. He received further education in Glasgow and Toronto. He taught at the Presbyterian College of Montreal, where he was said to have lectured on Gaelic language and literature for some fifteen years and eventually came to reside in Cornwall, Ontario.²⁴ He wrote text 3.6.

MacNeacail, Pàdraig ("The Right Reverend Patrick J. Nicholson"): Born in 1887 at Beaver Cove, Cape Breton. Ordained in Toronto in 1916. He was a professor of Physics at St. Francis Xavier University from 1916 to 1944 and served as President from 1944 to 1954. He edited the Gaelic column "Achadh nan Gàidheal" for *The Casket* newspaper of Antigonish from 1920 to 1945.[25] He recorded a variant of text 2.1. He passed away in 1965.

MacPhàrlain, Dòmhnall (Dòmhnall Dhùghaill 'ic Gilleasbaig 'ic Dhùghaill 'ic Phàdraig, "Donald MacFarlane"): Born in 1861 in Southwest Margaree, Cape Breton, where he lived all of his life. He taught school for twenty years and then began to work as a merchant. He passed away in 1950. He composed song-poem 8.10.

MacRisnidh, Fionnlagh ("Finlay McRitchie"): Born in Barbhas Ìochdrach (Lower Barvas), Isle of Lewis, Scotland, in 1841. His family emigrated in 1843 to Lingwick, Quebec. He lived the latter part of his life on Red Mountain, where he died in 1923.[26] He composed song-poem 6.7.

Moireach, Uilleam ("William Murray"): Born in Fionnlairig (Finlarig) near Killin, Perthshire, Scotland, in 1834. He emigrated to Toronto in 1854 and thence to Hamilton two years later. He was the official poet for Comunn Gàidhlig Hamilton for over twenty-six years and composed a great deal of poetry in both English and Gaelic. He passed away in 1923.[27] He composed song-poem 6.10.

Moireastan, Dòmhnall (Dòmhnall Fìdhlear, "Donald Morrison"): Resident of Kenyon (now North Glengarry), Ontario. Flourished in the 1820s and 1830s. He composed song-poem 5.6.

Moireastain, Murchadh (Murchadh mac Coinnich Bhàin Iain 'ic Fhionnlaigh, "Murdo Morrison"): Born on the Isle of Berneray in 1842. His family emigrated to Ferguson Lake, Cape Breton, when he was nine months old and he lived there for the rest of his life.[28] He composed song-poem 7.10.

NicGill-Ìosa, Anna ("Anna Gillis"): Born in Mórar, Scotland, about the year 1759. She married Iain Ruadh MacDhòmhnaill, a native of Cnòideart (Knoydart), in 1777 and they emigrated on the boat *McDonald* in 1786 to Canada, accompanied by Father Alexander "Scotus" Macdonell. They arrived in Cornwall, Ontario, on the first of October that year. They later relocated to St. Raphael's, Glengarry, Ontario. She passed away there in 1847 and was buried at St. Raphael's Church.[29] She composed song-poem 4.1.

SINCLAIR, ALASDAIR MACGILL-EAIN ("REVEREND ALEXANDER MACLEAN SINCLAIR"): Born in 1840. He was raised in Gleann a' Bhàird, Antigonish County, Nova Scotia by his mother's family, including his grandfather Iain MacGill-Eain (see above). Iain passed away when Alasdair was eight years old but had a huge effect on him. Alasdair graduated from teacher training in 1861 but went to Halifax to be trained for the ministry (in the Presbyterian Church) in 1863; he finished in 1866. He served as minister in Pictou County until 1888 when he relocated to Prince Edward Island. He retired in 1906 and returned to Nova Scotia in 1907. He passed away in 1924 in Hopewell, after writing and publishing many articles and books about Gaelic literature, tradition and history.[30] He composed song-poems 3.7 and 9.5.

Maps

These are the locations (a) where the authors of these texts lived, or (b) that are the subjects of these texts, or (c) were the homes of the subjects addressed by the texts.

Nova Scotia Mainland	Chapter
Antigonish:	6.2, 8.3, 9.5
Bailey's Brook:	6.12
Giant's Lake:	3.4
Glenbard:	3.7, 8.2
Halifax:	10.2
Highfield (Antigonish Co.):	3.1, 5.5, 6.4
Maryvale:	7.4
New Glasgow:	6.1
Pictou:	7.1, 7.2, 10.1
South River:	6.6
St. Andrews:	7.3
Upper South River:	10.3, 10.4

Cape Breton	5.7, 5.12
East Bay:	6.8
Ferguson Lake:	7.10
L' Ardoise Highlands:	8.8, 10.10
St. Andrew's Channel:	3.8
St. Ann's:	8.7
SW Margaree:	8.10
Upper Grand Mira:	5.8
Upper Margaree:	10.9
Whycocomagh:	7.11

Prince Edward Island	4.6, 5.7, 5.10

MAPS

Ontario   Chapter
    Bruce County: 10.5
    Hamilton: 6.10, 8.4
    Loch Huron: 8.1
    MacGillivray Township (North Middlesex): 6.5
    Middlesex: 7.5
    Oakville: 3.5
    Orilla: 6.9
    Ottawa: 10.6, 10.8
    Tiverton: 4.7
    Toronto: 8.5, 8.6, 9.1
    West Elgin: 7.7

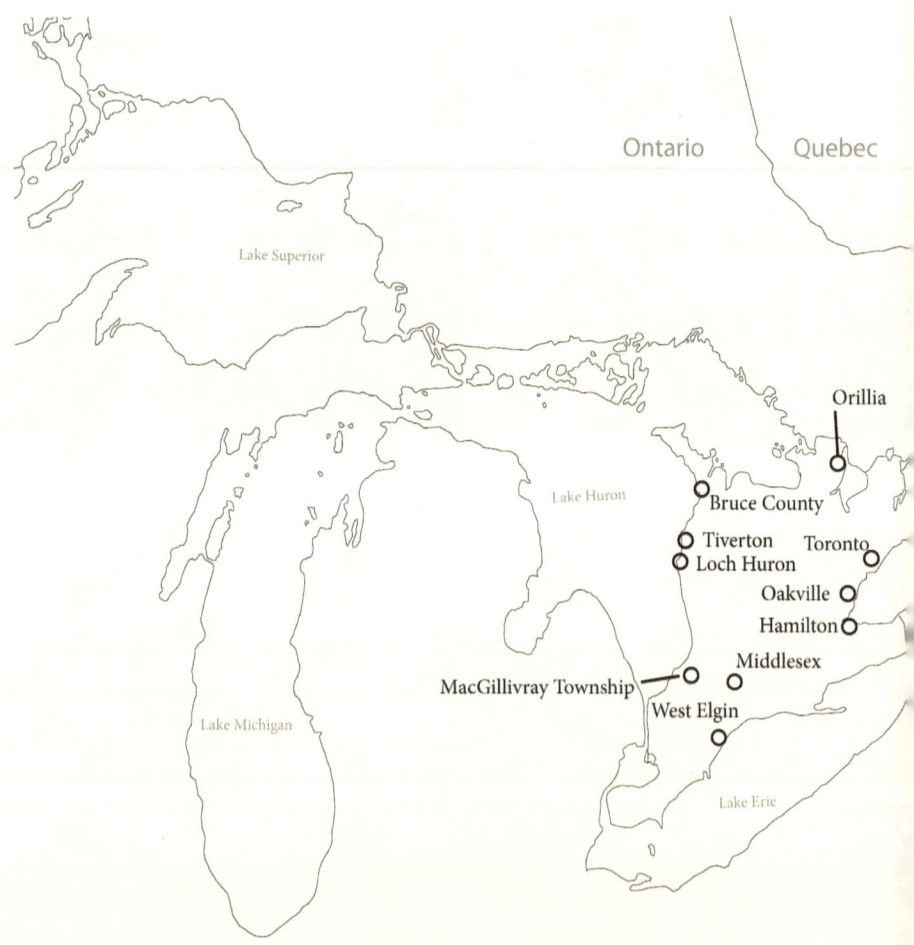

MAPS

Quebec	Chapter
Lennoxville:	6.13
Marston:	4.9
Megantic Township:	5.9
Montreal:	3.3, 7.6, 9.3
Red Mountain:	6.7
Springhill/Nantes:	5.15

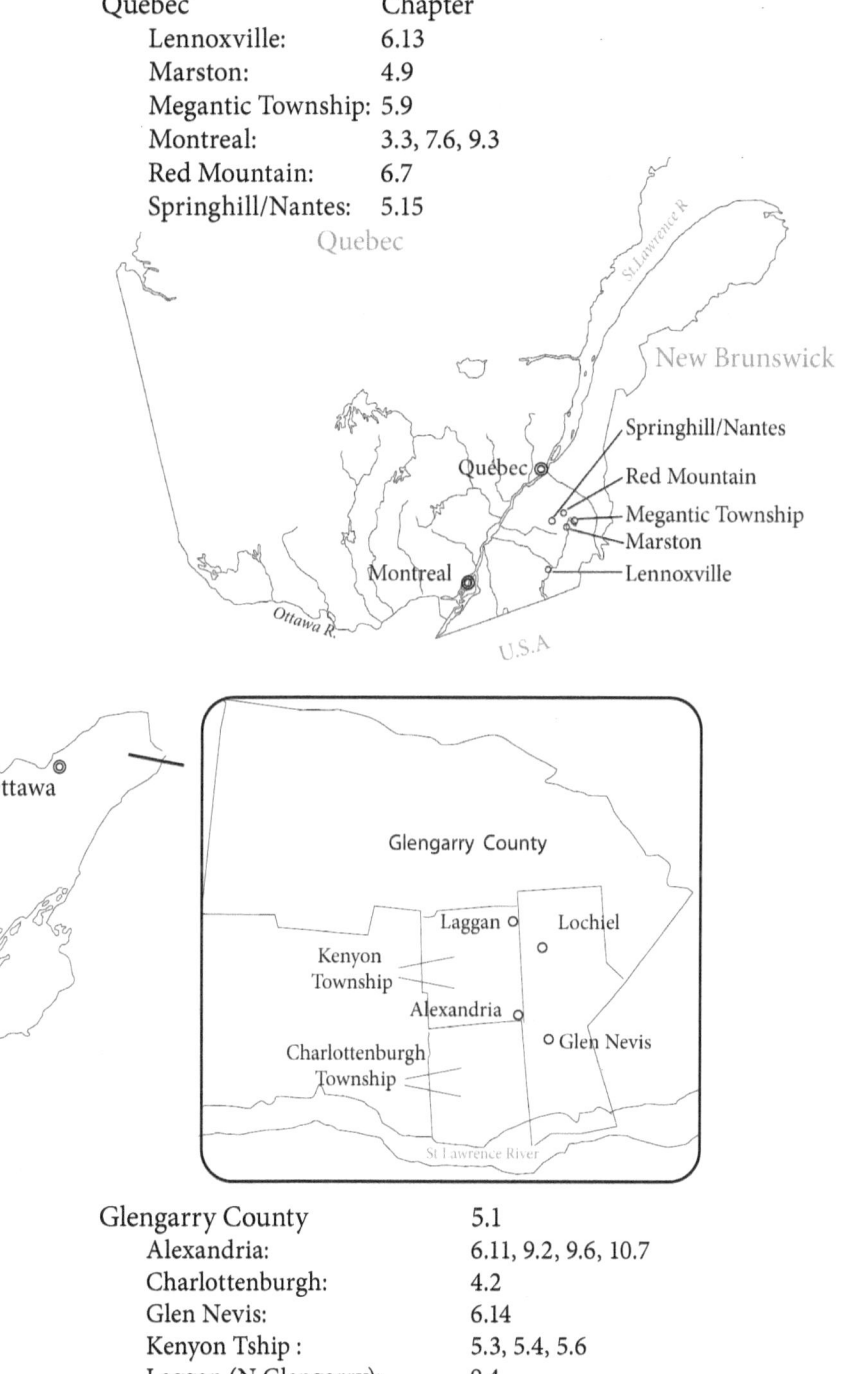

Glengarry County	5.1
Alexandria:	6.11, 9.2, 9.6, 10.7
Charlottenburgh:	4.2
Glen Nevis:	6.14
Kenyon Tship :	5.3, 5.4, 5.6
Laggan (N Glengarry):	9.4
Lochiel (N Glengarry):	3.6

SEANCHAIDH NA COILLE

	Chapter
British Columbia	
Vancouver:	7.8, 9.7
North-West Territories	2.5
Alberta	
Clandonald:	5.13

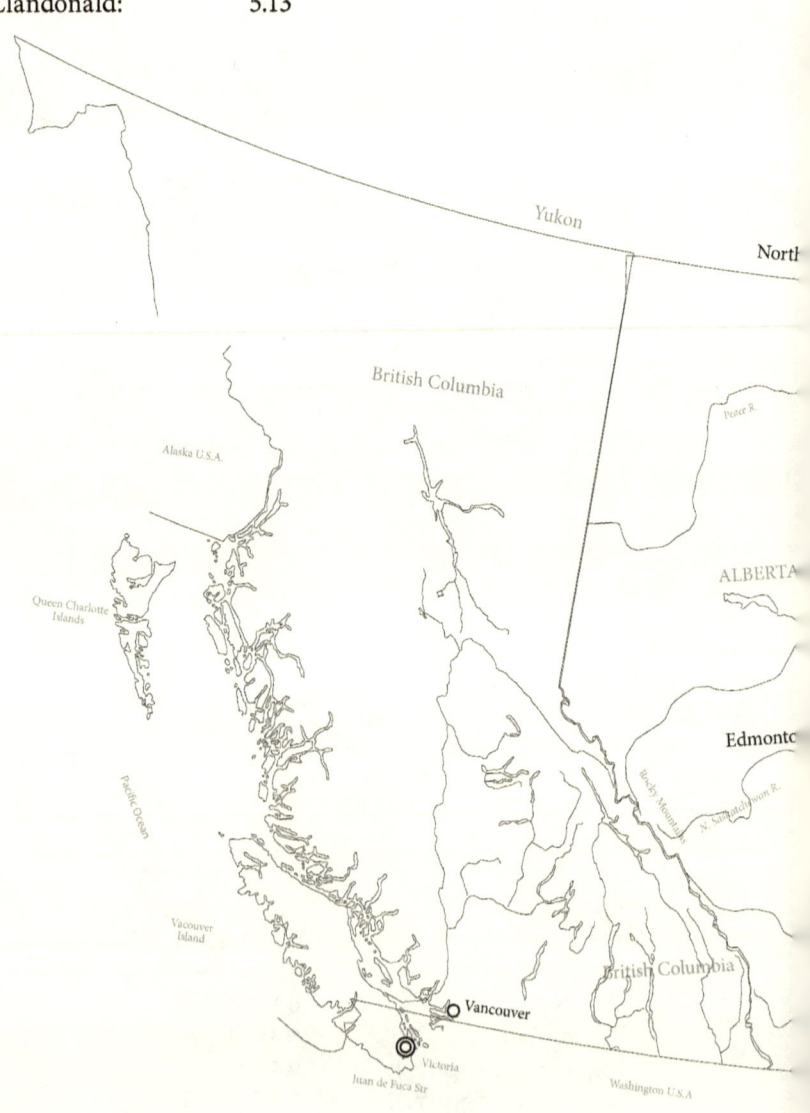

MAPS

Saskatchewan	Chapter
Moosimin:	8.9
Saltcoats:	5.10
Manitoba	
Lake Winnipeg:	7.9
St. Andrew's:	4.10
Winnipeg:	5.14

Notes

Notes to Foreword

1. It's fine. It's just pork/mutton meatloaf.

2. We live in Arizona.

3. Though every Lithuanian I spoke to was convinced that they're coming back.

Notes to Chapter 1

1. Dembling, "Gaelic in Canada."

2. Kennedy, *Gaelic Nova Scotia*, 28; Dunbar, "Understanding Canadian Multiculturalism."

3. Bitterman, "On Remembering," 257.

4. Newton, "How Scottish Highlanders Became White."

5. The term "Highlands" is the standard short-hand for the Gaelic-speaking area of the mainland—slightly more extended than the topographical upland territory—as well as the Western Isles.

6. MacGregor, "Gaelic Barbarity"; Newton, *Warriors of the Word*, 48-50, 59-79.

7. MacInnes, *Dùthchas nan Gàidheal*, 18-27, 31-47; Newton, *Warriors of the Word*, 44-46, 50-58, 67-76.

8. Grant, *Essays on the Superstitions*, 27-29.

9. Shaw, *Gaelic in Prince Edward Island*, 21.

10. Kemp, *The Beneficial Influence*, 3-4, 6, 7, 9-10, 11, 12.

11. Newton, "Scotland's Two Solitudes Abroad."

12. MacInnes, *Dùthchas nan Gàidheal*, 35-39; McLeod, *Divided Gaels*, 22-36; Newton, *Warriors of the Word*, 50-54; Stroh, *Uneasy Subjects*, 53-68.

13. From a photocopy of an unsourced Glengarry newspaper clipping given to me by Kenneth McKenna.

14. Meek, *Caran an t-Saoghail*, 405.

15. Ibid, 409.

16. MacKinnon, "Gaelic in the Bruce," 16.

17. Innes and Hillars, "A Mixed-Media Folklore Trove," 190-91.

18. Newton, Dunbar, Ó hAllmhurain and Williams, "Introduction."

19. Cregeen, *Recollections*, 108, 238.

20. Mac a' Phearsain and Linkletter, *Fògradh, Fàisneachd, Filidheachd*, 100-102.

21. Mann, *Margaret Macdonald*, xi.

22. Dunbar, "Understanding Canadian Multiculturalism"; Newton, "Bards of the Forests."

23. "Gaelic" does not appear at all in the index, but references to Gaelic exist on pages 8 and 39.

24. Mann, *Margaret Macdonald*, 4.

25. Kennedy, "Lochaber No More."

26. Newton, *Warriors of the Word*, 89-90; Ó Cathasaigh, "The literature of medieval Ireland," 13-14, 17-19.

27. Gillies, "Clan Donald Bards."

28. Friseal, *Leabhar nan Sonn*, 35.

29. Sinclair, "Gaelic in Nova Scotia," 254.

30. MacInnes, *Dùthchas nan Gàidheal*, 275.

31. This categorization is explained in Ross, "The Sub-Literary Tradition," 217-18.

32. Campbell and Collinson, *Hebridean Folksongs*, vol. 1, 19-20.

33. Shaw, "Observations on the Cape Breton Gàidhealtachd," 76.

34. An updated and revised edition can be found in MacInnes, *Dùthchas nan Gàidheal*, 265-319.

35. Black, *An Lasair*, xix.

36. Coira, *By Poetic Authority*, xi.

37. McLeod and Bateman, *Duanaire na Sracaire*, xxxvii.

38. Clancy, "Mourning Fearchar." There are at least two surviving poems composed in Antigonish County, Nova Scotia, that refer to Maol Ciarain.

39. Ní Annracháin, "Metaphor and Metonymy," 164-65, 172.

40. MacInnes, *Dùthchas nan Gàidheal*, 317. See also Stroh, *Uneasy Subjects*, 56-57, 80-83.

41. Dunbar, "The Emigrant Generation," 25.

42. Newton, *Warriors of the Word*, 311.

43. Meek, *Caran an t-Saoghail*, xxxi; MacInnes, *Dùthchas nan Gàidheal*, 172-74, 372-78; MacLeod, "The cianalas code," 67-72.

44. *Sydney Record*, April 23, 1921, 9.

45. Black, *An Lasair*, xi.

46. Ibid, xiii-xiv.

47. There are several quintessential descriptions of céilidhs, such as those in Newton, *Warriors of the Word*, 102-104. For a description of céilidhs in the Eastern Townships of Quebec, see Bennett, *Oatmeal and the Catechism*, 145-60.

48. MacKellar, "The Educational Power," 316.

49. Black, *An Lasair*, 410-11; MacInnes, *Dùthchas nan Gàidheal*, 116-17, 174; Newton, *Warriors of the Word*, 41, 103, 120-21, 359-61.

50. *Sydney Post-Record*, March 20, 1937, 11.

51. McMillan, "The First Settlers," 172.

52. Campbell, *Popular Tales*, vol. 1, 42, 17.

53. *Oban Times* August 17, 1901.

54. There is some discussion of this in Innes and Hillars, "A Mixed-Media Folklore Trove," 195.

55. University of Edinburgh, School of Scottish Archives, Original Track ID SA1970.292.A9.

56. Matheson and MacLeod, *Scottish Tradition*, Track 14.

57. Meek, "Gaelic Communities," 154.

58. Dunn, *Highland Settler*, 36.

59. Kennedy, *Gaelic Nova Scotia*, 42-53.

60. Meek, "Gaelic Communities," 169, 172.

61. MacGillivray, *The History of Antigonish*, 64.

62. Some of the texts in this volume were written down by the author and did not go through the "sifting process" of oral transmission, and thus may be more individualistic and idiosyncratic than those that were transcribed after circulation through community performance.

63. Black, "Gaelic Orthography," 253-54.

64. To be specific, I have retained the use of the apostrophes and the distinctions between the grave and acute accents. GOC essentially eliminates the use of the apostrophe on the basis that it causes confusion in English. This is a false premise that creates unnecessary ambiguities. Apostrophes are indeed inconsistent in English for historical reasons, but these cases do not apply to Gaelic, where they always and only represent elided vowels. The exclusion of apostrophes has resulted in the creation of ghost words that do not appear in dictionaries and can be very confusing to the learner. For example, if the three words "do mo athair" appear consecutively, they would be rendered in GOC as "dom athair." There is no word "dom" in the dictionaries. This is more logically rendered as "do m' athair."

Notes to Chapter 2

1. Newton, *Warriors of the Word*, 28-32, 66-69.

2. Hugh Cheape, Sabhal Mòr Ostaig, 2008, from an unpublished research paper.

3. Dodgshon, *From Chiefs*, 237-38; Newton, *Warriors of the Word*, 126-27, 144-45.

4. Newton, *We're Indians*, 70-73.

5. Campbell, *Travels*, 4.

6. Richards, *The Highland Clearances*, 77-89.

7. Walker, "Agents of Dispossession," 844, 846.

8. Mac a' Phì, *Am Measg nam Bodach*, 23-24.

9. Richards, "Scotland and the Uses," 109.

10. Quoted in Hunter, *The Making*, 64.

11. Quoted in Richards, "Scotland and the Uses," 110.

12. *Glengarrian*, October 11, 1895.

13. Meek, *Tuath is Tighearna*, 10. For further discussion, see Kennedy, "Lochaber no more," 275-81 and Hunter, *The Making*, 10-24.

14. Kennedy, "Lochaber no more," 276-77, 280.

15. Craig, *On the Crofters' Trail*, xv, xvi.

16. Dòmhnallach, "Whose Land is it Anyway?"

17. Rankin, *Às a' Bhràighe*, 11.

18. Campbell, *Songs Remembered in Exile*, 30, 218.

19. MacInnes, *Dùthchas nan Gàidheal*, 34-47; Newton, *Warriors of the Word*, 67-70.

20. Stewart and Stewart, *Cochruinneacha taoghta*, vol. 1, 90-93.

21. Matheson, *Òrain Iain mhic Fhearchair*, 290.

22. It was probably not until later that people assumed that the song was connected to the stratagem to remove Aonghus.

23. Macinnes, Harper and Fryer, *Scotland and the Americas*, 172.

24. Newton, *We're Indians*, 43-46; idem, *Warriors of the Word*, 58.

25. *Mosgladh*, 1.3 (Summer 1923): 60-62.

26. Richards, *The Highland Clearances*, 76, 123, 332.

27. MacLeod, *Òrain Dhonnchaidh Bhàin*, 346-49.

28. MacCoinnich, *Orain Ghaidhealach*, 103-109.

29. MacKenzie, *The History of the Highland Clearances*, 129.

30. Ibid, 128.

31. Meek, *Tuath is Tighearna*, 54-56.

32. *The Casket*, May 4, 1933, 8.

33. It was given the title "Cumha Gàidheil" when it appeared in print, though whether this was the title given by the author or editor is not stated.

34. Line missing in original source.

35. *The Casket*, January 6, 1927, 8.

Notes to Chapter 3

1. The use of tartan as a visual marker to symbolize a pan-Scottish identity rooted in the presumed archaisms of the Scottish Highlands.

2. Newton, *Warriors of the Word*, 141-45.

3. MacKillop, *More Fruitful*, 7, 8.

4. Ibid, 132.

5. Newton, "Jacobite Past, Loyalist Present."

6. Clyde, *From Rebel*, 175, 181; MacKillop, *More Fruitful*, 63, 75.

7. MacKillop, *More Fruitful*, 58-59, 236.

8. Dziennik, " 'Cutting heads'," 243.

9. MacKillop, *More Fruitful*, 44.

10. Devine, *The Scottish Nation*, 294.

11. Cameron, *The Clan Cameron*, 36.

12. MacKillop, *More Fruitful*, 226. See also Clyde, *From Rebel*, 163.

13. Clyde, *From Rebel*, 163; MacKillop, *More Fruitful*, 60-61.

14. Richards, "Scotland and the Uses," 84-85.

15. Dziennik, "Whig Tartan,"122.

16. Newton, "Paying for the Plaid."

17. MacInnes, *Còmhraidhean*, 31, 32, 33.

18. MacLeod, *Òrain Dhonnchaidh*, 512-14.

19. Newton, "Paying for the Plaid."

20. Shaw, "(E)migrating Legends," 54.

21. *The Casket*, February 5, 1914, 8.

22. *The Casket*, February 28, 1929, 8.

23. MacInnes, *Dùthchas nan Gàidheal*, 360, 362.

24. *The Casket*, March 2, 1939, 8. When it was printed in *Mosgladh*, 1.4 (1923-1924), it was stated as having been first printed in the February 1851 issue of *An Cuairtear Òg Gàidhealach* (of which no copies seem to survive) and was not given a title other than "Òran." Sinclair, *Clàrsach*, seems to be the earliest assignment of a title to the piece and the reprint of the text in *The Casket* may have simply followed Sinclair's designation.

25. Newton, *Warriors of the Word*, 200-201.

26. MacInnes, *Dùthchas nan Gàidheal*, 53.

27. Sinclair, *Clàrsach*, 314-16; *Mosgladh*, 1.4 (Winter 1923-1924): 36; *The Casket*, March 2, 1939, 8.

28. Nilsen, "Some Notes," 131.

29. *Cuairtear nan Coillte*, March 13, 1842, 3.

30. McKillop, *Temperance Odes*, 87-90.

31. Newton, *Warriors of the Word*, 56.

32. Original text: "sodhadh."

33. *The Casket*, August 5, 1920, 8.

34. *The Scottish Canadian*, July 2, 1891, 4.

35. By a man with the surname MacEalair; this was probably Gilleasbaig MacEalair of text 6.10.

36. Dembling, "Gaelic in Canada," 206-7.

37. *The Scottish Canadian*, July 9, 1891, 4.

38. Nilsen, "A' Ghàidhlig," 99, 106.

39. The memorial he mentions is probably the tablet commemorating the founding of the St. Columba Presbyterian Church at Kirkhill, which was erected in 1894 (see Harkness, *Stormont*, 122). It is possible that his speech, which was printed in 1896, was actually delivered in 1894. Alternatively, he may have delivered an annual commemoration speech at the site in 1896.

40. MacDonell, *Sketches*, 304.

41. Colley, *Britons*, 5.

42. Newton, *Warriors of the Word*, 1-4, 71-72.

43. *Glengarrian*, January 17, 1896.

44. Sinclair, *Gaelic Lessons*, 59.

45. *Sydney Post-Record*, September 4, 1935, 9.

46. *The Casket*, February 14, 1924, 8.

Notes to Chapter 4

1. MacLean, *The People*, 113.

2. Harper, *Adventurers*, 201-202.

3. MacDonald, *Gesto Collection*, 113.

4. MacKenzie, *Highland Clearances*, 266.

5. Mac a' Phearsain and Linkletter, *Fògradh*, 152-55.

6. Gibson, *Traditional Gaelic Bagpiping*, 170-71.

7. MacDonell, *Emigrant*, 11-12.

8. Devine, "The Flight," 647-48, 657.

9. Newton, *Warriors of the Word*, 41-42, 73-79.

10. Hunter, *A Dance*, 204-209.

11. *The Scottish-Canadian*, February 25, 1892.

12. *The Scottish-Canadian*, March 10, 1892.

13. Hunter, *The Making*, 223.

14. Hunter, *A Dance*, 215-17.

15. Hunter, *The Making*, 278-79.

16. MacDonell, *Emigrant Experience*, 131.

17. Ibid, 134-37.

18. Bueno, *Brasil*, 36.

19. *The Casket*, April 27, 1893.

20. McLean, *The People*, 112-16.

21. Newton, *Warriors of the Word*, 304-308.

22. From a photocopy of an unsourced newspaper clipping I received from Kenneth MacKenna; also found in the collection of Gaelic poems made by James McCrimmon in Archives of Ontario F775, R272786, MU2136 File 1939.

23. MacKay, *Urquhart and Glenmoriston*, 571.

24. Sinclair, *Reminiscences, historical and traditional*, 53.

25. *The Casket*, October 18, 1934, 8.

26. The Reverend Dr. Alasdair MacGill-Eain Sinclair probably transcribed Dòmhnall Donn's song from Ailean or his son for one of his books of Gaelic poetry. See Campbell, *Songs Remembered in Exile*, 209, 212.

27. Sinclair, *The Gaelic Bards*, 117.

28. MacInnes, *Dùthchas nan Gàidheal*, 236-37, 240, 274.

29. Watson, *Bardachd*, line 6810.

30. Although this is the only example of this usage of which I am aware.

31. It is likely that the place referred to as "Làirig" is Làirig Leacach in Lochaber, on the path between Loch Tréig and Coire Choingligh. See Livingstone, "Lochaber Place Names," 267-68.

32. St. Francis Xavier University Library, Ridge Manuscripts, vol. 1: 192-94; Rankin, *Às a' Bhràighe*, 74-76.

33. Harper, *Adventurers*, 112.

34. Ibid, 122.

35. Dunn, *Highland Settler*, 31-32.

36. MacDonald and MacDonald, *MacDonald Collection*, 370.

37. Thanks to Michael Kennedy for providing the information that led me to this conclusion.

38. *Mac-Talla*, 7.46 (June 16, 1899): 1.

39. Original: "dà dhollar an acair air a shon."

40. *The Scottish Canadian*, July 1903, 205-207.

41. MacDhùghaill, *Ceann-Iùil*, 6-7, 17-19.

42. Bennett, *Oatmeal*, 8-24. For another song-poem on the Gabhsainn migration in 1863, see MacDonald, *Gesto Collection*, 40.

43. *Stornoway Gazette*, May 10, 1963

44. Bartlett, *The First World War*, 45-46.

45. *Stornoway Gazette*, May 10, 1963; Bartlett, *The First World War*, 43-45.

46. MacDonell, *Emigrant Experience*, 149-50.

47. MacKinnon, A short history, 12.

48. *The Scottish Highlander*, February 28, 1889.

49. His hand-written notes for the booklet are among his manuscripts in the Archives of Ontario, F1015 – MU 1089, Envelope 4.

50. La Bhruinn, *Machraichean Móra Chanada*, 4-5, 7, 15, 18-19, 36-37, 52, 55.

Notes on Chapter 5

1. Dunbar, "The Poetry of the Emigrant Generation," 25.

2. Kennedy, "'Lochaber no more'," 280-82.

3. *Sydney Record*, November 6, 1920, 9.

4. Newton, "Coille Mhòr Chailleann."

5. MacDhùghaill, *Ceann-Iùil*, 45.

6. *Mosgladh* 3.3 (January 1931): 1.

7. Newton, "'Going to the Land'," 237-38.

8. Newton, "The Macs meet the 'Micmacs'," 82, 85, 91, 93.

9. Newton, "Unsettling," 159, 160, 162.

10. Newton, *Warriors of the Word*, 237-42, 290-91; idem., "The Caledonian Forest."

11. Newton, "Celtic Cousins."

12. Archives of Ontario File 1939, "Misc. Collection of Gaelic Poems by James McCrimmon."

13. Friseal, *Leabhar nan Sonn*, 86.

14. Alexander MacLennan has suggested to me that this line may refer to the hunter lying prone on the ground, in hiding, while hunting deer, which contrasted with the older method of killing deer in the Highlands.

15. Mac-Ille-Mhaoil, *Òrain*, 12-13.

16. Caimbeul, *Nuadh Òrain Ghailach*, 101.

17. Innes and Hillers, "A Mixed-Media," 190.

18. Archives of Ontario, Alexander Fraser papers (F1015 – MU 1089).

19. MacGillivray, *History of Antigonish*, 117.

20. Black, *An Lasair*, 476.

21. *An Cuairtear Òg Gàidhealach* 1.5 (March 1851): 43.

22. Dunbar, "The Poetry of the Emigrant Generation," 46-47.

23. *Mac-Talla* 3.34 (February 23, 1895): 8.

24. *Fear-Tathaich nam Beann* 6 (June 1848): 176-80; 8 (August 1848): 231-41.

25. *An Solus Iùil*, 1.7 (June 1926): 53.

26. *The Casket*, July 4, 1935, 8.

27. The original text is "Oil-thaigh Mhorin." I have interpreted "Morin" as an irregular spelling of the Gaelic diminutive form of "Mary" and thus assume that this refers to Collège Sainte-Marie in Montreal.

28. *The Scottish Canadian*, November 13, 1890, 5.

29. Harper, *Emigration from Scotland*, 103; Bueltmann, Hinson and Mortin, *The Scottish Diaspora*, 85.

30. *Sydney Post-Record*, April 28, 1937, 7.

31. *Mac-Talla* 2.5 (July 29, 1893): 3.

32. MacFhionghain, "Na Gàidheil."

33. R. A. MacDonell, "British Immigration Schemes"; Harper, *Emigration from Scotland*, 101-108; *Inverness Courier*, September 8, 2009.

34. Harper, *Emigration from Scotland*, 106.

35. Newton, *Warriors of the Word*, 141-45.

36. Campbell, *Popular Tales*, vol. 1, 15-16.

37. Mackay, "Am Breadabair agus an Gille Glas"; Campbell, *More West Highland Tales*, 394-409.

38. *The Casket*, February 14, 1929, 8.

39. Hunter, *A Dance*, 172-93.

40. Ibid, 194.

41. Campey, *An Unstoppable Force*, 106-10.

42. Harper, *Emigration from Scotland*, 100.

43. There is something corrupt about the original text which reads "mu thuairean leith."

44. *Sydney Post-Record*, January 12, 1938, 12.

45. *Clachan Crìche*, 14.

46. Ibid, 14-16.

Notes on Chapter 6

1. MacInnes, *Dùthchas nan Gàidheal*, 281.

2. Dunbar, "Poets of the Emigrant Generation," 86, 87.

3. MacInnes, *Dùthchas nan Gàidheal*, 265.

4. Dunn, *Highland Settler*, 70.

5. Black, *An Lasair*, xx.

6. Newton, *Warriors of the Word*, 181-85.

7. Ó Baoill and Bateman, *Gàir nan Clàrsach*, 54-59.

8. MacPhie, *Pictonians*, 37; Patterson, *A History*, 123, 465.

9. Patterson, *Memoirs*, 103.

10. Ibid, 104.

11. *Mac-Talla nan Tùr*, 65-67; *Mac-Talla* 9.35 (March 1, 1901): 272. The song is normally performed in overlapping couplets (1-4, 3-6, 5-8, etc.), but I have grouped these together into quatrains to simplify its presentation.

12. Johnston, *A History*, vol. 1, 431.

13. Ibid, 518.

14. Nilsen, "The Priest in the Gaelic Folklore," 180-85.

15. Johnston, *A History*, vol. 1, 437.

16. *Mosgladh*, 4.18 (April 1932): 5.

17. Campbell and Collinson, *Hebridean Folksongs*, 21.

18. *Cuairtear nan Coillte*, April 5, 1842, 5.

19. No air has yet been identified by this name (see Rankin, *Às a' Bhràighe*, 152, 187), although the name of at least one bagpipe tune ("Cumha Mhorair Chlann Dòmhnaill") comes close.

20. Shears, *Dance to the Piper*, 61-62.

21. Dunn, *Highland Settler*, 75-77.

22. Nilsen, "Some Notes," 133-34.

23. The original Gaelic text of this hymn was later published in *The Casket* April 9, 1939, 8.

24. *The Casket*, May 3, 1860.

25. *History of the County of Middlesex*, 36.

26. McCoinnich, *Oranean*, 6-8.

27. *The Casket*, October 30, 1913, 8.

28. MacKay, *Oscar and Finlay*, 241.

29. *The Weekly Examiner* (Sherbrooke, Quebec), April 15, 1887. My edition has benefited from McKay, *Oscar and Finlay*, 254-55.

30. Black, *An Lasair*, 54-59.

31. Johnston, *A History*, vol. 2, 88, 96, 118.

32. Black, *The Gaelic Otherworld*, 3, 294, 407, 701, 732.

33. *The Casket* November 1, 1928, 8.

34. Campey, *The Scottish Pioneers*, 104, 108.

35. From a photocopy of an unsourced newspaper clipping given to me by the late Kenneth McKenna which had an illegible date in the 1890s.

36. Friseal, *Leabhar nan Sonn*, 71.

37. *Mac-Talla* 2.41 (May 5, 1894): 1.

38. Ibid, 8.

39. Newton, *Warriors of the Word*, 52.

40. The community of Elphin in the Lanark Highlands of Ontario seems like a good candidate, except that it is some 160 kilometres to the west, and not the north, of Alexandria.

41. From a photocopy of an unsourced newspaper clipping given to me by the late Kenneth McKenna.

42. Mann, *Margaret Macdonald*, 10-11.

43. Ibid, 12.

44. Ibid, 41-42.

45. Dennis, *More About Nova Scotia*, 205.

46. *The Casket*, February 7, 1901, 8.

47. MacDonell, *Emigrant Experience*, 92-95.

48. MacÌomhair, *Òrain Ghailig*, 3-4.

49. This metre came to be commonly referred to as "strophic" in the early 20th century, but following the work of William Matheson, John MacInnes, Roibeard Ó Maolalaigh, and others, I accept the identification of this metre as iorram. See Newton, *Warriors of the Word*, 113.

50. *Alexandria News*, September 11, 1908, 4. A photocopy of this page was given to me by the late Kenneth McKenna.

Notes to Chapter 7

1. Pestana, *Protestant Empire*, 6.

2. Ibid, 16, 30.

3. MacLean and Dorgan, *An Leabhar Mór*, 118.

4. Newton, *Warriors of the Word*, 28-30, 65-66.

5. McIntosh, *Island Spirituality*, 41.

6. Ibid, 49.

7. MacInnes, *Dùthchas nan Gàidheal*, 364-72, 440; Newton, *Warriors of the Word*, 39-40; Stroh, *Uneasy Subjects*, 201-11; McIntosh, *Island Spirituality*, 51-54.

8. MacInnes, *Dùthchas nan Gàidheal*, 440.

9. Ibid, 370.

10. Phillips, *The Cousins' Wars*, xv, xxii-iii.

11. Meek, "Scottish Highlanders, North American Indians."

12. Meek, "Craobh-Sgaoileadh a' Bhìobaill," 144.

13. Kennedy, *The Days of the Fathers*, 1, 2.

14. For some Scottish Gaelic examples, see Dunbar, "The Poetry of the Emigrant Generation," 42-43.

15. Juster and Gregerson. "Introduction," 4-5.

16. Mac a' Phearsain and Linkletter, *Fògradh, Fàisneachd agus Filidheachd*, 190, 191, 192, 193, 195, 196, 199.

17. Dunn, *Highland Settler*, 92, 93.

18. Kennedy, *Gaelic Nova Scotia*, 123-28.

19. Patterson, *Memoir*, 257-58.

20. Quoted in Dunn, *Highland Settlers*, 100.

21. Quoted in Nilsen, "A' Ghàidhlig," 99.

22. Innes and Hillers, "A Mixed-Media Folklore Trove," 199.

23. Sinclair, *Dàin Spioradal*, 146.

24. MacGregor, *Dàin a chomh[n]adh crabhuidh*, 88.

25. My edition has benefited from the previous work on this poem in Meek, "Craobh-Sgaoileadh."

26. MacLeod, *Òrain Dhonnchaidh Bhàin*, 238-43.

27. Meek, "Craobh-Sgaoileadh," 143.

28. Ibid, 162.

29. MacGriogair, *Dàin a chòmh[n]adh cràbhaidh*, 103-10.

30. Johnston, *A History of the Catholic Church*, vol. 2, 141-42, 217, 232-33.

31. Mac Dhomnuill 'ic Eoghain, "Duthaich an Aigh," 204-205.

32. Mac na Ceàrdadh, *An t-Òranaiche*, 454-55.

33. Original text: "Le choim–na uachdraran."

34. Original text: "meanabhag."

35. *The Casket*, May 26, 1853. The original text has a number of mistakes and irregularities that make this edition and translation speculative in places.

36. This seems to refer to the nicknames of priests based on ancestral origins. I have not identified the individuals referred to.

37. *The Casket*, October 8, 1857.

38. McColl, *Some Sketches*, 14-15.

39. MacKay, *Pioneer Life in Zorra*, 276, 277, 278-79.

40. Archives of the Presbyterian Church in Canada: http://www.presbyterian-archives.ca/FA4000N.pdf (accessed December 30, 2014).

41. McCoinnich, *Oranean*, 1-6.

42. *The Scottish-American Journal*, October 2, 1884, 8.

43. Mac na Ceàrdadh, *An t-Òranaiche*, 39.

44. Mitsheall, *Drùchd nam Beann*, 57-61.

45. *Mil nan Dàn*, 105-108.

46. *An Solus Iùil*, 1.7 (June 1926): 54-55.

47. *An Solus Iùil*, 1.1 (August 1925): 1.

48. Bennett, *Oatmeal and the Catechism*, 139-41.

49. Campbell, *Songs Remembered*, 11.

50. Murray, *The History*, 117.

51. Morrison, *Òrain Fuinn*, 50-54.

52. Newton, *Warriors of the Word*, 303-308.

53. *An Solus Iùil*, 1.9 (September 1926): 65.

Notes to Chapter 8

1. Newton, *Warriors of the Word*, 52-55, 67-69; McLeod, "Language Politics"; Stroh, *Uneasy Subjects*, 140-46.

2. Smith, *Towards the Human*, 37.

3. Thomas, *The Welsh Extremist*, 26, 29, 30.

4. Quoted in Bumstead, "The Cultural Landscape," 389.

5. Dembling, "Gaelic in Canada," 209.

6. MacGregor, *Historical and Descriptive Sketches*, 70.

7. *The Highlander*, November 21, 1879.

8. *Mac-Talla*, 3.36 (March 9, 1895): 4.

9. Dòmhnallach, "An Iomlaid Amaideach," 1, 2.

10. *The Scottish-American Journal*, March 31, 1905.

11. McLeod, "Language Politics"; Stroh, *Uneasy Subjects*, 140-46.

12. *Fear na Céilidh*, 2.2 (September 1929): 12.

13. Newton, "'Becoming Cold-Hearted,'" 112-14.

14. *Mac-Talla*, 11.22 (May 1, 1903): 172-73.

15. Nilsen, "Some Notes," 131.

16. Newton, "'Becoming Cold-Hearted,'" 89-91.

17. Ó Baoill and Bateman, *Gàir nan Clàrsach*, 198-207.

18. McLeod and Bateman, *Duanaire na Sracaire*, 44-47.

19. *The Scottish-American Journal*, June 4, 1902, 5.

20. *The Scottish-American Journal*, July 21, 1909, 8.

21. Newton, "'Becoming Cold-Hearted'," 72, 87-88.

22. *Mosgladh*, 4.25 (November 1932): 4.

23. Sinclair, *Gaelic Lessons*, 66-72.

24. Dunbar, "Understanding Canadian Multiculturalism," 120.

25. Ibid, 141.

26. Sinclair, "Gaelic in Nova Scotia," 258.

27. Kennedy, *Gaelic Nova Scotia*, 31-39, 50-53.

28. Ibid, 58-59.

29. *Mosgladh*, 1.1 (Spring 1922): 44.

30. *Sydney Post-Record*, March 1, 1939, 7.

31. Cox, "Gaelic and the Schools," 36.

32. MacLennan, "The Early Settlement," 120.

33. Born in 1841 on the Isle of Arran, Scotland; served in the assembly 1875 to 1878.

34. *The Scottish-American Journal*, April 26, 1877, 3.

35. MacKinnon, "Gaelic in the Bruce," 14-15.

36. Nettle and Romaine, *Vanishing Voices*, 141.

37. Friseal, *Leabhar nan Sonn*, 99-100.

38. Sinclair, *Clàrsach na Coille*, 166.

39. Ibid, 163-66.

40. Nilsen, "Some Notes," 133-35.

41. *An Cuairtear Òg Gàidhealach*, 1.4 (April 1851): 65.

42. McLeod, "Language Politics," 112.

43. This was originally printed in *The Canadian Scotsman* in 1882, although I have used the text as reprinted in *Sydney Record*, May 28, 1921, 9.

44. Friseal, *Leabhar nan Sonn*, 35, 37-38, 48-50.

45. *The Scottish Canadian*, July 23, 1891, 4.

46. It should be noted that it was normal for people to share beds in old Highland houses and that there was not necessarily any erotic overtones to such experiences.

47. Bailey, "Chicago World's Fair."

48. Dunn, *Highland Settlers*, 132-34; Bennett, *Oatmeal and the Catechism*, 279-84; McLeod, "Language Politics," 126-30.

49. *Mac-Talla*, 11.12 (December 12, 1902): 96.

50. *Sydney Record*, November 20, 1920, 9.

51. MacKinnon, *A short history*, 6-7, 6, 11, 2.

52. Black, *The Gaelic Otherworld*, 558.

53. *Teachdaire nan Gàidheal* 1.4 (April 15, 1925): 8; *Sydney Post-Record*, August 10, 1935, 12.

54. *Mosgladh*, December 1933, 5; MacDhùghaill, *Smeòrach nan Cnoc*, 98-99.

Notes to Chapter 9

1. Newton, *Warriors of the Word*, 44-79.

2. Newton, "Scotland's Two Solitudes," passim.

3. *An Solus Iùil*, 1.10 (November 1926): 77.

4. Sinclair, *Gaelic Lessons*, 46.

5. Sullivan, "Scots by Association," 48.

6. Strang, *Glasgow and its Clubs*, 106-23.

7. McCullough, " 'For the Good and Glory,'" 204.

8. Newton, "Becoming Cold-Hearted," 98-107.

9. McCullough, " 'For the Good and Glory,'" 201, 206, 208.

10. Stroh, *Uneasy Subjects*, 181-89.

11. Newton, "Paying for the Plaid," 66.

12. MacLeod, *Òrain Dhonnchaidh Bhàin*, 512.

13. Fairney, "The Branch Societies," 69.

14. MacLeod, *Òrain Dhonnchaidh Bhàin*, 514.

15. See, for example, Gibson, *Traditional Gaelic Bagpiping*; Kennedy, *Gaelic Nova Scotia*, 157-76.

16. Newton, "Paying for the Plaid," 69.

17. Fairney, "The Branch Societies," 73.

18. Rules of the Highland Society.

19. The exact identity of this group is something of a mystery, given that 1858 is twenty years before other sources indicate that Comunn Gàidhlig Thoronto was founded. It may be that this was a short-lived society that was resurrected later or that this was an association with another name in English that the Gaelic source has obscured.

20. A handbill in the Alexander Fraser papers (F1015 – MU1091) in the Archives of Ontario. This statement was also sent to the Scottish newspaper *The Highlander* and was printed in their March 30, 1881 issue.

21. *The Canadian-American Gael* 1 (1943-1944): 25.

22. *Sydney Post-Record*, October 27, 1937, 10.

23. *Oban Times*, February 20, 1909.

24. *Vancouver Daily World*, December 14, 1910, 21.

25. *Sydney Post Record*, November 24, 1934, 9.

26. *Mac-Talla*, 2.8 (19 August 1893): 5.

27. MacDhùghaill, *Smeòrach nan Cnoc*, 24

28. McLeod, "Language Politics," 98-102.

29. MacDhùghaill, *Smeòrach nan Cnoc*, 88.

30. Bitterman, "On Remembering," 259-60.

31. From Annual Report: Review of the Work for the Year 1887-88.

32. Dòmhnallach, "Cor na Gàidhlig," 118; Alexander Fraser papers (F1015 – MU1091) in the Archives of Ontario.

33. *Teachdaire nan Gàidheal* 2.2 (April 1926): 3; *The Canadian-American Gael* 1 (1943): 20.

34. *Mac-Talla*, 6.35 (February 25, 1898): 273.

35. Newton, *Warriors of the Word*, 267.

36. *An Gàidheal* 1 (1872): 186; *Glengarrian* August 13, 1897.

37. MacInnes, *Dùthchas nan Gàidheal*, 275-76.

38. Newton, *Warriors of the Word*, 148-54.

39. Ibid, 48-50.

40. *An Gàidheal* has "bho 's leith"; the newspaper clipping seems to read "fos leatha."

41. *An Gàidheal* 1 (1871): 53-54; also on a photocopy of an unsourced Glengarry newspaper clipping given to me by Kenneth McKenna.

42. Crouse, "The establishment," 24.

43. Constitution and By-Laws: 33-34.

44. Constitution and By-Laws: 36.

45. It is possible that this correspondent was the son of the poet Alasdair MacGilleMhaoil whose poems appear in this volume.

46. *Mac-Talla*, 2.5 (July 29, 1893): 3.

47. Linkletter, *Bu Dual Dha*, 177-82.

48. Dunn, *Highland Settler*, 119, 127, 132-33.

49. *The Casket*, December 14, 1899, 8; *Mac-Talla* 8.23 (December 15, 1899): 184.

50. Probably Eóghann MacLachlainn (Ewen MacLachlan c.1775–1822).

51. I am unsure of the proper Gaelic form of this place name: Inbhir Aoidh (Inverie) in Knoydart is probably intended.

52. From a photocopy of an unsourced newspaper clipping given to me by Kenneth McKenna.

53. Newton, " 'Did You Hear,'" 93-95.

54. Black, *An Lasair*, 412-23.

55. Smith, *Towards the Human*, 24, 25.

56. *Sydney Post-Record*, January 14, 1939, 11; my transcription of an audio recording made by Sidney Robertson Cowell of Iain Cuineagan in Berkeley, California in 1940 (now in the Library of Congress and available online in the California Gold collection).

Notes to Chapter 10

1. The information in this paragraph and the following two is largely taken from *A History of the Vote in Canada*, chapter 1.

2. Dunbar, "The Poetry of the Emigrant Generation," 106.

3. McColl, *Some sketches*, 19-20.

4. MacKay, *Pioneer Life in Zorra*, 140, 141.

5. Matheson and Matheson, *O Cheapaibh nan Craobh*, 7, 8.

6. *Mac-Talla*, 4.42 (April 25, 1896): 8.

7. Ó Baoill and Bateman, *Gàir nan Clàrsach*, 120-23.

8. Creighton and MacLeod, *Gaelic Songs*, 209.

9. *Mac-Talla*, 2.41 (May 5, 1894): 1.

10. Phillips, *The Cousins' Wars*, 597.

11. The silent subsumption of Gaelic identity under the "British" rubric, and the assumption that British implies "anglophone" in Canadian multiculturalism, is discussed in Dunbar, "Understanding Canadian Multiculturalism."

12. Dunbar, "The Poetry of the Emigrant Generation," 106.

13. Ibid, 107.

14. Sinclair, *Clàrsach*, 142-45. My edition has also benefited from the work in Dunbar, *The Poetry of John Maclean*.

15. Quoted in Kennedy, *Gaelic Nova Scotia*, 50.

16. *Sydney Post-Record*, May 8, 1920, 9; Sinclair, *Gaelic Lessons*, 54.

17. P. B. Waite, "Thompson, Sir John Sparrow David," in Dictionary of Canadian Biography, vol. 12, University of Toronto/Université Laval, 2003,

http://www.biographi.ca/en/bio/thompson_john_sparrow_david_12E.html (accessed January 13, 2015).

18. Campbell, *Highland Songs of the 'Forty-Five*, 132-37.

19. I have interpreted the ethnonym "Iùdhaich" (Jews) as a derogatory term implying betrayal, given that there were no people of Jewish ancestry actually living in the area at the time.

20. St. Francis Xavier University, Ridge Manuscripts, vol. 1: 221-3.

21. MacGilleMhaoil was born in St. Andrews, Antigonish County. Thanks to Jocelyn Gillis of the Antigonish Heritage Museum for identifying all of the people who appear in this cryptic poem and enabling me to interpret it.

22. Howell, "W. S. Fielding and the Repeal Elections."

23. St. Francis Xavier University, Ridge Manuscripts, vol. 1: 170-75.

24. Debates of the Senate, 298; *Mosgladh*, 1.4 (1923-1924): 19.

25. Kennedy, *Gaelic Nova Scotia*, 36-37.

26. People of European ancestry, anyway. There is little acknowledgement of the First Nations of Canada or their languages.

27. A form of his original Gaelic speech is printed in Debates of the Senate, 302-303. It appears to have been transcribed from hand-written notes by someone who did not have any knowledge of Gaelic. An attempt to make a Gaelic edition of it was printed in *Mosgladh* 1 (1923-4): 17-18, but the results are not entirely satisfactory or complete. I have made an attempt to improve the transcription and edition.

28. MacGillivray, *Dictionary of Glengarry Biography*, 528.

29. From a photocopy of an unsourced newspaper clipping given to me by Kenneth McKenna.

30. Brown, *The Illustrated History*, 420-23.

31. Angus, *Canadian Bolsheviks*, 25.

32. Ibid, 27, 30.

33. Fisher, *The Glasgow Encyclopedia*, 277.

34. Camshron, *Na Baird Thirisdeach*, 289.

35. Archives of Ontario, Fraser Fonds (F1015 – MU 1090, envelope 1); Camshron, *Na Baird Thirisdeach*, 292-94.

36. MacDhùghaill, *Smeòrach nan Cnoc*, 54-55.

37. Brown, *The Illustrated History of Canada*, 433-35.

38. *The Casket*, September 14, 1925, 8.

Notes from Conclusions

1. Black, *An Tuil*, 729.
2. Harper, "Stephen Harper reflects on."
3. Toom, "John A. Macdonald."
4. Daschuk, *Clearing the Plains*.
5. Stanley, "John A. Macdonald's Aryan Canada."
6. Parsons, *The Rule of Empires*, 447.
7. Bailyn and Morgan, "Introduction," 11-14.
8. Phillips, *The Cousins' Wars*, 579.
9. See, for example, Black, *An Lasair*, 36-37, 40-41, 44-45, 48-49, 52-53, 60-61, 88-89.
10. Fraser, "The Gael in Canada," 211.
11. Colley, *Britons*, 5.
12. At least those who did not also have non-European ancestry. There is a significant amount of Scottish Gaelic ancestry among Canada's First Nations.
13. Smith, *Towards the Human*, 49, 50.
14. Sullivan, "Scots by Association," 51.
15. *Mosgladh*, 1.1 (Spring 1922): 17.
16. Mac a' Phearsain and Linkletter, *Fògradh, Fàisneachd, Filidheachd*, 210, 211.
17. Smith, *Decolonizing Methodologies*, 29, 34.

Notes to Biographies

1. Mac a' Phearsain and Linkletter, *Fògradh, Fàisneachd, Filidheachd*, 18-27.
2. *Mosgladh* 4.18 (April 1932): 6.
3. *The Celtic Monthly* 20 (1912): 1-2.
4. Sinclair, *Reminiscences, historical and traditional*, 51-2.
5. Thanks to William Lawson at Seallam! of Harris for information that supplements that of *Stornoway Gazette,* May 10, 1963.
6. McColl, *Some sketches of the early highland pioneers*, 56.
7. Black, *An Lasair*, 499-500.
8. Rankin, *Às a' Bhràigh*, 7-37.
9. Camshron, *Na Baird Thirisdeach*, 289-90.
10. Màrtainn, *Clachan Crìche*, 10-18.

11. MacDhùghaill, *The Emigrant's Guide*, 134-37.

12. *Fear na Céilidh,* 1.8 (October 1928): 59; MacLeòid, *Bàrdachd*, 50.

13. MacKillop, *Collected Verse*, iv-v.

14. *The Scottish-American Journal* April 18, 1894, 8.

15. http://www.historicplaces.ca/en/rep-reg/place-lieu.aspx?id=11015 (accessed July 16, 2014).

16. MacKinnon, *A short history*, 18.

17. *The Casket,* February 3, 1944, 8; *An Gàidheal,* May 1944.

18. MacKinnon, *A short history*, 18.

19. Sinclair, *Clàrsach na Coille*, xiii-xx.

20. Dunbar, "The Poetry," 27-8, 30; Shears, *Dance*, 61-62.

21. Gillies, *The Collected Works*, 192-4.

22. MacÌomhair, *Òrain Ghàilig*; McKay, *Oscar and Finlay*, 84.

23. *Mac-Talla*, 4.43 (May 2, 1896): 8; *The Casket*, January 13, 1927, 8; *Fear na Céilidh* 1.7 (September 1928): 56; MacLeòid, *Bàrdachd*, 60.

24. Nilsen, "A' Ghàidhlig," 99, 106. Some notes about him and his effort to establish the teaching of Gaelic as a regular course at the college appear in *Mac-Talla*, 4.47 (May 30, 1896): 1.

25. Nilsen, "P. J. Nicholson," 315.

26. McKay, *Oscar and Finlay*, 241.

27. Clark, *Selections from Scottish Canadian Poets*, 96.

28. Moireasdain, *Òrain Fuinn*, 7.

29. Information relayed to me by Dr. Sister Margaret MacDonell, given to her by J. R. Mcgillis, Edmonton, Alberta and L. T. Welch, Cornwall, Ontario.

30. Linkletter, *Bu Dual Dha*.

References

ANGUS, IAN. *Canadian Bolsheviks: The Early Years of the Communist Party of Canada*, 2nd ed. Bloomington, IN: Trafford Publishing, 2004 [1981].

BAILEY, KATHRYN. "Chicago World's Fair." http://digitalresearch.lib.unc.edu/exhibits/show/chicagoworldexpo/chicago-world-s-fair-essay/essay (accessed January 7, 2015).

BAILYN, BERNARD AND PHILIP MORGAN. "Introduction." In *Strangers within the Realm: Cultural Margins of the First British Empire*, 1-31. Chapel Hill: University of North Carolina Press, 1991.

BARTLETT, NIALL SOMHAIRLE FINLAYSON. "The First World War and the 20th Century in the History of Gaelic Scotland: A Preliminary Analysis." Masters Thesis, University of Glasgow. 2013.

BENNETT, MARGARET. *The Last Stronghold: Scottish Gaelic Traditions of Newfoundland*. Edinburgh: Canongate, 1989.

———. *Oatmeal and the Catechism: Scottish Gaelic Settlers in Quebec*. Montreal and Kingston: McGill-Queen's University Press, 2003.

BITTERMAN, RUSTY. "On Remembering and Forgetting." In *Myth, Migration and the Making of Memory*, 253-65. Ed. Marjory Harper and Michael Vance. Edinburgh: John MacDonald Publishing, 1999.

BUENO, EDUARDO. *Brasil: uma História*. São Paulo: Ática, 2003.

BLACK, RONALD. *An Lasair: Anthology of 18th Century Scottish Gaelic Verse*. Edinburgh: Birlinn, 2001.

———. *An Tuil: Anthology of 20th Century Scottish Gaelic Verse*. Edinburgh: Polygon, 1999.

———. "Gaelic Orthography: The Drunk Man's Broad Road." In *The Edinburgh Companion to the Gaelic Language*, 229-61. Edinburgh: Edinburgh University Press, 2010.

———. *The Gaelic Otherworld*. Edinburgh: Birlinn Ltd, 2005.

BROWN, CRAIG. *The Illustrated History of Canada*. Toronto : Key Porter Books, 2007.

BUELTMANN, TANJA, ANDREW HINSON AND GRAEME MORTON. *The Scottish Diaspora*. Edinburgh: Edinburgh University Press, 2013.

BUMSTEAD, J. M. "The Cultural Landscape of Early Canada." In *Strangers within the Realm: Cultural Margins of the First British Empire*, 363-92. Ed. Bernard Bailyn and Philip Morgan. Chapel Hill: University of North Carolina Press, 1991.

CAIMBEUL, DONNCHADH. *Nuadh Òrain Ghailach*. Cork: J. Cronin, 1798.

CAMERON, JAMES. *For the People: A History of St Francis Xavier University*. Montreal and Kingston: McGill-Queen's University Press, 1996.

CAMERON, JOHN. *The Clan Cameron: A Brief Sketch of its History and Traditions*. Kirkintilloch: Herald, 1894.

CAMERON, WILLIAM. *Drummer on Foot*. Ed. Raymond MacLean and Duncan MacFarlane. Antigonish: Casket, n.d.

CAMPBELL, JOHN FRANCIS. *More West Highland Tales*, vol. 1. Edinburgh: Birlinn, 1994 [1940]).

———. *Popular Tales of the West Highlands*. 2 vols. Edinburgh: Birlinn, 1994 [1860].

CAMPBELL, JOHN LORNE. *Òrain Ghàidhealach mu Bhliadhna Theàrlaich / Highland Songs of the Forty-Five*. Edinburgh: Scottish Gaelic Texts Society, 1984 [1933].

———. *Songs Remembered in Exile*. 2nd Ed. Edinburgh: Birlinn, 1999 [1990].

——— and FRANCIS COLLINSON. *Hebridean Folksongs*. 3 vols. Oxford: Oxford University Press, 1969-1981.

CAMPBELL, PATRICK. *Travels in North America*. Ed. William Ganong. Toronto: The Champlain Society, 1937.

CAMPEY, LUCILLE. *An Unstoppable Force: The Scottish Exodus to Canada*. Toronto: Natural Heritage Books, 2008.

———. *The Scottish Pioneers of Upper Canada, 1784–1855*. Toronto: Natural Heritage Books, 2005.

CAMSHRON, EACHANN. *Na Baird Thirisdeach / The Tiree Bards*. Stirling: The Tiree Association, 1932.

CLANCY, THOMAS OWEN. "Mourning Fearchar Ó Maoilchiaráin: texts, transmission and transformation." In *Cànan & Cultar / Language and Culture: Rannsachadh na Gàidhlig 3*, 57-71. Ed. Wilson McLeod, James Fraser and Anja Gunderloch. Edinburgh: Dunedin Press, 2006.

REFERENCES

Clark, Daniel. *Selections from Scottish Canadian Poets*. Toronto: Imrie, Graham & Co., 1900.

Clyde, Robert. *From Rebel to Hero: The Image of the Highlander, 1745-1830*. East Linton, Scotland: Tuckwell Press, 1995.

Coira, M. Pia. *By Poetic Authority: The Rhetoric of Panegyric in Gaelic Poetry of Scotland to c.1700*. Edinburgh: Dunedin Press, 2012.

Colley, Linda. *Britons: Forging the Nation, 1707-1837*. New Haven, CT: Yale University Press, 1992.

Constitution and By-Laws of the Celtic Society of Montreal. Montreal: W. Drysdale & Co., 1885.

Cox, Lori. "Gaelic and the Schools in Cape Breton." *Nova Scotia Historical Review* 14 (1994): 20-40.

Craig, David. *On the Crofters' Trail*. Edinburgh: Birlinn, 2006.

Cregeen, Eric. *Recollections of an Argyllshire Drover and other West Highland Chronicles*. Ed. Margaret Bennett. Edinburgh: John Donald, 2004.

Creighton, Helen and Calum MacLeod. *Gaelic Songs in Nova Scotia*. Ottawa: National Museums of Canada, 1979.

Crouse, Liam. "The establishment of Celtic societies." *History Scotland* (Sept/Oct 2013): 24-31.

Daschuk, James. *Clearing the Plains: Disease, Politics of Starvation, and the Loss of Aboriginal Life*. Regina: University of Regina Press, 2013.

Debates of the Senate of the Dominion of Canada, 1890. Ottawa: Brown Chamberlin, 1890.

Dembling, Jonathan. "Gaelic in Canada: new evidence from an old census." In *Cànan & Cultar / Language & Culture: Rannsachadh na Gàidhlig 3*, 203-14. Ed. Wilson McLeod, James E. Fraser and Anja Gunderloch. Edinburgh: Dunedin Academic Press, 2006.

Dennis, Clara. *More about Nova Scotia: My Own, My Native Land*. 2nd ed. Toronto: Ryerson Press, 1944.

Devine, T. M. "The Flight of the Poor: Highland Emigration to Canada in the Mid-Nineteenth Century." In *Celtic Languages and Celtic Peoples: Proceedings of the Second North American Congress of Celtic Studies*, 645-60. Ed. Cyril Byrne, Margaret Harry and Pádraig Ó Siadhail. Halifax, NS: St Mary's University, 1992.

———. *The Scottish Nation: A History, 1700-2000*. London: Penguin, 1999.

Dodgshon, Robert. *From Chiefs to Landlords*. Edinburgh: Edinburgh University Press, 1998.

Dòmhnallach, Dòmhnall. "Cor na Gàidhlig an America." *An Deò-Gréine* 8.8 (1918): 117-19.

DÒMHNALLACH, DÒMHNALL IAIN. "Whose Land is it Anyway?" *Bella Caledonia* March 12, 2014. http://bellacaledonia.org.uk/2014/03/12/whose-land-is-it-anyway/ (accessed January 20, 2015).

DÒMHNALLACH, TORMAD. "An Iomlaid Amaideach," *Teachdaire nan Gàidheal* 5.8 (1933): 1, 2.

DUNBAR, ROBERT. "The Poetry Of John Maclean, 'Bard Thighearna Chola', 'Am Bard MacGill-Eain'." PhD dissertation, University of Glasgow, 2005.

———. "The Poetry of the Emigrant Generation." *Transactions of the Gaelic Society of Inverness* 64 (2008): 22-125.

———. "Understanding Canadian Multiculturalism and Cultural Diversity in a 21st-Century Context from a 'Celtic' Perspective." In *Celts in the Americas*, 117-144. Ed. Michael Newton. Sydney, NS: Cape Breton University Press, 2013.

DUNN, CHARLES. *Highland Settler: A Portrait of the Scottish Gael in Cape Breton and Eastern Nova Scotia*. Wreck Cove, NS: Breton Books, 1991 [1953].

DZIENNIK, MATTHEW. "'Cutting Heads from Shoulders': The Conquest of Canada in Gaelic Thought, 1759-1791." In *1759 Revisited: The Conquest of Canada*, 240-66. Ed. Phillip K. Buckner and John Reid. Montreal and Kingston: McGill-Queen's University Press, 2012.

———. "Whig Tartan: Material Culture and its Use in the Scottish Highlands, 1746-1815." *Past and Present* 217 (Nov 2012): 117-47.

FAIRNEY, JANICE. "The Branch Societies of the Highland Society of London." In *Rannsachadh na Gàidhlig 5* / Fifth Scottish Gaelic Research Conference, ed. Kenneth Nilsen, 67-77. Sydney, NS: Cape Breton University Press, 2010.

FERGUSSON, DONALD. *Fad air Falbh as Innse Gall / Beyond the Hebrides*. Halifax: Lawson Graphics Atlantic, 1977.

FISHER, JOE. *The Glasgow Encyclopedia*. Edinburgh and London: Mainstream Publishing, 1994.

FRASER, ALEXANDER. "The Gael in Canada." *Transactions of the Gaelic Society of Inverness* 23 (1902): 209-19.

FRISEAL, ALASDAIR. *Leabhar nan Sonn*. Toronto: Uilleam Briggs, 1897.

GIBSON, JOHN. *Traditional Gaelic Bagpiping: 1745-1945*. Edinburgh: NMS Publishing, 1998.

GILLEASBUIG MAC DHOMNUILL 'IC EOGHAIN. "Dùthaich an Àigh." *Guth na Bliadhna* 5.3 (Summer 1908): 197-222.

GILLIS, RANNIE. *The Collected Works of Malcolm H Gillis*. North Sydney, NS: Northside Printers, 2004.

GILLIES, WILLIAM. "Clan Donald Bards and Scholars." In *Cànan & Cultar / Language & Culture: Rannsachadh na Gàidhlig 4*, 91-108. Ed. Gillian Munro and Richard Cox. Edinburgh: Dunedin Academic Press, 2010.

GRANT, ANNE. *Essays on the Superstitions of the Highlanders of Scotland*, vol. 1. London, 1811.

HARKNESS, JOHN G. *Stormont, Dundas and Glengarry: A History, 1784-1945*. Dundas: Mundy Goodfellow Printing Company, 1946.

HARPER, MARJORY. *Adventurers & Exiles: The Great Scottish Exodus*. London: Profile Books, 2004.

———. *Emigration from Scotland Between the Wars: Opportunity or Exile?* Manchester: Manchester University Press: 1998.

HARPER, STEPHEN. Stephen Harper reflects on Canada's first prime minister, Sir John A. Macdonald. Canada.Com, January 12, 2015. http://www.canada.com/life/Stephen+Harper+reflects+Canada+first+prime+minister+John+Macdonald/10715813/story.html#__federated=1 (accessed January 18, 2015).

History of the County of Middlesex, Canada: From the Earliest Time to the Present. Toronto: Goodspeed, 1889.

A History of the Vote in Canada. 2nd Ed. Ottawa: Office of the Chief Electoral Officer of Canada, 2007. http://www.elections.ca/res/his/History-Eng_Text.pdf (accessed January 18, 2015).

HOWELL, COLIN. "W.S. Fielding and the Repeal Elections of 1886 and 1887 in Nova Scotia." *Acadiensis* 8, no. 2 (1979): 28-46.

HUNTER, JAMES. *A Dance Called America: The Scottish Highlands, the United States and Canada*. Edinburgh: Mainstream, 1994.

———. *The Making of the Crofting Community*. 2nd ed. Edinburgh: Birlinn, 2000.

INNES, SÌM AND BARBARA HILLERS. "A Mixed-Media Folklore Trove: Celtic Folklore Collections in Harvard Libraries." *Proceedings of the Harvard Celtic Colloquium* 31 (2011): 173-203.

JOHNSTON, REV. ANGUS ANTHONY. *A History of the Catholic Church in Eastern Nova Scotia*. 2 vols. Antigonish: St Francis Xavier University, 1960.

JUSTER, SUSAN AND LINDA GREGERSON. "Introduction." In *Empires of God*, 1-18. Ed. Susan Juster and Linda Gregerson. Philadelphia: University of Pennsylvania Press, 2011.

KEMP, REV. ALEXANDER. *The Beneficial Influence of a Well-Regulated Nationality*. Montreal: Beckett, 1857.

KENNEDY, JOHN. *The Days of the Fathers in Ross-shire*. Toronto and Montreal: James Campbell & Son, 1867.

KENNEDY, MICHAEL. *Gaelic Nova Scotia: An Economic, Cultural, and Social Impact Study*. Halifax: Nova Scotia Museum, 2002.

———. "Lochaber no more: A Critical Examination of Highland Emigration Mythology." In *Myth, Migration and the Making of Memory: Scotia and Nova Scotia c.1700-1990*, 267-97. Ed. Marjory Harper and Michael E. Vance. Edinburgh: John Donald, 1999.

LA BHRUINN, ALIGHINN. *Machraichean Móra Chanada: Dorus Fosgailte do'n Ghaidheal*. Ottawa: Ughdarras Àrd-Uachdranachd Chanada, 1907.

LINKLETTER, MICHAEL. "Bu Dual Dha Sin (That was His Birthright): Gaelic Scholar Alexander Maclean Sinclair (1840-1924)." PhD dissertation, Harvard University, 2006.

LIVINGSTONE, COLIN. "Lochaber Place Names." *Transactions of the Gaelic Society of Inverness* 8 (1888): 257-69.

MAC A' PHEARSAIN, SEONAIDH AILIG AND MÌCHEAL LINKLETTER. *Fògradh, Fàisneachd, Filidheachd: An t-Urr. Donnchadh Blàrach (1815-1893) ann am Mac-Talla / Parting, Prophecy, Poetry: Rev. Duncan Blair (1815-1893) in Mac-Talla*. Sydney, NS: Cape Breton University Press, 2013.

MAC A' PHÌ, EÓGHAN. *Am Measg nam Bodach*. Glasgow: An Comunn Gàidhealach: 1938.

MCCOINNICH, ALISTEAR RUADH. *Oranean*. Parkhill, Ontario: Parkhill Gazette, 1882.

MACCOINNICH, COINNEACH. *Orain Ghaidhealach*. Edinburgh, 1792.

MCCOLL, HUGH. *Some Sketches of the Early Highland Pioneers of the County of Middlesex*. 2nd ed. Ottawa: Canadian Heritage Publications, 1979 [1910].

MCCULLOUGH, KATIE. "'For the Good and Glory of the Whole': The Highland Society of London and the Formation of Scoto-British Identity." In *The Shaping of Scottish Identities: Family, Nation, and the Worlds Beyond*, 199-213. Ed. Jodi Campbell, Elizabeth Ewan and Heather Parker. Guelph: Centre for Scottish Studies, 2011.

MACDHÙGHAILL, EACHANN. *Smeòrach nan Cnoc 's nan Gleann*. Glasgow: Alexander MacLaren & Sons, 1939.

MACDHÙGHAILL, ROIBEART. *Ceann-Iùil an Fhir-Imrich*. Glasgow: J & P Campbell, 1841.

MACDONALD, KEITH NORMAN. *The Gesto Collection of Highland Music*. Leipzig: O. Brandstetter, 1895.

MACDONELL, J. A. *Sketches Illustrating the Early Settlement and History of Glengarry in Canada*. Montreal: Wm. Foster, Brown and Co., 1893.

MACDONELL, MARGARET. *The Emigrant Experience*. Toronto: University of Toronto Press, 1982.

MacDonell, R. A. "British Immigration Schemes in Alberta." *Alberta Historical Review* 16, no.2 (1968): 5-13.

MacFhionghuin, Eòin. "Na Gàidheil an Ceap Breatunn." In *Cape Breton, Canada*, 72-81. Ed. C. W. Vernon. Toronto: Nation Publishing, 1903.

MacGilleain, Iain. *Dàin Spioradail*. Ed. Alexander Sinclair. Edinburgh: MacLachlan & Stewart, 1880.

MacGilleMhaoil, Alasdair. *Òrain le Alasdair MacGilleMhaoil an Gleann-a-Garaidh, an Canada-Àrd*. Inverness: John Murdoch at the Highlander Office, 1882.

MacGillivray, Ronald. *The History of Antigonish*. Ed. Raymond MacLean. Antigonish: The Casket, 1976.

MacGillivray, Royce. *Dictionary of Glengarry Biography*. Alexandria, Ontario: Glengarry Historical Society, 2010.

MacGregor, James. *Dàin a chomh[n]adh crabhuidh*. Glasgow: 1819.

McGregor, J. *Historical and Descriptive Sketches of the Maritime Colonies of British America*. London: Longman, Rees, Orme, Brown and Green, 1828.

MacGregor, Martin. "Gaelic Barbarity and Scottish Identity in the Later Middle Ages." In *Mìorun Mòr nan Gall, 'The Great Ill-Will of the Lowlander'?: Lowland Perceptions of the Highlands, Medieval and Modern*, 7-48. Ed. Dauvit Broun and Martin MacGregor. Glasgow: University of Glasgow, 2007.

Mac-Ille-Mhaoil, Alasdair. *Òrain le Alasdair Mac-Ille-Mhaoil an Gleann-a-Garaidh, an Canada-Ard*. Inverness: The Highlander Office, 1882.

MacInnes, Duncan. *Còmhraidhean an Gàidhlig 's am Beurla*. Glasgow: Alexander MacLaren and Sons, 1880.

MacInnes, John. *Dùthchas nan Gàidheal: Selected Essays of John MacInnes*. Ed. Michael Newton. Edinburgh: Birlinn, 2006.

MacInnes, Allan, Marjory-Ann Harper, and Linda Fryer. *Scotland and the Americas, c. 1650-c.1939: A Documentary Source Book*. Edinburgh: Scottish History Society, 2002.

McIntosh, Alastair. *Island Spirituality: Spiritual Values of Lewis and Harris*. Isle of Lewis: Island Books Trust, 2013.

MacÌomhair, Cailean. *Òrain Ghailig*. Sydney, NS: Mac-Talla Publishing Company, 1902.

Mackay, Margaret A. "Am Breabadair agus an Gille Glas." *Tocher* 42 (1989): 390-97.

McKay, Thomas A. *Oscar and Finlay: Bards of Scottish Lingwick*. Arlington, VA: n.p., 2000.

MacKay, William. *Urquhart and Glenmoriston*. Inverness: Northern Counties Publishing, 1914.

MacKay, W. A. *Pioneer Life in Zorra*. Toronto: William Briggs, 1899.

MacKellar, Mary. "The Educational Power of Gaelic Poetry." *The Celtic Magazine* 10 (1885): 313-19.

MacKenzie, Alexander. *The History of the Highland Clearances*. Stirling: Eneas MacKay, 1914 [1883].

MacKenzie, Archibald. *History of Christmas Island Parish*. n.p., 1926.

MacKillop, Andrew. *'More Fruitful than the Soil': Army, Empire and the Scottish Highlands, 1715-1815*. East Linton: Tuckwell Press, 2000.

MacKillop, Archibald. *Collected Verse of "The Blind Bard of Megantic"*. Winnipeg: n.p., 1913.

———. *Temperance Odes and Miscellaneous Poems*. Quebec: Thompson and Company, 1860.

MacKinnon, Archibald Roderick. "Gaelic in the Bruce." *Bruce County Historical Society Yearbook* 13 (1967): 13-20.

MacKinnon, James N. *A Short History of the Pioneer Scotch Settlers of St. Andrews, Sask*. Regina: Courier, 1921.

———. *Moosomin and its pioneers*. Moosomin, Saskatchewan: World-Spectator, 1937.

MacLean, Malcolm and Theo Dorgan. *An Leabhar Mór / The Great Book of Gaelic*. Edinburgh: Canongate Books, 2002.

MacLellan, Lauchie. *Brìgh an Òrain / The Songs and Tales of Lauchie MacLellan*. Ed. John Shaw. Montreal and Kingston: McGill-Queen's University Press, 2000.

MacLellan, Vincent. *Fàilte Cheap Breatainn*. Sydney, NS: The Island Reporter, 1891.

MacLennan, John. "The Early Settlement of Glengarry." *Transactions of the Celtic Society of Montreal* (1884-87): 113-21.

McLeod, Angus. *Òrain Dhonnchaidh Bhàin / The Songs of Duncan Ban Macintyre*. Edinburgh: Scottish Gaelic Texts Society, 1978.

MacLeod, Michelle. "The cianalas code: bridging traditional song and modern verse." *Scottish Gaelic Studies* 26 (2010): 67-86.

McLeod, Wilson. *Divided Gaels: Gaelic Cultural Identities in Scotland and Ireland c.1200-c.1650*. Oxford: Oxford University Press, 2004.

———. "Language Politics and Ethnolinguistic Consciousness in Scottish Gaelic Poetry," *Scottish Gaelic Studies* 21 (2003): 91-146.

——— and Meg Bateman. *Duanaire na Sracaire / Songbook of the Pillagers: Anthology of Medieval Gaelic Poetry*. Edinburgh: Birlinn, 2007.

MacLeòid, Calum Iain M. *Bàrdachd a Albainn Nuaidh*. Glasgow: Gairm, 1970.

―――. *Sgialachdan a Albainn Nuaidh*. Glasgow: Gairm, 1969.

MacMillan, C. "The First Settlers in Glengarry." *The Scottish Canadian* 9 (1904): 167-76.

Mac na Ceàrdadh, Gilleasbuig. *An t-Òranaiche / The Gaelic Songster*. St Andrew's, NS: Sìol Cultural Enterprises, 2004 [1879].

MacPherson, Iain S. " 'Like a peeling on the water': Songs of dislocation and displacement in the Prince Edward Island Gaelic context." *Scottish Gaelic Studies* 23 (2007): 179-200.

MacPhie, John. *Pictonians at Home and Abroad: Sketches of Professional Men and Women of Pictou County its History and Institutions*. Boston: Pinkham Press, 1914.

Mann, Susan. *Margaret Macdonald: Imperial Daughter*. Montreal and Kingston: McGill-Queen's University Press, 2005.

Màrtainn, Dòmhnall. *Clachan Crìche: Taghadh de Bhàrdachd Tholastaidh (1850-2000)*. Tolastadh mu Thuath: Comann Eachdraidh Tholastaidh mu Thuath, 2005.

Matheson, Trueman and Laurinda. *O Cheapaich nan Craobh / The Poetry of the Keppoch Bard*. St Andrew's, NS: Sìol Cultural Enterprises, 2008.

Matheson, William, ed. *Òrain Iain mhic Fhearchair / The Songs of John MacCodrum*. Edinburgh: Scottish Gaelic Texts Society, 1938.

――― and Morag MacLeod. *Scottish Tradition 16: William Matheson, Gaelic Bards and Minstrels*. Edinburgh: Greentrax Recordings, 1993.

Meek, Donald. *Caran an t-Saoghail / The Wiles of the World*. Edinburgh: Birlinn, 2003.

―――. " 'Craobh-Sgaoileadh a' Bhìobaill agus an t-Soisgeil': A Gaelic Song on the Nineteenth-Century Christian Missionary Movement." In *Fil súil nglais / A Grey Eye Looks Back*, 143-62. Ed. Sharon Arbuthnot and Kaarina Hollo. Ceann Drochaid, Scotland: Clann Tuirc, 2007.

―――. "Gaelic Communities and the Use of Texts." In *The Edinburgh History of the Book in Scotland*, Volume 3: Ambition and Industry 1800-1880, ed. Bill Bell, 153-72. Edinburgh: Edinburgh University Press, 2007.

―――. "Scottish Highlanders, North American Indians and the SSPCK: Some Cultural Perspectives." *Records of the Scottish Church History Society* 23 (1989): 378-96.

―――. *Tuath is Tighearna / Tenants and Landlords*. Edinburgh: Scottish Gaelic Texts Society, 1995.

Megaw, B. R. S. "Goat-Keeping in the Old Highland Economy." *Scottish Studies* 7 (1963): 201–09 and 8 (1964): 213–18.

Mil nan Dàn. Edinburgh: Oliver and Boyd, n.d.

Mitsheall, Donnchadh I. *Drùchd nam Beann or Mountain's Dew*. Rodney, Ontario: West Elgin Mercury Office, 1887.

Morrison, Murdoch. *Òrain Fuinn is Cladaich: Gaelic Poems and Songs*. Glasgow: Alexander MacLaren and Sons, 1931.

Murray, Rev. John. *The History of the Presbyterian Church in Cape Breton*. Truro, NS: News Publishing, 1921.

Nettle, Daniel and Suzanne Romaine. *Vanishing Voices: The Extinction of the World's Languages*. Oxford: Oxford University Press, 2000.

Newton, Michael. "Bards of the Forests, Prairies and Skyscrapers: Scottish Gaels in the Americas." In *Celts in the Americas*, 76-93. Ed. Michael Newton. Sydney, NS: Cape Breton University Press, 2013.

———. " 'Becoming Cold-Hearted Like the Gentiles Around Them:' Scottish Gaelic in the United States 1872-1912." *eKeltoi* 2 (2003): 63-131.

———. "Celtic Cousins or White Settlers? Scottish Highlanders and First Nations." In *Rannsachadh na Gàidhlig 5 / Fifth Scottish Gaelic Research Conference*, 221-37. Ed. Kenneth Nilsen. Sydney, NS: Cape Breton University Press, 2010.

———. "Coille Mhòr Chailleann ann am Beul-aithris nan Gàidheal." In *Cruth na Tìre*, 180-194. Ed. Wilson McLeod and Máire Ní Annracháin. Dublin: Coiscéim, 2003.

———. "'Did you hear about the Gaelic-speaking African?': Scottish Gaelic Folklore about Identity in North America." *Comparative American Studies* 8.2 (2010): 88-106.

———. " 'Going to the Land of the Yellow Men': The Representation of Indigenous Americans in Scottish Gaelic Literature." In *Irish and Scottish Encounters with Indigenous Peoples*, 236-52. Ed. Graeme Morton and David Wilson. Montreal and Kingston: McGill-Queen's University Press: 2013.

———. "How Scottish Highlanders Became White: The Introduction of Racialism to Gaelic Literature and Culture." In *Celts in the Americas*, 283-97. Ed. Michael Newton. Sydney, NS: Cape Breton University Press, 2013.

———. "The Great Caledonian Forest of the Mind: Highland Woods and Tree Symbolism in Scottish Gaelic Tradition." *Scottish Studies* 37 (2014): 164-73.

———. "The Macs meet the 'Micmacs': Scottish Gaelic First Encounter Narratives from Nova Scotia." *Journal of Irish and Scottish Studies* 5.1 (Autumn 2011): 67-96.

———. " 'This Could Have Been Mine': Scottish Gaelic Learners in modern North America." *eKeltoi* 1 (2005): 1-37.

———. "Unsettling Iain mac Mhurchaidh's slumber: the Carolina lullaby, authorship, and the influence of print media on Gaelic oral tradition." *Aiste* 4 (2014): 143-66.

———. *Warriors of the Word: The World of the Scottish Highlanders*. Edinburgh: Birlinn, 2009.

———. *"We're Indians Sure Enough": The Legacy of the Scottish Highlanders in the United States*. Saorsa Media, 2001.

———, ROBERT DUNBAR, GEARÓID Ó HALLMHURÁIN AND DANIEL WILLIAMS. "Introduction: The Past and Future Celt." In *Celts in the Americas*, 5-17. Ed. Michael Newton. Sydney, NS: Cape Breton University Press, 2013.

NÍ ANNRACHÁIN, MÁIRE. "Metaphor and Metonymy in the Poetry of Màiri nighean Alasdair Ruaidh." In *Fil súil nglais / A Grey Eye Looks Back: a Festschrift in honour of Colm Ó Baoill*, 163-174. Ed. Sharon Arbuthnot and Kaarina Hollo. Ceann Drochaid, Scotland: Clann Tuirc, 2007.

NILSEN, KENNETH. "A' Ghàidhlig an Canada: Scottish Gaelic in Canada." In *The Edinburgh Companion to the Gaelic Language*, 90-107. Ed. Moray Watson and Michelle Macleod. Edinburgh: Edinburgh University Press, 2010.

———. "P. J. Nicholson and 'Achadh nan Gaidheal.'" In *Bile ós Chrannaibh: A Festschrift for William Gillies*, 315-28. Ed. Wilson McLeod, Abigail Burnyeat, Domhnall Uilleam Stiùbhart, Thomas Owen Clancy and Roibeard Ó Maolalaigh. Ceann Drochaid, Scotland: Clann Tuirc, 2010.

———. "Some Notes on on Pre-Mac-Talla Gaelic Publishing in Nova Scotia" in *Rannsachadh na Gàidhlig 2000*, 127-140. Ed. Colm Ó Baoill and Nancy McGuire. Aberdeen: An Clò Gàidhealach, 2002.

———. "The Priest in the Gaelic Folklore of Nova Scotia." *Béaloideas* 64/65, (1996/1997): 171-94.

Ó BAOILL, COLM AND MEG BATEMAN. *Gàir nan Clàrsach / The Harp's Cry: An Anthology of 17th Century Gaelic Poetry*. Edinburgh: Birlinn, 1994.

Ó CATHASAIGH, TOMÁS. "The literature of medieval Ireland to c.800: St Patrick to the Vikings." In *The Cambridge History of Irish Literature*, vol. 1, 9-31. Ed. Margaret Kelleher and Philip O' Leary. Cambridge: Cambridge University Press, 2006.

PARSONS, TIMOTHY. *The Rule of Empires: Those Who Built Them, Those Who Endured Them, and Why They Always Fail*. Oxford: Oxford University Press, 2010.

PATTERSON, GEORGE. *A History of the County of Pictou, Nova Scotia*. Montreal: Dawson Brothers, 1877.

———. *Memoir of the Rev. James MacGregor*. Philadelphia: Joseph Wilson, 1859.

PESTANA, CARLA. *Protestant Empire: Religion and the Making of the British Atlantic World*. Philadelphia: University of Pennsylvania Press, 2009.

PHILLIPS, KEVIN. *The Cousins' Wars: Religion, Politics, & The Triumph of Anglo-America*. New York: Basic Books, 1999.

RANKIN, EFFIE. *Às a' Bhràighe: The Gaelic Songs of Allan the Ridge MacDonald*. Sydney, NS: Cape Breton University Press, 2004.

RICHARDS, ERIC. "Scotland and the Uses of the Atlantic Empire." In *Strangers within the Realm: Cultural Margins of the First British Empire*, 67-114. Ed. Bernard Bailyn and Philip Morgan. Chapel Hill: University of North Carolina Press, 1991.

———. *The Highland Clearances*. Edinburgh: Birlinn, 2000.

ROSS, JAMES. "The Sub-Literary Tradition in Scottish Gaelic Song-Poetry." *Éigse* 7 (1953/55): 217-39.

Rules of the Highland Society of Canada, A Branch of the Highland Society of London. Montreal: Armour and Ramsay, 1843.

SHAW, JOHN. "(E)migrating Legends and Sea Change." *Electronic Journal of Folklore* 37 (2007): 43-58.

———. *Gaelic in Prince Edward Island: A Cultural Remnant*. Ed. Michael Kennedy. Charlottetown: University of Prince Edward Island, 2002 [1987]. http://projects.upei.ca/iis/files/2014/07/Gaelic-Index.pdf (accessed January 20, 2015).

———. "Observations on the Cape Breton Gàidhealtachd and its Relevance to Present-Day Celtic Studies." In *Proceedings of the First North American Congress of Celtic Studies*, 75-87. Ed. Gordon MacLennan. Ottawa: University of Ottawa, 1988.

SHEARS, BARRY W. *Dance to the Piper: The Highland Bagpipe in Nova Scotia*. Sydney, NS: Cape Breton University Press, 2008.

SINCLAIR, ALEXANDER MACLEAN. *Clàrsach na Coille*. Glasgow: Archibald Sinclair, 1881.

———. *The Gaelic Bards from 1411 to 1717*. Charlottetown: Hazard & Moore, 1890.

SINCLAIR, REV. ALLAN. *Reminiscences, historical and traditional, of the Grants of Glenmoriston*. Edinburgh: Maclachlan & Stewart, 1887.

SINCLAIR, DONALD MACLEAN. "Gaelic in Nova Scotia." *Dalhousie Review* 30 (1950): 252-60.

———. *Gaelic Lessons for Beginners*. Sydney, NS: Post Publishing, 1939.

REFERENCES

SMITH, IAIN CRICHTON. *Towards the Human*. Edinburgh: MacDonald Publishers, 1986.

SMITH, LINDA TUHIWAI. *Decolonizing Methodologies: Research and Indigenous Peoples*. Dunedin: University of Otago Press, 1999.

STANLEY, TIMOTHY. "John A. Macdonald's Aryan Canada: Aboriginal Genocide and Chinese Exclusion." *Active History.CA: History Matters*. http://activehistory.ca/2015/01/john-a-macdonalds-aryan-canada-aboriginal-genocide-and-chinese-exclusion/ (accessed January 19, 2015).

STEWART, ALEXANDER AND DONALD. *Cochruinneacha Taoghta de Shaothair nam Bàrd Gàëlach. A Choice Collection of the Works of the Highland Bards, Collected in the Highlands and Isles*. Edinburgh: 1804.

STRANG, JOHN. *Glasgow and its Clubs*. London and Glasgow: Richard Griffin and Company, 1857.

STROH, SILKE. *Uneasy Subjects: Postcolonialism and Scottish Gaelic Poetry*. Amsterdam: Rodopi, 2011.

SULLIVAN, KIM. "Scots by Association: Clubs and Societies in the Scottish Diaspora." In *The Modern Scottish Diaspora*, 47-63. Ed. Murray Leith and Duncan Sim. Edinburgh: Edinburgh University Press, 2014.

THOMAS, NED. *The Welsh Extremist*. Cymdeithas yr Iaith Gymraeg, 1971. Online at: http://archif.cymdeithas.org/dadlwytho/ned-thomas-the-welsh-extremist.pdf (accessed December 31, 2014).

THOMPSON, ELIZABETH. *The Emigrant's Guide to North America*. Toronto: Natural Heritage Books, 1998.

TOOM, SARAH. "John A Macdonald: Son of Glasgow, 'Father of Canada.'" *BBC Scotland News* online http://www.bbc.com/news/uk-scotland-30782068 (accessed January 19, 2015).

WALKER, STEPHEN. "Agents of Dispossession and Acculturation. Edinburgh Accountants and the Highland Clearances." *Critical Perspectives on Accounting* 14 (2003): 813-53.

WATSON, WILLIAM. *Bàrdachd Ghàidhlig*, 3rd ed. Inverness: An Comunn Gàidhealach, 1959.

Index

Page numbers refer to the print version

Act of Proscription (1746) 40
Africa 306-308, 324, 327, 331
Alasdair Ailein Mhóir (Bàrd na Ceapaich) 465, 478
Alasdair mac Mhaighstir Alasdair 377, 399, 400
Alberta 253
  Clandonald 246-50
  Red Deer 252, 255
Anglo-conformity 12, 382-83, 385-86, 423, 468, 489, 505. 509-510
Anglo-Saxonism 5, 35-36, 509-510
authorship 28

Bannockburn (Battle of) 71, 79-80, 96-97, 99, 470-71, 473
Beàrnaraigh (Isle of) 26
Bitterman, Rusty 2
Black, Ronald 505
Blair, Rev. Duncan. *See* Blàrach, Rev. Donnchadh.
Blàrach, Rev. Donnchadh 123, 319, 512, 515
Boid, Iain 268, 395, 515
Bonaparte, Napoléon 74, 81-82, 93-94, 110, 114
British Columbia 487
  Vancouver 26, 353, 381, 426-27, 429, 456-62

Campbell, John Francis. *See* Iain Òg Ìle.
Campbell, Patrick 34
Cameron of Lochiel 72
Canadian Pacific Railway 125, 128, 171, 246
Casket (newspaper) 60, 96, 215, 246, 515, 522
Catholic Church 6, 225-26, 235-36, 244, 246-50, 268, 316, 478
céilidh(s) 16, 22-24, 27-28, 375-76, 387-88, 390, 414
chain migration 121
"A' Choille Ghruamach" (The Gloomy Forest) xii, 8, 20-21, 185-86, 237, 245

civil-savage dichotomy 3-4, 34-36, 70, 71-72, 84, 89, 189, 316-19, 324, 444, 513
Clan Donald 46-48, 50-51, 129-30, 132, 247, 313-14, 325, 330
Clanranald 289
Clàrsach nam Beann 398-99, 401
Clearance(s) 34-40, 230, 239-40
clothing 41-43, 75, 79-80, 82, 87, 90, 97, 148, 173, 389-91, 393, 423, 452- 455, 471, 473
Cnòideart (Scotland) 121, 129, 132, 311-12, 314
Companach an Òganaich 276
Cox, Laurie 384
Craig, David 39
Craig, James 434
Creegen, Eric 10
croft(s) 124
Cromwell, Oliver 71
Cuairtear nan Coillte (newspaper) 83, 274
Cuairtear nan Gleann (newspaper) 83, 161, 380, 389, 396, 518
An Cuairtear Òg Gàidhealach (newspaper) 199, 276, 395, 515
Culloden (Battle of) 20, 33, 228, 323

Dennis, Clara 306
Dòmhnall Donn Bhoth-Fhionntainn 143
Dòmhnallach, Dòmhnall Iain 39
Dòmhnallach, Dòmhnall Reverend 221
Douglas, Thomas (Earl of Selkirk) 68, 122, 250, 372
Dunbar, Professor Robert 184, 382
Dunn, Professor Charles 132, 198
Dunvegan, Fairy flag of 290

Eden, Garden of 377, 400-401, 431, 435, 437, 439-41, 475-77
Edinburgh (Scotland) 7, 172, 174, 328, 454, 456
emigration agent(s) 125-26, 128, 47

Falkirk Tryst 76
Fear na Céilidh (newspaper) 377, 519
Fear-Tathaich nam Beann (newspaper) 204, 210

INDEX

Fian 17, 109, 302, 324-25, 330, 392, 394, 418-19, 428, 432-33, 445
File *See* Literati (Gaelic)
First Nations 9, 187-89, 204, 208, 213-14, 225-26, 250-51, 254, 316-17, 357-61, 506, 510, 513-14, 549
Fraser, Alexander. *See* Friseal, Alasdair.
Fraser, Simon 251, 254
francophones (Canadian) 76-77, 139, 252, 254, 467, 475-77, 487-93, 500, 502
Fraser, Simon of Lovat 70
French (language) 101, 111, 219, 221, 383-86, 488-92, 509
French (people) 70, 80-82, 93-94, 108-109, 139-40, 142, 205-206, 210, 508-509
Friseal, Alasdair 14, 154, 175, 193, 196, 401, 515-16
Friseal, Tòmas 263-64
Friseal, Bishop Uilleam 268, 289, 333-34

Gaelic orthorgraphic conventions 30, 533
Gaelic College (Cape Breton) 425, 519
Gaelic Societies
  Antigonish (Nova Scotia) 444
  Bruce County (Ontario) 484
  Comunn Gàidhealach Caitligeach Chanada 417
  Comunn Gàidhlig Chanada 516
  Glasgow (Scotland) 422
  Glengarry (Ontario) 434
  Hamilton (Ontario) 299, 429, 522
  Highland Society of Canada 424
  Inverness (Nova Scotia) 427-28
  London (England) 76, 422-24
  Montreal (Quebec) 405, 439-42, 519
  Sydney (Nova Scotia) 383
  Toronto (Ontario) 381, 398, 399-400, 402, 424-25, 429, 516
  Vancouver (British Columbia) 426, 429
  Winnipeg (Manitoba) 425
Gàidheal (definition) 6
Gàidhealtachd (definition) 7
Gall (definition) 6-7
Galltachd (definition) 7
Gillanders, James 59-60
Gillis, Anne. *See* NicGill-Ìosa, Anna.
Gleann Moireastain 138

Glenmoriston (Scotland). *See* Gleann Moireastain.
goats 35
Gordon-Cathcart, Lady Emily 128, 171-72, 174, 247
Grannd, Dòmhnall Òg 434
Grannd, Iain 138, 516
Grant, Anne of Lagan 4
Greumach, Iain 167, 516

Harris (Island of, Scotland) 222-23, 258-59
Hudson Bay Company 250-51

Iain Òg Ìle 25, 247
Indian Rebellion of 1857 92
Ireland 9, 13, 18, 21, 33, 128, 168-69, 270-71, 273, 319, 380, 392, 394, 407, 451, 454, 456, 467, 491-92, 508
Islay (Island of, Scotland) 246, 295

Jacobitism 40, 70, 470
Jacobite Rising of 1745 33, 41, 205, 211, 228, 290, 292, 478
Jura (Island of, Scotland) 35

Kennedy, Michael 38
Knoydart (Scotland). *See* Cnòideart.

Lewis (Isle of, Scotland) 26, 167, 169, 219-20, 222-23, 224, 251
literacy 22-23, 25, 27, 126, 161, 318, 378-80, 390, 440-42, 519
literati (Gaelic) 13-14, 21, 185, 261-63, 521
Lochaber (Scotland) 129, 145, 443
London (England) 52, 57, 72, 328, 332
Lowlands (of Scotland) 3, 7-8, 34, 143, 176-77, 180-81, 229, 238, 422, 451
Lowlanders (Scottish) 4, 7-8, 36-38, 41, 87, 90, 135, 137, 143, 145, 292, 316, 325, 329-30, 333, 373-74, 396, 421-22, 510

Mac a' Ghobhainn, Dòmhnall 315
Mac a' Ghobhainn, Iain Crichton 371, 457
Mac an t-Saoir, Father Dòmhnall 246
Mac an t-Saoir, Donnchadh Bàn 52, 75, 76, 111, 115, 323, 399-400, 431-32

MacAonghuis, Tòmas R. 484-85, 487-93
Mac a' Phearsain, Iain 405, 516
Mac a' Phearsain, Maighstir Lachlainn 283-84, 340-47
MacCaluim, Seumas 154
MacCodruim, Iain 24-25, 44, 516
MacCodrum, John. *See* MacCodruim, Iain.
MacCoinnich, Alasdair Ruadh 282, 340, 516
MacCoinnich, Coinneach 52, 517
MacColl, Evan. *See* MacColla, Eóghann.
MacColla, Eóghann 398-99, 401-406, 431, 517
MacDhòmhnaill, Ailean "the Ridge" 40, 142, 517
MacDhòmhnaill, Alasdair "the Ridge" 25, 477, 517
MacDhòmhnaill, Father Anndra 246
MacDhòmhnaill, Aonghus "the Ridge" 40
MacDhòmhnaill, Bishop Alasdair Mór 37
MacDhòmhnaill, Dòmhnall (Tiree/Ottawa) 496, 517
MacDhòmhnaill, Dòmhnall D 305-308
MacDhòmhnaill, Doctor Dòmhnall D 302, 311, 450, 518
MacDhòmhnaill, Captain Dòmhnall Gorm 76
MacDhòmhnaill, Iain Liath 132, 518
MacDhòmhnaill, Murchadh D. 256, 377, 518
MacDhòmhnaill, Rev. Tormad 375
MacDhùghaill, Roibeart 161, 187, 518
Macdonald, Angus L. 466
MacDonald, Alexander "the Ridge." *See* MacDhòmhnaill, Alasdair.
MacDonald, Alexander "Sandfield" 434
MacDonald, Bishop Alexander. *See* MacDhòmhnaill, Bishop Alasdair Mór.
MacDonald, Allan of Kingsborough 45
Macdonald, Donald "Daniel". *See* MacDhòmhnaill, Dòmhnall D.
MacDonald, John A. 1, 103, 106, 125, 478-79, 482, 484, 505-507
MacDonald, John "Sandfield" 465
MacDonald, Flora 45, 419, 420
Macdonald, Margaret 11-12, 306-308

MacEalair, Gilleasbaig 298-99, 467-68
MacFhearghuis, Coinneach A. 410, 502, 518
MacFhilip, Gilleasbaig 91, 347, 439, 518
MacFhionghain, Alasdair 276
MacFhionghain, Aonghus 353, 519
MacFhionghain, Bishop Cailean 289, 333-38
MacFhionghain, Dòmhnall Òg 171, 519
MacFhionghain, Eòin G 227, 369, 519
MacFhionghain, Seumas 413, 519
MacGilleBhràth, Dùghall "the Old Squire" 285, 520
MacGilleBhràth, Iain (Am Pìobaire Mór) 78, 118, 199, 275-82, 520
MacGilleBhràth, Iain Òg 338, 520
MacGilleBhràth, Raonall 28
MacGill-Eain, Iain (Am Bàrd MacGill-Eain) 8, 20-21, 185-86, 380, 389, 469, 519
MacGill-Eain, Iain mac Theàrlaich Òig 40
MacGill-Eain, Maighstir Seathan 377
MacGill-Fhaolain, Aonghus Y. 466, 505
MacGilleMhaoil, Alasdair 194, 520
MacGilleMhaoil, Aonghus 442
MacGilleMhaoil, Maoileas 465
MacGill-Ìosa, Calum 499, 520-21
MacGregor, Rob Roy 96, 98, 99-100
MacGriogair, Rev. Seumas 263-64, 320, 322-23, 521
MacInnes, John 16, 17, 18
McInnes, Thomas R. *See* MacAonghuis, Tòmas R.
MacÌomhair, Cailean 308, 521
Macintyre, Duncan Ban. *See* Mac an t-Saoir, Donnchadh Bàn.
MacÌosaig, Alasdair 118
Mackay, Dr. Margaret 247
McKellar, Archibald. *See* MacEalair, Gilleasbaig.
MacKenzie, Alexander 59
Mackenzie, Sir Alexander 1, 103, 106, 251, 254
McKenzie, Archibald 385
MacKenzie, Kenneth. *See* MacCoinnich, Coinneach.
MacKenzie, William L. 298
MacKillop, Archibald. *See* MacFhilip, Gilleasbaig.

INDEX

MacKinnon, Jonathan G. *See* MacFhionghain, Eòin.
MacLachlainn, Iain Alasdair 311, 451, 453-55
McLachlan, John A. *See* MacLachlainn, Iain Alasdair.
MacLean, John. *See* MacGill-Eain, Iain.
MacLennan, Hugh 1
MacLeòid, Dòmhnall 456, 521
MacLeòid, Monsignor Niall 289
MacLeòid, Tormod 389
MacMhuirich, Lachlann 215, 289, 521
MacMhurchaidh, Mìcheal 77
Mac na h-Innse, Reverend Dr. Niall 108
MacNeacail, Pàdraig 15, 40, 60, 215, 522
MacNiven, Archibald 147-49
MacPhàrlain, Dòmhnall 417, 428, 522
Macpherson, James 17, 109
McPherson, Rev. Lachlan. *See* Mac a' Phearsain, Maighstir Lachlainn.
MacRisnidh, Fionnlagh 286, 522
Mac-Talla (newspaper) 150, 224, 227, 236, 245, 299, 301-302, 319, 378-81, 406-10, 427, 429-30, 442-43, 519
Manitoba 128, 171, 174-75, 178, 181, 222, 251
  Lake Winnipeg 357, 358
  Portage La Prairie 381
  St. Andrew's 171
  Winnipeg 250-56, 425
Maol Ciarain 17, 42, 44
Meek, Donald 38
Mitseall, Donnchadh 349
Moireach, Uilleam 299, 522
Moireasdan, Iain 474-77
Moireastan, Dòmhnall 201, 522
Moireastain, Murchadh 362 522
Montreal Presbyterian College 321
Mosgladh (newspaper) 381, 383, 417-420, 511
Mull (Island of, Scotland) 20-21, 147, 185, 186, 274-75

New Brunswick 385, 480
New York 33
NicGill-Ìosa, Anna 129, 133, 522-23
Nicholson, Right Reverend Patrick. *See* MacNeacail, Pàdraig.
North Carolina 33, 45

North Uist (Island of, Scotland) 44, 222-23
North West Company 250
Northwest Territories 62
Nova Scotia 45, 62, 79, 139, 246, 285, 382, 414, 469, 474, 480, 487-88, 499, 512, 521
  Antigonish 95, 276, 395, 444, 465, 480
  Arichat 335, 337
  Arisaig 286
  Bailey's Brook 305-306, 480
  Barney's River 11, 185, 186
  Bras d' Or 207, 211-12, 236, 245
  Bridgeville 382
  Caledonia 199-201
  Cape Breton 23, 27, 76-77, 148, 187, 203-14, 241, 384-85, 457
  Dunmaglass (Dùn Mac Glais) 305
  East Bay 289
  Giant's Lake 95
  Inverness 427-28, 499-500
  Knoydart (Cnòideart) 289
  Lake Ainslie 487
  Louisbourg 77, 205, 211
  Margaree 499
  Musquodoboit 200-201
  Pictou 62, 76, 123, 232, 320, 469, 480
  Port Hood 206
  St. Ann's 378-79, 406, 409-10
  St. Andrews 333, 335
  Sydney 206, 211-12, 232, 421
  Williams Point 333

Oisean 17, 42, 44, 109, 112, 116, 301-302, 325, 330, 392, 394, 431, 433, 440-41, 448, 450
Ontario 121, 193, 222-23, 303
  Alexandria 434-35, 437, 450, 452, 454, 493, 518
  Bruce County 8, 386-87
  Cornwall 373
  Dunvegan 373
  East Williams 340
  Finch 465
  Glengarry County 8, 24, 37, 108, 110, 114, 189, 194, 373, 381, 385, 442, 450, 466, 493, 495, 519
  Glen Nevis 311
  Glenroy 132
  Hamilton 100, 299, 398

Huron 340, 341, 344, 347
Kenyon 7, 197-98, 201
Kingston 274, 405-406
Laggan 442
Lake Huron 387
Lochiel 108-16
McGillivray Township 282, 516
Middlesex 340, 463, 516
Oakville 100-101
Orillia 295
Ottawa 378, 496, 517
Pictou 123, 263-64
Stormont 466
Tiverton 154
Toronto 14, 515-16
Zorra 464
orality and oral tradition 10, 12, 15, 22-24, 27-28, 139, 299, 379-80, 387, 390, 395-96, 411, 414, 493, 532
Ossian. *See* Oisean.
Otherworld (Celtic paradise) 129-32

panegyric code 16-17, 19
Plains of Abraham (Battle of) 70, 102, 104, 106-107, 486-87, 490, 492, 509
Potato Blight (of 1840s) 124
Prince Edward Island 4-5, 150, 188, 203-205, 209-10, 214, 224-26, 232, 241, 373, 480
Protestant Church 5, 18, 108, 219-20, 225-26, 235, 244, 295-96, 316-317, 321, 324, 385, 431, 443-44, 463, 496, 507
Protestant Church of Canada 340

Quebec 70, 91, 93, 274-75
  Eastern Townships 167, 256, 308
  Lennoxville 308-10
  Lingwick 168
  Marston 258-59, 516
  Megantic 219
  Montreal 5, 91, 439-42
  Scotstown 516
  Spring Hill (Nantes) 377, 518
  Winslow 168

racialism 10, 35, 354, 512
religion 224-27, 235, 264, 315-70, 510
Romans 71, 79, 80, 82, 96, 98, 100, 108, 111, 114

Sagart Àrasaig. *See* MacGilleBhràth, Raonall.
Saskatchewan 257, 259
  Moosomin 413
  Saltcoats 221-23
The Scottish American (newspaper) 380
Scottish Immigrant Aid Society 246
seanchaidh (definition) xii
Selkirk, Earl of. *See* Douglas, Thomas.
Sellar, Patrick 11, 36, 60
Seven Oaks, Battle of 250
Shaw, Dr. John 4
Sinclair, Rev. Dr. Alasdair MacGill-Eain xii, 116, 444, 469, 523
Sinclair, Rev. Dr. Alexander MacLean. *See* Sinclair, Rev. Dr. Alasdair MacGill-Eain.
Sinclair, Dòmhnall MacGill-Eain 382
Siosal, Eóghann 398
Skye (Island of, Scotland) 45, 150, 152, 203-204, 209, 276, 308
Society in Scotland for the Propagation of Christian Knowledge 316, 324
An Solus Iùil (newspaper) 361, 421
St. Andrew's Day 5, 434-44
Stephen, Sir George 171, 173, 175
Stornoway (Island of Lewis, Scotland) 150, 152-53, 257-60

tacksmen (fir-bhaile) 33, 124
tartanism 2, 68, 73-74, 426, 450-51, 469, 509, 511, 534
An Teachdaire Gaelach (newspaper) 389-90, 396
Thompson, John Sparrow David 477
trees xii, 177, 180, 187-89, 193-94, 208, 212-13, 215-19, 233, 242, 290

United Church of Canada 361-69
Upper Canadian Rebellion of 1837 108, 299

Vikings (and Norse) 71, 80, 82, 290, 292, 295

Wallace, William 71, 96, 97, 98, 99
whiteness 3, 145, 431

Yukon 62

Other Celtic/Gaelic Titles from CBU Press

As a' Bhraighe / Beyond the Braes: The Gaelic Songs of Allan the Ridge MacDonald (1794-1868). Effie Rankin, 2004.

Beartan Briste Agus dàin Ghàidhlig eile / Burstbroken Judgementshroudloomdeeds and Other Gaelic Poems. Rody Gorman, 2011.

A Better Life: A Portrait of Highland Women in Nova Scotia. Teresa MacIsaac, 2006.

Bearing the People Away: The Portable Highland Clearances Companion. June Skinner Sawyers, 2013.

The Cape BretonFiddle Companion. Liz Doherty, 2015.

The Cape Breton Fiddle: Making and Maintaining Tradition. Glenn Graham, 2006.

Celts in the Americas. Michael Newton, editor, 2013.

Dance to the Piper: The Highland Bagpipe in Nova Scotia. Barry Shears, 2008.

Famhair: agus dàin Ghàidhlig eile / Giant: and Other Gaelic Poems. Lodaidh MacFhionghain and Lewis MacKinnon, 2008.

Fògradh, Fàisneachd, Filidheachd / Parting, Prophecy, Poetry. Rev. Duncan Blair in Mac-Talla. Edited and translated by John A. MacPherson and Michael Linkletter, 2013.

Fonn, the Campbells of Greepe: Music and a Sense of Place in a Gaelic Family Song Tradition. Campbell Family, Acair, 2013.

The Naughty Little Book of Gaelic: All the Scottish Gaelic You Need to Curse, Swear, Drink, Smoke and Fool Around. Illustrated by Arden Powell. Sydney, NS: Cape Breton University Press, 2014.

One With the Music: Cape Breton Step Dance Tradition and Transmission. Mats Melin, 2015.

Rannsachadh na Gaidhlig 5: Fifth Scottish Gaelic Research Conference. Ken Nilsen, 2010.

Reeling Roosters and Dancing Ducks: Celtic Mouth Music. Heather Sparling, 2014.

Rudan Mì-bheanailteach is an Cothroman, Dàin : Intangible Possibilities, Poems, le Lodaidh MacFhionghain / by Lewis MacKinnon.

Seanchaidh na Coille / The Memory-Keeper of the Forest: Anthology of Scottish-Gaelic Literature of Canada. Michael Newton, editor, 2015.

About Michael Newton

MICHAEL NEWTON's PhD is in Celtic Studies from the University of Edinburgh. He has written many articles about Scottish Gaelic tradition, culture, history and literature, in Scotland and in North America. He is the author of the best-selling *The Naughty Little Book of Gaelic: All the Scottish Gaelic You Need to Curse, Swear, Drink, Smoke and Fool Around* (CBU Press 2014). Michael has also written or edited several other books, including *We're Indians Sure Enough: The Legacy of Scottish Highlanders in the Unites States* (2001), *Calum and Catriona's Welcome to the Highlands* (2006), *Warriors of the Word: The World of the Scottish Highlanders* (2009) and *Celts in the Americas* (2013). In April 2014, Michael was recipient of the inaugural Saltire Award from the Scottish Heritage Centre, St. Andrews University, Laurinburg, NC.

Also by Michael Newton

The Naughty Little Book of Gaelic: All the Scottish Gaelic You Need to Curse, Swear, Drink, Smoke and Fool Around. Illustrated by Arden Powell. Sydney, NS: Cape Breton University Press, 2014.

Bho Chluaidh gu Calasraid / From the Clyde to Callander: Gaelic Tales, Songs and Traditions from the Lennox and Menteith. Revised edition. Glasgow: Grimsay Press, 2010.

Warriors of the Word: The World of the Scottish Highlanders. Edinburgh: Birlinn, 2009.

Sgeulachdan an Dà Shaoghail. Glasgow: Sandstone Press, 2007.

"We're Indians Sure Enough": The Legacy of the Scottish Highlanders in the United States. Self-published, 2001.

A Handbook of the Scottish Gaelic World. Dublin: Four Courts Press, 2000.

As Editor

Celts in the Americas. Sydney, NS: Cape Breton University Press, 2013.

Dùthchas nan Gàidheal: Selected Essays of John MacInnes. Edinburgh: Birlinn, 2006.

Scotia 27: Proceedings of Highland Settlers Conference, 2003.

www.ingramcontent.com/pod-product-compliance
Lightning Source LLC
Chambersburg PA
CBHW032012230426
43671CB00005B/53